Alan Simpson's Windows Vista™ Bible Desktop Edition

Alan Simpson's Windows Vista™ Bible Desktop Edition

Alan Simpson & Bradley L. Jones

Wiley Publishing, Inc.

Alan Simpson's Windows Vista™ Bible, Desktop Edition

Published by
Wiley Publishing, Inc.
10475 Crosspoint Boulevard
Indianapolis, IN 46256
www.wiley.com

Published by Wiley Publishing, Inc., Indianapolis, Indiana

Published simultaneously in Canada

ISBN: 978-0-470-04640-1

Manufactured in the United States of America

10 9 8 7 6 5 4 3 2 1

For general information on our other products and services or to obtain technical support, please contact our Customer Care Department within the U.S. at (800) 762-2974, outside the U.S. at (317) 572-3993 or fax (317) 572-4002.

Library of Congress Cataloging-in-Publication Data is available from the publisher

WILEY

About the Authors

Alan Simpson is the author of more than 90 computer books, on topics ranging from Windows to word processing and Web-page design to databases. His books have been translated into more than a dozen languages and have sold millions of copies throughout the world. Prior to becoming a full-time author, Alan taught computer science at the college level and served as a computerized-training consultant to the U.S. Air Force and U.S. Navy.

Bradley L. Jones is an international bestselling author with more than a dozen books ranging from fixing PCs to Windows to learning how to use various programming languages. He is also the site manager of a number of high-profile web sites and discussion forums for Jupitermedia. Sites include Developer.com, JavaScripts.com, DevX, and many more.

In addition to his books, articles, and site work, he is also active in the community as a leader with local user groups. In addition to his many credits, he has also been recognized as a most valuable professional (MVP) by Microsoft Corporation.

Credits

Acquisitions Editor
Katie Mohr

Development Editor
Kelly Dobbs Henthorne

Technical Editor
Dan DiNicolo

Production Editor
Felicia Robinson

Editorial Manager
Mary Beth Wakefield

Production Manager
Tim Tate

Vice President and Executive Group Publisher
Richard Swadley

Vice President and Executive Publisher
Joseph B. Wikert

Project Coordinator
Heather Kolter

Graphics and Production Specialists
Carrie Foster
Denny Hager
Jennifer Mayberry
Barbara Moore
Amanda Spagnuolo

Quality Control Technicians
Laura Albert
John Greenough

Proofreading and Indexing
Aptara

Anniversary Logo Design
Richard Pacifico

Contents

Part II: Programs, Documents, and Folders   63

Part III: Using the Internet　　　　　　171

Part V: Getting Organized, Staying Organized   471

Chapter 19: Managing Files and Folders 473

Chapter 20: Finding Things on Your Computer 505

Part VI: Have It Your Way   **621**

Chapter 26: Personalizing Your Desktop **643**

Chapter 27: Using Parental Controls. **675**

Chapter 28: Speech, Writing, and Other Accessibility Features. **697**

Chapter 29: Expanding Your System. **715**

Chapter 30: Disaster Prevention and Recovery **733**

Part VII: Connecting Your Computers   755

Chapter 31: Design and Create Your Own Network 757

Chapter 32: Sharing Things on a Network. 779

Acknowledgments

Every book is a team effort—especially this one. But, before giving thanks where thanks are due, I want you to know that we're not trying to pass the buck here. Alan Simpson and I typed every word and captured every screen. So if you don't like something, blame us, but primarily blame me, Brad! This book was a composition of work done by both Alan and myself; however, in this edition, I took on the task of building the book to teach you about Windows Vista, so if a feature is off, then it is likely my fault unless Microsoft changed the feature after releasing the product.

I would like to acknowledge Microsoft for keeping me on my toes with this book. The Windows Vista product kept changing right up to the point when Microsoft released it. Even when they said they were releasing a "release candidate" (which is supposed to be a final version of the product), they still managed to change things. A number of icons, a few words, plus signs instead of triangles, and many other features all changed right before the product released. The good news is that this book was not finalized until after Windows Vista was released to manufacturing. This means that this book will have the icons, words, and other features correct—many other books released before this book are likely to have them wrong. If something isn't correct in this book, then again, it is my fault and you can e-mail me about the error at VistaBook@Jones132.com. I'd be glad to hear about it so I can get it fixed for future printings. Between Dan DiNicolo and I, along with several others, we have been through the book several times, so I believe you'll find the content to be solid!

But there's a lot more to creating a book than typing the words and making the pictures. And, for all the other countless tasks, we hereby sincerely thank the following persons:

Katie Mohr along with Alan Simpson deserve thanks for bringing this project to me. Kelly Henthorne and Dan DiNicolo for helping make this book read as well as it does, thanks to their flawless editing and suggestions. Thanks also go to the entire team at Wiley who made the process flow so smoothly.I'd also like to personally thank Richard Swadley and Joe Wikert. You'll see their names listed near the front of this book along with a bunch of editors. Richard has been instrumental in positively affecting my career more than anyone else. His guidance, suggestions, and recommendations have been greatly appreciated. Joe was one of the first people to take a chance with me well over a decade ago. His initial trust in my abilities is what launched my foray into writing. Both continue to support me by allowing me to be involved with projects like this book.

And, of course, all my love and thanks to my family for tolerating weeks of neglect as I pounded furiously at a keyboard and grumbled about Microsoft changing things in Vista yet again!

—Brad
(Bradley L. Jones)

Introduction

We wish we could have titled this book something like . . .

How to use your PC to access the Internet, do e-mail, play with pictures, print things, deal with ZIP files, download music from the Internet, e-mail pictures, open e-mail attachments, burn CDs and DVDs, talk long-distance for free, make movies, and more, without going crazy in the process

. . . but that was too many words.

Books aren't cheap, so you want to always make sure that you get a book that's appropriate for your needs. Which brings us right to. . . .

Who This Book Is For

In a nutshell, this book is for people who are clueless about computers and want to stop being that way. It's a book for people who have Windows Vista on their computers, but aren't sure why, or what they're supposed to do with it. It's a book about using your computer to do the things that most people want to do, including (but not limited to) those activities described in the aforementioned title-with-too-many-words.

This is a book for people who have never touched a computer in their lives or have just enough experience to want to touch their PC extremely hard with a sledgehammer. It's a book for people who either don't realize yet, or have come to realize the hard way, that when it comes to using a PC, the following is dead-bang true:

> Guessing doesn't work.

This is not an upgrade book for people who've been using Windows for the last 10 years. It's not a book for people who have already read one of our earlier Windows books and want to pick up where that book left off. If you can read the following sentence and picture clearly how, when, and why you want to do what it says, this may *not* be the right book for you:

Right-drag the selected items to the destination folder, drop, and then choose Copy Here or Move Here, depending on which you want to do, from the shortcut menu.

This is a book for people who can read the above sentence and honestly say, "I have no idea what he's talking about."

How to Use This Book

I cannot tell a lie. If you try to skip the first hundred or so pages in this book and jump to a particular topic in the middle or end, you will not be a happy camper. Despite what anyone tells you, the same is true of all books. So here's the reality check on how you should use this book:

Part I: "Beginner's Crash Course"—This is an absolute must for anyone who has never used a PC, doesn't know a right-click from a drag, a shortcut key from a toolbar, or a dialog box from a drop-down list. If the expression, "look it up in Help," doesn't help you, reading Part I is a must.

Part II: "Programs, Documents, and Folders"—This part is an absolute must for anyone who doesn't know a program from a document, a folder from a file, or a cut from a paste. If you wonder why things keep disappearing from your screen, and you can't get them back, this part is your lifesaver.

Part III: "Using the Internet"—Now we're getting into things that aren't so critical for using your computer. After all, you can do many things with a computer without using the Internet. But, if you want to do things like browse the Web; send and receive e-mail; chat with friends; and keep your computer safe from worms, viruses, and hackers, this is the place to go.

Part IV: "Fun with Multimedia"—If you're interested in pictures, music, movies, or DVD, this is the place to look. But, be forewarned; if you skip Parts I and II before you get here, the experience will be more along the lines of "struggling with multimedia." Sadly, you have to know a little bit about what you're doing before the fun can begin.

Part V: "Getting Organized, Staying Organized"—If you've ever lost a file that you created or downloaded, you need to read this part. If you want to see something on your computer, you have to know *where* that something is first. Also, if you plan to use CDs, DVDs, floppy disks, your hard disk, or ZIP disks, this it the place to look.

Part VI: "Have It Your Way"—This part belongs to the must-know department. It is useful if you have trouble seeing things on your screen, want to add some programs to your PC, or need to solve a PC problem.

Part VII: "Connecting Your Computers"—You can ignore this part if you will never own more than one computer and if you never have to use a computer that's part of a network. This part is a bit more technical than the other parts of the book. If you're not into *technical*, you can use this part for its auxiliary backup purpose as a guaranteed cure for insomnia.

Write Us

If you need to get in touch with Alan, it would be best to go to his web site at

`www.coolnerds.com`

Don't worry: Alan doesn't do ads; He doesn't do pop-ups; He doesn't sell things. To tell you the truth, he doesn't do much of anything on his web site. But, if you go there and click the Write to Alan link, he'll get your message. (See Chapter 10, if you don't know how to get to `www.coolnerds.com` or what a link looks like.)

You can also e-mail Alan at `alan@coolnerds.com`, but we wouldn't recommend that. Because he has no way of knowing who is going to write when, he can't set up his spam filter to expect your e-mail. If you don't go through his web site, there's a good chance your message will be inadvertently blasted into junk mail oblivion before he ever sees it.

If you'd like to get in touch with Bradley, you can give e-mail a try. You can use the address `VistaBook@Jones123.com`.

See you online,

Alan & Brad!

Beginner's Crash Course

Wouldn't it be great if you could just sit down at a computer and do whatever you wanted, without having to *learn* anything first? Those of you who have already tried the "just-do it" approach to using your computer probably know all too well the meaning of hair-pulling frustration. Simply stated, guessing doesn't work. So you finally decide to follow the directions, only to discover strange hieroglyphics like right-click the folder's icon and choose Properties. Huh?

Sad, but true, you have to know what you're doing just to understand the directions, assuming that you can find some directions. Part I is about all the basic skills and buzzwords you need to follow directions and to find information when you need it. If you can stay awake through these first three chapters, you'll finally be able to read the hieroglyphics. If all goes well, you'll keep more of your hair.

Getting Started

On the cover of this book, we promise that even beginners will be able to understand it. As a beginner, you need to know some basic things right off the bat. For example, to understand what Windows Vista is, you first have to understand what software is. And to understand what software is, you have to first know what hardware is. Let's start with first things first.

Getting to Know Your Computer's Hardware

Your personal computer (PC) is a system consisting of many individual components. Not everybody has exactly the same PC or exactly the same components. But regardless of whether you're using a desktop computer or a notebook, your PC will probably have most of the components shown in Figure 1-1.

With Windows Vista, you have all the support for using a desktop computer, a notebook computer, or even a *Tablet PC*. A Tablet PC is a newer style of portable computer that is primarily a screen without a keyboard or mouse. Rather, a special pen can be used to interact with the computer. In prior releases of Windows, you had to get a special version to use the added features of a Tablet PC. With Vista, these features are available in all the editions.

Whether you use a desktop system, your computer is likely to have a floppy disk drive, into which you can insert a floppy disk. With any style of computer, you probably have a CD or DVD drive as well, into which you can insert CDs and DVDs. Floppy disks, CDs, and DVDs are often referred to as removable media, because you can stick a disk into these drives, use the disks, and remove them from the drives when you don't need to use the disks anymore.

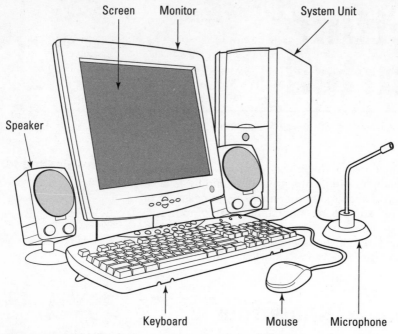

Screen   Monitor   System Unit

Speaker

Keyboard   Mouse   Microphone

Figure 1-1: Major hardware components of a typical PC

Inside your computer is another disk drive called the *hard drive*. This disk drive also goes by several other names, including *hard disk*, *fixed disk*, *primary drive,* or just C:. Your hard disk is an example of *nonremovable media*, so-named because you can't take the hard disk out of its drive. In fact, you can't even see the hard drive, because it's inside the system unit, as illustrated in Figure 1-2.

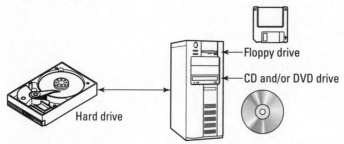

Floppy drive

CD and/or DVD drive

Hard drive

Figure 1-2: Disk drives on a typical PC

Using Your Mouse or Touchpad

The easiest way to operate your computer (especially if you can't type worth beans) is with your mouse. Most mice have two buttons; some mice have a wheel between the buttons. The mouse button on the left is called the *primary mouse button*. The mouse button on the right is called the *secondary mouse button* (see Figure 1-3). In a nutshell, you use the primary (left) mouse button when you want the computer to do something. You use the secondary (right) mouse button when you want to see your options before you do anything.

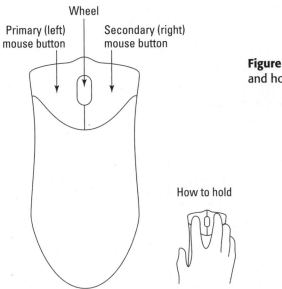

Figure 1-3: A typical mouse and how to hold it

As you move the mouse around (without holding down either of the mouse buttons), the mouse pointer on the screen moves in the same direction that you move the mouse.

Caution When moving the mouse, keep the front of the mouse aimed toward the screen. Don't twist or turn the mouse. If the mouse gets out of reach, just pick it up off the table, and set it down in a more comfortable position.

A mouse is an example of a *pointing device*, a gadget that enables you to point to and click things on the screen. If you're using a notebook computer, your pointing device might not be a mouse. It might be a touchpad or trackball. But it will still have a primary (left) and secondary (right) mouse button. Additionally, your touchpad might also support the functionality of a scroll wheel, even though it doesn't have one. This is generally supported by moving your finger up or down on the right side of the touch pad next to the edge. Some touch pads have markings to show that they support scrolling.

If you have difficulty using your notebook's pointing device, the best place to look for information is the documentation that comes with your computer.

Some standard terminology describes things you can do with the mouse. You'll see these terms used in all sorts of instructions — not just in this book. Boring as the terms may be, you might want to spend a little time getting to know them, so you can understand any written instructions you come across.

✦ **Mouse pointer:** The little arrow, hand, or bar on the screen that moves in whatever direction you move the mouse.

✦ **Point:** To move the mouse pointer so that it's touching some item. For example, the phrase "point to the Start button" means move the mouse pointer so that it's resting on the Start button in the lower-left corner of the screen, as shown in Figure 1-4.

Figure 1-4: Pointing to the Start button

> **Tip**
>
> Pointing to an item often displays its screen tip (also called a tooltip), like the words "Start" in Figure 1-4. Whenever you're clueless about what some little symbol on your screen represents, point to it to see whether it has a screen tip.

✦ **Click:** Point to the item and then tap (don't hold down) the primary (left) mouse button.

✦ **Double-click:** Point to the item; tap the primary (left) mouse button twice, as quickly as you can.

✦ **Right-click:** Point to the item; tap the secondary (right) mouse button.

✦ **Drag:** Point to the item and then hold down the primary (left) mouse button while moving the mouse.

✦ **Right-drag:** Point to the item and then hold down the secondary (right) mouse button while moving the mouse.

✦ **Drop:** Release the mouse button after dragging or right-dragging.

Using Your Keyboard

Like the mouse, the keyboard is a means of interacting with your computer. Most of it is laid out like a typewriter. If you already know how to type, you're in luck. If you don't know how to type, we can't help you there. But you can at least take solace in that you need the keyboard only to type text. You can use the mouse for nearly everything else.

Aside from the regular typewriter keys, you need to recognize some additional keys and areas on the keyboard. Figure 1-5 shows an example of a standard keyboard, although your keyboard probably won't look exactly like the one in the figure. But you should be able to find all the keys pointed out, even if your keyboard is arranged a little differently from the example in Figure 1-5.

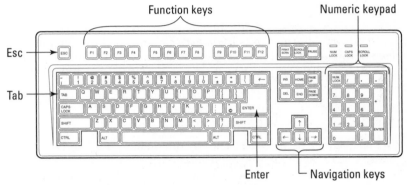

Figure 1-5: A sample of a standard computer keyboard

Navigation Keys and Numeric Keypad

The arrow keys and keys labeled Home, End, and so forth are the *navigation keys*. As you'll discover throughout the book, you can use those keys to move around in certain types of programs. The *numeric keypad* contains a set of numbers and math symbols laid out exactly as they would be on a standard adding machine. For people who are already quick with a standard adding machine, the numeric keypad offers a familiar way to type lots of numeric information into the computer.

On some keyboards, the navigation keys aren't separate; they are combined with the keys on the numeric keypad. In that case, use the Num Lock key on the keyboard to decide which keys you want to use. When the Num Lock key is on, the numeric keypad acts just like an adding machine's keypad. When the Num Lock key is off, the navigation keys take over, and the numeric keypad no longer types numbers.

On a notebook computer, the numeric keypad may be on top of the regular keys. In this case, there is generally a button that you can press to toggle between the regular letters and the numbers.

 Caution If you are typing on a notebook computer and numbers are showing up instead of letters, then you most likely have the numeric keypad activated. Look for a Num Lock key and press it.

Function Keys

The keys labeled F1, F2, F3, and so forth on your keyboard are called *function keys*. The F1 key is the Help key — you can press that key at any time for help. The exact purposes of the remaining function keys depend on what program you happen to be using.

The Windows and Application Keys

▦ Some computer keyboards have a couple of extra keys specifically designed for Windows. One, named the *Windows key*, shows the flying window logo as shown at top left. If your keyboard has that key, you'll most likely find it between the Alt and Ctrl keys on the left side of your keyboard. If your keyboard has an *Application key*, shown at bottom left, that one will likely be near one of the Windows keys on your keyboard or between the Alt and Ctrl keys on the right side of your keyboard.

The Windows and Application keys are entirely optional, so don't fret if your keyboard doesn't have them. Anything you can do with one of those keys, you can also do with the mouse or even some other keys. For example, if you have a Windows key on your keyboard, you can tap it to make the Start menu appear. Whether you have a Windows key or not, you can also make the Start menu appear by clicking the Start button or by pressing Ctrl+Esc. Which brings us to that little plus sign. . . .

Typing Those *key1* + *key2* Things

Often when working with computers, you'll see an instruction to press some *combination keystroke: key1+key2*. When you see a combination keystroke like that, it means "hold down *key1*, tap *key2*, and release *key1*." Here are some examples:

- **Ctrl+Esc** means "Hold down the Ctrl key, tap the Esc key, and release the Ctrl key."

- **Alt+Tab** means "Hold down the Alt key, tap the Tab key, and release the Alt key."

- **Shift+Enter** means "Hold down the Shift key, tap the Enter key, and release the Shift key."

- ▦**+D** means "Hold down the Windows key, tap the D key, and release the Windows key."

You'll learn about useful combination keystrokes as we go through the book. For now, it's sufficient to know that any time you see a plus sign (+) between two key names, *key1+key2*, that means "hold down *key1*, tap *key2*, and release *key1*."

That's about all the hardware you need to know to get started. Throughout this book, we will cover a few more hardware topics as well—such as attaching a second monitor to your computer. For now, let's talk about the software next.

Getting to Know Your Computer's Software

Let's say someone hands you two identical-looking video cassette tapes. You put one tape into the VCR, press Play, and the movie *Ben Hur* starts playing. You take that tape out, put in the second tape, and press Play, and the movie *Pippi Longstocking* starts playing. The two cassette tapes look exactly alike. So why does one show Ben and the other Pippi? The cassette tapes are only the *medium* (hardware) on which information is stored. The movie itself is in the *software* that's recorded onto that medium.

Like a movie on a video tape or like songs on a CD, computer software is invisible. You can't see it or touch it, because it's just information recorded onto some medium. In the case of programs that are already installed on your computer, that medium is generally your computer's hard disk.

What Is Windows Vista?

Windows Vista is a type of software known as an *operating system* (abbreviated *OS*). One thing that's unique about an operating system is that it's the only software that a computer is required to have. If you try to start a computer that has no operating system installed on it, you get nothing. If the computer has only an operating system and nothing else, that's fine. But it has to have an operating system to do anything at all, even start.

The operating system is also your computer's *platform*, the foundation upon which all other programs run. To illustrate what I mean by that, you can't go to the store, buy any old graphics program off the shelf, and expect it to work on your computer. It has to be a graphics program for Windows Vista. A graphics program for some other operating system, like the Mac OS, Linux, or UNIX, just won't work on a Windows computer. The reverse is also true. For example, to get a graphics program for a Macintosh computer, you have to get one that runs on the Mac OS.

Why Learn Windows Vista?

Besides all that technical stuff, the operating system also determines how you operate the computer. When you first start your computer, everything you see on your screen is Windows Vista. To use your computer, you really need to learn how to use Windows Vista.

Understanding the Different Home Editions of Windows Vista

Windows Vista actually comes in several editions. Each edition has features specific to it. In many cases, the features may overlap. This book assumes that you are using one of the two home editions, Windows Vista Home Basic Edition or Windows Vista Home Premium Edition. If you are using the Premium Edition, then you will have a few additional features that are not in the standard Home Basic Edition. These will be noted throughout this book. Some of the features in the Home Premium Edition that aren't in the basic include the following:

✦ The Aero Interface (explained in Chapter 2)

✦ Windows Media Center for music, photos, video, and television

✦ Windows DVD maker

✦ Windows Movie Maker (High Definition)

✦ Premium Games

✦ TabletPC support

✦ Handwriting recognition

✦ Windows Sideshow support

✦ Presentation Features

If you are not familiar with some of the preceding features, don't fret. Most will be covered throughout this book!

The business editions of Vista have features that are tailored more to business users. For the person who wants everything, there is also a Windows Vista Ultimate Edition that has it all, but also costs a little more.

It doesn't matter if your long-term goal is to e-mail pictures to friends, make your own music CDs, browse the Internet, or write the great American novel. In order to do anything at all with your PC, you first need to learn to use Windows Vista (assuming, of course, that your computer's operating system is Windows Vista).

Starting Windows Vista

Because Windows Vista is your computer's operating system, you don't have to do anything special to start Windows. All you have to do is start the computer (also known as *booting up*). We assume you already know how to do that. But, since there is a right way and lots of wrong ways to start a computer, let's go through the steps:

STEPS: Start Windows Vista

1. Turn on any device that's connected to the computer first (printer, modem, monitor, scanner, whatever you have).

2. Push the eject button on the floppy disk drive just to see whether there's a disk in there. If a floppy disk pops out, remove it.

3. Turn on the main power switch on the computer, and wait.

4. If you see a Welcome Screen similar to the one shown in Figure 1-6, click whichever name or picture represents your user account. If you don't see the Welcome screen, don't worry about. Just ignore this step.

When the computer is fully *booted up*, you should see the Windows desktop and taskbar. I can't say exactly what those will look like on your computer. The desktop is basically the entire screen and may appear as a photo, a solid color, a pattern, your computer manufacturer's logo, or boxes called window dialog boxes with information displayed. The taskbar is the colored strip along the bottom of the screen, as in the example shown in Figure 1-7. You may also have a sidebar displayed as shown in this figure.

 Caution If you see a message about an abnormal termination when you first start your computer, make sure you learn the right way to shut down your computer as described near the end of this chapter. If you see a message about an "invalid system disk," remove any floppy disks or CDs from their drives and then press the Enter key.

Figure 1-6: The Windows Vista Welcome screen

Windows desktop

Sidebar

Start button   Taskbar   Notification area

Figure 1-7: The Windows Vista desktop

The next section briefly describes all those things pointed out in Figure 1-7.

The Start Button

Windows may be the only program that starts automatically when you first turn on your computer. But it's certainly not the only program on your system. To start any other program, use the Start button. When you first click the Start button, the *Start menu* opens. The left side of the Start menu provides access to a few of the programs on your computer. The right side lists places (mostly *folders*) you're likely to visit often. Figure 1-8 shows an example, although yours might not look exactly like the one in the figure.

Note   A *menu,* in the computer sense, is like a menu from a restaurant in that it provides a list of items from which you can choose.

The left side of the Start menu actually shows icons for only a few of the programs installed on your computer: mostly programs that you use a lot or, if your computer is brand new, just some useful programs for beginners. As you'll see in a moment, you'll use the All Programs menu to start any program that isn't listed down the left side of the Start menu.

Programs   Places

Figure 1-8: The Start menu

One other feature on the Start menu is worth noting. On the bottom left is an Instant Search box. By typing into this box, the Start menu will search for a program, files, e-mails, and other items that match what you enter. This makes it easier to find something on the menus that you might not initially see. It also makes it easy to find other items on your computer.

The Windows Desktop

The Windows desktop gets its name from the fact that it's roughly equivalent to the desktop of a real desk. Your real desktop is where you do your non-computer work. The Windows desktop is where you do your computer work. Doing work on a computer usually means opening, and using, some program. Each program you open sits on the desktop, like a piece of paper on a real desktop.

If you're sitting at your computer now and want to see an example, perform the following steps to open the Calculator program that comes with Windows Vista:

STEPS: Starting Calculator

1. Click the Start button (in the lower-left corner of the screen).

2. Click the All Programs option. The menu on the left will change to the All Programs menu.

3. In the All Programs menu, click Accessories.

4. The Accessories folder will expand to show the accessory programs in the menu, click Calculator (see Figure 1-9).

A calculator opens on the desktop, in a window. The calculator hasn't replaced the desktop. It's just sitting on top of the desktop, as a real calculator would sit atop a real desktop.

Figure 1-9: Click Start; choose All Programs ⇨ Accessories ⇨ Calculator

The Taskbar

Usually, you open a program to perform a task. For example, you open Calculator to perform a math task. If you think of each open program as a task, the taskbar is the tool that enables you to manage those tasks. Each program you open has a title bar at the top, which shows the program's *icon* (symbol) and usually the name of the program as well. For each open program, you'll find a corresponding button on the taskbar that shows the same icon and name. Figure 1-10 shows the Calculator program you opened earlier, along with its taskbar button.

The taskbar is especially handy when you have several open programs piled up on the desktop at once. To bring any of those open programs to the top of the pile, you just have to click the program's taskbar button. You'll learn more about managing open program windows in Chapter 4.

Calculator's title bar

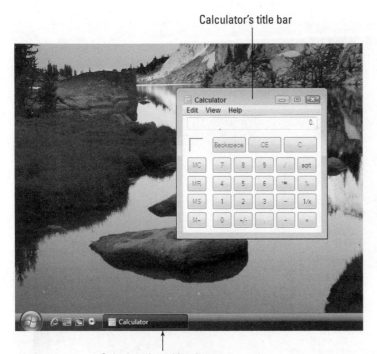

Calculator's taskbar button

Figure 1-10: Calculator on the desktop and its taskbar button

Tip   You can also make an open program window disappear, and reappear, by clicking its taskbar button.

To close an open program, click the Close (X) button (shown at left) in its upper-right corner.

If you are using Windows Vista Home Premium edition and you have a high-powered graphics card, then you will have the ability to use the Windows Aero interface, which can display smart icons. Smart icons allow for additional information to be displayed when you hover over an icon. This concept also applies to the taskbar and other areas. Figure 1-11 shows what you would see when the mouse is hovering over the Calculator taskbar button with Windows Vista Aero. You should also notice in Figure 1-11 that the title bar and some of the bottoms look different. More on Aero will be presented throughout this book.

Figure 1-11: Hovering over the Calculator taskbar button with Windows Vista Aero

The Notification Area

As you could see in Figure 1-8, the Notification Area is on the right side of the taskbar. It has the time of day and some weird little icons that represent services currently running on your computer. Its name comes from the fact that, when Windows or some other program has a suggestion for you, a little message pops up from that area, as in the example shown in Figure 1-12.

Figure 1-12: A sample notification message

When you see one of those notifications, you have several choices.

✦ Read the message, and, if you want to pursue what it's offering, click the text of the message.

✦ If you want to reject what it's offering, click the X button inside the message to close it.

✦ If you want to ignore the message, you can simply leave it alone and it should disappear after a few minutes.

If you don't understand what a notification means, your best bet would be to close it. The message will come back from time to time. You can try out whatever it's offering after you've learned more. For now, that's the gist of how some of the items on the desktop work. You'll be seeing, and using, all of those things in upcoming chapters, as well as each time you use your computer.

Using Icons

The little pictures you see all over the place in Windows are called *icons*. Every icon is a little emblem, or symbol, for something larger. That something larger could be anything — a program, a folder, a video, a song, a typed document — things you'll learn about in upcoming chapters. Using small icons to represent larger things helps keep the clutter on your desktop to a minimum. Figure 1-13 shows some examples of icons, in no particular order.

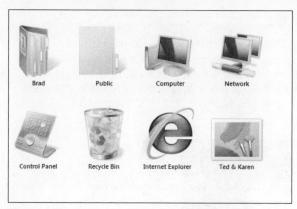

Figure 1-13: Some sample icons in no particular order

Opening Icons

You can open some icons by clicking them once. But most of the time, you'll need to double-click an icon to open it. Remember that *double-click* means to point to the icon and then tap the left mouse button twice, as quickly as you can. If you pause too long between the clicks, the icon won't open.

> **Note** As mentioned earlier, Windows Vista has a new feature called Live Icons. Applications that support this feature will have icons that can provide a small preview for the application to which the icon links. You will need the Home Premium edition in order to see this feature.

Shrinking a Big Thing Back to Its Icon

 Exactly what does open depends on what the icon represents. If you open an icon by accident, or don't know what to do with the thing that opens, just close it. Closing an item shrinks it to its original icon. To close, click the Close button (the X button shown at left) in the upper-right corner of whatever it is you want to close. Or, if your hands happen to be on the keyboard, you can press Alt+F4.

Organizing Icons

If you've already been using icons for a long time, and in fact they're getting pretty messy, you can easily whip them into alphabetical order. Just right-click some empty space between any icons (but not *on* any icon). From the shortcut menu that appears (shown on the left in Figure 1-14), choose Sort By ⇨ Name (shown in to the right in Figure 1-14). The icons will be neatly arranged into (roughly) alphabetical order.

For example, certain built-in Windows icons stick to the upper-left corner of your screen, so that they're always in the same place. The built-in icons have assigned names, for example, Recycle Bin. Any icons other than built-in ones will be alphabetized starting after the last built-in icon.

Right-click some empty space between icons; then choose by Sort By > Name

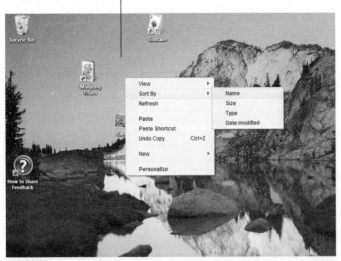

Figure 1-14: Right-click an empty spot and choose Sort By ⇨ Name.

Changing the Icon Size

In addition to sorting the icons, you can also change their size. Icons displayed on the desktop can generally be displayed in two sizes, medium and large. If you want them to take up the least amount of space, you can make them medium sized. If you want to see them easier, you can make them large.

Changing the size is similar to arranging them. Right-click some empty space between any icons (but not *on* any icon). From the shortcut menu that appears choose View ⇨ Large Icons to display large icons. Choose View ⇨ Medium Icons to display medium icons. If you don't like the newly displayed size, you can simply change the size back.

Working Common Controls

Throughout your work in Windows, you'll be presented with various *controls* on the screen. A control on the screen is like a control in a car. For example, in a car, the brake is a control you work with your foot. The steering wheel is a control you work with your hands, as are the controls for the radio, windshield wipers, and headlights. In Windows, the controls on your screen are things you work with your mouse or keyboard. In this section we'll look at some examples of controls you're likely to come across in Windows quite often.

Using Scroll Bars

Scroll bars appear on your screen whenever there's more text, or more information, than will fit in the space available. The scroll bar enables you to scroll
around and see any text that's not currently visible. There are vertical scroll
bars that let you move up and down and horizontal scroll bars for moving left
and right. The scroll bar has buttons at both ends, and a scroll box within it,
as shown in Figure 1-15.

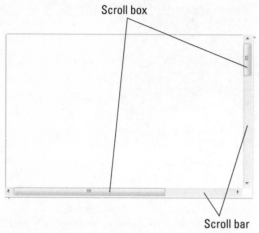

Figure 1-15: Horizontal and vertical scroll bars

The size of the scroll box relative to the size of the scroll bar tells you roughly
how much information is currently out of view. For example, looking at the vertical scroll bar in Figure 1-15, you can see that the scroll box occupies about
the top 25 percent of the scroll bar. That means that currently you're viewing
only the top 25 percent of whatever text is shown to the left of the scroll bar.
To scroll through text that's out of view, use the scroll bar to scroll down. To
operate the scroll bar using your mouse:

- ✦ Click the button at the bottom to scroll down one line.

- ✦ Click the button at the top to scroll up one line.

- ✦ Click an empty area on the scroll bar, beneath the scroll box, to move
  down a page.

- ✦ Click an empty area on the scroll bar above the scroll box to scroll
  up a page.

- ✦ If your mouse has a wheel, you can click the scroll bar; then spin the
  mouse wheel to scroll up or down. If you're using a notebook computer with a touchpad, then you might also be able to click on the
  scroll bar and then slide your finger up and down on the right edge
  of the touch pad to scroll up and down.

- ✦ Drag the scroll box to any place on the bar to go to that part of the list.

Tip Drag means "hold down the mouse button while moving the mouse." In a scroll bar you want to put the mouse pointer on the scroll box, hold down the left mouse button while dragging the scroll box along the scroll bar; and then release the mouse button when you get to wherever you want to go.

Working scroll bars with the mouse can be a bit more challenging, because there might be several scroll bars on the screen at the same time. The keyboard will work only one of them. For example, to use the scroll bar in a list box control, you first have to move the focus to that control. Anyway, here are the keys you use to scroll around using the keyboard:

✦ ↑: Scroll down a line

✦ ↓: Scroll up a line

✦ →: Scroll right a little

✦ ←: Scroll left a little

✦ **Page Down (PgDn):** Scroll down a page

✦ **Page Up (PgUp):** Scroll up a page

✦ **Home:** Go to the top

✦ **End:** Go to the end

Hiding and Showing Details

To keep your screen from getting too cluttered, Windows often hides some information on the screen. There are plenty of examples sprinkled throughout Windows, and we'll point them out as they arise. But those of you who like to explore on your own should be aware of how these buttons work, so you can recognize them and use them as they appear on your screen.

The button you use to show or hide information usually has some sort of arrow on it, or < and > symbols, sometimes pointing up and down. Figure 1-16 shows some general examples of Show/Hide buttons.

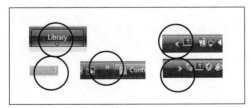

Figure 1-16: Examples of show/hide buttons

The Show/Hide buttons are simple to use—just click the button. If items are currently hidden, clicking the button will take them out of hiding. If items are currently displayed, clicking the button will put them back into hiding.

A similar capability exists in certain types of lists, where you can hide or show details (list items) under a heading. Again, we'll point out examples as they arise. But you intrepid explorers out there should keep an eye out for these things. If you don't notice them, or don't know how to use them, you're not seeing all the information that's available to you. Using the ▷ and ◢ buttons in a list is easy:

✦ If items are currently hidden, click the ▷ sign to expand the list.

✦ If items are currently displayed, click the ◢ sign hide the list.

Figure 1-17 shows a general example.

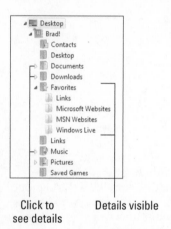

Figure 1-17: Use ▷ and ◢ buttons in lists to show and hide details.

Click to   Details visible
see details

Using Dragging Handles

A *dragging handle* (sometimes called a *sizing handle*, or even just a *handle*) is a control that enables you to move or size an item by dragging. Dragging handles come in various shapes and sizes, but as a rule they tend to look like little nonskid areas, as in the examples shown in Figure 1-18. We'll point out specific examples as we go through the book. For now, when you see a little nonskid area like one of the examples shown in the figure, know that it's not just there for decoration. Like everything you see on your screen, it's a control that serves some purpose.

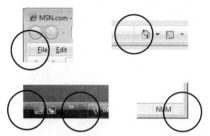

Figure 1-18: Examples of dragging handles

About Disabled (Dimmed) Controls

As you explore your computer and start noticing controls all over the place, you'll probably notice that some of them appear to be dimmed, as in the examples shown in the right side of Figure 1-19. If you click one of those dimmed controls, nothing happens. Why? Because the control is currently *disabled*. In other words *dimmed* stands for disabled. It's important to understand this, especially for beginners, because they often click away madly at disabled controls, thinking the control will somehow wake up and start working, That's not the way it works.

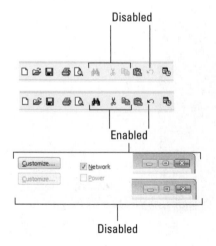

Figure 1-19: Examples of enabled and disabled controls

A disabled control is not indicative of something that's broken or needs fixing. It's simply a control that's not relevant at the moment. When circumstances change such that the control becomes useful, the control will automatically become enabled. You'll see many examples of enabled and disabled controls throughout this book. For now, it's enough to know that when you see a dimmed control, don't bother clicking it. If it's dimmed, it's simply not relevant at the moment. And no amount of clicking the disabled control will wake it up.

The Right Way to Turn Off Your Computer

Before you get any deeper into learning about your computer, now is a good time to learn the right way to shut down your computer when you're ready to call it a day. There are lots of ways to turn off a computer. But there's really only one right way and plenty of wrong ways. The right way is to shut down Windows first. Here's how:

STEPS: Shutting Down Windows

1. Click the Start button to pull up the start menu.
2. Click the power button (see Figure 1-20).
3. Watch the screen and wait.

 Note   Your computer might be set to sleep instead of shut down. To guarantee that your computer turns off, you can click the show button to the right of the Power button to show a menu. This menu is shown in Figure 1-20. Click Shut Down to select it.

Click Start   Click Power Button Click for other shut off options

Figure 1-20: Shutting down your computer

Don't expect the computer to shut down immediately. Windows has some housekeeping to do first, and that will take a few seconds. If you see any messages asking a question, as in the example shown in Figure 1-21, waiting won't work. You'll need to respond to the message before the shut down will complete.

Figure 1-21: Message that's asking a question

 The sample message shown in Figure 1-21 is asking whether you want to save the document you've recently created or changed. For more information on saving documents, see Chapter 6.

After you've responded to any questions that might have appeared on the screen, and Windows has finished its housekeeping, one of two things will happen. If you have the type of computer that Windows can shut down by itself, the monitor will go blank, any fan noise you normally hear will stop, and the computer will shut down. You don't have to push any buttons to turn off the computer.

If you have the type of computer that Windows can't turn off by itself, you'll see the message "It is now safe to turn off your computer" on the screen. In that case, you'll need to turn off the computer yourself, using its main power switch.

 On a computer that doesn't shut down automatically, you might have to hold the main power button for three or four seconds before the computer shuts down. That's to prevent the computer from being shut down accidentally when someone just brushes up against the button.

Summary

That about wraps it up for the basic skills you need to start your computer, use your mouse and keyboard, start programs, close programs, and turn off your computer. The part about starting and using programs in this chapter is, admittedly, a bit thin. There's a lot more you can do with program windows, as you'll learn in Part II. But for now, you're off to a great start and are ready to move to Chapter 2, where you'll learn some more critical basic skills.

✦ Your computer hardware is the stuff that you can see and feel.

✦ The main hardware devices you use to operate the computer are a pointing device such as a mouse and keyboard.

✦ Your computer software is the invisible instructions that tell the computer how to behave and what to do.

✦ All of the software in your computer is stored on your computer's hard disk.

✦ Windows Vista is a special type of software known as an operating system (OS).

✦ When you first start your computer, the Windows desktop will appear on the screen, along with the Start button, taskbar, and notification along the bottom of the screen.

✦ To start any program that's installed on your computer, click the Start button; then click All Programs.

✦ To close any large open object on your screen, click the Close (X) button in its upper-right corner.

✦ To shut down Windows properly before turning off your computer, click the Start button, and then click the Power Button.

Workin' It

Y ou work most of the gadgets in your life through controls — controls for your TV, your VCR, your car, your camera, your microwave, and your dishwasher. You work your computer through controls as well. However, most of the computer's controls aren't things you work directly with your hands. Instead, they're things on the screen you work with your mouse or keyboard.

Windows has thousands of controls — some (like the Start button) you'll see all the time. Others you'll see rarely. The controls you need to use often will be visible often. Controls that you rarely (if ever) need are a little more hidden away, and you have to go looking for them. Before we get to the details of working all these little controls, let's step back and take a look at the bigger picture to help us see that there's some rhyme and reason to the way it all works.

Understanding Objects and Properties

The room you're sitting in right now is filled with *objects* (objects is just a fancy name for things). Your chair is an object; your desk is an object; each picture hanging on the wall is an object. Every object in the room has certain *characteristics*, or properties, that further define that object. Properties include size, shape, weight, color, materials, and so forth. Often, you can change an object's properties without really changing the object. For example, you can paint an object to change its color without actually changing what the object is or what it does. Properties tend to personalize an object.

Most of the little doodads you see on your screen are objects, too. The Windows desktop is an object, as is each icon on the desktop. The Start button and taskbar are objects, too. Like objects in the real world, objects on the computer screen have properties. Each object has properties such as size, shape, and color. These properties can be changed to personalize the object.

Usually, the quickest way to get to an object's properties is to right-click the object of interest and then click Properties in the shortcut menu that appears near the mouse pointer, as in the examples shown in Figure 2-1.

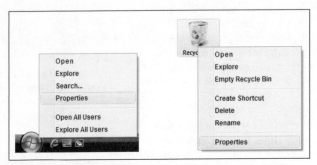

Figure 2-1: Right-click an object and choose Properties.

When you right-click an object and choose Properties, that object's Properties dialog box opens. A dialog box is a set of controls that enables you to change the properties of whatever object you right-click. (More on dialog boxes in a moment.) First, we want to talk about objects that aren't visible on your screen and how you can use the Control Panel to set their properties.

Introducing Control Panel

The objects you see on your screen at any given time aren't the only objects available to you. In fact, some objects that make up your computer system never appear on the screen. For example, your mouse is an object, and your keyboard is an object. If your computer has a modem, that modem is an object, too. But you can't very well right-click a mouse, keyboard, or modem, because those physical objects exist outside your computer, not on your screen. But most of those physical hardware objects have properties (not in the sense that you can change their size, shape, or color but in the sense that you can change how they behave).

So, if you can't get to an object or its properties by right-clicking an icon, how can you do so? The answer is the Windows *Control Panel*. In the real world, control panel refers to all the primary controls on a specific machine. For example, all the controls for your microwave make up the microwave's control panel. All the controls you use to drive your car make up the car's control panel. To open Windows Control Panel:

STEPS: Open Control Panel

1. Click the Start button.

2. On the right side of the Start menu, click Control Panel.

When Control Panel first opens, it will either open to the Control Panel Home page or in Classic view. Figure 2-2 shows an example of each view. At the left side of each window, you should see options titled Control Panel Home and Classic view. The text describing the view you are currently seeing will be in bold and have a dot to the left of it. To switch to the other view, you can click the other text. In the Control Panel Home view, options are categorized; whereas the Classic view has nearly everything listed together.

Control Panel Home (Category view)

Classic view

Figure 2-2: Control Panel open to the Control Panel Home and in the Classic view

Control Panel Home View and Classic View

The Control Panel Home view and the Classic view both provide access to the same objects and their properties. The difference between the two is how you get to a specific object's properties. From the Control Panel Home view, you drill down from the general categories to the specific items you want to find. That is, first you click whichever category name looks the most promising (for whatever it is you want to do at the moment).

For example, suppose you want to change the properties of a hardware device, like your mouse and keyboard. If you click the category name Hardware and Sound, Control Panel shows icons and options for working with your printer and other devices, as in Figure 2-3.

Tip　If you want to back up from wherever you land in Control Panel, click the Back button (shown to the left) on the Control Panel toolbar. Also, you can move, size, and close Control Panel using the same tools and techniques that other windows provide. See the section "Arranging Open Program Windows" in Chapter 4 for more information.

Either clicking an icon or clicking the text describing what you want to do opens the Properties dialog box for that device. For example, clicking the Mouse icon or any of the text to the right of the mouse icon results in the Mouse Properties dialog box opening, which provides controls for changing your mouse properties.

Figure 2-4 shows Control Panel in Classic view, where you don't drill down through categories to get to an object's icon. Instead, all the icons are just shown in plain view. For example, you can see the icons titled Game Controllers, Mouse, Printers, Keyboard, Phone and Modem Options, and Scanners and Cameras in both views.

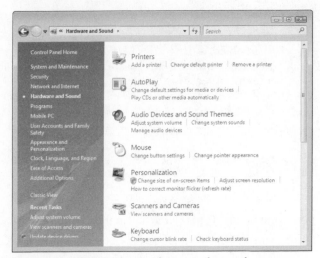

Figure 2-3: Clicking the Hardware and Sound category leads to these icons and options.

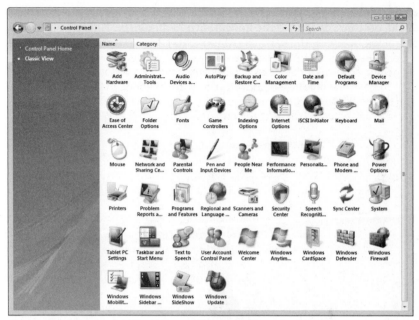

Figure 2-4: Classic view just shows all the uncategorized icons.

Classic view refers to the view used in older versions of Windows. The Control Panel Home view wasn't available in Windows until the release of Windows XP, where it was first called Category view because items are categorized. In Classic view, you might have to double-click (rather than just click) an icon to open it. But the results will be the same as clicking in Category view—the Properties dialog box for that object will open.

There is no right view, wrong view, good view, or bad view. There are just different views. Choosing one over the other is simply a matter of personal preference.

Anyway, no matter how you get to an object's properties, those properties are displayed in a dialog box, which in turn contains controls that enable you to change the object's properties. Different objects have different properties, and there are tons of them. But there are some definite basic skills and concepts you can learn that will apply to all objects and all dialog boxes.

Using Dialog Boxes

A dialog box is a set of options for you to choose from. You carry on a dialog with the box by making selections from the options it presents. There are many dialog boxes in Windows, but they all have certain things in common, such as a title bar at the top and some controls that you use to make your selections.

Some dialog boxes have a Preview area, which gives you a sneak peek at how changing an option will change the appearance of an object. Figure 2-5 shows a sample dialog box with the various components pointed out.

Tip   You can move a dialog box just as you would a window — by dragging its title bar. See the section "Moving a Program Window" in Chapter 4 for more information.

Controls   Title bar

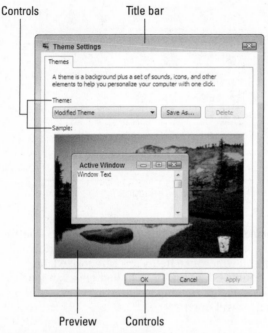

Preview   Controls

Figure 2-5: A sample dialog box

The controls in a dialog box are like the controls in a car or on any other gadget, except, of course, that you don't work the controls of a dialog box with your hands. You work them with your mouse or keyboard. It's usually easiest to use the mouse, since most of the time you just have to click a control to operate it. If you use your keyboard, it's a little trickier because you first have to move the *focus* to the control you want to operate. Press the Tab key to move to the focus of the next control in a dialog box. Press Shift+Tab to move back to the previous control. The control that currently has the focus will be highlighted in some manner, usually with some sort of border around it or perhaps as selected text (that is, light text against a dark background).

The way you work a control depends on what type of control it is. In the sections that follow, we'll look at the various types of controls you'll come across. If you want to follow along on your own computer, use the Taskbar and Start Menu Properties dialog box. To get to it, right-click the Start button and choose Properties.

My Dialog Boxes Look Different!

Windows Vista introduced a new visual style called Windows Aero. Windows Aero adds fancy graphics and effects to the Windows Vista desktop and dialogs. It includes glasslike, transparent window frames, 3D graphics, animated transitions, and more. The following figure shows an example of a dialog displayed using the Windows Aero style.

As you can see in the figure, the title bar is somewhat transparent. Additionally, the buttons on the top, top right of the title bar are also placed and presented differently than what is seen in the standard interface. Regardless of the look, the buttons still operate in the same way.

Windows Aero is not available in Windows Vista Home Basic. You have to have Windows Home Premium, a Business Edition, or Windows Vista Ultimate. Additionally, you have to have a high-powered graphics card with at least 128 MB of RAM. If you have a machine that can support Windows Aero, then some of the effects are nice.

In this book the standard graphical interface is generally used for the figures. In cases where the Windows Aero interface does something different, that will also be presented.

Using Tabs

Some dialog boxes contain more options than will fit within the box. In that case, the options will be separated into different tabs within the dialog box, as in Figure 2-6. To view the options on a tab, just click the tab. If your hands happen to be on the keyboard, you can press Ctrl+Tab to switch from one tab to the next.

Figure 2-6: Tabs in a dialog box

Using Option Buttons

Option buttons (also known as radio buttons) enable you to choose one of two or more mutually exclusive options. The name *radio button* comes from the older-style car radios. With a radio, you want to listen only to one station at a time. When you push the button on a radio to listen to a station, the button that previously was pushed in pops out, and you hear only the station whose button you pushed. The same thing happens with option buttons in a dialog box. When you choose one option, any previously selected option will be cleared.

For example, if you click the Start Menu tab in the Taskbar and Start Menu Properties dialog box, you'll see two option buttons named Start Menu and Classic Start menu, as shown in Figure 2-7. The two options are mutually exclusive because you can choose one or the other but not both.

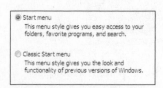

Figure 2-7: Examples of option buttons

Operating option buttons from the keyboard takes a bit of dexterity. First, press Tab or Shift+Tab to get the focus to the currently selected option. Then press the arrow keys (↑, ↓, ←, →) to select the option you want. When the option you want is selected, press the Tab or Shift+Tab key to move to the previous or next control.

Using Check Boxes

Check boxes are options that can either be selected (checked) or not selected (clear). If you click the Taskbar tab in the Taskbar and Start Menu Properties dialog box, you'll see several check boxes, as in Figure 2-8.

Figure 2-8: Examples of check boxes

Clicking a check box reverses its current setting. For example, if the check box is currently selected (checked), clicking it clears (unchecks) the check box. If the check box is clear, clicking it selects (checks) the check box.

If you're using the keyboard, you'll have to press Tab or Shift+Tab as necessary to move the focus to the check box you want to change. Then you can press the spacebar to select or clear the check mark.

Tip   If you want your taskbar to look and act like the examples shown in this book, select and clear the check boxes on your Taskbar tab to match those shown in Figure 2-8.

Using Spin Boxes

A spin box is a little box into which you can type a number or increase/decrease the number currently shown in the box using buttons. To see an example of a spin box:

1. In the Taskbar and Start Menu Properties dialog box, click the Start Menu tab.

2. Make sure the Start menu option (not Classic Start Menu) is selected; then click the Customize button to the right of the Start menu option.

A new dialog box appears, titled Customize Start Menu opens. The control near the middle of the dialog box is a spin box (see Figure 2-9).

Figure 2-9: Example of a spin box

There are three ways to work a spin box:

✦ Click the up arrow at the right of the box to increase the number.

✦ Click the down arrow at the right of the box to decrease the number.

✦ Click inside the box (where the number is displayed). Use the Delete (Del) key to delete the number(s) already shown in the box; then type a new number.

From the keyboard, you first have to use the Tab or Shift+Tab keys to move the focus to the spin box control. Then use the ↑ arrow to increase the number shown or ↓ to decrease it.

Using Drop-Down Lists

A drop-down list is sort of like a menu, where initially only the currently selected option is visible. There are a couple of examples on the Customize Start Menu dialog box. When you first look at a drop-down list option, you see only the currently selected option, as in the top drop option in Figure 2-10. To choose a different option, click the drop-down button at the right side of the control, as in the bottom list on Figure 2-10. You can then click the option you want to select.

Figure 2-10: A drop-down list control closed (top right) and open (bottom right)

 When a drop-down list has the focus, you can spin the mouse wheel to select an option from the drop-down menu without actually opening the drop-down menu. This can be a handy way to select an option. But it can be a real "gotcha" if you do it by accident and don't realize your mistake. To avoid the mistake, it's a good idea to move the focus away from a drop-down list right after making your selection. Just click outside the drop-down list, or press Tab or Shift+Tab to move to the previous or next control.

To operate a drop-down list from the keyboard, first use Tab or Shift+Tab to move the focus to the control. When the control has the focus, you have several options. You can type the first letter or letters of the selection you want to jump to that part of the drop-down menu. Or you can use the ↑, ↓ keys to scroll through options. Or you can press Alt+↓ to open the drop-down list, then use the ↓ and ↑ keys to move up and down the list. To select an option from the list, highlight it and press the Enter key.

Using List Boxes

A list box is a list of options to choose from, like a drop-down list. However, the list is in plain view, not hidden. If you're following along on your own computer and want to see an example of a list box from the open Taskbar and Start Menu Properties dialog box, follow these steps:

1. In the Taskbar and Start Menu Properties dialog box, click the Start Menu tab.

2. Make sure Start menu is selected (not the Classic Start menu); then click the Customize... button just to its right. A new dialog box titled Customize Start Menu opens.

The box at the top of the Customize Start Menu dialog box that contains options such as Computer, Connect To, and Control panel (see Figure 2-11) is an example of a list box control (although not all list boxes contain option buttons and check boxes).

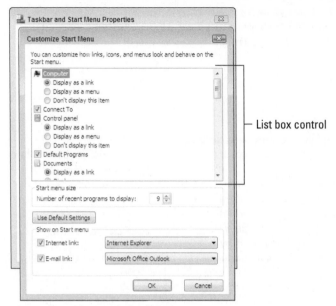

List box control

Figure 2-11: A sample list box

To operate a list box control using your mouse, first click the control to give it the focus. Then you can move through options using the scroll bar at the right side of the control. To select an item from the list, just click it so it's highlighted. If the option has a check box or option button associated with it, you can work that control in the usual manner as well — by clicking it.

To work a list box from the keyboard, press Tab or Shift+Tab as necessary to move the focus to the list box control. Then you can use the following navigation keys to move around within the list:

✦ ↓: Go to the next item in the list.

✦ ↑: Go to the previous item in the list.

✦ **Page Down (PgDn):** Move down a page in the list.

✦ **Page Up (PgUp):** Move up a page in the list.

✦ **Home:** Go to the top of the list.

✦ **End:** Go to the end of the list.

The term *page* refers to the total number of items visible at the moment. For example, suppose the list contains 30 options, but only 6 are visible at a time. You're currently viewing the first six items. Each time you pressed Page Down (PgDn) in that control, you'd see the next six items in the list, until you got to the bottom of the list.

The idea is to move the highlighter to the option in the list that you want to choose. If the option you've highlighted does not have a check box or option button associated with it, just press the Enter key to select the currently highlighted option from the list. Otherwise, use the spacebar to clear or select the check box or option button.

Using Sliders

A slider control enables you to choose a setting along a range of values. A slider is basically a bar along which you can place a little button. Figure 2-12 shows some examples of sliders, with each one's sliding box indicated by an arrow. Not all sliders are exactly the same. But the way you use them is similar to the way you use a scroll bar. Here are the ways to use a slider control:

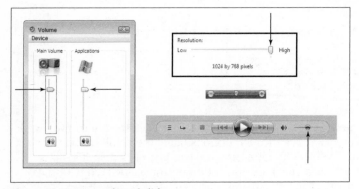

Figure 2-12: Examples of sliders

✦ Drag the slider box along the bar (that is, rest the mouse pointer on the box; hold down the left mouse button while moving the mouse left or right). When the box is where you want the setting, release the mouse button.

✦ Click anywhere along the bar to move the box to, or toward, that part of the bar.

✦ If there are buttons at the ends of the bar, click to do whatever the button offers. (Point to the button to see its name.)

To work a slider control from the keyboard, press Tab or Shift+Tab as necessary to move the focus to the slider control. Then you can use the following navigation keys to adjust the control:

✦ ↓ or →: Go to the next item in the list.

✦ ↑ or ←: Go to the previous item in the list.

✦ **Page Down (PgDn):** Move the slider down or to the right.

✦ **Page Up (PgUp):** Move the slider up or to the left.

✦ **Home:** Go to the top or to the far left.

✦ **End:** Go to the end or to the far right.

Getting Help in Dialog Boxes

 The labels that appear next to controls in a dialog box are brief and usually not very explanatory. In some dialog boxes, you can get more information. To get this added help, you can do one of two things. If the dialog box has a Help button in the upper-right corner, you can click it. Alternatively, you can press the F1 button.

A new window will open containing information about the dialog box, as in the example shown in Figure 2-13.

> **Tip**
>
> As you'll learn in Chapter 3, there are many ways to get help while you work in Windows.

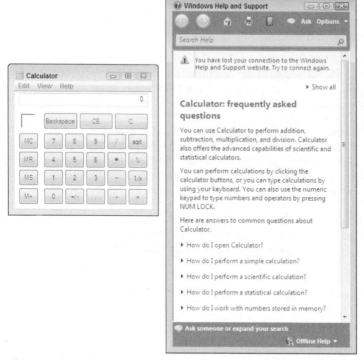

Figure 2-13: Getting basic help

Using Buttons

Buttons are the easiest controls of all to work, because you just have to click them. Each button has a label that describes what the button does, as in the examples shown in Figure 2-14. Some buttons can contain the additional functionality of being combined with a list box. An example of such a button is on the right side of Figure 2-14.

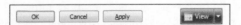

Figure 2-14: Examples of buttons — Standard buttons on the left; a list button in the middle; and a combo-list button on the right.

A dialog box can contain any number of buttons. Some buttons you're likely to see often, and their purposes, are summarized here:

✦ **OK:** Activates all options you choose in the dialog box and then closes the dialog box.

✦ **Apply:** Activates all options you choose in the dialog box but does not close the dialog box. This button is disabled when there are no new selections in the dialog box to apply.

✦ **Cancel:** Closes the dialog box without applying current selections. Any settings you changed since opening the dialog box (or since the last time you clicked the Apply button, whichever is most recent) will be cancelled out.

Caution Clicking the Close (X) button in the upper-right corner of a dialog box is not the same as clicking its OK button. Like clicking the Cancel button, clicking the Close button closes the dialog box without activating any selections you made in the dialog box.

✦ **Restore Default:** This button, when available, resets all options in the dialog box back to the original factory settings — the settings that were in place when Windows Vista was first installed on your computer.

If you're following along on your own computer, you can click the OK button in the open Customize Start Menu dialog box now to close it. Click the OK button in the Taskbar and Start Menu Properties dialog box to close it as well.

In Figure 2-14, the View button on the right is a special case that you will see a lot in Windows Vista. This is actually a button combined with a list box. Although the area labeled View is a button, the arrow to the right side of the button is a list box containing a list of options that are related to the button. Clicking the button will perform the button's action. Clicking the down arrow will list options from which you can choose one.

What's the Default?

In any computer documentation you read, you're likely to come across the term *default* or *default setting*. They both refer to a setting—a choice that's already been made for you. For example, as you explore dialog boxes, you'll notice that all of the controls in all the dialog boxes already have some setting, even if your computer is brand new. Those settings are the defaults.

Typing Text and Passwords

A text box is a control into which you type text. Text box controls can appear anywhere, not just in dialog boxes. Figure 2-15 shows some examples of text boxes.

Figure 2-15: Examples of text boxes

A text box appears whenever you need to type text. But you can type in only one text box at a time. The cursor (a blinking vertical line) shows where the next text you type will appear. So before you type in a text box, make sure the cursor is on the box in which you want to type. To move the cursor into a text box, just click the text box. Or, if you're using the keyboard, press Tab or Shift+Tab as necessary to move the cursor to the text box.

Once the cursor is in the text box, just type normally. If you make a mistake, you can use the Backspace key to erase characters to the left of the cursor. When you're done typing in the text box, press Enter. Or, if there's a Go button next to the text box, you can just click that text box instead.

 Tip　You can also paste text from the clipboard into a text box, which can save a lot of typing. See Chapter 8 for more information.

Changing Text in a Text Box

You can use the navigation keys to move the cursor through any text that's already typed into a text box. The basic keys you'll use are:

✦ **Home:** Move the cursor to the beginning of the text.

✦ **End:** Move the cursor to the end of the text.

✦ **→:** Move the cursor to the next character.

✦ **←:** Move the cursor to the previous character.

You can also click the mouse wherever you want to place the cursor.

 Caution You can't use the → key to move the cursor past the last character of existing text. If you need to insert a blank space at the end of a line, press the spacebar, not the → key.

To insert text at the cursor position, just type the new text. For example, let's say the vertical bar that follows represents the cursor, which I moved into position using the mouse or the → and ← keys:

```
Ala|impson
```

Suppose I now type **n S** (that is, a lowercase n, a blank space, and an uppercase S). That text will be inserted at the cursor position as follows:

```
Alan Simpson
```

You can also delete text near the cursor using the following keys:

✦ **Backspace:** Delete the character to the left of the cursor.

✦ **Delete (Del):** Delete the character to the right of the cursor.

Changing Chunks of Text

It's not necessary to change text one character at a time. You can work with chunks of selected text. The first step to using this technique is being able to distinguish selected text from regular unselected text. That's usually pretty easy because any text that's selected will be highlighted, usually as white letters against a blue background. Figure 2-16 shows some examples of regular text and selected text.

Figure 2-16: Examples of unselected and selected text

In some cases, the text in a text box will be selected automatically as soon as you move the cursor into the box. In most cases, it won't be. But it really doesn't matter; you can select, or unselect, text in a text box at any time using these techniques:

✦ *mouse*: Drag the mouse pointer through the text you want to select.

✦ **Shift+** → : Select character to right of cursor.

✦ **Shift+←:** Select character to left of cursor.

✦ **Shift+End:** Select text from cursor to end of line.

✦ **Shift+Home:** Select text from cursor to start of line.

✦ **Home:** Unselect selected text; move cursor to start of line.

✦ **End:** Unselect selected text; move cursor to end of line.

Let's look at an example of how you might use text editing to save some typing. Suppose you want to visit a web site at www.amazon.com and need to type that address into the address bar of your web browser. Currently, the address bar contains the address www.microsoft.com as at the top of Figure 2-17.

You really need to change only *microsoft* to *amazon* here, because the rest of the text is the same in both addresses. So, rather than retyping the whole thing or using the Backspace key, you can just drag the mouse pointer through the word *microsoft*, because that's the only part you need to change, as in the middle of Figure 2-10. When text is selected, any new text you type is instantly replaced by whatever you type. So, if you just type **amazon**, the entire new address will be typed as at the bottom of Figure 2-17.

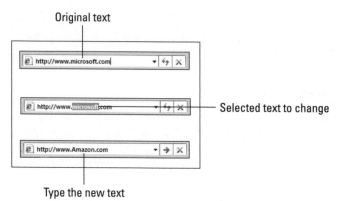

Figure 2-17: Changing just a chunk of text

The techniques described here are just some of Windows' standard text editing techniques. You'll learn more about those techniques in the section "Selecting Text to Change," in Chapter 7.

Combo Boxes and AutoComplete

Some text boxes are actually combo boxes, meaning they're both text boxes and drop-down menus. The drop-down menu usually contains a history of items you've typed into the text box in the past. As soon as you start typing in the text box, the menu drops down, showing the first item that matches the letter (or letters) you typed into the text box, as in the example shown in Figure 2-18.

Type first character(s) into text box   To choose an item, click on it

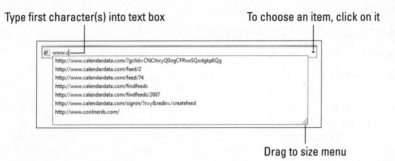

Drag to size menu

Figure 2-18: The sample menu that appears when typing in an AutoComplete text box

If you see, in the menu, the text you were intending to type, you can just click that text in the drop-down menu. That way, you don't have to type the whole thing. If the drop-down menu has a little sizing handle in its lower-right corner, you can drag that handle to resize the menu to your liking. If it has a scroll bar along its right edge, you can use that to scroll through other options on the menu.

Tip

To delete an item from the AutoComplete drop-down menu, point to it and press the Delete (Del) key on your keyboard.

Typing Passwords

Some text boxes are for typing passwords. When you type a password into a text box, you don't see the actual characters you've typed. Instead, each character is represented by a black circle or an asterisk. The purpose of the dots or asterisks is to prevent shoulder surfing, where someone learns your password just by looking over your shoulder.

Passwords are case-sensitive, meaning that uppercase and lowercase letters are not considered to be the same. For example, if your password is *meatball*, you must type it exactly that way each time it's required. If you type **Meatball** or **MEATBALL** or **MeatBall** or anything else, it won't work. Your best bet is to use only lowercase letters in any password you create, so you don't have to memorize the case of each letter in your password.

Other than the little dots and the case-sensitivity, typing a password is no different from typing anything else. You can even use the techniques described to make changes and corrections in a password text box. When all you can see is little dots rather than the characters to type, however, it's pretty tough to edit. If you type your password wrong, you might as well just type it again from scratch.

Summary

In this chapter, we've looked at fundamental, universal skills that you probably use each time you sit at your computer. Let's review the major points we've covered:

✦ Most items on your screen are objects, each with its own unique set of properties (characteristics).

✦ Hardware components such as your mouse and keyboard can be considered objects with properties as well.

✦ To tailor an object to your needs, adjust that object's properties via its Properties dialog box.

✦ There are hundreds of objects and thousands of properties. But you work all these things through a standard set of controls consisting of things such as buttons, check boxes, and so forth.

✦ On the screen, you can often take a shortcut to an object's properties just by right-clicking the object and choosing Properties.

✦ Selections you make in a dialog box are not actually applied to the object until you click the OK or Apply button.

✦ If you open a dialog box, and then change your mind about any settings you've changed, click the Cancel button to close the dialog box without implementing your changes.

Getting Help When You Need It

This book isn't your only resource for getting help when you need it. You can get a ton of information right on your screen through Windows Vista Help and Support. If you have an Internet connection already and know how to use your web browser, you can get support online as well. In this chapter, we'll take a look at the various resources available to you for getting the information you need, when you need it.

Using Help and Support

To get to that information, click the Start button and choose Help and Support from the right side of the Start menu. Optionally, you can press the Help key (F1). However, if you're using a program other than Windows at the moment, pressing F1 is more likely to open the help for that program rather than the help for Windows Vista.

Tip   If you have a Windows keyboard, pressing ⊞+F1 will always bring up the Windows Vista Help and Support dialog box.

Before we show you what the Help and Support dialog box looks like, a note of warning: Computer manufacturer's who sell machines with Vista preinstalled are allowed to change the Help and Support area to promote their own products. This means that when you open the Help and Support window, it might not look like the example you're about to see. (That's OK; it still works. It just looks different.) If you installed Windows Vista yourself, or your computer manufacturer didn't change anything, Help and Support will look something like the example shown in Figure 3-1.

For general information, you can click any text in the window. For example, if you click Windows Basics under Find an *answer*, you'll be taken to a new page that focuses on Windows basic skills. The new page, like most pages in Help and Support, lists a number of subjects and topics that enable you to dig deeper. Figure 3-2 shows what you might see when you click the Windows Basics link.

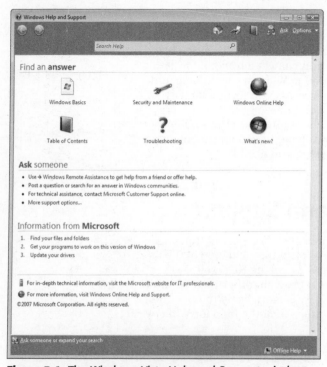

Figure 3-1: The Windows Vista Help and Support window

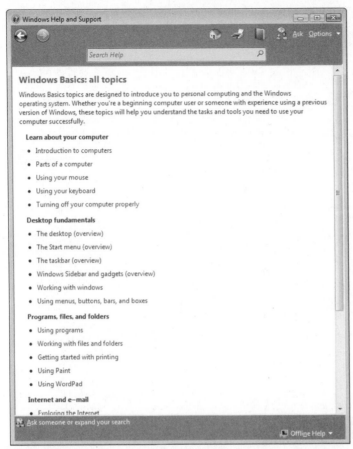

Figure 3-2: Results of choosing Windows Basics from the Help and Support window.

Another area within the main Help and Support page that you can dig into is the Contents area. It lists topics and subjects that can be drilled into for more details. Figure 3-3 shows the initial page within the Table of Contents.

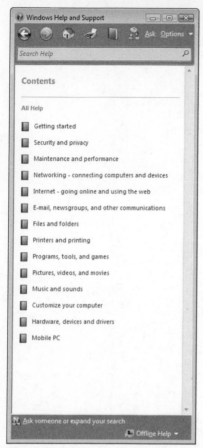

Figure 3-3: The Help and Support
Table of Contents

As you click topics and subject headings, you can move deeper into the help system and get to more specific information. Clicking a topic presents detailed help information on the topic. Clicking a subject heading presents a new list of subtopics and subjects. Figure 3-4 shows the Help and Support window after selecting *Contents* and then selecting *Files and folders* (see Figure 3-4).

Note   Overall, this is the same information you can get to from the other links on the Help and Support page.

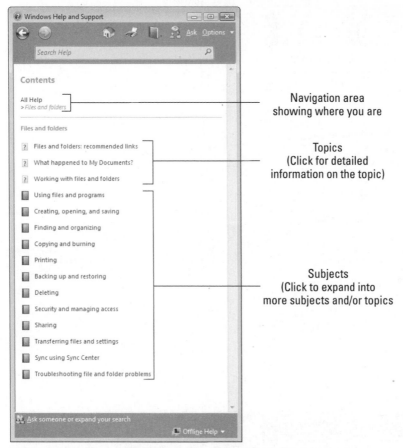

Figure 3-4: Topics and Subject areas within Help and Support

Searching for Specific Information

You can learn a lot just by clicking help topics and exploring what's available. But more often than not, you'll probably want to search help for specific information on a specific topic. That's where the Search box comes in. You can type any word or phrase into the Search box and click the magnifying glass find button or press Enter to search for that word or phrase. After a brief delay your Search Results will be displayed. If there are a lot of results, then the ones Windows Vista considers the best will be displayed. If there are too many results, then they may be broken into multiple pages. For example, Figure 3-5 shows the results of typing folder as the text to search for.

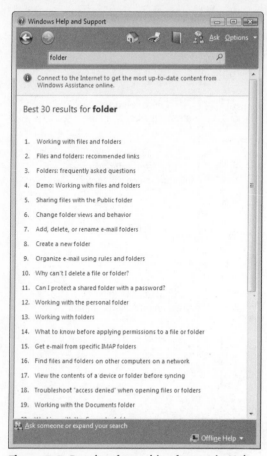

Figure 3-5: Results of searching for text in Help and Support

The search will list items it believes matches what you entered. The items most likely to match what you are searching for will be listed first. From the list, you'll be able to click any item and get the help topic that relates to it. For example, if you click Create a new folder (item number 8 in Figure 3-5), the Help and Support window will show instructions on how to create a folder, as shown in Figure 3-6.

Tip
You can move and size the Help and Support window as you would any other program window. See the section "Arranging Open Program Windows" in Chapter 4 for more information.

Figure 3-6: Results of clicking Create a new folder

Getting Around in Help and Support

The Help and Support window contains a number of icons and options that can help you navigate and find what you are looking for. You can see the location of each of these in Figure 3-7. Knowing what each does can help you get the most out of Help and Support.

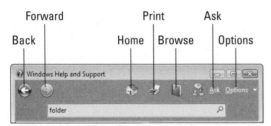

Figure 3-7: The Help and Support toolbar

Here's what each button does:

✦ **Back:** After you've navigated to another page in Help, the Back button will be enabled. Click it to return to the page you were viewing prior to the current page.

✦ **Forward:** After you click the Back button, the Forward button becomes enabled. Click it to return to the page you just backed up from.

✦ **Home:** Click this button to return to the Help and Support home page (the page that appears when you first open Help and Support).

✦ **Print:** Use this button to print the current help topic.

✦ **Browse Help:** Use this button to go the Help and Support Table of Contents. You'll go the topic within the table of contents closest to the topic you are viewing.

✦ **Ask:** Use this button to see other options for getting help.

✦ **Options:** Repeats some of the preceding options and provides a few options changing the look and feel of the Help and Support Center.

Troubleshooting

Help and Support also provides a list of troubleshooting items that can help you solve specific problems. If your computer offers the standard Help and Support options, you can get to the troubleshooting items by selecting Troubleshooting on the Help and Support home page. (If you're on some other page, just click the Home button on the toolbar.)

When you click Troubleshooting, you'll be taken to a set of instructions for diagnosing and solving a problem. Just read and follow the instructions that appear on the screen. The troubleshooting items are categorized into common areas where you might have trouble. When you click an item, just like with the regular help and support items, you will drill down into more specific information. The final results of the troubleshooting items, however, will be suggestions for specific tasks to do to try to solve an issue.

Getting Guided Help

Help and Support also includes Guided Help. Guided help is interactive help features that can either be fully automated or you can be guided step-by-step. A blue compass indicates guided help items.

Guided help shows you what you need to do including buttons to click or places to navigate. This makes it extremely simple to accomplish a task or learn how to do something.

You can find a number of guided help items by going to Help and Support. Remember, you get to Help and Support by clicking on the Start button and then selecting Help and Support on the right side. When in Help and Support you should find an option titled Guided Help that lists the guides within Window Vista. You can also see guided help items in other areas of Help and Support. They are identified by the words *guided help* at the end of a help topic as shown in Figure 3-8.

When you select a guided help task, a window will be displayed similar to the one in Figure 3-9.

As you can see, you are being asked to select either *Do it automatically* or *Show me step-by-step as shown in Figure 3-9* If you select Do it automatically, you will watch as the guided help shows you how to accomplish the task from beginning to end. If you choose step-by-step, then guided help will still show you how to accomplish the task; however, you will be prompted each step of the way. Either way, you'll be guided through the task and shown exactly how to accomplish it.

Figure 3-8: A list of help items including some that are Guided Help

Figure 3-9: Using a Guided Help item

Windows Vista Maintenance Help

On the Help and Support home page, you will also find a maintenance option. Clicking the Security and Maintenance link takes you to the Windows Vista Safety Checklist similar to what is shown in Figure 3-10. If you are using a version of Windows other than Home Premium, then the display will be slightly different.

The security and maintenance items will help you to take advantage of making sure your computer is as secure as possible. Many improvements were made in Windows Vista to make it more secure for you. The options in this window provide you with help on many of the security items. These items range from parental control to updating your system with Windows Update to using Windows Defender to protect against viruses. Most of these items are important enough that they are covered throughout the rest of this book.

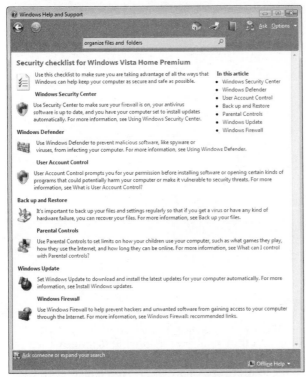

Figure 3-10: The Help and Support Security and Maintenance window for Vista Home Premium edition

Asking for Help

On the toolbar in the Help and Support window there is an icon called Ask. Clicking this icon is the same as clicking the More Support Options link within the Ask someone section of the Help and Support home page. Figure 3-11 shows the list of other types of help you can get from this selection.

If you don't find the help you need within the other areas of Help and Support, then these options may be the answer for you. You will find information for contacting Microsoft customer support directly—either online or by phone. Additionally, there are options you can click for help online.

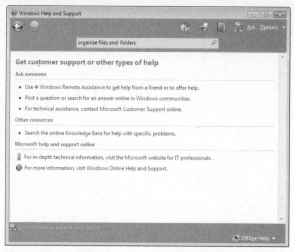

Figure 3-11: The help you get with Asking

Getting Help Online

Windows Help and Support should always be your first resource for getting help with Windows Vista. But if you can't find what you're looking for there, then getting online help is a great option. To do this, you'll need an Internet connection (see Chapter 9) and a web browser (see Chapter 10). You'll also need to know how to use your web browser. Many of you probably already know how to browse the World Wide Web, so we'll just go ahead and explain how to use Microsoft web site now. If you're not an Internet user yet, you can always return to this section after you've connected your computer to the Internet.

The Ask area of Help and Support includes a number of options for online help. The Microsoft Customer Support option will take you to a web site where you can find additional customer support help from Microsoft.

You will also find a link in the Ask area to the Windows communities. This is a place on the World Wide Web where you can post a specific question and other people can then offer suggestions.

The final place worth noting for online help is the Windows Online Help area that is also listed in the Ask window. This page is similar to the Help and Support area within Windows Vista; however, it may be more up-to-date. You'll find support for the programs and features of Windows Vista at this web site.

Cross-Reference You'll learn more about using the World Wide Web and Internet in Part 3 of this book.

Help and Support links to online help. If your computer is not hooked up to the Internet, then you can turn off the online help by first going to the Help and Support page. Then select Options from the taskbar, followed by Settings. You can turn off online help in the dialog window that will then be presented (see Figure 3-12).

Figure 3-12: Turning on or off online help

Closing Help and Support

When you've finished using Help and Support, you can close it as you would any other program window: by clicking the Close button in its upper-right corner. The window will disappear (as will its taskbar button). You can reopen it at any time by clicking the Start button and choosing Help and Support.

Getting Help with Your Computer

If you're already online and using the Web, your computer manufacturer's web site is also another valuable resource for you to get to know. We can't tell you exactly where that site is, because we don't know who manufactured your computer. But you can usually find a link to it somewhere in Help and Support or on the Start menu. Or, if your computer manufacturer happens to be one of those listed below, you can use the address shown next to the manufacturer name:

- ✦ **Acer Computers:** http://support.acer.com
- ✦ **Dell Computers:** http://support.dell.com
- ✦ **eMachines:** www.emachines.com/support
- ✦ **Gateway Computers:** http://support.gateway.com/support
- ✦ **Hewlett-Packard (and Compaq):** http://support.hp.com
- ✦ **IBM/Lenovo:** www-307.ibm.com/pc/support/
- ✦ **Sony Vaio:** www.vaio.net
- ✦ **Systemax:** http://support.Systemax.com
- ✦ **Toshiba:** http://pcsupport.toshiba.com/

If all else fails, you can always check the printed documentation that came with your computer. Or take a wild guess, using the address `www.manufacturerName .com` (where manufacturerName is your computer manufacturer's company name) as a web site address. The guess might not work. But it's worth a try.

Other Sources of Help

Besides the sources of help we've just discussed, there are others that you've already seen in this book and will see elsewhere. Some sources of help just pop up on the screen as screen tips. But sometimes that's all you need. Here's a quick summary of your other sources of help:

✦ Often, just pointing to an item provides enough information to get you going, as in the examples shown in Figure 3-13.

✦ Right-clicking an item displays a shortcut of things you can do with that item, which is often helpful in itself. The Properties option on that menu (if available) opens the Properties dialog box for that item, which in turn provides more information and more options.

✦ In a dialog box that has a ? button, you can click that button, then click any option with which you need help.

✦ In a program, you can choose Help from that program's menu bar to view help options for that particular program.

✦ Pressing the Help key (F1) usually brings up help that's relevant to whatever you're doing at the moment.

Even more ways of getting help will be pointed out as you progress through the book. But be aware that there's a lot of information available to you every time you sit down at the computer. You simply need to know what you're look- ing for and where to look for it.

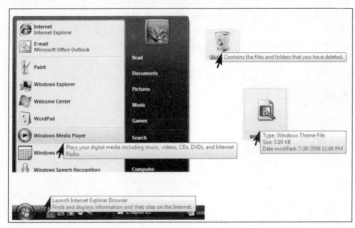

Figure 3-13: Just pointing to an item often shows brief, descriptive text.

Summary

When you're sitting in front of your computer staring at the screen, wondering "now what do I do?" or trying to figure out what some message means, you're not as helpless as you might think. You can get information at any time through Windows Help and Support, from the Microsoft web site, and plenty of other places. Here's a quick review of the main topics in this chapter.

✦ To open the Help and Support window, click the Start button and choose Help and Support, or press the Help key (F1).

✦ If you have trouble finding something within Help and Support, then use the search feature to find it.

✦ For solving issues with your computer (troubleshooting), go to the Troubleshooting area of Help and Support.

✦ If all else fails, use the links within the Ask section of Help and Support to get help online.

✦ Your computer manufacturer probably offers support through the company's web site. Check the documentation that came with your computer for more information.

✦ The Help key (F1), pointing to items, and right-clicking items are all handy methods of getting instant help, although the help is usually just brief text.

Programs, Documents, and Folders

✦   ✦   ✦   ✦

In some ways, a computer is like a stereo or VCR. A stereo plays music; a VCR plays movies; and a computer plays *programs*. Just as thousands of CDs and movies are available for your stereo and VCR, you can *run* (not play) thousands of programs on your computer. There are programs for e-mail, programs for photos, programs to make movies, programs to manage your bank account, programs for all kinds of things. To use them, you have to know where they are and how to work them.

A lot of programs enable you to create and manage *documents*—things such as letters, reports, pictures, songs, and movies. Like the documents printed on paper in your filing cabinet, all your computer documents are in *folders*. In a way, your computer is just a filing cabinet with muscle. But we're getting ahead of ourselves. It's no surprise that Part II is all about using programs and working with documents.

Running Programs

The reason we buy a CD player is to listen to music recorded on CDs. The reason we often buy a DVD player is to watch movies recorded on DVDs. The main reason we buy a computer is to run programs. Thousands of programs are available for Windows — for example, programs for sending and receiving e-mail, browsing the Web, typing documents, touching up photos, producing your own movies, talking toll-free to someone anywhere in the world, and so on.

If you can think of something a computer might be able to help with, there's probably at least one program on the market to help you do that job. Not all programs are exactly alike, so there's no way to come up with a single book to describe them all. But some general skills and concepts do apply to most programs. Those skills and concepts are the main topics of this chapter.

Starting Programs

A computer program is a set of instructions that tells the computer how to behave. Your computer already has lots of programs installed on it. We know this because you have Windows Vista, which is a program itself. Windows Vista comes with lots of free programs for doing some of the things presented as examples at the start of this chapter.

All of the programs currently installed on your computer are generally accessible from the Start menu. When you first click the Start button, the left column of the Start menu displays a list of programs you've used frequently in the past. Or, if your computer is brand new, there are a few sample programs listed down the left side of the Start menu. To view your entire collection of installed programs, click All Programs in the Start menu. That opens up the All Programs menu.

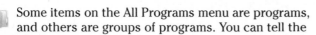 Some items on the All Programs menu are programs, and others are groups of programs. You can tell the

groups by their similar icons. When you click a program group, it expands to show the programs in that group, and perhaps more groups. For example, when you click the Start button, choose All Programs, and choose Accessories, you end up with something that looks like Figure 4-1. We say "something like" because not everybody has exactly the same programs on his or her computer — just as not everybody who owns a CD player owns exactly the same CDs.

 Tip If your computer is brand new, you might consider just looking around in all the various program groups available to you. You'll probably discover that there are a lot more programs on your computer than you realized!

To start a program from the All Programs menu, you just click its name or icon on the menu. Optionally, if you see an icon for the program on the Windows desktop or in the Quick Launch toolbar, you can click (or double-click) that icon to start the program. Regardless of how you start a program, it will most likely be in its own window on your desktop (more on that in a moment).

You'll see many examples of starting and using programs throughout this book. To make it easy for you to follow the sequence of menu options that you need to choose to launch a particular program, we'll use an abbreviated format like this:

Click the Start button and choose All Programs ⇨ Accessories ⇨ Calculator.

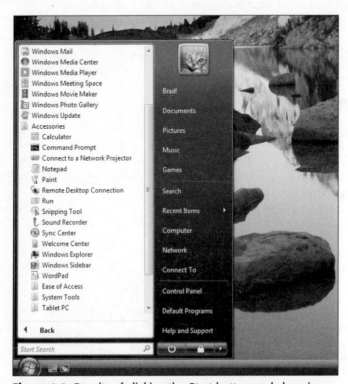

Figure 4-1: Results of clicking the Start button and choosing All Programs ⇨ Accessories

Think of the ⇨ symbol as meaning *then click*. For example, that sample instruction is a short way of saying "Click the Start button; then click All Programs; then click Accessories on the All Programs menu; then click Calculator in the Accessories menu."

Finding a Lost Program

If you know that you have a program but you can't immediately find it on the All Programs menu or the groups within the menu, then don't fret. Windows Vista includes Quick Search right on the Start menu. Within this search box, you can enter part of a program's name, and Windows Vista will search for programs and files.

As an example, if you weren't sure where the Calculator program was, you could start typing *calculator*. Figure 4-2 shows the search box with just *ca* entered. As you can see, Windows Vista has already narrowed down the choices to just a few, including the Calculator program. What you see as a result of searching on the letters ca on your computer may differ. If there are still too many items showing, type a few more letters, and that should help narrow the search

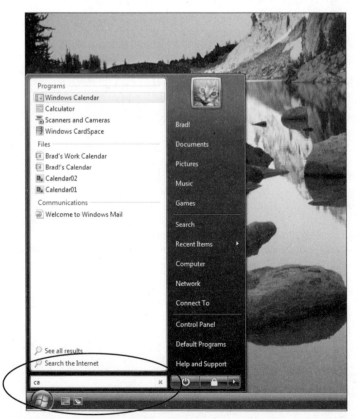

Figure 4-2: Results of entering ca into the Start menu's search option

Taking Control of Program Windows

In the olden days of personal computing (the 1970s and 1980s), people used an operating system called DOS. With that operating system, you could run only one program at a time. When you started a program, it filled the entire screen. If you wanted to use some other program, even if just for a moment (like to check your e-mail), you had to save your work, close the program you were in, run the other program, do whatever you needed there, close that program, and reopen the first program. Not a very convenient way to do things.

Microsoft Windows changed all of that by allowing you to open as many programs as you want. Rather than taking over the entire screen, each program you start opens in its own *program window* (or just *window*, for short), sort of like one sheet of paper on a regular desktop.

Learning how to control all those open windows on your desktop is an important part of learning to use your computer. After all, if you can't control what's visible on your screen, you can't really get much done with a computer. So let's take a look at the many ways in which you can manage open program windows on your Windows desktop.

If you want to follow along in this chapter, and try things out on your own computer, you'll need to open a few programs to use as examples. Follow these steps now:

1. Click the Start button and choose All Programs ➪ Accessories ➪ Paint.

2. Click the Start button and choose All Programs ➪ Accessories ➪ WordPad.

3. Click the Start button and choose All Programs ➪ Accessories ➪ Calculator.

 Note   If you can't complete a preceding step because you're missing a program, don't fret. You can open Photo Gallery (Start ➪ All Programs ➪ Photo Gallery) or Movie Maker (Start ➪ All Programs ➪ Windows Movie Maker) to use a sample program instead.

After you've completed these steps, you'll have three open program windows on your desktop. Don't worry about the purpose of each program or how each is arranged on the screen. You'll just be using those programs as examples for learning skills that apply to all program windows.

Tools Found in Most Program Windows

If you look at all the open program windows on your computer screen, you'll notice they have certain things in common: a title bar at the top and a menu bar beneath that (see Figure 4-3). Some programs have a toolbar beneath the menu bar. Some programs have a status bar along the bottom of their windows. Each open window will also have its own button in the taskbar. The icon and name of the button match the icon and name in the title bar of the program that the button represents.

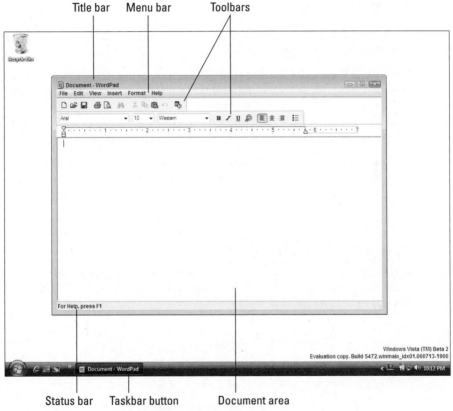

Figure 4-3: Components of most program windows

The items you see in the program are not there solely for decoration. In general, Windows never puts anything on your screen purely for decoration. Each item in the program window has a specific role:

✦ **Title bar:** Displays the program's icon and name and provides tools for moving and sizing the window. For example, dragging a program's title bar moves the window.

✦ **Menu bar:** Provides access to the tools and features of the program contained within that window. Clicking an option on the menu bar displays a menu.

✦ **Toolbar:** Provides one-click access to the program's most commonly used features. This enables you to get at the feature without having to use the menu bar. Not all programs offer toolbars. Additionally, not all tool bars are necessarily shown at the same time.

✦ **Document area:** If the program enables you to work with documents (text, pictures, or video), the currently open document will appear here.

✦ **Status bar:** The exact role played by the status bar varies from one program to the next. Many programs don't have a status.

✦ **Taskbar button:** A program window's taskbar button enables you to show or hide the window on the desktop by left clicking on it. You can right-click a program's taskbar button for other options related to that program.

About the Active Window

Whenever you have two or more programs open on your Windows desktop, only one can be the *active window*. There are three ways you can tell which window is active at the moment:

✦ The active window is almost always at the top of the stack. No other program window will cover or obscure the active window.

✦ The active window's title bar is colored more brightly than the other (inactive) windows' title bars.

✦ The active window's taskbar button is pushed in.

For example, in Figure 4-4, the Calculator is in the active window. You can tell because no other program window covers the Calculator (it's on the top of the stack), the Calculator title bar is darker than the title bars for Paint and WordPad, and the Calculator taskbar button looks pushed in.

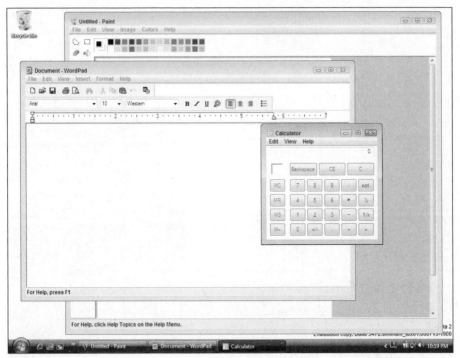

Figure 4-4: The Calculator window is in the active window.

If it's difficult to imagine how Calculator is on the top of the stack from Figure 4-4, imagine that there were a way to modify the desktop so that the windows appeared in a 3D space. And imagine that you could lift each program window off the desktop a little. If you are running the Windows Aero interface as described in Chapter 2, then you can actually cause this to happen by pressing and holding down the Windows key (⊞) and then pressing the Tab key. The result is a 3D image like the one in Figure 4-5 where you can see that the Calculator window is at the top of the stack, that the inactive windows are below that, and that the desktop (as always) is at the bottom or behind the windows.

If you press ⊞+Tab again, you'll change which window is at the top of the stack. Note that if you are running Windows Vista Home Basic edition, or if you don't have the graphics power in your computer to support the Aero interface, then pressing these keys will not give the 3D graphics. Rather, nothing will happen if you don't have the Aero interface.

Figure 4-5: The active window is always at the top of the stack.

Looking at Figure 4-5, if you were to click the Paint button in the taskbar, the Paint window would jump to the top of the stack, and Calculator and WordPad would each move down a level. Remember, the program at the top of the stack is in the active window.

So what difference does it make if a program is in the active window or an inactive window? There are a couple of unique things about the active window:

✦ Anything you type applies to the active window only.

✦ Hovering the mouse pointer over a button or other item to see its screen tip works only in the active window. Hovering over an item in an inactive window does nothing.

In other words, before you can really do anything with an open program, you need to make sure it's in the active window. That's easy to do, and you can use whichever of the following methods is most convenient at the moment:

✦ Click any visible portion of the program's inactive window to make it the active window.

✦ Click the inactive window's taskbar button.

✦ From the keyboard, hold down the Alt key and press the Tab key until the program's icon is selected and its name is visible, as in Figure 4-6; then release the Alt key.

✦ If you are using the Aero interface, then, as stated earlier, hold down the Windows (⊞) key and press the Tab key until the program's window is at the top of the 3D stack of windows.

Figure 4-6: Box for switching among open programs from the keyboard

It doesn't matter which method you use; the result will be the same—the program you specify will jump to the top of the stack on your screen and become the active window, ready for either mouse or keyboard input from you.

As a side note, if you are using the Windows Aero interface, then when you hover the mouse pointer over a taskbar button, you will get a small pop-up preview of what the window contains, even if it is not the active window. Figure 4-7 illustrates this pop-up.

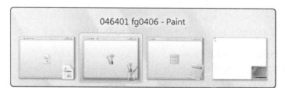

Figure 4-7: Taskbar button previews provided with Aero

Arranging Open Program Windows

Program windows don't have to be scattered and sized haphazardly around the desktop. You can tidy them up with just a couple of mouse clicks. But you have to *right-click the taskbar* first. Before you try, you should know that the phrase doesn't mean "right-click anywhere you feel like it along the bottom of the screen." It means "right-click some empty portion of the taskbar."

When the taskbar is full of buttons, there's not much empty space to right-click. But you can right-click the current time instead to achieve the same result, as illustrated in Figure 4-8. Anyway, after you've right-clicked an appropriate area of the taskbar, you'll see the shortcut menu shown in the same figure.

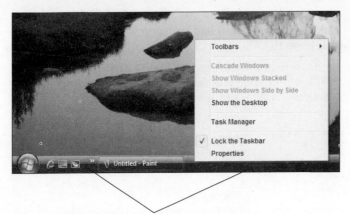

"Right-click the taskbar" means to right-click on an empty spot on the bar or on the current time

Figure 4-8: Where to right-click the taskbar, and the menu you'll see

To quickly arrange all the program windows currently open and visible on your desktop, choose (click) one of the following options in the shortcut menu:

✦ **Cascade Windows:** Neatly stacks the open program windows like sheets of paper, with each window's title bar visible.

✦ **Show Windows Stacked:** Arranges windows like tiles (no overlapping), with large windows stretched horizontally across the screen.

✦ **Show Windows Side by Side:** Arranges windows like tiles (no overlapping), with large windows stretched vertically on the screen.

The Paint and Calculator windows are both a little unusual in that you can size them freely. So if you really want to try these options on your own screen, you will do well to try some other open windows. Follow these steps:

1. Close Calculator by clicking its Close button or by right-clicking its taskbar button and choosing Close.

2. Close Paint, again by using its Close button or taskbar button and choosing Close.

3. Click the Start button and choose Documents.

4. Click the Start button and choose Control Panel.

Now you have three open windows on your desktop again, each with its own taskbar button. Figure 4-9 shows how those three windows arrange themselves when you choose the Cascade option or one of the Show Windows options.

Tip If you change your mind right after cascading or tiling windows, you can right-click the taskbar and choose the Undo Cascade or Undo Show option from the shortcut menu that appears. Or just press Ctrl+Z.

Cascading   Side by Side

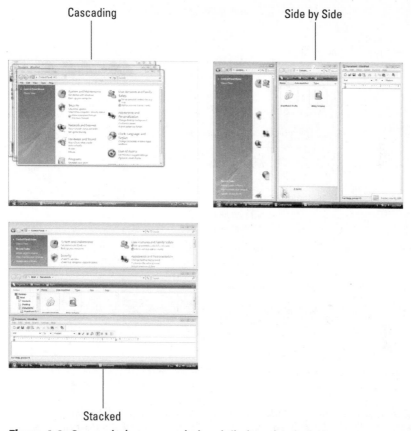

Stacked

Figure 4-9: Open windows cascaded and tiled on the desktop

Maximizing and Minimizing Program Windows

There are lots of ways to control the size of most program windows. You can quickly *maximize* a window so it fills the entire screen. You can also *minimize* a window so it's temporarily off the screen. And you can make most program windows any size between those two extremes.

Maximizing and minimizing open program windows is easy. You can use the buttons at the right edge of the title bar, the title bar itself, or the program window's taskbar button. You can also restore a maximized window to its previous size using the same tools (Figure 4-10). Here's what each button does:

Caution   Some windows prevent or limit how much you can change their size. For example, Calculator's Maximize button will be disabled because Calculator's window can't be resized. There are also limits on how small you can size Paint's window. If you want to try out these techniques, use something other than Calculator or Paint. For example, you could close Paint and WordPad. Then click the Start button and choose Documents; click the Start button again and choose Control Panel to bring the Documents window and Control Panel onto the screen.

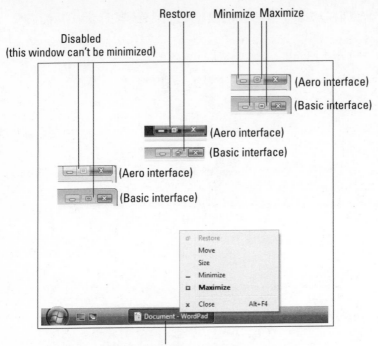

Figure 4-10: Minimize, Maximize, and Restore buttons and options

✦ **Minimize:** To *minimize* an open program window, click its Minimize button (shown at left), or click its taskbar button (if it's currently the active window). Or right-click its taskbar button and choose Minimize. The window disappears, leaving behind only its taskbar button. Click its taskbar button, or right-click its taskbar button and choose Restore to bring the window back to the desktop.

✦ **Maximize:** To maximize a program window, click its Maximize button, double-click its title bar, or right-click its taskbar button and choose Maximize. A maximized window fills the entire screen, covering the entire desktop and all inactive program window.

✦ **Restore:** To restore a maximized or minimized window to its previous size, click its Restore button, or right-click its taskbar button and choose Restore. The window goes to its previous size (which might be only slightly smaller than the maximized size). You can also restore a maximized window by double clicking on its title bar.

See the Desktop by Minimizing All Open Windows

If you ever want to get to your Windows desktop in a hurry, it's not necessary to minimize each open window individually. Instead you can:

✦ Right-click the taskbar and choose Show the Desktop.

✦ Or, press ⊞+D.

✦ Or, click the Show Desktop button in the Quick Launch toolbar, as shown in Figure 4-11.

Tip If you don't see a Quick Launch toolbar on your desktop, right-click the taskbar and choose Toolbars ⇨ Quick Launch from the shortcut menu that appears. If there's a Show/Hide button symbol (>>) on your Quick Launch toolbar, click that to see other buttons on that toolbar.

Figure 4-11: Showing the desktop

Every open program window is instantly minimized, leaving behind a clean desktop. As usual, you can restore any program window by clicking its taskbar button. Optionally, you can restore just the previously open windows, or all program windows, in one fell swoop. Here's how:

✦ Right-click the taskbar and choose Show Open Windows.

✦ Or click the Show Desktop button on the Quick Launch toolbar again.

✦ Or press ⊞+D again.

Sizing a Window

As mentioned, most program windows can be any size between minimized and maximized. Calculator's program window is one of a few that has a fixed size. So if you're going to try out this stuff on your own computer, please don't try it out on Calculator. Use any other open program window on your desktop instead.

There's another catch. You can't size a window while it's maximized or minimized; you can't see the borders around the window at either of those extreme sizes. So if the window is maximized or minimized, you have to restore it to its previous size first.

When the program window is at an in-between size, you'll notice it has a border all the way around it. In some windows, you'll see a little sizing handle—a nonskid surface of sorts—in the lower-right corner. When you can see those edges and corners, sizing the window is easy. Follow these steps:

1. Move the mouse to the any edge or corner of the window's border, or to its sizing handle if available, until the mouse pointer changes to a two-headed arrow, as in one of the examples shown in Figure 4-12.

Move mouse pointer to any
edge or corner, then drag

Figure 4-12: To size a window, drag any edge or corner.

2. Hold down the left mouse button while moving the mouse in the direction you want to stretch that corner or edge.

 Tip If you change your mind while sizing a window, press the Esc key before you release the mouse button to return the window to its original size.

3. When the window reaches the size you want, release the mouse button.

 Tip If you want to start with all windows of equal size, right-click the taskbar and choose Cascade Windows.

Moving a Program Window

You can easily move a window to any place on the screen. You simply have to drag the window by its title bar. However, you can't move a maximized window or minimized window. Here are the exact steps:

✦ If the window you want to move is currently maximized, shrink it a bit (click its Restore button or double-click its title bar).

✦ If the window you want to move is minimized, click its taskbar button to restore it to the screen.

1. Move the mouse pointer to the title bar of the window that you want to move, as in the example shown in Figure 4-13.

Move mouse pointer to title bar, then drag

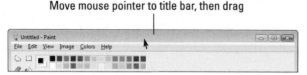

Figure 4-13: To move a window, drag its title bar.

2. Hold down the left mouse button while moving the mouse to drag the window to some new location. Then release the mouse button.

It's easy—at least once you realize that you can't move a maximized window, and don't even bother trying to move those!

Working the Menu Bars

As mentioned, many programs have a menu bar stretched across the top. Every program's menu bar is different, as each program's menu bar gives you control of that particular program (or the document you're working on in that program). But even though the *commands* (options) on the menus vary, the way you work them doesn't. You can use the techniques described in this section to work any program's menu bar.

Each option across the menu bar represents a hidden *pull-down menu*. To see the pull-down menu, just click an option in the bar. For example, if you click the Edit option in WordPad's menu bar, you'll see the Edit menu shown in Figure 4-14.

To choose an option from a pull-down menu, just click it. Some menu options will lead to a submenu of more options, which you can click in the same manner.

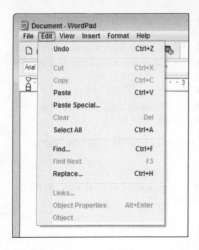

Figure 4-14: A sample pull-down menu

If you open a menu by accident and just want to back out without making a selection, just click some empty space outside the pull-down menu. Or press the Escape (Esc) key.

As with controls in a dialog box, some options on a pull-down menu may be disabled (dimmed) because they're not relevant at the moment. For example, in Figure 4-14, the options Cut, Copy, Paste, Paste Shortcut, Copy to Folder, and Move to Folder are currently disabled. Clicking those options would have no effect.

The little combination keystrokes (*key1+key2*) you see on the menu are *shortcut keys*. If your hands happen to be on the keyboard, you can skip reaching for the mouse and choosing an option from the menu by pressing the shortcut key instead. For example, pressing Ctrl+A at the keyboard is identical to choosing Select All from the Edit menu.

You can also work the menu bar from the keyboard without using shortcut keys. It's a little tricky, but here's how it works:

1. Look for an underlined letter in the menu option you want to choose. If you don't see an underlined letter, hold down the Alt key.

2. When you see the underlined letter, hold down the Alt key and type the underlined letter. For example, to open the File menu (where F is the underlined letter), press Alt+F.

3. When the pull-down menu is open, you can use the ↓, ↑, →, and ← arrow keys to move around through options. Or type whatever letter is underlined in the option you want to pick.

4. When the option you want to choose is highlighted, press the Enter key to select that option.

To close a menu without making a selection, press the Escape (Esc) key.

Watch Out for Collapsible Menus!

Some programs use *collapsible menus*, where initially the menu shows only frequently used commands (to keep the menu short) or shows only the number
of items that will fit on the screen. Keep an eye out for those, because you may
not be seeing all the options available on the menu. When you see a little
show/hide button on the bottom or the right side of a menu or toolbar, as in
the example shown in Figure 4-15, click it to expand the menu. Then you'll see
all the commands. You can click the show/hide button a second time to collapse the menu to its smaller size.

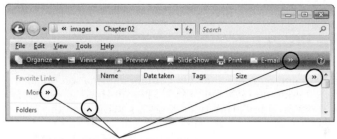

Additional menu and toolbar options

Figure 4-15: A collapsible pull-down menu

Using Toggles on Menus

Some options on menus act as *toggles*. A toggle is an option that can have
only one of two possible settings: On or Off. When a toggle option is set to On,
its option on the menu shows a check mark, as in the example at the left in
Figure 4-16. When the option is set to Off, the check mark isn't there, as on the
right side of the same figure.

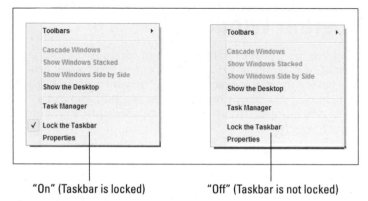

"On" (Taskbar is locked)   "Off" (Taskbar is not locked)

Figure 4-16: A toggle option on a menu

Clicking a toggle option in a menu switches the option to the opposite setting. For example, if you open a menu, see a check mark next to an item, and click that item, the option will be turned off and the check mark removed. (Had you just closed the menu without clicking the toggle option, the setting would remain on.)

The same is true when the setting is currently turned off. Clicking such an option would turn the setting on and place the check mark next to the item on the menu.

 Note While check marks are the standard for indicating an option is on, other symbols may be used as well.

Getting Help in Programs

Keep in mind that there are thousands of programs available for your computer. Windows Vista Help and Support does not contain information on all those programs. In fact, it contains only help that's relevant to Windows Vista. If you need help with some program other than Windows Vista, then the Windows Vista Help and Support won't do you much good. It's better to choose Help from that program's menu bar. Then choose whichever option seems to offer general help. That will usually be the first option on the menu, as in the examples shown in Figure 4-17.

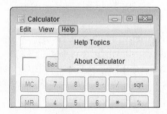

Figure 4-17: Choose Help from any program's menu bar for help with that program.

Closing Program Windows

Although it's often convenient to have multiple program windows on your desktop, you don't want to get too carried away. Having too many open program windows is like having too many sheets of paper on your real desk. It just becomes clutter. Also, having too many programs open at a time can cause your computer to slow down—a lot. So when you're finished with a program for the time being, you'll want to close it.

Just as there are umpteen ways to do everything else, there are lots of ways to close a program window:

✦ Click the Close button in the title bar of the program you want to close.

✦ Right-click the taskbar button of the program you want to close and choose Close.

✦ To close the active window, press Alt+F4.

Saving Your Work Before Closing

If you've left behind any unsaved work in the program you're closing, a dialog box like the one shown in Figure 4-18 will open. It means that you've created or changed a document without saving that work. You have three choices in the dialog box:

Figure 4-18: Warning that you've left unsaved work behind

✦ **Save:** If you choose Save, the Save As dialog box will open. Navigate to the folder in which you want to save the document, type a file name, and click the Save button.

> **Cross-Reference** You'll learn all the details of using the Save As dialog box in Chapter 6. If you need to save a file now, type a file name into the File name: text box and then click the Save button.

✦ **Don't Save:** The program will close without saving your work. There is no way to recover the unsaved work.

✦ **Cancel:** The program and document will remain open.

Closing Multiple Windows

For most programs, you're not limited to having just one copy on the desktop at a time. You can open multiple instances of most programs. If you've ever browsed the World Wide Web, you may have seen an example of multiple program windows in the form of pop-up ads. You get these irritating ads popping up, each in its separate Internet Explorer window.

Many (but not all) programs provide a handy way for you to close all open instances of a program, saving you from the irritating task of closing them one by one. The trick is simple — right-click the program's taskbar button and choose Close Group, as in Figure 4-19.

Figure 4-19: Closing all open instances of a program

Summary

This chapter has focused on fundamental, universal skills for managing open program windows on your desktop. Here's a quick recap of the important points:

✦ To start any program installed on your computer, click the Start button, and choose All Programs; then get to, and click, the name or icon of the program you want to start.

✦ Each program you start opens in its own program window on the desktop. Program windows on the Windows desktop can stack up, like sheets of paper on a real desktop.

✦ If you can't find a program, you can use the Quick Search option on the Start menu.

✦ When two or more programs are open, only one is in the active window. Only the active window accepts keyboard input and is always on the top of the stack.

✦ To make any program's window active, click any visible portion of that program window, click the program's taskbar button, or press Alt+Tab until the name of the program is highlighted. If you are using the Windows Aero interface, you can also press ⊞+Tab until the program is at the top of the stack.

✦ To quickly arrange open program windows into a neat stack, right-click the taskbar (or current time) and choose Cascade Windows.

✦ The menu bar across the top of a program window provides access to all the tools and features of that program.

✦ To get help in a program, choose Help from its menu bar, or press Help (F1) while the program is in the active window.

✦ To close an open program, click its Close button.

Navigating Your Folders

Windows Vista, all your programs, and all information in your computer right now are stored in *files* on your hard disk. Some files contain programs or components of Windows Vista. We can categorize all of those as *system files*, because they're the files that make up the entire software component of your computer system.

System files are practically invisible to you. This makes sense, since there are thousands of them, with all kinds of strange, unrecognizable names. The contents of system files would have no meaning to a human, because they all contain computer code — instructions that make the computer behave in certain ways.

There's no need, ever, for you to open, delete, rename, change, or even see any of the system files. Windows Vista takes care of all the system files automatically, behind the scenes, and it's best if you just stay out of it.

Understanding Documents

Although there's no need for you ever to get involved with system files, there is one type of file you will create and use regularly — documents files (or just documents, for short). Unlike system files, which contain computer code, documents contain information for humans to view. A document might be written text, a photograph, a song, or a video. It really doesn't matter. All that matters is that the document contains stuff for humans, not computers, to view.

A currently closed document is generally represented by an icon. With Windows Vista, most documents will have a representation of either a generic document or of the actual content in the file. To open a document, double-click its icon.

Figure 5-1: Examples of icons that represent documents

In Figure 5-1, you can see that the first item is a picture, the second a Microsoft Word document, the third a text document, the forth a video, the fifth an MP3 music file, and the last one a song. As you can see, the graphic on each item represents what the document contains.

When you *open* a document, the document appears on the screen, but it doesn't appear all by itself. A document always opens within the document area of some program. For example, a picture might open in the Photo Gallery Viewer program, as shown on the left side of Figure 5-2. A typed document might open in the WordPad program, as shown on the right side of Figure 5-2.

We use different programs for different types of documents because of the tools that a program offers. For example, the menu bar across the top of the Photo Gallery Viewer program window and the toolbar on the bottom offer tools specifically designed for working and viewing pictures. The menu bar and toolbars across the top of the WordPad program offer tools for working with text. Those tools operate on the document currently open in the program.

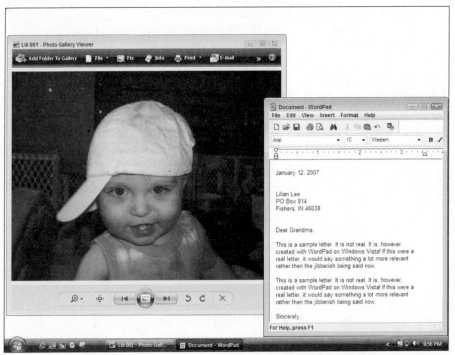

Figure 5-2: A picture in the Photo Gallery Viewer (left) and a typed document in WordPad (right)

Exactly what program opens when you open a document depends on many factors, as we'll discuss in Chapter 6. For now, remember that unlike programs, which open by themselves, documents always open within some program.

There's probably room on your hard disk for thousands of documents. As time goes by, your collection of documents will grow. So will your need to keep them organized, so you can find what you want, when you want it. To keep your documents organized, you can arrange them into folders, as you would in a file cabinet.

All About Folders

Like paper files, files on a disk are stored in *folders*. If you think of a disk as a filing cabinet, a folder is like a manila file folder in the cabinet — it's a container in which you store documents (files). Figure 5-3 illustrates how the computer terms *disk*, *folder*, and *document* (or file) relate to a filing cabinet.

Like unopened programs on your Start menu, unopened folders and icons are represented by icons. Folders that contain documents usually have a manila file folder image in their icons. The manila folder will often hold representations of some of the files within the folder. An empty folder will have an empty manila folder representing it. Examples of folders are shown in Figure 5-4. To open a folder, double-click its icon. The contents of the folder appear on the screen.

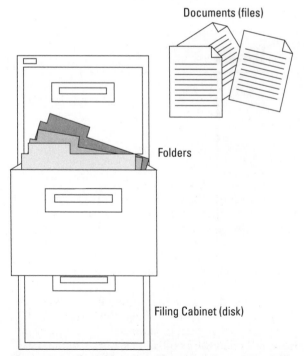

Figure 5-3: Like folders in a file cabinet, computer folders are containers for storing documents (files).

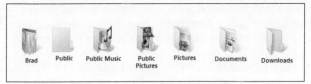

Figure 5-4: Examples of icons that represent folders

 Note   If the contents of a folder are not shown as icons, don't worry. Later in this chapter, you will learn how to change the presentation.

How Folders Are Organized

Unlike folders in a file cabinet, folders on a disk are arranged in a somewhat *hierarchical* order. In other words, a folder can contain still more folders. We can't say how all the folders on your PC are organized — that all depends on whether or not you've created any folders of your own. But if you forget about all the system folders and look at the ones most usable to a human being, the hierarchy would look similar to Figure 5-5.

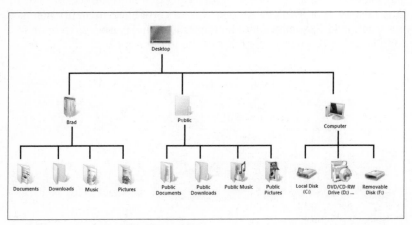

Figure 5-5: A sample folder hierarchy

You'll notice that icons such as Desktop, Computer, and the various drive icons don't look like manila file folders. That's because they're not document folders. That is, they're not containers for storing documents. Rather, they're special folders that contain icons to useful resources other than documents, such as icons for your floppy disk and CD drive. Icons that do show the manila file folders are the ones specifically designed for storing your documents.

It's not necessary to learn what each folder in the hierarchy represents at this point. For the moment, stay focused on navigating through the hierarchy, as you'll learn next. But, just so you know that each icon does, indeed, represent something useful that will be described in the book, here's a brief summary of some of the icons shown in Figure 5-5:

✦ **Desktop (folder):** This special folder contains a copy of every short-cut icon on your Windows desktop (but is not the same as your Windows desktop, because it doesn't have a background picture or taskbar). This folder is especially handy after you've learned to create desktop shortcuts to frequently used programs, folders, and documents, as discussed in the section "Creating your own Shortcuts" in Chapter 25.

✦ **Brad:** This is actually a folder specific to one of your author's machine It is a *personal folder* that is named after the account that was used to sign into Windows Vista. The name of this folder will be different on your computer and will depend on what account you used to sign into the computer. You can learn more about accounts in Chapter 25.

✦ **Documents:** This document folder is where you can store any document you create or download. If the document is a picture or song, however, you might want to store it in the Pictures folder or the Music folder instead.

✦ **Pictures:** A good place to store pictures, including any pictures you copy from a digital camera or scanner. See "Using Your Pictures Folder" in Chapter 15 for more information.

✦ **Music:** A good place to store songs you copy from CDs (see the section "Using Your Music Folder" in Chapter 16).

✦ **Public Documents:** The same idea as the Documents folder, except that documents in this folder are accessible to everyone who has a user account on this computer (see Chapter 24), as well as people on the same local area network (see Chapter 31).

✦ **Public Pictures:** Same idea as Public Documents but particularly well suited to storing pictures.

✦ **Public Music:** Same idea as Public Documents but particularly well suited to storing music.

✦ **Computer:** Provides access to all the disk drives in your computer, including your floppy disk drive, CD drive, and entire hard disk, as well as other resources.

✦ **Floppy Disk Drive (A:):** If there's a floppy disk in the floppy disk drive, opening this icon will display the contents of the disk. If the floppy drive is empty when you double-click this icon, you'll see a message asking you to insert a disk— You can click the Cancel button instead (see the section "Using Floppy Disks and Zip Disks" in Chapter 22).

✦ **Local Disk (C:):** Represents your entire hard disk, including *system folders,* which are best left alone (see Chapter 21).

✦ **DVD/CD-RW Drive (D:):** This could be labeled *CD drive* or *DVD drive,* depending on the type of drive installed in your computer. But if you insert a disk into that drive and double-click this icon, you'll see the contents of that disk (see the section "Using CDs and DVDs" in Chapter 22).

✦ **Removable Disk (F:):** Represents a removable disk being attached to your system. This can be a thumb drive, or some other removable media drive. (Chapter 22 covers more on this.)

You may also see additional Document folders for other types of documents such as video and television recordings. In general, such icons describe what is best stored within their folders.

Parent Folder and Subfolders

Figure 5-5 shows the logical arrangement of folders, but it doesn't necessarily make clear that folders lower in the hierarchy are contained within the folder above them. For example, the Public Documents, Public Downloads, Public Music, and Public Pictures folders shown in that hierarchy are actually contained within the Public folder.

When one folder contains still other folders, we refer to the containing folder as the *parent*, sort of like in a family tree. For example, in Figure 5-5, Public is the parent to Public Documents, Public Downloads, Public Music, and Public Pictures. The personal folder labeled Brad is the parent to Documents, Downloads, Music, and Pictures.

The folders within the parent are usually referred to as *subfolders* but can also be called *child folders* or *children*. In other words, Public Documents, Public Downloads, Public Music, and Public Pictures are subfolders of (or children of) the Public folder because they're contained within the Public folder.

You'll never actually see your folders laid out in a hierarchical diagram like the one shown in Figure 5-5. That's just an illustration of the hierarchical arrangement of files. But if you open a folder that's the parent of other folders, you'll see icons for those subfolders within the parent folder.

Let's look at an example. In Figure 5-5, you see a folder called Brad. This is a special, personal folder named after the account you used to sign into the computer. When you click the Start button, you will see a similar name at the top of the right side of the menu. This should be directly above a link for Documents. Click this name, and you will open the folder.

A window opens, showing you the contents of your personal folder. We can't say exactly what your folder contains, but chances are it will contain folders similar to those shown in Figure 5-5 under the Brad folder. But since Documents, Music, and Pictures are subfolders that are built into Windows Vista, you should see at least the icons for those folders. If your folder contains any documents, you'll see icons for those documents as well. Note that the name of the folder whose contents you're currently viewing (Brad in this example) appears near the top of the window that's showing you the contents of the folder (see Figure 5-6).

If you double-click the icon for the Music or Pictures folder, that folder will open. The name at the top of the window will change to include whatever folder you opened, and the large pane will show the contents of that folder.

Current folder you are viewing   Contents of the folder

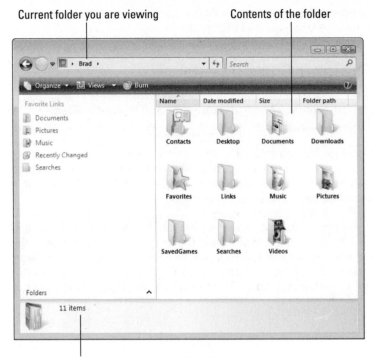

Information about the current folder if nothing is selected
or the item selected if something is selected

Figure 5-6: The folder for your account name contains icons for Documents, Downloads, Music, and Pictures folders (and possibly more).

 Tip   You can right-click any icon in the main pane to see a shortcut menu of things you can do with the folder or file that the icon represents. Additionally, you can single-click on any icon to see information displayed at the bottom of the window about that item.

Obviously, there's more than just a title and some icons in Figure 5-6. All that other stuff you see in Figure 5-6 is part of a program named *Windows Explorer* (or just *Explorer*, for short). And as its name implies, it's a program for exploring the contents of your entire computer.

 Note   If you don't see icons like those shown in Figure 5-6, don't worry. You'll learn how to change the display to icons later in this chapter!

Using Windows Explorer

Windows Explorer is a program for exploring the contents of folders on your computer. Any time you open a folder, Windows Explorer is the program that's showing you the contents of that folder. Thus, no matter what folder you're viewing at the moment, the Navigation pane and toolbar will always operate the same, because those items belong to Windows Explorer, not to the particular folder you happen to be viewing at the moment.

Windows Explorer Components

Only icons that appear in the main pane of Windows Explorer are contained within that folder. The toolbar, search, details pane, and Navigation pane, shown in Figure 5-7, all belong to the Windows Explorer program.

 Tip Don't confuse Windows Explorer with Internet Explorer. Internet Explorer lets you explore things that exist beyond your computer, on the Internet. Windows Explorer is a program for exploring all the things that exist within Windows Vista (generally on your computer).

 Note Unlike most programs, Windows Explorer never displays its own name in the title bar. The title bar in Windows Explorer is left blank. However, the title bar does provide all the standard tools and techniques for moving, minimizing, maximizing, restoring, and closing the program, as discussed in Chapter 4. You can also size Windows Explorer by dragging any corner or edge.

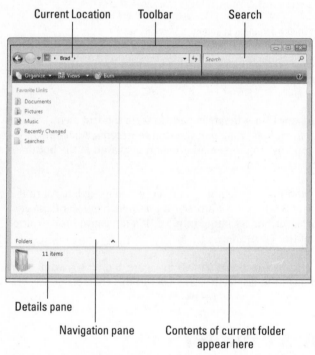

Figure 5-7: Windows Explorer program window components

The Windows Explorer Toolbar

The toolbar, which appears near the top in Windows Explorer, provides access to commonly used options for organizing, displaying, and working with folders and documents. What options are actually displayed can change based on what folder you have opened and what item you have selected.

Most of the buttons on the toolbar have labels. Some buttons will show only a little picture. To see the name of an unlabeled button, just point to it. The button's name will appear in a screen tip, as in the example at left.

We'll talk about specific buttons in the sections later in this chapter. For now, note that the toolbar might also contain some disabled (dimmed) controls or menu items. That simply means that the functionality doesn't make sense at the current time.

Explorer's Search

As with many areas within Vista, Windows Explorer also includes a search box. This box enables you to enter any text, and Windows Vista will search for all occurrences of that text. The content area will list any documents that are found that contain the search text you enter. The search will actually look at more than just document names — it will search within documents, too.

For now, I'm going to focus on other areas of Windows Explorer. In Chapter 20, you will learn the details of doing advanced searches to find nearly anything on your computer.

The Windows Explorer Detail Pane

At the bottom of the Windows Explorer window is the Details pane. Within this pane you find additional information about the current item selected. If no item is selected within the content area, then you will discover information about the current folder being viewed in Windows Explorer.

The Windows Explorer Navigation Pane

The Navigation pane contains still more useful links for navigating through folders and for working with icons contained within the current folder. Options in the Explorer bar are divided into two primary categories. In Figure 5-7, you can see that these are named Favorite Links and Folders. You can click any item in the Navigation pane to show or hide the options under that heading or to display the item's contents in the contents area.

The Navigation pane is optional and will disappear if you size the window down to where it's too small to be displayed. If the Navigation pane never appears in Windows Explorer on your computer, no matter how large you make its window, you can perform the following steps to make it visible.

STEPS: Turn the Explorer Navigation Pane On or Off

1. Click the Organize toolbar icon. This will display a menu.

2. Select Layout ➪ Navigation Pane. If the Navigation pane was not shown before, then it will be shown. If it was shown before, then it will be turned off.

The Windows Explorer Menu Bar

Like many programs, Windows Explorer has a menu bar that can be displayed across the top. The menu bar provides tools (*commands*) for working with items visible in the main content pane of the window. You didn't see this in Figure 5-7 because by default it is not turned on. You can, however, turn it on by doing the following:

1. Click Organize on the Windows Explorer toolbar. This will present a drop-down menu.

2. Select Layout ➪ Menu bar from this menu. The menu bar will be added to your Windows Explorer window as shown in Figure 5-8.

After you turn on the menu bar, it will be displayed every time you open Windows Explorer again. You can turn it back off again by following the steps above.

 Tip   If the menu is off, then you can temporarily show it by pressing the Alt key.

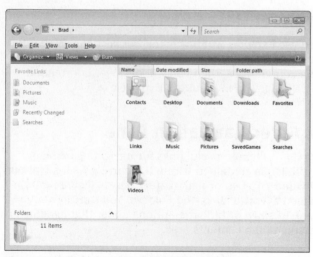

Figure 5-8: The menu bar in Windows Explorer

The menu bar in Windows Explorer works just like any other program's menu bar. See the section "Working the Menu Bars" in Chapter 4 for all the ways you can use menu bars.

The Preview Pane

Another area of Windows Explorer that is not turned on by default is the preview pane. The preview pane does exactly what its name suggests — it provides a quick view of what is in the currently selected item. This pane can be turned on in much the same way as the menu bar in the previous section:

1. Click Organize on the Windows Explorer toolbar. This will present a drop-down menu.

2. Select Layout ⇨ Preview Pane from this menu. The preview pane will be added to your Windows Explorer window as shown in Figure 5-9.

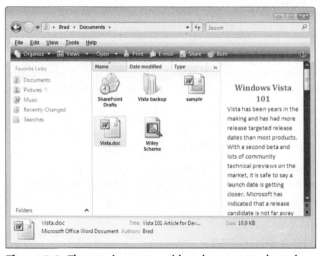

Figure 5-9: The preview pane with a document selected

The Windows Explorer Taskbar Button

Just like with any other program you open, when you open Windows Explorer, you also open a taskbar button. The taskbar button never shows the name Windows Explorer or Explorer. Instead, it shows only the name of the currently open folder. For example, when you are viewing the contents of Documents, the taskbar button show *Documents*.

If you open many folders, each will have its own taskbar button. Eventually, however, Windows may decide to collapse all those separate buttons into one taskbar button, as in Figure 5-10. (It does this to prevent making the taskbar buttons too small to see.) When that happens, the Windows Explorer taskbar button will show its own name, as well as a number. The number indicates how many folders are currently open.

Figure 5-10: Multiple open folders grouped onto a single taskbar button

When you click the Windows Explorer taskbar button, you'll see a menu of all open folders (see Figure 5-10). Click any folder name to bring that folder to the top of the stack on the screen. Optionally, you can use the taskbar button as follows:

✦ Right-click the Windows Explorer taskbar button, and cascade, stack, set side by side, minimize, or close all the open folders.

✦ Click the Windows Explorer taskbar button; then right-click any individual folder name on the menu to restore, move, resize, minimize, maximize, or close that folder.

Navigating Through Folders

Because all the folders in your system are connected in a hierarchical manner, you can easily get to any folder when you're in Windows Explorer. There are lots of ways to open the more commonly used folders. For example, if you click the Start button, you'll see icons on the right side of the menu for opening Documents, Computer, and other folders, as in the example shown in Figure 5-11. Just click any folder name to open that folder. You might also see icons on your Windows desktop titled Documents or Computer. You can double-click either of those to open that folder.

When you're looking at the contents of any folder, you can navigate to any other folder in the hierarchy. That is, you can get to any folder you want from whatever folder you happen to be in at the moment.

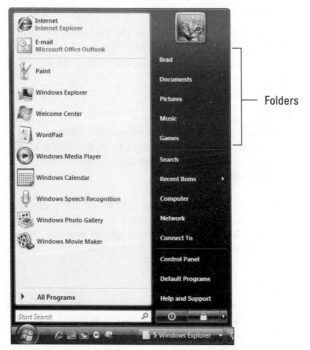

Figure 5-11: Folders you can open from the Start menu

Opening a Subfolder

To open a subfolder, you might have to get to its parent folder first. Since your personalized folder is the parent of your Music and Pictures folders, you'll see icons for that folder within your personalized folder. The personalized folder is the top folder shown on the Start menu (see Figure 5-11). To open a subfolder, just double-click its icon or name.

When you double-click the icon for Music or Pictures, you'll open that folder. The top text box within Windows Explorer changes to show the name of whichever folder you opened as well as the parent folder. In addition, the main pane shows the contents of that folder. Referring back to Figure 5-5, by opening Music or Pictures, you moved down the hierarchy — from a parent folder to a subfolder. By looking at the text box at the top of Windows Explorer, you see that the hierarchy is also displayed for you.

Tip　To open a subfolder in a new, separate Explorer window, hold down the Shift key and double-click the folder's icon. Choosing a different folder's name from the Start menu will also open that folder in a separate Explorer window.

Moving Up the Hierarchy

So, how do you move up the hierarchy? As mentioned in the previous section, the hierarchy is displayed in the text box near the top of Windows Explorer. You can always move straight up to the parent of the current folder by clicking the parent's name in the text box.

Jumping Across the Hierarchy

The Favorite Links category in the Navigation pane also provides some short-cuts to commonly used folders. Just click any folder name to open that folder. This is handy when you want to make a lateral move, for example, from the Documents to your Pictures folder or vice versa.

Tip If you can't see the Navigation pane on your computer, then use the Organize menu to select Layout ➪ Navigation Pane. If you don't see the Favorite Links listed or if it is blocked by a Folders option, use the show/hide buttons to collapse the Folders list.

Navigating with the Address Bar

The text box that has the current folder listed is an address bar. You can click its drop-down list arrow (the arrow pointing downward) to see a list of folders to which you can jump. The listed folders are ones you've been to before.

You an also click the arrows between items in the address bar. The right-pointing arrow to the right of an item will display subfolders for that item. You can then click a subfolder to go to it.

Finally, if there is a double arrow (<<) to the left of the navigation items, you can click it to get a list of the major folders on your system such as Documents, your personalized folder, Desktop, the Recycle Bin, and more. Clicking one of the items will take you directly to that folder.

The Back and Forward Buttons

As soon as you've navigated to another folder in Windows Explorer, the Back button in the toolbar will be enabled. The back button is the arrow that points to the left. You can click that button to go back to the folder you just came from. After you've clicked the Back button, the Forward button will be enabled, and you can click that button to return to the folder you just backed out of. The Forward button is the arrow that points to the right.

Different Ways to View Icons

Like many programs, Windows Explorer enables you to choose how you want to view the information it's presenting. As in most programs, those options are on the View menu in the menu bar. However, you can also click the down arrow within the Views button in the Explorer toolbar (as shown in Figure 5-12) to choose a view. Be careful, clicking the Views button anywhere other than the down arrow simply changes the view to the next one on the menu.

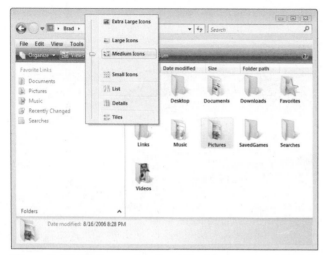

Figure 5-12: Choose a view from the View menu or Views toolbar button.

> **Tip** Although you can click the Extra Large, Large, Medium, or Small Icons options to select a specific icon size, you can also drag the slider control that is on the left side of the menu to adjust the icon size. Moving it toward the top increases the size of the icon. Moving it toward the bottom decreases the icon size.

Each view shows the same information — the contents of the current folder. The view affects only *how* the information is displayed, not *what's* displayed. We'll look at some examples in the sections that follow. Also, icons work the same no matter what view you're in. For example, double-clicking an icon opens the folder or file that the icon represents. Right-clicking an icon shows you other options for the file or folder that the icon represents.

The Icon View

We've been showing an icon view in the figures in this chapter. In general, the Medium Icons view has been shown. The icon view shows each file or folder's icon and name, nothing more. This is the typical way to view icons.

In addition to the Medium Icons view, there are three other icon views: Extra Large Icons, Large Icons, and Small Icons. Figure 5-13 shows a folder displaying Extra Large Icons. Figure 5-14 shows the Small Icons view.

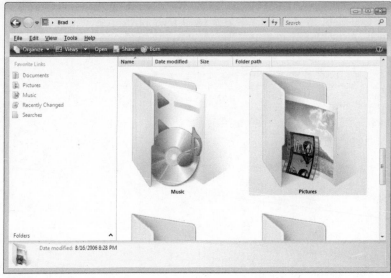

Figure 5-13: Sample icons shown in Extra Large Icons view

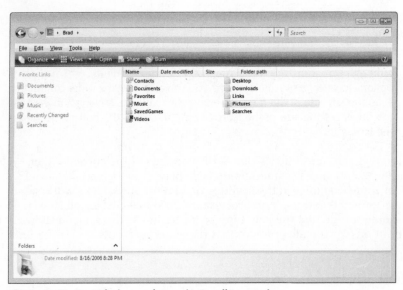

Figure 5-14: Sample icons shown in Small Icons view

The Tiles View

The Tiles view also shows the icon and name of each file and folder. But in addition to the icons, there's a bit of added information with each icon's name. The exact information shown varies with different types of documents. However, information such as the name of the program that opens the file and the size are typical, as in the example shown in Figure 5-15, which displays the Sample Pictures folder that is within the Pictures folder.

Figure 5-15: Sample icons shown in Tiles view

The List View

The List view shows tiny icons, and the full name, of each folder and file. It's mostly useful for viewing folders that contain hundreds of icons, because it makes it easy to read through their names alphabetically, as in the example shown in Figure 5-16. (It's unlikely that your computer has a folder that contains that many subfolders right now.)

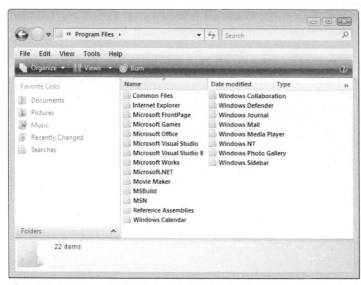

Figure 5-16: Many folder icons shown in List view

The Details View

The Details view shows tiny icons and lots of detailed information about each subfolder and file in the current folder (see Figure 5-17). Because the folder in Figure 5-17 contains mostly subfolders, the first column shows the icon and name. The other columns can vary depending upon the type of content that is primarily in the folder you are viewing. Generally, this includes the date the file was modified, the file's size (folders don't display a size), and the path (where the file is located on the hard drive).

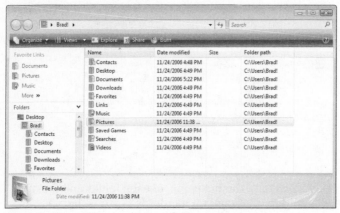

Figure 5-17: Sample icons shown in Details view

As mentioned, if the primary content type is not folders, then the information displayed in Details view will be different. Figure 5-18 shows the Details view for the Sample Pictures folder that is shown in Figure 5-15. As you can see, the detailed information displayed relates more to pictures.

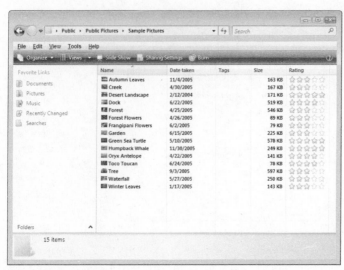

Figure 5-18: Details view of the Sample Pictures folder

Tip If there are more columns than can fit in the Explorer window, you'll see a horizontal scroll bar beneath the columns. Use the scroll box to scroll left and right through the columns.

Working with Columns

The Details view is unique in that all the information is presented in columns with specific headings at the top. The column headings are actually useful tools in themselves. For example, you can sort (or alphabetize) the list by clicking any column heading. The first time you click a heading, items are placed in *ascending order* based on that column, and the heading shows an up-pointing triangle. Ascending order means *A to Z* in the case of text or *smallest to largest* in the case of numbers. Or if you sorted the Date Modified column, ascending order would mean *oldest to newest*.

Sorting Columns

Clicking the same column heading will reverse the items in descending order, the column head showing a down-pointing arrow to indicate the sort order. Descending order means *Z to A* in the case of text, *largest to smallest* for numbers, and *newest to oldest* for dates.

Sizing Columns

You can also change the width of any column heading by placing the mouse pointer on the bar at the right side of the column heading. The mouse pointer changes to a two-headed arrow, as in Figure 5-19. When you see that two-headed arrow, hold down the left mouse button and drag left or right to size the column.

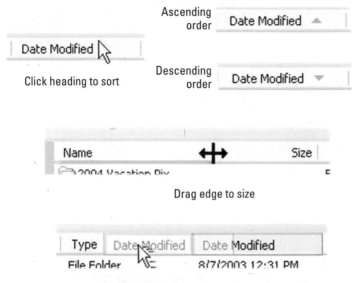

Figure 5-19: Using column headings

Moving Columns

As illustrated at the bottom of Figure 5-19, you can also move an entire column left or right by dragging the entire column heading. That is, point to the middle of the column heading. Then hold down the left mouse button and drag left or right. Release the mouse button when the column is where you want to put it.

Tip The techniques shown in Figure 5-19 are universal; they work with any column headings in any program, not just with the Windows Explorer Details view.

If you find that your customizations are lost when you come back to a window, then make sure the Remember each folder's view settings option is turned on. To make Windows remember each folder's most recent view, choose Tools ➪ Folder options from the menu bar. In the Folder Options dialog box that opens, click the View tab. Scroll down the list of Advanced Settings, and select Remember each folder's view settings. Then click OK.

Choosing Columns in Details View

As mentioned earlier, the columns visible to you in Details view will vary, depending on what folder you're viewing. For example, when viewing a folder that contains pictures, you may see column headings relevant to pictures. When viewing a folder that contains music, you may see column headings relevant to music, as in Figure 5-20.

Figure 5-20: Details view column headings in a folder that contains songs

If the columns that appear in Details view aren't the ones you want to see, you can choose others. From the menu bar in Explorer, choose View ➪ Choose Details. A dialog box titled Choose Details appears, as in the example shown in Figure 5-21.

Choose the columns you want to see by selecting them. To make a column visible in Details view, select its name. To hide the column in Details view, clear the check box next to the column name. Use the scroll bar to scroll through all your options.

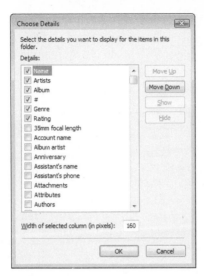

Figure 5-21: The Choose Details dialog box

The other controls in the dialog box are optional. You can set a width for the currently selected column using the Width of selected column option near the bottom of the dialog box. But, as described a moment ago, you can also size the column while you're in Details view. You can move the currently selected item up or down the list by using the Move Up and Move Down buttons. But you can also arrange columns however you wish when you're in Details view.

When you've finished making your selections, click OK to return to the Details view. Use the horizontal scroll bar at the bottom of the Explorer's window to scroll left and right through the columns.

Arranging Icons in Explorer

You can sort the icons in the main pane of Explorer by:

✦ **Name:** Folders are listed in alphabetical order, followed by files listed in alphabetical order.

✦ **Size:** Files are listed from smallest to largest size, after folders.

✦ **Type:** Files are listed in alphabetical order by type, after folders.

✦ **Date Modified:** Files are listed from oldest to newest, based on the date and time that you last saved the file.

You may see other options on the menu; it just depends on the particular folder you're in. For example, if the Music folder is active, you'll see options for arranging icons by Artist or Album Title. You can get to the sorting options using whichever of the following methods (shown in Figure 5-22) is most convenient:

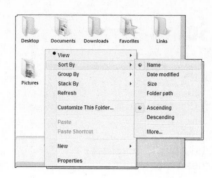

Figure 5-22: Two ways to get to the Sort By menu

✦ Choose View ➪ Sort By ➪ *option*.

✦ Right-click some empty space between icons and choose View ➪ Sort By ➪ *option*, where *option* is any option available on the menu.

You'll also see some toggles and other group options on the View menu. Here are the other options you can change:

✦ **Groups By:** If selected, icons are shown in groups with group headings (particularly useful when viewing many icons arranged by Type).

✦ **Stack By:** If selected, icons are stacked into groups rather than showing all icons individually.

✦ **Auto Arrange:** If selected, icons will be sorted automatically, so they're always in order when you first open the folder.

✦ **Align to Grid:** If selected, icons align to an invisible grid as you drop them on the screen. This keeps the icons neatly aligned, even when you move them yourself. (To move an icon, just drag it to some new location within the folder; then release the mouse button.)

Closing Windows Explorer

You can close Windows Explorer, and hence the folder you're currently viewing, as you would any other program window: Click the Close button in its upper-right corner, choose File ➪ Close from its menu bar, or press Alt+F4 if it's in the active window. The window will close and the taskbar button will disappear.

If you have many folders open simultaneously, and their buttons have collapsed into a single taskbar button, you can right-click that taskbar button and choose Close Group.

Summary

There's a lot more you can do with Windows Explorer than what you've learned in this chapter. But most of its other features make sense only after you've created and stored some documents on your hard disk. You'll learn how to do that in Chapter 6. And we'll resume our discussion of Windows Explorer in Part V. For now, you might want to practice moving up and down the folder hierarchy shown in Figure 5-5. Just open any folder from the Start menu, and navigate up and down through the folders shown in Figure 5-5. A little hands-on practice goes a long way toward helping you remember things.

Before we move on, here's a quick review of the main topics covered in this chapter:

✦ A document, in the computer sense, is like a written document, even though it could be a picture, song, or video as well. Each document is stored in its own file. (You'll learn more about documents in Chapter 6.)

✦ Like documents in a filing cabinet, document files are organized into folders on your disk.

✦ Your hard disk already has some built-in folders, such as Documents, Pictures, and Music, for storing your documents.

✦ You can open many folders right from the Start menu.

✦ When you open a folder, you're actually opening a program named Windows Explorer (or Explorer, for short), which in turn displays the contents of the folder.

✦ Windows Explorer contains tools that enable you to navigate to other folders on a disk. In fact, you can get to any folder from any other folder.

Working with Documents

Many programs are designed to let you create, view, edit, print, save, and open documents. As mentioned in Chapter 5, a document in the computer sense is much like a document in the real-world sense — it's basically anything that might otherwise be printed on paper and perhaps stored in a filing cabinet. Although a computer document might just as well be a song or movie, it doesn't have to be something printed on paper.

Understanding Document Types

Until now, we've been referring to types of documents in a very broad sense, such as texts, pictures, music, and videos. In fact, many different types of documents exist within each of those broad categories. There are lots of different types of text documents and lots of different types of pictures.

This has to do with the way the computer industry evolves. People come up with new programs, new ways to do things, and even new document formats, always trying to make things better. Some of these things catch on; some don't. The ones that catch on tend to be supported by many different programs.

The main thing that defines a document's type is its *format*, which has to do with the way in which information is stored in the file. Different types of documents are stored in different formats. Any given program will be able to open files in at least one format. Most programs can open files from many formats. There isn't, however, any program that can open all types of documents correctly.

Showing/Hiding File Name Extensions

When you double-click a document's icon, Windows opens both the document and some program that's capable of displaying that type of document. Or, at least it tries to do that. (More on that in a moment.) But how does Windows know what format the document is in, so it can open the appropriate program? The answer to that question is the *file extension*.

Every document file has an extension at the end of its file name. The extension is a dot (period) followed by one or more characters. Figure 6-1 shows an example.

File name

Extension

Figure 6-1: An icon, file name, and extension

Figure 6-2 shows an example of some icons in an Explorer window. On the left, file name extensions are invisible. On the right, they're visible. (Folder names never have extensions, because they're not files; they're containers in which you store files.) On your own screen, you might, or might not, see extensions on your document file names. Whether or not file name extensions are visible on your screen is something you get to decide for yourself.

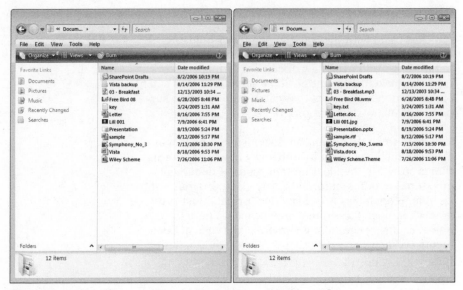

Figure 6-2: Files with extensions hidden (left) and visible (right)

To choose whether you want to see, or not see, file name extensions, follow these steps:

1. If you're not already in Windows Explorer, open it now (click the Start button and choose Documents, since Explorer is the program that shows you the contents of all folders).

2. From Explorer's menu bar, choose Tools ⇨ Folder Options. The Folder Options dialog box opens. If your menu bar is not displayed (you learned how to turn it on in Chapter 5), then select Organize on the toolbar and select Layout ⇨ Menu Bar.

3. In the Folder Options dialog box, click the View tab shown in Figure 6-3.

4. Now you have two choices:

   • If you want to hide file name extensions, choose the Hide extensions for known file types option.

   • If you want extensions to be visible, clear the Hide extensions for known file types option.

5. Click the OK button.

You can repeat Steps 1–5 at any time to either show or hide file name extensions.

Caution   Never change a file name extension, as doing so might prevent you from being able to open the file. Keeping file name extensions hidden is an ideal way to keep yourself from accidentally changing a file name extension.

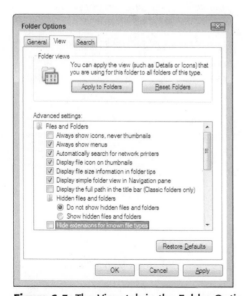

Figure 6-3: The View tab in the Folder Options dialog box

Even when file name extensions are hidden, you might occasionally come across a file that shows its extension anyway. That's because the option hides extensions only for known files. A *known file* is one for which Windows already knows what program to use to open that file. An *unknown file* is a document that isn't associated with any program on your computer. An unknown file will always display its file name extension.

Common Document File Types

Thousands of different programs are available for Windows, capable of creating hundreds of different types of documents. It wouldn't make sense to learn them all—most document types are so rare that you may never come across them. Some common document types, however, you're almost certain to come across eventually. Those types are listed and briefly described in Table 6-1.

Table 6-1
Common File Name Extensions and Document Types

Extension	General Type	Format	Opens with
MP3	Audio	MP3	Windows Media Player and other players
WMA	Audio	Windows Media Audio	Windows Media Player and Windows Movie Maker
JPG or JPEG	Picture	Joint Photographic Experts Group	Internet Explorer and most graphics programs
GIF	Picture	Graphics Interchange Format	Internet Explorer and most graphics programs
BMP	Picture	Bitmap	Most graphics programs
PPT or	Presentation	PowerPoint Show PowerPoint Player	Microsoft PowerPoint or PPTX
XPS	Text	Microsoft XPS Document	Microsoft XPS Viewer
PDF	Text	Portable Document Format	Adobe Acrobat Reader
RTF	Text	Rich Text Format	Microsoft Word/WordPad
DOC or DOCX	Text	Document	Microsoft Word or WordPerfect
MPG or MPEG	Video	Motion Picture Experts Group	Windows Media Player and other players
WMV	Video	Windows Media Video	Windows Media Player
HTM, HTML	Text	Web page	Internet Explorer or any web browser

For a beginner, all this business of multiple document types can seem pretty intimidating. However, when you create a document and save it, the program you're using at the moment will suggest an appropriate format for you, and 99 percent of the time, you can just use the suggested format. We'll talk about why you might want to choose another type one percent of the time in the section "Changing the Document Type," later in this chapter. For now, let's focus on how you go about creating a document in the first place.

Tip You can look up just about any file name extension at www.filext.com.

Using a Program to Create a Document

As you know, you can start any program installed on your computer from the Start menu. Most programs that enable you to work with documents contain a large document area, where the document you're working with at the moment is displayed. For example, WordPad is a small word-processing program that enables you to create letters, reports, and other textual documents. To open WordPad, click the Start button and choose All Programs ➪ Accessories ➪ WordPad.

When WordPad opens, the large white area you see is a blank document. It is, essentially, an empty sheet of typing paper on which you can type. Surrounding the empty document is the WordPad program window, which contains all the usual accoutrements of program windows, as discussed in Chapter 4 (see Figure 6-4).

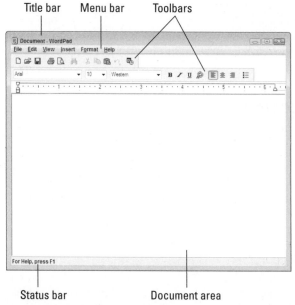

Figure 6-4: The WordPad window, containing a blank document

Cross-Reference As you'll learn in Chapter 7, there are lots of ways to edit text in WordPad.

To add text to the blank sheet of paper you see in WordPad, just start typing. In fact, that's how you create a document in WordPad — you type text. If you're following along on your own computer right now, feel free to type any text at all into your blank document. Even if you type just one sentence, you will have created a document. You can use that as an example as you learn to save and open documents in the sections that follow.

Saving a Document

As you create a new document, it exists in the computer's Random Access Memory (RAM). RAM is different from a disk in that there are no moving parts, and changes can be made very quickly. Storing an open document in RAM, rather than on the hard disk, is what enables you to quickly and easily make changes to the document.

Although RAM is king when it comes to speed, it has one major drawback that disks don't have: RAM is *volatile*. That means that the moment the power goes off, everything in RAM instantly disappears, as though it never existed. It doesn't matter if the power went off intentionally (you turned off the computer) or unintentionally (a power outage). The document disappears either way.

In fact, the document also disappears the moment you close the program that you're using to create the document. This is not a good thing if you had planned on keeping the document around for a while. To keep a document around for a while, you have to *save* it. When you save a document, you take an exact copy of the document on your screen and stick it in a file on the hard disk. The hard disk is not volatile. Whatever you put there stays there forever (unless you delete it).

How to Save a Document

To save the document you're currently working on, do whichever of the following is most convenient at the moment:

✦ Choose File ⇨ Save from the program's menu bar.

✦ Click the Save button (if available) on the program's toolbar.

✦ Press Ctrl+S.

If you've created and typed a short document already in this chapter and you're looking at it right now on your screen, you can use any of the preceding methods to save what you've typed so far. If this is the first time you've saved the document, you'll be taken to the Save As dialog box, discussed next.

Using the Save As Dialog Box

The Save As dialog box appears anytime you save a new document (as well as when you download a new file or save an e-mail attachment). It does so because it's up to you to keep your own files organized. You stay organized by using the Save As dialog box to tell Windows *where* to put the file (in what folder) and *what* to name the file. This is not unlike choosing a particular manila file folder in a file cabinet to store a document you're currently holding in your hand.

The Save As dialog box is a mini Windows Explorer in that you can navigate to any folder in your system. Using the Save As dialog box is usually a three-step process as illustrated in Figure 6-5 and summarized here.

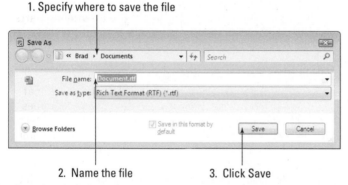

Figure 6-5: Three steps to saving a document from the Save As dialog box

Step 1: Choosing a Folder to Save In

Your first job in the Save As dialog box is to tell Windows *where* you want to store the file. The Save In option shows which folder that will be. If you're a beginner, the smart thing to do is always choose your Documents folder to save things in. That way, you'll know where every file is. You can organize your documents into smaller subfolders at any time in the future.

Often, Documents will be the default folder anyway. That is, Documents will already appear as the folder name in the address box. If some other folder name appears there instead, you can always change it to your documents folder. To navigate to another folder in the Save As dialog box, start by clicking the Browse Folder option near the bottom. That expands the Save As dialog window shown in Figure 6-6.

The expanded Save As dialog box looks very similar to Windows Explorer in earlier chapters. It has the same layout with the addition of the ability to save a file. Navigation within the Save as folder area is identical to that of Windows Explorer as well.

Click these to select   Click to show other folders
a Favorites folder   where you've been

Current folder   Double click to go to any subfolder

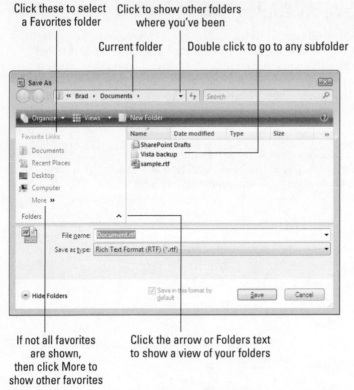

If not all favorites   Click the arrow or Folders text
are shown,   to show a view of your folders
then click More to
show other favorites

Figure 6-6: The expanded Save As dialog box for browsing folders

On the left side of the main area, you will see a navigation pane that lists favorite links. You probably want to save your files in some primary areas on your machine — Documents, Pictures, Music, or any of the other favorite areas. Alternatively, you can click the Folders option to expand the subfolder containing a list of folders on your computer. You can then navigate through those to find the location in which you'd like to save your file.

After you've navigated to the location where you'd like to save your file, simply click it. The address bar at the top of the page will change to show the new location. If you are satisfied with the file name, you can then click the Save button to save the file to your new location.

If you can't open a folder directly from the lists, you can probably get to a nearby parent. For example, if you created a folder named Vacation 2007 in your Pictures folder, you could get to it quickly by clicking the Start button and choosing Pictures. In the Pictures folder that opens, double-click Vacation 2007 to open that folder.

Tip   The name of the folder that appears in the text box at the top of the Save As dialog box is where your document will be saved when you click the Save button. That name is also the name of the current folder; the larger pane always shows the contents of whatever folder is selected.

Tips on Choosing a Folder for Storing a Document

Here are some general tips, especially geared toward beginners, on choosing a folder in which to store a document:

✦ If in doubt, use Documents for general documents, Pictures for pictures, and Music for music.

✦ Do not choose Recent Items or Recent Places as a folder for storing files. These folders play a special role we will describe later in this chapter.

✦ There's no need to save a new document to a floppy disk or CD. Store all documents on your hard disk; use floppies and CDs for backups or distribution only.

✦ Avoid the temptation to put the file on the desktop. You don't want your desktop to become so cluttered with icons that it becomes a disorganized mess.

Step 2: Naming a Document

After you've navigated to the folder in which you want to store the document, the next step is to give it a name using the File Name option near the bottom of the dialog box. You'll want to come up with a name that will make it easy to identify the document just from its icon. The name can be up to 256 characters in length. But as a rule, stick with shorter names that are easy to type and remember.

The file name you enter can contain letters, numbers, spaces, underscores (_), hyphens (-), and apostrophes ('). Avoid using all other punctuation marks and special characters.

Often, a default file name is already given in the File name text box. It will be a generic name such as Document or Image. You'll want to replace that name with a more meaningful name. You can use any of the techniques discussed under "Renaming Files and Folders" in Chapter 19 to enter or change the file name.

If the default file name in the File name text box already has an *extension* at the end (a period followed by one or more letters), don't change that extension! As you'll learn later, the file's extension tells Windows what type of information is in the file. If you change the extension, Windows will get the wrong information from the extension, and the file may not open.

To avoid changing the extension, you can click just to the left of the period to put the cursor there. Drag the mouse pointer to the left to select all the text to the left of the period, as in Figure 6-7. Then type the new name. The new name will replace the selected portion of the name, leaving the extension intact.

Figure 6-7: Renaming a document while leaving the extension as is

Finally, be aware that every file within a folder must have a unique name. So don't try to give two different files the same name. You can make part of each file name the same, as in Vacation01, Vacation02, Vacation03, and so forth.

Step 3: Saving the Document

After you've completed Steps 1 and 2, that's usually all you need to do. You can ignore any other options in the dialog box and click the Save button. We'll talk about when, and why, you might want to use the Save As Type option in the Save As dialog box in the section "Changing the Document Type," later in this chapter.

Save Your Work Often!

When you save a document, you're saving a copy of that document as it exists in the computer's memory at that moment in time. Any changes you make after saving the document are *not* saved until you save the document again. So when you're happy with a change you've made to a document, you'd be wise to save the entire document right then and there; don't risk losing the change.

In the long run, the smart thing to do is save a new document at the moment you create it. Don't wait until you've put a bunch of work into it. That way, the document has a name and a place. As you work on the document, use any of the standard Save techniques (summarized again here) to save your work every five minutes or so:

✦ Click the Save button on the program's toolbar (if available).

✦ Choose File ➪ Save from the program's menu bar.

✦ Press Ctrl+S.

If you save your work every five minutes, the most work you can lose is five minutes' worth. On the other hand, if you spend six hours working on a document but never save it, you stand to lose all six hours of work.

Troubleshooting Saves

Normally, when you save a file, it just gets saved, and the Save As dialog box closes. If there's a problem, you'll likely see an error message like the example shown in Figure 6-8. You'll need to fix the problem to proceed. Here are some common error messages, what they mean, and how to solve the problem:

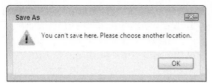

Figure 6-8: A sample error message

✦ **You cannot save in the folder specified:** The folder you've chosen can't be used to store files. Solution: Click OK, and choose the Documents folder; then click Save. The document will be stored in your Documents folder.

✦ *File name* **already exists. Do you want to replace?:** The file you're about to save has the same name as a file that's already in the folder. If you choose Yes, you'll replace that file with the one you're saving, and the original file will be lost forever. Solution: Choose No, change the file name of this document, and click the Save button again. The document you're saving will be placed under the file name you provide; the original file will keep its original name.

✦ **The file name is invalid:** There's an invalid character, such as a punctuation mark in the file name you entered. Solution: Click the OK button, remove the invalid character(s) from the file name, and click Save.

✦ **Please insert a disk into drive A:** You've selected the floppy drive as the place to save the file, but there is no floppy disk in the drive. Solution: You have two choices here. The best would be to click the Cancel button, choose Documents as the location to save the file instead, and click the Save button. Otherwise, insert a floppy disk with sufficient empty space into the drive and wait a few seconds for the Save As dialog box to close.

✦ **You have files waiting to be written to CD:** You chose your CD-R or CD-RW drive as the place to save the file. Solution: Save the file again; this time, choose Documents as the folder. To learn how CD and DVD disks work, see Chapter 21.

Closing a Document

Saving a document that's currently open ensures that all your recent changes get stored to the disk. But saving the document doesn't close it. The saved program remains open and visible on your screen so that you can do some more work. But there's no need to keep the document on-screen until you're completely finished. You can close the document at any time and then reopen it at any time in the future to work on it some more or print it.

Closing a document takes it off your screen, freeing up space so that you can work with other programs or documents without the additional clutter. The easy way to close a document is to just close the program that's displaying the document, using whichever of the following methods you feel is most convenient for you:

✦ Click the Close (X) button in the upper-right corner of the program window.

✦ Or choose File ➪ Exit (or File ➪ Close) from the program's menu bar.

✦ Or if the document's program is the active window, press Alt+F4.

If you've made any changes to the document since the last time you saved it, you'll be prompted whether you want to save those changes. Click Yes to save the document as it appears on the screen now. Or click No to abandon any changes you've made since you last saved.

 If the program you're using supports multiple document interface (MDI), you can close the document and leave the program open. For more information, see the section "Working with Multiple Document Windows," near the end of this chapter.

If you're following along online, go ahead and close your document and the WordPad program window now. Choose Yes if asked about saving your work. In the next section, you'll learn now to reopen a document you've saved to your hard disk.

Opening Documents

After you've created a saved a document, you can open it at any time to view it, edit it, or print it. This is the same idea as going to your file cabinet and retrieving some document you stored there for safekeeping. Your computer document will open on the screen however, contained within the *default program* for the type of document you've opened. (We'll discuss the meaning of *default program* a little later in this chapter.)

As with most things, there are several ways to open a document. Choosing one method over the other is simply a matter of deciding which is most convenient at the moment. The sections that follow describe the different methods.

Opening a Recent Document

If the document you want to open is one you've worked on recently, you may be able to open it right from the Start menu. To do so, click the Start button, and choose Recent Items, as in Figure 6-9; then click the name of the document you want to open.

The document will open, most likely in the same program you used to create it.

Figure 6-9: The Recent Items menu; your Recent Items menu will obviously have different items!

 Tip

To alphabetize the Recent Items list, right-click any document name and choose Sort By Name.

Where's My Recent Documents?

If you don't see a Recent Items option on the right side of your Start menu, just perform the following steps to add that option:

1. Right-click the Start button and choose Properties. The Taskbar and Start Menu Properties dialog box opens.

2. If the Start Menu tab is not selected, then select it.

3. Make sure the *Store and display a list of recently opened files* option is selected.

4. Click the OK button in the Taskbar and Start Menu Properties dialog box.

5. Click the Start button, and you should see Recent Items listed on the right side of the Start menu.

Opening a Document from Its Folder

You can always open a document from whatever folder you put it in. This works for downloaded files and saved e-mail attachments, as well as for documents you created yourself. The trick is simply to open the folder in which the file is contained. You can do that by clicking the Start button and choosing the folder's name. Or, if the folder's name isn't on the Start menu, open the folder's nearest parent; then navigate down from there.

For example, let's say you created a folder named 2004 Vacation inside your Pictures folder. You want to open that folder from the Windows desktop. Click the Start button and choose Pictures to get to your Pictures folder. Then double-click the 2004 Vacation folder's icon in the main pane of Windows Explorer.

 If you have no idea what we're talking about in the preceding paragraph, see the sections "How Folders Are Organized" and "Navigating Through Folders" in Chapter 5.

When you see the icon for the file you want to open, just double-click it. The document will open in the default program that is associated with that type of document (assuming there is such a program on your computer).

Using the Open Dialog Box

If the program you'll be using to view or edit the document is already open, you can use its Open dialog box to open a document. You can get to a program's Open dialog box using one of the following methods:

✦ From the program's menu bar, choose File ➪ Open.

✦ Click the Open button on the program's toolbar, if available.

✦ Press Ctrl+O (if the program is in the active window).

The Open dialog box looks a lot like the Save As dialog box and offers the same navigation tools. Opening a document from the Open dialog box is usually a simple two-step process:

1. Navigate and select the folder in which the document is contained.

2. In the main pane, double-click the document's icon. (Or click the document's icon and then click the Open button.)

Figure 6-10 summarizes these basic steps. Note that the Open dialog box contains the same navigation tools as the Save As dialog box, described earlier in this chapter. For example, suppose you're in the Open dialog box and want to jump to your Documents folder. In that case, choose Documents from the address box drop-down list, or click Documents from the Favorite Links section of the navigation pane at the left side of the dialog box (if available).

1. Navigate to the folder containing the document

2. Double click the icon for the file to be opened

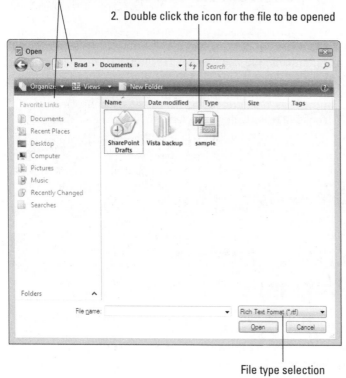

File type selection

Figure 6-10: The Open dialog box

After you've opened the folder that contains the document, you should see that document's icon in the main pane. If you don't, take a look at the Files Type drop-down menu near the bottom of the Open dialog box (see Figure 6-10). That selection limits the icons visible in the main pane to files of that type. To see all the files in the current folder, choose All Documents (*.*) from the Files Type drop-down list.

 Tip   To alphabetize the icons in the main pane, right-click an empty space between icons and choose Sort by ⇨ Name. To change your view of the icons, click the Views button in the dialog box.

As mentioned, when you see the document's icon, you can just double-click it to open it. Or click the icon and click the Open button in the dialog box. The document will open in the document area of your program.

Where's My File?

Suppose you're in the Open dialog box and you navigate to some folder in which you're certain you stored a file. But there's no sign of the file in that folder. What to do? The first thing to remember is that the only document icons visible in the main pane are those whose document type matches that selected in the Files Type drop-down list. If a file seems to be missing, choose All Files (*.*) or All Documents (*.*) from the Files Type drop-down list to see all icons. Or choose the file type that matches the type of file you're looking for.

All of the preceding methods have one thing in common: They will open the document in the default program for that document type. That might be the same as the program you used to create the document, but then again it might not be. So it's time to get this whole business of the *default program* for a document squared away so that you're the one in control of things.

Opening a Document in a Different Program

As we've mentioned before, when you open a document, it opens in whatever program is set as the *default program* for that document type. That default program might not be the only program on your computer capable of opening the document. You might have several programs on your computer that can open a certain type of document.

To see which programs can open a document, go to the document's icon on the Recent Items menu. Or use the method described under this chapter's "Opening a Document from Its Folder" section to get to the document's icon through Windows Explorer. When you see the document's icon, don't double-click it. Instead, right-click the icon and choose Open With. If two or more programs on your system can open the document, you'll see their names listed on the Open With menu, as in the example shown in Figure 6-11.

After you've clicked Open With, click the name of the program you want to use to open the document. That document will open in that program.

Be forewarned that if you just take a wild guess at choosing a program to open some document, the document may open but appear only as meaningless gobbledygook on the screen. If that happens, you should close the program and document. If the program asks if you want to save any changes made to the document, definitely choose No, because you really don't want to save the meaningless gobbledygook version of the document that's on the screen at the moment.

Figure 6-11: Example of an Open With menu

Changing the Default Program

If you find that you always have to right-click a particular type of document and choose Open With to get it to open in the program you want, you can change the default program. That is, you can change which program opens automatically when you double-click the document's icon.

Choosing a new default program for a file type is fairly easy. First, find a document that's the appropriate type. (You may need to make file name extensions visible for this part.) When you find a document of the appropriate type, follow these steps:

1. Right-click the icon and choose Open With.

2. In the Open With menu, click Choose Default Program. The Open With dialog box shown in Figure 6-12 opens.

3. Click the name of the program you want to use as the new default program for this type of document.

4. Select the check box Always use the selected program to open this kind of file.

5. Click OK.

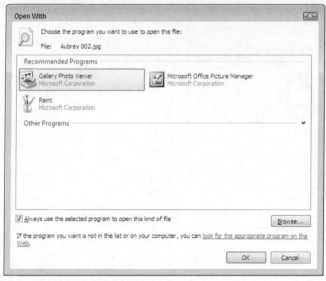

Figure 6-12: The Open With dialog box

From now on, whenever you double-click a document that's of the same type (that is, has the same file name extension) as the one you right-clicked in Step 1, you can still right-click the icon and choose Open With to open the document in any program you want. All you've done here is define what program opens when you double-click the icon.

Note If there is not a default program already associated to a document, then you will see Open With. . . (notice the three dots) instead of just Open With. When you click Open With. . ., you end up with an Open With dialog box similar to Figure 6-12.

When Windows Can't Open a Document

If you create a document yourself, you can surely open it by using whatever program you used to create the document. But if you download a document from the Internet, or if someone sends you a document by e-mail, there's no guarantee that you already have a program installed that can open that document.

When you try to open a document for which there is no default program defined, you'll see a dialog box like the one shown in Figure 6-13.

The dialog box is saying, "There is no default program for opening this type of document. What do you want to do about that?" In this example, we're trying to open the document Guidelines.pdf. So what that dialog box is saying, more specifically is, "There is no known program installed on your computer that can open a PDF file." You have three choices on how to handle the situation:

Figure 6-13: The options that appear when Windows can't open a document

✦ **Use the web service to find the appropriate program** and then click the OK button. Choosing this option takes you to a Web page where you can learn which program or programs are available for opening this document. (This requires that you also know how to use your web browser and perhaps how to download and install programs.)

Tip   To open a PDF document, you need a program named Adobe Reader. You can get that program for free by visiting www.adobe.com and clicking the Get Adobe Reader button on their home page. After you've started the installation, be sure to choose the Open button in the File Download dialog box that appears.

✦ **Select a program from a list of installed programs** and then click the OK button. If you think one of the programs already installed on your computer might be able to open the document, choose the second option; then choose a program from the Open With dialog box that opens. (This requires that you have enough experience with the programs on your computer to be able to make a reasonable guess about which program will be able to open the document.)

✦ **Click Cancel.** Choose this option if you can't decide what to do. The dialog box will close and no further attempt will be made to open the document.

Whether or not you'll be able to get anywhere using the first two options really depends on your experience level. For a beginner, the simple solution might be to ask whoever sent you the file what program is needed. If the person who sent you the file is an experienced user, he or she may be able to send you a copy of the document in a format you can open.

Changing the Document Type

Once in a while, you may need to change a document's type yourself. For example, let's say you send someone a document you created in Microsoft Word, but the recipient can't open the document because he or she does not own Microsoft Word. How can you save the same document in some other format that your recipient can open?

One thing is for sure: Simply changing the file name extension will not work. You never want to change a file's extension, because if you do, the extension on the file name will no longer accurately describe the format of the data in the file. And possibly, no program will be able to open the document! What you need to do is open the original document; then save a new copy of the same document in a different format. Here's how:

1. Open the document in the usual manner (by double-clicking its icon, for example).

2. From the menu bar of the program that opens the document, choose File ➪ Save As. The Save As dialog box opens.

3. Navigate to the folder in which you want to store the converted document (for example, choose Documents from the Favorite Links list).

4. Enter a name for the converted document (do not type a file name extension in the File Name text box).

5. Click the Save As Type drop-down list button; then click the file type you want to use for this copy of the document. The exact file types available to you will depend on the program you're using at the moment. Figure 6-14 shows a couple of examples.

 Caution   If file name extensions are visible, the extension that appears in the File Name text box will reflect whatever type you choose from the Save As Type drop-down list. As always, you never want to change the extension that appears in the File Name text box.

6. Click the Save button in the Save As dialog box.

Why Can't I Convert to PDF?

Portable Document Format (PDF) is a popular format for distributing documents over the Internet. This has to do with the fact that a portable document looks the same across operating systems, including Windows, Macintosh, Linux, UNIX. But to create PDF files, you need to purchase and install Adobe Acrobat. Or you can sign up for a service that enables you to do that online at www.adobe.com. You can *read* (view) PDF files with the free Adobe Reader software. But you can't *create* or edit PDF documents with Adobe Reader.

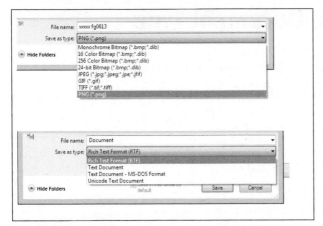

Figure 6-14: Sample Save As Type drop-down lists from
Paint and WordPad

Now you can close the program and open the folder in which you stored the
converted document. If you made this conversion to send the document to
someone else, make sure you send the converted copy of the document, not
the original.

Working with Multiple Document Windows

Some programs provide a multiple document interface (MDI), which enables
you to have several documents open at the same time. Each document
appears within its own document window inside the program's window. A document window is similar to a program window, except that it has no menu bar
or toolbar. A document window doesn't need those things, because the program displaying the document already has all the menus and tools needed to
edit the document.

For example, take a look at Figure 6-15. There, the open program is Microsoft
Excel 2007 (as indicated by that name in the title bar). The menu bar and toolbar for that program appear just below the title bar.

Currently, we have three documents (each a spreadsheet) open in that program. Two of the documents are visible. The third document is currently minimized within the program window and appears near the lower-left corner of
the program window. Note that unlike a minimized program window, which
appears on the taskbar, a minimized document window appears within the
program's document area.

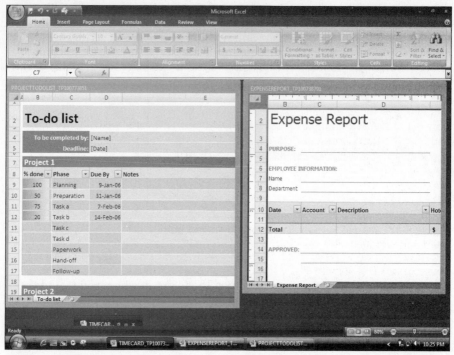

Figure 6-15: Some programs enable you to work with several open documents simultaneously.

Managing document windows isn't too different from managing program windows. Perhaps the trickiest thing is getting a document at maximum size back to its normal size. If the program does contain a maximized document window, you'll see the Minimize/Restore/Close buttons for the document just above the upper-right corner of the document, as shown in Figure 6-16. You can click the Restore button (the one in the middle) to shrink the document window a bit.

An application that supports MDI might include a Windows option on the program's menu bar for tiling and cascading the document windows within the program.

Minimize/Maximize/Close
program window

Figure 6-16: Minimize, Restore, and Close buttons for a minimized document window

Minimize/Restore
document window

If you minimize a document window, it will most likely end up looking like a tiny title bar. In some programs, however, the document window might shrink to a tiny icon within the program window. Either way, you can always restore a minimized document window by double-clicking the icon or bar. Optionally, choose Windows from the menu bar, and click the name of the minimized window to restore it.

You can also move and size document windows as you would a program window. To move a document window, drag it by its title bar. To size a document window, drag any corner or edge, just as you would with a program window.

Summary

This chapter has covered fundamental, universal skills for working with document files. As you gain experience with computers, you'll discover hundreds of different document types. As intimidating as that might sound, you'll also discover that the skills you've learned in this chapter will apply to just about every document you create or download. To recap this chapter's content:

✦ Every document file has an extension at the end of its name. Windows uses this extension to determine with which program to open a document.

✦ You can make file name extensions visible or invisible through the Folder Options dialog box.

✦ To save a new document, choose File ➪ Save from the program's menu bar. Alternatively, click the Save button on its toolbar or press Ctrl+S. The Save As dialog box opens.

✦ To keep your documents organized, use the Save As dialog box to specify where you want to save the file and what you want to name it.

✦ To open a recently saved document, click the Start button, and choose Recent Items; then click the name of the document you want to open.

✦ You can also open a document from its folder or by choosing File ➪ Open from a program's menu bar.

✦ The program that opens when you double-click the icon for a document is the default program for all documents of that type.

✦ To open a document in a program other than the default program, right-click the document's icon and choose Open With.

Type, Edit, Copy, and Paste

No matter what you do with your computer, some typing will almost always be involved. Even if you plan to work with pictures, music, or video, there will be plenty of times when you'll need to type e-mail messages and such. If you can't type worth beans, the whole issue of typing can be a real pain. Although we can't well teach you to type, we can definitely show you how to get things done with minimal typing. For those of you who can type, we can show you techniques that will make your work go more quickly.

You can find, of course, hundreds of programs that enable you to type, ranging from the simple little Notepad program that comes with Windows Vista to huge, full-blown word-processing or desktop-publishing programs such as Microsoft Word and WordPerfect. Obviously, we can't cover all those products in a single book or single chapter. But we can cover *standard text-editing techniques*. Because such techniques are universal, you can use them virtually anyplace you type text — from tiny text boxes to instant messages, from e-mail messages to entire books.

If you want to follow along on your own computer and try out some of the things described in this chapter, use the WordPad program that comes with Windows Vista. WordPad is a simple word processor (as compared with behemoths such as Word and WordPerfect) that enables you to type quite fancy documents. To start WordPad, click the Start button and choose All Programs ⇨ Accessories ⇨ WordPad. WordPad's program window (and taskbar button) will open, showing you a new, blank sheet of paper to type on.

Note With Windows Vista, the need to type has actually been reduced because alternatives to typing are available. If you are using a Tablet PC or a convertible PC (a notebook computer that operates as a tablet as well), then you are able to use a special stylus, or pen, to write instead of type. Additionally, Windows Vista includes speech recognition software that enables you to use a microphone and speak instead of typing. Although Windows Vista provides support for both of these, only speech recognition will be covered in this book. You'll find more on it in Chapter 28.

Typing on a Screen

If there's any one thing that makes typing on a computer different from typing on paper, it's this: On a typewriter, you press the Return key (the equivalent of the Enter key on most computer keyboards) at the end of each line you type. On a computer, you don't do that. Instead, you just keep typing past the right margin, even past the right edge of the screen, if necessary. As you type, the text will automatically *word wrap* to the next line. That means it will break the line between two words, not in the middle of a word.

On a keyboard, you don't press Enter until you get to the end of a paragraph. If you want to insert a blank line before typing the next paragraph, you'll press Enter a second time. If you're typing a list of short lines, you'll need to press Enter at the end of each of those short lines. But other than that, the rule is *don't press Enter until you've typed the entire paragraph*. Figure 7-1 shows an example where the ↵ symbol shows where the Enter key was pressed. (That symbol wouldn't show up on the screen or in print.)

Now you might think, "What difference does it make if I press Enter at the end of each line?" It makes a huge difference; if you add or delete any text in a paragraph, the text can reformat itself correctly only if the paragraph was typed correctly. If you press Enter at the end of each line and then go back and make changes to the text, you're going to have a real mess on your hands!

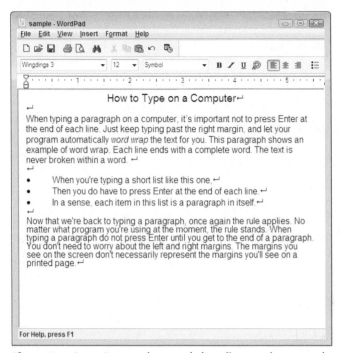

Figure 7-1: Press Enter only to end short lines and paragraphs and to insert blank lines.

Indenting and Aligning Text

On a computer, pressing the spacebar repeatedly to indent or align text is generally not a good idea (especially if you're using a *proportional font*, where each character's exact width varies). The width of multiple blank spaces becomes somewhat unpredictable, and what you see on a printed page might not match what you saw on the screen.

To indent text, it's better to use the Tab key. If you don't see a key labeled Tab on your keyboard, look for the key with two opposing arrows, pointing left and right (⇆). You should find it just to the left of the letter Q or thereabout.

> **Tip** In some programs, you can outdent the first line of text in a paragraph by pressing Shift+Tab at the start of the paragraph.

To center text, or align text to the right margin, use your program's text align features. In WordPad, you'll find buttons for centering and aligning text in the toolbar (see Figure 7-2). If you don't see similar buttons in a program you're using, consider searching that program's Help for the word *align*.

> **Tip** If you're using WordPad and don't see the formatting toolbar, choose View ⇨ Format Bar from WordPad's menu bar.

Text-Align buttons

Figure 7-2: Use text-align tools and the Tab key to indent, center, or right-align text.

Setting Margins

Another common mistake beginners often make is thinking that the margins that appear on the screen represent the margins that will appear on the printed page. That's usually not the case. If you try to force margins onto the page by indenting every line or pressing Enter at the end of each line, you can end up with a real mess on your hands. On the screen, you don't have to make any allowance whatsoever for margins.

The margins on the printed page will be determined solely by the margin settings in page setup. Although this may not be true for every program ever created, it's almost universally true that you get to those settings by choosing File ➪ Page Setup from that program's menu bar. Most Page Setup dialog boxes will have options similar to those shown in Figure 7-3. (That Page Setup dialog box is the one that appears when you choose File ➪ Page Setup from WordPad menu bar.)

The margin settings are clearly visible in Figure 7-3. As you make changes to the margin settings, the preview document at the top of the dialog box will change to show the current setting. Again, don't expect the margins to be visible on the screen. Margins are often hidden on the screen because there's really no need for them on the screen. Showing them would just waste valuable screen space.

Figure 7-3: The WordPad Page Setup dialog box

Tip
As always, your selections in the dialog box aren't applied until you click the OK button in that dialog box.

Choosing a Page Orientation

The Orientation option you see in Figure 7-3 refers to how text is printed on the page. The normal mode is Portrait (vertical), so named because it's the orientation artists use to paint portraits. The Landscape option flips the page sideways, like the way an artist might paint a landscape. The Landscape setting is useful for printing extra-wide tables that won't fit within the normal Portrait orientation. If you choose Landscape from the dialog box shown in Figure 7-3, the preview document at the top of the dialog box will show you what we mean.

Printing Text

Printing text (or anything else, for that matter) is usually simple. As a rule, you can use whichever of the following techniques is most convenient at the moment:

✦ Choose File ➪ Print from the program's menu bar.

✦ Click the Print button in the program's toolbar.

✦ Press Ctrl+P.

Cross-Reference
See Chapter 8 for a thorough discussion of printing.

Navigating Text

If you're lucky enough to type everything perfectly on the first try, you're a lucky person indeed. Most of us have to go back and fix a bunch of little errors before we can print our text. To make any change to existing text, you first have to get the *cursor* to where you want to make the change. Some programs might refer to the cursor as the *insertion point*, so named because it shows, on the screen, where the next text you type will be inserted. Whatever you call it, it usually looks like a small, blinking vertical line.

Before you try these techniques, however, be aware that they work only in text you've already typed. You can't move the cursor freely about the blank page using these techniques. You can only move through text that's already in the document. To position the cursor using the mouse, just point to where you want to place the cursor and click the left mouse button. The cursor will move to that exact spot the moment you click. You can also use the navigation keys listed in Table 7-1 to move the cursor through existing text.

 Caution The specific program you're using at any given moment might not support all the keys listed in Table 7-1. The keys listed first are the most common of the bunch.

Table 7-1
Universal (or Almost Universal) Keys for
Moving the Cursor Through Text

Key	Where It Moves the Cursor
→	One character to the right
←	One character to the left
↑	Up one line
↓	Down one line
Home	Beginning of the line
End	End of line
Ctrl+Home	Top of document
Ctrl+End	End of document
Page Up (PgUp)	Up a page (or screen)
Page Down (PgDn)	Down a page (or screen)
Ctrl+←	One word to the left
Ctrl+→	One word to the right
Ctrl+↑	Up one paragraph
Ctrl+↓	Down one paragraph

Key	Where It Moves the Cursor
Ctrl+Page Up (PgUp)	To top of previous page
Ctrl+Page Down (PgDn)	To top of next page
Alt+Ctrl+Page Up (PgUp)	To top of visible text
Alt+Ctrl+Page Down (PgDn)	To bottom of visible text

Tip　　To add a blank space to the end of your text, press the Spacebar. To end the line of text, press Enter.

Selecting Text to Change

As you'll learn throughout this book, the concept of *select, then do* is almost universal in Windows programs, especially when it comes to working with text. The term *select* in this context means *highlight*. As an example, Figure 7-4 shows where we've selected some text and then changed the font, size, and alignment using buttons on the WordPad toolbar. Notice how only the selected text gets the changes.

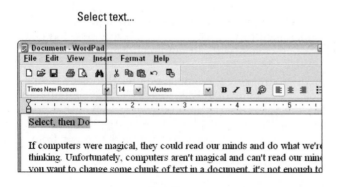

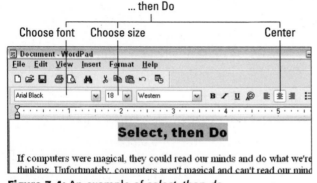

Figure 7-4: An example of *select, then do*

The most common text-selection methods are:

✦ Click at a starting point and then drag the mouse pointer through the text you want to select.

✦ Hold down the Shift key while pressing any of the navigation keys listed in Table 7-1.

The following methods are also widely available. However, not every program may support these methods (if in doubt, search the Help option in the program you're using at the moment):

✦ **Select one word:** Double-click the word.

✦ **Select one sentence:** Hold down the Ctrl key and click the sentence.

✦ **Select one line:** Move the cursor into the white space to the left of the line; then click in that space.

✦ **Select one paragraph:** Triple-click the paragraph.

✦ **Select multiple paragraphs:** Drag through all of them. Or click where you want to start the selection. Then hold down the Shift key and click to where you want to extend the selection.

✦ **Select a rectangular chunk of text:** Hold down the Alt key and drag the cursor through the text.

If you make a mess of things while selecting text and need to start over, just click any text within your document to deselect all the currently selected text. Or press the ↑, ↓, ←, or → key by itself (without holding down the Shift key).

If you use Adobe Reader, dragging the mouse pointer through a chunk of text might not select text immediately. Instead, you may end up only scrolling through text. Click the Select Text button (shown at left) in that program's menu bar first. Then drag the mouse pointer through the text you want to select. If you don't see that button, choose View ➪ Toolbars ➪ Basic from Adobe Reader menu bar.

Changing Text

There are lots of ways to change text in most programs. For tiny corrections, you can use the following keys:

✦ **Backspace:** Deletes the character to the left of the cursor.

✦ **Delete (Del):** Deletes the character to the right of the cursor.

✦ **Insert:** Switches between Insert and Overwrite modes.

Why Can't I Change This Text?

Not every program that displays text is an *editor*. Just because you can see text in a program doesn't mean you can change text in that program. Some examples of programs that show text, but don't let you edit it, are your *web browser*, as well as any *viewer* or *reader* program like Adobe Reader.

If you want to use text from some other document in a document you're working on yourself, you can (usually) select text in your browser, viewer, or reader. Then copy and paste that text into WordPad or whatever program you're using at the moment to create your document. After you've pasted the text into your document, you can edit it as much as you want. It's not different from text you've typed yourself, when it's in your editing program. Copying and pasting is covered in detail later in this chapter.

Tip   Most keys on your keyboard can *autotype*, which means rather than tapping a key a bunch of times, you can just hold the key down for a second or two. The key will start behaving as though you were tapping away at it madly. Release the key when you're done. If you overdo it, press Ctrl+Z to undo the change.

The Insert key acts as a toggle, which means you don't tap it repeatedly to do something. Tap it once to switch from Insert more to Overwrite mode or from Overwrite mode to Insert mode. Here's the difference between the two modes:

✦ **Insert mode:** Any new text you type is inserted into existing text at the location of the cursor, without changing any of that text.

✦ **Overwrite mode:** Any new text you type replaces text that's already at the cursor position.

Deleting and Replacing Large Chunks of Text

To delete or replace a large chunk of text, select the text you want to get rid of by using any of the techniques described in "Selecting Text to Change" earlier in this chapter. To delete all the selected text, press the Delete (Del) key. To replace all the selected text with something new, just start typing the new text. The selected text will disappear instantly, and the new text will take its place. If you make a mistake, press Ctrl+Z to undo the change.

Styling Text

Most word-processing programs enable you to change the style of your text. The buzzwords for text style are *font* (the design of the letters); *weight* (**bold-face** and *italic* are examples of weights); *effects* (underline, ~~strikethrough~~); size (generally measured in *points*, where 1 point is equal to about ½ inch); and, of course, *color*. Figure 7-5 illustrates some examples of these buzzwords.

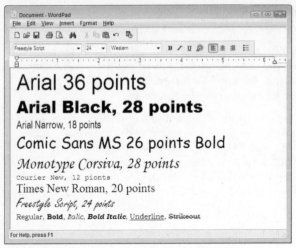

Figure 7-5: Examples of fonts, sizes, and weights

 Caution Notepad, a simple text editor, doesn't enable you to change fonts. You need to use WordPad or some other word-processing program if you want to style your text.

To change the font of text in your program:

STEPS: Change the Style or Color of Text

1. Select the text you want to stylize and then . . .

   • Choose options on the program's formatting toolbar (if available).

   • Or choose Format ➪ Font from the program's menu bar. In the dialog box that opens, make your selections; then click OK.

Figure 7-6 shows the formatting toolbar and Font dialog box from the WordPad program. Other programs will have similar, or perhaps more, options to choose from.

If your computer is new, you'll be limited to choosing from among those fonts that come with Windows Vista. However, literally hundreds, if not thousands, of fonts are available for Windows. If you go to www.google.com and search for **free Windows fonts**, you'll find many examples. But before you download any fonts from a web, make sure you read the instructions for installing the fonts at that site. There's really no general technique that applies to all fonts from all manufacturers.

Format Bar   Font dialog box

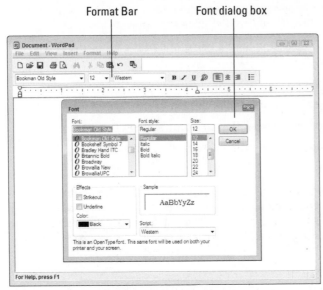

Figure 7-6: Formatting options in WordPad

If you just want to **boldface**, *italicize*, or underline a selected chunk of text, you can use the shortcut keys that follow:

✦ **Ctrl+B:** Boldface

✦ **Ctrl+I:** Italic

✦ **Ctrl+U:** Underline

Copying, Moving, and Pasting Text

Any place you can type text, you can also *paste* text. That boils down to this: If there's a chunk of text somewhere on your screen that you want to include in some document you're currently working on, you'd be crazy to retype it all. It's better to just copy and paste (or cut and paste) the text from its current location into your document. The basic procedure works like this:

STEPS: Copy and Paste Text

1. Select the text you want to copy.

2. To copy the selected text, use one of the following methods:

   • Press Ctrl+C.

   • Right-click the selected text and choose Copy.

   • Choose Edit ➪ Copy from that program's menu bar.

   • If available, click the copy button on the toolbar.

3. In the document you're writing, place the cursor where you want to insert the copied text. (You can just click the appropriate spot.)

4. Paste the text you copied in Step 2 using one of the following methods:

   - Press Ctrl+V.

   - Right-click near the cursor and choose Paste.

   - Choose Edit ⇨ Paste from that program's menu bar.

   - If available, click on the paste button on the toolbar.

You can use a similar technique to copy pictures and paste them into text, provided that the program you're using allows it. Most programs, including WordPad, do. Notepad, on the other hand, does not. To really appreciate the value of copying and pasting, it helps to look at some examples, as we'll do in the sections that follow.

Copying from One Document to Another

Assume you're working on a paper and doing your research on the World Wide Web. You want to copy chunks of text from various web pages to use as your source material. Here's what you do:

Cross-Reference Chapter 10 describes the World Wide Web and related topics.

STEPS: Copy Text from a Web Page to Your Documents

1. In your web browser, select the text you want to copy.

2. Press Ctrl+C, click the copy button, or choose Edit ⇨ Copy from your web browser's menu bar.

3. In your document (the one you're writing), click where you want to put the copied text, so the cursor shows where the next text will appear.

4. Press Ctrl+V, click the paste button, or choose Edit ⇨ Paste from your word-processing program's menu bar. The copied text appears where you pasted it, as shown in Figure 7-7.

You can use the same basic technique to copy from just about any document to another. But don't expect it to work with every single document you come across. For example, people who create PDF documents (the kind you open with Adobe Reader) can lock their documents to prevent copying. If a document is locked, you'll likely see a message asking for a password when you try to copy. The only person who knows that password is the person who created and locked the document.

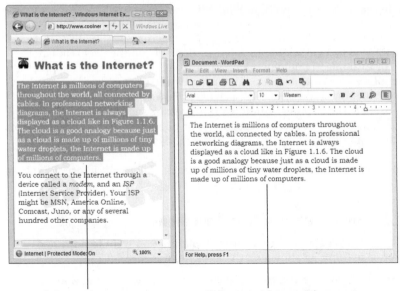

1. Select and copy text
(Ctrl + C or right click and choose Copy)

2. Paste text into your document
(Ctrl + V or right click and choose Paste)

Figure 7-7: Copying text from a web page to a WordPad document

Twenty-first Century Term Papers

My daughter, who is in high school, has developed a very fancy technique for doing her term papers. First, using Microsoft Word, she sets up a document that will print on index cards. Then she searches the Web for pages on her topic. As she browses through web pages, she copies chunks of text, and each page's URL, to a separate index card. When she has enough information, she prints the index cards.

Next, she opens a new, blank document and starts copying chunks of text from the index cards into her new document, in roughly the order she wants them to appear in the finished product. When that step is finished, she has her rough draft (albeit a completely plagiarized rough draft).

Finally, she creates the paper by adding, changing, and deleting text in the rough draft to make the text her own. Or, in some cases, she may use a quote directly and copy the web site information into her bibliography. And of course, Microsoft Word takes care of any misspellings or grammatical errors automatically. The whole process takes about ¹⁄₁₀ the time I had to spend writing those awful papers in high school!

Copy and Paste a Picture

Most modern programs enable you to include pictures with your text. Exactly how fancy you can get with your pictures depends on the program you're using. For example, if you're working in Notepad, it's impossible to paste a picture into your document. If you're using WordPad, you can paste a picture into your document. But you can't make text flow around the picture. If you're using a more sophisticated word processor such as Microsoft Word or WordPerfect, you can put a picture into your document, make text flow around the picture, and do a whole bunch of other fancy stuff.

We can illustrate this by way of an example using Microsoft Internet Explorer and WordPad, two programs built into every copy of Windows Vista.

STEPS: Copy a Picture into a Document

1. In Internet Explorer, right-click the picture you want to copy and choose Copy, as shown on the left side of Figure 7-8.

2. In the document you're typing, click the spot where you want to paste the picture.

3. Press Ctrl+V, or right-click near the cursor and choose Paste, or choose Edit ⇨ Paste from that program's menu bar.

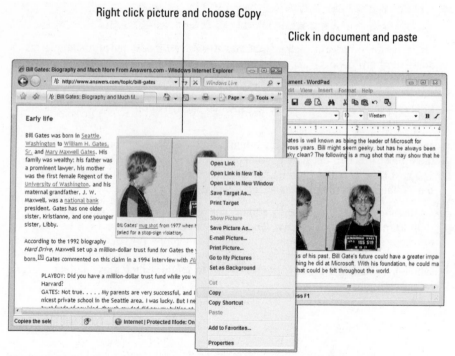

Figure 7-8: Copying a picture from a web page to a WordPad document

Tip In Step 3, you can just as easily paste the picture into a graphics program. There, you can crop it, touch it up, resize it, save it to your hard disk, or whatever. See Chapter 15 for more information on working with pictures in graphics programs.

In WordPad, that's about all you can do. If you're using a fancier word-processing program, try right-clicking the picture in that program to see what your other options are. Or search that program's Help for picture or graphic.

Move a Chunk of Text within a Document

You can use cut and paste to move a chunk of text within a document or from one document to another. The only difference is that when you cut, rather than copy, the original text is deleted right after the copy is made. So when you paste the text, only the pasted copy remains. Here are the steps:

Caution You can copy text from nearly any document you want. But you can only cut text from documents that you have the ability to edit. If Cut won't work, try Copy.

STEPS: Move Text

1. Select the text you want to move.

2. Press Ctrl+X, click the cut button, or right-click the text and choose Cut, or choose Edit ➪ Cut from the program's menu bar.

3. Move the cursor to where you want to place the text you just cut.

4. Press Ctrl+V, click the paste button, right-click and choose Paste, or choose Edit ➪ Paste from the program's menu bar.

The text is inserted at the location where you placed the cursor in Step 3.

Dragging and Dropping Text

You've seen ways to copy, cut, and paste text. Text can be copied or cut and then pasted in another way — by using the drag-and-drop technique. To use this technique, complete the following steps.

STEPS: Cutting or Copying with Drag and Drop

1. Select the text or image that you want to copy or move. You can do this in the manner shown earlier in this chapter.

2. Click the selected item with the right mouse button and hold that button down. Drag the item to the new location. The new location can be within a different window or within the same window provided the resulting spot is within a document you can edit.

3. Release the mouse button. A pop-up menu will be displayed. You can select either Move Here or Copy Here from the menu. If you drop the item in the wrong place, you can press Ctrl+Z to undo the action.

As a caution, if you drag and drop content from a web page to another document, Windows might display a dialog box similar to the one shown in Figure 7-9 for you to confirm that you want to copy something from the Web. Because you don't necessarily know what could be included when you copy something from the Web, you want to proceed with caution (unless you know the site).

Figure 7-9: Use caution given if you drag content from a web page.

Adding Special Characters to Text

Your keyboard has all the letters, numbers, and punctuation marks you need to type just about anything. But once in a while, you may need to use a special character, like a copyright or trademark symbol, in your text. Many programs have this capability built into them. But there's one program you can use with just about any program. The program's name is Character Map, and the following steps demonstrate how you use it to insert a special character into text you're currently typing.

STEPS: Insert a Special Character

1. In your document, position the cursor where you want to insert the special character(s).

2. Click the Start button and choose All Programs ➪ Accessories ➪ System Tools ➪ Character Map. The Character Map program opens (see Figure 7-10).

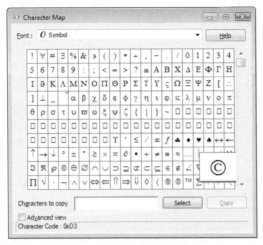

Figure 7-10: Windows Vista Character Map

3. If you don't see the character you want:

   • Use the scroll bar to the right of the characters to see additional characters.

   • Or choose a different font from the Font drop-down list (Figure 7-10 displays the font named Symbol).

 Tip   If it's hard to see a character in Character Map, click the character to magnify it.

4. To select a character to use, click it; then click the Select button. You can repeat this step to select as many characters as you need.

5. Click the Copy button.

6. In your document, click where you want to place the special character(s).

7. Press Ctrl+V, or right-click near the cursor and choose Paste, or choose Edit ⇨ Paste from the program's menu bar.

The character is inserted into your document at the cursor position.

What's Character Map?

Character Map is an optional Windows Vista component and therefore might not be installed on your system. If you can't find Character Map, you can install it using the techniques described in Chapter 29. In the Windows Components Wizard described there, you'll find Character Map under Accessories and Utilities ⇨ Accessories.

Saving Your Text

The moment you start typing text into a blank sheet of paper in a program, you've created a document. As discussed in Chapter 6, just because it's a document and on your screen doesn't mean it's been saved. If you plan to revisit the document, you'll need to save it. You can use all the standard techniques described in the sections "Saving a Document" and "Closing a Document" in Chapter 6 to save your work and close your document. If in doubt as to where you save the document, go for the most obvious and simple solution — your Documents folder.

Tip   When working on a lengthy document, remember what I say in Chapter 6 — save your work often!

Likewise, you can open your document at any time by using any of the techniques described in the section "Opening Documents" in Chapter 6. There's nothing to it.

Summary

In this chapter, you've learned fundamental, universal techniques for creating, editing, printing, and saving text. Of course, hundreds of programs are available for Windows Vista that enable you to type and edit text, and there's no way to test them all. The techniques discussed in this chapter, however, will almost certainly work in any program you use. If in doubt, try it out.

If all else fails, choose Help from the program's menu bar, and search for whatever word or phrase describes what you want to do. Before we move on to Chapter 8, here's a quick recap of the main skills you've acquired in this chapter.

✦ When typing paragraphs, don't press Enter at the end of each line (only at the end of each paragraph).

✦ To print text, press Ctrl+P, or choose File ➪ Print from the program's menu bar, or right-click the text and choose Print. If a Print dialog box opens, click its Print or OK button.

✦ To change text, you must first move the cursor (or insertion point) to where you want to make the change. You can click the spot or use the navigation keys on the keyboard.

✦ To style, delete, copy, or move text, you first need to select the text so your program knows which text to work with.

✦ If you need to get text from one program window to another on your computer, don't retype. Use copy and paste instead.

✦ To add a special character to your text, click the Start button and choose All Programs ➪ Accessories ➪ System Tools ➪ Character Map.

Printing Documents

If your computer has a printer attached, you can
print any document currently open and visible on
your screen. Even though tens of thousands of programs enable you to print documents, and hundreds of
makes and models of printers exist, the way you go
about printing a document is almost always the same.
In the same way, you can also create a file that you
can send or share with others, which they can view or
print, but not otherwise modify.

In this chapter, you'll learn fundamental, universal skills
that you can apply to printing just about any document,
from any program.

 Note   A faxing program is included in the Windows Vista
Business and Windows Vista Ultimate editions. It
is not included in the Vista Home or Vista Home
Premium editions.

Printing a Document

Although we can't say that we've used every one of the
programs available for Windows Vista, we have used a
lot of them. So far, they all support the first three
options listed here:

✦   Click the Print button in the program's
       toolbar.

✦   Choose File ➪ Print from the program's
    menu bar.

✦   Press Ctrl+P.

If you use the first method, the document will likely just
start printing within a few seconds. Using either of the
other methods is likely to display the Print dialog box,
where you can choose options to specify exactly how
you want to print the current document. What that Print
dialog box looks like depends on the program you're

using and your printer's capabilities. Figure 8-1 shows a couple of sample Print dialog boxes. The one on the left belongs to Microsoft Paint; the one on the right to Microsoft Word 2007.

 Caution Don't expect any document to start printing immediately. There's always some prep work that needs to be done, and that will take a few seconds.

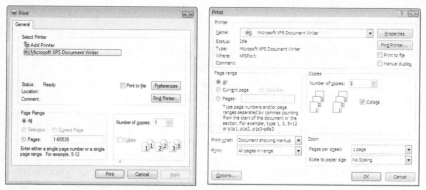

Figure 8-1: Examples of two Print dialog boxes

Common Printing Options

As you can see in Figure 8-1, you have a lot of options to choose from before you start printing. Here's a quick overview of the options you're likely to come across and most likely to use:

✦ **Select Printer:** If you have access to multiple printers (as when you're connected to a network), choose the printer you want to use. You will also see an item called Microsoft XPS Document Writer in the list of printers. This will be covered later in this chapter.

✦ **Page Range:** Choose which pages you want to print, ranging from All (the entire document), the current page (the page visible on your screen), Selection (only the text and pictures you selected in the document prior to getting here), or Pages (define a specific page, like 1, or a range of pages, like 2–5, to print only pages 2, 3, 4, and 5).

✦ **Manual Duplex:** Print pages back to back on printers that don't have the capability to do that automatically. (*Duplex* is a nerd word for *back to back*.) When you choose this option, odd-numbered pages will be printed first. You'll then be prompted to reinsert those pages, so the remaining pages can be printed on their backs.

✦ **Number of Copies:** Specify the number of copies to print.

✦ **Collate:** If this is selected, and you print multiple copies, pages are collated. If you print multiple copies, and clear the Collate option, you'll get multiple page 1s, followed by multiple page 2s, and so on.

After you've made your selections in the Print dialog box, click the Print button, or OK button, to start printing. Or you can choose additional options that are unique to your printer, as discussed next.

Tip   If your Print dialog box has a ? button in its upper-right corner, you can click that button; then you can click any option in the dialog box for more information.

Choosing a Print Quality

The general options that appear in the Print dialog box are almost universal. Depending on the make and model of your printer, you might have some other options to choose from. For example, you might be able to control the print quality of a document, opting for a quick draft or a time-consuming but better-quality job. To get to those settings, click the Properties or Preferences button in the Print dialog box. The dialog box showing preferences or properties for your printer opens. Figure 8-2 shows what this dialog box looks like when you print to an HP PhotoSmart 7760 printer.

Here's a description of what each option in the sample dialog box offers:

✦ **Orientation:** Portrait prints in the normal vertical orientation; Landscape prints horizontally across the page.

✦ **Page Order:** Front to Back prints pages from lowest page number to highest. It keeps printed pages in correct order if those printed pages come out of the printer face up. Back to Front prints pages from last to first, which keeps them in order if the printed pages come out face up.

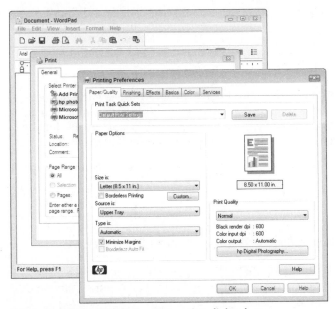

Figure 8-2: Sample Printer Properties dialog box

✦ **Pages per Sheet:** If you specify a number greater than 1, multiple pages are reduced to fit on the page. For example, choosing 2 prints two document pages on each piece of paper, making each document half its actual size.

✦ **Paper Source:** If your printer has more than one paper-feeder, use this option to choose which one you want to use. For example, if you can keep regular paper in one printer bin, and envelopes in a second bin, choose the second bin whenever you want to print envelopes.

✦ **Media:** Enables you to specify the type or quality of paper you're printing on, such as Plain Paper or Premium Photo Paper.

✦ **Quality Settings:** Enables you to choose a print quality. The higher the quality, the longer the job takes (and probably the more ink that gets used). Use Draft or Normal for printing day-to-day documents. Use High when printing a prized photo on photographic paper.

✦ **Color:** Enables you to print a color document in black and white, to conserve color ink. It might also speed up the whole process on some printers.

After you've made your selections in the Printer Properties dialog box, click OK to return to the Print dialog box. There you can choose additional options. Or click its Print or OK button to start printing.

Previewing What You're Printing

Many applications that enable you to print will also let you preview what you are printing before actually sending the information to the printer. To get a sneak peek at what the printed document will look like, you use the Print Preview option. Try choosing File ➪ Print Preview from a program's menu bar to see whether it offers this feature. Some of the programs you have opened in earlier chapters offer this preview. Figure 8-3 shows the print preview from within the Microsoft Paint program. Paint can be found in the All Programs ➪ Accessories folder.

You can use buttons in the Print Preview window to view the document at different magnifications. If your document is multiple pages long, you can also switch between the pages to preview each page. When you are finished with the preview, you can close the preview or print the document.

In addition to the Print Preview option, many programs will also offer the ability to make some changes to the setup of the page you want to print. To change margins and such, choose File ➪ Page Setup from that program's File menu. Like Print Preview, not all programs will have this option. If they do, you should end up with a dialog box with options similar to the Page Setup dialog boxes from Microsoft Paint and WordPad shown in Figure 8-4.

You can use the Page Setup dialog box to adjust a number of settings. This usually includes the margins on the page as well as whether the paper is used in landscape or portrait mode.

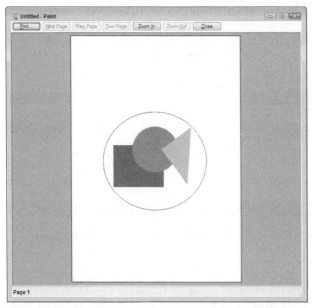

Figure 8-3: The Print Preview dialog box in Microsoft Paint

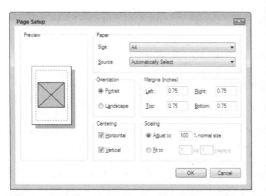

Figure 8-4: The Page Setup dialog boxes from Microsoft Paint and WordPad

Stopping the Printer, Managing Print Jobs

As mentioned, a document rarely starts printing right away, because there's some work to be done first. Part of that organization involves sending the document to the *print queue* as a *print job*. If there are other print jobs waiting to be printed, your document gets in line and waits to be printed. You can use the print queue to manage print jobs. For example, you can stop printing a document or clear all documents waiting to be printed via the print queue.

Initially, all you see of the print queue is a tiny printer icon in the notification area. When you point to it, the screen tip shows the number of documents waiting to be printed (see Figure 8-5). When you double-click that tiny icon, the print queue opens, as in the example shown Figure 8-5.

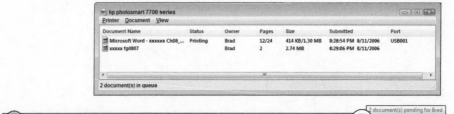

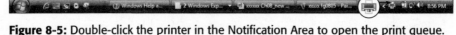

Figure 8-5: Double-click the printer in the Notification Area to open the print queue.

The print queue shows the names of any documents waiting to be printed. To pause or cancel a specific print job, right-click the document name in the print queue and choose one of the following options from the shortcut menu:

✦ **Pause:** Stops printing the document until you restart it.

✦ **Restart:** Restarts the paused print job.

✦ **Cancel:** Cancels the print job so it doesn't print and removes the job from the print queue.

✦ **Properties:** Provides detailed information about the print job. You can also set the document's priority. The higher the priority, the more likely the print job is to butt in line ahead of other documents waiting to be printed.

You can get to the same options by using the Document command in the print queue's menu bar. Whatever option you choose is applied only to the selected (highlighted) print jobs. To select one print job, just click it. To select additional print jobs, hold down the Ctrl key while clicking them. If you want to control multiple print jobs, make sure you select them all before making a selection from the Document menu in the print queue.

What Print Queue?

If you're printing to a shared printer connected to another computer in your local network, things won't work quite as described here. The file you print will be sent to the *print server's* print queue. The print server is the computer to which the shared network printer is physically attached through a cable. To cancel a network print job, you have to open the print queue on the print server computer, and then cancel the print job there.

How Do I Stop This Thing?

Don't expect a paused or canceled print job to stop right away. It may print several more pages, even after you've canceled a print job. That's because the print queue sends chunks of a document to the printer's *buffer*. That buffer, in turn, holds information waiting to be printed. Canceling a print job prevents any more data from being sent to the buffer. But the printer won't stop printing until its buffer is empty (unless, of course, you turn the printer off).

You can use commands on the print queue's menu bar to manage all the documents currently in the queue, as follows:

✦ **Printer ➪ Pause Printing:** Pauses the current print job and all those waiting in line. To resume printing, choose the same options to clear the check mark that appears next to the Pause Printing option.

✦ **Printer ➪ Cancel All Documents:** You guessed it — cancels the current print job and all those waiting to be printed.

You can close the print queue as you would any other window — by clicking the Close button in its upper-right corner or by choosing Printer ➪ Close from its menu bar. To get help with the print queue while it's open, choose Help from its menu bar.

That covers the main options for printing documents. You can also manage printers (as a whole) and fax devices using the Printer folder, described in the next section.

Managing Printers and Faxes

You can manage your printers and faxes using the Printers and Faxes folder, available in Control Panel. To open the folder:

STEPS: Open the Printers and Faxes Folders

1. Click the Start button and choose Control Panel instead and complete Steps 2 and 3 as follows.

2. If the Control Panel Home dialog box is displayed, click Printer under the Hardware and Sound category. If Classic View is displayed instead of the Control Panel Home dialog box, then double-click the Printers icon.

3. The Printers folder opens. You'll see something similar to Figure 8-6; however, the printer icons may look different on your screen.

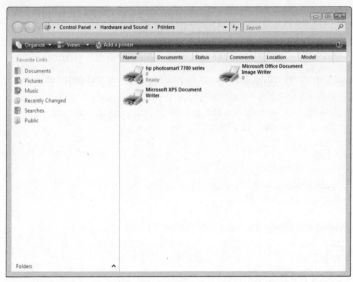

Figure 8-6: The Printers folder with no printer selected (in Tiles view)

Within the Printers and Faxes folder, you'll see an icon for each printer, fax, or other printing device to which you have access from this computer. If you click a specific printer's icon, the toolbar near the top of the window will show options for working with that particular printer (see Figure 8-7). If you click some empty space just outside an icon, so that no icon is selected, the Explorer bar will show the options shown on the right side in Figure 8-7.

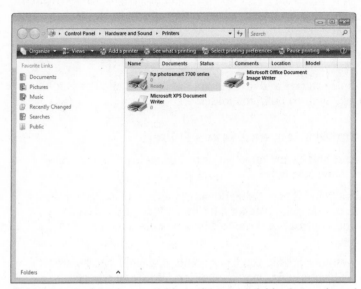

Figure 8-7: Explorer bar available in the Printer folder for a selected printer

The Explorer bar options are largely self-explanatory. The options here are available if you select (click) a printer in the main folder:

✦ **See what's printing:** Open the print queue for the selected printer.

✦ **Select printing preferences:** Lets you change the selected printer's default settings, to be used for all future print jobs.

✦ **Pause printing:** Pauses all print jobs in the selected printer's print queue.

✦ **Share:** Shares the printer so that other computers in the network can use it, if your computer and printer are on a network.

✦ **Rename this printer:** Lets you change the name displayed for the selected printer.

✦ **Delete this printer:** Removes the printer's icon from the folder.

✦ **Set printer properties:** Lets you change the selected printer's properties.

✦ **Go to manufacturer's web site:** Brings a limousine to your front door so you can visit the printer manufacturer's web site. (Yeah, sure.)

The *Add a printer* option is discussed later in this chapter.

Changing the Default Printer

The *default printer* is used to print a document when you don't specify a printer. For example, if you just click the Print button in a program's toolbar to print, without going to the Print dialog box first, the document will be printed to the default printer. In the Printers folder, the default printer is identified with a check mark, as shown in Figure 8-8.

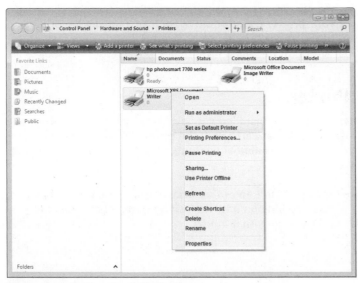

Figure 8-8: Setting the default printer

To change the default printer, right-click the icon for the device you want to use as the default, and choose Set as Default Printer from the shortcut menu (see Figure 8-8).

Using a Different Printer for One Job

If you have access to multiple printers from your computer, you're not limited to using the default printer. You can send any document to a specific printer (or a fax device or file for printing later) from the Print dialog box without changing the default printer. To do so, open to the Print dialog box from your program (that is, choose File ⇨ Print from the program's menu bar or press Ctrl+P). When the Print dialog box opens, click the item in the Select Printer area that represents the printer you want to use. Some printer dialog boxes might present a drop-down list for you to choose from instead. Figure 8-9 shows these two methods for selecting a different printer.

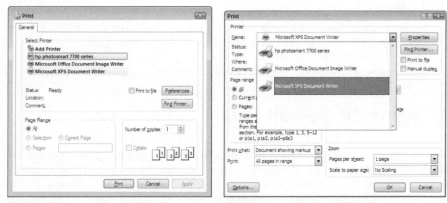

Figure 8-9: Examples of choosing a printer for the current print job only

After you've chosen your printer (or alternative such as a fax device or file), you can choose additional options if you want. To start printing (or faxing), click the Print or OK button in the same Print dialog box.

Installing a Printer

If you have a printer, but it's not installed yet, your best bet is to install it according to the instructions that came with the printer. Trying to install something through guess work is almost guaranteed to turn into a hair-pulling exercise in frustration.

If following the directions just isn't an option, wing it and hope for the best. The best scenario to use depends on how the printer connects to the computer, as discussed in the sections that follow.

Traditional Cable or USB?

If you can connect your printer to the computer using either a traditional paral-
lel/LPT type cable or a USB/FireWire cable, go with the traditional LPT cable
(even though it might seem a tiny bit quicker with the USB/FireWire cable). It's
really best to reserve your USB and FireWire cables for things that you need to
plug and unplug often, like digital still and video cameras. If you run out of USB/
FireWire ports and start plugging/unplugging the printer often to make room for
temporary devices, the likelihood of printer problems will surely rise. You don't
need problems.

USB, IEEE 1394 FireWire, or Infrared Connection

If your printer connects to your computer through a USB port, an IEEE 1394
(a.k.a. FireWire) port, or through an infrared connection, the installation procedure should go like this:

1. Close all open programs on your Windows desktop, so you have a
   nice, clear desktop to work with.

2. Plug the printer into the wall; connect the printer to the computer
   with its USB or FireWire cable. If it's an infrared printer, aim the
   infrared beam toward the infrared receptor on the computer.

3. Turn on the printer, and wait a few seconds.

You should see a message in the Notification Area that tells you the device is
connected and ready to use. You're done. The printer is installed and ready
to go.

 Tip   Figure 18-4 in Chapter 18 and Figure 29-5 in Chapter 29 show examples of
various ports found on computers.

Parallel and Serial Port Connections

If your printer is a typical plug-and-play printer that connects to the computer
through an LPT or COM port, the best approach is as follows:

1. Save any unsaved work, shut down windows, and turn off your
   computer.

2. Plug the printer into the wall; connect the printer to the computer's
   LPT or serial port, turn on the printer, and turn on the computer.

3. When Windows restarts, wait for the Found new hardware wizard to
   appear, and follow the instructions it provides.

 **Cross-
Reference**   For more information on installing new hardware, see Chapter 29.

It's difficult to say what will happen beyond this point. The printer may well just install and be ready for use without your taking any further action. An icon for the printer will be created in the Printer folder and will be available for selection in your Print dialog box.

Note When installing a new printer, a security dialog box may pop up asking whether it is okay to install a driver. A driver is software that enables your computer to talk to the printer, so it will be necessary to say that this is okay.

Sharing Unmodifiable Documents with Others

With Windows Vista, you have the ability to create a file in the XPS format. This file can then be given to others or printed from another machine. The file is like a snapshot of a document just as if it had been printed; except that it is still in an electronic format that you can share with others. Just like a printed copy, however, an XPS file cannot be changed.

You create an XPS file by using the XPS Document Writer. The XPS Document Writer acts like a printer installed in Windows Vista. As such, any program that prints will have access to it. In fact, if you look at Figure 8-9, you will see the Microsoft XPS Document Writer listed with the other print options.

After a document has been written as an XPS file, you can share it with others. To view an XPS file, you will need an XPS viewer. Fortunately, Windows Vista includes a reader — Internet Explorer.

When an XPS document is opened in Internet Explorer, a few extra tool buttons are included. These buttons enable you to add permissions as well as a digital signature to an XPS file to help secure it. Figure 8-10 shows a picture that was printed from Paint as an XPS image. This is a sample picture that comes with Vista.

Note A more popular file format for sharing files is the PDF file format from Adobe. There are programs that will also generate PDF formatted files that can be shared; however, these programs do not come with Windows Vista by default. XPS is a Microsoft alternative to the PDF format.

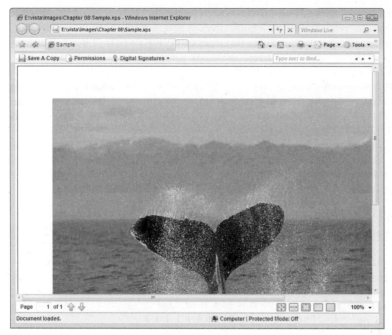

Figure 8-10: XPS Viewer in Internet Explorer

Printing the Screen

If you were around in the olden days of computers with text screens, you might remember a time when you could print whatever was on the screen just by pressing the Print Screen (PrtScn) key. (This was a so-called *screen dump*.) It doesn't work that way in Windows. You cannot print the screen directly to the printer. But you can *capture* the screen, paste it into a graphics program, and print it from there. Here's how it works:

STEPS: Print the Screen

1. Get the screen to look the way you want.

2. To capture the entire screen, press the Print Screen key. To capture only the active window, dialog box, or message, press Alt+Print Screen.

3. Open your favorite graphics program. (If you don't have one, you can use Paint in a pinch. Click the Start button and choose All Programs ➪ Accessories ➪ Paint.)

4. Press Ctrl+V, Ctrl+Insert, or choose Edit ➪ Paste from the graphics program's menu bar.

A snapshot of the screen (or whatever you captured) opens in your graphics program. If you view it at 100% magnification, it might look more like a hole through your graphics program or something hovering over it. If your graphics program allows it, shrink it a bit to get a closer view.

Tip   In some graphics programs, you can spin your mouse wheel to change the image's magnification. In others, you have to choose some option from the program's View menu, such as View ➪ Zoom. In Microsoft Paint, you can see a full screenshot effectively by choosing View ➪ Zoom ➪ Custom ➪ 50%.

To print the screen, print the picture as you would any other document (click the Print button in the program's toolbar, or press Ctrl+P, or choose File ➪ Print from your graphics program's menu bar). To save the image as a file, perhaps to include it in some other document later, save it as you would any other file. That is, click the Save button on the toolbar, or press Ctrl+S, or choose File ➪ Save from the menu bar, as discussed under "Saving Documents" in Chapter 6.

Tip   If you plan to use the screenshot as a picture in a web page, save it as a JPEG or Portable Network Graphics (PNG) file (if possible), using the Save As Type option in the Save As dialog box.

Troubleshooting Common Printer Problems

Here are some common printer problems and what you can do about them:

✦ **My pages come out in the wrong order:** Change the Page Order option to the opposite settings. For example, if it's currently set to Front to Back, change it to Back to Front. See "Choosing a Print Quality," earlier in this chapter, for more information.

✦ **The printer doesn't print:** If you recently paused all printing, open the print queue and choose Printer ➪ Pause Printing to clear the check mark from that option and resume printing. However, other problems may cause this— the printer is turned off, it's out of paper, out of ink, not connected to the printer, not properly installed, and more. You have to check all those trouble spots. Refer to the instructions that came with your printer for details.

✦ **The printer won't stop/start:** Make sure you're giving it enough time. (See "Printing a Document" and "Stopping the Printer, Managing Print Jobs" earlier in this chapter.)

✦ **The wrong document/page printed:** You probably chose File ➪ Print from the wrong program's menu bar. Click the document you want to print, to make sure it's in the active window. Then press Ctrl+P to print that document.

✦ **The same document prints over and over again:** You may have clicked the Print button too many times. Open the print queue and cancel any print jobs you don't want.

✦ **My document supposedly printed, but I don't see the pages:** If your computer is on a network, the document may have printed to some other printer. Check the other printers. See "Changing the Default Printer," earlier in this chapter, for more information.

✦ **My printed pages suddenly look blotchy:** Most likely, your printer is about to run out of ink. You're just getting the last few sputters.

✦ **My pictures don't look so hot:** Try printing on photographic paper, on a higher-quality print setting, if possible. See "Choosing a Print Quality," earlier in this chapter, for more information.

✦ **The printer suddenly went bonkers:** If you suddenly start getting gobbledygook from your printer, turn it off. On your computer, open the print queue and cancel all documents waiting to be printed. To play it extra safe, shut down the computer as well. Then start the printer first, start the computer second, and try again.

 Tip   Be sure to try the Troubleshoot printing option in the Printers and Faxes folder, as another potential resource for fixing a problem.

Faxing Documents

With the growing use of the Internet and e-mail, most people no longer send faxes. In prior versions of Windows, if you needed to send documents to fax machines (because the recipient doesn't have a computer), you could fax files directly from your computer to a fax machine. You could also fax a file to another computer.

Now, as a rule, you'll want to avoid sending faxes; instead use e-mail attachments for sending documents to other computers. Similarly, if someone is going to send you a document, have the person send it as an e-mail attachment, not as a fax. The reasons are described in the sidebar "Can't Edit a Faxed Document."

You don't need a fax machine to send and receive faxes with your computer. But you do need some kind of connection to the outside world. The usual setup is to use a *fax modem* that connects your computer to a phone line.

If you don't have a fax modem, you can have one installed or buy one and install it yourself if you're comfortable with that sort of thing. You can find fax modems at any computer or large office supply store. To shop around online, go to any web site that sells such things (for example, www.amazon.com, www.cdw.com, www.tigerdirect.com) and search the keyword *fax modem*.

Can't Edit a Faxed Document

FAX is short for facsimile, because it works by sending a facsimile copy (a photo-copy) of the document through the phone lines. When you send that photocopy to another computer, it gets essentially a photograph of the original document.

For example, let's say you fax a WordPad document or Microsoft Word document to some other computer user. You are sending a *photo* of that document. When the recipient opens the document, it will be in a graphics program. This, in turn, makes it impossible to edit the document using Microsoft Word, WordPad, or any other word-processing program.

If you decide to use e-mail and you don't want someone to edit a document, then you can still avoid the need to send a fax by sending an XPS version for them to view rather than the original document.

 Caution   Even if your computer came with a modem, there's no guarantee that it's a fax modem. To learn more about your modem, see the documentation that came with your computer, or visit your computer's manufacturer's web site.

As an alternative to using a fax modem, you can use the Internet to send and receive faxes. If you want to explore that route, skip to the section titled "Faxing Without a Fax Modem," later in this chapter.

In addition to a connection to the outside world, you also need fax software. Unfortunately, one of the changes with Windows Vista is that not all editions have fax software included. In fact, neither Home edition includes fax software. As such, you will have to upgrade to a Business edition or the Ultimate edition of Vista, or you will have to buy a third-party fax program in order to do faxing.

Using the Fax Console

Because several versions of Vista do not include the Windows fax software, we will only provide a brief look at the program. If you are running a version that includes the program, then you'll be able to launch it from the Start menu. From there, select All Programs ➪ Accessories ➪ Windows Fax and Scan. This brings up the Windows Fax and Scan program shown in Figure 8-11.

You should also be able to open the Fax and Scan program from within the Control Panel.

Open the Printer folder and double-click the Fax icon in that folder. This also opens the dialog box shown in Figure 8-11.

Figure 8-11: The Windows Fax and Scan program opened for the very first time in Windows Vista

When the Fax and Scan console opens, you'll see several folders on the left-hand side. Click any folder name to see its contents. If you haven't sent or received any faxes yet, all the folders will be empty. After you get going with faxes, here's what each folder will contain:

✦ **Incoming:** Contains faxes currently being received.

✦ **Inbox:** Contains faxes that have been received.

✦ **Draft:** Contains faxes you've created and saved, but not yet sent.

✦ **Outbox:** Contains faxes waiting to be sent.

✦ **Sent Items:** Contains faxes that have been successfully sent.

The Fax and Scan window is a Fax Central of sorts, in the sense that every fax you send and receive will end up there (unless you opt to print incoming faxes but not have them sent to the console). So anytime you need to look at a received fax, review faxes you've sent in the past, and so on, the Fax and Scan window is the place to go. As in any program, there are plenty of options in the menu bar and toolbar that you can use to manage faxes.

Like most programs, the Fax and Scan window has its own Help, which you can get to by pressing F1 while Fax Console is the active window or by choosing Help from the Fax Console's menu bar. To close the Fax Console, click its Close button or choose File ⇨ Exit from its menu bar.

Sending a Fax

The easiest way to send a fax from your computer is to use the Send Fax Wizard. There are lots of ways to start that wizard. Use whichever method here is most convenient at the moment:

✦ If you're in the Fax and Scan window, click the New Fax button in the toolbar.

✦ From the menu bar, choose File ⇨ New ⇨ Fax (or Fax from Scanner....).

✦ If you want to fax the document you're currently creating in a program that supports faxing, choose File ⇨ Send. If that option isn't available, choose File ⇨ Print from that program's menu bar. In the Print dialog box that opens, choose Fax the "printer" to use; then click OK.

The first page of the Send Fax Wizard opens. The rest is largely self-explanatory. When you are prompted to enter a fax, you will see the New Fax window shown in Figure 8-12.

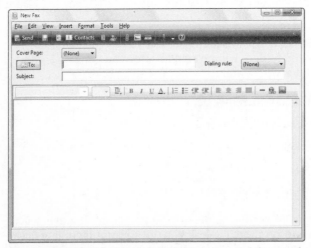

Figure 8-12: The Recipient Information page of the Send Fax Wizard

You can enter the name of the person that will receive the fax or click the To button to select a name from your address book. You can also enter a subject and fax message. If you have sent e-mails before, you should find this format relatively familiar.

You also have the option of setting a cover page and dialing rules. A number of options are available, and a wizard will walk you through the creation if you choose to add one. The same is true with the Dialing rules.

After you have created your fax, you can click the Send button or press Alt+S to send the fax. If you don't have a fax modem or other faxing service set up, then you are likely to be prompted to set this up. You can check the status of a fax by looking in the Outbox or Sent Items folders on the left side of the Fax and Scan window.

Faxing Without a Fax Modem

You can bypass the whole fax modem/phone line business and use the Internet to send and receive faxes. This isn't really a Windows Vista thing *per se*. It's a service you subscribe to on the Internet. But once you've established an account, you can certainly use Windows Vista to send and receive faxes with that account. Exactly how you do that depends on which service you use. To learn more about these services, visit either of the following web sites:

✦ **eFax:** www.efax.com

✦ **Venali:** www.venali.com

If you use Microsoft Office, you may be able to sign up for a fax service right from an Office application. For example, if you open a document in Microsoft Word 2007 and choose File ➪ Send ➪ Internet Fax Service (see Figure 8-13), you can work your way to the Office Marketplace, which may provide more offerings by the time you read this.

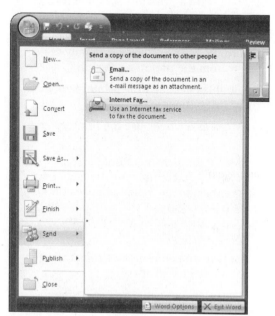

Figure 8-13: Using, or getting more information about, Internet fax services from Word 2007

More on Faxing

Faxing with a computer is actually a large topic — one that could fill a small book as opposed to part of a chapter in a book. Because most of the Windows Vista editions do not install a fax program by default, or do not include a fax program, the coverage has been brief. With so many topics available to cover, some things had to be left short. To supplement the basics you've learned here, you can search the Windows Help and Support pages for more details.

Summary

As mentioned, there are hundreds of makes and models of printers on the market and thousands of programs that can print documents. But despite the countless possibilities, some things are so common that you can safely assume they're true for whatever printer you own and whatever program you're using. Likewise, there are lots of ways to send and receive faxes with a computer and lots of different fax modems on the market. Again, the skills you've picked up in this chapter should be enough to at least get you started. Here's a quick recap of the main points made in this chapter:

✦ To print the document that's currently open and visible on your screen in some program, click the Print button on the program's toolbar, or choose File ➪ Print from that program's menu bar, or press Ctrl+P.

✦ When you print a document, you create a print job, which in turn is sent to the print queue before the printer actually goes to work.

✦ Most programs enable you to view what a printed document will look like before you actually send it to the printer. This is generally done by selecting File ➪ Print Preview from the program's menu.

✦ To manage current print jobs, double-click the little printer icon in the notification area to open the print queue.

✦ To manage printers and fax devices as a whole, use the Printer folder in Control Panel.

✦ To print a snapshot of your screen, first press the Print Screen (PrtScn) key, or press Alt+Print Screen to capture only the active window. Then open your favorite graphics program and choose Edit ➪ Paste from its menu bar, press Ctrl+V, or press Ctrl+Insert. Use the Print and Save options on that program's menu bar to print the image or to save it as a file on your hard disk.

✦ If you want to share a document with someone else but don't want them to modify it, you can print an XPS file to share.

✦ If your computer has a fax modem installed and if you are using Windows Vista Ultimate Edition, or a Business edition, you can use the Windows Vista Fax and Scanning Services to send and receive faxes.

✦ To send and receive faxes without a fax modem, use an Internet service such as eFax (www.efax.com) or Venali (www.venali.com).

Using the Internet

The Internet is home to every bit of knowledge known to humankind, all just a few mouse clicks away. No more paper mail, stamps, and two-week waits. Letters and pictures arrive anywhere in the world instantly, without costing a cent. No more long-distance bills or plain old voice phones. Now you can see whom you're talking to, talk all day, and Ma Bell will never even know it. Best of all, it's legal!

If only there were a way to use all that Internet stuff without having to learn anything first. If only. . . . Time to face up to the awful truth—it takes more than an Internet account to use the Internet. Or, put another way, if you don't know what you're doing online, you might as well be offline. So guess what Part III is about. . . ?

Getting Online

As just about everyone knows, the Internet is an enormous collection of computers connected by cables. The two most widely used services that the Internet provides are e-mail and the World Wide Web. Plenty of other lesser-known services are available, however, such as instant messaging and file sharing, and you'll learn about them in this part of the book.

Nobody actually owns the Internet, other than perhaps the American taxpayers who paid for it during the Cold War. On the Internet as a whole, there is no censorship — anything goes on the Net. Nobody polices the Internet looking out for your best interests. You need to protect yourself from any threats out there. It's the Wild, Wild West of the twenty-first century. And if you're easily shocked, you'll no doubt find some things pretty shocking out there.

What Is the Internet?

The Internet consists of millions of computers throughout the world, all connected by cables. In networking diagrams, the Internet is always displayed as a cloud, as in Figure 9-1. The cloud is a good symbol for the Internet; just as a cloud is made up of millions of tiny water droplets, the Internet is made up of millions of computers.

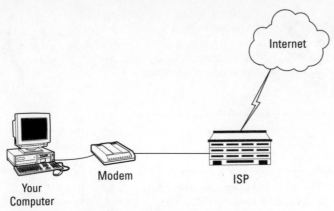

Figure 9-1: A modem and ISP provide your computer's connection to the Internet.

You connect to the Internet through a device called a *modem* (or *router*) and an *ISP* (Internet Service Provider). A modem or router is a gadget that connects your computer to a phone line or cable. An ISP is a company that provides the connection between your modem and the Internet.

Your ISP might be MSN, America Online, Comcast, Yahoo!, AT&T, or any of several hundred other companies. In a sense, it really doesn't matter, because there is only one Internet. ISPs all basically work the same way. They rent a large amount of *bandwidth*, say $10,000 or $100,000 a month worth. The lightning bolt in Figure 9-1 represents that expensive high-bandwidth connection. The ISP sells smaller *chunks* of that bandwidth to lots of customers, with the intent of making a profit.

What Is Bandwidth?

Bandwidth, measured in kilobits per second (Kbps or Kb), is a measure of how much information at a time can be sent through the line that connects your computer to your ISP. For example, a dial-up account tops out at about 48 to 50 Kbps. That's roughly 48,000 to 50,000 bits per second (bps). That sounds like a lot. Since any given file can contain millions of bits, however, it's really not that fast.

The lower the bandwidth, the longer the wait for things you've requested from the Internet. For consumers, accounts generally cost anywhere from $10.00 to $20.00 a month for a 56K dial-up account, to maybe $20.00 or $50.00 a month for a broadband connection. Here's the difference:

✦ **Dial-up:** Connection to your ISP goes through a standard modem and traditional telephone lines. (Your phone line is busy if anyone tries to call while you're online.) The maximum speed of a dial-up account is usually in the 48 to 50 Kbps range. Even though your modem may be rated at 56K, the phone lines can't move traffic quite that quickly.

✦ **Broadband:** Connection to your ISP is through cable (the type used by cable TV companies), or special Digital Subscriber Lines (DSL) owned by the phone companies, that can move data at faster than 50 Kbps. You connect to a broadband account using a modem or *router*. You can get just about any connection speed you want.

A typical broadband cable account moves data at about 750–1,000 Kbps. So wait times are relatively brief. What might take several minutes to accomplish with a dial-up account takes only a few seconds with a broadband account.

Clients and Servers

Most of the computers on the Internet at any given time are *clients*. That is, they are consumers of what the Internet has to offer. Your computer is most definitely a client.

Other computers on the Internet are *servers*. Servers provide the services that clients are using. Nobody sits at a server and does work. Rather, the server just sits online and answers requests coming from clients. For example, a *web server* is a computer that holds a web site people visit. All day and night, the web server sends its web pages to whoever happens to request those pages. That's the web server's only job.

Online and Offline

The term *online* means connected to the Internet and ready to use its services. The term *offline* means not connected to the Internet. (That is, the cable connecting your modem to your ISP is not active at the moment.) When you're online, you have access to *remote resources* and *local resources*. When you're offline, you have access to *local resources* only.

A *resource* is anything useful. *Remote resources* are things that are not on your computer but instead are on other computers. You need to be online to access remote resources. Local resources are things that are in your own computer, such as your hard disk, floppy disk, CD drive, and all your files. You have access to local resources any time your computer is turned on. You don't have to be online to access local resources.

With a dial-up account, you have to make some small effort to get online. The shape this effort takes depends on your ISP. The typical scenario is that you open a program, and the modem starts to howl and make weird noises. Then you type your user name and password, which identify who you are and verify that you really are that person, because presumably you're the only person in the world who knows that password.

When you're online, you can use the Internet (for example, do e-mail, browse the Web). To go offline, you might have to close the program you initially started. Or you may be able to right-click the little connectoid icon in the notification area (if available) and choose Disconnect. At that point, you're offline and can no longer get to current things on the Internet.

With a broadband account, there's no such logging in and out. If the computer is on, and the modem is on, you're online. If the computer is off, or the modem is off, you're offline. No dialing, no weird phone noises, no signing in. Contrary to popular belief, this is not a bad thing. It's a good thing, and we'll talk about why it's not dangerous to be online all the time in Chapter 13.

Downloading and Uploading

One thing people do a lot of on the Internet is download stuff. The term *download* means to copy something from some other computer to your own computer. The term *upload* means the opposite: to copy something from your computer to some other computer on the Internet. To upload, you need to have some sort of space on the Internet to which you can copy files. (More on that later in this part of the book.) For now, it's sufficient to know the difference between downloading and uploading.

 Tip   If you envision the Internet as a cloud, it's easy to keep the terms straight. *Download* means to copy something down from the cloud onto your computer. *Upload* means to copy something from your computer up to the cloud.

Getting an Internet Account

Most people who buy a computer just sort of stumble into their first Internet account by double-clicking some icon on their screens. AOL and MSN sell lots of Internet accounts through that method. If you want to be more choosey, you need to do a little homework. If you look up Internet service provider (ISP) in your local yellow pages, you'll probably find you have lots of companies and account types from which to choose.

For broadband accounts, many people go through their local phone company. That way, the charges just get added to the phone bill, and you don't have an extra monthly bill to pay. Or, if you already have cable TV, you can probably get a fast cable account through your cable provider. Again, they'll tack the additional charges onto your cable bill so you don't have another monthly irritant to contend with.

Although some tools in Windows Vista are designed to help you set up an Internet account, the truth is that people rarely need them or use them. The typical scenario is more like this: You choose an ISP, and you set up an account with that ISP; then one of three things happens:

✦ Your ISP comes to your house and sets everything up for you (that's ideal).

✦ Your ISP sends you some sort of instructions, and you follow those instructions to set up your account.

✦ Your ISP sends you some program that you run on your computer, and the program sets up your account.

Because hundreds of ISPs are available, and they don't all follow a standard set of rules, I can't give you any more details than those, other than to tell you that your ISP is motivated to make setting up your account as easy as possible, because they'd rather not pay a whole staff of people to sit on the phone lines and talk their customers through the set-up procedure.

Connecting to the Internet

When you have an Internet account, there's a little icon called a *connectoid* (connection ID) that represents your connection in your Network Connections folder. If you don't have an Internet connection yet, but *do* have an account, you might be able to get connected to your ISP through this folder. As we mentioned earlier, however, it's rarely necessary to do this, because your ISP will try to simplify the process as much as possible.

Windows Vista includes a wizard for connecting to the Internet. If your ISP didn't provide a setup disk or process, then you can use the Connect to the Internet wizard. You'll still need to have an ISP and a modem to connect. To run the wizard, do the following:

1. Click the Start menu and select Control Panel.
2. Select Network and Internet.
3. Select Connect to the Internet under Internet Options.

Alternatively, you can also get to the same location by doing the following:

1. Click the Start menu and select Connect To. This will display any known Internet and network connections.
2. At the bottom of the dialog window displayed, select Setup a connection or network. As shown in Figure 9-2, this will display a list of connection options from which you can choose. (Your options might be slightly different.)
3. Select Connect to the Internet and then click the Next button.

If you follow either of the steps above, you will be placed into the Connect to the Internet wizard as shown in Figure 9-3. The wizard asks for the type of connection you have. You can click the icon that represents the connection you are using. This wizard can also be used to connect to a hotspot. A hotspot is simply a wireless network. For example, you can find hotspots at restaurants, hotels, and other places. You can also set up your own wireless network (hotspot).

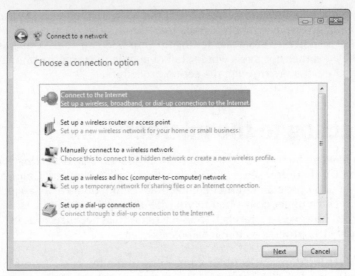

Figure 9-2: Selecting a connection type to set up

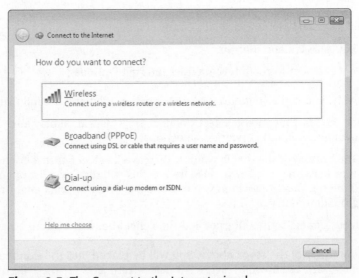

Figure 9-3: The Connect to the Internet wizard

After you've selected your connection, you can continue to follow the wizard. What you see next depends on the type of connection you select.

Wireless Network Setup with the Wizard

If you selected to set up a wireless connection, then you will see a dialog box that lists the wireless connections. Figure 9-4 shows the wireless connections that are within range of the computer shown.

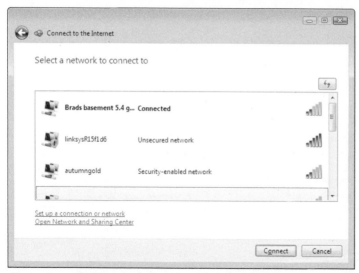

Figure 9-4: Wireless Network Connection page of the Connection wizard

Note If you don't see any wireless networks, then you should make sure that you have a wireless modem. If you do, you should then verify that your modem is turned on. Many newer notebook computers include a switch that lets you turn off a wireless modem when you aren't using it so that it won't drain your battery.

On the list of wireless connections, you can click the connection to select it. You can then click the Connect button. The computer will try to connect to the network. If the network is a secured network, you will need to enter a password to gain access.

Broadband and Dialup Network Setup with the Wizard

If you selected Broadband or dialup, then you will get a different window asking for information about your connection as shown in Figure 9-5.

You will need to enter the user name the ISP gave you as well as your password. You'll want to give the connection a name in case you need to access information about it again later. Finally, you'll have to decide if you want to share the connection as discussed earlier in this chapter. If you are going to share the connection, then select the check box that allows others to use it.

If you don't have an ISP yet, then you can click the link at the bottom of the window labeled I don't have an ISP. This will give you additional information. If the additional information doesn't help, then you will need to contact an ISP provider independently. If offers for Internet service aren't coming to you from your cable company or the phone company, then you can always open the phone book and look up ISP.

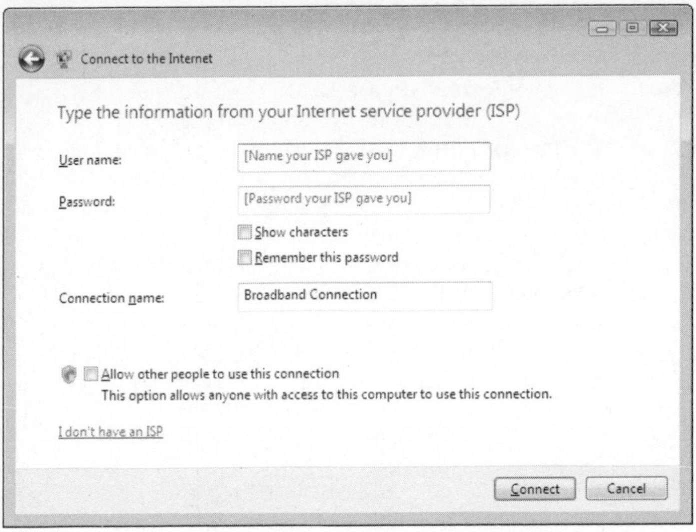

Figure 9-5: Entering information about a broadband connection

If you are setting up a dial-up connection, then you will see an additional link on the dialog box presented in Figure 9-5 titled Dialing Rules. You can click this link to set up information about your phone (see Figure 9-6).

Figure 9-6: The dialing rules window for entering your local information

In this dialog box, you can enter location information that will be used when dialing your phone. This includes things like area code and any additional numbers you might need to dial to get a phone connection.

Network and Sharing Center

A few additional areas within Windows Vista are worth reviewing now. Additionally, you can learn a lot more about networking and network connections in Chapters 31 and 32. The first area to see is the Network and Sharing Center.

You can access the Network and Sharing Center in one of a couple of ways. The quickest is to right-click on the network icon in the notification area. This is the icon of two computer screens. When you right-click this icon, you see a pop-up menu. The last item in the menu is Network and Sharing Center. Clicking the link opens the Network and Sharing Center shown in Figure 9-7.

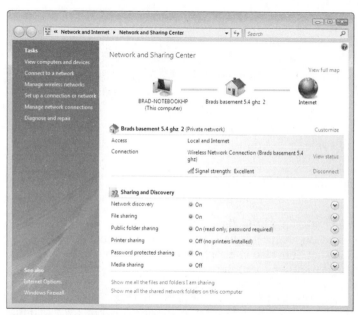

Figure 9-7: The Network and Sharing Center

An alternate way to access this window is to do the following:

1. Open the start menu by clicking on the Start menu icon.

2. Right-click the Network option on the right side of the start menu. This will display a pop-up menu.

3. Select Properties from this menu. This opens the Network and Sharing Center.

Your window won't look exactly like the example shown, because there are thousands of products on the market that enable you to connect to the Internet. But let us briefly explain what a few things represent.

This window provides you with information about your network and Internet connection. For example, you can see that the computer used in Figure 9-7 (BRAD-NOTEBOOKHP) is connected to the Internet through a wireless connection called Brads Basement 5.4 gHz. If you were to click the View full map link, you would actually get a better picture of this network (see Figure 9-8).

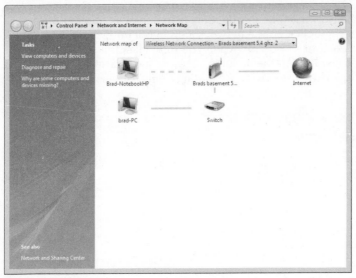

Figure 9-8: A network map of Brad's network

The full network map makes it a little clearer how my Internet connection is working. As you can see in Figure 9-8, Brad's computer is connecting to a wireless router to the Internet. It is also connected via the wireless router to a switch that connects it to other computers that are also on the network.

The important thing to note about the Network and Sharing Center and the network map is this: If you are connected to the Internet, then this will be indicated by the icons on these pages. If you are having trouble with your Internet connection, you can check out the icons to see whether something is amiss.

Cross-Reference
Chapters 31 and 32 go into much more detail about using networks and about sharing files and devices on a network. It isn't critical that you know how all this works in order to use the Internet. It only matters at this point if you run into an issue with your Internet connection.

Internet Options

One other window deserves a brief mention now. This is the Internet Options window. This window provides you with a number of advanced options for configuring your Internet connection and other settings that relate to how you use the Internet. Some of the options available will be covered within the next few chapters. In general, if you need to change something about how you are using the Internet, this is likely the place to look. On the other hand, you don't want to change something in the Internet options unless you are sure of what you are changing.

To get to the Internet Options, you can access the Network and Sharing Center as shown in the previous section. On the lower left side you will find a link called Internet Options under the See also section. You can also get to these options by opening the Start menu and then selecting the Control Panel. From the Control Panel home page, select Network and Internet followed by Internet Options. You'll see is a dialog box similar to the one shown in Figure 9-9.

Figure 9-9: The Internet Options/Properties dialog box in Windows Vista

As stated, you'll return to this dialog box within the next few chapters. You can use it to set default programs for Internet Explorer to use to open files, to set security and privacy when you are using the Internet, to create your default home page (or pages), to implement some parental controls on web pages, and more.

You can also use this dialog box as a starting point to set up an Internet connection. To do this, select the Connections tab. Within that tab, click the Setup button. This starts the Connect to the Internet wizard you learned about earlier.

Troubleshooting a Network Connection

Before you try to troubleshoot your Internet account, the first thing you need to realize is that much of the information you need is available only from your ISP. Windows Vista does contain some network troubleshooting tools that *might* be able to help.

Your best resource when it comes to troubleshooting an Internet connection, however, will always be your ISP — only your ISP knows the specifics of the service they provide. Nonetheless, the Network Troubleshooter just might be able to help. To get to it:

1. Open your Network and Sharing Center folder using any of the methods described previously.

2. Under Tasks on the left side of the window, click Diagnose and repair. This runs the Windows Network Diagnostics.

 Tip   You can also get to the Diagnose and repair link by right-clicking the network icon in the notification bar in Windows Vista.

You may be asked for more information. Follow any prompts and suggestions. Windows Vista will do its best to try to resolve any network issues on its own. If the troubleshooter can't help you resolve the problem, your best bet is to call your ISP.

Summary

Getting your computer connected to the Internet is largely a matter of setting up an account with an Internet Service Provider (ISP) and doing whatever they tell you to do to make the connection work. The main points made in this chapter include:

✦ The Internet is a network of millions of connected computers throughout the world.

✦ Some computers on the Internet act as *servers*, in that they provide the very services the Internet offers.

✦ Other computers, like yours and mine, are clients, in that they use those services as consumers.

✦ Bandwidth is a measure of how quickly information can get from your ISP to your computer. Low (or narrow) bandwidth means slower traffic and more wait time. Broadband offers higher speeds and less wait time.

✦ Your Network and Sharing Center holds the icon that represents the modem (or router) you use to connect to the Internet.

✦ The Network and Sharing Center also provides access to the Windows Network Diagnostics, which can help with a problematic Internet connection.

✦ When it comes to troubleshooting a network connection, your ISP is your best resource, because only they know the specifics of the service they provide.

Browsing the World Wide Web

The Internet offers many services, including the wildly popular Word Wide Web (the Web for short). The Web provides an easy point-and-click interface to a vast amount of information, free software, technical support, and just plain fun. Even if you haven't been on the Internet yet, you've undoubtedly seen web site addresses — those www.whatever.com things — in ads, letterheads, or elsewhere. In this chapter, you'll learn how to get to those addresses and much more about using the Web.

We mention in Chapter 9 that most of the computers on the Internet are clients, whereas others are servers. Servers are called *web servers* because they serve up web pages to Internet clients. Each web server is host (home) to one or more *web sites*. A web site consists of one or more pages of information and has a unique address on a web server. That address is often called a URL (Uniform Resource Locator). Most URLs look something like www.sopmething.tld or http://something.something.tld, where *something* can be any name and *tld* is one of the top-level domains shown in Table 10-1.

Table 10-1
Examples of Top-Level Domains and URLs of Web Sites

Top Level Domain	Type	Example URL
.com	Commercial	www.amazon.com
.edu	Education	www.sdsu.edu
.gov	Government	www.fbi.gov
.org	Nonprofit organization	www.redcross.org
.net	Network	www.comcast.net
.mobi	Mobile	www.businessweek.mobi
.aero	Aviation (Aeronautics)	www.dsm.aero
.museum	Museum	www.Australian.museum
.mil	Military	www.army.mil

When you first enter a web site, you're taken to that site's *home page*. From that page, you'll find links to other pages within the same site or even links to pages in other web sites.

Using Microsoft Internet Explorer

To use the Web, you need two things: an Internet connection and a web browser. The latter is a program that enables you to access the World Wide Web. Several makes and models of web browsers are on the market, including Microsoft Internet Explorer, MSN Explorer, Mozilla Firefox, and Netscape Navigator. If you've already been browsing the Web, you've probably been using one of those web browsers.

In a sense, all web browsers are the same. You type some URL into the address bar and press Enter. The web browser fetches the web page at that URL from the Internet and displays it on your screen. All browsers access the same Web and Internet, and they generally work with whatever Internet connection is available.

The main web browser that comes with Windows Vista is called Microsoft Internet Explorer, often abbreviated IE or MSIE. The Internet Explorer icon looks like a blue lowercase *e*, as in the example shown at left. Since Internet Explorer is a web browser, your computer has to be online to use it effectively. So if you have a dial-up account and want to start Internet Explorer you may need to get online before opening the browser. Just go ahead and connect to the Internet in whatever way you normally do. Don't disconnect or go offline before starting Internet Explorer. (Broadband users don't have to do anything before starting Internet Explorer.)

When you're online, you can start Internet Explorer using one of the following methods:

✦ Click the Launch Internet Explorer Browser button (e) in the Quick Launch toolbar.

✦ Double-click the Internet Explorer icon on your desktop.

✦ Click the Start button and choose Internet Explorer from the left side of the Start menu.

✦ Click the Start button and choose All Programs ⇨ Internet Explorer.

Assuming you're online, Internet Explorer will open and take you to your *default home page*. That's just a fancy name for the first web page you see when you open your web browser. As we'll discuss later in this chapter, you can make any web page you want your default home page.

 Tip You can move and size the Internet Explorer program window as you would any other. When open, Internet Explorer also has a taskbar button.

Getting to a Web Site

To get to a web site, you type its URL into the Internet Explorer address bar. When you click the URL that's already in the address bar, that URL is automatically *selected* (highlighted), as in the example shown in Figure 10-1.

Figure 10-1: The Internet Explorer address bar, with the URL selected

Any new text you type will automatically replace the selected text. So it's not necessary to press Backspace or Delete before typing a new URL.

 Tip If the URL starts with `http://www`, you don't have to type the `http://` part.

Using AutoComplete

Internet Explorer will remember URLs you've typed in the past. When the URL you're typing now matches ones you've typed in the past, a *history menu* will drop down, showing those previous URLs. When that happens, you can:

✦ Ignore the menu and keep typing. Each new character you type will reduce the number of items in the menu to those that match what you've typed so far.

✦ Click any item URL in the history menu to put it into the address bar.

Copy and Paste a URL

When somebody sends you a URL through some sort of text message, like certain e-mail messages and discussion boards, the text is likely not a hyperlink. That is, it isn't colored or underlined, and clicking it will do nothing. When that happens, it's not necessary to retype the URL into your browser's address bar. You can use standard copy and paste to copy it. Here's how:

1. Start with the mouse pointer just outside the URL; hold down the left mouse button, and drag the mouse pointer through the URL. Make sure the entire URL is selected, as in the example that follows.

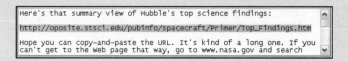

2. Press Ctrl+C or right-click the selected text and choose Copy.

3. Click in your web browser's address bar, or drag the mouse pointer through the URL that's currently in the address bar, so all text is selected.

4. Press Ctrl+V to paste. The URL you copied replaces the selected text in the address bar, as in the following example.

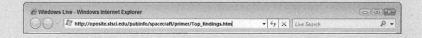

5. Press Enter or click the Go button (the arrow pointing to the right).

That's all there is to it.

You can see all the URLs in the history by clicking on the down-pointing triangle on the right of the address box. You can empty the history menu at any time by clicking the Clear History button in the Internet Explorer Internet Options dialog box, as discussed later in this chapter.

Tip   The AutoComplete feature is optional. To turn it on or off from the Internet Explorer toolbar choose the Tools button and select Internet Options. Click the Advanced tab. Under the Browsing category in the list that appears, you can select the check box next to Use Inline AutoComplete to turn this feature on (checked) or off (not checked).

Changing a URL

If you want to change the current URL rather than replace it, don't type anything. Instead, point to the place within the selected URL where you want to type changes. Then click the spot to place the cursor in that location. When you see the cursor, you can start making your changes using standard text-editing techniques.

See the section "Changing Text in a Text Box" in Chapter 2 for standard text-editing techniques.

After you've entered a valid URL and pressed Enter or clicked the Go button, the status bar at the bottom of the screen will present messages to inform you of the browser's progress. You'll also see a progress bar in the status bar that shows how much of the page has loaded. When the Done message appears in the left side of the status bar at the bottom of the browser, the page is fully loaded.

If you don't see the Address bar or status bar in Internet Explorer, choose the Tools button, then select Toolbars followed by the name of any unchecked toolbar you want to see.

Weird Ways to the Web

There are a couple of other ways to get to a web site besides using the Internet Explorer menu bar. As you may recall from Part I of this book, Windows Explorer is the program that enables you to explore the contents of your computer. Internet Explorer is the program you use to explore resources on the Internet, outside your computer.

If you happen to be in Windows Explorer, and its address bar is visible, you can type a URL right into the address bar and press Enter. Windows Explorer will automatically open Internet Explorer with that address.

You can also place an Address bar in your taskbar and just type any URL. First, right-click an empty area of the taskbar or the current time and choose Toolbars ➪ Address. An address bar appears on the Windows taskbar. If you can see only its label, you'll need to unlock the taskbar and widen the bar, as shown in Figure 10-2. Or you can drag it up to the desktop and make it a free-floating toolbar. See the section "Personalizing Your Taskbar" in Chapter 26 for details.

Figure 10-2: An Address bar in the Windows taskbar

When the address bar is in place, you can type any URL and press Enter or click the Go button (the arrow pointing to the right) to go to a web site. Your web browser will open to display the web page.

To copy the URL that's currently in your address bar to an e-mail message, or any other document, click the URL so the whole URL is selected; then press Ctrl+C. Click where you want to paste the URL; then press Ctrl+V or right-click the spot and choose Paste.

Navigating the Web

When you're at a web site, you may not have to do much more typing of URLs. After you're at a page, you can click any *hyperlink* (also called a *link*) to go to whatever page the link represents. Hyperlink text can be anything—it need not be a URL. But it will most likely be underlined and either blue or magenta. In general, blue indicates a link to a web page you've never visited. Magenta identifies pages you've already visited.

A picture, or even a portion of a picture, can be a hyperlink too. You can't tell just by looking whether a picture is a hyperlink or not. You have to point to it. If the mouse pointer changes to a hand, as in any of the examples shown in Figure 10-3, it's a hyperlink. The hand means *click here to go*. If the status bar in your web browser is turned on, the URL that the hyperlink will take you to appears in the lower-left corner of your browser window, as shown in the same figure.

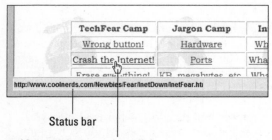

Status bar

Mouse pointer on a hyperlink

Figure 10-3: Pointing to hyperlinks, and the Internet Explorer status bar

Using Hyperlinks

When you know the mouse pointer is touching a hyperlink, you just click to follow the hyperlink (that is, to go wherever the hyperlink points you). Depending on how the link was set up, it will either open the new page in the current copy of Internet Explorer, or open it in a new window containing Internet Explorer. If it opened in the same window, then you can click the Back button in your web browser to return to the page you just left. More on the Back button a little later in this chapter.

Opening a Page in a New Window

If you want to keep the web page you're viewing at the moment visible on the screen, and also go to a linked page, don't click the hyperlink. Right-click it instead and choose Open in New Window from the shortcut menu that opens (see Figure 10-4). The current page will be left alone, and the new web page opens in a new Internet Explorer browser window, which you can move and size independently of the first.

Figure 10-4: Right-clicking a hyperlink

When you have two separate browser windows open, you can right-click the current time and choose Show Windows Side by Side to put the browser windows side by side. Or choose Cascade Windows from that same menu to stack the browser windows like sheets of paper.

If you open lots of separate Internet Explorer program windows, their taskbar buttons may combine into one button. You can click that one large taskbar button to see a menu of all open web pages. Click any page in the menu to bring that web page to the top of the stack.

 Tip　If you get lots of pop-ups, and want to close all open web pages in one fell swoop, right-click the Internet Explorer taskbar button and choose Close Group. See "Closing Multiple Windows" in Chapter 4 for an example.

Opening a Page in a New Tab

If you want to open a page while still keeping the page, plus you want to avoid cluttering your desktop with numerous copies of Internet Explorer windows, then you can choose to open a link in a new tab within the current Internet Explorer window rather than opening it as a new window. Like opening a link in a separate window, you don't click the hyperlink. Rather, right-click it and choose Open in New Tab from the shortcut menu that opens (see Figure 10-4 again). The new web page opens in a new tab within the Internet Explorer browser (see Figure 10-5). The title of the new page is displayed on the new tab. You can click on the tabs to switch between the two web pages.

If you get more than one tab, then you can get a preview of all the tabs at once. To do this, click the Quick Tabs button in the tab bar. This displays previews of all open pages. Figure 10-6 shows four tabs with four different pages. You can click any of the images in the Quick Tabs view to open that tab and its web page in full view.

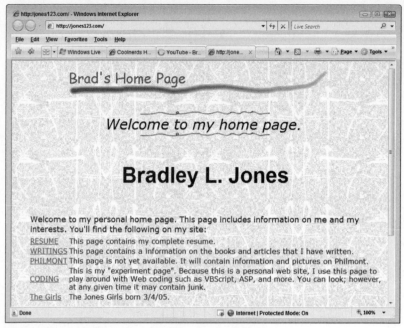

Figure 10-5: Multiple tabs with different web pages

Quick Tabs

Tab List

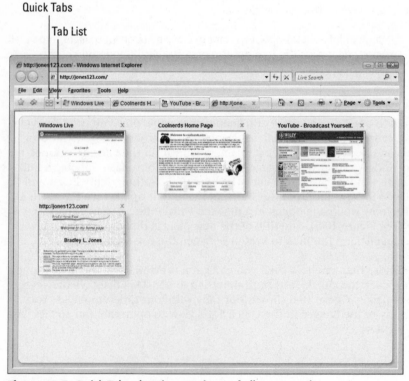

Figure 10-6: Quick Tabs showing previews of all current tabs

You can also click the Tab List icon to list the titles of all the web pages you have open in tabs. With just a few tabs open, this might not be necessary; however, if you get a large number of open web pages, then this can come in handy for getting quickly to the page you want.

> **Tip** You can also press Ctrl+Q while in Internet Explorer to display the Quick Tabs view.

Other Hyperlink Tricks

Quite a few items on the shortcut open when you right-click a hyperlink. Remember that in the menu, the word *page* means the web page you're currently looking at. The word *target* refers to whatever the hyperlink points to. For example, if clicking the hyperlink displays a video, *target* refers to that video. If clicking the hyperlink takes you to a web page, *target* refers to that web page you'd land at. So with that in mind, here's what the options in the shortcut menu (shown earlier in Figure 10-4) offer:

✦ **Open:** Opens the resource that the link refers to. (It's usually another web page, but it could be a movie, song, picture, or file you download — anything.)

✦ **Open in New Tab:** As mentioned previously, opens the resource in a new tab within the current Internet Explorer window.

✦ **Open in New Window:** As mentioned previously, opens the resource in a new, separate Internet Explorer window.

✦ **Save Target As:** Rather than showing you the resource, this option opens the Save As dialog box so you can download the resource to your own hard disk. (That is, you can download the resource. More on downloading later in this chapter.)

✦ **Copy:** You can select text on a web page and copy the text. Or you can right-click a picture on a web page and copy that picture. But you can't copy a hyperlink. So this option is disabled on hyperlinks.

✦ **Copy Shortcut:** Creates a shortcut to the target resource, which you can then paste to the Windows desktop or into any folder (right-click the spot and choose Paste Shortcut).

✦ **Cut and Paste:** You can't edit other peoples' web pages (and they can't edit yours). So the Cut and Paste options are disabled, as they would enable you to edit the page.

✦ **Add to Favorites:** Creates a *favorite* to the target resource. See the section "Tracking Favorite Web Sites," later in this chapter.

✦ **Properties:** Shows general information about the link, including the URL that the hyperlink points to.

Other Navigation Tools

The Standard toolbar in Internet Explorer, shown in Figure 10-7, provides some handy tools to help with your browsing.

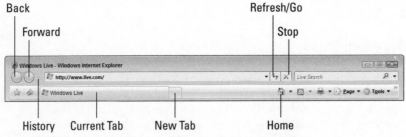

Figure 10-7: Standard buttons toolbar in Internet Explorer

Looking at the first few buttons, you have:

- ✦ **Back:** After you've navigated from one page to another, you can click the Back button to return to the previous page.

- ✦ **Forward:** After you've clicked the Back button at least once, you can click the Forward button to return to the page you just backed out of.

- ✦ **Refresh:** Downloads the current page from the web server again, so you can see recent changes to that page.

- ✦ **Stop:** If a page is taking too long to load, or you think you clicked the wrong link, clicking the Stop button will stop the download and make it easier to navigate back to the preceding page or another page.

- ✦ **Current Tab:** The currently displayed web page.

- ✦ **New Tab:** Clicking this area switches you to a new tab where you can enter a new address and open a new web page. You can switch between any open tabs by clicking on the tab.

- ✦ **Home:** Takes you to your default home page.

The Back and Forward buttons are *session-specific*. A session begins when you first open a tab in your web browser and ends when you close that tab or the browser. So when you first open your browser or first open a new tab, both Back and Forward will be disabled, because you haven't been to any other pages yet in this session. But as you navigate around within the tab, the Back and Forward buttons enable you to move among those pages you've visited during the current session.

Behind the Scenes

As you browse the Web, you might get the impression that you're viewing web pages from afar — on computers outside your own on the Internet. That's true to some extent. But here's how it really works. When you type a URL and press Enter, your web browser sends a tiny *packet* of information to the web server that says, "Send your web page to me." The web server sends its web page across the Net, right into your modem and computer.

As the web page arrives, your web browser writes it a file in your Temporary Internet Files folder. What you see on your screen is that downloaded file. In other words, by the time you see the entire web page, you're looking at a copy on your computer. You're not even connected to the web server any more.

When you click the Back button to return to a page you were just at, Internet Explorer doesn't bother to download that page all over again. Instead, Internet Explorer just pulls the *cached* copy out of your Temporary Internet Files folder file and shows it on your screen. That's much quicker than downloading it from the web server again. It also reduces Internet traffic a lot, because there are millions of peoples navigating around through web pages every minute of every day.

Refreshing a Page

The one drawback to using cached copies of web pages is that if the original page changes while you're viewing your cached copy, those changes won't be reflected in the copy you're viewing. It's pretty unlikely that a web page is going to change dramatically during one of your browser sessions. But if you suspect a page you're viewing at the moment might be out of date, click the Refresh button in the toolbar. This tells Internet Explorer, "Go get the current copy of this web page off the Internet, and replace my cached copy with the new copy."

 Tip If your eyes aren't as good as they use to be, then you might want to take a closer look at a web page. In the bottom left corner, you will see a zoom level for the browser. This defaults to 100%. If you want a bigger (or smaller) view of the page, you can click this area and adjust the zoom level up or down. You can also press the Ctrl and plus keys simultaneously to zoom in or the Ctrl plus the minus key to zoom out.

Printing a Web Page

To print the web page you're currently viewing, use any of the standard techniques for printing documents — that is, press Ctrl+P or click the Print button on the Internet Explorer toolbar.

 Tip To copy chunks of text and pictures from web pages to a new document that you can edit and print independently, see the section "Copying, Moving, and Pasting Text" in Chapter 7.

Some web pages are divided into frames—multiple sections that you can scroll through independently. Some frames might contain ads or a table of contents, or something else you don't particularly want to print. If you want to print the contents of just a single frame within a page, anywhere in the text within that frame first, you can press Ctrl+P or choose File ⇨ Print, or right-click the text and choose *Print* to bring up the Print dialog box. When the Print dialog box opens, click its Options tab to reveal the options shown in Figure 10-8.

Figure 10-8: Options tab of the Internet Explorer Print dialog box

To print only the frame you clicked in, choose the Only the selected frame option. You could also choose the option All frames individually, to ensure that each frame's content is printed on a separate page.

Be careful of the Print all linked documents option. It prints the current web page, plus all the web pages that this page provides links to. It could end up being a heck of a lot of pages if the current page contains a lot of links. As an alternative, you can choose the Print table of links option, which will print just the hyperlinks in the page without printing the actual pages to which those links refer.

Note When Internet Explorer prints a web page, it will generally shrink it a little bit to get it to fit on the paper. If some text is cut off at the right margin, even after printing individual frames, then choose Print preview from the print toolbar menu. On the Print preview page, select Shrink to Fit from the drop-down menu in the Print Preview toolbar.

Revisiting Previous Sites

Internet Explorer keeps track of all the sites you've visited in the current session and previous sessions. As mentioned, when you type a URL into the address bar, URLs of sites you've recently visited appear in the drop-down menu. You can also view a history of recently visited sites using any method that follows:

✦ If the menu bar is showing, choose View ➪ Explorer Bar ➪ History. You can display the menu bar by clicking the Tools button on the toolbar and selecting Menu Bar from the menu that is displayed.

✦ Press Ctrl+Shift+H.

✦ Click the History menu button in the Standard buttons toolbar (see Figure 10-9) and then select History.

The History pane appears at the left side of the Internet Explorer window (see Figure 10-9).

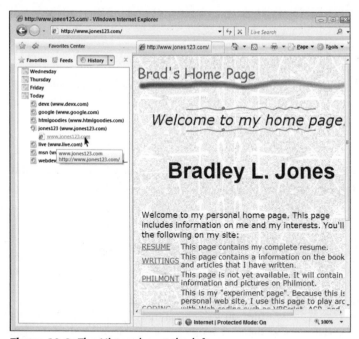

Figure 10-9: The History bar at the left

Using the History Bar

Using the History pane is simple. Click any heading to expand or hide the items beneath the heading. For example, in Figure 10-9, when clicking the Today heading and jones123, you're pointing to a page icon that reads jones123; the URL shows in the tooltip. Clicking that item takes you to the web page.

Notice the little toolbar near the top of the History bar. If you want to rearrange the list, click the down arrow on the right side of the History button. On the menu that appears, click a new sort order, such as By Order Visited Today.

To search through your history list for web pages that contain some keyword, select Search History from the History button menu. Under Search for in the box that opens, type any word or phrase; then click Search Now. The resulting list of pages will contain your search text. To get back to seeing all items in the history, click the down arrow in the History button and choose any view.

Closing the History Bar

To close the History bar, do any of the following:

✦ Click the X in the upper-right corner of the History bar.

✦ Click the History button on the Internet Explorer toolbar and select History.

✦ Press Ctrl+Shift+H.

✦ If the menu bar is showing, choose View ➪ Explorer Bar ➪ History.

Closing the History bar doesn't change its contents in any way. It just gets the History bar off the screen and out of your way. You can reopen the History bar at any time.

Getting Rid of Cookies, Files, and History

When you're browsing around the Web, Internet Explorer keeps track of where you've been in a couple of ways. It keeps track of every URL you've been to and adds it to your history list. It also puts a copy of every web page you visit in the Temporary Internet Files folder on your hard disk, making a copy of every web page you visit. Furthermore, it keeps track of many, if not all, of the pages you've visited in your Temporary Internet folder. Finally, Internet Explorer can keep track of your doings through cookies.

The name *cookies* comes from an old story where some kids decide to explore some spooky forest or something. To make sure they can find their way back, they leave a trail of cookie crumbs. This turns out to be a bad idea, because animals eat the crumbs. But that part's not relevant to cookies on the Internet. The idea of leaving a trail behind is the only part that matters.

An Internet cookie is a tiny text file in a folder named Cookies on your hard disk, placed there by some web site to act as sort of a crumb trail to your computer. Some cookies are *session cookies*, also called temporary cookies. Session cookies exist only for the duration of the current browsing session. As soon as you close your web browser, all session cookies vanish. A *persistent* cookie stays on your hard disk, even after you close your web browser.

Some cookies, which go by the highly technical name of *unsatisfactory cookies*, are put on your computer by third-party web sites. These web sites are often advertisers who track the type of web sites you visit, sending you ads according to your browsing habits. In other words, they invade your privacy. You can regain your privacy at any time by deleting your history, your temporary files, your cookies, or any combination thereof. Here's how you did it in previous versions of Windows. You can still do it this way in the current version; however, I'll show you an easier method in a moment:

1. From the Internet Explorer toolbar, click the Tools button and then select Internet Options from the menu.

2. On the Internet Options dialog box that opens, click the General tab as shown on the left side in Figure 10-10.

Note   On the general tab of the Internet Options dialog box is a Settings button. You can click it to specify how Internet Explorer handles temporary files (although the default settings are usually fine) as well as to set the number of days to keep pages in your history.

3. Within the General tab, click the Delete button within the Browsing history section. This opens the second dialog box shown on the right side of Figure 10-10.

An alternative method for getting to the Delete Browsing History dialog is to click on the Tools button in the toolbar and select Delete Browsing History from the pop-up menu. This will open the dialog as shown on the right side of Figure 10-10.

The rest is fairly obvious:

✦ To delete cookies, click the Delete cookies button; then click Yes.

✦ To delete temporary Internet files, click the Delete files button; then click Yes.

✦ To clear your history of visited sites, click the Delete history button; then click Yes.

✦ To delete data that may have been saved from forms you've entered, click the Delete forms button; then click Yes.

✦ To delete any passwords that might be stored on your system, click the Delete passwords button; then click Yes.

✦ To delete all temporary files, you can click the Delete all button at the bottom of the form; then click Yes.

Click Close after making your selection(s) in the Delete Browsing History dialog box. If you used the longer method of getting to the dialog box, then you will also need to click OK to close the Internet Options dialog box.

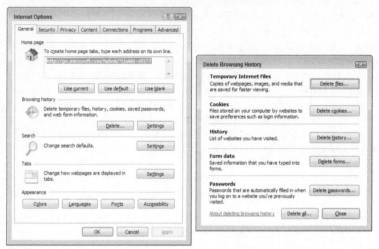

Figure 10-10: The General tab of the Internet Options dialog box (left) and the Delete Browsing History dialog (right)

Changing Your Default Home Page

The default home page is the first web page you come to when you open Internet Explorer. Most likely, you're going to want to change your default home page to something you really do need to visit often. For example, if you search the Web a lot using Google, you might want to make Google your default home page. You should note that in Internet Explorer 7 you can actually have more than one home page. Each home page you specify will be placed into its own tab. To define a new default home page:

1. In Internet Explorer, go to the page you want to make a home page (for example, www.live.com).

2. When you're at the page, choose the down arrow next to the Home icon on the toolbar (see Figure 10-7).

3. From the pop-up menu, click Add or Change Home Page.

4. Click one of the options that fits what you want to do:

   • Select the option Use this webpage as your only home page, if you want the page in the current tab to be the only home page.

   • Select the option Add this web page to your home page tabs, if you want the current page to be an additional home page. When you have more than one home page, then, when you open the browser or when you click the Home button, all the web pages that you have marked as home pages will be opened—each in its own tab. If you have a lot of home pages, it might take a while to load them all.

- Select the option Use the current tab set as your home page, if you want to replace any pre-existing home pages with all of the tabs you currently have opened. If you only have one tab open, you won't see this option.

5. Click Yes to accept your selection.

From now on, whenever you open Internet Explorer or click the Home button, you'll first be taken to the pages you set.

Tracking Favorite Web Sites

As you follow links and explore the Web, you're sure to find sites you'll want to revisit. You can make the return trip easier by adding the site to your Favorites while you're there. Here's how:

1. While viewing the page you want to add, do one of the following:

- Press Alt+Z

- 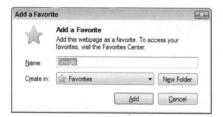 Click the Add to Favorites button (the button with a plus sign on top of a star) on the toolbar.

- Choose Favorites ➪ Add To Favorites from the Internet Explorer menu bar if it is displayed.

2. Select Add to Favorites from the pop-up menu. You'll see the Add Favorite dialog box, shown in Figure 10-11. If you want to add all of the currently opened tabs to your Favorites, then you can select Add Tab Group to Favorites instead.

3. Type a name for this favorite item or accept the suggested name. If you selected to add a Tab group, then you are naming a folder that will contain each of the pages from each of the currently opened tabs.

4. Click the Add button.

As a shortcut, you can go to the page you want to add to Favorites and then press Ctrl+D. Internet Explorer adds the page to your Favorites list without displaying the Add Favorite dialog box.

Figure 10-11: The Add Favorite dialog box

Viewing Your Favorite Sites

To return to a favorite site, you don't need to retype its URL. Instead, you can just use any of the following techniques to view your collection of favorites; then click the site you want to visit:

✦ In Internet Explorer, click the Favorites button (the star) in the toolbar to view the Favorites pane.

✦ Press Ctrl+I.

✦ Choose View ➪ Explorer bar ➪ Favorites from the Internet Explorer menu bar if it is displayed.

✦ Click Favorites on the Internet Explorer menu bar; and then click the name of the site you want to visit.

✦ Click the Start button and choose Favorites from the right side of the Start menu.

 Cross-Reference If your Start menu doesn't offer a Favorites option, see "Personalizing Your Start Menu" in Chapter 26.

If you use one of the first three options, the left side of the Internet Explorer window displays your favorites (see Figure 10-12).

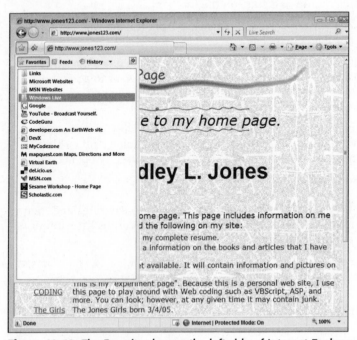

Figure 10-12: The Favorites bar on the left side of Internet Explorer

Items in the list with manila file folder icons are folders. Clicking a folder opens it, so you can see the favorites within the folder. Clicking a folder a second time closes it again. All the other icons represent favorite web sites. Clicking a favorite takes you straight to that web site.

To move an item in the favorites list, just drag it to some location. That is, point to the item you want to move, hold down the left mouse button, drag the item to its new position, and release the mouse button.

Organizing Your Favorites

As your collection of favorites grows, you might want to organize it into folders. That way, you won't be faced with a huge list of favorites each time you open your Favorites bar. To organize your favorites, select Favorites ➪ Organize Favorites from the Internet Explorer menu bar. You'll be taken to the Organize Favorites window shown in Figure 10-13.

Figure 10-13: The Organize Favorites window

The bottom of the dialog box provides instructions, buttons, and information. The top shows you your current folders (all with folder icons) and favorites.

Creating a Favorites Subfolder

The first step to creating a subfolder is to make sure you're at the right level within the hierarchy. For example, if you want to create a folder at the same level as the folders you first see, you have to make sure the highlighter is either on a closed (not expanded) folder icon or on a specific favorite icon, as on the left side of Figure 10-14. On the other hand, if you want to create a subfolder within an existing folder, you need to open that parent folder first. For example, if you want to create a subfolder within an existing folder, you first have to open that parent folder by clicking it. On the right side of Figure 10-14, I've opened the Kid Sites folder. So if I were to create a folder there, it would be a subfolder within Kid Sites.

Assuming you're in that Organize Favorites window, here are the steps to creating a new folder for your favorites:

1. If you want to create a subfolder within a folder, open that folder by clicking its name. Otherwise, make sure the highlighter is on a closed folder or favorite icon.

2. Click the New Folder button. A folder named New Folder appears, its name selected and ready to be edited.

3. Type a name for the folder, and press Enter.

That's all there is to it.

Starting Your Favorites Collection

If you're new to the Web and want to visit some useful web sites that you might want to add to your favorites, here's a few to help you get started. Not everyone will want to add all of these to his or her favorites, of course. But you're likely to find some sites you'll want to revisit:

✦ www.Dictionary.com: Look up a word in a dictionary or thesaurus, or translate text from one language to another www.eBay.com: The ever-popular buy-and-sell-anything-and-everything site.

✦ www.fandango.com: Find out what movies are playing in your local theaters, their start times, and other movie-related information.

✦ www.FirstGov.gov: The U.S. Government's official web site.

✦ www.Google.com: A popular site for searching the World Wide Web.

✦ www.MapQuest.com: A great resource for maps and driving directions.

✦ http://search.Microsoft.com: Search the Microsoft web site for technical support.

✦ www.OnlineConversion.com: Convert all types of measurements, such as feet to meters or gallons to ounces.

✦ www.USPS.com: The United States Postal Service, including a Calculate Postage option to figure out the cost of shipping an item.

✦ www.YouTube.com: A site with videos that have been submitted by people from all over the world.

✦ www.WindowsCatalog.com: A catalog of hardware and software products for Windows XP.

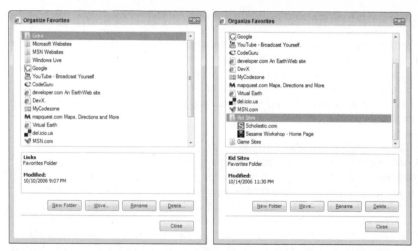

Figure 10-14: Creating a folder or a subfolder within the Kid Sites folder

Moving, Changing, and Deleting Favorites

To move a favorite or folder icon in Organize Favorites, you can just drag it and drop it wherever you want to place it. If you want to move an item into a folder you've created, you can just drag the item and drop it right onto the folder's icon. Or you can click the item you want to move and click the Move to Folder button. In the Browse for Folder dialog box that opens, click the name of the folder to move the favorite to. If you're trying to pull the favorite out of a folder back up to the first list, click Favorites at the top of the folder list. Click the OK button.

To change the name of a favorite or folder, click the item; then click the Rename button. Or right-click the item and choose Rename. The name will be selected (highlighted). Type the new name, or edit the existing name using any of the standard text-editing techniques. To edit, you'll need to position the cursor by clicking the spot where you want to put the cursor or by pressing the ← or Home key to move the cursor to the left. Press Enter when you're done.

To delete a favorite or folder, click its name; then click the Delete button, or press the Delete (Del) key. Optionally, you can right-click the item and choose Delete. If asked "Are you sure . . .?" choose Yes.

 Tip   If you delete a favorite or favorite folder by accident, you can get it back by restoring it from the Recycle Bin. See "Using the Recycle Bin" in Chapter 19 for details.

Closing Up Favorites

To close the Organize Favorites window, click its Close button. To close the Favorites bar, click the Close (X) button in its upper-right corner. Or click the Favorites button on the Internet Explorer toolbar, or press Ctrl+I.

Choosing and Creating Favorites Folders on-the-Fly

The Organize Favorites window is good for organizing favorites you've already created. You can also create folders, and put new favorites into folders, on the fly. For example, let's say you're at a web page you want to add to your favorites. Click the Add to Favorites icon, or choose Favorites ⇨ Add to Favorites from the Internet Explorer menu bar. The Add Favorite dialog box opens as shown in Figure 10-11.

To put the favorite you're about to save into an existing folder, just click the drop-down list button next to Create in and you'll see a list of your existing favorites folders. Pick the name of the folder you want to use and then click Add. If you want to create a new folder, you have to think about where you want to put it. If you want to put it at the same level as Links and any other folders, click Favorites at the top of the list first. But if you want to create a subfolder within one of your existing folders, click the parent folder's name first. Then click New Folder button, type a folder name, and click Create to create the new folder. You will then need to click Add to add the new favorite link into the new folder.

Creating Desktop Shortcuts to Web Pages

You Favorites folder isn't the only place you can store links to favorite web sites. You can put a shortcut icon to a web site right on your Windows desktop. That way, to revisit the site, you don't even need to open your web browser. Just double-click the site's icon on your desktop and you're on your way. The first step is to get to the web site using Internet Explorer. Then do one of the following:

✦ Choose File ⇨ Send ⇨ Shortcut to Desktop from the Internet Explorer menu bar.

✦ Drag the tiny icon to the left of the URL in the address box out to the desktop and drop it there (see Figure 10-15).

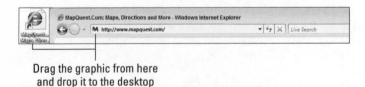

Drag the graphic from here
and drop it to the desktop

Figure 10-15: Create a desktop shortcut by dragging.

When you're at the Windows desktop, you can just double-click that new icon to open your web browser and get to the web page that the icon represents.

General Browsing versus Secure Browsing

Browsing the Web is usually an anonymous endeavor. When you visit a web page, the web server that sent you a page has no idea of who you are or specifically where you are. All the web server can do is hand the web page off to the Internet and assume it will get to you. Other than an address on the Web, you are anonymous to the web site.

When you shop online, you need to enter some personally identifiable information, such as your name, address, e-mail address, and maybe even credit card information. In other words, you need to enter some information that you don't necessarily want to make public. While it's extremely unlikely that any information you transfer over the Internet would ever become public, a highly knowledgeable Internet nerd could grab some information off the Internet and dig around it looking for credit card information and such.

To be absolutely sure that it's impossible (not just remotely possible) for your credit card information to be lifted off the Internet, legitimate businesses use a technology know as Secure Sockets Layer (SSL) to encrypt sensitive information as it crosses the Internet. In the unlikely event that someone does get ahold of that encrypted information, it won't do them any good. They'll only see a bunch of meaningless gobbledygook, and there's no way to decipher that information into anything useful. Only the web site that you're dealing with can make sense of the encrypted information.

To alert you to when you are entering, or leaving, a secure site, Internet Explorer displays a couple of little messages on your screen. The URL for a general, anonymous web site usually begins with the letters http://, where http stands for Hypertext Transfer Protocol. The URL of a secure site, where it's safe to send sensitive information, usually starts with the letters https://, where the s stands for *secure*.

When you leave a general http:// site and are about to enter a secure https:// site, Internet Explorer shows a lock to the right of the URL in the address bar as shown in Figure 10-16. The lock indicates that you are on a secure site, so if you're about to enter sensitive information, like a credit card, it's safe for you to provide that information. When you leave a secure (https://) site and go to a regular http:// site, the lock disappears.

If you click the lock icon next to the address bar, you will be provided with a security report about the site you are viewing. If you are unsure about whether the site is legitimate, this will help you determine if the site is certified and more.

When you start downloading files from the Web, you're likely to come across other types of security warnings. We'll discuss those in the downloading section later in this chapter.

Figure 10-16: Security alerts for a secure connection — the lock icon and the https address

 Caution   Note in Figure 10-16, the current web page displays an "Important Message." Many web pages will have similar messages stating that the site is a secure site. Just because the site says it is secure, doesn't make it so. The best way to validate that a site should be secure is looking for the lock as shown above.

Searching the Web

The World Wide Web contains just about all public knowledge. You can find anything on the Web; you just need to know how to look for it. Internet Explorer offers you several ways to search for information on the Internet. Perhaps the handiest is the built-in Live Search. This search feature is at the top right of the window ready for you to use. You simply need to type in what you want to find and press the search button (the spyglass to the right). The more specific you are when entering your search text, the better off you'll be. For example, if you search for just the word *Mustang*, you'll get links to about a zillion web pages that have the word mustang in them, including web pages about the horse breed, the car, and any other page that happens to contain that word. However, if you search for *Ford Mustang*, that will narrow it down considerably. If you search for *1966 Ford Mustang convertible*, that will narrow it down even more. The more specific you can be, the better results you'll get.

After you've typed the word or phrase you want to search for, click the Search button. After a brief delay, you'll see a message indicating how many relevant web pages were found, followed by the titles of the web pages. As usual, you can click any underlined text or any web site preview picture to visit that site.

 Caution   Spelling counts big-time in searches. The search is based on exactly the characters you type into the Find a Web page text box. If a search results in nothing, click the New button and check your spelling.

If you don't find what you're looking for, you can enter different text into the Live Search text box and try again. If you don't find anything, check to make sure your spelling is correct.

If instead of looking for web pages with a search word, you want to actually find that word on the current page, you can do this as well. You should enter the word or words into the Live Search text box. Instead of clicking the search icon, click the down arrow to the right of it to display a menu. From the menu, select Find on this Page. A small dialog box similar to the one shown in Figure 10-17 will be displayed with your search term in it. Click Next to find the next occurrence of the search term found. The search will start from the location of your cursor.

Figure 10-17: Finding a search term on the current web page

Searching Without the Search Bar

The World Wide Web is home to many *search engines*. These are Web sites that regularly scan the entire World Wide Web for new pages and then create an index to those pages, similar to the index in the back of a book. Since the Web contains billions of pages, the index is enormous — somewhere along the lines of an index for a million different books. There are lots of search engines to choose from, including www.google.com, www.altavista.com, www.yahoo.com, www.infoseek.com, www.lycos.com, and www.hotbot.com, just to name a few.

Quite a few search engines actually use Google as their index source. Google is one of the most popular search engines on the Internet. People often use its name as a verb, as in "I googled *<some word or phrase>*." In English, that translates to "I went to www.google.com and searched for *<some word or phrase>*." To get to Google, just type its URL (www.google.com) into your web browser's address bar and press Enter.

When you get to the Google home page, type the word or phrase you're looking for into the Search box; then click the Google Search button. After a few seconds, you'll see the results of your search, as in the Example shown in Figure 10-18, where my search resulted in 3,710,000 matching results. Each underlined title is a hyperlink that you can click to visit the referenced page. If there are multiple results, you'll find links for accessing other pages at the bottom of the current page.

In Google's search results, you can use the tabs above the links to narrow the search results to certain types of results. For example, clicking the Images tab takes you to pictures that relate to the search text. Clicking the News tab displays news articles that relate to the search text.

Figure 10-18: Results of searching the Web using Google's search engine

If your searches keep producing thousands, or millions, of pages and you want to try to narrow things down using Google Advanced Search. Just return to the Google home page at www.google.com, click the Advanced Search link near the top of the page, and fill in the blanks on the form that appears.

Downloading from the Web

Downloading means copying a file from the Internet to your own PC. There's tons of stuff you can download—programs, updates to existing programs, documents, music, video—you name it. Exactly how you do a download really depends on what you're downloading from where. (Things can just never be simple, ya know.)

Downloading and Installing Programs

As you learn in Part I of this book, programs are tools you use to open, edit, and create documents. All the programs currently installed on your computer are accessible from your All Programs menu. When you download a program from the Internet, it's not sufficient to just download a file. You also have to *install* the program. The installation process configures the program to run on your system and adds a startup icon for the program to your All Programs menu (and possibly a shortcut icon to your desktop).

Chapter 29 talks about general issues to take into consideration before installing any program. The following list briefly summarizes these issues; refer to Chapter 29 for details:

✦ Consider creating a Restore Point before installing any new software (program) or hardware. The advantages to doing so are discussed in the section "Playing It Safe with Installations" in Chapter 29.

✦ Close all programs currently open (except your Web browser in this case), and save any work, if prompted. It's not necessary to close little programs whose icons appear only in the notification area.

✦ Just downloading a program isn't enough to get it working on your computer. You have to install the program as well, as explained shortly.

✦ Be careful of free programs. Many such programs make their money from advertising revenues they generate by allowing pop-up ads on your screen—lots of irritating, never-ending pop-ups.

To download a program, start with a link on a web page that gives you access to the program. There are plenty of sites that enable you to download software; www.tucows.com and www.microsoft.com/downloads come to mind. If you need to download and install Adobe Reader, you go to www.adobe.com, and find and click the link shown at left.

Once you've clicked the link that begins the download process, you'll need to follow any instructions that appear on the screen. We can't help you much with that, because there's no standard set of rules that all web sites follow. But it should be a simple matter of filling in some blanks and answering some questions.

When you're downloading a program, you might come across a dialog box similar to the one shown in Figure 10-19. Be aware that the message at the bottom isn't telling you that there's a problem with the file. It's just telling you that the type of file you're downloading *could* contain something bad, like a virus or worm. The dialog box is basically asking you to make a judgment call. Eventually, you're likely to come to a dialog box like the example shown in Figure 10-19:

Figure 10-19: This dialog box often appears when you download a program from the Internet.

The basic rule of thumb for making the judgment call is where the program is coming from. If it's from a controlled web site like www.tucows.com, or any legitimate software company like Adobe, Corel, Microsoft, and so on, it's probably safe. If you were offered this program through some unrequested pop-up or junk e-mail, its source is much more dubious. You could still save the file, then scan it for viruses before opening it (assuming you have anti-virus software on your computer, as discussed in Chapter 13). If you're familiar with the company that's providing the program, you can choose Open and just install the program. Anyway, here's how the buttons in the dialog box work:

Tip   If file name extensions are visible, a program you're downloading will likely have an .exe extension. That stands for *executable*. That means the file is a program containing instructions that the computer can execute. Most documents don't contain executable code. See the section "Showing/Hiding File Name Extensions" in Chapter 6 for information on showing/hiding file name extensions.

✦ **Run:** If you choose Run when downloading the program, the program will be installed automatically. There won't be any leftover files you need to delete.

✦ **Save:** The installation program will be saved to your hard disk. To install the program, you need to open (double-click) that downloaded file and follow its instructions. When the download is complete, you can delete the file you downloaded.

✦ **Cancel:** If the dialog box shown in Figure 10-19 popped up for no apparent reason (that is, you weren't downloading anything), some advertiser might be trying to sneak a program onto your computer. Click Cancel to prevent any unwanted downloads.

If you choose Run, there's nothing left to do but follow instructions on the screen until the download is complete. At that point, the program will be installed and accessible from your All Programs menu.

If you choose Save rather than open, a Save As dialog box (perhaps titled as File Download) like the one shown in Figure 10-20 will likely open. Even if the dialog box is titled File Download, it works just like the Save As dialog box discussed in Chapter 6. Your job is to choose a folder for the downloaded file. When you're downloading a program, there's no need to change the file name or Save As Type. But you should at least look at the file name so you know what to look for when the download is complete.

Figure 10-20: The Save As dialog box appears when you're downloading files from the Web.

If you've already created a folder for storing all downloaded files, you can choose that folder name from the Save In drop-down list. For example, Figure 10-20 shows a folder named Downloads. Optionally, you can choose Desktop from the Save In drop-down list to put the icon right on your desktop. You won't need to keep the downloaded file for long, so the desktop is a handy place to put it.

After the download has finished, you'll need to get to the icon for the file you downloaded. Double-clicking that icon will begin the installation process. Just follow the instructions on the screen. When the installation is complete, you generally don't need the file you originally downloaded anymore. Opening that file again would just start the installation process over. You need only to install a program once, not every time you want to use it. So you can go ahead and right-click that icon and choose Delete to get rid of it.

When the installation is done, you'll be able to start the program by clicking the Start button, choosing All Programs, and looking around for the startup icon for that program. Also, any documents that refused to open before should open now. For example, if you downloaded and installed Adobe Reader, double-clicking a PDF file should open the document in Acrobat Reader without any problems.

Downloading Documents

Documents are different from programs in that you never have to install a document. You don't start documents from the All Programs menu either. Rather, you store documents in document folders such as Documents, Pictures, or Music. Opening a document automatically opens the program required to view that document (assuming you have an appropriate program installed on your computer for opening that type of document).

Document downloads can begin like program downloads, where you click some link that offers the document. Many PDF documents can be downloaded this way. You can also download just about anything visible on your screen. For example:

✦ To copy a picture you see on a web page, right-click the picture and choose Save File As.

✦ To save the entire web page you're currently viewing, click the Page toolbar button and Save As.

✦ To download the picture, song, or video that a link points to, right-click that link and choose Save Target As (the word *target* means *the file that this hyperlink leads to*).

Tip   If you're unable to copy a picture by right-clicking and choosing Copy, you can also take a picture of the entire screen with the picture visible. Then paste the screenshot into a graphics program and crop out whatever you don't want. See the section "Editing Pictures with Paint" in Chapter 15 for more information.

A Note on ZIP Files

Some of the files available for download on the Web are compressed (or *zipped*), so they'll download more quickly. These files typically have the extension .zip on their file names. Before you can use such a zipped file, you need to *extract* its contents. See Chapter 23 for details.

When you download a document, you might see the following options:

✦ **Open:** Opens the document in an appropriate program so you can see the document but does not save a copy of the document to your computer. If you want to save the document, you have to choose File ➪ Save As from that program's menu bar; then use the Save As dialog box to specify a folder and file name for the document.

 Caution When you open streaming media and protected content, the file will play on your screen, but there won't be any way to save it. The Save As option on the File menu will be disabled.

✦ **Save:** Displays the Save As dialog box, so you can specify a folder and file name for the documents you're downloading. The document probably won't appear on the screen. But when the download is complete, you can open the downloaded document as you would any other document — by double-clicking its icon.

 Tip Unlike programs, which have an .exe file name extension, a document will have some other extension. That extension, in turn, defines the format of the file and the programs that can open the file. See the section "Understanding Document Types" in Chapter 6 for more information.

Playing Online Music and Video

The Internet is home to a fair amount of streaming media, which is basically music you can listen to or videos you can watch without actually downloading or saving anything. When you click a link that plays music or a video, Internet Explorer will do its best to play the media.

What happens when you follow a link to a media file depends on a lot of things. If the media is a standard song file (such as an MP3 file) and you are running Windows Vista with its default settings, then Internet Explorer will open Windows Media Player to play the song. In some cases, a site may have embedded a player in the page. In those cases, the media will be played in their player.

Cross-Reference Chapter 16 covers the details of using Windows Media Player, so we won't cover them here. To see all the details of playing media, see Chapter 16.

If the media file is not a format currently recognized by Windows Vista, then you will be prompted with a dialog box similar to the one shown in Figure 10-21. This dialog box asks if you want to save the file or if you want Internet Explorer to look for a program online that can open the file.

Figure 10-21: The dialog box when you click an unrecognized (by Windows Vista) media type

Figure 10-21 shows a sound file selected that is in the Real Media format from the BMGMusic.com web site. Windows Vista doesn't recognize this format. When you click the Find button, Internet Explorer will attempt to find a program that will open the file type. Rather than downloading the program, Vista opens a new tab and loads a page for a program that is (hopefully) the best match. In the case of the Real Media file shown in Figure 10-21, the Find button opened www.Real.com, which is where the Real Media player can be downloaded.

Although some video formats such as Windows Media Video (WMV) will be played by Windows Media Player without you needing to do anything special, not all video formats will. One video format that has become very popular is Adobe Flash Player. If you go to a site such as YouTube.com, you will not see the videos until you install Flash as an add-in to Internet Explorer. If you run into a situation where you need Flash, the page is likely to provide a link to the Adobe page so you can download the player. After you install the player, you will be able to watch videos with Internet Explorer. It is worth noting that Flash is also used for many ads and fancy graphics on web sites, so there is a good chance that if you use the web a lot, you will end up installing Flash Player at some point.

Troubleshooting Web Browsing

When your computer is connected to the Internet, web browsing is fairly easy and straightforward. There are a couple of fairly common problems, however, that you'll want to know how to handle, summarized as follows.

Page not Found Error

If you attempt to go to a web page and only get a Page not Found error message, you have typed the site's URL incorrectly. Note that when typing a URL, you always use forward slashes (/), not backslashes (\). In other words, a URL like `http://www.microsoft.com/downloads` will work just fine, whereas typing `http:\\www.microsoft.com\downloads` will produce a `Page not Found` error. Also, note that URLs never contain blank spaces.

 Tip   You're also likely to get a Page not Found error if you're not online when you attempt to go to a web page.

Do You Want to Debug?

Once in a while, you'll come across an error message that says there is something wrong with the page you're trying to view. The message will read, "Do you wish to debug?" You should always answer No, because only the person who created the web page can actually debug (fix) it.

People who create web pages are supposed to fix everything before they put the pages online. If this were a perfect world, you would never see the "Do you want to debug?" message, because all the errors that need debugging would already be fixed. But, it's not a perfect world so this happens.

Typically, clicking the No button tells Internet Explorer to do the best it can with the stuff that is working in the page. And hopefully, you won't even notice any difference. If it's a more serious problem than that, there's really nothing you can do about it. Only the site's *web master* (the person in charge of the Web site) can fix such errors.

 Tip   If you get those "Do you want to debug?" errors often, downloading and installing the Java Virtual Machine can help. Go to `http://java.sun.com` and click the link to download the free Java VM. Follow the instructions on the screen (click Yes at the Security Warnings).

Using the Internet Explorer Troubleshooter

For tougher web-browsing problems, try the Internet Explorer troubleshooter. Here's how:

1. Click the Start button and choose Help and Support.

2. In Help and Support, click Troubleshooting.

3. You can select any of the troubleshooters that seem to apply such as Repair Internet Explorer or any of the e-mail or web items.

 Caution   If your computer manufacturer changed the Help and Support Center so that you don't see the Fixing a Problem option, type **Internet Explorer Troubleshooter** into the Search box and press Enter. Then click Internet Explorer Troubleshooter under Suggested Topics in the left pane.

Internet Explorer Help and Support

There's tons of information available to you to learn more about Internet Explorer and fix problems. Whether you're online or not, you can always start Internet Explorer and use its built-in Help. Just choose Help ⇨ Contents and Index from Internet Explorer's menu bar. Then use the Contents, Index, or Search tabs in the Help window that opens to locate topics of interest to you.

If you are online, you can get more information from Microsoft's online Help and Support. For an overview of support options and access to the Microsoft Knowledge Base, choose Help ⇨ Online Support from the Internet Explorer menu bar. If the web site you're taken to is too confusing, go to www.microsoft .com/ie and have a look around there.

Tip If you're looking for general information, tips, or techniques for browsing the Web, go to www.microsoft.com/ie, click Using Internet Explorer in the left column, and start browsing from there.

Summary

This chapter has been something of a whirlwind tour of the World Wide Web and the Internet Explorer browser that comes with Windows Vista. The techniques presented here represent the most important everyday skills you need to use the Web successfully. To recap:

✦ To browse the World Wide Web, connect to the Internet and start your web browser program (Internet Explorer, if you don't have a preference).

✦ Every site on the World Wide Web has a unique address, or URL, often in the format http://www.whatever.com.

✦ To go to a specific web site, type its address (URL) into the Address text box near the top of the web browser window and press Enter.

✦ You can browse the Web by clicking *hyperlinks* — hot spots that appear on the various pages you visit.

✦ To keep track of your favorite web pages, add them to your Favorites list. That is, visit the web page and click the Add to Favorites icon then select Add To Favorites from the menu bar.

✦ To revisit a favorite page at any time, open the Favorites menu and click the name of your favorite page.

✦ To search for specific information on the Web, use the Live Search box at the top of Internet Explorer or use a search engine.

✦ To *download* a file means to copy it from a computer on the Internet to your own PC.

✦ For more information on using Internet Explorer to browse the Web, choose Help ⇨ Contents and Index from the Internet Explorer menu bar, or visit the Internet Explorer web site at www.microsoft.com/ie.

Sending and Receiving E-mail

It seems that just about everyone knows what e-mail is these days. The *e* stands for *electronic*. With e-mail, you type a letter or message on your computer, send it to the recipient's e-mail address, and it ends up in the recipient's e-mail inbox a few seconds later. You can attach pictures and other files to the message so the recipient gets those, too. It's a lot faster than the postal service and doesn't cost a cent.

To use e-mail, you need an Internet connection and an e-mail address. All e-mail addresses follow the format *someone@somewhere.tld*, where *someone* is your user name and *somewhere.tld* is a domain name. For example, Alan Simpson's e-mail address is `alan@coolnerds.com`. You also need an e-mail client, a program capable of sending and receiving e-mail. If you're already using e-mail, you already have all those things.

Introducing Windows Mail

Windows Vista comes with an e-mail client named Windows Mail. If you're already sending and receiving e-mail, it's not necessary to know anything about Windows Mail. You can skip this chapter, keep using e-mail the way you have, and not miss out on anything. On the other hand, if your ISP requires that you use Windows Mail as your e-mail client and they're offering a POP3 account (Post Office Protocol 3, the traditional means of doing Internet e-mail), you'll need to get the information shown in Table 11-1 from your ISP so you can set up Windows Mail. Note that the second column of Table 11-1 shows only examples of how that information might look. You need to fill in the third column with the actual information provided by your ISP.

Table 11-1
Information You Need to Set Up Windows Mail for POP3 E-mail

Information Needed	Example	*Write Your Information Here*
Your e-mail address	somebody@somewhere.com	
Your e-mail username	Somebody	
Your e-mail password	********	
E-mail account type	POP3 or HTTP	
Outgoing (SMTP) mail server	smtp.somewhere.com	
Incoming (POP3) mail server	mail.somehere.com	

 Tip   You can also use Windows Mail with MSN and Hotmail accounts as well as with Windows Live mail. The only information you'll need for such accounts are your e-mail address (must end in @msn.com or @hotmail.com) and your e-mail password.

Setting Up Your E-mail Account

If you're going to use, or at least try out, Windows Mail, and you feel confident that you have the information you need from your ISP, you can set up your e-mail account in several ways:

1. Click the Start button and choose All Programs ➪ Windows Mail.

2. If you see a message asking if you want to make Windows Mail your default e-mail client, you can choose Yes if you think Windows Mail will be the only program you'll use for e-mail. Otherwise, click No.

3. If you've never used Windows Mail, the Internet Connection Wizard will open automatically to help you set up an account. If you see the Internet Connection Wizard, skip to Step 5.

4. When Windows Mail opens, you can set up a new account by choosing Tools ➪ Accounts from its menu bar. In the Internet Accounts dialog box that opens, click the Add button and choose E-mail Account. Click the Next button.

5. Answer all question presented by the Wizard, clicking the Next button at the bottom of each page, until you get to the page with the Finish button.

Be sure to read the information on each Wizard page carefully, and type your answers accurately. Any misinformation or simple typographical errors will start to haunt you the minute you try to send or receive any e-mail messages.

There's just no margin for guessing, sloppiness, or error when it comes to setting up your e-mail account.

After you've set up your e-mail account, the Folders pane will display a set of folders for your account. The exact folders that appear varies with different types of accounts, as in the example shown in Figure 11-1. The most common, and most useful, folders are summarized as follows:

✦  **Inbox:** Every e-mail message that you receive initially appears in your Inbox. If messages don't arrive automatically, click the Send/Receive button on the Windows Mail toolbar to bring your Inbox up-to-date.

✦ **Outbox:** On some e-mail accounts, this folder gathers e-mail messages waiting to be sent. To send messages waiting in the Outbox, click the Send/Receive button.

✦ **Sent Items:** Maintains a history of all e-mail messages you've sent.

✦ **Deleted Items:** Contains messages you've deleted from your Inbox (or any other folder) but haven't completely removed from your hard disk yet.

✦ **Drafts:** Contains e-mails you've written and saved, but not yet sent.

✦ **Junk E-mail:** Contains messages that were flagged as junk mail.

Figure 11-1: Windows Mail with a couple of new e-mail accounts set up

Sending E-mail with Windows Mail

When Windows Mail is open, you can use any of the following techniques to get started on sending an e-mail message to someone:

✦ Click the Create Mail button on the Windows Mail toolbar.

> **Tip** To add a fancy background to your message, click the down-arrow button on the Create Mail button; then click a stationery name.

✦ Choose Message ➪ New Message from the Windows Mail menu bar.

✦ Press Ctrl+N when a mail folder is open.

✦ Select File ➪ New ➪ Mail Message from the Windows Mail menu bar.

A New Message window for composing your e-mail message appears on the screen. To compose your message, fill in the address portion of the window as explained in the following steps.

1. Type the recipient's e-mail address into the To: box. If you want to send the message to several people, you can type several addresses separated by semicolons (;).

   • Optionally, to send carbon copies of the message to other recipients, put their e-mail addresses in the Cc: box. Again, you can separate multiple e-mail addresses by semicolons.

   • Optionally, to send blind carbon copies of the message to other recipients, type their e-mail addresses into the Bcc: box, again separating multiple addresses with semicolons.

> **Tip** A blind carbon copy sends the e-mail message to the recipient with all other recipients' names hidden. This protects the privacy of other recipients and makes the e-mail look as though it was sent to the recipient directly. If you don't see a Bcc: box at the top of the New Message window, choose View ➪ All Headers from the New Message window's menu bar.

2. In the Subject: box, type a brief subject description of the message. This part of the message appears in the recipient's Inbox and is visible prior to opening the message.

3. Type your message in the larger editing window below the address portion. You can use all the standard typing and editing techniques described in Chapter 7. Figure 11-2 shows an example of a simple text message typed in the New Message window.

If you want to add any fonts, pictures, or hyperlinks to your e-mail message, keep reading! Otherwise, you can skip to the "Sending the Message" section.

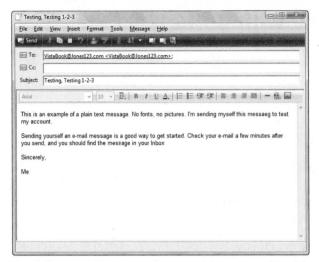

Figure 11-2: A plain-text e-mail message, addressed and ready to send

Composing Fancier E-mail Messages

E-mail messages can be *plain text* or *rich text* (also called HTML). Plain-text messages contain only plain text. Rich-text messages can include fonts, pictures, and hyperlinks, like the example shown in Figure 11-3.

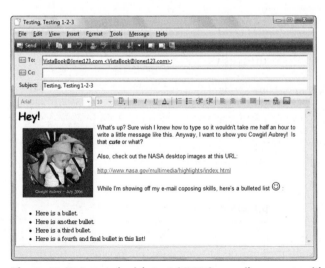

Figure 11-3: A sample rich-text (HTML) e-mail message with a picture and fonts

To compose a rich-text e-mail message, use formatting buttons on the toolbar, just above the message text. If you don't see a formatting toolbar, choose Format ➪ Rich Text (HTML) from the New Message window's menu bar. You can type your text normally. Then apply formatting using the "select then do" method described in Chapter 7 and summarized in the sections that follow.

> **Tip** If you've installed Microsoft Word, Microsoft Excel, or Microsoft PowerPoint on your computer, you can use the Spelling button on the Windows Mail toolbar (or press F7) to correct misspellings in your e-mail message.

Using Fonts and Alignments

As an example of using fonts and alignments in an e-mail message, suppose you want to put a large, centered heading at the top of your message (or anywhere in your message). Type the line of text and press Enter. Then select the same line of text using any of the text-selection techniques described in Chapter 7 (for example, just drag the mouse pointer through the text you want to format). Then choose your font, size, color, and the Center button in the toolbar, as illustrated in Figure 11-4.

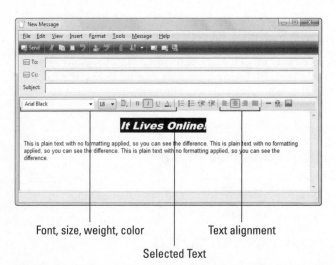

Font, size, weight, color   Text alignment

Selected Text

Figure 11-4: Text selected and formatted using buttons on the toolbar

Typing a List

Numbered and bulleted lists are useful ways of organizing text. For example, you might want to show some numbered steps or a list of points or options in your text. To do so, type each item in the list, pressing Enter once at the end of each line, as at the top of Figure 11-5.

Next, select all the lines of text (and only those lines) as in the center of Figure 11-5. An easy way to do this is to simply start with the mouse pointer just outside the last item in the list; then drag the mouse pointer up and to the left so that all items (and only the items) you want to put into list form are selected (highlighted).

Click the Formatting Numbers or Formatting Bullets button in the New Message toolbar. Optionally, to indent or outdent the list, click the Decrease Indentation or Increase Indentation button in the toolbar. The bottom part of Figure 11-5 shows the selected list after clicking the Formatting Numbers and Increase Indent buttons in the toolbar.

1. Type the list

2. Select the list   3. Choose List/Index options

Figure 11-5: Typing a numbered or bulleted list

Inserting a Picture

You can insert a small photo or picture into the body of your e-mail message, like the Cowgirl Aubrey picture shown back in Figure 11-3. You'll have to make sure you're using the Rich Text (HTML) format. Then follow these steps:

Tip   Use Insert ➪ Picture to insert small pictures only. As described later in this chapter, you can *attach* large pictures and photos to messages.

1. Move the mouse pointer to about where you want to place the picture.

2. Do one of the following:

   - Click the Insert Picture button in the New Message toolbar (shown at left).

   - Choose Insert ⇨ Picture from the New Message menu bar.

3. In the Picture dialog box that opens, navigate to the folder that contains the pictures you want to insert. Then double-click the picture's icon, or click the picture's icon and click the Open button.

   The image will be placed in your e-mail. If you'd like to adjust the alignment so that text wraps or add a border, then you need to take a few additional steps:

4. Right click the image and select Properties from the menu that is displayed. You'll get the Picture property dialog box.

5. If you want the picture to appear to the left of text (like the picture in Figure 11-3), choose Left from the Alignment drop-down list. Or choose Right to make the picture align to the right of adjacent text.

6. If you want to put a border around a picture, enter a thickness (in pixels) in the Border Thickness option (for example, the number **1** will put a nice, thin border around the picture).

7. If you chose the Left or Right alignment option, use the Horizontal and Vertical options to put some space between the text and the picture (a setting of **5** is usually plenty).

8. Click the OK button.

If you want to change any of the options you chose, right-click the picture and choose Properties again. If you change your mind and want to delete the picture, click the picture and press Delete (Del).

Inserting a Hyperlink

A hyperlink is a clickable URL. If you simply type a URL into a message, Windows Mail will automatically make it into a hyperlink. Optionally, you can copy a URL from your web browser's address bar or a web page and paste it into your e-mail message. (The latter saves a lot of time and possible typographical errors.)

If you want to create a "Click here" type of link, where plain-English words rather than a URL are visible in your message, follow these steps instead:

1. Type the text you plan to use as a URL (for example, the words "Click here").

2. Select the text that will act as a hyperlink.

3. Click the Create a Hyperlink button (shown at left) in the New Message toolbar, or choose Insert ➪ Hyperlink from the New Message menu bar.

4. In the Hyperlink dialog box that opens, type (or paste) the URL of the Web site into the URL text box, as in Figure 11-6.

Figure 11-6: Making selected text a hyperlink

5. Click OK in the Hyperlink dialog box.

The text you selected in Step 1 will be colored and underlined as a hyperlink. The recipient of your e-mail message need only click that link to visit the site.

Attaching Files to E-mail Messages

An e-mail message isn't a document — it's, well, a *message*. The main difference is that unlike documents, which are stored in regular document folders like your Documents folder and Public Documents, e-mail messages are stored in your e-mail client's folders.

If you want to send someone a document via e-mail, attach the document to the message. The document can be anything: something you typed, a photograph, a song, a video, and so on. But there is one big catch: Most ISPs won't let you attach any more than 1 or 1.5 megabyte (MB) worth of files to a single message. (One megabyte equals roughly 1,000K.) Songs and videos tend to be larger than that, so they're not always good candidates for e-mail.

Tip Many people use ZIP files (Chapter 23) to compress one or more large files into a single, smaller file that's easier to e-mail. You can also use the Send a File or Photo option in Windows Messenger (discussed in Chapter 12) to send someone a file of any size.

A Shortcut for E-mailing Photos

Here's a handy shortcut for e-mailing pictures that will automatically shrink large photos to a more manageable size for your recipients. The shortcut method works with Windows Mail, Outlook Express, Outlook, and a few other e-mail clients. But it doesn't work with all e-mail accounts. So whether or not this option will work for you depends on the program you use as your e-mail client.

Here's how the shortcut works. Let's say you're browsing around your folders and haven't even opened your e-mail client. You come across a document file you want to e-mail (we'll use a photo as an example, but the method works with any type of document file). Rather than opening your e-mail client, just right-click the file's icon and choose Send To ➪ Mail Recipient as follows.

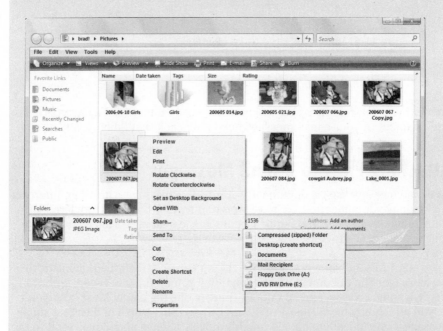

To attach multiple files to an e-mail message using the shortcut method, select the files you want to send; then right-click any one of them and choose Send To ➪ Mail Recipient. If the attachment is a large picture (or pictures), you'll be given the option to make your picture(s) smaller. Click OK and choose any size (640×480 is plenty big). If no sizing options appear, it just means that all photos you've attached are already smaller than 640 pixels wide and 480 pixels tall.

Attached documents don't appear in the body of the e-mail message. They just follow the message along on the Internet to the recipient's e-mail Inbox. The file names and sizes of the attachments will appear just above the text, as in Figure 11-7.

Attachments

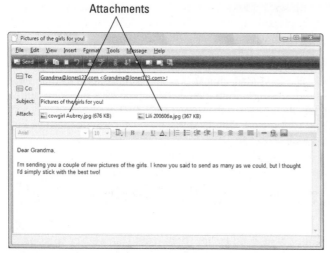

Figure 11-7: Two photos attached to an e-mail message

Sending the Message

🖅 Send When your message is addressed, composed, and ready to go, click
the Send button in the upper-left corner of the New Message to send
the e-mail. If Windows Mail is configured to send mail immediately, and you're
online, the message will be sent to the recipient, and a copy will be added to
your Sent Items folder.

How E-mail Works

Here's a quick rundown of how e-mail works. Let's say you send an e-mail to
somebody@somewhere.com (a hypothetical e-mail address). When you send
the message, your e-mail client hands it off to your modem, which in turn sends
it to your ISP's *outgoing mail server*. That mail server is a program that has only
one job in life — to accept e-mails coming in from all of the ISP's customers and
then hand them right off to the Internet.

When the Internet gets the message you sent, it looks at the domain name in
the recipient's address and transfers the message over to the *incoming mail
server* at the recipient's domain. In the somebody@somewhere.com example,
the Internet would hand the message off to the incoming mail server for
somewhere.com.

The incoming mail server is a program that stores all of the e-mail messages
pouring in from the Internet. Then, like a postal worker, it puts each message in
the appropriate customer's Inbox. So the next time somebody@somewhere
.com checks her e-mail, the message is sitting in her Inbox, waiting to be read.

If you're not online, or Windows Mail isn't configured to send messages immediately, the message will be placed in your Outbox. Click the Send/Receive button on the Windows Mail's toolbar to send the message from your Outbox to
the recipient.

Tip   To set options in Windows Mail, choose Tools ➾ Options from its menu bar.
The option to send messages immediately when you click the Send button
is on the Send tab. If you clear, rather than select, that option, all newly sent
messages will be sent to your Outbox until you click the Send/Receive button in Windows Mail's toolbar.

Reading Your E-mail with Windows Mail

E-mail messages that people send to you are initially stored on your ISP's mail
sever computer. To see them, you need to get them from that server to your
own computer. Depending on how Windows Mail is configured, you may have
to click the Send/Receive button to retrieve your mail. Either way, all new messages will be added to your Inbox. So you need to click the Inbox folder
(shown in Figure 11-8) to see your messages.

Cross-
Reference   See the section "Customizing and Configuring Windows Mail," later in this
chapter, for details on configuration.

Inbox

Body of currently selected message header

Figure 11-8: Inbox, message headers, and one message

The Windows Mail program window and taskbar button work the same as with any other program. You can use these buttons to:

✦ Move, size, minimize, and maximize the Windows Mail program window using all the standard techniques described under "Taking Control of Program Windows" in Chapter 4.

✦ Choose Help ⇨ View Help from the Windows Mail menu bar, or just press F1, to get help with the program.

✦ Sort message headers, and arrange column headings, using the standard column-heading methods described under "Working with Columns" in Chapter 5.

✦ ↔ Drag the bar that separates any two panes to size the panes.
↕

The Inbox is split into two panes. The top pane shows *message headers* — who sent it, the subject, and the date and time that you received the message. Headers for new messages you haven't read yet are in boldface. Click any message (once) to see its contents in the lower *preview* pane.

To see the contents of a message in more detail, double-click the message header. The message opens in a new window, as in the example shown in Figure 11-9. Items in the toolbar provide quick access to the most commonly used menu commands, summarized as follows.

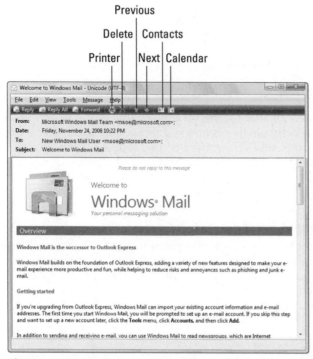

Figure 11-9: Viewing an open e-mail message in its own window

✦ **Reply:** Click to send a reply to the sender (only). Then type your reply and click Send.

✦ **Reply All:** Click to reply to everyone who received this message. Type your reply and click the Send button.

✦ **Forward:** If you think a friend should see this e-mail, click the Forward button, type the new recipient's e-mail address, and click Send to pass the message along.

✦ **Print:** To print the message, click the Print button, which is the small picture of a printer.

✦ **Delete:** If you never want to see this message again, click the Delete button, which is the button with the red X. However, remember that deleting isn't the same as closing. When you delete a message, you say goodbye to it forever. When you close a message, you just get it off the screen, but it stays in your Inbox.

✦ **Previous:** The up-arrow button, which displays the previous message from the header list.

✦ **Next:** The down-arrow button, which displays the next message in the header list.

To close the open message and return to your Windows Mail window, click its Close (X) button at the right side of its title bar. Or you can size and arrange the preview window and Windows Mail so you can see both on the screen at the same time.

Tip

> To reply to, or forward, a message that isn't open, right-click the message header and choose one of the Reply or Forward options on the shortcut menu that appears.

Opening Attachments

Before I tell you how to open an attachment, be advised that e-mail attachments are how the vast majority of viruses and worms are spread. As discussed under "Viruses, Worms, and Trojan Horses" in Chapter 13, you should open an attachment only if you know whom it's from and what it is. So please don't practice what you learn here with the first e-mail attachment that comes along. Send an e-mail and attachment to yourself, and practice with that.

Checking Your Attachment Security

Windows Mail has some serious virus protection built into it, in the form of "you can't open this attachment because it's the type of file that *could* contain a virus." That's different from the kind of virus protection discussed in Chapter 13, which is a little more choosey. Virus-protection programs usually only block attachments that *do* contain a virus. (More on that topic in Chapter 15.)

Before you try to open any attachments, you'll want to check, and possibly change, the Windows Mail security settings. Here's how:

1. From the menu bar in Windows Mail, choose Tools ➪ Options.

2. In the Options dialog box that opens, click the Security tab.

3. To be warned when some program attempts to send e-mail through Windows Mail, choose "Warn me when other applications try to send mail as me."

4. To block all potentially unsafe e-mail attachments, choose "Do not allow attachments to be saved or opened that could potentially be a virus" (see Figure 11-10).

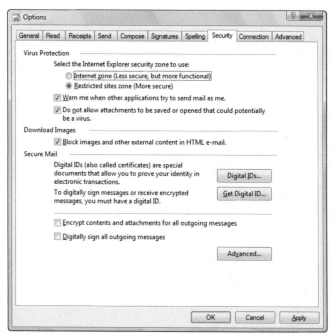

Figure 11-10: Virus-protection options in the Windows Mail Options dialog box.

5. Click the OK button.

Viewing (Opening) an Attachment

Recall that all new incoming e-mail messages are generally stored in your Inbox. While viewing your e-mails, you can tell which ones have attachments by the little paper clip icon that appears next to message headers. When you click such a message, a large paper clip appears above the message text (see Figure 11-11).

Attachments

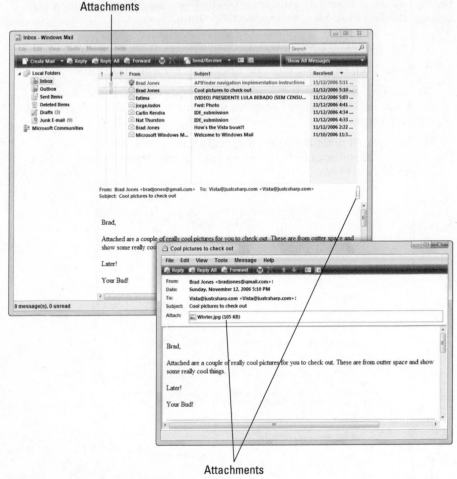

Attachments

Figure 11-11: Paper clips indicate e-mail attachments.

Assume that you've clicked the message header for a message that has a file attached. You know who sent you this attachment, the message looks legitimate, and you feel it's safe to open the attachment. You can use any of the following techniques to open an e-mail attachment in Windows Mail:

✦ Click the message header; then double-click the paper clip icon to the left of that message header.

✦ Click the message header; then click the large paper clip in the lower preview pane.

✦ Double-click the message header; then double-click the attachment file name just above the body of the message that opens.

Windows will attempt to open the attachment as a regular document. If you have a program that can open the attached document, the document will open. If you'd like to print the attachment, choose File ➪ Print from the program's menu bar. If you'd like to save the attachment as a document on your own hard disk, choose File ➪ Save As from the program's menu bar. When the Save As dialog box opens, make sure you navigate to your Documents folder or some other folder before clicking the Save button.

Caution Sometimes, when you open an attachment, all you get is a blank message with another attachment. So you have to double-click the attachment to open its attachment. You may have to repeat this several times — it all depends on how many AOL users forwarded it to each other before you got it.

If the attachment is a ZIP file, it will have a .zip extension. A ZIP file consists of one or more files compressed for fast transport across to the Internet. If you receive a ZIP file, you're probably better off saving it (as discussed in a moment) than trying to open it. After you've saved the ZIP file, you can extract its contents, as discussed in Chapter 23.

If you don't have an appropriate program for the document you're trying to open, you'll see the Windows cannot open this file dialog box, described under the section "When Windows Can't Open a Document" in Chapter 6. There are a couple of solutions to the problem. You can reply to the sender, asking him or her to send the file to you in a different format, or ask the sender if he or she knows of a suitable program that you can download and install for free.

Tip To view PDF files, you'll need to download and install Adobe Reader from www.adobe.com.

Saving Attachments

Attachments are generally saved with e-mail messages, which means you can't use them as freely as documents stored in regular folders like your Documents folder. If you want to keep an e-mail attachment around, and use it as a normal document, you need to *save* the attachment.

Saving an attachment isn't the same as opening it. That is, saving an attachment won't trigger any viruses. So if you have anti-virus software, you can save any suspicious attachments first. Then scan them for viruses *before* you open them. (If the scanning program finds a virus, just delete the infected file; do not open it!) To save an attachment:

1. In Windows Mail, open the e-mail message to which the file is attached by double-clicking its message header.

2. Click the large paper clip icon in the preview area. Then:

- To save a single attachment, right click its name. In the menu that opens, click Save As. In the Save Attachment As dialog box that opens, navigate to the folder in which you want to save the attachment.

- To save all attached files, click Save Attachments (see Figure 11-12). In the Save Attachments dialog box that opens, click the Browse button; then navigate to the folder in which you want to save the attachments.

3. Click the Save button in the dialog box.

After you've saved the attachment, it will be just like any document you created yourself. So you can use Windows Explorer to navigate to the folder in which you placed the attachment. Then double-click any attachment's name to open it. You can also delete the original e-mail message and attachment if you want. The copy on your hard disk is its own separate file and won't be affected by anything you do in Windows Mail any more.

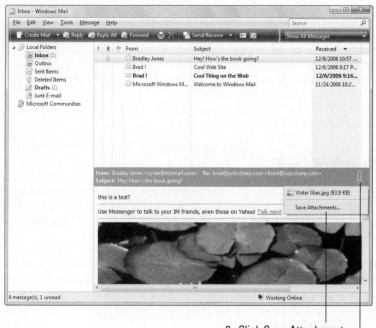

2. Click Save Attachments

1. Click the Paperclip

Figure 11-12: An e-mail message with multiple attachments

I Can't Save or Open Any Attachments!

As mentioned, the built-in Windows Mail virus protection blocks any file that *could* contain a virus, not just files that *do* contain viruses. As such, you may not be able to open some perfectly innocent files, like photos.

When Windows Mail blocks an attachment, clicking the large paper-clip icon in the preview area reveals only disabled (dimmed) options, as in the example that follows:

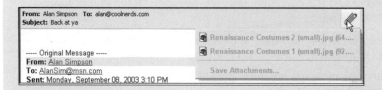

If you open the e-mail message, you won't see the usual file names above the body of the message. Instead, you'll see a bar that reads "OE removed access to the following unsafe attachments in your e-mail" (where OE stands for Windows Mail), as in the example that follows:

If you're sure the attachment is safe, and you do want to open it, you can repeat Steps 1–4 in the section "Checking Your Settings," earlier in this chapter. But clear, rather than select, the Do not allow attachments to be saved or opened option in Step 4 to turn off virus protection. Don't forget to turn that option back on if you want to continue to use it in the future.

Managing E-mail Messages

As time goes by, your collection of e-mail messages will grow. To manage those messages, you can organize them into folders, delete the junk mail or any messages you don't need any more, and so on. You do most of these managerial tasks in the list of message headers in the Windows Mail program window.

Selecting Messages

In the list of message headers, you can work with individual messages or groups of messages. To work with multiple messages, you first need to *select* the messages you want to work with. You can use the same techniques you use to select multiple icons (described in more depth under "Working with Multiple Files and Folders" in Chapter 19). For example, you can first click any message header to select only that message. Then, do one of the following:

✦ To select more message headers, hold down the Ctrl key while clicking additional messages you want to select.

✦ To extend the selection through a group of messages, hold down the Shift key and click the header to which you want to extend the selection.

✦ To select from the currently selected message to the end of the list, press Shift+End.

✦ To select from the currently selected message to the top of the list, press Ctrl+Home.

✦ To select all message headers, press Ctrl+A or choose Edit ➪ Select All from Windows Mail's menu bar.

You can also Ctrl-click to unselect selected messages. For example, suppose most of the messages in your Inbox are junk mail and you just want to get rid of them without even opening them up. You can click the first message header, then press Ctrl+A to select all the message headers. Next, hold down the Ctrl key and click the messages you *don't* want to delete, as in Figure 11-13. Pressing the Delete key in that figure would delete all the selected messages.

Select All messages, then ...

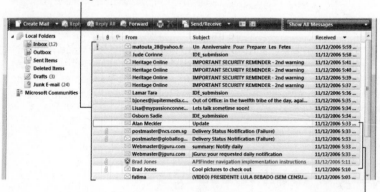

... Ctrl+Click the headers you don't want to select

Figure 11-13: A quick way to select most (but not all) messages

Tip   You can use a *spam filter* (see Chapter 13) to help keep junk e-mail messages from ever reaching your Inbox. Additionally, Windows Mail will filter some junk automatically into the Junk E-mail folder. This practice is covered later in this chapter.

Deleting Messages

Deleting messages is simple. If you want to delete a single message, you can right-click its message header and choose Delete. Optionally, you can select the headers of the messages you want to select, as in the example shown in Figure 11-13. Then use one of the following techniques to delete the selected messages:

✦ On your keyboard, press the Delete (Del) key or Crl+D.

✦ Click the Delete button on the Windows Mail toolbar.

✦ Choose Edit ➪ Delete from the Windows Mail menu bar.

✦ Right-click any selected message and choose Delete.

The message isn't permanently deleted from your hard disk. It's just moved into your Deleted Items folder. So if you ever delete an e-mail message by accident, here's how you can get it back:

1. Click the Deleted Items folder.

2. If you want to undelete several messages, you may select them all first.

3. Right-click the message (or any selected message) and choose Move to Folder, then select Local Folders ➪ Inbox.

There are a couple of disadvantages to using the Deleted Items folder. For one, the messages in that folder are still on your hard disk, taking up space. Each message is a trivial amount of disk space. But when you store thousands of them in that folder, it adds up. So once in a while, it would be good to empty the Deleted Items folder. When you do, you won't be able to recover any messages that where there. So you want to make sure there's nothing important in the Deleted Items folder. To empty the folder:

✦ Choose Edit ➪ Empty 'Deleted Items' Folder from the Windows Mail menu bar.

✦ Or right-click the Deleted Items folder and choose Empty 'Deleted Items' Folder.

 Caution The term *permanently delete* always means just that — to forever remove the item from your hard disk. There's no changing your mind after you've permanently deleted an item.

You'll have one last chance to change your mind, in the form of a dialog box that asks "Are you sure you want to permanently delete these message(s)?" Click Yes only if you're certain you're willing to part with the selected messages forever.

Keep Your Messages to Yourself

If you have one computer in a household with several users, having one e-mail address for everyone can get very old, very fast. It's not necessary to pay extra to your ISP to set up extra e-mail accounts. Nor is it necessary to try to set up and manage multiple e-mail identities. The best way to handle the multiple-users problem is to create a *user account* for each family member (see Chapter 25).

After you've set up a user account for a family member, you can then set up a free MSN or Hotmail e-mail account for each member and a separate .NET Passport for each user (see Chapter 12). That way, each family member has his or her own e-mail account, Documents folder, and personal settings. And best of all, it keeps everybody's e-mail entirely separate. (If you're the administrator, however, you can always spy on people and see what they're up to.)

Grouping Messages into Folders

You're not limited to using the folders that first appear when you open Windows Mail. You can create as many folders as you want. For example, you can keep a number of subfolders under your Inbox to store messages that you might need to refer to later (see Figure 11-14). When you get an order-confirmation message from a web site where you've purchased something, that message can go into your Orders folder until the package arrives. You can also organize your messages by the person or company that sent you the message, by project if you work online—whatever makes sense for your situation.

Figure 11-14: Custom subfolders beneath the Inbox folder

Before you create a folder, you need to decide which folder will be its parent. For example, if you want to create subfolders for your Inbox, as in Figure 11-14, Inbox will act as the new folder's parent. Once you've decided on a parent folder, use whichever technique that follows is most convenient to create a new folder:

1. Open Windows Mail if it isn't open already. Then do one of the following:

   - Right-click the folder that will act as the parent folder and choose New Folder.

   - Choose File ⇨ New ⇨ Folder (or press Ctrl+Shift+E). In the Create Folder dialog box that opens, click the folder that will act as parent to the new folder.

2. Type the name of the new folder and then press Enter or click the OK button (if you're in the Create Folder dialog box).

If you change your mind about a folder's name, right-click that folder, choose Rename, type your new name, and press Enter. You can also delete a folder. But be aware that if there are any messages in that folder, you'll delete those as well. Aside from that, deleting a folder is pretty much the same as deleting anything else: right-click the folder you want to delete and choose Delete.

Moving Messages into Folders

An easy way to move a message from your Inbox to one of your subfolders is to drag the message header so that the mouse pointer is sitting right on top of the folder in which you want to put the message. Then release the mouse button.

Optionally, you can right-click any message and choose Move to Folder. Or, to move a bunch of messages into a subfolder, select their message headers first. Then right-click any selected message and choose Move to Folder. In the Move dialog box that opens, click the folder in which you want to put the selected message(s); then click OK.

Marking Messages as Read or Unread

As mentioned, headers for any new messages you receive are shown in boldface. When you click a message header to view its contents in the preview pane, or double-click a message to open it, the bold text turns to regular text, indicating that you've read the message. (Actually, you have to leave the highlighter on the message header for a few seconds before the boldface goes away.)

You can manually mark a message header as "read" or "not read" by right-clicking the message header and choosing Mark as Read or Mark as Unread. Or select a group of messages first; then right-click any one of them, and choose a Mark As option.

Tip A boldface folder name with a number to the right contains unread messages. The number indicates how many unread messages are in the folder.

For example, suppose you read an important message, but can't deal with it right away. You want to make its header bold again to call attention to it next time you open Windows Mail. To make the read message look like an unread message, right-click its header and choose Mark as Unread.

Using Windows Contacts

Windows Vista provides a handy program that enables you to store and manage peoples' names and addresses. This program is appropriately called Windows Contacts. You also can use Windows Contacts as an address book to fill in the e-mail addresses of your mail recipients automatically when you compose a new message or when you reply to or forward a message. By way of introduction to the program, we'll show you how you can add *contacts* (peoples' names and addresses) automatically from Windows Mail.

Tracking Names and Addresses Automatically

It's not entirely necessary to manually add names and addresses to your Address Book. You can automatically add peoples' names and addresses using any of the following techniques. You can have Windows Mail automatically add the name and e-mail address of anybody you reply to in an e-mail message by following these steps:

1. Make sure you're in the Windows Mail program window.

2. Choose Tools ➪ Options from the Windows Mail menu bar.

3. In the Options dialog box that opens, click the Send tab.

4. Select (check) Automatically put people I reply to in my Address Book.

5. Click the OK button in the Options dialog box.

A slightly less automated technique (but one that still saves you some typing) is to add the e-mail address of the person who sent you a message. There are a couple of ways to do that. In the Windows Mail list of message headers, right-click the message header and choose Add Sender to Contacts, as near the top of Figure 11-15. Or, if the message is already open and you're reading it, right-click the name next to From and choose Add to Contacts from that submenu, as in the lower half of the same figure.

If a Properties dialog box opens, click its OK button. Later, you can go back and add information if you like, as discussed shortly.

Note   You can also add the sender, everyone included on an e-mail, or the person the e-mail is to. To add one of these to Windows Contacts, select Tools ➪ Add to Contacts from the menu within the Message window. You can then choose the appropriate choice from the menu displayed.

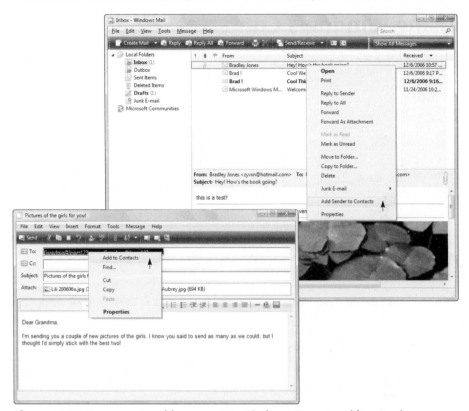

Figure 11-15: Two ways to add a contact to Windows Contacts without typing

Opening Windows Contacts

You can open Windows Contacts at any time to view, change, delete, or print information. From Windows Mail, you just have to click the Contacts button (shown at left), which appears on the Windows Mail toolbar. Alternatively, you can press Ctrl+Shift+C, or choose Tools ➪ Windows Contacts from the menu on the Message window. You can start Windows Contacts without going through Windows Mail. Just click Start in the lower-left corner of your screen and choose All Programs ➪ Windows Contacts. Either way, your Contacts will open, looking something like Figure 11-16. In this case, we've already added one contact whose name, e-mail address, and phone numbers appear in the main pane.

Figure 11-16: Windows Contacts is open with the first contact selected.

Note Items added to Windows Contacts are stored in files on your computer. These files have an extension of .contact. If you have changed the file options to show extensions, then you may see .contact listed after the names of your contacts listed in the Windows Contacts main window.

Managing Contacts

Your list of contacts will grow. Keeping it up-to-date and organized is going to take some management on your part: things like adding contacts, changing and deleting contacts, putting together groups of people so you can send them all an e-mail, like a family newsletter or something. Let's start with adding and changing contacts.

Adding and Changing Contacts

You may (or may not) have already added some contacts to your address book from Windows Mail and other programs. You can add contacts at any time. And you can change contact information at any time. It's simple:

✦ If you want to add a contact to Windows Contacts, click the New Contact button in its toolbar. Alternatively, you can select File ➪ New ➪ Contact from the Windows Contacts menu.

✦ If you want to change or add information to an existing contact (such as one that was added automatically), right-click the contact's line in the main pane of Windows Contacts and choose Open.

If you add a contact, you'll come to a Properties dialog box similar to the one in Figure 11-17, but all the text boxes will be empty and there will not be a summary tab. If you right-click an existing contact and choose Open, you'll come to the same dialog box. But you might have to click the Name and E-mail tab to see the options shown in Figure 11-17.

Figure 11-17: The Name and E-mail tab of the Contact Properties dialog box

The rest is easy. Fill in the blanks with whatever information you want. For example, click the Home tab and type the home address and telephone number. Or click the Work tab and type a work address and phone number. (You can do both.) You can fill in additional information, if appropriate, on the other tabs. Then click OK.

Gotcha

When you open a contact to add or edit the information, make sure that you select Open. If you select Properties, you will get a different dialog box that won't allow you to enter or update all the personal information.

Deleting Contacts

Deleting a contact permanently removes that contact's information from your address book and your hard disk. There's no changing your mind after you delete a contact. So be careful with what you delete. Other than that, deleting a contact is pretty much the same as deleting anything else. Use whichever method is most convenient at the moment:

✦ In the Windows Contact main pane, right-click the contact you want to delete and choose Delete.

✦ Click the contact you want to delete and click the Delete button on the Windows Contact toolbar, or press the Delete key.

Optionally, you can select multiple contacts using any of the techniques you'd use for selecting multiple icons in Windows Explorer. Then delete them all in one fell swoop by clicking the Delete button in the toolbar or by pressing the Delete key.

After selecting Delete, you will be asked to confirm that you want to move the contact to the Recycle Bin. Click Yes to finalize the deletion process.

 Note Deleting a contact actually places it into the Recycle Bin. As such, you can restore the contact if you have not emptied the Recycle Bin. See "Restoring Accidentally Deleted Files and Folders," in Chapter 19 for more on restoring from the Recycle Bin.

Printing Contacts

You can print your contact information in a variety of formats. If you want to print information for just one contact, select that contact's line by clicking on it. If you want to print information for all contacts, you can click any contact in the list. If you want to print information for several contacts, select those contacts first. You can select multiple contacts using any of the standard techniques for selecting icons in Explorer.

Next, click the Print button on the Windows Contacts toolbar or choose File ➪ Print from the menu bar. A Print dialog box opens. To print all contacts, choose All Contacts. Otherwise, choose Selected Contacts to print only the currently selected contacts. Then choose a print style—Memo, Business Card, or Phone List. Finally click the Print button and wait a few seconds.

Creating Groups and Mailing Lists

There may be times when you want to send sort of a form letter to a group of people. They might be people in your family, co-workers on a project, or members of a group. When it comes time to send a message to all these folks, you probably won't want to type all their e-mail addresses individually. It's easier to just send the message to the group as a whole, especially if you have to do it often.

To send a message to a group, you have to define who is in the group. To do so, click the New Contact Group toolbar button in Windows Contacts. A Properties dialog box opens. On the Contact Group tab, give the group a name of your own choosing. For example, in Figure 11-18, the group is named My Mailing List.

Next, click the Add to Contact Group button. In the Add Members to Contact Group dialog box that opens, click any name in the main area then click the Add button to add that person to the group. You can select any number of names first, using any standard technique for selecting multiple icons. Then click the Add button to add them all to the Contact Group. If you change your mind about an address in the right column, right-click that name and choose Remove. When the Contact Group contains the names of everyone you want in your mailing list, click the OK button. The contact names appear as group members, as in the example shown in Figure 11-18.

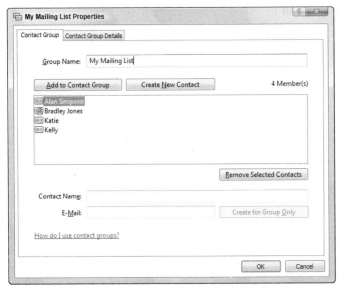

Figure 11-18: A new group named My Mailing List

Click the OK button in the Properties dialog box for the group. You'll return to the address book, where you'll see the group name added with all the individual names. If you ever want to change the group, right-click its name in the address book and choose Open.

Using the Address Book to Send E-mail

You can send an e-mail message to anyone in your address book, including all members of a group. Start your e-mail message in the normal manner, but don't type anything in the To: box of the mail. Use the Contacts button instead. Here are the specific steps:

1. If you haven't already done so, start Windows Mail.

2. Click the Create Mail button on the Windows Mail menu bar to create a new, blank e-mail message.

3. Click the Contacts button to the left of the To: box. The Select Recipients window opens.

4. To add a group or contact name to the To: portion of the e-mail message, click the person name or group name; then click the To: button. You can use the same technique to add names or groups to the Cc: and Bcc: boxes of the message. Figure 11-19 shows a message that will be sent to people in the My Mailing List group only.

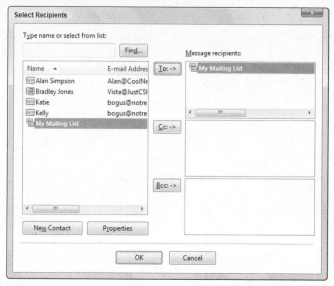

Figure 11-19: About to send an e-mail message to all members of the My Mailing List group

5. Click the OK button to return to your message. The recipient addresses (or group name) appear above the subject line.

6. Type the Subject and main body of the message; then click the Send button.

That's it. The e-mail message will be sent to all intended recipients.

Customizing and Configuring Windows Mail

Windows Mail has a many optional settings, all accessible through its Options dialog box. To get to the dialog box, choose Tools ➪ Options from the Windows Mail menu bar. As you can see in Figure 11-20, the dialog box offers many tabs and many options. I think most are self-explanatory. If not, you can always press F1 or use Windows Mail Help to get more information. In the sections that follow, we'll look at some of the main options available to you.

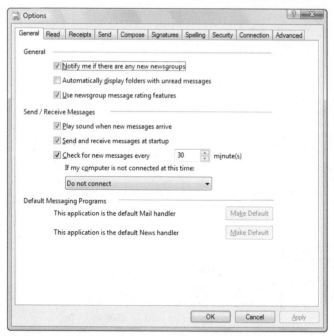

Figure 11-20: The General tab of the Windows Mail Options dialog box

General Options

The General tab of the Options dialog box offers options that enable you to choose whether to play a sound when new messages arrive, whether to check for new messages automatically, and how often to check.

Read Options

The Read tab in Options, shown on the left side of Figure 11-21, contains options that enable you to control how Windows Mail gets new messages from your ISP's web server. You can choose whether to mark previewed messages as read and how long to wait before marking them. You also can choose the font used to display your messages.

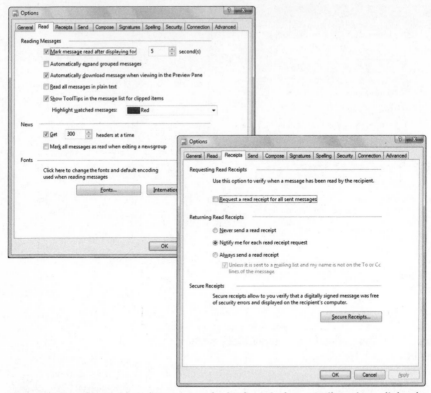

Figure 11-21: The Read and Receipts tabs in the Windows Mail Options dialog box

Receipt Options

A *read receipt* is a message that you get, automatically, as soon as someone opens an e-mail message you've sent. Use read receipts when you need to know that your recipient has received your message. Secure receipts require a digital signature, described later in this chapter.

Send Options

The Send tab offers options that control how the messages that you write are sent. As you can see in the left side of Figure 11-22, you can choose whether or not to save copies of sent messages to your Sent Items folder, to send messages immediately when you click the Send button (as opposed to just putting them in your Outbox). The Mail Sending Format option defines the format of each new e-mail message you create. If you want to be able to use fonts and pictures in your e-mail messages, choose HTML as your mail sending format.

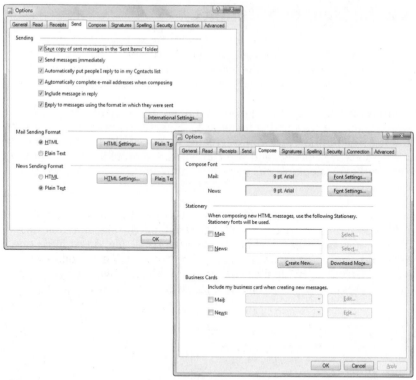

Figure 11-22: The Send and Compose tabs in the Windows Mail Options dialog box

Compose Options

The Compose tab in the Windows Mail Options dialog box, shown on the right in Figure 11-22, enables you to choose options for formatting e-mail messages. For example, you can choose a default Compose Font for all new messages. You can choose a custom stationery to use as a background for your messages. And finally, you can choose whether or not to include your business card with each message you send. (You'll need to add yourself to Windows Contacts for this option to work.)

Caution   The News options in Windows Mail are for working with Usenet newsgroups, not with e-mail. Most people use their Web browsers for newsgroups these days, which makes Windows Mail's options irrelevant. For e-mail, stick to the Mail options in the dialog box.

Automatic Signature Options

Windows Mail can automatically insert a signature at the bottom of every e-mail message you send, saving you the time and trouble of doing so. To create an automatic signature, click the Signatures tab in the Windows Mail Options dialog box, shown on the left side of Figure 11-23.

Click the New button to create a signature. Initially, the signature is named Signature #1. You can change that name to My Signature or whatever you want, using the Rename button. After you've created a new, empty signature, the Edit Signature options are enabled, and you can type a signature in the Text box. It can be as simple or as complex as you want, but it can contain only text (no pictures or fonts).

As an alternative to typing a signature, you can choose the File option; then use the Browse button to specify the file that contains the signature information. The file must either be a text (TXT) file or an HTML file. A text file is one you create and save using a text-only editor like Notepad (which comes with Windows Vista). And an HTML file is one you create using Hypertext Markup Language (HTML) and may contain fonts, pictures, hyperlinks, and such.

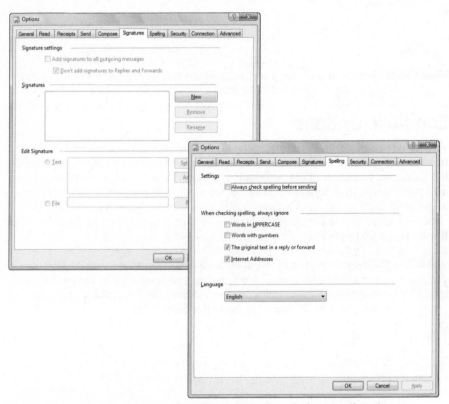

Figure 11-23: The Signatures and Spelling tabs in the Windows Mail Options dialog box

About Virtual Business Cards (vCard)

A vCard is a virtual (electronic) business card. To create one, you need to add yourself to your Windows Contacts. Then click your own address information in the Windows Contact main pane and choose Send Contact. This opens an e-mail and attaches the contact information to it. You can send a vCard from any of your other contacts in the same way.

You can also choose to export a vCard to a file that you can then attach to an e-mail. To do this, select the contact for whom you want to create a vCard. Then click the Export button in the Windows Contacts taskbar. This displays an Export dialog box that will enable you to select a file format. Select vCard and click the Export button. Next, you need to select a location to place the exported vCard. Navigate to the folder where you want to save it and click OK. The information is exported. Click OK to end the process and then close any windows that remained open.

If you receive a message with a vCard attached, the vCard appears in your message as a Rolodex card icon. You can then click or right-click the vCard icon and choose Open or Remove from the shortcut menu that appears. For more information, choose Help and Support from the Start menu and then search for vCard.

 Note HTML is a large topic and is beyond the scope of this book. You can learn what HTML is about from the World Wide Web Consortium (W3C) web site at www.w3C.org. A brief introduction to the topic is available at www.w3 .org/MarkUp/Guide.

When you've defined a signature, you need to select the check box Add signatures to all outgoing messages under Signature Settings near the top of the dialog box. This adds the signature to all your messages. You can choose whether or not you want that signature added to your replies and forwarded messages as well.

If you don't opt to add the signature to all outgoing messages, you can manually insert the signature any time you're in the New Message window or when you're typing a reply or forwarding a message. Just move the cursor to where you want to insert the signature. Then choose Insert ➪ Signature from the menu bar above the message.

E-mail Spelling Options

The Windows Mail Spelling options, shown on the right side of Figure 11-23, enable you to choose how to handle spell-checking in your messages. Windows Mail doesn't have its own built-in spell checker. Instead, it uses the Microsoft Office spell-checker, if available, on your computer. If you don't have Microsoft Office (or at least, Microsoft Word, Microsoft Excel, or Microsoft PowerPoint), spell-checking won't be available to you as an option in Windows Mail.

E-mail Security Options

The Security tab in the Windows Mail Options dialog box, shown on the left in Figure 11-24, offers the Virus Protection options described earlier in this chapter, as well as more advanced features. The Internet Explorer security zone options define what's acceptable in e-mail messages. Your options are:

✦ **Internet zone (Less secure, but more functional):** Allows objects that are generally secure, such as Java applets and signed ActiveX controls to be opened and executed in e-mail messages.

✦ **Restricted sites zone (More secure):** Severely restricts allowable e-mail content by preventing access even to objects whose security risk is minimal.

Tip   For more information on Internet security zones, select Help and Support from the Start menu and then search for the word **zone**.

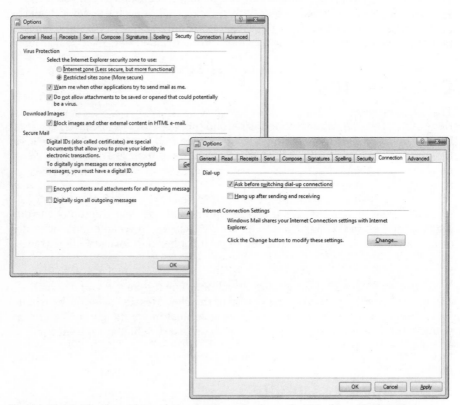

Figure 11-24: The Security and Connection tabs from the Windows Mail Options dialog box

The Warn me when other applications try to send mail as me option provides an alert when some program (not you) attempts to send e-mail without your knowing it. That's exactly how most viruses spread themselves from computer to computer — by e-mail copies of themselves to people in your Contacts, using your e-mail client as the sending program. Selecting this option won't prevent you from picking up a virus. But it will help you realize when you've picked one up, so you can start taking steps to remove the virus (see Chapter 13).

As mentioned in the section "Checking Your Attachment Security," earlier in this chapter, the Do not allow attachments option on the Security tab puts extremely tight controls on the types of attachments you can open. If you select this option, Windows Mail will block access to any attachment that *could* contain a worm or virus. But unlike an anti-virus program, this option can't discriminate between those files that actually *do* contain a virus and those that don't.

The Secure Mail options all concern digital signatures, a technology that enables you to verify your identity in e-mail transactions. Use the Get Digital ID button to create a digital ID. Use the Digital IDs button to manage existing digital IDs (if any).

Connection Options

The Connection tab of the Windows Mail Options dialog box, shown on the right in Figure 11-24, provides options for automatically connecting to your ISP when you request mail. If you don't have a dial-up Internet account, the Dial-Up options might be disabled. That's because the dial-up options make no sense with broadband accounts, which don't use traditional phone lines to provide your connection.

Advanced Options

The Advanced options tab includes a number of options that enable you to control features such as whether to convert contact attachments to vCards, whether to insert a signature at the bottom of a reply, whether to associate your Windows user account picture with your Windows Contacts information, and more.

Within the Advanced options tab is a Maintenance and Troubleshooting section. Clicking the Maintenance button in this section presents you with maintenance options.

The Maintenance options provide a few settings for automatically managing e-mail messages. The first option, Empty messages from the Deleted Items folder on exit, keeps your Deleted Items folder from becoming huge. If you select that option, all messages in your Deleted Items folder will be deleted automatically as soon as you close Windows Mail. The disadvantage to choosing that option is that it limits your ability to undelete an accidentally deleted message. After a message has been removed from your Deleted Items folder, it no longer exists on your hard disk and hence cannot be retrieved.

The Compact messages option, if selected, tells Windows Mail to compress and compact older messages to conserve disk space. You can set how often Windows Mail will compact the older messages. If you get lots of messages and tend to delete them, then you might want to compact more frequently.

Dealing with Junk Mail

You may have noticed another folder in Windows Mail called Junk E-mail. You can see this folder in Figure 11-1 of this chapter as well as in many of the other figures. The longer you use an e-mail address, the more likely you are to notice this folder because it will start collecting e-mail.

Although we stated earlier that all e-mail goes to your Inbox, that is not entirely true. You can set a number of options within Windows Mail to help screen junk e-mail and SPAM. When Windows Mail sees something it believes to be junk, it will automatically move it to the Junk E-mail folder, thus helping to keep your Inbox focused on e-mails that are more relevant to you.

The junk mail filtering is not perfect. As such, you'll want to skim through the e-mails in the folder to make sure nothing important gets stuck there. You can select the level of protection you want the junk mail filter to provide. To set the level, click Tools ➪ Junk E-mail Options from the Windows Mail menu. This displays the Junk E-mail options dialog box, shown in Figure 11-25.

In the Options dialog box, you have the ability to select the level of protection you want. If you select No Automatic Filtering, then you are taking total control of junk mail. By default, the level is set to Low in order to only move the most obvious junk. Even at the low setting, however, some good mail may still get filtered.

You can go as far as setting your level of protection to Safe List Only. With this setting, you must specify exactly who can send you e-mail. You do this by clicking the Safe Senders tab in the Junk E-mail Options (see Figure 11-26). On this tab, you can click the Add button to enter e-mail addresses. E-mails from these addresses will be left in your Inbox. Any addresses not on this list will be moved to the Junk E-mail folder if you have Safe List Only protection.

If you are using a setting other than Safe List Only, then any names on your Safe Senders list will never be filtered. By contrast, if you add e-mail addresses onto the Blocked Senders tab, those addresses will always be filtered regardless of your protection level settings. The Blocked Sender tab works exactly like the Safe Sender tab.

You can also set protection settings for International addresses and to help protect you from phishing scams. Phishing scams are e-mails and web sites that attempt to get you to provide confidential information or money by pretending to be a site or person they are not. By default, phishing protection is turned on for e-mail.

Figure 11-25: The Junk E-mail options for Windows Mail

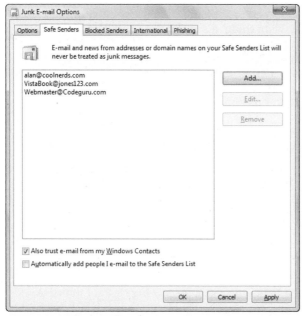

Figure 11-26: The Safe Senders list in the Windows Mail Junk E-mail options

Troubleshooting E-mail

Troubleshooting e-mail can be a tricky proposition, because there are so many players involved. But by far, the best resource for fixing e-mail problems is your Internet Service Provider (ISP); they're the only ones who know the specifics of the e-mail service you're using. You can either call them for advice or visit the Support page they provide on their web site.

There's also an E-mail Troubleshooter built into Windows Vista, which can help with problems at your end. To get to the troubleshooter:

1. Click the Start button and choose Help and Support.

2. Click Troubleshooting.

3. Click Troubleshoot problems with Windows Mail.

 Caution If your computer manufacturer has removed the Fixing a Problem option from your Help and Support, type **troubleshoot Windows Mail** in the Search box in Help and Support. Then click the Go button or press Enter. Under Suggested Topics, click Troubleshoot problems with Windows Mail.

When you select this option in Help and Support, you will be presented with a number of common problems with Windows Mail. Select the one that is closest to your issue and follow the instructions on the screen.

Summary

E-mail isn't really a Windows Vista thing. It's an Internet thing and a service provided to you by your ISP. Exactly how you do your e-mail is entirely up to your ISP. Windows Vista plays almost no role. Windows Mail is just one of many possible e-mail clients. Whether or not it's required, or even an option, with your particular e-mail address is entirely up to your ISP. Here's a quick recap of what you've learned in this chapter:

✦ E-mail is a service of the Internet and is provided by your ISP. Different ISPs offer different types of services.

✦ Windows Mail is an e-mail client — a program for sending and receiving e-mail messages. Windows Mail is optional and isn't even supported by all ISPs.

✦ Regardless of the program you use for e-mail, all new e-mail messages you receive end up in your e-mail Inbox.

✦ If you use Windows Mail as your e-mail client, you use the Create Mail button in its menu bar to write new e-mail messages.

✦ Windows Contacts is a handy program for storing contact information (peoples' names and addresses). It's integrated with Windows Mail, so you can use it to create mailing lists and address new messages.

✦ All options for configuring and customizing Windows Mail are in its Options dialog box, which you can get to by choosing Tools ➪ Options from the Windows Mail menu bar.

✦ When it comes to troubleshooting e-mail problems, your best bet is to go to your ISP. Only they know the specifics of the e-mail service they provide.

✦ Although Windows Mail can't eliminate all junk mail, there are a few tools in place to try to help eliminate some.

Chatting and Interacting Using the Internet

◆   ◆   ◆   ◆

◆   ◆   ◆   ◆

If you've been using Windows Vista for a while, you
may have noticed the phrase Windows Live used
here and there. You may have also noticed references
to a Windows Live ID or a .NET Passport. You may have
even seen a notice suggesting you create a Windows
Live ID or .NET Passport. You may have already followed through and created a passport for yourself.
Alternatively, you might have totally ignored any
requests to create such an ID.

It really doesn't matter, because you can set up a
Windows Live ID at any time. The real question for
many is "What is a Windows Live ID, and why would
I want one?" This chapter aims to resolve those
questions.

For starters, a *Windows Live ID* is basically a type of
Internet account that provides access to services
that go beyond what an ISP can provide. These added
services include instant messaging; live toll-free voice
and video conversations with anyone, anywhere in
the world; the ability to transfer files of any size; and
Remote Assistance, where you can give a trusted expert
access to your computer to fix a problem.

.NET Passport versus Windows Live ID

In prior versions of Windows, Microsoft used the term .NET Passport instead of Windows Live ID. You will find both phrases used with web sites and programs. A Windows Live ID should work anywhere a .NET Passport is requested.

What Is a Windows Live ID?

Everyone who has a Windows Live ID has a unique user name. Rather than force everyone to make up some name, Windows Live ID lets everyone use his or her e-mail address as a user name. The advantages to that approach are twofold: It's easy to remember your own user name, because it's the same as your e-mail address; and no two people have the same e-mail address. So by using e-mail addresses, the uniqueness of each person's user name is guaranteed.

In order to set up a Windows Live ID, you need to know your own e-mail address, and you need to know how to send and receive e-mail using that e-mail address. Using your e-mail address as your Windows Live ID user name will not affect the way you do e-mail. Even after you've set up your Windows Live ID, you'll continue to do e-mail exactly as you always have in the past.

 Caution Don't be afraid to use your existing e-mail address as your Windows Live ID user name, even if your e-mail address ends in @aol.com, @earthlink.com, or anything else. Your Windows Live ID won't change or interfere with your e-mail account in any way.

You'll also have to think up a password. The password has to be at least six characters and should not contain any blank spaces. Also, passwords are case-sensitive, meaning that uppercase and lowercase letters are not treated the same. So when you create your password, use all lowercase letters so you don't have to remember the case of each letter.

If you have a favorite password you use for all your accounts, you can use that one, which is easier than trying to remember a bunch of different passwords for a bunch of different accounts. Before you even get started, I suggest that you write down your e-mail address and password. It might sound a little goofy at first, but you'd be amazed at how many people set up their Windows Live ID and two days later can't get into their own accounts because they've forgotten their user name, password, or both.

✦ My Windows Live ID User Name (my e-mail address, too):

_____

✦ My Windows Live ID password: _____

Creating E-mail Accounts for Other People

When setting up your own Windows Live ID, you want to use your own e-mail address as your user name. If you want to create new e-mail addresses for other members of your family, to keep their e-mail separate from your own, you can create a new e-mail address on the fly while creating their Windows Live IDs. However, it would be best to create a separate Windows Vista user account for each family member first. Then associate each new e-mail address and Windows Live ID you create with each family member's user account. See Chapter 25 for more information on creating using accounts.

Creating Your Windows Live ID

Creating a Windows Live ID for yourself is fairly easy. If you want, you can wait until after you install a program that requires a Windows Live ID (like the programs later in this chapter). Your best bet will be to go ahead and create one now. To create your Windows Live ID, just follow these steps:

 Caution You need only set up your Windows Live ID once, not each time you intend to sign in to your account. If you've already created a Windows Live ID, skip the steps presented here and go to the section titled "Opening Windows Live Messenger" later in this chapter.

1. Open Internet Explorer and go to www.Live.com. This is the Microsoft Live site and home to Windows Live. The Windows Live page displays Live Search that you can use to search the Internet.

2. In the upper-right corner, click Sign in. This takes you to a page similar to Figure 12-1.

3. If you already have a Windows Live ID, then you can sign right in. Additionally, if you have an e-mail account provided by Microsoft, you can use that to sign in and as a Windows Live ID. If you don't have a Microsoft e-mail address, then click the link on the left side: Sign up for Windows Live!

4. When you click the link, a new page is displayed. The page asks whether you already have an e-mail address. Assuming you do, choose Yes, and click Continue. This displays the credentials dialog box in Figure 12-2.

    Note If you do not have an e-mail address already, you can select no and follow the instructions to sign up for a Hotmail address from Microsoft.

5. On the Credentials web page type your e-mail address and password exactly as you wrote them in this book earlier in this chapter. Follow all the instructions on the page carefully. Scroll down and click the Continue button.

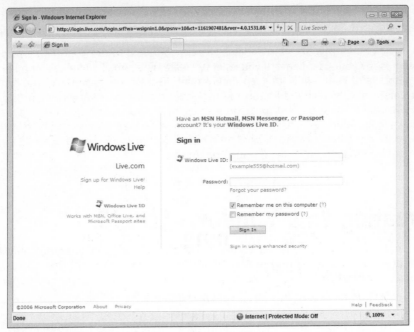

Figure 12-1: The sign-in page for Windows Live

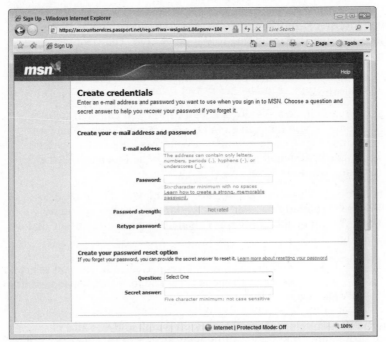

Figure 12-2: The credentials page for setting up a Windows Live ID

6. The page that is displayed next is for creating an MSN account. You'll need to fill out this page in order to continue. Fill in the information and click Continue.

7. You will now be presented with the agreements that you need to accept in order to complete the creation of your Windows Live ID. Enter your e-mail address into the page and click I Accept.

Assuming you did everything correctly, you should now be at a page that says you have completed the creation of an MSN account. While this is done, you still need to click Continue one more time. This takes you back to the Windows Live page, and you will be signed in. At this point, your e-mail address is set up as a Windows Live ID. It can also be used as a .NET Passport ID as well.

Installing and Opening Windows Live Messenger

Probably the main reason most people set up a Windows Live ID is so they can use the Windows Live Messenger program. As you'll learn in this chapter, Windows Messenger provides access to all sorts of Windows Live services. Among those services is the ability to send and receive messages from others.

Unlike previous versions of Windows, Vista does not include the messenger program preinstalled. As such you will need to download and install it. To download Windows Live Messenger, click the Start button and select All Programs ➪ Windows Live Messenger Download. This takes you to a web page where you'll be able to download the program for free.

On the page that you are taken to, select Get it free. This presents you with the File Download dialog box. Select Run to run the program. Alternatively, you can select Save to save the download file on your machine. You can then double-click the file that is downloaded to run it, and start the install.

After you start the install, you will need to follow the installation wizard. The following steps walk you through this wizard:

1. On the first page, click Next > to start the wizard.

2. In order to install Windows Live Messenger, you need to agree to the terms of use and the privacy statement. After you've read the terms listed on this page, click the I accept the Terms of Use and Privacy Statement option and then click Next to continue.

3. The next page (shown in Figure 12-3) enables you to select additional options and features you'd like to install. Each option listed on the page includes a description of what it does. If you are unsure, you should click the option to remove the check box and thus prevent the selection from being installed. None of the options are required.

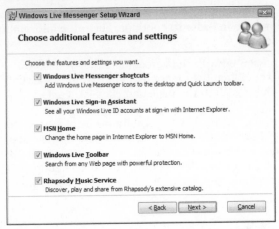

Figure 12-3: The additional options and features you can install when setting up Windows Live Messenger

4. At this point, Windows Live Messenger will install. You will see a progress bar showing the status of the install. You may also get prompted by the User Account Control (UAC) dialog box to confirm that you started this installation. Press Continue on the UAC dialog box if it displays and then wait for the progress of the install to complete.

5. When the installation is completed, a message is displayed stating that Windows Live Messenger has been installed. Click Close to end the setup and to start Windows Live Messenger.

If all went okay, then you have installed Windows Live Messenger. If you look on your Start Menu, you will find that Windows Live Messenger is now listed on the All Programs menu. When the installation wizard is complete, it will also start Windows Live Messenger.

Running Windows Live Messenger

Whether the wizard starts it, or whether you select All Programs ➪ Windows Live Messenger from the Start menu, what you will see the first time you start it is shown in Figure 12-4.

In the window you will need to enter your e-mail address, the one you just set up as a Windows Live ID, and your password. You can then click the Sign in button. At this point, a couple of windows are likely to open as shown in Figure 12-5.

Figure 12-4: The initial sign-in screen for Windows Live Messenger

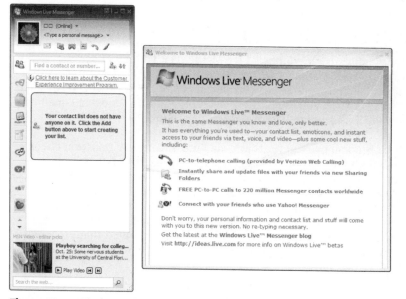

Figure 12-5: Windows Live Messenger running for the first time

Sign Me in Automatically

In some situations, you'll see an option that reads *Sign me in automatically* at a Windows Live ID prompt. If you choose that option, you'll be able to sign in to your account without typing your user name and password. This is perfectly safe if you're the only person who uses this computer. But on a public computer, or a computer you share with other people, choosing that option will allow other people to sign in to your Windows Live ID. As a rule, that isn't a good idea.

Windows Messenger is similar to other programs in that it has its own title bar, toolbar, and other controls. You can move and size the window using all the techniques described in the section "Taking Control of Program Windows" in Chapter 4. Before you get started using Windows Messenger, there may be a couple more things to attend to.

Windows Firewall Has Blocked...

The first time you run Windows Live Messenger, you may have a dialog box pop up that says Windows Firewall has blocked some features of this program. The dialog box will provide information and links to information on what it means to unblock the program. To get all of the features of Windows Live Messenger, you will need to click the Unblock button. If you are concerned with keeping the tightest security, then click the Keep blocking button.

E-mail Address Not Verified

When you first start using Windows Live Messenger, you might see the "E-mail Address Not Verified" message. E-mail verification involves guaranteeing that you do, indeed, own the e-mail address you specified. How do you verify such a thing? It's easier than you might think. Windows Live ID sends an e-mail message to the e-mail address you gave as your user name.

Your job is to keep an eye out for that e-mail message every time you check your e-mail. All you have to do is check your e-mail as you always do (ignore the Go to my e-mail inbox option in Windows Live Messenger for now). Eventually, you should get an e-mail message from Microsoft with "Confirm your e-mail address for the Microsoft Passport Network" (or something similar) in the Subject line. When you get that message, open it and follow the instructions it provides. After you do that, you'll have verified that you are, indeed, the owner of the e-mail address, and the "E-mail Address Not Verified" message in Windows Messenger will disappear.

A New Version of Windows Live Messenger Is Available

Windows Live Messenger regularly gets new updates and other revisions. As such, there's a good chance that when you open Windows Live Messenger, there is a chance you'll see a message that reads "A new version of Windows Live Messenger is now available. Click here for more information." You'll be given the option to update (for free) your current copy of Windows Live Messenger.

Then you'll get the standard security warning that appears whenever you download and install any program. Just follow the instructions on the screen until the update is complete. After you've finished this whole hullabaloo with e-mail verification and updates, everything will be ready to go, and you can forget all about setting up your account and verifying your e-mail address. From here on out, you can just sign in and use Windows Live Messenger as described in the sections that follow.

Instant Messaging with Windows Messenger

Instant messaging is a lot like a telephone, in that your conversation takes place in *real time*. Unlike the phone, which costs money, communication via Windows Live Messenger is free. It doesn't matter where in the world the other person is located. Also, with the phone, you're limited to voice communications. With Windows Live Messenger, you can type messages back and forth or use voice. Throw in a *Web cam*, and you can see each other during the conversation as well.

There are some limitations to instant messaging, however. The person you want to communicate with also needs to have a computer, an Internet connection, a Windows Live ID, and a compatible message program such as the Windows Live Messenger program, MSN Messenger, or Yahoo! Messenger. You can have others download Windows Live Messenger and install it. If they are using Windows XP, then they will have Windows Messenger on their system by default.

Setting Up Your List of Contacts

A *contact* in Windows Messenger is any person with whom you plan to do instant messaging. To create a contact, you just need to know that person's Windows Live ID user account name (which is the same as his or her e-mail address). Then follow these steps:

1. Click the Add a Contact button on the Windows Live Messengers toolbar. The Add a Contact dialog box is displayed with the General dialog box presented as shown in Figure 12-6.

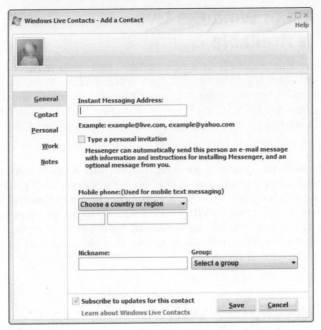

Figure 12-6: The Add a Contact form for Windows Live Messenger

2. Type the complete e-mail address into the *Instant messaging Address* field for the person you plan to communicate with.

3. When you save this form, Windows will send a request to the contact to connect with you. Windows Live messenger sends a generic message. You can, however, click the Type a personal invitation option if you want to include a personal message with the request that will be sent to the person. When you select this option, a text box is displayed that you can use to enter your message.

4. Optionally, you can enter a nickname for this person. If entered, you will see the nickname on your contacts list. If you don't enter a nickname, then you will see the contact's e-mail address.

5. You don't need to enter the other information about the contact. In most cases, this information will be pulled from the person's public profile if he or she has one. You can click Save to continue.

6. When you click the Save button, the person is added to your Windows Live Messenger main window as a contact. Additionally, you'll be able to tell the person's current status. You can repeat the steps to add as many contacts as you want. Each contact you create appears in the main pane beneath the menu bar. For example, Figure 12-7 shows three contacts: Alan, CSharpGuy, and Melissa. As you can see, one of these still appears as an e-mail addresses.

Tip When you have a conversation with someone, his or her e-mail address in Windows Live Messenger might be replaced by his or her *display name*. This information may come from the profile information the person keeps on his or her own computer.

Starting a Conversation

Windows Live Messenger lists your contacts in two groups: those currently online (and therefore available for instant messaging) and offline (those not online). For example, in Figure 12-7, the contacts named CSharpGuy and Melissa are online and the other contact is offline. (Click the Online or Offline heading to show or hide items under each heading.)

Figure 12-7: Contact groups

Tip ⇓⇑ If your contacts are shown in groups other than Online/Offline, choose the Manage your contacts button and select Sort by Status.

You can start a conversation with anybody who is currently online by sending an instant message. Just double-click the online contact's name, or right-click the name and choose Send An Instant Message to get started.

A Conversation window opens, like the example shown in Figure 12-8. The Conversation window is separate from the Windows Messenger main window and has its own separate taskbar button. You can move and size the Conversation window like any other program window and independently of the main window.

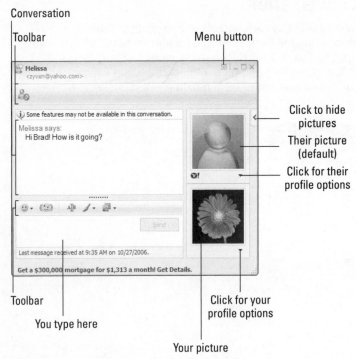

Figure 12-8: The Conversation window, with a conversation in progress

To send a message to someone, fill in the lower portion of the window near the Send button; then press Enter or click the Send button. Whatever you typed moves up into the Conversation area and also appears in the Conversation area of whomever you're talking to. Figure 12-8 shows the Conversation window with a conversation between two people just getting started.

While typing in the Conversation window, you can use all the standard text-editing techniques described in Chapter 7. When you press Enter, however, you don't start a new paragraph. Instead, you send the message (the same as clicking the Send button). If you want to start a new line or paragraph without sending the message, press Shift+Enter or Ctrl+Enter (once or twice).

Adding Emoticons

Emoticons (emotion icons) are little symbols you can use to express emotions in your typed messages. To add an emoticon to your message, just make sure the cursor is positioned where you want to place the icon in your text. Click the Emoticons button; then click the icon you want to insert. You can edit emoticons like text. For example, to delete an emoticon from your message, move the cursor just to the right of that icon, and press the Backspace key.

 Caution   If you don't have an Emoticons button just above where you type your text, choose the menu button in the title bar then select Tools ➪ Show Emoticons.

You can also type emoticons using special combinations of keystrokes. For example, typing : D or : d displays the happy-face emoticon. Typing : - (or : (types the sad-face emoticon and so forth. Table 12-1 lists many of the emoticons and the optional keys you can use to type them.

Table 12-1
Conversation Emoticons and Optional Keys to Type Them

Emoticon	Name	To type
	Happy	**:-D** or **:d**
	Sad	**:-(** or **:(**
	Wink	**;-)** or **;)**
	Angel	**(A)** or **(a)**
	Angry	**:-@** or **:@**
	Cool	**(H)** or **(h)**
	Confused	**:-S** or **:s**
	Crying	**:'(**
	Embarrassed	**:$** or **:-$**
	Surprised	**:-O** or **:o**
	Tongue out	**:-P** or **:p**
	Watchu Talking About?	**:-|** or **:|**

Continued

Table 12-1 *(continued)*

Emoticon	Name	To type
	Smile	**:-)** or **:)**
	Crying (animated)	**:`(**
	Sick	**+o(**
	Secret	**:-***
	Lips sealed	**:-#**
	Nerdy	**8-|**
	Doubtful (animated)	**:^)**
	Boring (animated)	**|-)**
	Eye roll (animated)	**8-)**
	Star	**(*)**
	Thumbs down	**(N)** or **(n)**
	Thumbs up	**(Y)** or **(y)**
	Rose	**(F)** or **(f)**
	Wilted rose	**(W)** or **(w)**
	Kiss	**(K)** or **(k)**
	Love	**(L)** or **(l)**
	Broken heart	**(U)** or **(u)**
	Bat	**:-[** or **:[**
	Dog	**(&)**

Emoticon	Name	To type
	Cat	**(@)**
	Dude hug	**({)**
	Girl hug	**(})**
	Hands across (girl)	**(X)** or **(x)**
	Hands across (guy)	**(Z)** or **(z)**
	Messenger	**(M)** or **(m)**
	Bright idea	**(I)** or **(i)**
	Coffee	**(C)** or **(c)**
	Time	**(O)** or **(o)**
	Birthday	**(^)**
	Party	**<:o)**
	Gift	**(G)** or **(g)**
	Music	**(8)**
	Telephone	**(T)** or **(t)**
	Picture	**(P)** or **(p)**
	Movie	**(~)**
	Mail	**(E)** or **(e)**
	Beer	**(B)** or **(b)**
	Martini	**(D)** or **(d)**
	Moon	**(S)**

Tip

To see the complete set of emoticons, including animated ones, go to `http://messenger.msn.com/Resource/Emoticons.aspx`. To see all other add-ons and some more freebies, go to `http://messenger.msn.com`.

Choosing a Message Font

You can choose a font, size, and color for the text you type. Just click the Font button above where you type your message. In the Change My Message Font dialog box that opens, choose the Font, Style, and Size you want to use. Use the Effects options to choose Strikeout font, underline, or a color. Then click OK.

Tip

In Figure 12-8, the text is Comic Sans MS, Regular, 14 point size.

Pasting to the Conversation Window

As you know, anywhere you can type, you can also paste. The typing area of the Conversation window is no different. For example, you can select (drag the mouse pointer through) any chunk of text from a document, web page, e-mail message or whatever, and press Ctrl+C to copy it. Then either right-click in the typing area of the Conversation and choose Paste, or click the exact spot in the typing area where you want to paste the copied text and press Ctrl+V.

Caution

You can't paste a picture to the typing area — only text. If you try to paste a picture, Paste will be disabled on the shortcut menu, and pressing Ctrl+V will do nothing. But you can always send a picture as a file, as described later in this chapter.

If you use Microsoft Internet Explorer as your web browser, you can copy and paste a hyperlink from a web page into your message. In Internet Explorer, right-click the hyperlink you want to copy and choose Copy Shortcut. Then right-click in the typing area of your Conversation and choose Paste. The actual URL will show. But it will be *hot* (meaning that the recipient can get to the site just by clicking the link in the message you send).

When Someone Contacts You

Just as you can add contacts to your copy of Windows Messenger, your friends can add you to their list of contacts. If you're online and signed in to your Windows Live ID when someone else adds you to his or her list of contacts, you'll see the dialog box shown in Figure 12-9. If the person is someone you're interested in conversing with, choose the first option. If it's some knucklehead you can do without, choose the second option. Then you can decide whether or not you want to add that person to your own list of contacts, and click OK.

Figure 12-9: Someone is adding you as a contact in his or her copy of Windows Live Messenger.

When you've allowed someone to contact you via Windows Live Messenger, you'll be alerted when that person sends you an instant message, via the Notification Area message shown in Figure 12-10. The taskbar button for the conversation window will also change color and blink. Click that taskbar button to open the Conversation window and have your conversation.

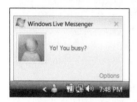

Figure 12-10: Yoo-hoo — someone wants to have an instant message conversation.

> **Tip** Like most windows in Vista, Windows Live Messenger has a menu bar; however, it is turned off by default. You can turn the menu on by clicking the Show Menu icon and then selecting Show Menu Bar.

Inviting Others to Join In

Up to five people can join in on an instant message, provided you're typing messages back and forth (only two people when you get voice or video involved, however). To invite someone to join your conversation, go to I want to... in the sidebar and select Invite Someone to this Conversation. Or choose Actions ➪ Invite a Contact to Join This Conversation from the Conversation Window menu bar. In the Add Someone dialog box that opens, click the name of the person you want to add. Or click the Other tab, and enter the new person's Windows Live ID user name (usually the same as the person's e-mail address). Click OK.

Inviting Others to Get Lost

If anyone starts being a pain in a conversation, you can prevent that person from sending you more messages. To block anyone in the current conversation, click the Block button on the toolbar; then click the name of the person you want to block. There are other ways to block people, as you'll learn in the section "Managing Your Contacts," later in this chapter. But the Block button on the toolbar is a quick and easy way to kick someone out of the current conversation.

Ending a Conversation

To end a conversation, just close the Conversation window. The Windows Live Messenger window will remain open, so you can still start or accept other conversations. To go offline entirely, so nobody can reach you, choose File ➪ Sign Out from the menu bar in Windows Live Messenger or right-click the Messenger icon in the Windows notification bar and select Sign Out from there.

Your *Do Not Disturb* Options

If you stay online, but don't actually use your computer for about 10 minutes, Windows Messenger will automatically change your status to Away, like Melissa's status back in Figure 12-7. You can set your own status message at any time. Whatever you choose will appear next to your name in all the Windows Messenger programs that have you as a contact.

To change your status:

✦ Click the menu button and choose File ➪ My Status, as in the top part of Figure 12-11. Then click the status message you want to display next to your name.

✦ Or right-click the little Windows Live Messenger icon in the Notification Area and choose My Status, as in the bottom part of Figure 12-11; then click the status message you want to display.

If you find that Messenger has changed your status to Away automatically and you want to change that, just use either of the preceding techniques to change your status to Online (or to whatever you want). If you want Windows Messenger to stop showing you as Away after 10 minutes of inactivity, you can disable or change that setting using its Options dialog box, described in the section "Configuring Windows Messenger," later in this chapter.

 Tip   If you want to see (who is online) without being seen, set your status to Appear Offline. You'll be able to see who is online. But everyone else will think you're offline.

Regardless of your status, you can still see who is online at the moment by opening Windows Live Messenger. If you want to disconnect altogether, right-click the same Windows Live Messenger icon in your Notification Area and choose Sign Out. You won't be logged in to your Windows Live ID anymore. All your contacts will see you as Offline.

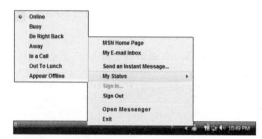

Figure 12-11: Change your status from Windows Messenger's File menu or its Notification Area icon

To get back online to communicate with your contacts, you'll need to right-click the Windows Live Messenger icon in your Notification Area and choose Sign in from the menu that appears.

Transferring Files and Photos

While you're in a conversation with someone, you can send files to each other. Unlike e-mail, which tends to put a limit on the size of the file you can attach to a message, there really is no size limit on transferring files in a conversation. Of course, the larger the file, the longer it will take to transfer, especially if either party in the conversation is using a dial-up connection.

STEPS: Send/Receive Files in a Conversation

1. If you haven't already done so, start a conversation with the person to whom you want to send a file.

2. Click the Show Menu button, then select *Actions ⇨ Send a Single File or Photo.*

3. The Send a File dialog box that opens is the same as an Open dialog box, in the sense that you first have to get to the folder that contains the file or files you want to send. For example, to send a picture from your Pictures folder, choose Pictures from the Favorite Links.

4. Double-click the file you want to send.

5. The recipient gets an invitation to accept the file. If the recipient clicks Accept, the file will be transferred.

Caution Sometimes a file will have trouble transferring when you click Accept. If this happens, try using the Save As option. Save the file to your machine, then open it.

Tip You can also send a file by simply dragging its icon into the conversation area and dropping it.

Assuming you're the sender of the file, there's nothing left to do. The file is transferred and that's the end of it.

If someone sends you a file using this method, you'll be given the option to Accept or Decline the transfer. When you choose Accept, the file will be copied to your computer; then you'll see a message like the one shown in Figure 12-12.

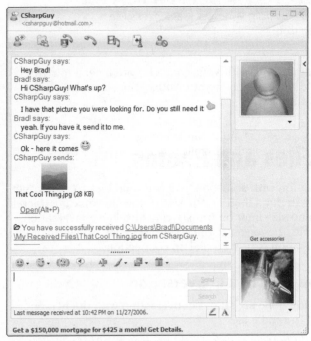

Figure 12-12: This person has received a file transferred by someone in a conversation.

The big chunk of underlined text is the path to the transferred file. The `C:\Users\Brad!\Documents\My Received Files` is the *path* to the My

Received Files folder in Brad!'s Documents folder. That Cool Thing.jpg is the name of the file. The entire path is a hyperlink. So if you click it, the file will open in whatever program is appropriate for that file type.

 Tip   If you miss the opportunity to click the link in the message, click the Show Menu button and then select File ⇨ Open Received Files from the Windows Messenger menu bar to open the folder where all your received files are stored.

If you don't have a program capable of opening the file you've received, you'll get the "Windows Cannot Open This File" message described in the section "When Windows Can't Open a Document" in Chapter 6. You'll either need to send the file in a format you can open or to download and install (if possible) a program capable of opening that file type.

You can also get to your My Received Files folder at any time (even when you're not using Windows Live Messenger) by opening your Documents folder and then double-clicking the My Received Files folder in Documents. When you open (double-click) the My Received Files folder, you'll see all files you've received through Windows Live Messenger file transfers. (You can then move those files to more appropriate folders, using any of the techniques described in Chapter 19.)

Toll-Free Talking

If you're not a big fan of typing messages, you can communicate with other Windows Messenger users by voice. But you'll need one extra piece of computer hardware to do that—a microphone (and speakers, to hear what the other person is saying). If you don't have a microphone for your computer, you can buy one at any computer store. Microphones that you wear on your head are generally better than the ones you just set on your desktop, because having the microphone close to your mouth helps cancel out all the background sound in the room.

There are several USB microphone headsets that you might want to check out next time you're shopping online or at a computer store. USB is good, because it means you just have to plug it into your computer to use it. There's no complicated installation to go through. The first time you use your microphone, you'll need to run the Audio Tuning wizard to get the best performance from Windows Messenger. Here's how:

1. Open Windows Live Messenger, if it isn't already open, by double-clicking the Windows Messenger icon in the Notification Area or by clicking the Start button and choosing All Programs ⇨ Windows Live Messenger.

2. Click the Show Menu button, then select bar in the Windows Messenger window, choose Tools ⇨ Audio and Video Setup.

3. Follow the instructions that appear on each page of the wizard. Click the Next button after completing each page.

4. On the Speaker Setup page, you'll want to confirm that your speakers are working by clicking the Play Sound button. If you are using headphones instead of computer speakers, then make sure that you select the check box indicating you are using headphones. Click the next button when you are done with your speaker settings.

5. The next page asks you to set up your microphone. You should talk into your microphone to verify that the volume is appropriate. The wizard shows how well your microphone is receiving using a colored status bar. Click the Next button to continue to the Webcam setup page.

6. The Webcam setup page shows a preview of what your webcam is seeing, assuming you have a webcam attached. This enables you to position your camera as well as set any additional options for your camera. Click the Finish button once you have set your web cam options.

After you've installed a microphone and have run the Audio and Video wizard, you're ready to talk online. This is easy to do:

✦ If you're already having a conversation with someone in the Conversation window and want to switch to voice, either click the Call a Contact button and choose Call Computer from the menu that is displayed. Alternatively you can click the Show Menu button and select Actions ➪ Call ➪ Call Computer.

✦ If you're not already in a typing conversation with someone, open Windows Live Messenger normally. Then right-click the name of the Online contact you want to talk to and choose Call ➪ Call Computer. The contact receives a message that you're ready to talk and will reply if ready.

The recipient gets a text message that shows your name followed by ". . . is calling you. Answer (Alt+C) Decline (Alt+D)." You'll then get some feedback as to whether the recipient accepted or declined. Assuming the person accepted, you can just start talking.

To adjust the volume of the other person's voice, drag the Speakers slider up or down beside the corresponding avatar (see Figure 12-13). If the other person has trouble hearing you, try increasing the volume of your microphone by using the Microphone volume control slider. (That person could, however, turn up his or her speakers.)

When you're ready to end a voice conversation, you can close the messenger window, click Hang Up, or click the phone icon. It's easy!

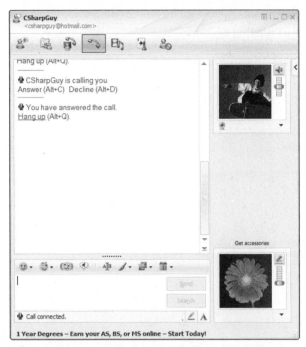

Figure 12-13: Volume controls appear to the right of the avatars (pictures) in a voice conversation.

Calling Phones

You can also use Windows Live Messenger to call telephones. To do this, however, is not toll-free like calling a computer. Rather, you will need to set up an account with Verizon. To set up an account, or to call someone if your account is already set up, click the Show Menu button and then select Actions ➪ Call ➪ Call a Phone.

Voice Conversations versus Telephone Calls

Anyone with a computer, sound card, speakers, and a microphone can have voice conversations using the techniques described under "Toll-Free Talking," earlier in this chapter. Those voice conversations always involve two or more computers (no telephones) and are always free of charge.

Telephone conversations are different in several ways. For one thing, there's a standard telephone, a cell phone, or some other non-computer communications device involved in the conversation. For another, telephone calls are never free of charge. In fact, you can't even use Windows Messenger to make phone calls unless you sign up with a supported provider such as Verizon.

If you have already set up an account, then you can use the Windows Live Call keypad to dial the number. If you have not set up an account, then you will need to click the Learn More or Continue button (as shown in Figure 12-14) and then follow the instructions for setting up a Verizon Call account.

Figure 12-14: The Windows Live Call dialog box for calling phones

Twenty-First Century Toll-Free Videophone

You can use your toll-free Windows Live Messenger voice communications to use voice plus live video communications, provided that you have a web cam. A web cam is a small, inexpensive digital video camera that doesn't record video. Rather, it just sits on top of your computer monitor and shows your face live to the person with whom you're conversing in Windows Messenger.

Video communications work best with broadband Internet connections, such as cable or DSL. You can still use a web cam with a dial-up account and modem, but the picture won't be as smooth as, say, regular TV. The video will look a little jerky, like pictures sent from astronauts in the early days of the space program. Not a big deal — you can still see and hear each other.

If you've never seen or heard of a web cam, you can check out some available products at any computer store or large office supply store. Optionally, you can go to any online store that sells computer stuff and search for *web cam*.

You don't need anything particularly fancy, though. Any USB web cam compatible with Windows Vista will do. A few models have built-in microphones, which saves you from having to install both a microphone and the camera.

After you've installed a web cam, you can start a video conversation with someone in the same way that you start a voice conversation. That is, if you're already in a typing conversation with someone, you can just click the Start or Stop a Video Call button or click the Show Menu button and select Actions ➪ Video ➪ Start Video Call. If you're not already in a conversation with someone, open Windows Live Messenger, right-click any contact who is online, and Video ➪ Send my Webcam. The recipient will get an invitation that he or she can accept or decline. If the recipient accepts, you'll automatically get both voice and video once the connection is made.

When you're in a voice and video conversation, as in Figure 12-15, you can use the sliders by the video images to adjust the volume of your conversation. If you're having a bad-hair day, and don't particularly want to be showing it off on your web cam, you can click the Camera button under the video Conversation window to keep talking without sending your video image.

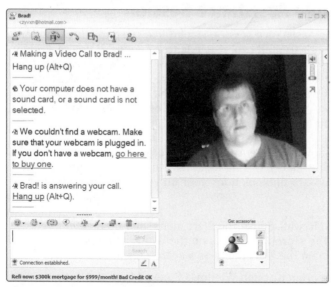

Figure 12-15: Having a video conversation in Windows Messenger

You might find the messages in Figure 12-15 interesting. The user actually made a video call to someone else even though they didn't have a video camera themselves. The result is that they can see the video of the person they called, but that person will not see any video.

Using Remote Assistance

Remote Assistance is a special feature of Windows Live Messenger where you can have a typing, voice, or video conversation going on. But you can also turn control over to a trusted expert. The expert can then see your screen on her screen. And she can work your computer using her own keyboard or mouse. This is why we use the term *trusted expert*. You wouldn't want to turn your computer over to a crook or knucklehead.

Unfortunately, there aren't any free experts floating around, helping people with their computers. The only trusted expert you're going to be able to get is someone you know and who (you can hope) knows a lot about computers. It could be your son or daughter, brother-in-law, or computer guy at the office — anyone with a Windows Vista computer and an Internet account.

> **Caution** Remote assistance is definitely slow if either party has a dial-up account. Leave the video off, and maybe even the voice off, to free up bandwidth for all the other activity involved in controlling your computer from afar.

Starting a Remote Assistance Session

 Starting a Remote Assistance session is a lot like starting any other conversation. First, your trusted expert needs to be online. If you're already in a Conversation window with the person, click the *See a list of activities* button and select *Request Remote Assistance*. Otherwise, in Windows Messenger's main window, right-click the online contact who'll be your trusted expert, and choose Request Remote Assistance. Either way, a Conversation window opens, and an invitation is sent to the recipient.

If you've not used Windows Remote Assistance before, then you may get a message saying your firewall is blocking Remote Assistance. In order to use this feature, you will have to unblock it for your firewall. You can do this using the following steps:

1. Open Windows Firewall. Select the Start menu, and then enter Firewall into the search box. Click on the Windows Firewall option that is displayed on the Start menu as a search result.

2. Click Allow a program through Windows Firewall from the options on the left side of the Windows Firewall dialog box. This displays the Windows Firewall Settings page with the Exceptions tab selected.

3. Check Remote Assistance to make it an exception to the firewall.

4. Click Ok to save the change.

5. Close the Windows Firewall window.

Now, with Remote Assistance allowed through your firewall, you'll get some feedback to that effect if the recipient accepts the invitation. You will then be asked to set up a password for the person to use to connect to your computer as shown on the left side in Figure 12-16. The person will get a dialog box that requires them to enter this password as well, as shown on the right side in Figure 12-16.

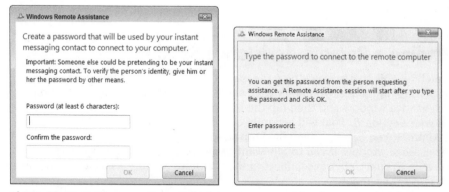

Figure 12-16: Setting up a Remote Assistance password for the person helping you.

Then it will take a while to get your screen over to the expert's screen. Eventually, you'll get a dialog box confirming the invitation. Click Yes to chat with the expert. When the expert attempts to take control of your screen (by clicking Take Control), you'll see the dialog box shown in Figure 12-17.

Figure 12-17: Are you ready to turn control of your computer over to this trusted expert?

Assuming you click Yes, you won't notice too much change on your screen. There will be a dialog box/chat area for Windows Remote Assistance, as shown in Figure 12-18. You can use the controls in the dialog box to converse with your expert or to end the remote assistance. The other change will be that Casper the Ghost will be working your screen. Well, it might seem like a ghost. It's actually your trusted expert working your computer with her mouse and keyboard. Before the expert can actually start working on your screen, she will have to request permission and you will have to say Yes.

Figure 12-18: The Windows Remote Assistant dialog box that will display on your screen when you are getting assistance from a trusted expert

Ending a Remote Assistance Session

You'll be able to see everything the expert is doing. If you think your expert is getting into places you don't want them to be, click the Windows Remote Assistance window and then tap the Escape (Esc) key at the upper-left edge of your keyboard. That will instantly cut off the expert's control of your computer. You can also click the Stop sharing icon in the Windows Remote Assistance window. If you totally want to disconnect from the expert (not even be able to chat), click Disconnect in the Windows Remote Assistance window or close the window.

You'll be lucky to find such a trusted expert somewhere. Unfortunately, there are no businesses out there that provide free trusted experts you can contact on the fly when you have a question or problem. And truthfully, very few people have any compu-nerdy friends or relatives to call upon. But if you have someone in mind, Windows Remote Assistance is the way to go for fixing problems without taking the computer anywhere.

Sharing Multiple Files

Windows Live Messenger enables you to share a number of files with others. The easiest way to do this is by creating a sharing folder. A sharing folder is simply a folder that you can create using Windows Live Messenger that will be shared between both you and the contact you designate.

To create or open a sharing folder, click the Share File icon and select Open Your Sharing Folder. Alternatively, on the Show Menu button, select Actions ⇨ Create or open a sharing folder. If a contact isn't already selected, then you will need to select a contact to share a folder. A message will be sent via the Windows Live Messenger meeting requesting to share folders. When accepted, the Sharing Folder window will be displayed similar to Figure 12-19.

You can now use the Shared Folder window to share files with your contact. You can use the buttons and controls in the window, or simply drag and drop files into the Window. A copy will be created on your contact's machine as well.

Figure 12-19: A shared folder between two contacts

Managing Your Contacts

Windows Live Messenger's main window shows all the contacts you've added through the Add a Contact option. There are two ways to view those contacts: You can group them simply as either Online or Offline, as in the example shown in Figure 12-7, or you can sort them by Groups. To change the sort order, click the Manage Contacts button or from the Show Menu button, choose Contacts ⟱ Sort Contacts By ⟱ Groups to see contacts organized into groups such as Coworkers, Family, Friends, or any other group name you want. With just a few contacts this might not seem necessary; however, as you increase your contacts, grouping them makes it easier to find who you are looking for. You can still easily tell which contacts are online and offline by the colors of their icons and the statuses to the right of their names. You'll see a few other options for sorting contacts in the menus as well.

Grouping Contacts

When viewing contacts by groups, you can click any group name to show, or hide, the contacts within that group. Initially, all your contacts will be in the Other Contacts group at the bottom of the list. To group your contacts, use one of these options:

✦ In the Other Contacts list, right-click the contact you want to group and choose Group Options ⟱ Move Contact To and the name of the group to which you want to add the contact. The contact is moved to that group.

✦ You can also choose to copy the contact from Other Contacts to a different group. If you do this, you will see that the contact is actually moved. A contact will only appear in the Other Contacts area if it isn't in any other group.

If you move a contact to a group, but later change your mind, there are a couple of ways to deal with the problem. First, make sure you can see all members of the group in which the contact is currently stored. Then right-click the contact's icon within the group. Since you're not in the Other Contacts list, you'll see an additional option that isn't availing in that list:

Remove Contact from Group: To remove the contact from the current group, click this option. The contact will be put back into the Other Contacts group and in any other groups to which the contact is a member.

Creating Groups

You're not limited to the few sample groups that first appear in Windows Live Messenger. You can create whatever groups you wish. To create a new group, right-click an existing group and choose Create New Group from the menu that appears; or click the Show Menu button and choose Contacts ⇨ Create a Group. The Create a Group window is displayed (see Figure 12-20). You can enter the new group name and then select the box next to any contacts you want to be in that group. Clicking Save will then create that group and move your selected contacts.

Figure 12-20: Creating a new Group for Instant Messenger contacts

If you make a mistake, right-click the group name and choose Rename Group. Edit the name, or type a new name. Then press Enter.

After you've created a group, you can use the Copy Contact To and Move Contact To options described previously to add contacts to your new group. You can also choose Edit Group, which will show a list of all your contacts like was done in the Create A Group window. You can then select the ones you want to add and save them.

Deleting Groups

To delete a group, first remove all contacts from the group. To remove a contact, right-click its icon within the group. Then move the contact to a different group, or delete it from the current group. After the group is empty, right-click its name and choose Delete Group. If you don't clear out the group first, then all of its contacts will be moved into the Other Contacts group.

Deleting a Contact

To delete a contact from all groups, right-click the contact you want to delete and choose Delete from the pop-up menu (or simply select the contact and press the Delete key). You'll see a dialog box asking whether you also want to block this person from sending messages to you. You can also remove the person as a contact on this dialog box. You'll need to select the appropriate boxes. When done with the dialog box, click the Delete contact button. The contact will be deleted from your instant messaging groups. If that isn't your intention, choose Cancel.

 Caution If you did not choose to remove the person from your contacts list in addition to deleting them, then they will be moved into the Non-Instant Messaging group. They will still be a contact, just not one you can send instant messages to.

Configuring Windows Messenger

Like most programs, Windows Live Messenger has an Options dialog box that you can use to control how the program behaves. You get to the Options dialog box the same way you do in many other programs — by choosing Tools ➪ Options from the Windows Messenger menu bar. In the sections that follow, we'll look at how you can use those options to control how Windows Messenger starts, your degree of privacy, and more.

Choosing Your Display Name and Font

Even though you add contacts to Windows Messenger through your contacts' e-mail addresses, your contacts' names usually appear in your list of contacts. Each user gets to choose a display name. When you choose Tools ➪ Options from the Show Menu button's menu, the first choice you come to (on the Personal tab) is your display name (see Figure 12-21).

Figure 12-21: The Personal tab of the Windows Live Messenger Options dialog box

The options on the Personal tab also enable you to choose your profile picture, as well as edit your profile. If you want to adjust how long the computer waits before displaying the Away status, you can adjust this in the My Status options. If you want to hide the fact that you have a web cam (assuming you have one), you can clear the option in the My Webcam section. When you've made the changes you want, you can click the Apply button to apply them, or you can click the OK button to apply the changes and close the window.

Changing Your Message Options

In the Options dialog box, you can click Messages on the left side to see the different options for customizing your messages. The first option you'll see is to change the font you use for instant messages. Click the Change Font button if you want to change the font, its style, its size, and its color. Click OK to save the font changes.

On the Message options, you can also determine if emoticons are displayed, if messages have the contacts name before them, if you can receive voice clips, and more. You can also select whether you should keep a history of your conversations on your computer. Again, you can select the options you want and click the Apply button to apply them or the OK button to apply them and close the options window.

To Autostart or Not to Autostart

From the Options dialog box, you can select General on the left side to be able to change a number of general settings for Windows Live Messenger shown in Figure 12-22.

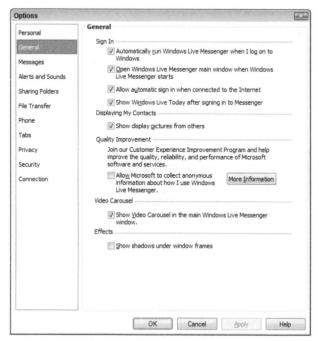

Figure 12-22: The General options within the Windows Live Messenger Options dialog box

If you want to automatically start Windows Live messenger when you log into your computer, then you will want to review the Sign In options:

✦ **Automatically run Windows Live Messenger when I log on to Windows:** If selected, this ensures that the Windows Live Messenger icon appears in the Notification Area when you first log into your computer. If you disable this option, Windows Live Messenger won't start automatically and won't appear in the Notification Area. You'll need to click Start and choose All Programs ➪ Windows Live Messenger when you want to run the program.

✦ **Open Windows Live Messenger main window when Windows Live Messenger starts:** This option causes the Live Messenger window to automatically open when you start the live messenger program. If this option is not selected, then only the icon in the notification tray will be shown when the program loads.

✦ **Allow automatic sign in when connected to the Internet:** If you are not continuously connected to the Internet, then this option will automatically log you into Windows Live Messenger whenever the Internet is available.

✦ **Show Windows Live Today after signing in to Messenger:** When you opened Windows Live Messenger, you may have noticed that a second window also opened up. This is the Windows Live Today page that has news and other information. If you don't want this window displayed when you log in, then don't select this option.

In addition to the Sign In options, there are several other options on the general tab. The other important option is Show display pictures from others. This enables you see the display pictures from your contacts.

Showing/Hiding Message Alerts

If you select Alerts and Sounds from the left side of the Windows Live Messenger Options window, then you will get options for controlling how you receive alerts. As you can see in Figure 12-23, your options include:

✦ **Display alerts when contacts come online:** If this is selected, you'll see a little message in the Notification Area each time one of your contacts signs in to his or her Windows Live ID. (You must also be signed in yourself.) Clearing this option prevents the Notification Area message from being displayed.

✦ **Display alerts when message is received:** If this is selected, you'll see a message in the Notification Area whenever someone invites you to join an instant-messaging session. If you clear this option, the Notification Area message won't be displayed.

✦ **Display alerts when e-mail is received:** If this is selected, you'll see a message in the Notification Area whenever someone sends an e-mail to your e-mail account — the account you used for your messenger ID. If you clear this option, the Notification Area message won't be displayed.

✦ **Display alerts when a Sharing Folder is updated:** If you have a sharing folder with a contact and if this is selected, you'll see a message in the Notification Area whenever that person updates a file in the sharing folder. If you clear this option, the Notification Area message won't be displayed.

Using the settings in the lower half of this dialog box, you can also change the sounds that occur when different events happen. By checking an event listed in the box, you will get a sound when that event occurs. If you click on that event to highlight it, then you will see the name of the file listed under the Windows Live Messenger events box. You can press the right arrow button to play the sound, or you can click the Browse button to select a new sound to play when the highlighted event occurs. When you've made your adjustments, you can click the Apply button to save your changes or you can click the OK button to save your changes and close the dialog box.

Figure 12-23: The Alerts and Sounds options within the Windows Live Messenger Options dialog box

Choosing Where to Put Received Files

Anytime someone sends a file during a Windows Messenger conversation, that file is stored in a folder named My Received Files folder in your Documents folder. You can change that default folder to anything you want. For example, in Chapter 13, I talk about the option of putting all downloaded files in a Recent Downloads folder, so you can scan just those files for viruses rather than having to scan your entire hard disk.

To change where Windows Messenger stores your received files, click the File Transfer on the left side of the Windows Live Messenger Options window. You can then change the folder name by clicking the Browse button under File Transfer Options.

You can also select the Automatically share backgrounds and accept shared backgrounds check box, if you want to share (and receive) backgrounds with others. If you don't select this option, you can still share backgrounds, it just won't be automatic.

Maintaining Your Privacy

People use instant messaging differently. Some people use it in a very public manner, chatting with strangers in chat rooms, making information about themselves available to other people, and so forth. Other people don't want any public exposure at all. They want to use instant messaging to converse with people they know, and that's it. You can have it either way. It's all a matter of knowing which settings to choose. The Privacy tab in Windows Live Messenger's Options dialog box, shown in Figure 12-24, provides your privacy options.

Figure 12-24: The Privacy tab in the Windows Live Messenger Options dialog box

Blocking Known and Unknown Contacts

When you first open the Privacy tab, you'll see two lists: the Allow List and the Block List. People in the Allow List can see when you're online and can send you instant messages. People on the Block List can't see when you're online and cannot send you messages. To move a contact from one list to the other, click the contact name. Then click the Allow or Block button to move the contact to the opposite list.

The boldfaced item **All other** refers to umpteen million people in the world who have a Windows Live ID and are not my contacts. When Other Windows Live ID Users is in your Allow List, anyone can add you to his or her list of contacts and send you messages. If you move All other to your Block List, only the people in your Allow List can see when you're online and can contact you.

 Caution If you send an instant message to someone, but they don't receive it, ask that person to add you, or All others, to his or her Allow List. If you can't receive a message from someone, check your own Allow List.

See Who Has You as a Contact

If you're curious who has you listed as a contact in Windows Live Messenger programs, click the View button next to the See who has added you to their contact lists option on the Privacy tab. In the dialog box that opens, you can see the list of everyone who has added you.

Showing/Hiding Your Phone Number

When you right-click a contact in your Windows Live Messenger list and choose View ➪ Contact Card, you see some basic information about that person in a dialog box. That information might, or might not, include the contact's phone number. You can choose whether or not to make your own phone number visible to your contacts by clicking the Phone tab on the left side of the Windows Live Messenger Options window. To make phone numbers visible to your contacts, choose a Country/Region Code from the drop-down list. Then type any phone numbers you want to make visible. To prevent contacts from seeing your phone numbers, leave all the options empty.

Signing Off, Closing, and Terminating

Closing Windows Live Messenger doesn't automatically take you out of your Windows Live ID account. Instead, the program window just closes, but the Notification Area icon remains. To sign out altogether, so that nobody can send you messages or alerts, do either of the following:

✦ Click the Show Menu button in Windows Live Messenger and choose File ➪ Sign Out.

✦ Right-click that little messenger icon in the Notification Area and choose Sign Out.

When you're signed out, you cannot use any Windows Live ID features. To sign back in, double-click the Windows Live Messenger icon in the Notification Area. You can also right-click that icon and choose Sign In.

 Caution The gray pop-up ads that you might get, which show Messenger Service in their title bars, aren't related to your Windows Live ID or Windows Live Messenger. To get rid of those, see the section "Blocking Pop-Ups" in Chapter 13. Terminating your Windows Live ID won't disable those pop-ups.

Working with Windows Meeting Space

Although Windows Live Messenger enables you to interact in exciting ways, you can also use another program, Windows Meeting Space, to share documents, programs, and your desktop as well as to collaborate with up to 10 other people across your network or the Internet. When you share your desktop, you can let the other person actually control the programs and documents that you have on your desktop or you can simply let them view what is happening on your desktop. This is a great feature if you want to collaborate, share information, and more.

Caution If you are using the Windows Vista Home Basic edition, then you won't be able to do all of the features of Windows Meeting Space. With the Home Basic version of Vista, you can only view documents that are shared, you cannot edit or otherwise change anything on someone else's desktop. To do this, you need Windows Vista Home Premium, one of the business editions, or the Ultimate edition.

To use Meeting Space, you set up a meeting and then invite people to it. When in a meeting, you can change who is controlling the meeting regardless of whose desktop is being used.

Starting and Setting Up Windows Meeting Space

To start Windows Meeting Space go to the Start menu and select All Programs ➪ Windows Meeting Space. This launches the program.

The first time you run Meeting Space, you will need to perform some setup tasks. You'll be prompted to make changes to your Windows Firewall settings to allow Meeting Space to work. You'll need to allow this in order for Meeting Space to work. You will then be prompted to set up people nearby who are using computers on the same network as you do in the People Near Me dialog box shown in Figure 12-25.

Figure 12-25: The People Near Me setup dialog box for Windows Meeting Space

When you use People Near Me, it will inform you who is near you on the network. It will also allow them to see you. You'll need to decide what display name you'd like to be seen as to people that may be near you on your network. You'll also need to determine whether you want to be signed into People Near Me automatically, and who you want to be able to accept invitations for meetings from. After you've made your selections, click the OK button to continue. You'll only have to fill in the information for People Near Me the first time you log into Meeting Space.

When you've gone through the setup, Meeting Space will actually run as shown in Figure 12-26. The next time you select Meeting Space, you will go straight to the program and not have to deal with the firewall or People Near Me.

Figure 12-26: Windows Meeting Space with one locally active meeting

Starting a Meeting

With Meeting Space running, to start a meeting, you need to click Start a new Meeting. This changes the right side of the window to enable you to enter a meeting name and a password. After you've entered these, you can click the arrow icon to start the meeting. The arrow icon will not be active to click, however, until you enter both a meeting name and an arrow.

If you set up People Near You, then they will get a notice that a meeting has been created. When you load Meeting Space, you will see meetings that are near you as well. Figure 12-26 included a notice for a meeting that had been set up called Family Christmas Drawing. If you click that listing, you will be prompted to enter the password for the meeting. That prevents uninvited guests since they will need to know the password in order to join. When the password is accepted, you will be taken to the meeting space for that meeting as shown in Figure 12-27.

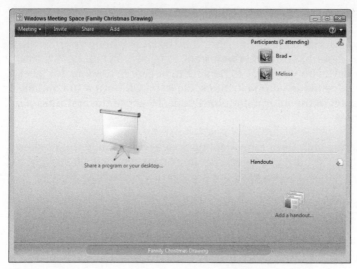

Figure 12-27: A meeting space with no sharing set up yet

Not everyone you want to attend a meeting is going to be on the same network as you. If you want to invite people that are somewhere else, then they can also join when connected to the internet. For them to join, you should send them an invitation file. Once you've created an invitation file, you can send it via Instant Messenger or e-mail. The person can then use its information with Meeting Space to join your meeting.

To create the invitation file, click the Invite option at the top of Meeting Space. This will display the Invite people dialog box as shown in Figure 12-29. You should then click the Invite others button near the bottom. This will allow you to send an invitation via e-mail or to create an invitation file. If you chose to create the invitation file, you will be prompted with the standard Save As dialog box that you can use to save the file that will be created. Once created, you can e-mail or send the file via instant message as you learned earlier in the prior chapter and earlier in this chapter, respectively.

When you receive an invitation file, you can simply open it. When you open the file, it will launch Meeting Space and prompt you for the password. After you enter the password, you will be taken into the meeting.

Sharing an Application or Your Desktop

With a meeting set up and people participating, you will want to share your desktop or an application. To start sharing, click the picture of a screen or the text below it that says Share a program or your desktop text. You will first be given a warning that if you share your desktop others will be able to see what is there. You will likely want to click the Don't show this message again check box to avoid the message in the future. Clicking OK will take you to a dialog box similar to Figure 12-28 for starting a shared session.

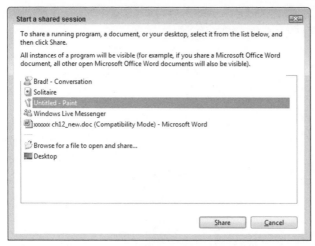

Figure 12-28: Selecting an application, file, or your desktop to share

In the dialog box you will see the applications you have running on your desktop. If you don't see an application listed that you want to share, then make sure you have it already running. To share an application, click it and select Share. To share your desktop click Desktop and then click Share. To share a file click the Browse for a file to open and share option and click Share. When sharing a file, you'll be prompted to open the file you want to share.

Tip You can also double-click the item in the Start a shared session list. This does the same as if you had selected it and clicked the Share button.

When you share an item, Meeting Space changes to tell you what you are sharing and to give you the option to stop sharing. In Figure 12-29, you can see that Microsoft Paint is being shared.

When you've selected to share the item, the Meeting Space window on everyone's machines will change to display the application, file or your desktop, depending on what you selected to share. Others will be able to see any actions that are taken with the shared application. In this case, you are sharing Microsoft Paint. In Figure 12-30, you see what other members of the meeting see. In this case, their Meeting Space changes to show a shared application.

Changing Who Controls a Shared Item

When you share an item in Meeting Space, in addition to the application you are sharing, your overall screen in Windows Vista will also change. Your application will show in its title bar that it is being shared. Additionally, across the top of your screen you will see a title bar showing that you are sharing the screen and application (see Figure 12-31).

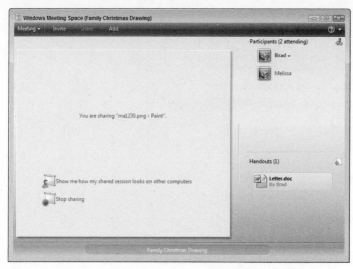

Figure 12-29: Meeting Space for the person sharing a file

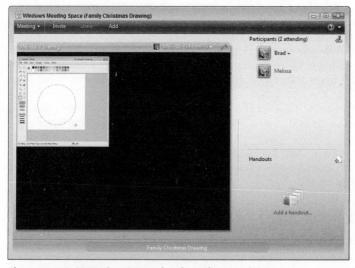

Figure 12-30: Meeting Space for the other participants

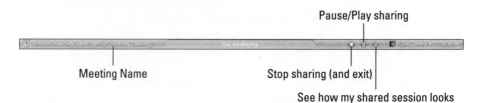

Figure 12-31: A title bar appears across the top of your desktop when you are sharing.

When you are sharing your application, you can make changes and everyone in the meeting will see them. If you want to let someone else make changes, then you can give them control of the item. Do this by clicking the Give Control option in the title bar shown in Figure 12-31. You'll be able to select from the list of participates that have the ability to take control. After you select a person, she will then have control to make changes. In fact, the person will be able to fully use the item even if she doesn't have the software for it installed on her machine. This is because the person is actually controlling the item on your computer.

When they are done, or when you are ready for that person to be done, you can click the same menu option again, which will have changed to say *xyz* is in control (where *xyz* is the user name of the person in control). From the drop down menu, you can select Take Control. Alternatively, you can press ⊞+ESC. This gives control back to you.

Other Sharing Options

In addition to changing who is in control, you have a few additional options in the title bar at the top of your screen when using Meeting Space. The Options drop-down menu contains a few options, but the more interesting ones are the three buttons to the left of Give Control:

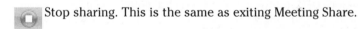 Stop sharing. This is the same as exiting Meeting Share.

Pause sharing. This temporarily suspends sharing, but not end your meeting. Those in the meeting will see a black screen with a pause icon rather than the shared information. The Pause button changes to a Play button that can then be clicked again to start sharing again.

See how my shared session looks. This changes your Meeting Space window to show you what the others are seeing. If you want to make sure things look okay from the viewer's perspective, then click this button to get a view of what they are seeing.

 Caution   If you are sharing a file or application and you then switch to another program you have running, then you might end up with a window on top of the shared window. If this happens, the user will see black space where you have the shared application covered. If you choose the option to see how your shared session looks, and if the Meeting Space window covers the shared application, you will also see that there is blackness where the Meeting Space window covers the shared application because Meeting Space is not likely the application you are sharing!

Sharing a Handout

Meeting space also enables you to share additional documents besides the one that is being viewed. You can click the Add a Handout link in the Meeting Space window to copy a file into Meeting Space. Others will then be able to open this handout and view it. One person at a time can even make changes.

Note The document inserted as a handout will be a copy of the original document. This means that changes others make to the document will not be reflected in your original and thus you don't have to worry about it being overwritten by another member of your meeting.

Ending a Meeting

A meeting can last as long as you'd like it to. When you are ready to leave the meeting, then you can click the Stop button if you are sharing an item, or you can simply close the Meeting Space Window. Either will cause you to exit the meeting.

Note that the meeting will continue without you! Just as if you left a meeting room with all the people in it, as long as there are still people in the meeting space, the meeting will continue. When the last person has left, then the meeting will end.

Still More Windows Live ID Stuff

There's even more to Windows Live ID than you've learned in this chapter. But these other features take place through the Internet or your web browser and aren't directly related to Windows Live Messenger. Here are more resources you can visit and take advantage of using your Windows Live ID:

✦ **Create your own web site:** Your Windows Live ID entitles you to create an MSN Group, which is much like a web site where you can post text, pictures, and such. For more information, visit http://groups .msn.com.

✦ **Create your own web space:** You can create a personalized space that shows your interests, pictures, music, and more. Stop by Windows Live Spaces at http://spaces.live.com.

✦ **Meet people:** Stop by a chat room, where you can meet new people and debate hot topics. Visit http://chat.msn.com to get started.

✦ **Play games online:** Want to show off your gaming skills online? Stop by at http://zone.msn.com to get started.

✦ **MSN on your cell phone or PDA:** For information on extending the reach of Windows Messenger to your cell phone, PDA (Personal Digital Assistant), or wristwatch, take at look at http://mobile.msn.com.

✦ **Windows Live ID help and support:** For general information, troubleshooting, and other Windows Live ID support, swing by http://messenger.msn.com/Help.

Summary

Here's a quick recap of the main points covered in this chapter:

✦ A Windows Live ID is a free account that provides Internet services that go beyond basic e-mail and web browsing.

✦ Windows Live Messenger is a program that enables you to communicate with other people in real time, by typing, talking, or videophone.

✦ You can also send and receive files of any size using Windows Live Messenger. Alternatively, you can share a folder with someone to share multiple files.

✦ Remote Assistance is a Windows Live Messenger feature that enables you to turn control of your computer over to a trusted expert on the Internet.

✦ To personalize Windows Live Messenger, choose Tools ➪ Options from its menu bar. You can click the Show Menu button to get to the menu bar options.

✦ To sign out of your Windows Live ID, right-click the little Windows Messenger icon in the Notification Area and click Sign Off.

✦ Windows Meeting Space enables you to connect with other people and share applications, files, or your desktop in real time. It even allows you to give them control of running the application on your computer from where they are.

Keeping It Safe

Using the Internet isn't an entirely risk-free adventure. Sadly, there are people in the world who get perverse pleasure from ruining other peoples' fun. The Internet provides ample opportunity to do that. Threats on the Internet take many forms, from relatively harmless, but irritating, *spam* (junk e-mail) to *viruses* and *worms* — programs designed to do bad things and make copies of themselves to boot.

Contrary to popular belief and hard-sell TV commercials, a dial-up Internet account is no safer than a broadband account. Millions of computers are on and online 24 hours a day, seven days a week, yet never victimized by any bad things online. And millions of people with dial-up accounts get all the bad things. The difference has nothing to do with the type of account you have or how fast your connection is. The only thing that can protect you is knowing what the threats are and how to defend yourself against them.

Viruses, Worms, and Trojan Horses

The most widely know threat on the Internet is the *computer virus*. Computer viruses aren't like viruses that humans and animals catch. Computer viruses are programs written by human beings. What makes a virus different from most other types of programs is that a virus is able to replicate itself. That is, a virus is a program that can e-mail copies of itself to other peoples' computers (via the Internet). The virus might do other bad things as well, such as erase files from your hard disk, perform attacks on other computers without your knowing it, or just play pranks on you.

A *worm* is very similar to a virus in that it's a program designed to do bad things, and you don't want it on your computer. A worm can also replicate itself. It just tends to do so using techniques other than e-mail. For example, a worm might slowly infect one file after the next on your computer, until things get so out of hand you can't even start or shut down the computer.

A *Trojan horse* is a potentially bad program. A Trojan horse doesn't replicate itself and most likely won't do any harm to your computer. For example, a program capable of digging lost passwords out of files is considered a Trojan horse. On the one hand, such a program can be a lifesaver if you save some document using a password, then forget the password. On the other hand, allowing such a program onto a corporate network could be bad news for corporate security, because people could use it to break into other peoples' password-protected files. In other words, whether or not the program is bad depends on how you intend to use it.

The majority of viruses are spread through e-mail attachments. For example, Figure 13-1 shows a bunch of e-mails, all of which contain viruses. Note that just because they're sitting in an e-mail Inbox doesn't mean that the computer is infected by the virus. For the virus to take effect, the recipient would have to open one of the infected attachments.

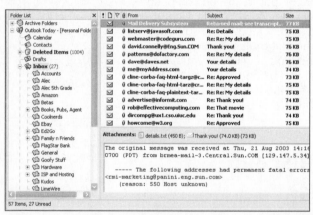

Figure 13-1: All these e-mail messages have viruses attached.

Of course, we wouldn't dream of opening any of those e-mail messages or their attachments. The right thing to do is to simply delete them without taking a peek at them. The question is, "What can you do to avoid opening virus-infected e-mail attachments?" A simple, free, low-tech solution to the problem is to ask yourself these three questions before you even consider opening an e-mail attachment:

1. Do I know, personally, who sent this e-mail attachment to me?

2. Was I expecting that person to send me this attachment?

3. Does the e-mail message itself describe what's in the attachment?

If the answer to any of the preceding questions is "no," your best bet is to just delete the e-mail message and forget about it. Getting rid of worms and viruses is no small feat. So there's no point in even taking a chance on a suspicious e-mail attachment. It is important to realize that the attachment doesn't have to be an executable program (one that has an .exe or .scr extension). It can be an image, a video, a song file, or several other types.

Just knowing whom the e-mail message is from isn't enough to guarantee its safety. Here's why. Let's say your friend Mabel picks up a virus from an e-mail attachment. She opens it, and her computer is infected, but she has no way of knowing this. While Mabel is innocently clicking around, the virus is busy sending copies of itself to people in Mabel's address book. Mabel doesn't know this — even if she's sitting there staring right at the screen while the virus is doing its thing. The virus will give no hint of its evil intent.

If your e-mail address is in Mabel's address book, there's a good chance the virus will eventually send a copy of itself to you. When you get the e-mail it may or may not even have Mabel's return address. If it has Mabel's return address, you have no way of knowing that she unwittingly sent you the virus. The moment you open the attachment, your computer is infected, too. And your computer will then start sending copies of the virus to people in your address book. You won't know it either. The virus just spreads from computer to computer, its hapless victims madly sending copies to each other without having a clue that they're sending and receiving viruses.

Many viruses today are smarter. When your friend Mabel got a virus, it is possible that the virus could grab your e-mail address and send a copy of itself to you. Additionally, it might also grab a different e-mail address out of Mabel's address book and use that address as the sending address. This means, you won't get an e-mail saying it is from Mabel, but rather it will be from someone else — someone pulled randomly from her contact list, and possibly someone else that you might also know. This means you can't assume that the return address is the address of the person that sent you the virus.

Some viruses are attached to e-mail messages intended to look real. For example, the first message header in Figure 13-1 looks like a typical bounce-back message (that is, a notification you receive when you send an e-mail that doesn't reach the intended recipient). However, upon closer examination of the e-mail message (in the lower pane), it turns out that yours truly never sent an e-mail to that address in the first place, so the message must be a fake, and the files attached to it are likely viruses.

Here's another example of where just knowing whom a message is from offers no protection at all. The e-mail messages in Figure 13-2, all from Support@ microsoft.com, are all viruses, too, for the following reasons:

✦ Brad hasn't sent an e-mail to Support@microsoft.com lately, so there is no reason for a reply.

✦ A legitimate software company like Microsoft, Adobe, Corel, or any other would *never* send unsolicited e-mails that contain attachments, even if the attachments were safe.

✦ The body of the first e-mail message, shown in the lower-half of
Figure 13-2, doesn't indicate what's in the attachment.

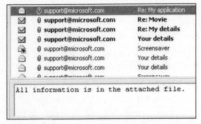

	support@microsoft.com	Re: My application
✉	₿ support@microsoft.com	**Re: Movie**
✉	₿ support@microsoft.com	**Re: My details**
✉	₿ support@microsoft.com	**Your details**
	₿ support@microsoft.com	Screensaver
	₿ support@microsoft.com	Your details
	₿ support@microsoft.com	Your details
	₿ support@microsoft.com	Screensaver

All information is in the attached file.

Figure 13-2: Virus-infected attachments
pretending to be from Microsoft

The fact of the matter is that none of the messages in Figure 13-2 are really from
Support@microsoft.com. They're not from Microsoft at all. The return address
in each of those messages is bogus. The best, and only, solution: to delete all of
those messages without even wasting time to look at their contents.

Tip   The Virus Protection feature of Windows Mail (see Chapter 11) will prevent
you from opening any attachment that *could* contain a virus. For example,
attachments with an extension of .exe, .pif, or .scr are all blocked. If your e-mail
address ends in @msn.com or @hotmail.com, your e-mail will be scanned for
viruses automatically, and any viruses will be destroyed before they even reach
your computer.

Installing Anti-Virus Software

The low-tech technique of avoiding opening suspicious e-mail attachments
isn't enough to protect you from all viruses, worms, and Trojan horses. That
technique just protects you from e-mail viruses. But just about any file you
download could be a virus, worm, or Trojan horse. To protect yourself from all
forms of viruses, you need to install *anti-virus software*. Windows Vista comes
with some software that will help protect you, but it doesn't come with any
sort of anti-virus program built into it. That's something you need to purchase
and install separately.

Of course, if you bought your computer with software already installed, there
may already be anti-virus software installed on your computer. To find out for
sure, you'd need to learn about the software that came with your computer.
And you can get that information only from that particular computer manufacturer. But then again, if you have anti-virus software installed already, that
program might display an icon in your notification area. Likewise, since all programs currently installed on your computer are accessible from your All
Programs menu, you could fire up your anti-virus program by clicking its icon
on the Start menu.

Tip Some popular anti-virus programs include Symantec Norton Anti-Virus (www.symantec.com), **McAfee VirusScan Online** (www.mcafee.com), and **Trend Micro PC-cillin** (www.trendmicro.com).

If you don't already have anti-virus software, it's not too tough to get it. It's just not free, and most require that you buy a subscription to keep it up-to-date. If you're looking for a reliable program you can buy and install without even getting up from your chair, consider McAfee VirusScan (www.mcafee.com).

Using Anti-Virus Software

Unfortunately, we can't teach you how to use your anti-virus program. There are just too many of them out there to even make an attempt. But as with any programs, you can learn to use your anti-virus software from its built-in help, the program manufacturer's web site, or the printed documentation that comes with the software. In general, you want to make sure the anti-virus software scans all incoming e-mail attachments and all files you download. Also, be aware that new viruses and worms hit the Net all the time, some able to sneak past your anti-virus software. Your best protection there is to make sure your anti-virus software is always up-to-date. Most anti-virus programs keep themselves up-to-date automatically. But you should learn to use that feature so you know that your program is up-to-date at all times.

Scanning Downloaded Files

Simply downloading an e-mail attachment or file that contains a virus or worm generally isn't enough to infect your computer. You have to open the attachment or file. One thing you can do, especially if you download a lot of free stuff, is store all downloaded files (and saved e-mail attachments) in one folder. For example, you can click the Start button and choose Documents. Then, in your Documents folder, click the Organize button on the toolbar and choose New Folder from the menu. A new, empty folder named New Folder appears. Type some new name, like Recent Downloads, and press Enter.

Just creating an empty folder isn't enough, though. You also have to remember to store all dubious files in that folder, and scan them, before you open any of them. As far as saving goes, that's just a matter of choosing Documents from the Save As or File Download dialog box's Save In drop-down list and double-clicking the Recent Downloads folder. When the folder name Recent Downloads appears next to Save In, click the Save button in the dialog box to save the file to that folder.

You certainly don't want to have to scan your entire hard disk for viruses every time you save an e-mail attachment or download a file. That takes too long. But you should be able to get your anti-virus software to scan only your Recent Downloads folder. For example, in McAfee VirusScan, you just click Scan my computer for viruses. Then, in the next window that opens, you choose the folder under Location to scan; then you click the Scan button.

If your anti-virus software detects a virus in a file, you should just delete that file. See if you can find a clean copy of the same file somewhere. Any file that passes that test is OK, which means you can open it or move it to a more permanent folder.

Caution   If you download free music and videos from the Internet, you should direct all files you download to your Recent Downloads folder. Scan them before opening them or moving them to a more permanent home.

Hackers and Crackers

A second threat on the Internet, though rare compared to viruses, are hackers and crackers. These are people (or more likely computers) that sneak stuff into your computer through open *ports* in your Internet connection. Hacking in real life isn't at all like it is in movies. In movies, some good-looking young kids take two or three guesses at some password and magically have access to the entire computer. In real life, it doesn't work that way at all. Nobody can break into your computer and steal things or even look around.

The kind of hacking that takes place on computers is almost always done by computers, not humans. Some human programmer creates a program that just wanders around the Internet looking for open ports, sneaking some virus-type program onto a computer's hard disk without the owner knowing it. This is a slow and tedious way to infect multiple computers and therefore isn't done much. But it is done, and you need to have some protection.

The type of program you use to protect your computer from hackers is called a *firewall*. It actually works on a very simple principle. Normally, your computer will just accept anything that comes in off the Internet, under the assumption that if there's something coming in from the Internet, you must have requested it. That's the very assumption that enables hackers to sneak things onto your computer.

Hackers versus Crackers

The press and the general public use the terms *hacker* and *cracker* interchangeably, despite the fact that doing so irritates the daylights out of computer programmers. In the programming world, *hacker* is a slang term for *programmer*. The vast majority of programmers in the world never write any code that would damage a computer or replicate itself, and they don't like being put in the same category as those who know just enough programming to take some existing virus and tweak it into something else (not at all impressive to a real programmer).

Programmers refer to people who do bad things with their programming skills as *crackers*, not hackers. *Cracker* has its origins in the idea of a safecracker, one who breaks into safes. But these programmers don't break into safes. They break into computers and networks where they don't belong, stealing corporate secrets or just wreaking random havoc.

A firewall is a program that keeps track of what you've requested from the Internet. As information from the Internet comes streaming into your modem, the firewall takes a look at everything coming in. If the information is something you requested, the information rides in normally. If the information is *not* something you requested, the firewall rejects the information, so it never reaches your computer. Figure 13-3 illustrates the basic concept.

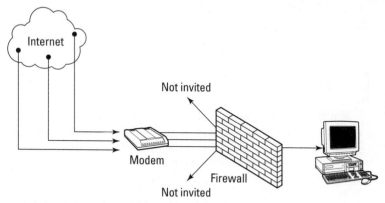

Figure 13-3: A firewall blocks any unrequested data from the Internet before it reaches your computer.

Fortunately, you don't have to go out and buy a firewall, because there's one built into Windows Vista. Chances are, it's been protecting your computer from hackers since the day you installed or purchased Vista. But it certainly can't hurt to take a look and make sure it's running. First, you have to open your Network Connections folder. You can do so using any of the following techniques:

✦ Click the Start button and enter **firewall** into the search box. Select Windows Firewall from the selections that are displayed.

✦ Click the Start button and choose Control Panel. From the Control Panel home, click the Security heading, then click the Windows Firewall heading.

✦ Click the Start button and choose Network. In the Network window, click the Network and Sharing Center button in the toolbar. When in the Network and Sharing Center, select Windows Firewall from the left side of the page.

✦ If you see a little Notification icon that represents your Internet connection, right-click that icon and choose Network and Sharing Center. From the displayed window, select Windows Firewall from the left side.

When you've selected one of these options, the Windows Firewall dialog box is displayed (see Figure 13-4). This dialog box will tell you if your firewall is on or off as well as give you links to configure other firewall settings.

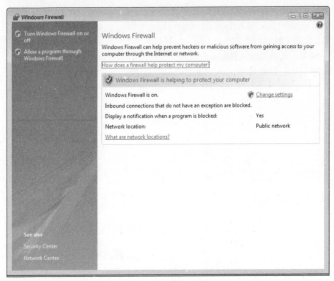

Figure 13-4: The Windows Firewall window

Note Windows Firewall with Advanced Security opens a different window than Windows Firewall. Figure 13-4 shows the standard Windows Firewall. More on the Advanced Security dialog box later in this chapter.

If your firewall is turned off, then you can turn it on by either clicking the Change settings link to the right of where you are told the firewall is off, or you can click the Turn Windows Firewall on or off link on the left side of the Firewall window. You can use this same method to turn off the firewall if it is on — something that we don't recommend you do since it protects you when it is on.

After you click the Change settings link, a new dialog box is displayed (see Figure 13-5). You should make sure the General tab is selected; from there you can turn on or off the firewall by selecting the corresponding option.

This dialog box enables you to not only turn on or off the firewall, but also configure a number of additional settings. On the Exceptions tab you can choose to make exceptions that will allow programs to get through the firewall. Unless you know you need to make an exception, best to leave the settings as they are defaulted.

The final tab in the Firewall Settings is the Advanced tab. It enables you to configure a few advanced settings. This tab also includes a button called Restore Defaults that enables you to restore the default values for firewall settings. This is something you most likely won't want to do since it may cause some programs to stop working if they require an exception to get through your firewall.

Your version of Windows Vista may also have a second program that you find when searching for Firewall in the Start menu. This is the Windows Firewall with Advanced Security program. If you choose this option, you are likely to see a dialog box similar to the one shown in Figure 13-6.

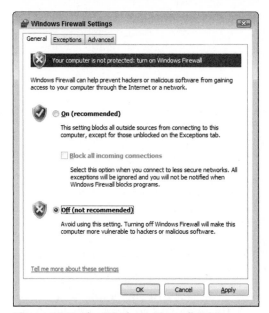

Figure 13-5: The Windows Firewall Settings dialog box, with the firewall turned off

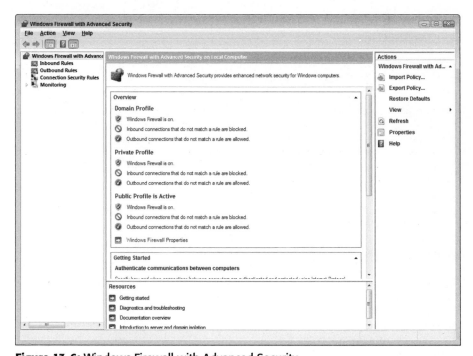

Figure 13-6: Windows Firewall with Advanced Security

You can also use this program to see whether your firewall is on. As you can see, the window is a bit more complicated than the standard Windows Firewall settings. For that reason, you may want to stick with the standard Windows Firewall dialog box for basic setup.

Dealing with Pop-up Ads: Windows Pop-up Blocker

Pop-up ads are uninvited messages or web pages that pop up on your screen while you're online. These ads aren't harmful to your computer, but sure can be harmful to your sanity. Plus, they eat up bandwidth, which means they cause all your other Internet stuff to slow down. If you have a dial-up connection to the Internet, the last thing you need is a bunch of pop-up ads eating up your bandwidth and slowing things down even more.

There are several ways for pop-up ads to find their way to your computer. Free software is one of the greatest offenders. Programs that you download and install for free often generate income for the program's creators through advertising revenues. While you're using the program, it just keeps popping up ads on your screen, hoping that you'll eventually respond to one. If you do respond to one, the program creator gets a little commission. The idea, of course, is to get thousands of copies of the free software out there to make thousands of little commissions.

 Spyware programs may also cause pop-ups. Spyware (also called malware or spybots) is covered later in this chapter.

You can use a pop-up blocker, described in the next section, to block those ads. But blocking them isn't the perfect solution, because the ads aren't blocked until they reach your computer. By that time, they've already consumed some of your bandwidth, causing everything else to slow down. If you have a dial-up account, which works with minimal bandwidth to begin with, you really can't afford to waste any of it on pop-up ads. So if you suspect that some freebie program is causing you to get flooded with pop-ups, you might consider uninstalling that program or at least keeping it closed when you don't need it.

Blocking Pop-ups

Even if you do avoid free software, you're bound to get some pop-up ads while you're browsing the Web. There's no way to make all those just go away, because any web page can open another web page the moment you open or close the first page. But you can use a pop-up blocker to get rid of them. In the past, people installed the Google toolbar to block pop-ups. Although the Google toolbar works and is free, Internet Explorer 7 has its own pop-up blocker—Windows Pop-up Blocker.

To use the Windows Pop-up Blocker, do the following:

1. Open Internet Explorer. You can do this by clicking its icon or selecting it from the Start menu.

2. Click the Tools button on the toolbar, then select Pop-up Blocker ➪ Turn On Pop-up Blocker. This turns on the pop-up blocker. To turn off the Pop-up Blocker, click the Tools button on the toolbar and then select Pop-up Blocker ➪ Turn Off Pop-up Blocker. The menu will only show either On or Off, depending on your current setting.

After you have turned on the Pop-up Blocker, Internet Explorer will block most pop-ups for you. A few pop-ups may still get through for a number of reasons. For example, you can create a list of excepted sites that can display pop-ups, plus as mentioned earlier spyware and other programs running may cause pop-ups unrelated to Internet Explorer.

When Internet Explorer encounters a pop-up, it will block it. When blocked, a message is displayed near the top of Internet Explorer in the Information bar informing you that a pop-up was blocked. Figure 13-7 shows the information bar after a blocked pop-up.

Figure 13-7: Turning the Windows Pop-up Blocker on or off

Note In a bit of irony, when Internet Explorer blocks a pop-up and displays the Information bar, it also displays a pop-up to let you know it blocked the pop-up.

You can select the check box to never see this ironic pop-up again.

Allowing Pop-ups

If you want to see the pop-up that was blocked, you can click the Information bar and select Temporarily Allow Pop-ups. This will let the pop-up through. If you trust a site and want to allow all pop-ups from it, then select Always Allow Pop-ups from This Site. This will add the pop-up to a list of allowed sites.

Although the menu will let you add sites to an exception list that will let you see their pop-ups, you have to add them one at a time. If you want to add a number of sites, or if you want to remove a site from the exception list, then you should go to the Pop-up Blocker Settings. The Pop-up Settings Dialog box (shown in Figure 13-8) can be accessed by either clicking the Information bar after a pop-up has been blocked and then selecting Settings ➪ More Settings or by clicking the Tools button and then selecting Pop-up Blocker ➪ Pop-up Blocker Settings.

Figure 13-8: The Pop-up Blocker Settings dialog box

Extortion Pop-ups

You should ignore any ad that tells you your computer is at risk and that you need to do something right away about it. As an example, a bogus ad is shown in the following figure.

This ad is a bald-faced lie, designed to raise your anxiety to extort money from you. Your computer will never make public any personal information about you or your bank account or credit cards. It's not possible to broadcast IP addresses over the Internet, so your computer is not doing that now and never will. Even if it were possible to broadcast over the Internet, the information wouldn't help anybody anywhere attack your computer. Everything in this type of ad is a lie.

If an ad raises your anxiety level one iota, close the ad and forget about it. Don't buy anything from a pop-up ad, or junk e-mail either, for that matter. Any product that promises to make your computer safer, fix your computer with one mouse click, double the speed of your computer or Internet connection, or make your computer crash proof is dubious at best.

In fact, when you close such ads, you should also be careful. Many sinister ads will switch the functionality of Yes with No or of Ok with Cancel. As such, you may end up accepting when you didn't mean to. The best way to avoid this is to use the close button – the X button on the top right corner – to close the window rather than any buttons that the pop-up displays.

The Pop-up Blocker Settings dialog box enables you to enter addresses in the text box Address of website to allow. You can then press the Add button to add it to the list of sites that are allowed to display pop-ups. You can see in Figure 13-8 that I've allowed four sites to display pop-ups.

If you decide you want to remove a site from the exceptions list, you select it in the Allowed sites list and click the Remove button. You can block all sites by clicking the Remove all button.

Adjusting the Pop-up Blocking Settings

You can adjust a few settings regarding what pop-ups are blocked. You may have noticed in Figure 13-8 that there were a few check boxes and a drop-down list button. Using the check boxes, you can turn on or off the information bar as well as turn on or off the sound that plays when a pop-up is blocked.

Using the Filter level button, you can set how strict the pop-up blocker is. By default, the blocker is set at Medium. If you want to block all pop-ups, then you can change this setting to High. If you change the setting to Low, then sites that are secure will also be allowed to display pop-ups. Regardless of the setting you choose, sites on your exception list will still be allowed to display pop-ups.

Tip   Regardless of your setting, if you truly want to see a pop-up, then you can override the block by holding down the ALT+CTRL keys when a page is loading.

Dealing with Spam (Junk E-mail)

Junk e-mail isn't harmful to your computer, but it sure can be harmful to your sanity. There's really nothing built into the Windows Vista operating system, per se, for dealing with junk e-mail. This is something you need to do through your *e-mail client* (the program you use to send/receive e-mail messages). There are hundreds of e-mail clients out there, so I can't tell you specifically how to work yours unless you are using Windows Mail that came with Vista. If your e-mail client has the ability to block junk e-mail, you should be able to find information on that by searching that program's help for *spam* or *block*.

When you block junk mail, you are generally not stopping it from getting to your computer. Rather, you are having your mail program identify the mail message and move it out the way or delete it. This blocking results in the mail being filtered away from your attention so that you can focus on what are hopefully more important messages.

Blocking Spammers in Windows Mail

If you use Windows Mail (Chapter 11) as your e-mail client, and you have a POP3 mail account, then you can block junk mail. When you get a junk e-mail message from someone and don't want to get any more from them, you can add them to your blocked senders list. This causes future e-mails from that sender to be put into a junk mail folder. To add an e-mail sender to the blocked list, follow these steps.

STEPS: Blocking an E-mail Sender

1. Select the message by clicking it in the inbox, or by opening it.

2. Choose Message ➪ Junk E-mail ➪ Add Sender to Blocked Sender List. You can also choose Add Sender's Domain to Blocked Senders List. This causes all e-mails from the same domain to be blocked.

3. Choose OK from the dialog box that appears.

Future messages from that sender or sender's domain will be blocked. If you want to block an e-mail address and you don't have a message to start from already, you can still block it. Start by selecting Tools ➪ Junk E-mail options from the Windows Mail menu. This open the Junk E-mail options window. Select the Blocked Senders tab as shown in Figure 13-9.

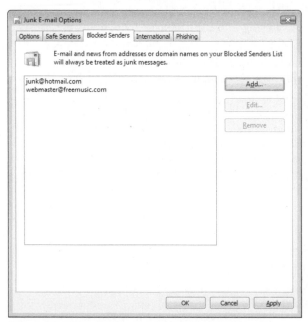

Figure 13-9: The Windows Mail Junk mail page for blocking spammers and other senders

Clicking the Add button opens a dialog box that enables you to enter an e-mail address. You can enter as many addresses as you like. Each will be blocked when mail is received. Again, a blocked e-mail message is one that is automatically moved to the junk mail folder.

If you find you want to unblock one of the addresses on your list, you can select it and click the Remove button to remove it from the list. This stops blocking that address. When you are done with your changes, you can click OK to save your changes and exit the window.

Marking Safe Senders in Windows Mail

In addition to blocking spammers, you can also declare certain e-mail addresses as always safe. You might wonder why you would do this. There are two good reasons. The first is to ensure that e-mail from a given address is never blocked. The second is that you can change settings in Windows Mail to only allow people you deemed safe — e-mail from everyone else can be treated as junk.

To mark an e-mail address as safe, you follow similar approaches to marking them as spam.

STEPS: Marking an E-mail Sender as Safe

1. Select the message by clicking it in the inbox, or by opening it.

2. Choose Message ➪ Junk E-mail ➪ Add Sender to Safe Sender List. You can also choose Add Sender's Domain to Safe Senders List. This causes all e-mails from the same domain to be considered safe.

3. Choose OK from the dialog box that appears.

Future messages from that sender or sender's domain will avoid the junk mail filters. If you want to block an e-mail address and you don't have a message to start from already, you can still mark a sender as safe. Start by selecting Tools ➪ Junk E-mail options from the Windows Mail menu. This opens the Junk E-mail options window. Select the Safe Senders tab as shown in Figure 13-10.

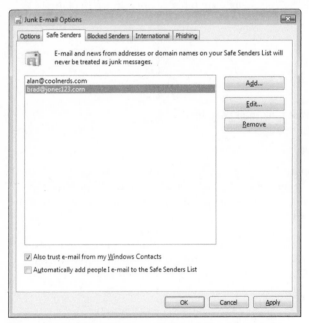

Figure 13-10: The Windows Mail Junk E-mail page for marking e-mail addresses as safe

Clicking the Add button opens a dialog box that enables you to enter an e-mail address. You can enter as many addresses as you like. Any e-mails from these addresses will always be considered safe and never moved to the junk mail folder. If you decide later that an address is not safe, you can come back, select it, and click the remove button to take it off the list. Clicking OK will save the changes and close the window.

There are two additional options on the Safe Sender tab that are worth noting. These are options you can select to turn on or clear to turn off. You can automatically include anyone in your Windows Contacts list as a safe person by clicking the first box. Chances are, if they are worthy of being a contact, then they are worthy of sending you an e-mail. The second option is a little bit more precarious. Checking the second option automatically adds as a safe sender, anyone you send an e-mail to.

Setting the Level of Spam Protection in Windows Mail

Blocking and unblocking junk e-mail message one sender or one domain at a time can be a long, tedious, never-ending battle. If you want to beef up your spam-killing abilities, you can change the level of protection that Windows Mail's junk filter does.

Setting the protection level can also be done in the Junk Mail Options window. Select Tools ➪ Junk E-mail Options to display the Junk E-mail options window, then select the Options tab. This displays the information shown in Figure 13-11.

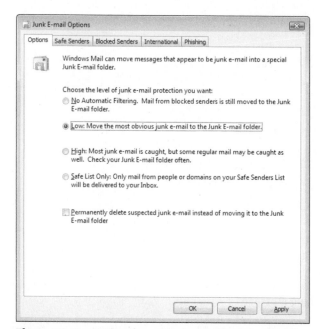

Figure 13-11: Setting the safety level of your junk mail filtering

As you can see in Figure 13-11, there are several different levels. Choose the one that best fits your needs, then click the OK button. The Low option is generally a good starting point. If you find you are getting too much junk mail, you can switch your settings to High; however, some e-mails that are not junk might get treated as junk.

For the greatest level of security, you can use the Safe List Only option; however, if your long-lost aunt decides to send you an e-mail about including you in her will, then you won't get the message if she isn't in your safe list!

Avoiding Phishing

A lot of junk e-mails are phishing schemes. A phishing scheme is a fake e-mail or web site that appears to be real but isn't. Generally these e-mails tell you that your account is about to expire, that your password was changed accidentally, or some other situation where you need to come to a web site and get things corrected quickly. The ultimate goal of these fake mail messages and sites are to get you to enter your IDs and passwords or even to give credit card information. The sites and messages are set up to look very real. Figure 13-12 shows an example of a phishing message. Needless to say, this e-mail is not from Paypal.

Figure 13-12: A sample phishing message

Even though they may look very real, they are not. The people sending these messages and running the fraudulent sites behind them will take your information and then use it to break into your sites. In the case of a bank account, they will quickly withdraw as much of your money as they can.

Because many phishing sites look very real, they are often hard to detect. Windows Mail does, however, work to give you some protection from phishing.

When you start using Internet Explorer, you will find that you often see a dialog box similar to the one in Figure 13-13 pop up. This dialog box is displayed for your protection.

Figure 13-13: The phishing filter prompt

You can simply select *Turn on automatic Phishing Filter* to turn on the phishing filter. When on, it will do its best to help you avoid phishing sites.

You can also make a change in Windows Mail to have recognized phishing e-mails treated as junk. To do this, within Windows Mail, select Tools ➪ Junk E-mail Options from the menu, then select the Phishing tab as shown in Figure 13-14.

You can see that there are two key options for phishing. The first should be selected by default. It helps to prevent fraudulent links from being displayed in e-mails. For example, if someone is trying to get your eBay login, then they may show what looks like a legitimate a link in the e-mail message, for example, www.eBay.com; however, this link may actually be connected to some other site. By selecting the first option, Windows Mail helps make sure links go where they say they go.

The second option is relatively obvious. If you select it, then any e-mails that are recognized as phishing attempts will automatically be moved to your junk mail folder.

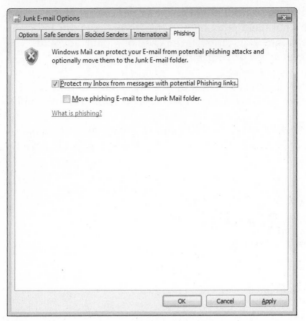

Figure 13-14: Setting the phishing options in Windows Mail

Adware, Spyware, and Windows Defender

Adware and spyware are types of programs that don't do any harm to your computer. But they do keep track of your browsing preferences and then send that information to advertisers, who in turn use it to tailor ads to your tastes.

Although XP did not originally have software built in to help defend against spyware and adware, Microsoft has since released Windows Defender. Windows Defender is also a part of Windows Vista and is defending you from adware and spyware.

You can use Windows Defender in a number of ways. It can do scans on a regular basis — in fact the default is to do a quick scan every day at 2 a.m. It can also do a more robust scan on a regular basis. Finally, it can be set to protect you all the time you are on the computer. The protection can be to alert you or to take immediate action.

Running Windows Defender

To run Windows Defender, from the Start menu select All Programs ➪ Windows Defender to open the program (see Figure 13-15).

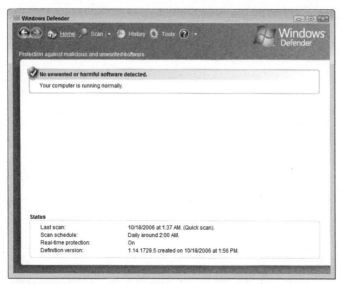

Figure 13-15: The Windows Defender home page

When you see a window similar to the one in Figure 13-15, Windows Defender is running and your machine is protected. This window also tells you information about the last scan and what definition version is being used.

The definition version is critical to watch. New adware and spyware are created all the time. Microsoft and its partners work to identify and create definitions for those that are risks. These updates are added to the definition files regularly. To keep your computer safe, you need to make sure you get any new updates to these definitions. Your definition files will be updated before each scan provided your computer has access to the internet. You'll want to make sure you keep your computer up to date.

Doing Scans on Demand

Although Windows Defender will do regular scans, you can also have it do a scan on demand. You can have it do a quick scan, a full scan, or a custom scan. A quick scan checks the most common areas where adware and spyware are likely to hide on your computer, and checks for the most likely definitions. A full scan will do a complete check of your computer on a more complete list of definitions. A custom scan enables you to select the files and folders that get scanned by Windows Defender.

To run a scan on demand, select the Scan button in Windows Defender. You can then select Quick Scan, Full Scan, or Custom Scan. The Quick and Full Scan buttons will open a window and immediately start a scan. As the scan is happening, you'll see what file is being scanned and the scan status (see Figure 13-16). While the scan is occurring, you can actually switch to another window and work.

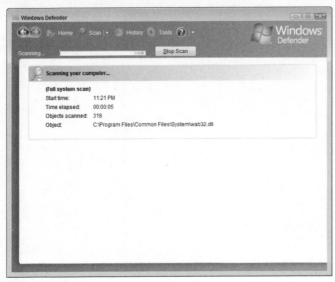

Figure 13-16: A scan in progress

You can stop a scan at any time by clicking the Stop Scan button. If you let the scan progress, it will identify any issues your computer might have.

You can do a custom scan by clicking the Scan button and then selecting Custom Scan. This enables you to select the specific drives and folders you want to scan.

Changing Windows Defender Settings

Although Windows Defender defaults to running a scan every day at 2 a.m., you can change this time to anything you want. Do this by clicking the Tools button, followed by selecting Options from the displayed window. This displays the options window shown in Figure 13-17.

From the Windows Defender options page in the Automatic scanning area, you can change the automatic scan to happen only on a certain day of the week, or daily. You can also set the time of day and whether a quick scan or full scan is done. If you choose to clear the check box Automatic scan my computer, then you will turn off automatic scans — something I don't recommend unless your computer isn't having new software installed and isn't connected to a network or the Internet. You can also turn on or off whether the computer checks for new definitions. Again, it is recommended that you check this option.

The last option within the Automatic scanning area is Apply default actions to items defected during scan. This option allows Windows Vista to determine the best course of action when adware or spyware is found. Although you can have Windows Defender prompt you any time a bad file is found, you might find it better to simply let Defender make the decisions. You can also control the default actions that Windows takes.

Figure 13-17: The Windows Defender options

In the bottom half of the options you can set the default action for adware and spyware that is found. Actions can be set based on the severity of the found items. Some items found may not really do anything (low severity) whereas others may do tracking or possibly even do damage (high severity). You can choose to have Defender take one of three actions:

✦ **Default action (definition based)** — The action is based on what the definition recommends.

✦ **Ignore** — You may choose to ignore a level of adware or spyware.

✦ **Remove** — You can have found adware or spyware deleted.

If in doubt, simply leave the action levels at the default action level and let Windows Defender take care of things.

Dealing with Found Adware and Spyware

When adware or spyware is found, you can have one of four things can happen. You can have Defender ignore what is found, remove what is found, allow what is found, or quarantine what is found.

If you choose to ignore something that is found, you are basically allowing the software to be installed or executed. If you set Defender to ignore a specific item, then that is what it will do. It will, however, only ignore it until it tries to do something unsafe (such as try to change a secured setting), or until the next time you run a Windows Defender scan that sees the software.

If you choose to remove what is found, then that is what will happen — the program will be deleted. It will no longer be on your computer, so it will no longer be a threat.

If you choose to allow what is found, or more correctly, if you choose to Always Allow an item, then that is again what will happen. The software will be marked as allowed and Windows Defender will ignore it from that point forward. You should be very careful of always allowing a program that Windows Defender flags in a scan. You should only do this if you are completely sure that the program will not cause any issues.

When you flag an item as always allowed, it will be added to a list that Defender will check. You can review this list of always allowed items at any time. Do this by selecting the Tools button in the Windows Defender toolbar. From the Tools and Settings window, select Allowed Items. This displays a window similar to the one in Figure 13-18.

Figure 13-18: The Allowed Items that are ignored if found by Windows Defender

The list in Figure 13-18 is empty, which is recommended. Should you have items in your allow list and decide that you no longer want Defender to ignore it, then you can remove it from the list. Do this by clicking it to select it, and then click the Remove from List button. The item will no longer be ignored by Defender.

The fourth option you have with adware or spyware that is found is to place it in quarantine. Quarantine moves the software to a safe location on your computer. It doesn't allow it to be installed or executed. Quarantine doesn't allow it to interact with anything else on your computer. It is isolated so that it can't hurt your system. It also isn't simply deleted so that you'll have a chance to review it to see if it is something that is actually okay.

Like items that are always allowed, you can also review items that are quarantined. To see these items, once again select the Tools button from the Windows

Defender toolbar. Then select Quarantined Items. This displays the list of quarantined items in a window that is similar to the always allowed window shown in Figure 13-18. You'll be able to remove or restore any items on the quarantine list by selecting them and clicking the corresponding button.

The Windows Defender Software Explorer

Windows Defender also includes Software Explorer. Software Explorer enables you to monitor the software that is running on your computer. Software Explorer will show you four different lists of software and the status of each program on the lists. The lists include software that is run when your computer starts, programs currently running, network connected programs, and WinSock Service Providers.

In Figure 13-19 you see Software Explorer showing the programs that are a part of Windows Startup. You can also get additional details on each program by clicking it. In Figure 13-19, you can see that Windows Defender is one of the programs that ran at Windows Startup. Since it is selected, the right side includes additional details about the program.

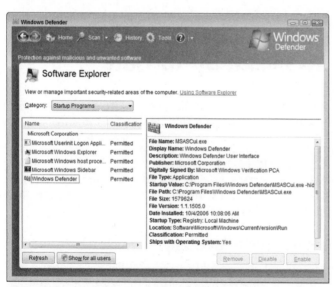

Figure 13-19: Software Explorer showing the Startup programs

You can change which list of programs is displayed by changing the Category list. Additionally, you can remove some items by clicking the Remove button when the item is selected. If an item can't be removed, then the Remove button will be protected.

 Note   The Software Explorer is an advanced area within Windows Vista.

Parental Controls

The no-censorship nature of the Internet makes it a very risky place for kids, indeed. If you've spent much time at all on the Internet, you've probably come across some materials that are definitely not kid-friendly. Keeping kids from gaining access to that stuff is no small feat. Even a perfectly innocent Internet search can produce links that lead to adult material. For example, a search for Ford Escort wouldn't likely turn up anything too dicey. But a search for Escort can lead to a variety of escort services whose sites are certainly not appropriate for kids.

The Smart Parent web site, www.SmartParent.com, is specifically designed to help educate parents on the best ways to safeguard children on the Internet. There you'll find lots of resources on programs you can download and install, services you can sign up with, and more. More importantly perhaps, you'll have a solid, reliable resource for chatting with other parents, to ask questions and to deal with the problem in the most effective way possible.

Chapter 27 also contains a lot of information on the parental controls provided by Windows Vista and explains how to limit computer usage, restrict programs, and more.

Keep Windows Vista Up-to-Date

The whole business of Internet security is something of a cat-and-mouse game between the legitimate software vendors and the *evildoers* (to borrow George Bush's term). The good guys keep coming up with new and better ways to block the evildoers. But the evildoers just keep coming back and find new ways around the protections. And so it goes, on and on.

Keeping your copy of Windows Vista up-to-date is a good way to make sure you always have the latest-and-greatest security in place. It's also free and easy to do. Just enable automatic updating. Here's how.

STEPS: Keep Vista Secure Automatically

1. Click the Start button and choose All Programs ➪ Windows Update to launch the Windows Updates window shown in Figure 13-20. (You can also get to the Windows Update window by selecting the Control Panel and then select System and Maintenance followed by Windows Update.)

2. Click the Turn on now button. Figure 13-20 shows that Windows Updates is not turned on. Clicking the Turn on now button will turn on automatic updates.

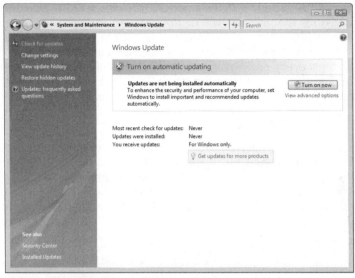

Figure 13-20: Turning on Windows Updates

3. Select the Change settings check box on the right side of the page. This displays the dialog box shown in Figure 13-21. You can use this dialog box to change a number of settings.

Figure 13-21: Setting how Windows Update will operate

4. Verify that the Install updates automatically check box is selected. This ensures that updates will be downloaded and installed. You can determine how often by changing the values of the drop-down buttons. You can choose to do it once a week on a given day, or you can do updates every day. You can also select the time that the updates occur. If you leave your computer turned on, then you can set the updates to happen at a time when you are not using the computer.

5. Click the OK button.

Now all you have to do is keep an eye out for a notification message in the Windows Toolbar. Don't expect it to appear right away. Some updates are huge and take a long time to download, especially if you're using a dial-up account. But all of that time-consuming stuff will take place in the background without you having to wait around. When you see a message stating that updates have been downloaded, just click it and follow the onscreen instructions to install the update.

 Tip You don't have to worry about viruses and such in the files you download from Microsoft or from any other legitimate software company's site.

Getting Everything Up-to-Date

In addition to updating Windows Vista, you can also turn on updates for other programs such as Microsoft Office. To turn on updates for other products, return to the Windows Update window shown in Figure 13-20. (Remember, select Start ➪ Control Panel and then select System and Maintenance followed by Windows Update.)

On the Windows Update page, you will find a yellow box with a link titled Get updates for more products. Clicking this link opens a web page that will walk you through installing Microsoft Update. When completed, the Windows Update page will also update Windows as well as other Microsoft products.

Windows Vista Security Center

There is a program that I could have covered first in this chapter but instead choose to cover last because I thought it good to focus on the individual items that you need to know about to keep your computer safe. In Windows Vista, Microsoft has provided the Windows Vista Security Center to help consolidate the key safety programs for you.

You can access Security Center by selecting the Control Panel from the Start menu. From the Control Panel, select the Security section and then select Security Center. This displays the Windows Vista Security Center (see Figure 13-22).

 Tip You can get to the Security Center quicker by entering **Security** into the search box on the Start menu. This displays Security Center as one of the options you can select.

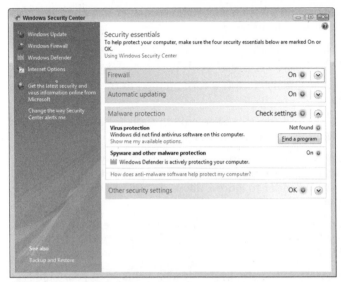

Figure 13-22: The Windows Vista Security Center

The Security Center gives you a quick view of your security setting. You can select items on the page to change their settings. When you click an item, it will expand to show you additional information about its settings. If you want to adjust a setting, you can click any of the links on the left side of the page. Changing the settings is exactly the same as you saw earlier in this chapter.

You might also see the Security Center at other times when you are using your computer. If you want to adjust when you see Security Center, then click the Change the way Security Center alerts me link on the left side of the page. From the dialog box that is displayed, you will be able to choose whether you are notified when your computer might be at risk.

Keeping your computer secure is important, so making sure you are notified when you are at risk is important. It is best to let Security Center inform you of such risk rather than to turn off the notifications.

Summary

Keeping your computer safe and secure online is all about knowing what the threats are and how to avoid them. In this chapter, you've learned all the threats and the different ways of dealing with them. To summarize:

✦ Viruses, worms, and Trojan horses are bad programs spread through files and e-mail attachments.

✦ To avoid picking up viruses spread through e-mail attachments, be very choosey about the e-mail attachments you open.

✦ To get complete protection from all viruses, consider installing and learning to use anti-virus software.

✦ To protect your computer from hackers (or crackers), make sure Windows Vista Internet Connection Firewall is enabled.

✦ To block pop-up ads, make sure you turn on the Internet Explorer pop-up blocker.

✦ Some e-mail clients and services have built-in tools for blocking spam (junk e-mail). Windows Mail also includes features you can use.

✦ Adware and spyware are programs designed to spy on your web-browsing habits to better target ads displayed on your computer. You can use Windows Defender to ignore, allow, delete, or quarantine adware and spyware.

✦ Phishing sites try to trick you into disclosing private, personal information. Internet Explorer and Windows Vista help to identify phishing issues for you.

✦ Using Windows Vista Automatic Updating also helps keep your computer more safe and secure.

Fun with Multimedia

◆ ◆ ◆ ◆

◆ ◆ ◆ ◆

Downloading music, burning CDs, e-mailing pictures, making DVDs—people talk about this stuff like they talk about boiling water. *Everybody* knows how to boil water. What, ya kiddin'? Have you ever tried to guess your way through getting pictures out of a digital camera or scanning some prints into your computer? Ever tried to download a song from the Internet for free or make a CD you can play in your car, just by clicking whatever looks relevant on your screen? If so, you might wonder who's kidding whom.

What's up with all that MP3, CD-R, CD-RW, DVD+RW, MPEG, and JPEG stuff anyway? And, by the way, thanks for sending me that ZIP file attachment. Was I supposed to do something with that? Such are the questions on the minds of the uninitiated everywhere.

Well, prepare to be initiated, as we bravely head into Part IV, which we actually have the nerve to title "*Fun* with Multimedia."

Using Your Camera and Scanner

Cameras and scanners are *devices* for getting pictures into your computer. A digital camera stores its pictures electronically rather than on film. When you copy pictures from the camera, each photo becomes a file on your computer's hard disk.

A scanner is a photocopy machine attached to a computer. Each image you scan can be stored in a file on your hard disk, just like a photo from a digital camera. As you'll learn in this chapter, you can use the Windows Vista Scanner and Camera Wizard to get pictures from your camera, scanner, or even a photo CD.

Tip Don't be alarmed if a picture ends up being sideways on your screen. As you'll learn in Chapter 15, you can easily rotate it to the correct orientation after you've copied it to your hard disk.

About Pictures

Every picture on your computer is a document. As such, it's stored as a file in a folder somewhere — exactly where, of course, is up to you. A couple of folders on your hard disk, however, are especially well suited to storing pictures:

+ **Pictures:** Contained within your personalized folder, this folder is the default place in which pictures will be placed. Generally, it is only you that has access to pictures in your Pictures folder.

+ **Public Pictures:** This is similar to the Pictures folder, except everyone has access to the pictures in the Public Pictures folder.

For now, the important skill to have is the ability to open your Pictures or Public Pictures folder when you need it. Here are your options:

✦ Click the Start button and choose Pictures.

✦ In your personal folder, double-click the icon for your Pictures folder.

✦ If you're in any folder, you can click Pictures or you can choose Public and then Public Pictures in the favorites section of the Navigation Pane on the left side of Windows Explorer to hop to that folder (see Figure 14-1).

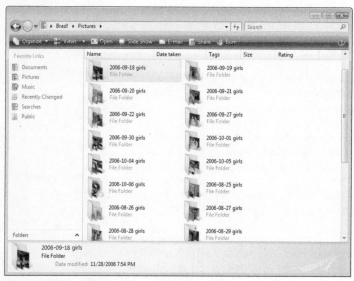

Figure 14-1: A sample Pictures folder

Figure 14-1 shows an example of a Pictures folder. In that example, Pictures contains several subfolders. Each subfolder contains a group of pictures. Your Pictures folder won't look like the example, but don't worry about that. As long as the title bar shows Pictures or Public Pictures, you're in the right folder.

If you used prior versions of Windows, then you might have noticed that the Pictures folder (called My Pictures in prior versions) and Public Pictures folder (called Shared Pictures in prior versions) had extra view options you could use to view pictures and their icons in Explorer. These added views included filmstrip view and thumbnails. In Windows Vista, the picture folders are like any other folder. You still can get similar views using the larger or extra large icon views. For more on changing views, see "Different Ways to View Icons" in Chapter 5.

The one difference you will notice in these folders is in the toolbar. A View Slideshow button is displayed on the toolbar if the folder contains primarily pictures. You can use this button to play a slide show containing the current folder's images. This slide show is displayed using the Photo Gallery, which will be covered in Chapter 15.

Looking at Figure 14-1, you can see that images on the computer have been somewhat organized. The Windows Picture Import feature helps you organize your pictures into subfolders like that. You'll learn how to use this wizard later in this chapter. You can also create your own folders, selecting the New Folder option after clicking the Organize button in the Explorer toolbar.

 See "Creating Your Own Folders" in Chapter 19 for the goods on creating your own folders.

Viewing Picture Icons

As discussed in Chapter 5, any time you view the contents of a folder, Windows Explorer is the program providing the view. So when you're viewing the contents of your Pictures or Public Pictures folder, you have access to all the tools described in Chapter 5. For example, you can choose a view for displaying icons. In Pictures or Public Pictures, you're likely to find Large or Extra Large views to be most useful. To choose a view, use one of the following methods:

✦ Click the left side of the View button on the Explorer toolbar to cycle to the next view format.

✦ Click the down arrow on the right side of the Views button in Explorer's toolbar; then click the view you want to use.

✦ Right-click some empty space between icons in the main pane and choose View from the shortcut menu; then click a view name.

✦ If your menu bar is displayed, select View and then click the name of the View you want to display.

You'll learn more about your Pictures folder in Chapter 15.

 If you need a reminder on the different views available to you, see the section "Different Ways to View Icons" in Chapter 5.

Types of Pictures

You might think a picture is a picture and therefore all pictures are the same type of file. Alas, it's not that simple. Pictures come in many different formats. As with any file, the picture's file name extension describes the format of the information in the file. Table 14-1 lists many of the picture types available.

Table 14-1
File Extensions Representing Different Types of Pictures Used on PCs

Filename Extension	Format
.iff	Amiga
.art	AOL Art File
.dxf	Autodesk Drawing Interchange
.gif	CompuServe Graphics Interchange
.cgm	Computer Graphics Metafile
.cmx	Corel Clipart
.cdr	CorelDraw Drawing
.lbm	Deluxe Paint
.cut	Dr. Halo
.eps, .ai, .ps	Encapsulated PostScript
.fpx	FlashPix
.img	GEM Paint
.hgl	HP Graphics Language
.jpg, .jif, .jpeg	Joint Photographic Experts Group
.kdc	Kodak Digital Camera
.pcd	Kodak Photo CD
.pic	Lotus PIC
.pct	Macintosh PICT
.mac	MacPaint
.drw	Micrografx Draw
.msp	Microsoft Paint
.psp	Paint Shop Pro
.pic	PC Paint
.psd	Photoshop
.pbm	Portable Bitmap
.pgm	Portable Greymap
.png	Portable Network Graphics
.ppm	Portable Pixelmap
.raw	Raw File Format

Filename Extension	Format
.sct, .ct	SciTex Continuous Tone
.ras	Sun RasterImage
.tif, .tiff	Tagged Image File Format
.tga	Truevision Targa
.gem	Ventura/GEM Drawing
.clp	Windows Clipboard
.emf	Windows Enhanced Metafile
.wmf	Windows Meta File
.rle	Windows or CompuServe RLE
.bmp	Windows Bitmap
.dib	Windows Device Independent Bitmap
.wpg	WordPerfect Bitmap or Vector
.dcx	Zsoft Multipage Paintbrush
.pcx	Zsoft Paintbrush

 Tip File name extensions are visible only when the check box Hide extensions for known file types is cleared. See the section "Showing/Hiding File Name Extensions" in Chapter 6 for specifics.

Don't let all the different file types intimidate you. Some are so rare that you may never come across them. When saving a file, you'll rarely be presented with so many options. The simple rule is, if in doubt choose JPEG, which works with nearly everything, even e-mail. If JPEG isn't an option, you can use GIF or Windows Bitmap (BMP), which are also widely supported.

Copying Pictures from a CD

If you get pictures developed and saved onto a CD, you'll be able to view and print them right from the CD. But if you want to be able to change them in any way, you'll need to copy them to your hard disk first. That's because the pictures will most likely be on a CD-ROM (the ROM stands for Read Only Memory). You can't change the contents of a CD-ROM in any way. So you can't change a picture on a CD-ROM.

 Tip You don't need a digital camera to take digital photos. You can have your regular film developed and delivered to you on CD-ROM or use a disposable camera such as the Kodak PLUSDigital.

You can copy the pictures from the CD-ROM to your Pictures folder or to any folder on your hard disk, for that matter. Once the pictures are in a folder on your hard disk, you can edit, print, and view the photos freely without the CD-ROM. To copy the pictures, you can use any method described in Chapter 22, the main chapter in this book on CDs. Or you can use the built-in wizard for importing pictures as described in the steps that follow.

STEPS: Copy Photos from a CD

1. Put the photo CD-ROM into your CD-ROM drive and wait a few seconds. Then:

   - If it's a Kodak Picture CD, you'll most likely see a slideshow of your pictures, of the Kodak Photo CD program, or the Kodak Picture CD program opens. If either happens, skip the remaining steps and go to the sidebar titled "Using a Kodak Picture CD."

   - If you see the dialog box asking what you want to do with the CD, click Import pictures using Windows. Then go to Step 2. Otherwise, you'll automatically be taken to Step 2.

Cross-Reference If absolutely nothing happens within a minute of inserting the CD into its drive, you can access the disk directly from its icon in the Computer folder that you can access from the Start menu. See the section "Using CDs and DVDs" in Chapter 22 for more information.

2. The Scanner and Camera Wizard opens and begins the import process. The first step is to count the number of images on the disk. You'll then be prompted to tag the images as shown in Figure 14-2. You can enter a descriptive term into the Tag field. This word (or words) will be associated to your images.

Figure 14-2: Tagging images during the picture import process

3. If you want to change some of the options for importing your images, then click the options link. This opens the options dialog box shown in Figure 14-3. If you don't want to change any options, then click the Import button and go to Step 4.

Figure 14-3: Changing settings while importing pictures

There are a number of options you may want to modify. Any settings you change will apply to future imports of images and video from CDs or DVDs as well as this import. After you have set your options, click the OK button to continue the import. The options you may want to adjust are:

- **Import to** — This is the default directory where images will be placed. This is Pictures unless you choose the Browse button and select a different location. You can change this to any folder including the Public Pictures folder.

- **Folder name** — The pictures you import will be placed in a sub-folder of the one you specified in the Import to option. If you select this option, you will see that you have a variety of naming options that can use the tag you entered, the date imported, or the date the image was taken, or a variety of combinations of this information. If you select an option such as Date Taken + Tag, then pictures will be organized by the date the image was taken and the tag you entered in Step 2.

- **File name** — This option controls how the import names the images it imports. You can use the Tag or the original file name. If the images on your CD are in folders, you can choose to keep those folder names as well.

- **Other options**—There are several additional options you can select to turn on (or clear to turn off). This includes the ability to automatically erase images from the camera and to open the images in Windows Photo Gallery after they are imported. If you select Rotate pictures on import, then you will see an additional dialog box during the import similar to Figure 14-4. In this dialog box you will be able to rotate any images.

If you change any options, the import wizard will restart from the beginning.

4. The Import pictures and video wizard will load each item based on the options that were defaulted or that you set. You'll see each image displayed briefly as it is being imported.

5. If you did not select the option to remove the images or the option to display them in the Windows Photo Gallery, then when the images are imported, the wizard exits. If you choose to view them in the gallery, then the gallery will be loaded with your images. Figure 14-4 shows pictures that were just imported in the Windows Photo Gallery.

Figure 14-4: The Windows Photo Gallery with recently imported images. The gallery is covered in detail in Chapter 15.

After the images are imported, the wizard closes. You can remove the CD now and put it someplace for safe keeping. From now on, you'll do all your work on the copies in the folder on your hard disk. The CD is just a backup of your original photos, in case you ever want to copy an original photo to your hard disk again.

Using a Kodak Picture CD

When you insert a Kodak Picture CD into your CD drive, you'll most likely see a slide show of the pictures on the CD. Clear the check box Show Opening Slideshow, or press the spacebar on your keyboard. You should come to the main program for managing a Kodak Photo CD. Here's how to proceed:

1. Click the first option, My Pictures (shown as follows), on the main menu.

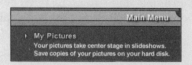

2. Click the Save As option on the next page that appears.

3. Click the Select All button near the upper-left corner of the Kodak window, as follows.

4. Under Choose picture size, choose Large (for printing), since this will give you the best originals to work with.

5. Click the Save button in the Kodak program, shown as follows.

In the Save As dialog box that opens, navigate to the folder in which you want to store the pictures. For example, to put the pictures in your Pictures folder, click the Pictures favorite at the left side of the Save As dialog box.

Change the file name to whatever you want to name this group of pictures. Click the Save button in the Save As dialog box. When copying is done, you'll see a dialog box telling you how many pictures were copied. Click its OK button. Then you can close the Kodak program (large X near its upper-right corner) and remove the CD. Keep the CD in a safe place as a backup of your original photos. From now on, you can work with the copies of the photos in a subfolder within your Pictures folder.

The folder(s) that the pictures are in is a subfolder of your Pictures folder unless you changed the default in Step 4 above. You can get there by going to your Pictures folder as shown earlier in this chapter. You can then click the appropriate subfolder based on the options you set during the import.

If you try to import the images from the same CD-ROM again, then the wizard will look for new images. The wizard will not import the images you already copied.

We'll talk about techniques for viewing, printing, and editing pictures in Chapter 15. For now, it's time to talk about getting pictures from a digital camera.

Getting Pictures from a Digital Camera

If your digital camera is a recent model supported by Windows Vista, and that camera connects to your computer with a USB or FireWire cable, you can use the Import Pictures and Video wizard to get pictures from your camera to your hard disk. Here's the basic procedure.

STEPS: Get Pictures from a Digital Camera

1. Connect the camera to the computer through the USB or FireWire cable.

2. Turn on the camera and wait a few seconds. Little messages might appear in the notification area as Windows gets ready to copy from the camera. Then you might see a dialog box asking what you want to do. This is the same dialog box you see when copying images from a CD-ROM. Click Import pictures using Windows. Now you can follow the same steps starting at Step 3 for importing images from a CD-ROM shown in the previous section.

If you want to have Windows remove the pictures from the camera when it has finished copying them, choose the option Always erase from camera after importing, as shown earlier in Step 3 for importing images from a CD. Alternatively, you can select the check box Erase after importing while the images are being imported (see Figure 14-5). This also removes them from the camera.

Figure 14-5: Selecting the check box deletes the images from the camera after they are copied.

After the pictures are imported, the import window shown in Figure 14-5 closes. If you had the Windows Photo Gallery option selected, then it would open with your newly imported images displayed. You can turn off and disconnect the camera. All of its pictures are now safely stored on your computer's hard disk. If you didn't tell Windows to delete all the pictures from the camera, you can do so using the controls on the camera.

We'll talk about techniques for viewing, printing, and editing pictures that you got from your camera in Chapter 15. For now, it's time to talk about getting pictures from a scanner.

Scanning Documents

A scanner is like a photocopy machine attached to a computer. Unlike a photocopy machine, which copies a document directly to paper, a scanner copies a document to a file on your hard disk. The document is a picture, which is fine in most cases. But if you scan text in the hopes of editing it with WordPad or some other word-processing program, it won't work. You'll have to convert the scanned document to text first, using *Optical Character Recognition (OCR)* software. Many scanners come with such software. You can also purchase and install OCR software yourself.

 Tip To see Windows Vista–compatible OCR products, from the Start menu go to All Programs ➪ Extras and Upgrades ➪ Windows Marketplace. You'll need to be connected to the Internet. In the search box on the page you can enter `scanner` or `OCR`. Either one will return a number of products. You can also shop online at any site that sells software (for example, `www.TigerDirect.com`, `www.cdw.com`) and search for `OCR software`.

How you install and use your scanner depends on its make and model. Most of that information will have to come from the printed documentation that came with the scanner. However, assuming the scanner is Vista-compatible, and is properly installed, you can use it to import pictures.

If you are using Windows Vista Business, Enterprise, or Ultimate Editions, then you will have Faxing and Scanning software included. If you are using Vista Home or Home Premium, then the Faxing and Scanning software is not included. You can upgrade to obtain the software or you can use software that comes with your scanner.

After you've scanned an image into the computer, it can be treated like any other image. Chapter 15 details how you can manipulate it.

Copying Pictures from a Web Page

If you browse the Web using Internet Explorer (see Chapter 10), and you come across a picture you'd like to keep, you can easily copy it to your hard disk. Here's how.

STEPS: Copy a Picture from a Web Page

1. Right-click the picture and choose Save Picture As, as in the example shown in Figure 14-6.

2. In the Save Picture dialog box that opens, navigate to your Pictures folder, if you're not taken there automatically.

Tip The Save Picture dialog box works exactly like the Save As dialog box discussed in section "Saving a Document" in Chapter 6.

3. Optionally, change the file name to something that will help you better identify the picture by name.

4. Click the Save button in the Save Picture dialog box.

You'll find the file in your Pictures folder (or in whatever folder you navigated to in Step 2). It will most likely be a JPEG, GIF, or PNG image, since they're the most widely used formats on the Web. You'll learn more about using your Pictures folder in Chapter 15.

If right-clicking a picture doesn't get you to a menu, you can take a snapshot of the entire screen. Then paste the screenshot into a graphics program like Paint and crop the parts you don't want. See the sections "Printing the Screen" in Chapter 8 and "Editing Pictures with Paint" in Chapter 15.

Figure 14-6: Copying a picture from a Web page

Installing Cameras and Scanners

If you tried getting pictures from a camera or scanner using the preceding techniques and couldn't get it to work, you should check the following. First, eliminate the obvious ones: Is the camera/scanner turned on? Is the camera/ scanner connected to the computer? If those things are OK, the most likely scenario is that the device does not connect to the computer through a USB or FireWire cable and hence needs to be installed.

The first step in installing *any* device to your computer is this: Follow the instructions that came with the camera or scanner. There are hundreds of makes and models of these items on the market, and they're not all the same. Although the general techniques described here and in Windows Help and Support might help, there's no substitute for following specific instructions for your specific device.

If you've been through that procedure and still can't get things to work, or for some reason you were unable to complete the installation procedure by following the manufacturer's instructions, the next step is to grab the software disk that came with your camera or scanner and put it into the appropriate drive. Then follow these steps:

1. Click the Start button and choose Control Panel.

2. From the Control Panel Home click Hardware and Sound, then select Scanners and Cameras.

3. The Scanners and Cameras window opens. If you have a scanner or camera installed on your computer, each will be represented by an icon, similar to the example shown in Figure 14-7.

Figure 14-7: The Scanners and Cameras folder

Caution   A device that connects through a USB or FireWire port won't appear in Scanners and Cameras, even when it's working perfectly. That's because such devices are installed and uninstalled on the fly and hence don't need a permanent icon in Scanners and Cameras.

4. Click the Add Device button. The first page of the Scanner and Camera Installation Wizard opens. Read the first page; then click Next.

5. The next wizard page asks what device you want to install. Here's how that works:

   • If you inserted a disk from your camera or scanner already, click the Have Disk button.

   • If you don't have a disk for your device, click the device manufacturer's name in the left column; then (if possible) click your specific make and model of printer in the right column. Click Next.

From this point on, you have to read and follow the instructions that appear on the screen as you go through the Wizard. If you still can't get your device installed, you'll probably have to use the software that came with the device to get pictures from that device. Only the instructions that came with your camera or scanner can tell you how to install and use that software.

Troubleshooting Cameras and Scanners

Lots of things can cause a camera or scanner not to work. After you've checked for the obvious reasons (see the previous section), and your equipment still doesn't work, check out the following.

If this is the first time you are using the device and you are having trouble, then you should make sure you followed any installation instructions that came with it. There may have been special software you needed to install, although generally most devices that connect to a USB connection don't need anything special.

If you still can't figure out the issue, then make sure that your scanner is properly installed as per the manufacturer's instructions. Also, try using the Vista installation feature to help. In most cases, if the scanner is installed, then it might include the ability to test the scanner. You can check a scanner's properties from the Scanners and Cameras window. The following steps walk you through this:

1. Click the Start button and choose Control Panel.

2. From the Control Panel Home click Hardware and Sound, then select Scanners and Cameras.

3. The Scanners and Cameras window opens. Click the scanner that isn't working in order to select it.

4. Click the Properties button. This displays properties for the device similar to Figure 14-8. Each device might have different properties, so what you see might look different from what is shown

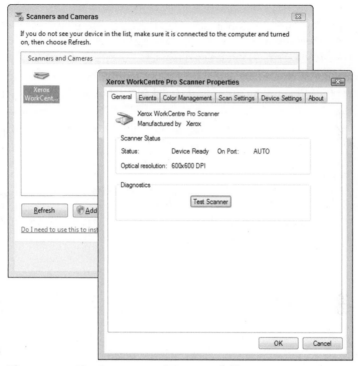

Figure 14-8: The Scanners and Cameras folder

5. Look for a button or link that says something like Test Scanner. If you find that button or link, click it and follow what you are told.

For beginners, the most common problem with scanners and cameras is assuming that all makes and models of these things are the same. They're not the same. You really need to learn the specifics of your exact camera or scanner. And the only places to get that information are the printed documentation that came with the device and the manufacturer's web site. Trying to hack things together through sheer guesswork is likely to turn into a frustrating experience!

Summary

That should be enough to get you started working with pictures. You'll learn the fun stuff about working with pictures in Chapter 15. For now, here's a quick recap of the most important points made in this chapter:

✦ Every picture is a document file. Like all files, pictures are stored in folders.

✦ Windows Vista comes with two built-in folders for storing pictures, Pictures for your pictures and Public Pictures for pictures you want to share.

✦ You can view and print photos on a CD or DVD. But if you want to change them, you need to copy them to your hard disk first, unless it is a rewritable disk.

✦ If your digital camera or scanner is Vista-compatible, you can use the import pictures and video wizard to get pictures right to your Pictures folder.

✦ To copy a picture from a web page, right-click the picture and choose Save Picture As.

Playing with Pictures and the Photo Gallery

✦ ✦ ✦ ✦

CHAPTER 15

In This Chapter

Using your Pictures folder

Using Windows Photo Gallery Viewer

See how to filter and find images using Windows Photo Gallery

Editing Photos with Windows Photo Gallery

Editing pictures with Paint

✦ ✦ ✦ ✦

Your computer can display and print all sorts of pictures, ranging from simple drawings to photographs and animations. The computer biz sometimes uses fancy terms such as *digital image* and *graphic image* to describe pictures, but basically a picture is a document stored in its own file on a computer disk.

As with any document, you can't just open a picture by itself. You need some sort of program to view a picture on your screen. Programs you use to create and edit (change) pictures are generally referred to as *graphics programs* or *graphics editors.* A graphics program like Windows Photo Gallery Viewer (which comes with Windows Vista) enables you to look at pictures but not change them. A graphics editor like the Paint program that comes with Windows Vista enables you to create, view, and edit (change) pictures. Finally, graphics programs like Windows Photo Gallery that also come with Windows Vista enable you to do some touch up work on digital photos and pictures.

Before we get into the programs, you need to get to the folder where your pictures are stored.

Using Your Pictures Folder

As with documents, you store pictures in folders. Windows Vista already has a couple of built-in folders especially well suited for storing pictures. Your

Pictures folder (which you'll find in your personalized Documents folder as well as in the Favorite Links area of the Windows Explorer navigation pane) is the easiest one to get to. There's also a folder named Public Pictures, which is the same idea as your Pictures folder. However, on a network or computer with multiple user accounts, pictures in the Public Pictures folder are available to everyone, whereas pictures in your Pictures folder are private, in the sense that only you can get to them.

There are several ways to get to your Pictures folders:

✦ Click the Start button and choose Pictures.

✦ Click the Start button, choose your personalized folder, and double-click the Pictures icon.

✦ If you're already in a folder and see Pictures listed under the Favorite Links, click that option.

The contents of your Pictures folder are displayed in the Explorer window (discussed in Chapter 5), shown in Figure 15-1. You can choose a view (for example, Large icons or Tiles) from the View menu or the Views button in the toolbar.

Figure 15-1: A sample Pictures folder

If your Pictures folder contains subfolders, you can double-click any subfolder's icon to open it and see the pictures it contains. If you click one or more pictures, then the taskbar near the top of the window will contain a number of tasks specific to pictures. Here's a quick overview of what each of those offers:

✦ **Slide Show:** Clicking this option makes the background go blank and then displays each picture in the folder, one at a time, in slide-show fashion on the background. See the "Using Slide Show" section later in this chapter.

✦ **Preview:** This option enables you to choose a program to view the selected item. This is initially Paint or Windows Photo Gallery; however, you can choose a different default program as well.

✦ **Print:** See the "Printing Pictures" section that follows.

✦ **Email:** Send the selected files as an attachment on an e-mail.

✦ **Share:** Share the selected items with others on your computer or network.

✦ **Burn:** Enables you to copy all (or selected) pictures to a CD. See Chapter 22 for skills and concepts required to make this work.

The same options are also available in your Public Pictures folder, as well as in any subfolder contained within Pictures or Public Pictures folders. When you're in your Pictures folders, you can quickly switch to Public Pictures, if you like, by clicking Public ➪ Public Pictures under Favorite Links in the Windows Explorer navigation bar. It works the other way, too. If you're in your Public Pictures folder, you can click Pictures in the Explorer navigation pane to go to your Pictures folder.

Tip

If your computer is connected to a network, or other people have user accounts on the same computer, you may want to share some photos with other users. Put those photos in the Public Pictures folder. Keep the private ones in your Pictures folder.

Printing Pictures

You can print any picture, or group of pictures, right from the Explorer bar. First, get to the folder that contains the pictures you want to print and perform the steps that follow.

STEPS: Printing Pictures from a Folder

1. Open your Pictures folder or navigate to the folder that contains the pictures you want to print.

2. Select the pictures you want to print within the folder.

3. On the Explorer toolbar click the Print button. The Print Pictures dialog box opens (see Figure 15-2).

Tip

You can select the pictures to print before clicking the Print option. Use any of the techniques described in the section "Working with Multiple Files and Folders" in Chapter 19 to select the pictures you want to print.

4. In the dialog box, first select the printer you want to use. Depending on your printer selection, additional options may also be displayed as shown in Figure 15-2. You can adjust any of the displayed options such as paper size and quality.

Printer selection · Printer Options · Layout options

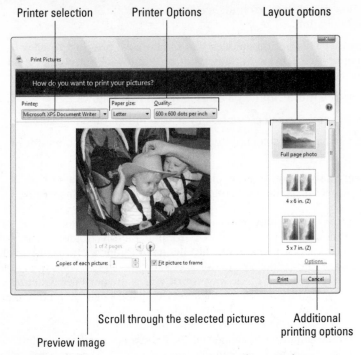

Scroll through the selected pictures · Additional printing options

Preview image

Figure 15-2: The Print Picture options in Windows Explorer

5. Select the layout you want to use for your images from the right side of the screen. Some layouts will allow for more than one picture to be printed on a single page. The actual options and amount of white space shown will vary based upon the printer and the paper size that you choose. When you select a different layout, the center, preview area will change to show the images in the selected layout.

6. Select the number of prints you want from each of the selected pictures. You can scroll through the selected pictures by using the arrows underneath the preview image.

7. Optionally, you can select the Options link. This displays the dialog box shown in Figure 15-3, which enables you to select an option for sharpening the image for printing as well as to modify the options displayed. You can also select additional links to get to the specific properties of your printer or to manage the color on your system. When you are done changing options, select OK to save them or Cancel to simply return to the Print Pictures dialog without saving the options changes.

8. With your options selected, click the Print button to print your pictures.

9. Printing should start within a few seconds. You'll see a status bar showing the images being sent to the printer. When printing is completed, the dialog box will close automatically.

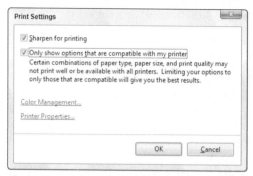

Figure 15-3: The Printing Options dialog box for Picture Printing

Making a Working Copy of a Picture

On your hard disk, you're free to make changes to your pictures. But before you do, know that it's always a good idea to keep a copy of the original picture on disk. Use other copies for touchup work, sizing, or any other changes. That way, if you ever manage to make a mess of things, you always have the original picture to work from. You can use any of the techniques described in Chapter 19 to move and copy pictures (since each picture is a file). But if you just want to make a quick copy of one picture:

1. Right-click the icon for the picture you want to copy, and choose Copy.

2. Right-click some empty space near the icon you just right-clicked, and choose Paste.

Optionally, you can point to the picture, hold down the Ctrl key, drag the picture a slight distance so the mouse pointer is touching some empty space between icons, and release the mouse button.

The new file will be named *OriginalName - Copy*, where *OriginalName* is the same as the file you copied. If you want to rename the copy, right-click it, choose Rename, and type a new name, or edit the existing name.

Rotating a Picture

If you hold a camera sideways when you take a picture, that picture will likely show up sideways on your screen. If the picture is in your Pictures folder (or any other folder on your hard disk, for that matter), you can rotate it. It's better to rotate a copy of the original picture rather than the original itself. So if you haven't already done so, you can make a copy. To rotate the copy:

1. Right-click the icon of the picture you want to copy.

2. Choose Rotate Clockwise to rotate the picture 90 degrees to the right or Rotate Counterclockwise to rotate 90 degrees to the left.

3. You might see a message recommending that you work with copies. Assuming you are working with a copy, click Yes to proceed.

That's it. If you rotate a picture the wrong direction, just rotate it the opposite direction twice to straighten things out.

Recording Details About Your Photos

If you're a serious camera buff, you can record details about each photo as part of the file's properties. Right-click any single photo's icon and choose Properties. Or, if you want to assign the same properties to several photos, select the appropriate icons first. Then right-click any selected photo and choose Properties. Either way, the Properties dialog box for the picture(s) will open.

Cross-Reference See "Working with Multiple Files and Folders" in Chapter 19 for more information.

In the Properties dialog box, click the Details tab. the properties you see depend on the type of file you're working with. But if you're working with a JPEG image, you should see the properties shown in Figure 15-4.

Figure 15-4: The Properties for a JPEG image (Details view)

The properties listed under Image are facts about the picture that you can't change. But you're welcome to fill in the blanks on many of the other items, such as Title, Subject, Tags (for searching), and so forth. Later, when looking through pictures, or after performing a search for all pictures on your hard drive, you can display that information in Details view.

For example, suppose you do a search for all pictures. When the search is complete, you can switch to Details view, choose the details you want to see, and arrange columns as suits your needs. You can click any column heading to sort the pictures on that column. Figure 15-5 shows an example, with the Title, Date taken, Dimensions, Rating, Tags, and Author properties visible.

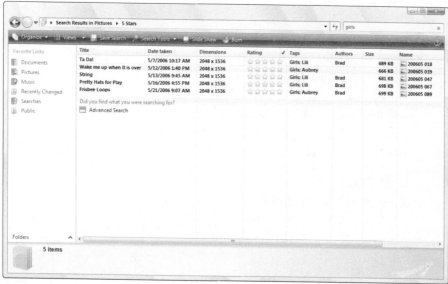

Figure 15-5: Pictures listed in Details view

 Tip   You can also fill in a star rating from one to five stars. The farther to the right you click, the higher the star rating. You can later search and filter based on this rating. Give your best pictures five star ratings so you can quickly filter them from the rest!

 Cross-Reference   See the section "The Details View" in Chapter 5 for information on using columns in Windows Explorer. See the section "Searching for Lost Files" in Chapter 20 for information on searching for files.

Using Slide Show

One of the other options you will see when viewing a folder with images is the Slide Show option. Clicking the Slide Show button within a folder such as the Pictures folder starts a slide show. This slide show initially covers your display and cycle through the images in the current folder. The entire screen will be taken up with the show.

You can continue to work while the slide show continues to cycle through images. You can do this because the slide show is actually running somewhat like your desktop. If you use Flip 3D (press the ⊞+Tab) or press Alt+Tab, you can switch to a currently running program. The slide show will continue in the background.

You can also adjust the settings of the slide show by right-clicking somewhere within an image that is being displayed. This action presents you with a menu with the following options:

✦ **Play**: If you have paused the slide show, this option starts it playing again.

✦ **Pause**: This option stops the slide show on the current slide.

✦ **Next**: This option advances the slide show to the next picture.

✦ **Back**: This option returns the slide show to the previous picture.

✦ **Shuffle**: This option causes the images to be randomly displayed if selected. If not selected, images will be presented in order.

✦ **Loop**: This option causes the images to continuously be displayed. After all the images have been displayed, they will be displayed again. If this option is not selected, then, when the last image displays, it will remain on the screen.

✦ **Slide Show Speed — Slow/Medium/Fast**: This option adjusts how fast the images are automatically advanced.

✦ **Exit**: This option closes the slide show.

Using the Photo Gallery

Windows Vista comes with a program that enables you to view and manipulate digital photos; it's called Photo Gallery and comes with a viewer for looking at your pictures. It also has several easy-to-use tools that enable you to do standard fixes and adjustments to photos. In fact, the tools will most likely be all you need to fix most photos that you take. If not, then you always have the option of purchasing a more robust photo editing software package.

Viewing Pictures

You can always use Large and Extra Large icons in Windows Explorer to view small representations of your photos and pictures. For a better view, you can use the Photo Gallery Viewer. To open the viewer, simply double-click on an image. If you have not changed your default settings in Windows Vista, then the Photo Gallery Viewer is what will be used to open your image.

The Windows Photo Gallery viewer shown in Figure 15-6 is a part of the Photo Gallery. Using the controls below the image, you can adjust how it is viewed. This includes the ability to zoom in and out, the ability to view the image in actual size or fit within the window, the ability rotate the image, and the ability to switch to the next or previous image in the current folder. You also have the ability to start a slide show or to delete the image. The buttons to do each of these are shown in Figure 15-6.

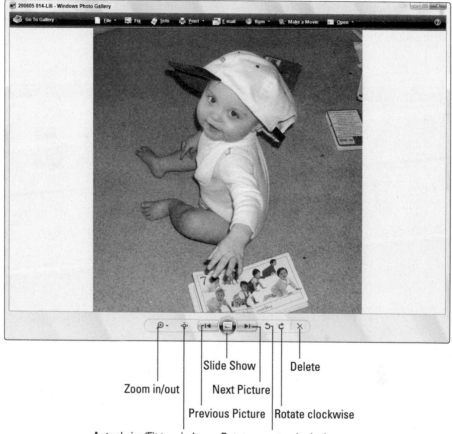

```
200605 014-Lili - Windows Photo Gallery
```

Go To Gallery	File ▾	Fix	Info	Print ▾	E-mail	Burn ▾	Make a Movie	Open ▾

Slide Show   Delete

Zoom in/out   Next Picture

Previous Picture   Rotate clockwise

Actual size/Fit to window   Rotate counterclockwise

Figure 15-6: The Windows Photo Gallery Viewer

When in the Photo Gallery Viewer, you can click the Go To Gallery link near the top of the window to go to the main page of the tool as shown in Figure 15-7. This page will allow you to view icons for all the images on your system. More importantly, it will allow you to sort, search, or filter images based on a number of criteria.

You can also get to this page by selecting Start ⇨ All Programs ⇨ Windows Photo Gallery. The result is the same — you'll have a page that lists the images on your computer in a categorized format.

When in the Photo Gallery, you can adjust what is shown and how it is shown. To adjust what is shown, simply click the options on the left side of the page. Based on what you select, more or fewer images will be displayed. For example, you can select All Pictures and Videos to see all the pictures and videos. If you want to narrow down the images, you can select one or more tags; you can choose a date or set of dates when the pictures were taken; you can choose a star rating; or you can choose different folders. When you make a selection, the images on the main part of the window will be filtered based on the selection. In Figure 15-8, the subfolder called 2006 was selected within the Date Taken folder. This causes the main page to display only the images taken in 2006.

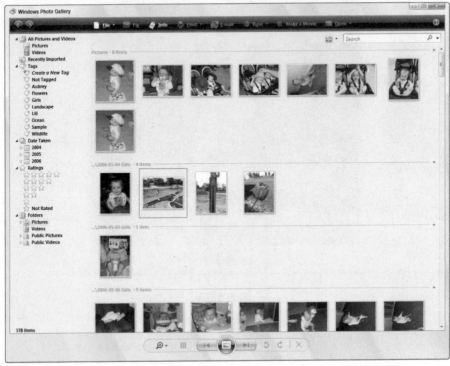

Figure 15-7: The main Windows Photo Gallery page showing all the images on a system

> **Tip**
>
> In Figure 15-8, you can also see that additional information is being shown in a preview window for one photo. Whenever you hover the mouse over a photo, the preview window will display, showing the additional information about an image.

In addition to filtering based on what is displayed on the left side of the Gallery, you can also change how the icons are displayed. You do this by clicking the icon to the left of the search box. This icon enables you to select a thumbnail view to use in the Gallery. Your options are as follows:

✦ **Thumbnails:** A small image of the picture.

✦ **Thumbnails with Text:** A small image of the picture along with a minor amount of information including the image's date and time.

✦ **Tiles:** A small image of the picture with the key information related to it. This includes displaying the file name, the date taken, the file size, the resolution, the rating, and the caption. In this view, you can click on some of the information (such as rating and caption) to add or change them.

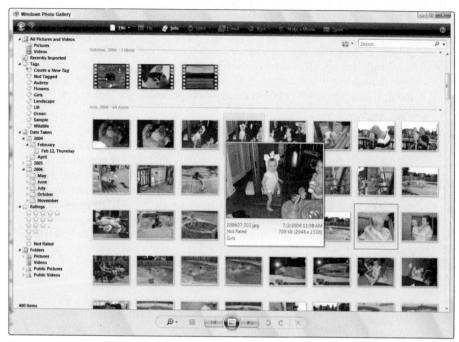

Figure 15-8: Filtering in the Gallery to show only pictures taken in 2006

You can also choose to group and sort the icons by clicking this icon and using the options on the menu. Alternatively, you can right-click an open area in the Gallery, and you'll get a similar menu for selecting the settings you want.

If your images scroll off the page, you can select the Table of Contents option to add a column to the page that lets you see all the groupings. You can then click on the group titles in the table of contents to have the main window scroll to display those picture icons.

Fixing Photos with the Photo Gallery

You can use the Gallery to find images you want to manipulate or fix. You can also use Windows Explorer to find images. When you have found an image you want to change, you can click on it, double-click on it, or if you are in the Gallery, you can also right-click on it and select Preview. Either way, you will end up back in the Windows Photo Gallery Viewer you saw in Figure 15-6.

With a picture selected, you can begin to make a number of changes. If you click the Fix button on the toolbar at the top of the Gallery Viewer, then a menu of fixing options will be displayed on the right side of the page. These options include the following:

✦ **Auto Adjust:** This automatically adjusts the exposure and color on an image. Oftentimes this can help fix poor lighting or a slightly blurry image. If this doesn't improve your image, then you can click the Undo button and manually adjust your photo with the other tools.

✦ **Adjust Exposure:** This option enables you to adjust the brightness and contrast in your image.

✦ **Adjust Color:** This option enables you to adjust the color temperature, the tint, and the saturation in your image. If you are not sure what these are, then you can either play with the settings or try using the Auto Adjust option mentioned previously.

✦ **Crop Picture:** This option enables you to cut out parts of the picture to focus on an individual area. When you first select to Crop an image, a frame is placed into it as shown in Figure 15-9. You can then adjust the frame using the mouse. You can also adjust the frame using the Proportion drop-down list in the crop options as well as by clicking on the Rotate frame icon. You should select a proportion for cropping that matches the size of photo you are likely to print. For example, selecting the 4 × 6 or 5 × 7 options helps to ensure the image will not be skewed when being printed since its digital size will match the printed proportions. After you have what you want to crop within the frame, you can click the Apply button to crop the image. The cropped image will replace the original one.

✦ **Fix Red Eye:** This option removes red eye from your images. After selecting this option on the right, you will need to select the eye you want to fix. You then drag the mouse pointer around the eye. The reddish areas will be adjusted to a darker color.

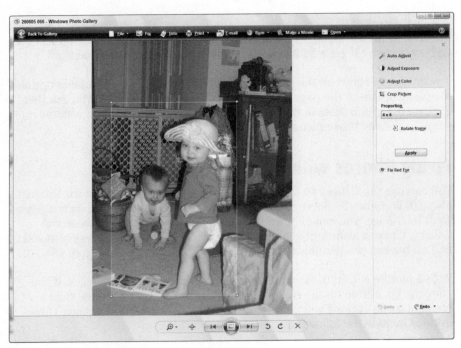

Figure 15-9: The cropping frame in Photo Gallery

If you make a change and decide you don't like it, you can click the Undo button to roll back to the prior status of the image. You can click the Undo button to reverse multiple changes as well—you are not limited to undoing just the last change.

Note As a reminder, you can also rotate the image by right-clicking it and selecting Rotate Clockwise or Rotate Counterclockwise from the menu that displays.

Sharing Photos from Photo Gallery

When you have your photos fixed, you likely want to share them. You can do this by printing them, e-mailing them, or burning them to a CD. You can do all of these by following the corresponding instructions throughout the rest of this book. In brief, here is how to do each directly from the Photo Gallery:

E-mailing a Picture

Click the E-mail icon in the toolbar of the Photo Gallery Viewer. This will prompt you to select a resolution for the image as shown in Figure 15-10. The larger the resolution, the larger the file that will be generated.

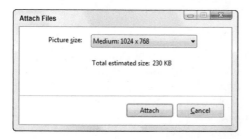

Figure 15-10: Picking a resolution to use for the image you are e-mailing

After you've selected a resolution, click the Attach button. This opens your mail program with the image as an attachment. You can add any text to your e-mail and send the image on its way. See Chapter 11 if you need to know more about sending e-mails.

Printing a Photo

You learned earlier that you can print an image directly from the Windows Explorer folder. Within Windows Photo Gallery, there is a Print button on the toolbar. When you click this button, you are given two options. One is to simply Print the image; the other is to Order prints.

If you select to print the image, then you will see the same dialog box that was shown earlier in this chapter. You'll be able to make the same selections and then print the image.

If you choose the Order prints option, then a dialog box opens that will look for recommended companies on the Internet from which you can order prints.

For example, when you click the Order prints option, you get the dialog box shown in Figure 15-11.

Figure 15-11: Ordering prints of photos

After you select the option you want by clicking on it, clicking the Send Pictures button will take you to the service. What happens at that point depends on the service selected. You should follow the instructions on the screen to work through the process. Be aware that these companies are going to charge you to print and mail your images to you.

Burning Pictures on a CD

Your other option for sharing photos is to put them on a disk. To do this, you can click the Burn icon on the Gallery toolbar. You will have the option of burning a data disk or a video disk. Make your selection and then follow the instructions on the screen. For more about burning disks, see Chapter 22.

Editing Pictures with Paint

Windows Photo Gallery is great for viewing, fixing, and sharing photos and pictures. If you want to create a picture or add something to a picture, then you should look at Microsoft Paint. Microsoft Paint is a simple little drawing program, which enables you to do some rudimentary things with pictures. Paint is also limited in terms of the types of pictures it can open. If a picture can be opened in Paint, you'll see that program in the picture's Open With menu. For example, to open a compatible picture in Paint, right-click the picture's icon in your Pictures folder (or whatever folder it's in), choose Open With, and click Paint, as in Figure 15-12.

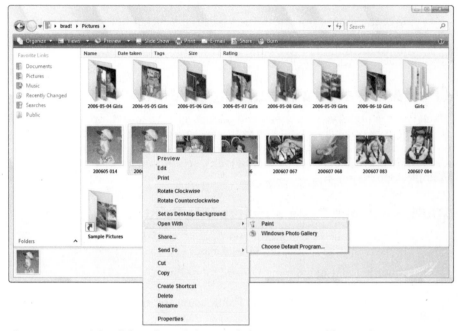

Figure 15-12: Right-click a picture's icon and choose Open With ➪ Paint.

Opening Paint

To open Paint with a new, empty document inside, click the Start button and choose All Programs ➪ Accessories ➪ Paint. The large, white area in the Paint document window is like a sheet of paper on which you can draw. If you want to work with a photo in Paint, it might be best to shrink that sheet of paper to a really tiny size first. That will prevent the photo from having a large white margin around it.

Can't Open in Paint

Paint can open pictures stored in the BMP, .DIB, JPEG, GIF, TIFF, and PNG formats. It cannot, however, open other types of pictures. If Paint won't open a picture, try double-clicking the picture's icon to see if any program can open the picture. Or right-click the picture's icon, choose Open With, and click some other program that appears on the menu. If you can't open the picture in any program, you don't have the right program for that type of file. If that happens, see the section "When Windows Can't Open a Document" in Chapter 6.

To shrink the sheet of paper in Paint, use whichever of the following techniques seems easiest to you:

✦ Choose Image ➪ Resize/Skew from the Paint menu bar. Under Resize, set the Horizontal and Vertical settings each to 1; click OK.

✦ Move the mouse pointer to the lower-right corner of the paper until the mouse turns to a two-headed arrow. Then drag that corner up, and to the left, until the white square is tiny.

Copy and Paste a Picture into Paint

When Paint is open, you can copy and paste a picture into it, provided you can get the picture open and visible on your screen. For example, suppose you're browsing the World Wide Web and come across a picture you want to copy and work with. You'd like to open it in Paint, so you can crop or size it, for example. Here's how you do that.

STEPS: Copy and Paste a Picture into Paint

1. When you can see the picture on your screen, right-click it and choose Copy, as on the left side of Figure 15-13.

2. From the Paint menu bar, choose Edit ➪ Paste.

A copy of the image will be visible in Paint, as on the right half of Figure 15-13.

Figure 15-13: Copying a picture from a web page into Paint

Cross-Reference To paste a snapshot of your computer screen into Paint, see the section "Printing the Screen" in Chapter 8.

Cropping a Picture in Paint

Often, when you take a picture, things don't turn out exactly as you planned. Sometimes there's too much background and not enough of the main subject. Cropping is a technique that enables you to get rid of extra background. To do this, you first need to open the picture in Paint. Then follow these steps.

STEPS: Crop a Picture in Paint

1. With your picture open in Paint, click the rectangular Select tool on the Paint toolbar (shown at left with its screen tip visible).

2. Move the mouse pointer to the upper-left corner of where you want to start cropping. Then hold down the left mouse button and drag a rectangle around the area you want to keep, as in Figure 15-14. If you make a mistake, press the Escape (Esc) key and try again.

Figure 15-14: The portion of picture to keep is selected (inside the white frame).

Tip
Like many programs, Paint supports *undo*. If you make a mistake, choose Edit ⇨ Undo from the Paint menu bar, or press Ctrl+Z, to undo your most recent action.

3. From the Paint menu bar, choose Image ⇨ Crop. The image will be cropped to your selected area.

4. Save your new image as a new name by clicking File ⇨ Save As. Type a new file name for the cropped image; then click the Save button in the dialog box. Be careful—if you use Save instead of Save As, you will overwrite the original image.

To open the cropped image or the original image, you can choose File ⇨ Open from Paint's menu bar. In the Open dialog box, navigate to the folder in which you stored the image, and double-click that picture's icon. The image opens. If you open the cropped image, you'll see it, as in the example shown in Figure 15-15.

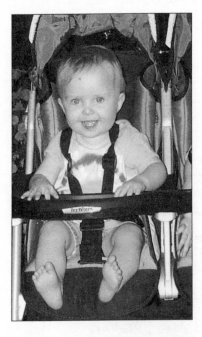

Figure 15-15: The cropped image created from Figure 15-14

Tip
If your original image is too big to see on the screen, you can select View ⇨ Zoom ⇨ Custom ⇨ 50% to display the image at half its original size. You can choose smaller percentages if the image still displays too big. This option does not change the picture in any way. Rather, it only changes how you see it on the screen. This makes it easier to select an area to crop. When cropped, you can select View ⇨ Zoom ⇨ Custom ⇨ 100% to return to the actual size of the image.

Sizing a Picture in Paint

Pictures from digital cameras and scanners can be *huge*. For example, a picture of Aunt Matilda's smiling face might be so huge on the screen that you see Aunt Matilda's left nostril only. Not too flattering, and not a particularly good thing to print, or to e-mail to your friends.

When you have a picture open in Paint, you can easily change its size. For example, you might want to make a copy of some huge photo that's only 50 percent the original size. Then use that smaller copy for e-mailing and printing.

 Caution It's best not to resize the original of a picture, because you may lose pic-ture quality when enlarging a photo. It's better to keep the original and work with a copy. Also, you can always shrink a large picture without los-ing picture quality. But when you enlarge a small picture, you often lose quality. The enlarged photo might be *pixilated*, a fancy term for *blotchy*.

STEPS: Resize a Picture in Paint

1. With your picture open and visible in Paint, choose Tools ➪ Resize/ Skew from the Paint menu bar. The Resize and Skew dialog box opens.

2. Under Resize, set the Horizontal and Vertical options to some per-centage size. For example, to make the picture half its current size, enter **50** in the Horizontal and Vertical text boxes under Resize.

3. Click the OK button in the Resize and Skew dialog box.

The picture resizes to your specifications. If you're not happy with the results, press Ctrl+Z or choose Edit ➪ Undo from the Paint menu bar. The picture will return to its previous size.

Adding to a Picture

Windows Paint includes a number of tools that enable you to draw and manip-ulate a picture. For example, you can add text to an image using the text tool as shown in Figure 15-16. The best way to see what paint can do is to open a copy of an image and simply start playing!

Printing and Saving a Picture in Paint

To print a picture currently open in Paint, use the standard technique. That is, do either of the following:

✦ Choose File ➪ Print from the Paint menu bar.

✦ Press Ctrl+P.

When the Print dialog box opens, you can choose options as appropriate for the picture (for example, if your printer enables you to choose a paper type and print quality, as discussed in the section "Printing a Document" in Chapter 8).

Figure 15-16: Manipulating a photo in Paint

To save the newly resized picture under a new file name, choose File ➪ Save As from the Paint menu bar. In the Save As dialog box that opens, navigate to the folder in which you want to store the picture, and enter a file name. Optionally, you can choose a file type from the Save As Type drop-down list. Click OK, and the picture is saved.

 Cross-Reference For more information on saving documents, see the section "Saving a Document" in Chapter 6.

Summary

This chapter has taught you some tools and techniques for working with pictures in Windows Vista. Here's a quick summary of the main points:

✦ To print pictures from a folder, navigate to that folder and click Print in the Explorer bar.

✦ To create a working copy of a picture, right-click its icon and choose Copy. Then right-click some empty space outside that icon and choose Paste.

✦ To rotate a picture, right-click its icon and choose one of the Rotate options on the shortcut menu.

✦ The Windows Photo Gallery Viewer enables you to view several different types of pictures.

✦ The Window Photo Gallery helps you sort and filter your pictures. Using it, you can find pictures based on dates, tags, ratings, and other information.

✦ Using the Windows Photo Gallery you can also make standard fixes to photos, including auto adjusting the settings, fixing exposure, adjusting color, cropping, and fixing red eye.

✦ Microsoft Paint, which also comes with Vista, enables you to crop and resize pictures.

Music and Video with Media Player 11

Music and video are examples of what's called
multimedia in the computer biz. Audio files
can contain any kind of sound, ranging from tiny sound
effects to entire songs from CDs. Video files can be anything from a small video clip to a movie you created
yourself. If your computer has a DVD drive, you can
watch DVDs.

Multimedia files (also called *media files* or *digital media*)
are documents. As such, they don't open by themselves.
They open in a program called a *media player.* Windows
Vista comes with a built-in media player, cleverly named
Windows Media Player. This chapter is about using
Windows Media Player 11 to listen to music and watch
videos.

Introducing Windows Media Player 11

As when starting any program, you can start Windows
Media Player from the Start menu, although the default
Quick Launch toolbar also has a button for launching
Media Player. So you can start Media Player at any time
using one of these options:

- ✦ Click the Start button and choose All
  Programs ➪ Windows Media Player.

- ✦ Click the Media Player button in the
  Quick Launch toolbar.

If this is the first time you've opened Media Player, you might see a message asking you to choose initial settings. You can choose:

✦ **Express Settings (Recommended)** — This gets everything ready for you to use Media Player with the littlest effort on your part. It will make Media Player your default player, add a shortcut to your Quick Launch bar, and much more. If you select this option, you can then click the Finish button.

✦ **Custom Settings** — This prompts you for a few additional tidbits of information in order to set up Media Player. You'll be able to configure download options, history options, and more. You'll also be able to determine whether a shortcut to Media Player is added to the Quick Launch menu and the desktop. Finally, you'll be able to determine whether media files should be played by Windows Media Player automatically or if only certain types of files should be played automatically by Media Player. You should provide the responses to each page of the wizard and click the Next button. You can click Finish on the last page.

If you're confused by all the options in the Custom setup, you can click the Next button on each page and click Finish on the last page. You can change your mind about any options you choose by clicking the Media Player Library toolbar button and then More Options from its menu.

When Windows Media Player finally opens, you'll probably see its program window, including the toolbar shown at the top of Figure 16-1. If you don't see the toolbar or if you want to see a classic menu, click the Layout options icon and select the appropriate item. Selecting Show Classic Menus brings the menu bar into view.

Media Player can be seen in Full or Compact modes. Figure 16-1 showed the full mode. Figure 16-2 shows the Media Player in Compact mode. You can switch between the two modes by clicking the icon shown in the figures.

Media Player is also unique in that it supports the use of *skins*. A skin is a whole different *interface* for a program. That is, a skin radically changes the appearance of a program on the screen, without changing that program's capabilities. Skins exist because people like to personalize things. If Media Player opens in a skin, you can easily switch to the Full mode (the normal program window) by right-clicking the skin and choosing Switch to Full Mode. You'll learn how to set a skin on Media Player later in this chapter.

Using the Features Taskbar

The Features taskbar provides access to the main features of Media Player. You can see this taskbar in Full Mode as shown in Figure 16-1.

Tip   As with any program window, you can double-click the Media Player title bar, or click its Maximize button, to size it to full-screen size. See the section "Arranging Open Program Windows" in Chapter 4 for details.

Layout options

View options

Features Toolbar

Seek bar

Click for Compact Mode

Player controls

Figure 16-1: Windows Media Player in Full mode

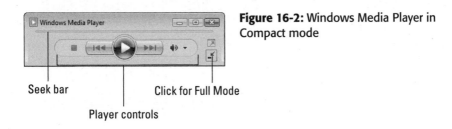

Figure 16-2: Windows Media Player in Compact mode

Seek bar

Click for Full Mode

Player controls

The first step in getting anything done in Windows Media Player is usually to click the appropriate button on the Features taskbar, depending on what you want to do at the moment:

✦ **Now Playing:** Lets you control the music you're listening to now, with an optional visualization. The visualization is a pattern of colors that changes with the music. You'll also be able to choose any playlist you want to listen to.

✦ **Library:** Takes you to the list of multimedia you have access to use. From the library, you can create lists of music to play, you can manage your content, and you can share your music.

✦ **Rip:** Lets you copy songs from a music CD to your hard disk and Media Library.

✦ **Burn:** Lets you copy any selection of songs to your own custom audio CD or to a portable diskless player.

✦ **Sync:** Lets you copy music to or from your portable music device such as an MP3 player.

✦ **URGE:** Numerous online services that you can use in conjunction with Media Player to download music and movies from the Internet. Nothing free here either, except trial runs.

You'll learn more about the major features summarized here later in this chapter and in Chapter 17.

Using the Play Controls

In Full Mode, Media Player's Play controls are along the bottom of the program window. Most work like the controls on a stereo or VCR. As usual, you can point to any button in the Play controls to see its name. Figure 16-3 points out the locations of the various controls. Here's what each does and how it works:

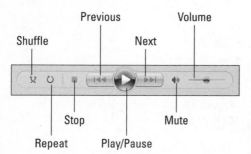

Figure 16-3: Windows Media Player's Play controls

✦ **Play/Pause:** Click to play the current song/video or to pause the current song if it's playing.

✦ **Stop:** Stop playing the current song or video and rewind to beginning.

✦ **Previous:** Go to previous song in the playlist (you'll find out what a playlist is in just a few moments).

✦ **Next:** Go to next song in the playlist.

✦ **Mute:** Turn off all sound. Click again to restore sound. If you get no sound from a playing song or video, click this button to make sure the speakers aren't muted.

✦ **Volume:** Adjust the volume of the song or video. Drag the sliding bar to the left to lower the volume before playing your first song or video. After something is playing, you can drag the slider to the right to increase the volume.

✦ **Shuffle:** Turns shuffle on and off. When on, songs from the current playlist are played in random order. When off, songs from the current playlist are played in the order they're listed. (You'll learn about playlists later in this chapter.)

✦ **Repeat:** Turns repeat on and off. When on, when Media Player reaches the end of the current playlist, it will start the playlist over.

There is also a line above the controls and below the main window area. This line is also on the Compact Mode version of the player. This is the seek line as shown in Figures 16-1 and 16-2. This line will be highlighted as a media file is played. Additionally, the line has a small slider control on it that shows the current status of the playing media. The farther to the right the control is, the farther into the media you are. You can actually click this control and drag it forward or backward to move forward or backward in the song or video.

Using Mini Mode in the Taskbar

Media Player 9 offers mini mode, where the Play controls rest on your Windows taskbar while the rest of Media Player stays hidden from view. To activate mini mode, follow these steps:

1. Right-click an empty area of the Windows taskbar (or the current time in the lower right corner of your screen) and choose Toolbars.

2. If the Windows Media Player option doesn't have a check mark next to it, click that option. If Windows Media Player is already selected (checked), press Esc to leave the setting unchanged.

The mini mode Play controls will only be visible when Windows Media Player is open but minimized. You can minimize the Media Player program window as you would any other program window — by clicking its Minimize button or by clicking its taskbar button until the window disappears from the desktop. After the window is minimized, you'll see the play controls in the taskbar (see Figure 16-4).

Figure 16-4: Play controls in the Windows taskbar in mini mode

If the taskbar is unlocked, you can move the play controls by dragging the handle just to their left. To get out of mini mode, click the tiny Restore button in the lower-right corner of the Play controls in the taskbar.

Tip If you don't see any dragging handles on your Windows taskbar, right-click the current time, and choose *Lock the Taskbar* to clear its check mark and unlock the taskbar.

Closing Windows Media Player

As with any other program, you can maximize, minimize, move, and size the Media Player program window. Like most programs, Windows Media Player also has a taskbar button when it's open. You can close Windows Media Player using any of the usual methods:

✦ Click the Close button in the upper-right corer of the Media Player program window.

✦ Choose File ➪ Exit from the Media Player menu bar if it is displayed.

✦ Right-click the Media Player title bar and choose Close.

✦ If Media Player is in the active window, press Alt+F4.

If Media Player is playing a song when you close it, the music stops, too. If you want to get Media Player off your desktop, but have it still play music, minimize its program window; don't close it.

We'll get back to Media Player in just a moment. Before we do, we need to talk about media files in general.

Using Your Music Folder

If you've been reading along in this book, you probably recall seeing a folder named Music in the Favorite Links area of Windows Explorer and within your personalized folders. There's also a folder named Public Music. Use Music for songs you want to keep to yourself (or if you're the only person who uses this computer). Use Public Music for songs you want to share with other people who use the same computer or other people in your local area network. To open your Music folder, use one of the following methods:

✦ Click the Start button and choose Music.

✦ Open your personal folder and double-click the Music folder's icon.

To get to the Public Music folder from your Music folder, in the Favorite Links area of Windows Explorer click Public ➪ Public Music. If your computer is new, both folders might be empty or nearly empty. But if you've already started building a media collection (a topic we'll discuss in Chapter 17), you'll likely see folders representing different artists (see Figure 16-5).

Figure 16-5: A sample Music folder that already contains music

If you double-click an artist's folder, like Newsboys, that folder will reveal albums and songs by that artist that you've copied to your Media Library, as in Figure 16-6.

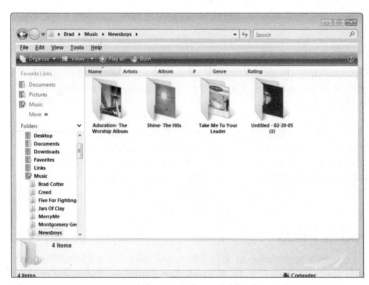

Figure 16-6: Contents of the Newsboys folder from Figure 16-5

If you double-click an album folder in Figure 16-6, you'll see an icon for each song on that album, as in Figure 16-7.

Figure 16-7: Contents of the Shine- The Hits folder from Figure 16-6

Depending on what you happen to be viewing at the moment, and whether or not you select and individual song, you'll see different options in the toolbar of Windows Explorer. The ones of interest now are summarized here:

✦ **Play:** Clicking this option will play the selected songs. You can select to use Windows Media Player or another media player if you've installed one.

✦ **Play All:** Clicking this option plays all the songs in the folder or plays all the selected songs or folders.

✦ **Burn:** Starts the process of creating a new custom audio CD from the selected songs or folders. See Chapter 17 for details on creating custom audio CDs.

Choosing the Play All (or Play) option would most likely open Windows Media Player to play the media files. But there's no guarantee that Media Player opens, because it depends on what type of file you're trying to play and what program is currently set as the default player for that file type. Let's start with the issue of file types that Windows Media can play.

Types of Media Files

Media files are documents and come in many formats. Windows Media Player can read a lot of file formats, but not all of them. For example, there are many video files on the Internet that are stored in the RAM and MOV formats, which Media Player can't read. You need to use RealOne (www.real.com) to read RAM files and Apple QuickTime (www.QuickTime.com) to play MOV files videos. But Windows Media Player can read all the media file types listed above Real Audio Movie and QuickTime Movie in Table 16-1.

Table 16-1
Types of Media Files

File Type	File Name Extensions	Description
Windows Media File	.asf, .asx, .dvr--ns, .wpl, .wm, .wmx, .wmd, .wmz	Various media types, often sent as streaming media across the Internet
Windows Media Audio	.wma, .wax	A preferred audio format for Windows Vista
Windows Media Video	.wmv, wvx	A preferred video format for Windows Vista
CD audio	.cda	Format used by music CDs played in stereos
Windows video file	.avi	General purpose video, sometimes compressed with DivX[1]
Wave sound	.wav	Best for tiny sound effects, bad for recorded music
Motion Pictures Experts Group	.mpeg, .mpg, mpe, .m1v, .mp2, .mpv2, .mp2v, .mpa	The most widely used format for video and DVD
MP3 audio	.mp3, .m3u	The most widely used format for storing recorded music
Musical Instrument Digital Interface (MIDI)	.mid, .midi, .rmi	Contains synthesized music only, cannot contain recorded sound
AIFF	.aif, .afc, .aff	General sound file
AU	.au, .snd	General sound file
RealAudio Movie	.ram	Cannot be played by Windows Media Player
QuickTime Movie	.mov	Cannot be played by Windows Media Player

[1] AVI files that are compressed with DivX might play sound, but no video. To play properly, you need to download the DivX codec or DivX Player from www.divx.com. See also www.divx.com/support/newbies.php.

If you're new to all of this, all those file types might be intimidating at first glance. But there are a couple of simple rules you can follow when given a choice of choosing one file format over another:

- ✦ **Music:** The MP3 and WMA formats are widely used and work great in Windows Vista and Media Player.

- ✦ **Video:** The MPEG and WMV formats are also widely used and also work great in Media Player.

So if you can remember those four main formats, MP3, MPEG, WMA, and WMV, you'll be ahead of the game in terms of knowing what to look for in media files.

> **Tip** File name extensions are visible only when the *Hide extensions for known file types* option in Folder Options is turned off. For details, see the section "Showing/Hiding File Name Extensions" in Chapter 6.

Searching Your Hard Disk for Your Media Files

Even if your computer is brand new, chances are there are a few sample media files you can play around with to learn. If you want to search your hard disk now to see the media files you already have, follow these steps:

1. Click the Start button and choose Search from the right side. This displays the search window as shown in Figure 16-8.

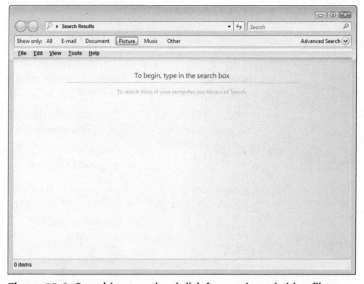

Figure 16-8: Searching your hard disk for music and video files

2. Click Music or Pictures in the Show only menu. If you want to search for Videos, then select All.

3. Enter * in the Search box. This is a wildcard that will look for everything. If you want to find Video files, enter ***.wmv** in the search box or enter ***.mpeg** depending on which video format you want to find.

4. If the search doesn't automatically start, then press the Enter key or click the Search button.

> **Tip** You can choose any drive or folder you want under the Advanced Search options. See Chapter 5 if you want to know more about searching.

The resulting search will include all files currently on your hard disk that contain the media type you indicated. There's more to a media file, though, than the file name and icon, as discussed next.

Media files that will play in Windows Media Player when you open them all have the document-icon look (the dog-eared sheet of typing paper) with Media Player's logo or a media logo on top, as in the example at left. If some other program, such as Music Match, is currently configured as your default media player, that program's icon will appear in place of Media Player's icon.

Opening a Media File

You open a media file in Explorer the same way you open any document. You can double-click the icon, in which case the file will open in the default player for the type of media file you double-clicked. You can also right-click the media file, choose Play or choose Open With and click the name of the program you want to play (or edit) the file with.

 Note   The default player is, simply, the program that opens automatically (by default) when you double-click a media file. If your media files open in some other program, you can close that program, right-click the same icon, and choose Open With ➪ Windows Media Player. Or make Windows Media Player the default for that type of file, as in the sidebar that follows.

When the media file starts playing, you can use the Play controls described earlier to control the volume of the sound, pause playback, rewind, and so forth. Use the Now Playing feature, described later in this chapter, to watch a video or a music visualization.

You're not limited to playing files currently on your computer's hard disk. You can play any standard music CD or DVD as well. You can also play sound and video clips available from the Web. We'll show some examples in the sections that follow.

Playing Music CDs

A music CD generally contains only music stored in the CDA format. That includes all CDs that you buy from a record store and play on a stereo or CD player. Playing a music CD is usually pretty simple:

 Caution   Playing a music CD is not the same as copying a music CD. When you play a music CD, you hear the music. But nothing gets copied from the CD to your computer's hard disk.

STEPS: Playing a Music CD

1. If you want to be able to see song titles, and you have a dial-up account, connect to the Internet so Media Player can download media information.

Make Media Player the Default for Music CDs

You can choose how your CD drive reacts when you insert a music CD into your CD drive. Click the Start button and choose Computer to open your Computer folder. In the Computer folder, right-click the icon for your CD drive (typically drive D:) and choose Open AutoPlay. In the AutoPlay dialog box that opens, select the Set AutoPlay defaults in Control Panel check box. This opens the Control Panel page for setting defaults for different media types as shown in the following figure.

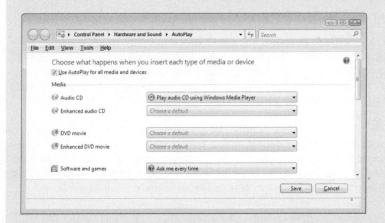

Pick the default for playing audio files for Audio CDs, and then click Save. After you've made the change, click the Save button in the dialog box. The next time you put a music CD into your computer's CD drive, Windows Media Player will open and start playing the CD.

Note   As discussed in the section "Where Media Information Comes From" in Chapter 17, you need to be online to get media information, such as song titles, from the Internet. That information isn't stored on most CDs.

2. Insert the music CD, label-side up, into your computer's CD drive, and wait a few seconds.

3. If you see a dialog box like the one in Figure 16-9, click Play audio CD using Windows Media Player, and click OK. Otherwise, ignore this step.

4. In Windows Media Player, click the Now Playing button in the Features taskbar.

5. Use the Play Controls in Media Player to adjust the volume, pause playback, mute the speakers, skip songs, and so forth.

Figure 16-9: Dialog box that might open when you insert a music CD into your CD drive.

After you have some music playing, you can learn about the Now Playing feature in Media Player.

Playing a Video

Video files come from all kinds of sources. Some are simply streaming video that comes from the Internet and you watch in Windows Media Player. As a rule, you can't save these as files. You can only watch them. Beyond streaming video, there are all sorts of videos stored in files and all sorts of ways to create them. People can e-mail them to you. People can send them to you on a CD or other disk. You can download videos (in files) from many web sites and file-sharing networks, such as Gnutella.

Tip   In Internet Explorer, the best and quickest way to download a video is usually not to open it at all, but rather to right-click and choose Save Target As. See Chapter 10 for details.

Icons for video files don't look much different from other icons. But if you're in Thumbnails view, MPEG and WMV movies will show the first frame of the video, as in the examples shown in Figure 16-10. To open a video, double-click its icon, or right-click its icon and choose Open With ➪ Windows Media Player.

Windows Media Player will open to play the video. Click the Now Playing button on the Media Player Features taskbar. You can use the Play controls, discussed earlier in this chapter, to adjust the volume, mute the speakers, pause, fast forward, and so forth. Use Now Playing features described later in this chapter to watch the video in Full Screen mode.

Tip   To avoid having your screen saver kick in and replace a playing movie, click the menu area under the Now Playing button (the little down-pointing arrow under the Now Playing words). From the menu that is displayed, select More Options. In the Options dialog box that is displayed, select the Player tab. Clear the Allow screen saver during playback check box and click OK.

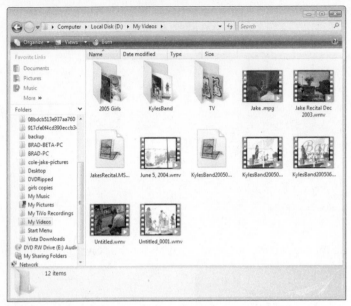

Figure 16-10: Sample icons for videos, in Explorer Thumbnails view

Watching a DVD

If your computer has a DVD drive, you can also watch DVDs with Windows Media Player. (You can't play a DVD in a CD drive.) DVDs on a computer play just as they do on a regular TV. To watch a DVD:

1. Insert a DVD disk, label-side up, into your computer's DVD drive, and wait for a few seconds.

2. If you see a dialog box like the example shown in Figure 16-11, click the Play DVD using Windows Media Player check box. Otherwise, skip this step.

3. Media Player should load and the movie should start playing. It will likely play in Full Screen mode. If you end up in Full Screen mode, you can click the Now Playing button on the Media Player Features taskbar so you can see the movie. Like a video file, a DVD plays in the large visual pane of Media Player, as in the example shown in Figure 16-12.

Use the Full Screen button or the Maximize/Restore Visual button, described in the next section, to choose your viewing.

Figure 16-11: Options like these may appear when you insert a DVD into your computer's DVD drive.

Figure 16-12: DVDs and videos play in the large pane of Now Playing.

Watching a VCD

A VCD (video CD) is similar to a DVD but contains less content or lower-quality content. Playing a VCD is similar to playing a DVD. When you insert the VCD into the computer, you are likely to see the AutoPlay menu as you did with a DVD. You can then select Play Video CD using Windows Media Player to play the VCD.

If the VCD doesn't do anything when you insert it into the CD drive, you'll need to give it a little kick from within Windows Media Player.

STEPS: Play a VCD

1. From Media Player, click the Library button. This displays your current library.

2. The item near the bottom of the menu on the left side should include your VCD. If the VCD indicates its contents, then the content name will be listed. If it does not, then something like Unknown Video CD will be listed. Click on this option to select it (or right-click and select Open).

3. The titles on the VCD should be displayed in the main library window. You can select any that you want to play.

Use the Play controls to control playback. Click the Now Playing button in the Features taskbar to watch the video.

Digital Media on the Web

The URGE button in Windows Media Player takes you to the URGE music store web site where you play music and video samples, buy music by the CD or song, and just play around in general. The first time you click URGE, you will be shown a licensing agreement and a notice that you need to download the store software. You will need to read the agreement and click the I Accept button to continue. This will start the download and setup of the Music Store software as shown in Figure 16-13.

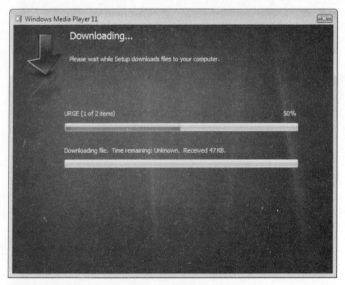

Figure 16-13: Downloading the URGE software

When the download completes, you will be asked whether you want to run the URGE software. Click Yes, and the install will complete. When the installation is completed, the program returns you to Windows Media Player. This time, however, when you click Urge — and subsequent times — the Urge page will be displayed.

If you click the down button below the URGE icon on the toolbar, a menu is displayed. From this menu, you can select the Browse all Online Stores option. Selecting this option presents you with stores you can choose from as shown in Figure 16-14. The content on this page is provided by the URGE site, so it may be different every time you come to this page.

Figure 16-14: Selecting an Online Store. You can filter the list of what is shown by clicking a Category on the left.

Note   After you select a different store from the Online Store, its icon might replace the URGE icon on the Media Player toolbar. You can get back to URGE if you want by clicking the down arrow to pull up the menu.

Using the online store, you can shop for media to download to your computer. Let me preface that with some warnings for newbies (beginners) who haven't done this sort of thing before:

✦ Digital media files are large and take time to cross the Internet. Don't expect much instant gratification here, especially if you're using a dial-up account. The progress indicator near the lower-left corner of Windows Media Player, shown at left, keeps you apprised of progress.

✦ When you see a link that offers a download in multiple speeds, dial-up users should always choose 56K. Broadband users can choose any speed.

✦ At any time, your web browser might pop open and cover up your Windows Media Player. You can use the taskbar buttons to switch back and forth between the two windows.

✦ When a video is playing, you might need to click Now Playing to see it. To return to the Web from there, click the Media Guide button. See "Using the Now Playing Feature," later in this chapter, for details.

✦ If you're looking for a Napster-type service, where things are free and anything goes, `WindowsMedia.com` isn't that place. Gnutella is, however. (See "Downloading Free Stuff from the Internet," later in this chapter.) If you want to see some free videos, check out `YouTube.com`.

As far as music and video go, things get a little more complicated when you start viewing and downloading from the Web. First, you need to be aware that there's a difference between *streaming media* and media files. Second, you need to understand digital licenses.

Streaming Media

There are two ways digital media is delivered over the Internet. One is *streaming*, which is like radio or TV. The music or video plays, but it's not saved in any format. It just plays, it's over, and that's it. Saving streaming media isn't an option, and that's kind of the whole point. If you don't want people making copies of your stuff, send it to them in streaming format so they can't save it.

Media files are things you *download* from the Internet and put on your hard disk. That's what *download* means: to copy a file from some other computer to your own computer. With downloading, you don't just watch once. You get to keep your own copy. But exactly what you can do with that copy depends on whether or not the file is protected, as discussed next.

Downloading Licensed Content

When you go through traditional web sites like URGE or the stores listed in the Online Store, downloading usually means buying. And what you get is the song or video, plus a *digital license*. The digital license enables you to keep a copy and play it on your computer, but only on your computer. You can't make copies to share with anyone else. That's why it's also called *protected content*.

How long you keep the license varies. If it's something you got for free, the license might expire after 30 days or whatever, at which point you can't use the file any more. If you purchase protected content, you'll more likely get to keep it forever. But still, you can't make copies or play it on any computer but the one it's on.

Whether or not you can copy protected content to a music CD or portable music player depends on the specific song you're downloading and from whom you're downloading it. Since this all happens on the Web, there's no way for me to tell you exactly what to expect. When you select a store from the Media Player's online stores, you will be transferred to that store on the Web. You can then use that site's features to obtain music, videos, or whatever other media it provides.

How to Download

Exactly how you purchase and download media depends on the web site you're using. The process is usually to add items to your shopping cart, pay for them, and start downloading. If you see a prompt asking you to run or save a media file, always click the Save button, as that's the only option that actually saves the file to your hard disk.

When you click the Save button, a Save As type dialog box opens. Use the standard techniques described in the section "Using the Save As Dialog Box" in Chapter 6 to navigate to your Music folder (or to any folder of your choosing), and save the file normally. Once the file is downloaded, you can open it as you would any other document.

Tip   When downloading files from legitimate companies doing business on the Web, you needn't be worried about viruses or worms. E-mail attachments and free stuff are the things you need to be concerned about.

Managing Digital Licenses

The digital licenses you get with protected media are critical. If you lose it, or accidentally delete it, you're out of luck. You won't be able to play the file ever again. For this reason, if you're going to be purchasing music online, you'll want to know what the licensing on the media is. You can check the licensing within Windows Media Player.

STEPS: Checking Digital Licenses

1. In Windows Media Player, go to the Library view by selecting the Library toolbar button.

2. Right-click the song or media file you want to check the digital rights for. Select Properties from the menu that is displayed.

3. In the Properties dialog box that is displayed, select the Media Usage Rights tab. This displays the rights for the selected song as shown in Figure 16-15.

4. Click OK to exit the dialog box.

Figure 16-15: The Media Usage Rights (Digital Rights) for a given song. This song can be freely shared.

Downloading Free Stuff from the Internet

There's nothing built into Windows Vista that enables you to download free music from the Internet. A few music stores are linked into Media Player, but each of those operates differently.

As to free downloads, you may have heard about the Gnutella network, which is a file-sharing service (also called a *peer-to-peer* or *p2p* network) on the Internet.

To use Gnutella, you need a *Gnutella client*, a program that enables you to share and download files from the Internet. There are several freebies around that you can download and start using right away, including LimeWire (www .LimeWire.com), Morpheus (www.Morpheus.com), iMesh (www.iMesh.com), and Kazaa (www.Kazaa.com).

Before you grab one of them, however, keep in mind that freeware (free software) often earns money through ad revenues. And it gets those revenues by displaying pop-ups on your screen. You can block the pop-ups. But they don't get blocked until they reach your computer, which means they're eating up bandwidth even though you don't see them. (*Eating up bandwidth* translates to *slowing everything down*.) So if you'd rather part with a few bucks than lose speed to pop-ups, consider purchasing a pop-up free program like LimeWire Pro (www.LimeWire.com).

Whatever program you get, you should learn to use it before you start downloading. In particular, you'll want to know what files you're sharing. It's illegal to share copyrighted music, so you want to know what files you're sharing at all times.

You'll need to know the folder that your downloads are being stored in. Ideally, you should configure the program to put all downloaded files in a Downloads folder, as discussed in Chapter 13. Nobody owns Gnutella; there's no censorship or monitoring. So there's no guarantee that what you downloaded is what you thought you downloaded. As for the no-censorship part, parents should be aware of that and consider blocking all adult material if your Gnutella client allows it.

When choosing an audio file to download, try to stick to MP3 and WMA formats, as you can add those to the Windows Media Player Media Library. The *bit rate* of a song is basically a measure of its quality. If you want to stick to CD quality or better, only download songs with bit rates of 128 Kbps or better.

When downloading video, try to stick with the WMV and MPEG formats. Other file formats can be *iffy*. Many shared video files in the AVI format are compressed using DivX. To play those, you need to download and install the DivX codec from www.DivX.com.

If you plan to add the song to the Windows Media Player Media Library, it would be best to move it to its permanent folder beforehand. Moving songs around after they're in Media Library can be *iffy* as well. Also, consider checking and correcting any media information attached to the file before adding the file to Windows Media Library. See "Media File Hidden Properties" in Chapter 17 for more information.

Finally, you'll need to choose the menu below the Library button and select Add to Library to have Windows look for newly downloaded files to add to your Media Library. Your Gnutella client won't update Windows Media Player's Media Library.

Good luck, and remember that the only places you're going to get information about the Gnutella client you chose are the Help within that program or the web site from which you downloaded the program.

Using the Now Playing Feature

When you have a song, video, or DVD playing in Media Player, you can use the Now Playing button in the Features taskbar to watch the video or a visualization of the music that's playing. The default screen within the Now Playing option is shown in Figure 16-16. As you can see, the Play controls at the bottom of the window are the same in all views. As usual, you can point to any button to see its screen tip.

In its basic form, the Now Playing page shows a movie or a visualization. Visualizations are graphics that beat to the music. You can expand what is shown in the Now Playing window by clicking on the menu under the Now Playing button and making a few choices.

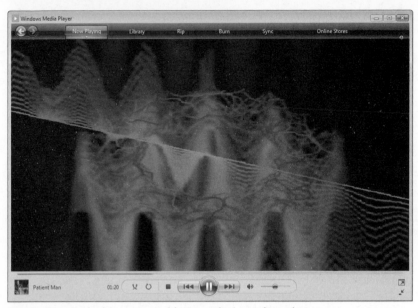

Figure 16-16: Playing a song with Now Playing selected

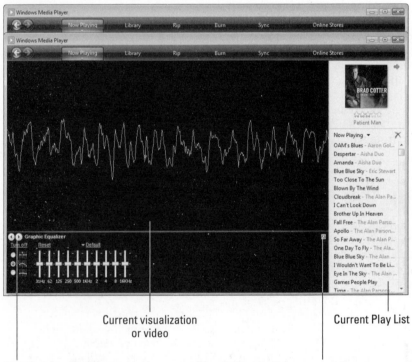

Current visualization
or video

Current Play List

Next/Previous Enhancement

Close button for Enhancement Pane

Figure 16-17: Tools available in the Now Playing feature of Windows Media Player

✦ **Playlist:** Shows album art and song titles from the current CD or playlist. If there are more songs then will fit on the screen, you can use the scroll bar at right. Double-click any song to play it, or right-click any song title for other options.

✦ **Visualization or Video:** If you're watching a video or movie, it appears in this large pane. If you're listening to music, a *visualization* plays here. A visualization is a pattern of shapes and colors that changes in response to changes in the music. You can right-click on a visualization to get a menu that enables you to change what visualization is being displayed.

✦ **Options:** Clicking the down arrow below the Media Player Now Playing toolbar button displays a menu of options that apply to the Now Playing feature you're in. They're all entirely optional and safe to play around with. Your options are:

- **Show List Pane:** This hides or list displays the Now Playing pane on the right side of the Now Playing window.

- **Enhancements:** Replaces the lower part of the visualization/video pane with sound and video enhancement tools, such as a graphic equalizer, color chooser, video settings, and other fun toys. To hide enhancements, click this button and click Show Enhancements (to clear the selection).

- **Visualizations:** Lets you choose a different visualization, turn off visualizations, or visit a web site where you can download more visualizations.

- **Plug-Ins:** Takes you to a web site where you can download plug-ins that extend the capabilities of Media Player 9. Things include audio special effects, DVD decoders (for watching DVDs in Media Player), MP3 creation tools (see Chapter 10), and more.

- **More Options:** Takes you to advanced configuration options for Media Player.

✦ **Full Screen On Off:** Click once to expand the visualization/video to show in Full Screen mode. You'll see some controls that fade away shortly. To get back to the Normal view, press any key on your keyboard, or move the mouse around a little. Then click the button again. (In Full Screen mode, the button's tooltip reads Exit Full Screen when you point to it.)

✦ **Playlist Options:** These are found in the Now Playing link at the top of the playlist. Not much offered when playing an audio CD. But when working with custom playlists, you may find these options useful for customizing the playlist without switching to the Media Library feature.

Radio Tuner and Premium Services

The URGE button was mentioned earlier. In addition to taking you to Online Stores, it also provides connections to radio stations. These radio stations, however, are also a premium service if accessed through URGE.

If you want to listen to the radio rather than to your own music, then click the Library button on the toolbar. On the left side, click on the URGE option to expand it. You will find a number of options displayed including Radio. I can't really tell you what you'll see when you click on the Radio button or any of the other premium media types under URGE. But things should be self-explanatory when you get there. When you get to the web site, you should be able to figure out what's going on just by reading the information presented on the web page that opens.

The Radio option takes you to a web site where you can listen to radio stations that broadcast over the Internet. (This doesn't work too well with dial-up Internet accounts.) On the page that opens, you'll be able to check out radio stations by category (for example, Top 40, Country, Rock) and search for radio stations by keyword.

Playing with Skins

Skins in Media Player are entirely optional and really exist only for amusement. Skins don't change what Media Player does. They just change the way it looks on the screen. To see available skins:

STEPS: Change Media Player's Appearance

1. If you haven't already done so, open Media Player and go to the Library view.

2. In the library view, show the classic menus by clicking the Layout Options button and selecting Show Classic Menus. You can also press Ctrl+M to display the menus. You can press the Alt key to get the menu to display temporarily.

3. From the menus you can select View ➪ Skin Chooser to display the Skin Chooser similar to what is shown in Figure 16-18.

4. If you find a skin you like, click the Apply Skin button.

 Note When you first open you the skin chooser, there may not be that many options on the left to pick from. Later in this chapter you'll see how you can download more skins.

Media Player instantly changes to the requested skin. Exactly how you use that skin depends on the skin. In most cases, you can figure out which control is which just by pointing to each one to see its name. To move the skin around on your desktop, point to some neutral area on the skin (not on a button or other control), hold down the left mouse button, and drag the skin around.

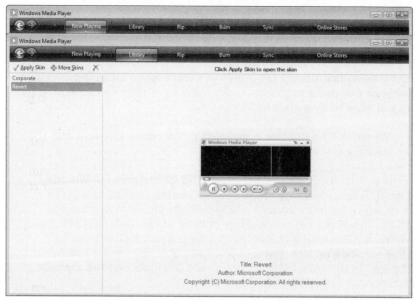

Figure 16-18: The Media Player Skin Chooser

To return to Full mode, use whichever of the following techniques is convenient and works with the current skin:

✦ Right-click the Skin and choose Switch to Full Mode.

✦ Point to buttons until you find one that switches to Full Mode, and click that button.

✦ Press Ctrl+1 (that's the number 1, not the letter l).

Downloading Skins

The skins that appear when you choose Skin Chooser are just some samples that come with Media Player 9. You can download other skins from the Microsoft web site. Here's how:

1. If Media Player is currently in a skin, switch to Full Mode.

2. Click the Skin Chooser button on the Media Player Features taskbar.

3. Click the More Skins button.

At the site, scroll through your options. There are several pages of skins to choose from, so don't limit yourself to the first page that opens. When you find a skin you like, click it. The standard File Download dialog box with the standard warnings opens. Anything you download from this site is sure to be safe, so you can just click the Open (or Yes) button to proceed. When the download is complete, you can click the Close button if you want to download more skins. If you want to apply the new skin immediately, click the View Now button.

Windows Media Center

In addition to Windows Media Player, some versions of Vista also include Windows Media Center. Windows Media Center is a much more comprehensive interface for using multimedia ranging from CDs to video including television. If you use your computer primarily for listening to or viewing music or videos, then you will want to consider the Media Center.

 Note Windows Media Center is included in the Home Premium and Ultimate versions of Windows Vista.

You can run it from the Start menu by selecting All Programs ➪ Windows Media Center. When you run Windows Media Center, you will change to a different interface than the normal Windows Vista interface as shown in Figure 16-19. The Media Center interface is more in line with something you could control with a remote control in that its primary features can be selected by scrolling up and down, or left and right. The simple interface makes it possible to control Media Center with a remote control, through your television, or even though an Xbox 360.

Figure 16-19: The interface to the Windows Media Center

Windows Media Center has a much nicer interface for working with your media. Additionally, it supports high definition and widescreen interfaces as well as the recording of television and more. When drilling down into the different media areas, you will generally get much more visual feedback. For example, Figure 16-20 shows the default page for music. As you can see, it isn't just a list of albums, but rather a scrollable list of the album covers that can easily be selected.

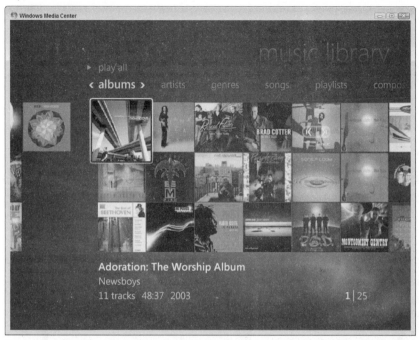

Figure 16-20: The Music Library view within Windows Media Center. You can see the albums I have on my machine.

An entire book could be written about using Windows Media Center. If you have a version of Windows Vista that has Windows Media Center, then run the program. You can then do the Express setup. There will be options to load your images, music, videos, and recorded television into the Media Center library. If you have a television card, there are also options for setting it up so that you can control recording television. If, however, you don't have a very powerful machine, then you might want to stick with the Media Player instead.

Summary

Whew! There's a load of information about music and videos for ya. Here's a quick recap of the main issues discussed in this chapter:

✦ Windows Media Player is a program that can play multimedia files (music and video).

✦ Music and video contents are stored in document files, just like text and pictures. Your Music folder is specifically designed to store music.

✦ A *music CD* is the type you buy in a music store and usually play in a stereo.

✦ You can play, copy, and create your own music CDs in Windows Media Player.

✦ You can download music and video from the Internet, using the URGE button, a pay service like `WindowsMedia.com` or a Gnutella client like LimeWire.

✦ Skins are an optional feature of Windows Media Player that enable you to change the appearance of the program, just for fun.

Managing Music, Making CDs

Windows Media Player is available on the versions of Windows Vista. Windows Media Player can do more than play music, video, and DVDs. You can use Windows Media Player to build up and maintain a collection of media files. For example, let's say that you have some favorite CDs you want to protect. You can copy all the songs from those CDs to your computer's hard disk and then put the original CDs you copy someplace safe, where they won't be used or damaged.

Then you can play the music directly from your computer. Or you can create your own custom audio CDs and use those for day-to-day play in your home stereo, car, or portable player. If you buy blank CD-R disks in quantities, you can get them for about 25 cents apiece (no big deal if you scratch up or lose one of those). Plus, the CDs you create can contain any combination of songs you like. You don't have to just make an exact copy of a given CD. You can make party CDs, mellow CDs, or whatever you like.

Media File Hidden Properties

Before we get to the specifics of building a Media Library, burning CDs, and such, a little background will help make an otherwise confusing experience a little more palatable. The first thing you need to remember is that all media files are document files. Media files stored in MP3, MPEG, WMA, and WMV format all have some *Summary properties* (also called *metadata*), which are very useful for cataloging and managing music and video. Some of those summary properties contain *media information*, such as the artist, title, and genre of a song.

Normally, you don't see the media information, because the summary properties are rarely displayed on the screen. But every media file of the types mentioned has summary properties. Here's how you get to them, assuming you're currently looking at the icon for a media file:

1. Right-click the file's icon and choose Properties.

2. In the Properties dialog box that opens, click the Details tab. This tab provides you with a listing of the additional information stored as shown in Figure 17-1. Depending on what you are viewing, you may have to scroll to see all of the different items.

Figure 17-1: A media file's Detail properties

You can actually add or change much of the information being presented. Different types of files will have different properties. As far as Windows Media Player is concerned, the main properties that form the media information are as follows:

✦ **Title:** The title of the song or video contained within the file.

✦ **Artist:** The musicians who perform the song (audio only).

✦ **Album:** The title of the album on which the song is published (audio only).

✦ **Genre:** General category such as Rock, Disco, Jazz, or Classical (for audio).

✦ **Rating:** The rating you give the music from one stars to five stars.

✦ **Author:** The person who created the video (video only).

That media information isn't hidden at all in Media Player. In fact, it's all in plain view when you're viewing your Media Library, as in the example shown in Figure 17-2. Note the column headings Title, Rating, Artist, Album, and Genre, each providing media information from a file's Summary properties.

Figure 17-2: Column headings in Media Player show media information from media files on a hard disk.

 Tip   In Windows Explorer, you can use Details view and then view the properties of a selected item to view media information. For more information, see the section "The Details View" in Chapter 5.

As you'll learn later in this chapter, you can use all that media information to sort, search, group, and categorize all your media files. But before we get to that, we need to talk about where media information comes from.

Where Media Information Comes From

You might think that media information comes straight from the CD you copied. But it doesn't really work that way with music CDs. (Remember, we're using the term *music CD* to refer to the type of CD you buy in the music store and play in a regular stereo or CD player.) Although the CD certainly contains all the music on the album, the only text on the CD is the artist and album name (often referred to as the CD's *tag* or *tag information*).

When you first insert a music CD into your computer, Media Player doesn't know what songs are on the CD. So instead of song titles, it may just show generic names like Track 1 for the first song, Track 2 for the second song, and so forth. However, if you're online when you insert the CD, and wait a few seconds, the song titles will magically appear, as you saw in Chapter 16.

What causes this bit of magic is a thing called the Compact Disk Data Base (CDDB). This is an enormous database on the Internet that has the name of every song title on just about every CD ever recorded by the music industry. While the CD you inserted doesn't contain song titles, it does contain just enough information for Media Player to find the CD in the CDDB and display its song titles. (Of course, this can happen only while you're online, because the database is on the Internet.)

Media Player might not be able to get media information for a given song or album for several reasons. If you're not online when you insert a CD, you will certainly prevent media information from appearing. However, it's also possible that the album just doesn't exist in the CDDB. Or, if you're working with a single song you downloaded from the Internet, the song might not contain enough information for the CDDB to accurately identify it. Also, the Media Player can only update songs stored in the WMA or MP3 format.

Finally, there are also some settings in Media Player that determine to what extent Media Player can look for information on the CDDB, so you need to be aware of those settings and make selections according to what you want done, as described next.

Getting Media Player to Fill in the Blanks

If you want Windows Media Player to be able to find media information on the Internet, you might need to make some selections in the Media Player Options dialog box. Here's how:

1. If you haven't already done so, start Windows Media Player. Then choose the menu under the Library button and select More Options.

2. In the Options dialog box that opens, click the Library tab to see the options shown in Figure 17-3.

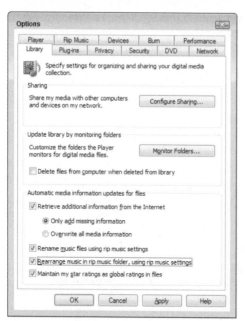

Figure 17-3: Library tab in the Media Player
Options dialog box

As you can see, you have several options for grabbing song titles and other
media information from the Internet. Here's what each option offers:

✦ **Monitor Folders:** Lets you choose which folders contain music that
should be watched for new media files. By default, Media Player monitors only your Music folder (which includes all subfolders within
Music). If you want to keep track of new media files, put them in
Music. Or, you can adjust some of the Monitor Folder settings.
Clicking the Monitor Folders button will bring up the Add to Library
dialog with additional options you might want to use. Click the
Advanced button to fully expand the dialog box. This gives you the
following options:

• **Add:** Add a new folder to be monitored. When new media files
are added to this new folder, they will be added to your Library.

• **Remove:** This will remove the selected folder from those that are
monitored. If a new media item is added to this folder after it has
been removed, then the item will not be automatically added to
the Library.

- **Add files previously deleted from library:** If a file has been removed from the library, then if this is not checked, it will not be added back to the library even if the folder it is in is monitored.

- **Skip files smaller than:** Lets you set a cut-off point for adding files to your Media Library. The default settings of 100 and 500 are sufficient to keep out small sound effects and tiny video clips.

✦ **Delete files from your computer when deleted from library:** As a rule, you want to leave this unselected. If you select this, deleting items from your Library will also delete the corresponding media file from your hard disk.

✦ **Retrieve additional information from the Internet:** This item must be selected if you want Media Player to be able to find media information for songs. When you select it, you can choose from the following options to determine how and when media information is updated using the options here.

- **Only add missing information:** If selected, Media Player will fill in blank media information only; it will not change existing media information. Use this option if you manually change media information and don't want Media Player to replace your manual changes.

- **Overwrite all media information:** Choose this option if you're willing to allow Media Player to fill in missing information and also to replace existing information. If you don't want Media Player to change information you've manually entered into a song's properties, clear this option.

- **Rename music files using rip music settings:** If selected, this option ensures that any song whose media information is changed will cause Media Player to rename the song accordingly.

- **Rearrange music in rip music folder using rip music settings:** If selected, this option ensures that any song whose media information is changed will cause Media Player to recategorize the song accordingly.

- **Maintain my star ratings as global ratings in files:** If this option is selected, then any star ratings you give music will be maintained along with the music file whether in the library or not.

If in doubt about how to choose settings in the dialog box, just go with the default settings shown in Figure 17-3. Choosing those options alone isn't sufficient to guarantee you'll get all the benefits of the CDDB. You also have to adjust your Media Player privacy and security settings as described next.

Media Player Privacy Settings

Clicking the Privacy tab in the Media Player Options dialog box reveals some options that determine how much information Media Player transmits across the Internet. If you want Media Player to be able to get media information online, you should select the first four options, as shown in Figure 17-4. Other settings on that tab aren't as critical. For detailed information on privacy settings, click the Read the privacy statement online link near the top of the dialog box.

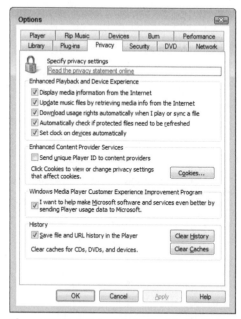

Figure 17-4: Privacy tab in the Media Player Options dialog box

After making your selections in the Options dialog box, click its OK button. You don't need to go through that rigmarole every time you want to copy CDs. Just once is sufficient.

Copying Music CDs to Your Media Library

A good source for music for your Media Library is the CDs you already own, as well as any you purchase in the future. If you record at the highest quality, you can store about 200 songs per gigabyte. Dollar-wise, a gigabyte (GB) is usually less than a dollar's worth of hard-disk space. How much hard disk space you're willing to use for music is entirely up to you. But given how inexpensive hard disk space is these days, even using 10GB to store 2,000 songs is no big deal.

Tip   If you don't know how much hard disk space you have available, open Computer. The amount of free space should be displayed under any available drives. If not shown, you can right-click the icon for your hard drive (C:), and choose Properties. See the section "Discovering How Much Hard Disk Space You Have" in Chapter 21 for more information.

It's not really possible to run out of disk space. No matter how much you use, you can always add more. For example, you can probably get a 100GB drive for about eighty bucks. And that drive has enough room to store about 20,000 high-quality songs.

Tip   If you just want to copy a music CD to a blank CD, it's not necessary to use Windows Media Player. You use Windows Media Library only when you want to create a collection of digital media on your computer's hard disk.

Preparing to Copy Music

Before you haul off and *rip* a CD (nerd slang for *copy the contents of a CD to your hard disk*), you'll want to choose some options by following these steps:

1. If Windows Media Player isn't open, go ahead and open it.

2. Choose the menu under the Library button and select More Options.

3. In the Options dialog box that opens, click the Rip Music tab to see the options shown in Figure 17-5.

4. Make your selections in the dialog box, using the sections that follow as your guide; click OK.

Figure 17-5: The Rip Music tab in the Media Player Options dialog box

Choosing a Location and Name for Songs

By default, all songs you copy from a CD will be placed in your Music folder. If you want to change this behavior, click the Change button in the Rip Music tab of the Media Player Options dialog box. You can then navigate to the folder you want to use. For example, if several people have user accounts on this computer, you might want to use Public Music instead. That way, everyone will be able to play the music from his or her user account or computer.

To choose your Public Music folder, click the Change button; then click Public ⇨ Public Music. Click the OK button in the Browse For Folder dialog box. The folder name will likely be something like C:\Users\Public\Music.

If you do change the folder, and want to make sure the files' media information is updated automatically, make sure you add the folder you selected to the monitored folders on the Media Library tab, as discussed under "Getting Media Player to Fill in the Blanks," earlier in this chapter.

By default, files you copy from music CDs will be named using just the track number and song title. For example, if the first song is titled *Smooth*, its file name will be *01 Smooth* on your hard disk. To change that, click the File Name button to open the File Name Options dialog box. You'll see a list of media information details such as Song title, Artist, and Album, which you can use to define the file name of each song you copy.

You can use any combination of the details listed to form each song's file name. Use the Separator option to choose a character to separate portions of names. To change the order of details, click any name to select it. Then click the Move Up or Move Down button to move it within the list.

For example, let's say you want to name each song in the format *song title-artist-album*. For example, if you copy the song titled *Smooth* from Santana's Supernatural album, its file name on your hard disk will be *Smooth-Santana-Supernatural*. To meet that goal, select only the details you want to include in the file name. Then put them in the order you want them to appear, and choose – (dash) as the separator, as in Figure 17-6. Click OK after making your selections.

Figure 17-6: The File Name Options dialog box

Choosing a File Format

Under Rip settings on the Rip Music tab, the Format drop-down list enables you to choose which format you prefer to use among the following:

✦ **Windows Media Audio:** Songs are copied to Windows Media Audio (WMA) format files and compressed to conserve disk space. You can choose the amount of compression using the Audio Quality slider in the same dialog box.

✦ **Windows Media Audio Pro:** Similar to the Windows Media Audio files except that the pro version has a more efficient format intended to create music files to be used where there is little storage space, such as phones.

✦ **Windows Media Audio (Variable Bit Rate):** Same as the preceding format, but the amount of compression varies with the complexity of the information being stored. However, the usual result is a better-quality recording and smaller file.

✦ **Windows Media Audio Lossless:** Same as the preceding format, but files are not compressed at all. The copied file's audio quality is the same as that on the original CD. The files are also huge. Files in this format are not widely supported and are generally used only by audiophiles and professionals. Files in this format can also be used to create High-Performance Media Access Technology (HighMAT CDs; see www.HighMAT.com for more information).

Rippin' MP3s

More current stereos and CD players can play MP3 files directly. The advantage of using MP3 formatted files is that rather than putting 80 minutes of music on a CD, you can put nearly 12 hours of music on one CD. Additionally, you don't have to use Media Players to format and create a CD that can play MP3s. Instead, you can simply gather a bunch of MP3 songs and copy them directly to a CD-R using the standard CD-copying techniques described in Chapter 21.

✦ **WAV (Lossless):** This format is generally for small sound files and recordings. It is not recommended that you use this format for standard music.

✦ **MP3:** This format has become a standard for digital players. The copied file's audio quality is not necessarily as good as the original CD; however, the files sizes can be small in comparison.

Copy Protect Music

If you choose this option on the Rip Music tab, you'll be able to play only copied music on the current computer. If you copy the song to another computer or try to play it on another computer, it won't play. This can be a big disadvantage if you have more than one computer. The purpose of the option, though, is to protect you from accidentally breaking any laws by sharing copyrighted music.

Not that it's easy to share copyrighted music. It's not like anyone can just come off the Internet and help themselves to your files. To share music on the Internet, you need to jump through quite a few hoops. So if you're not worried about accidentally sharing copyrighted material over the Internet, you can leave this option turned off.

 Note The Copy Protect Music option will be protected on formats that don't support copy protection. This includes WAV and MP3 formats.

Rip CD when Inserted

If selected, this option tells Windows Media Player, "As soon as you see a music CD in the CD drive, just start copying it." You can use this to copy several CDs in rapid succession. If you select the Eject option described next, it'll be like factory work. You insert a CD, wait for it to eject, put in the next CD, wait for it to eject, and so on, for as long as you can stand it. (Of course, you can use your computer for other things during that time, although I wouldn't recommend actually playing any CDs while copying them, as that might give Media Player too much to do and slow things down.)

With this option you have the ability to customize it further. If you want to limit when CDs are copied, but still have it happen automatically, you can choose the Only when in the Rip tab. This means that CDs will only be automatically copied when you have Media Player open and have clicked the Ripped toolbar button (the toolbar in Media Player, not the Rip Music tab in the Options dialog box).

Eject CD when Ripping Is Completed

If selected, this tells Media Player to eject the CD from the drive when it's finished copying. If you're near the computer when that happens, you can hear it. So you'll know as soon as the CD is ready.

Audio Quality

The Audio quality slider enables you fine-tune the format you selected from the drop-down list (unless you chose the Lossless quality, in which case no compression is allowed). The basic rule is that the higher the quality, the larger the file. If hard disk space is not an issue, go for the highest quality, as shown in Figure 17-5. Why quibble over a few megabytes more? Treat my ears to the best. (Not Lossless though, as that's a difficult format to work with.) Feel free to choose whatever quality you want.

 Tip   If you want more information on the formats — such as comparisons between some of the different types — then click the Compare formats online link. You'll need to be connected to the Internet for this link to work.

Digital or Analog?

Some CD drives and sound cards enable you to copy and create digital music CDs, while others support only analog. What your particular computer offers depends on your computer's CD drive, sound card, and a couple of little cables that connect the two inside your computer. Quality-wise, it really doesn't seem to matter much if you use digital or analog; it'll probably sound the same either way. But if you at least want to know what your options are, follow these steps:

1. If you're still in the Media Player Options dialog box, click the Devices tab. Otherwise, click the Library button and select More Options from the menu; then click the Devices tab.

2. Click the icon that represents the CD drive you use to copy music; then click the Properties button. The Properties dialog box for that drive opens (see Figure 17-7).

3. To copy in Digital, select Digital under the Copy option. You can also choose Error Correction, which allows Media Player to correct any flaws in the CDs (such as crackles and pops caused by scratches) to be corrected.

4. Click OK after making your selections.

Figure 17-7: The Properties dialog box for a sample drive

All the settings we've described up to now need only be set once. They will then be applied to all CDs you copy in the future. Just make sure you click OK in any open dialog boxes to save your settings and close the dialog boxes before copying your first CD.

Copying a Music CD

With all your settings in place, you're ready to start copying music CDs to your hard disk. The procedure is pretty straightforward:

1. If you have a dial-up modem, make sure you're online (so Media Player can get media information from the Internet).

2. Insert the CD you want to copy into your CD drive.

3. If you see a message asking what you want to do with the CD, you have two choices. If you want to start copying right away, click Rip music from CD using Windows Media Player; then click OK. If you want a moment to choose specific songs to play, click Play audio CD in Windows Media Player; then click OK. If nothing happens after you insert the CD, start Windows Media Player yourself from the All Programs menu or Quick Launch toolbar.

Note If some program other than Windows Media Player opens in Step 3, close that program and start Windows Media Player from your All Programs menu.

4. On the Windows Media Player features taskbar, click the Rip button.

5. If song titles don't appear right away, wait a few seconds. It can take a while with a dial-up account.

Tip   If the wrong titles appear, or no titles appear, you can manually change them after they are copied. If you want to change any media information before copying, use the techniques described in the section "Editing Media Information in Media Library," later in this chapter, to make your changes.

6. If you can hear the music playing, you can click the Stop button in the Play controls before copying. The CD will copy faster and more reliably if the drive doesn't have to worry about playing at normal speed while trying to copy at a higher speed.

7. Make sure that all songs you want to copy have a check mark next to them (see Figure 17-8). Clear the checkmark for any songs you don't want to copy. You can select the check box next to the Album column heading to select all of the songs on an album, or to clear all songs if they are currently all selected.

Figure 17-8: Ready-to-copy songs from a music CD

8. Click the Start Rip button and wait.

As each song is being copied, the Copy Status column will keep you apprised of progress. When all songs show *Ripped to Library* in the Copy Status column, the CD has been copied. If you set up Media Player to eject automatically, the CD will eject, and the main pane in Windows Media Player will go blank.

Otherwise, you can eject the CD yourself. You won't need to play the original CD anymore. Keep it as a pristine backup in case you ever accidentally lose the copy that's now on your hard disk.

Finding Copied Songs

You'll find the songs you copied from a CD in two places:

✦ In your Music folder (or whatever folder you chose as the location for copied media), as discussed in the section "Using Your Music Folder" in Chapter 16.

✦ In the Windows Media Player Media Library, which we'll discuss next.

You may want to copy several CDs before you start exploring Media Library, as it's a little easier to understand why it's valuable once you get a real collection of songs started. When you find a song, you can double-click it to play it. There's no need to put the original CD back in the drive.

Using Your Media Library

The Media Library button on the Media Player features taskbar takes you to your collection of songs. The examples you'll see here are from my own collection of nearly 5,000 songs. It'll take a while to make your own media collection that large. But you can better appreciate Media Library's value when there are lots of songs to manage. So I'll use that large collection as an example.

Keeping Your Media Library Up-to-Date

Songs you copy from CD using Windows Media Player are added to your Media Library automatically. Songs you download from file-sharing networks and songs you copy using other means aren't necessarily added to Media Library by default unless you store them in folders that you've identified for Media Player to use. To ensure that Media Library contains all the media currently on your hard disk, follow these steps:

 Tip The first time you use Media Player or Media Library, it may prompt you to do this automatically. Whether you do that or not, you can perform the following procedure at any time to add any songs that seem to be missing from your Media Library.

1. If you haven't already done so, open Windows Media Player.

2. From the Library button's menu, choose Add to Library. The Add to Library dialog box opens.

3. Click the Advanced Options tab to expand the dialog box as shown in Figure 17-9.

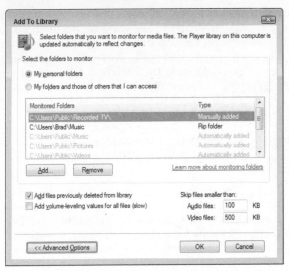

Figure 17-9: About to bring Media Library up to date

4. Make your selections from the dialog box. You can use the Add button to select additional folders. These folders will then be automatically checked for new media. If you want to search your entire hard disk for media files, then select the Add button, followed by Computer ⇨ Local Disk (C:), and then click the OK button.

5. After you've added the folders you want, click the OK button on the Add to Library dialog box. This starts the search for media (see Figure 17-10).

Figure 17-10: Adding additional media files to the library by searching the computer

6. Click the Close button when the search has completed.

Now when you view your Media Library, as discussed next, it should include all the media files from your hard disk.

Managing Your Media Collection

Whenever you want to work with your media collection, click the Library button on the Media Player taskbar. The screen splits into two or three panes. On the left are categories and on the right or in the middle are individual songs. If there is a third pane, it will be the list pane. You can turn on and off the list pane by clicking the Layout Options icon and selecting Show List Pane or Hide List Pane respectively.

The songs that appear in the right pane depend on the category you click. For example, if you click on Songs within the Library section, then the right pane will list every song in your collection.

When items within the library selection are selected in the left pane, you can sort songs by Title, Length, Rating, Artist, Album, or any other column heading. Just click the appropriate column heading once to sort into ascending order (A-Z or smallest to largest). You can also drag column headings left and right to arrange the columns to your liking.

Cross-Reference   See the section "Working with Columns" in Chapter 5 for more information on moving, sizing, and arranging items with columns.

There are several different categories within Library that you can select. In most cases, the list of songs will be displayed sorted by the option you pick. If the type you pick could have subsections then, you can click an item to drill into the choice. For example, in Figure 17-11, you can see the Album view.

Figure 17-11: The Media Player showing Albums on my computer

Tip   To widen or narrow the panes, drag the narrow bar that separates the two panes to the left or right.

Double-clicking an album such as American Town by Five for Fighting in Figure 17-11, displays all the songs on that album. So if, for example, you want to see songs only from The Posies album in the right pane, click that album cover or title.

Similarly, if you want to see the different genre of music on your computer, then click the Genre option in the left pane under Library. This will show your genre similar to Figure 17-12, only with your music.

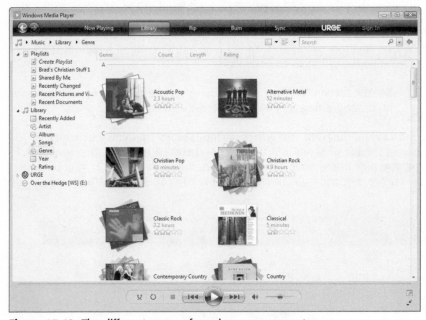

Figure 17-12: The different genre of music on my computer

You can then double-click on any genre to show a list of the albums and songs within it.

If you want to play an entire category of songs, right-click the category name and choose Play. To watch a visualization of the music, click the Now Playing tab.

Changing How You See Things

You might have noticed that the views of music that I've shown have been a mixture of album covers and song titles. Just like with Windows Explorer, you can change the view with the library. You do this by clicking the View Options button to the left of the search box. This enables you to choose from several display options:

✦ **Icon:** This option displays a cover icon with minimal additional information below.

✦ **Tile:** This option displays a cover icon with additional information to the right such as title, artist, genre, and rating. Figure 17-12 was using the Tile view.

✦ **Expanded Tile:** This view is like the Tile view with the addition of the list of songs being displayed. Figure 17-3 was using the Expanded Tile view.

✦ **Details:** This option does not display the cover art, but instead lists much more information about each item.

Depending on what you select, you may not have all of the different view options. For example, if you select the Song category, you will not have an Icon or Tile view.

Special Views

There are a couple of special views within the Library as well. If you click Library in the Navigation pane (the left side), then you will see something similar to Figure 17-13.

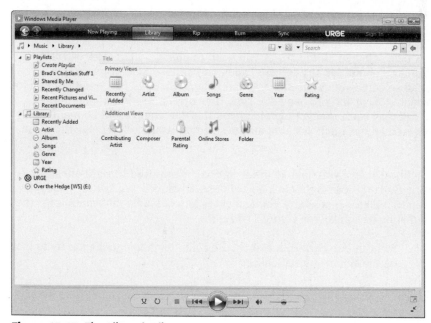

Figure 17-13: The Library's Library

The Library option only has an Icon view. The icons you can view are categorized into the Primary Views and Additional Views. The Primary Views are icons that lead to the same place as the categories under Library in the left navigation menu. Double-clicking one of them is the same as clicking the same option in the left pane.

The Additional Views provide some additional views that you can use to navigate your library. If the information is known, then these categories can be great ways to view your library. If the information isn't known, then your library will simply be lumped into a single Unknown category. Some of the available views include Parental Ratings, music you've gotten from online stores, a folder view showing what folders your music is stored in, and more.

Editing Media Information in Media Library

There's no guarantee that Media Player will be able to find media information for every song you copy or download to your PC. Sometimes you just have to go in there and manually type the correct information. But that's easy to do. When you see something incorrect in Library, just right-click the incorrect information, choose Edit, type the correct information, and press Enter.

If you want to make the same change to several songs, it's not necessary to do them one at a time. To make the same change to several song titles, simply select all of the songs, click the first song title in the list. Then press Shift+End, or hold down the Shift key and click the last item in the list, so all the titles are selected. Optionally, you can click the first song you want to change; then hold down the Ctrl key as you click other songs for which you want to make the same change.

After you've selected all the songs you want to change, right-click within the appropriate column for any selected song and choose Edit. For example, to assign all selected songs the same Artist name, right-click the Artist column for any selected song and choose Edit. Type the correct information and press Enter. You may see a dialog box telling you that the change will be made to all the selected songs. Click Yes, and all the selected songs will receive the same change.

When editing songs, you have another option, as opposed to right-clicking and choosing Edit. You can right-click and choose Advanced Tag Editor. That will take you to a dialog box where you can enter lots of media information for the selected song or songs (see Figure 17-14).

Tip   You can also right-click and choose Find Album Information to try to look up the album yourself online.

Figure 17-14: The advanced Tag Editor where you can change lots of settings on individual songs

Creating Custom Playlists

Custom playlists are a great way to organize your music by mood or style or favorite artist or whatever tickles your fancy. You can create playlists of any length to play on your computer. For example, you can put 12 hours or more worth of music into a single playlist and just let it play all day long.

Playlists are also a great way to create custom audio CDs. Choose any combination of songs up to 74 or 80 minutes in length (depending on which type of CD you plan to burn to), and just copy the playlist to a CD. You can then play that CD in any stereo or CD player.

Creating a custom playlist is pretty easy. First, follow these steps to create a new, blank playlist:

1. In Windows Media Player, click the Library button to go to the Library view. Click the Library button in the toolbar again to display its menu.

2. Click Create Playlist. Alternatively, you can simply press Ctrl+N to create a new playlist. The List pane is displayed on the right side of Media center and an untitled playlist is created and shown (see Figure 17-15).

Figure 17-15: Creating an empty playlist

3. In the list pane, the new playlist's name, Untitled Playlist, is highlighted so you can replace it with whatever you want to name this
   playlist. (I'm going to create a playlist named Rocking Holy Rollers
   CD for this example.)

4. Press Enter.

To see your new playlist name, click the arrow sign next to Playlists in Media
Library's left pane. When you click the playlist name, its contents appear in
the right pane. Initially, a new playlist will be empty.

 Note You can also create a new playlist by clicking the *Create Playlist* option
within the Playlist section of the Library Navigation pane on the left. This
will let you name the new playlist within the Navigation pane instead of the
List pane on the right. The end result is the same.

To add songs to your playlist, go back to your Artist, Title, Genre, and other categories, and click any name that will get you to the songs you want to use. For
example, for the Rocking Holy Rollers CD, you might start off by clicking the
Christian Rock genre to see what Holy Rolling songs you can get from there.

When you get to a song you want to add to your playlist, right-click its title in
the main pane and choose Add to followed by the name of the playlist you
want to add it to. If a playlist is currently selected, you will have an option to
add to it on the main menu as well as shown in Figure 17-16. If the List pane is
open, then you will see the song added to it on the right. When you are done
adding songs, click the Save Playlist button to save your playlist.

Figure 17-16: Adding a song to a playlist

If the purpose of this playlist is to burn a custom audio CD, you'll want to get about 73 to 79 minutes worth of music into your playlist, so as not to add more than the CD can handle.

It is worth noting that you can edit a playlist in the middle pane or the list pane on the right. To add songs, change order, and do most editing, you will want to edit the playlist in the List pane. You can move a playlist to the list pane by selecting it from the Playlist menu on the left navigation menu and then clicking the Edit in List Pane button at the bottom of the display in the middle pane.

To arrange songs in your playlist, just drag them up and down in the list of songs. That is, point to any song title and hold down the left mouse button while moving the mouse pointer up or down the list. Release the mouse button to drop the song back into the list at the current location.

When you are done editing the playlist in the List pane, you can click the X button next to the playlist name to close the playlist. Make sure to remember to save the list by clicking the Save Playlist button.

Creating Playlists Automatically

The preceding technique is just one way to create a playlist. You can also create playlists automatically by specifying *criteria* that define songs that need to be added to the playlist. The criterion could be a specific genre, artist, or whatever. You can even mix and match criteria. Here's how you create an Auto Playlist:

1. In Windows Media Player, click the Library button in the features taskbar to make the library view active.

2. Right-click Playlist in the left Navigation pane. This presents a menu of options.

3. Select Create Auto Playlist.

4. In the Auto Playlist name text box, type a name for this playlist.

5. Click the first + sign; then choose a criterion, such as Artist, Genre, or whatever.

6. Click right next to the new entry (where it says "click to set").

7. Repeat steps 4–5 to add multiple criteria.

8. Optionally, you can choose options next to the last two + signs to further restrict or expand the criteria. Figure 17-17 shows criteria specified for a new Auto Playlist named New Country, which contains songs from the Country genre that have been added to the library within the last 30 days.

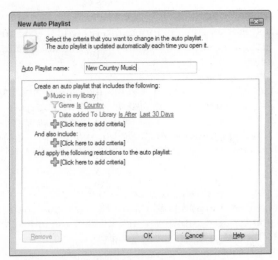

Figure 17-17: Defining a new Auto Playlist named New Country

9. Click the OK button.

Windows Media Player creates the playlist, highlighting its name in the left column. If you want to make changes to your Auto Playlist, you can right-click its name and choose Edit. Then change the criteria for that playlist and click OK.

To get rid of a sample Auto Playlist, right-click it and choose Delete. If a dialog box opens asking what you want to do, choose *Delete from Library only* in the dialog box that opens (if one does) and click OK.

If you're already playing songs in a playlist, you can temporarily add a song to that playlist while it's playing. As you're navigating the Library looking at songs, right-click any song title and choose Add to ➪ Now Playing. When you go back to Now Playing, you'll see all the songs you've added at the bottom of the playlist on the right side of the Now Playing window.

Creating a Custom Audio CD

Before you create a custom audio CD, make sure you understand the difference between different media types. This topic is discussed in some detail in Chapter 21. But as far as creating CDs to play is concerned, you need to be aware that there are three different types of blank CDs to which you can write data:

- ✦ **Audio CD-R (80 minutes):** Store up to 80 minutes of music on a single CD that can be played on any computer or stereo.

- ✦ **Data CD-RW (74 minutes):** Store up to 74 minutes of music on a single CD that can be played on any computer or stereo.

- ✦ **CD-RW:** Can be played only on computers with CD-RW drives and on the rare stereo that has the ability to read this type of CD. (Very few stereos can read CD-RW disks!)

For maximum flexibility, you'll want to stick with CD-R disks. Be aware that CD-Rs are WORM (Write Once, Read Many), which means that as soon as you burn *anything* to that disk, even if it's just one song, that's it. You cannot add songs later or change the contents of the CD in any way. You can't undo burning a log to the CD; and you can't undo burning CD-R either! So make sure you gather up 70 to 80 minutes of songs to copy before you even begin the process. Making a custom playlist first, as described previously, is a good way to approach the process.

STEPS: Create a Custom CD from a Playlist

1. Insert a blank CD-R into your CD drive, and wait a few seconds.

2. If you see a dialog box asking what you want to do with the blank CD, choose Burn an audio CD using Windows Media Player, and click OK. Then skip to Step 4.

 Caution Not all CD drives can burn CD-Rs. If you have any problems burning CDs, first make sure you have a CD-R drive installed on your computer!

3. If Windows Media Player isn't already open, open it. Click the Burn button on the Media Player features taskbar.

4. In the navigation pane on the left side of Media Player, right-click the name of the playlist you want to burn.

5. From the menu that is displayed, select Add to *burn list*. This adds the playlist to the burn list on the right side of the page (see Figure 17-18).

Figure 17-18: Choosing a playlist to copy to CD

6. You can see in Figure 17-18 that each song that will be burned is listed. You can also see exactly how much time remains on the CD that you are burning. If you add more songs then will fit on a single CD, then the Burn List will show where the break is and list each song in each disk. You can drag and drop songs to change the order and otherwise make any changes you want. You can click the Burn List button at the top of the list for options on sorting the list.

7. When your list is as you want it, make sure your blank CD is in the drive and then click the Start Burn button and wait.

As the songs are being copied, you'll see each go through a three-step process, where each song is analyzed, written, and completed. When the Status column shows Complete for every song in your playlist, you're done. You can remove the CD from its drive and play it in any computer, stereo, or CD player.

Note   If you want to create a CD of MP3 songs, then you should copy the MP3 files to the CD rather than do the burn process above. See Chapter 22 for information on copying files to a CD.

Copying Music to Portable Players

The technique you use to copy songs to blank CDs will also work for copying songs to portable music devices (commonly referred to as *MP3 players*). These are tiny, diskless stereos you can wear on your arm or attach to a belt. Joggers swear by them because no matter how much you jump around, the music won't skip. That's because there's no CD or moving parts in the player.

Exactly how much music you can store in a portable player depends on your player. You'll be able to get that information only from the instructions that came with your player. You'll no doubt get software and instructions for copying music to the player as well.

With a Vista-compatible portable player, you can use Windows Media Player to copy songs to the device. Just connect the device to your computer as per the device manufacturer's instructions. In Windows Media Player, select the Synch button on the Media Player features taskbar. You can then go through the same steps you would when burning a CD; however, instead of a Burn List, you have a Sync List.

When you connect your device to your computer, it will be added to the Navigation list on the left side. If there are already songs on the player that you need to erase, you can click the name of your player in the left pane to display its contents. Like your local library, you can display items on your player based on Artist, Album, Songs, Genre, and so on. When you display items, you can right-click them and choose Delete to remove them from the device. If you want to delete them all, select them all first. To do so, click any song in the list; then press Ctrl+A. Click right-click the mouse button on one of the items and choose Delete.

The rest is the same as copying to a CD. That is, choose your playlist under Items to Copy in the left pane. Then click the Start Sync button in the toolbar to copy the songs to the player.

More on Media Player

If this book were a couple thousand pages, I could go on and on about Media Player here. But alas, this isn't a book about Windows Media Player per se. It's a book about Windows Vista, and there are lots of other things that I need to cover. But there are plenty of resources available to you for learning more about Windows Media Player, including:

✦ **Media Player Help:** From the Media Player Classic menus, choose Help ➪ Windows Media Player, or simply press the F1 button when you are anywhere within Media Player.

✦ **Media Player Web Site:** From the Media Player Classic menus, choose Help ➪ Windows Media Player Online.

Summary

When it comes to playing music, there's a lot you can do with Windows Media Player. Here's a quick recap of the most important points from this chapter:

✦ Music files in the WMA and MP3 formats contain hidden *media information*, which Media Player uses to organize and categorize songs.

✦ Media information is rarely stored on music CDs. That information usually comes from the Internet.

✦ The Media Library feature in Windows Media Player provides access to all music on your computer's hard disk, organized by artist, album, star ratings, and genre.

✦ To build up your collection of songs, copy music CDs to your hard disk using Windows Media Player.

✦ You can create custom playlists from your media collection and copy those playlists to blank CDs and portable MP3 players.

Making Home Movies

Every movie or TV show you've ever seen is a collection of *scenes* organized into a story. Windows
Movie Maker is a program that lets you create profes-
sional-grade videos in a similar manner — by combining
your favorite scenes from home movies or even video
you download from the Web. Your movie can contain
full audio, additional background music, narration, and
a number of special effects to add a creative touch to
your production. You get to be cameraman, director,
and producer all wrapped into one.

The movies you create are stored in Windows Movie
(WMV) files. Just about anybody who has a Windows
PC will be able to play them. If you have the right
equipment, you can also copy your movies to video
tape, DVD, and CD.

Introducing Windows Movie Maker

Windows Vista includes the program Windows Movie
Maker. You can start Movie Maker by clicking the Start
button and choose All Programs ➪ Windows Movie
Maker. Using Movie Maker you can edit your own
movies.

Caution If you see a message indicating that your screen
resolution is set to 800×600 or lower, you'll probably want to increase that resolution to 1024×768.
See Chapter 26 for the steps.

Taking Control of Movie Maker

Producing a movie is very much a step-by-step process. More accurately, it is a task-by-task project. For example, the first task is to *get* some video to work with. Then the video needs to be organized into scenes (clips). You need to be able to watch clips, edit out junk you don't want, and maybe add narration or background music. Then the scenes need to be arranged into a movie and so on. To provide all the tools you need for every task, Movie Maker provides several different *panes* of information.

Tip

Like most program windows, Movie Maker has its own title bar, menu bar, and toolbar at the top, as well as its own taskbar button. So you can move and size its window like any other. There's a limit, however, to how small you can make the window.

Windows Movie Maker Panes

When the Movie Tasks pane is open in Movie Maker, the program might look something like the example shown in Figure 18-1. The panes pointed out in that figure are described in the following sections.

Figure 18-1: Windows Movie Maker, with its Movie Tasks pane open

Movie Tasks Pane

Options in the Movie Tasks pane provide quick access to all the tools and dialog boxes you need to make a movie. To show or hide the task pane, click the Tasks button in the toolbar, or choose View ➪ Tasks from the Movie Maker menu bar.

When the Movie Tasks pane is open, it shows a list of tasks, such as Import, Edit, and so forth. They enable you to step through the process of producing your movie in a task-by-task manner. You can click items within each of the headings to choose a specific task. Simply click the task name to get started.

You can hide the Movie Tasks pane the same way you show it; click the Task button or select View ➪ Task from the menu.

Storyboard/Timeline

The Storyboard/Timeline, also called the work area, is where you create your movie. You can also think of it as the creative area rather than the work area, because this is about having fun and making things. As you'll learn later, you create a movie by dragging clips (scenes) from the Contents pane into the work area, arranging them into whatever order you need to present a story or present a coherent movie.

The storyboard/timeline is where you create your movie. You'll be able to add background music, special effects, and narration to the storyboard/timeline as well. I'll get to the details of it all in a moment. For now, look at other major components of Movie Maker.

Collections Pane

A Movie Maker *collection* is like a folder; it's a container in which you store things. But you don't store files in a collection. You store video clips. You can also edit the clips there, doing things such as getting rid of junk you don't want in your movies and compiling small clips into individual panes.

The Collections pane, shown in Figure 18-2, shows you all your collections at once, so you don't have to use the Collections drop-down list to see their names. To make the Collections pane visible, click the Collections button on the toolbar, or choose View ➪ Collections from Movie Maker's menu bar. When the Collections pane is open, you can drag its right border left or right to size it.

Collections button ¬

Collections button

┌ Views button

Collections
drop-down list

┌ Collections pane

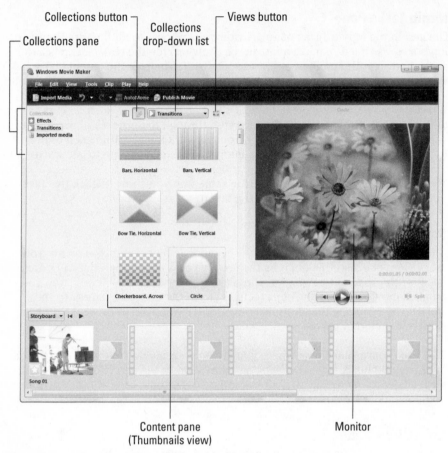

Content pane
(Thumbnails view)

Monitor

Figure 18-2: Windows Movie Maker, with the Collections pane open

Contents Pane

The contents pane, also shown in Figure 18-2, shows the contents of whatever collection is currently selected in the Collections pane or the Collections drop-down list. For example, in Figure 18-2, I've selected the Video Transitions collection in the Collections pane and the Collections drop-down list in the Collections pane. Each of the large icons in the Contents pane represents one transition from the Video Transitions collection.

The Contents pane in Figure 18-2 shows its icons in Thumbnails view. If you prefer, you can show those icons in Details view, where only textual information about each item appears. Use the Views button on the toolbar to choose Details or Thumbnails view for the Contents pane. Use the Arrange Icons By on the Views button to change the order of icons in the Contents pane.

Monitor

The monitor is where you can watch clips, transitions, or your entire movie so far as a work in progress. The first frame of the currently selected clip (if any) appears in the Monitor. To select a clip, click its name in the Contents pane. After you've selected a clip, you use the Play controls shown in Figure 18-3 and summarized as follows to watch the clip, split it, or to take a snapshot of the current frame:

Tip   The Video Transitions and Effects are really just special effects, not pictures. When you play a transition, you see it played out on generic photos. But when you actually *use* a transition in your movie, those generic pictures aren't included.

Name of clip

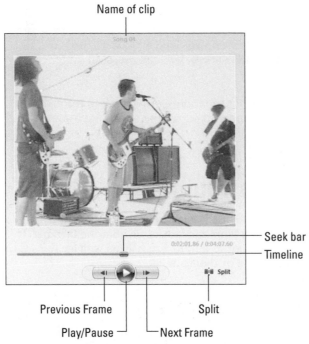

Seek bar

Timeline

Previous Frame   Split

Play/Pause   Next Frame

Figure 18-3: The Play controls in Movie Maker

- ✦ **Name of this clip:** Shows the name of the clip you're currently viewing in the monitor. Matches the name of the clip selected in the Contents pane.

- ✦ **Seek bar:** The handle moves along this bar as the clip is playing. You can drag that handle to the left or right to zoom to a particular spot in the video. This works best if you click Play, then Pause, then drag the handle while the clip is paused.

✦ **Play/Pause:** When the clip is paused or not playing, click this button to play the clip. When the clip is playing, click this button to pause it at the current position without rewinding.

✦ **Previous frame:** When the clip is paused, click this button to move one frame at a time to the left.

Tip   A video is actually a collection of still images, in the same way that movie film is a series of tiny pictures. Each picture in the video is a frame.

✦ **Next frame:** When the clip is paused, click this button to move one frame at a time to the right.

✦ **Split:** When a clip is paused, click this button to break it into two clips at the current frame.

In addition to the controls shown, you can also right-click in the preview area to get a menu that enables you to preview the video at 320×200, 640×480, or full screen. If you view the video at full screen, you can press Alt+Enter to return to the normal view.

You'll have plenty of chances to try out the tools as we progress through this chapter. But before you can make a movie, you really need to have some *content* (video, pictures, or music) to work with.

Getting Content for Your Movie

Before you can really start making movies, you need some content to work with. That content can be video from your camcorder or from the Internet. It can include still photos you might want to add to a movie, as well as any songs you want to use as background music or theme music.

Getting Video from Your Camcorder

To get video from a videotape into your computer, you don't import the video. Rather, you *capture* it. This means that you connect a digital camera, VCR, TV, or even stereo to your computer and play the video or music you want to capture. While it's playing, Movie Maker will capture it — that is, Movie Maker will copy all the sound and video playing into a file on your hard disk. You then work with the file on the hard disk.

Connecting the Camera

The first step to capturing content is to get the device connected to the computer. How you do this depends on what kinds of plugs are available on the device and what kinds of plugs are available on your computer. There are four main types of connections used for this sort of thing, shown in Figure 18-4.

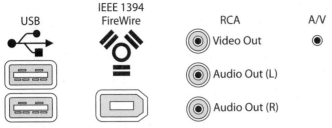

Figure 18-4: Four common plug types for connecting computers and cameras

 Tip   Stereo devices have two Audio Out plugs: one for the left speaker (L) and one for the right (R). Mono devices have only a single Audio Out plug.

✦ **USB:** Provides high-speed plug-and-play connections between just about any device and a computer. Some, but not all, newer video cameras have USB ports. You need a USB cable that can connect the USB port on the camera to the USB port on the computer. You don't need to connect anything except the one USB cable. (The USB plug on the camera may be smaller than the plug on the computer.)

✦ **IEEE 1394 (FireWire):** Provides a high-speed connection between a digital video camera and the computer. Not many video cameras, or computers, have FireWire ports. If your camera has a FireWire port but your computer doesn't, you can add a FireWire port to the computer. You don't need to connect anything except the FireWire cable. (The FireWire plug on the camera may be smaller than the FireWire plug on the computer.)

✦ **RCA Jacks:** These are available on just about every video camera, TV, VCR, and stereo. Computers rarely have matching jacks. But you can purchase hardware that can act as a *bridge* to the computer, as illustrated in Figure 18-5.

✦ **A/V (Composite video):** Some video cameras may have a single A/V or A/V Out plug instead of separate Video and Audio jacks. As with RCA jacks, you can usually connect an AV/Out port to a device that acts as a bridge to the computer.

Tip   The two best resources available to you for specifics on connecting your video camera to your computer are the printed manuals that came with each of those devices. We can talk only in general terms here, because there are hundreds of different makes and models of computers and video cameras!

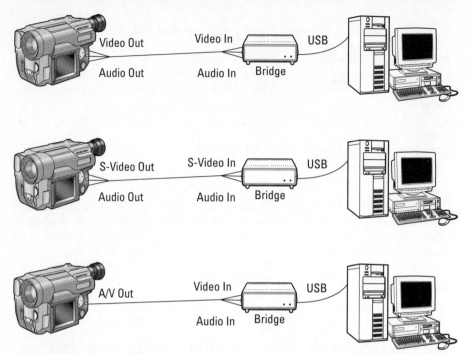

Figure 18-5: Using a bridge to connect a video camera to a computer's USB port

If your computer and camera both have FireWire ports or USB ports, it's a simple connection. You just need one cable to connect the two plugs on each end to the two devices. For example, connect the USB port on the camera straight to the USB port on the computer, and forget about any other plugs. In the case of a FireWire port, connect the FireWire port on the camera to the FireWire port on the computer. Ignore all other plugs.

If your camera has only RCA or A/V ports, and you don't have matching ports on your computer, you can buy a device that acts as a *bridge* between the camera and computer. Dazzle (www.dazzle.com) makes several products along these lines. Their primary products have RCA Video and Audio *In* jacks and also an S-Video *In* jack, on one side. You connect your camera to those. On the other side of the bridge, there's a simple USB port that connects to the USB port on your computer.

Tip The Dazzle DVD Recorder offers a high-speed USB 2.0 port, which you can connect to a USB port on the computer. The Dazzle Video Creator Platinum also provides capabilities such as the ability to output your finished movie to Apple iPods and Sony PSP. Check it out under the Consumer section at www.dazzle.com.

You can connect just about any camera using one of those bridges. For example, if your camera has standard RCA ports, connect the Video Out and Audio Out ports to the Video In and Audio In ports on the bridge, as shown at the top of Figure 18-5.

Tip S-Video provides better quality than standard RCA video. So if you have a choice, go with S-Video. (You can use one or the other, but not both at the same time.)

If your camera has S-Video, don't use the RCA Video port at all. Rather, use an S-Video cable to connect the S-Video Out on the Camera to the S-Video In on the bridge. Connect the Audio Outs on the camera to the Audio Ins on the bridge normally, as in the middle of Figure 18-5.

If your camera has a Composite A/V or A/V Out port, you'll need a cable that connects to that port on one end, then splits into three ports on the other end, as at the bottom of Figure 18-5. If you take the camera and bridge to a Radio Shack and tell them what you plan to do, they can probably hand you the cable right there and show you how to connect the two devices. The small plug on the single side of the cable will be divided into three bands, as in the example at left. One band is video; the other two are audio.

Using the Video Capture Wizard

You get video from a video camera, TV, or VCR by *capturing* it. The video actually plays on your computer screen, at normal speed, and your computer also captures a copy in a file as it's going by. It all happens in real time; if you're going to copy an entire 30-minute tape, it will take 30 minutes to copy it.

The first step is to turn the camera on in VCR mode (not Camera mode) and put the tape you want to capture into the VCR. Rewind the tape to the beginning. Or, if you're not going to capture the entire tape, wind the tape to a few seconds before the spot where you want to start capturing. (It's always better to capture a little too much than not enough.)

Tip Think of a captured video as a piece of material. If you cut it too long, you can always cut it shorter. If you cut it too short, you have a problem.

Turn the camera off, and set it aside for a moment. On your computer, close all open program windows, so you can work from a clean desktop. Then connect everything starting from the computer and working your way out to the camera. Connect the camera last. Don't turn the camera on until it's connected to the computer. Then keep an eye on the screen for a while, to see if Windows detects your camera. (That might take a few seconds.)

If Windows can detect your camera, Windows Movie Maker might start automatically. Or you might be given the option to start Movie Maker. Either method is OK. If Windows Movie Maker doesn't start within a minute or so, automatically, go ahead and start it yourself. Click the Start button and choose All Programs ⇨ Windows Movie Maker.

The Video Capture Wizard might automatically open as well. If so, you're ready to start capturing, as described in a moment. If the Record dialog box doesn't open automatically, just go ahead and open it using whatever method is most convenient:

✦ Choose File ➪ Import from Digital Video Camera from the Windows Movie Maker menu bar.

✦ In the Tasks pane under the Import section, click From digital video camera.

✦ Press Ctrl+R.

Depending on the camera you're using, the Video Capture wizard might present one or more pages of options. We'll look at some of the pages of the wizard in the sections that follow. Remember that after you complete a page of the wizard, you need to click Next to move onto the next page. If you click Next too soon, just click the Back button (the arrow pointing to the left) to return to the previous page. Don't be alarmed if some pages don't appear. The Wizard is smart enough to present only the options needed for your particular camera.

The first page of the Video Capture wizard will ask you for the device you are using to obtain the video. This page is asking where the video and audio feed that you plan to capture will be coming from.

The exact options available to you will depend on your computer and camera. You need to click the item that represents your camera or the plug to which the camera is connected. Click whichever icon represents your device. As a rule, once you click an icon, you can leave all other settings as they are and click the Next button.

The second page of the wizard, titled "Captured Video File," asks what you want to name the video you're about to capture and where you want to put it (Figure 18-6). Enter a short, descriptive name in the Name field. Under the Import to option, choose Videos (unless, for whatever reason, you want to put the video in some other folder). Then click Next.

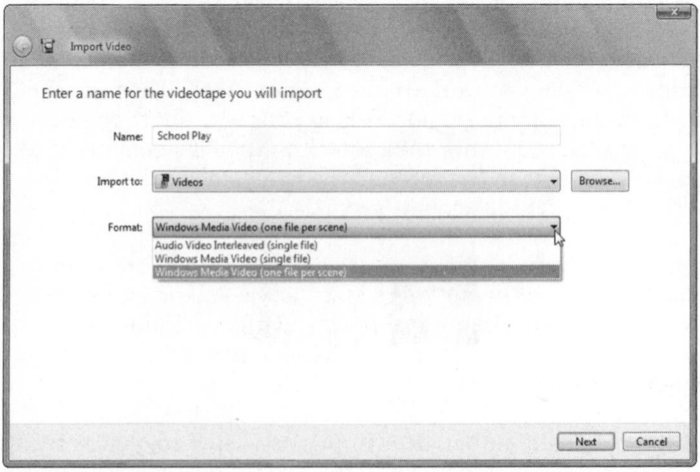

Figure 18-6: Naming your imported video and stating where to save it

On the page shown in Figure 18-7, you'll be able to state whether the entire video should be captured or if you want to import only parts. Select the option you want, and then click Next.

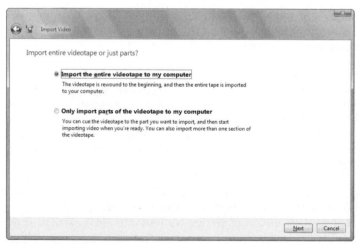

Figure 18-7: Selecting all or parts for importing a video

The next page is where the actual capture takes place (see Figure 18-8). From this page you can set a stop time by selecting the check box labeled Stop importing after (min). If you want to capture a fixed amount of video (for example, exactly 30 minutes), choose this option and set your time limit. Alternatively, you can leave it cleared and the video will record based on the option you selected in Figure 18-7.

Figure 18-8: The Capture Video page of the Video Capture wizard

Now you're finally ready to capture your video. Press the Play button on your video camera to get the tape going, and click Start Video Import in the dialog box. Whatever video plays in the monitor on your screen will also be captured into Movie Maker.

When you've finished capturing video, just click the Stop Video Import button in the dialog box; then stop the playback on the camera as well. Click the Finish button to complete the wizard.

The video you captured will be added to your Collections under whatever file name you gave the movie near the start of this process. When you click the collection's name in the Collections pane, or choose the collection's name from the drop-down list on the toolbar, you'll see an icon or icons that represent the captured video. To play a captured video or clip from the video, click its icon in the Contents pane, and click the Play button under the Monitor, as illustrated in Figure 18-9.

You can repeat the procedure to capture more content. Or you can just start building your movie from the content you captured. Before we get to that, however, let's look at another means of getting content into Movie Maker.

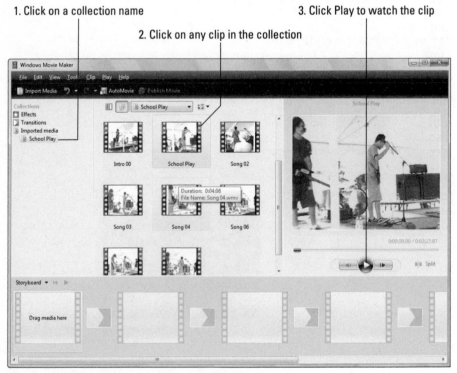

Figure 18-9: How to view a clip in a collection

Importing Video from Files

If you already have video stored in files on your hard disk, there's no need to capture that video. It's already been captured to a file. To get video from a file on your hard disk into Movie Maker, *import* the video. In addition to importing video, you can import music, such as songs you copied from an audio CD or downloaded from the Web. Those you can use as background music. You can also import still photos and include those in your movie production: The types of files you can import are summarized here:

 Note   You can't import protected content (digitally licensed) into Movie Maker.

✦ **Video:** .asf, .avi, .m1v, .mp2, .mp2v, .mpe, .mpeg, .mpg, .mpv2, .wm, and .wmv.

✦ **Still pictures:** .bmp, .dib, .emf, .gif, .jfif, .jpe, .jpeg, .jpg, .png, .tif, .tiff, and .wmf.

✦ **Audio:** .aif, .aifc, .aiff .asf, .au, .mp2, .mp3, .mpa, .snd, .wav, and .wma.

If you just want to practice and play around with Movie Maker to get your feet wet, you can use any sample video already on your hard disk. Chances are that you probably already have at least one sample video in your Videos folder. To find out, follow these steps:

1. Click the Start button and choose your personalized folder.

2. Double-click the Videos folder in your personalized folder to open that folder. Explorer shows the contents of your Videos folder.

If there are any videos in that folder already, you'll see their icons. You may also find a Sample Videos folder within your Video folder that contains samples you can use.

If you don't have any videos in your Videos folder, or if you think you have more video files elsewhere on your hard disk, you can use the Windows Search feature (discussed in Chapter 20) to search your entire hard disk for Video files. Then you can use any of the techniques described in the section "Moving and Copying Files" in Chapter 19 to move or copy found videos to your Videos folder.

Be aware that Movie Maker doesn't actually *store* copies of your video files. It simply creates pointers to your video files and uses those pointers to create your movie. If you import some videos into Movie Maker and later move those files, Movie Maker might lose track of them. So it's in your best interest to put all video files you'll be using to make movies into a permanent folder where you don't need to move them after you've imported them into Movie Maker.

 Tip   If your computer is on a network and you want videos to be accessible to all computers in the network, put them in your Public Videos folder rather than in your personal Videos folder.

When you know where the file you want to import is located, and its file name, you can follow these steps:

STEPS: Import a File into Movie Maker

1. If you haven't already done so, start Windows Movie Maker.

2. From Movie Maker's menu bar, choose File ➪ Import Media Items. (Optionally, you can click Videos under the Import section of the Tasks pane or you can click the Import Media button in the taskbar.)

3. A folder opens (most likely your Videos folder). If the file you want to import is in some other folder, navigate to that folder. For example, to import a photo, you can navigate to your Pictures folder. To import a song to use as background music, navigate to your Music folder.

4. Click the icon of the file you want to import. Optionally, you can select multiple files using any of the techniques described under "Working with Multiple Files and Folders" in Chapter 19.

5. Click the Import button and wait a moment.

After the file is imported, it is stored in its own collection with the same name as the file you imported. To view the imported video, or a clip from it, click the collection name, click a clip, and click the Play button as shown in Figure 18-9.

You can capture and import as many clips as you want. Your movie can contain clips from any number of collections. To create your movie, add clips to the Storyboard/Timeline, as discussed next.

Creating the Movie

A movie is a collection of clips. This is as true in Movie Maker as it is in real movies. In a real movie or TV show, scenes aren't shot in the order you see them at the theater. Instead, they shoot all the scenes based on location, set, costumes, who's in the scene, and so forth. All scenes are assembled into a story that (one hopes) makes sense.

In Movie Maker, you assemble your movie in the storyboard/timeline (also called the *workspace*), near the bottom of the Movie Maker window. There are two ways to view the contents of the workspace. Figure 18-10 shows examples of the two views and points out buttons that appear above the Storyboard/Timeline. The name and purpose of each button is summarized as follows:

✦ **Timeline:** Shows the first frame of each scene and the size of the clip relative to the overall movie and other clips.

✦ **Storyboard:** Shows each scene as the first frame in each clip only.

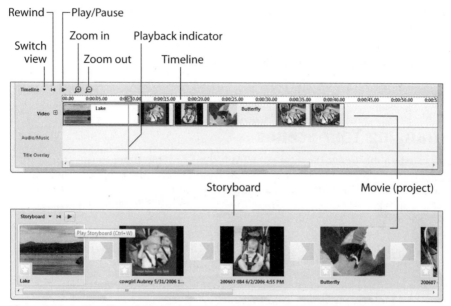

Figure 18-10: Timeline view (top) and Storyboard view (bottom) of a movie

Tip

To change the height of the Storyboard/Timeline, drag its upper border up or down.

✦ **Movie (project):** To create your movie, add clips to the storyboard/ timeline in the order you want them to be played. A work-in-progress movie is referred to as a *project*, to differentiate it from a finished movie.

✦ **Audio Levels:** Lets you adjust relative volume of audio from a video and any background music or narration you add.

✦ **Narrate:** Lets you add narration starting at the current Playback Indicator position.

✦ **Zoom in:** Magnifies the timeline (disabled in Storyboard view).

✦ **Zoom out:** Shrinks the timeline so you can see more scenes (disabled in Storyboard view).

✦ **Playback indicator:** (In Timeline view only) Shows the current position within the window. Drag the handle atop the indicator left/right to move through the movie. Point to the handle at top to see how many minutes into the movie the Playback Indicator is resting.

✦ **Rewind:** Rewinds the project to the beginning.

✦ **Play/Pause:** Plays the move from the current Playback Indicator position.

✦ **Switch view:** Click to switch from Timeline to Storyboard view or from Storyboard view to Timeline view.

Next, we'll look at how you use the tools and buttons to create a movie.

Arranging Your Scenes

You create a movie by copying clips from the Contents pane to the storyboard/ timeline. Clips are played in the order in which they appear in the storyboard/ timeline. You can add any clip from any collection to the storyboard/timeline using whichever technique of the following techniques is most convenient for you:

✦ Drag the clip from the Contents pane to where you want it to appear in the storyboard/timeline and drop it there.

✦ Right-click the clip that you want to add to the movie and choose Add to Storyboard or Add to Timeline.

✦ Click the clip you want to add to the movie and choose Clip ➪ Add to Storyboard or Add to Timeline from Movie Maker's menu bar.

✦ Click the clip you want to add and press Ctrl+D.

✦ Select several clips using Ctrl+Click, Shift+Click, or Edit ➪ Select All (Ctrl+A). Then drag any selected clip to the storyboard/timeline.

A copy of the clip appears in the storyboard/timeline. The clip isn't removed from the Contents pane. (That's so you can use the same clip in multiple movies.) If you change your mind about a clip after adding it to the storyboard/ timeline, you can do any of the following to back up:

✦ In the storyboard/timeline, right-click the clip you want to remove and choose Remove.

✦ In the storyboard/timeline, click a clip to select it. Then drag it left or right to move it within the movie. Or right-click the clip and press Ctrl+X to cut it. Then right-click the frame to the right of where you want to replace the clip and press Ctrl+V.

✦ To select multiple clips to move or delete, click one clip in the story- board/timeline. Then hold down the Ctrl key while clicking other clips you want to select.

✦ To select a range of adjacent clips, click the first one; then hold down the Shift key and click the last one you want to select. Or move the mouse pointer past the last clip in the movie; then drag the mouse pointer to the left through clips you want to select.

✦ To select all clips in the movie, right-click any click in the story-board/timeline and choose Select All.

✦ To clear the storyboard/timeline, choose Edit ➪ Clear Storyboard or Edit ➪ Clear Timeline from the menu bar, or press Ctrl+Delete (Del).

✦ To undo your most recent action, choose Edit ➪ Undo from the Movie Maker menu bar, click the undo button in the taskbar, or press Ctrl+Z.

You can add as many, or as few, clips to the storyboard/timeline as you want.

 Tip When dragging video clips to the timeline, make sure you drag them to the bar titled "Video," not the bar titled "Audio/Music or Title Overlay."

Previewing Your Movie

After you've dragged one or more clips to the storyboard/timeline, you can preview the entire movie at any time. If you use the Timeline view, you'll be able to see the Play Indicator move through the movie as the movie is playing in the Monitor. The Play and Rewind buttons that follow refer to the buttons in the storyboard/timeline shown in Figure 18-10.

✦ **Play/Pause:** Click the Play button in the storyboard/timeline to play the movie starting at the current Play Indicator position. Or choose Play ➪ Play Storyboard/Timeline from Movie Maker's menu bar, or press Ctrl+W (Watch). When the movie is playing, the Play button becomes a Pause button with a | | symbol on it. Click the Pause button to stop playback without rewinding the movie.

✦ **Rewind:** Click the Rewind button in the storyboard/timeline to move the Player Indicator to the first frame of the movie. Or choose Play ➪ Rewind Storyboard/Timeline from the menu bar, or press Ctrl+Q (Quit).

✦ **Play Indicator:** To move rapidly through the movie, drag the little box atop the Playback Indicator left or right. Or click a spot to the left or right of that little box to move the Play Indicator to that position.

If the movie is already playing, and you want to start over from the beginning, click the Pause button in the storyboard/timeline — then the Rewind button just to its left, then the Play button.

 Tip The various controls in the Monitor also work while you're viewing your movie.

Trimming Scenes

If a scene in your movie runs longer than you'd like, you can trim it from the front, back, or both. You need to drag the clip into the storyboard/timeline first. Then make sure you're in Timeline view. Click the scene you wish to trim; then click the Play button to start playing the scene. Click the Pause button in the Monitor when the scene is at about where you want to trim. You can then use the Previous Frame and Next Frame buttons to zero in on the exact frame where you want to set a *trim point*.

To trim all frames to the left of the current frame (within the selected clip), choose Clip ⇨ Trim Beginning. Or, to trim off all frames to the right of the current position, choose Clip ⇨ Trim End. Play the entire movie (or at least from before the trim point) to verify that you like the shortened scene. If you don't like the results, click the scene again in the timeline and choose Clip ⇨ Clear Trim Points. Then you can start over with new trim points if you like.

Tip   You can also delete trash from any clip by splitting the clip into two parts and deleting anything you don't plan to use.

Overlapping Scenes

It's OK to make scenes in the timeline overlap one another. Doing so will automatically produce a fade transition, where one scene (or song, or photo) will automatically fade out as the other is fading in. How long the fade transition lasts depends on how much overlap there is.

Tip   If the clips in the timeline are too small to see, keep clicking the Zoom (+ magnifying glass button) in the timeline to zoom in until you can see both clips well. Use the horizontal scroll bar under the timeline to scroll left and right.

To make two scenes overlap, make sure you're in Timeline view. Then click the scene to the right of the one you want to overlap it with. Drag that scene slightly to the left. Or choose Clip ⇨ Nudge Left to move the scene just a tiny bit to the left. Then drag the Play Indicator to the left of the whole overlap and click the Play button in the storyboard/timeline to see (or hear) the transition. If the transition is too short, you can nudge the scene on the right a little more to the left. If the transition is too long, nudge the scene on the right a little to the right.

The two scenes (clips) will partially overlap, as shown at the bottom of Figure 18-11. The word *Fade* appears in the transition bar where the scenes overlap. (Click the + or - sign to the right of the word *Video* to show/hide the Transition bar.) When you play the movie, the first scene on the left will slowly fade out as the scene on the right slowly fades in.

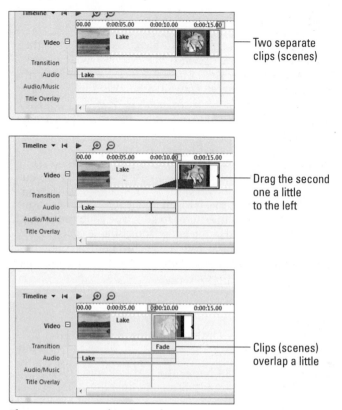

Figure 18-11: Overlapping two scenes in Timeline view

Spicing Up Your Movie

After you've dragged some clips to the storyboard or timeline, you can start spicing things up with some special effects, music, still photos, and titles. Let's start with some titles.

Adding Titles and Credits

Titles are textual information that you insert anywhere into a movie. For example, you can add titles to the beginning of the movie or credits to the end. You can even overlay textual information onto video as its playing. The process is easy:

1. If you plan to insert titles into, or between, clips in the movie, click the scene in the storyboard/timeline where you want to insert text.

2. Choose Tools ➪ Titles and Credits from Movie Maker's menu bar, or, in the Edit section in the task pane, click Titles or credits.

3. Choose where you want to place the text from the options that appear, such as Title at the beginning; Title before the selected clip; Title on the selected clip; or Credits at the end.

Making Photos from Videos

You can convert any single frame from a video clip to a regular still photo. This is true whether you plan to use that photo in your movie or not. The picture you create is no different from a picture you take with a regular still camera.

To get started, you need to click a clip in the Contents pane; then click the Play button in the Monitor to start playing the clip. When you get near a frame you want to copy to a photo, click the Pause button in the Monitor to pause the video. Use the Previous Frame and Next Frame buttons in the Monitor to get to the exact frame you wish to convert to a photo. Then select Tools ➪ Take Picture from Preview from the Movie Maker menu.

In the Save Picture As dialog box that opens, navigate to the folder in which you want to store the picture (for example, the Pictures folder), type a file name, and click Save. A copy of the picture is stored in the folder and also in a collection. If you don't intend to use the photo in a movie, you can delete it from the Contents pane by right-clicking and choosing Remove. A copy of the photo will remain in whatever folder you place the photo.

4. In the top box, add the main title. Optionally, add a subtitle in the lower box.

5. To choose a font and colors, click Change the text font and color. Choose your Font, Color, Transparency, Size, and Position.

 Tip The higher the transparency level, the more the background color or image will show through the text.

6. Optionally, click Change the title animation, and then select an option from the list that appears. To see how a title will look when played, click the Play button in the Monitor.

7. When you're happy with your title, click *Done, add title to movie.*

In Storyboard/Timeline view, each title will be presented as its own scene within the movie. (They're easiest to spot in Storyboard view.) To see the title play out within the context of the movie, just play the movie, using the Rewind and Play buttons in Storyboard/Timeline view, or the Play Indicator in Timeline view.

Adding Still Photos to Your Movie

If you have some photos you'd like to add to your movie, you can add those as well. The images can be any pictures stored in BMP, DIB, EMF, GIF, JFIF, JPE, JPEG, JPG, PNG, TIF, TIF, or WMF format. But before you start importing still pictures, you'd do well to set *default duration* for pictures. Here's how:

1. From the Movie Maker menu bar, choose Tools ➪ Options.

2. In the Options dialog box that opens, click the Advanced tab.

3. Set the Picture Duration to however long you want the picture to be *still* within the movie (usually three to five seconds is sufficient).

4. Click OK in the dialog box.

Now you're ready to import a picture. Here's how:

1. From Movie Maker's menu bar, choose File ➪ Import Media Items (or press Ctrl+I).

2. In the Import File dialog box that opens, navigate to the folder that contains the picture you want to insert.

3. Click the picture you want to insert (or select multiple pictures); then click the Import button.

The picture is added to the current collection, looking just like a video clip (although its name is the same as the name of the file you imported). To make the picture part of your movie, drag it down to wherever you want it to appear in the Storyboard/Timeline. When you play the entire movie, the photo will appear for its specified duration.

> **Tip**
>
> A movie doesn't *have to* contain video clips. You could create a movie containing just still photos along with background titles, special effects, background music, and/or narration. Then save the whole project as a movie, and you'll have a nice slideshow of your favorite photos to show off to your friends.

Adding Video Effects

A video effect is a special effect applied to a single scene within your movie. That single scene can be any video clip, title, or picture within the storyboard/timeline. Adding a video effect is simple:

1. Select (click) the scene within the storyboard/timeline to which you want to add a video effect.

2. Choose Effects under the Edit section of the Tasks pane, or choose Tools ➪ Video Effects from the Movie Maker menu bar. You can also select the Collections pane and click Effects. A list of video-effect names, such as 3D Ripple, Blur, Ease In, and so forth, appears.

3. To see an example of an effect, click the effect name and click the Play button in the Monitor. The effect will be played out against a generic picture.

4. When you find an effect you like, click its name; then press Ctrl+D to add the effect to the currently selected scene. Or drag the effect name to the scene to which you want to apply it. You can also right-click the effect in the Collections pane and select Add to Timeline from the menu that will display.

5. You can repeat Step 4 to add as many effects as you wish to the current scene.

In Storyboard view, any scene to which you've applied a video effect will show two colored stars rather than a single gray star (see Figure 18-12). To see the effect, click the scene name to which you applied the effect; then click the Play button in the Monitor. If you change your mind, right-click the scene in the storyboard/timeline and choose Video Effects. In the dialog box that opens, click the name of the effect you want to remove under Displayed Effects. Click the << Remove button; then click OK.

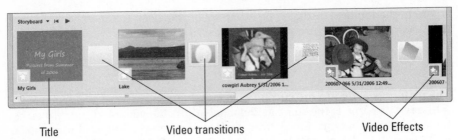

Title   Video transitions   Video Effects

Figure 18-12: Titles, video effects, and transitions in Storyboard view

Using Transition Effects

A transition effect is a special effect that takes place between scenes in the movie. It provides a segue from one scene to the next. You can place a transition effect before a scene, after a scene, or both. By default, each transition lasts 1.25 seconds. If you want to change that, choose Tools ➪ Options from the Movie Maker menu bar. On the Advanced tab of the Options dialog box, change the Transition duration to some other number of seconds (one to three seconds is usually sufficient). Then click OK.

You might find it easiest to add transition effects in Storyboard view. So if you're in Timeline view, press Ctrl+T or click the Timeline list button and select Storyboard. Then follow these steps:

1. Switch to the Transitions view in the Collections pane by doing one of the following:

    • Select Tools ➪ Transitions from the Movie Maker menu bar.

    • Click Transitions in the Collections pane from the list button.

    • Select Transitions from the Edit section of the Task Pane.

2. Optionally, choose View ➪ Thumbnails to see a large icon for each transition.

3. To see the transition played out against a generic picture, click its name; then click the Play button in the preview area.

4. When you find a transition you like, drag it to the small box before, or after, the scene to which you want to apply the transition.

Figure 18-12 shows an example with transitions added before and after the clip named Cowgirl Aubrey. To see a transition played out in your movie, play the entire movie. Or, in Timeline view, move the Playback Indicator just to the left of the transition; then click the Play button in the storyboard/timeline. To delete a video transition, right-click its little box in the storyboard and choose Remove.

Adding Narration or Background Music

You can insert audio clips into your movie in much the same way you insert video clips and still photos. For example, you could import into Movie Maker a favorite song that you copied from a CD or downloaded from the Web. Then use that song as background music for the whole movie. Or add little short clips of music to individual scenes, like they do in theater movies. The first step is to import the music in Movie Maker. Here's how:

Caution　Finalize the video portion of your movie before adding background sound or narration. If you add audio, but later remove a bunch of video from the movie, the audio may get chopped up as well.

1. Select Audio or Music from the Import section of the Tasks pane. Alternatively, from the Movie Maker menu bar, choose File ➪ Import Media Items.

2. In the Import File dialog box that opens, navigate to the folder that contains the song you wish to import (for example, your Music folder).

3. Double-click the name of the song to import.

The file is imported into the collection, its icon just a large musical note. To add the music clip to your movie, right-click it and choose Add to Timeline or Add to Storyboard. You'll see the song in the Audio/Music bar of the Timeline. If you click the + sign next to Video, you'll also see the audio that's already built into the video on the Audio bar (see Figure 18-13).

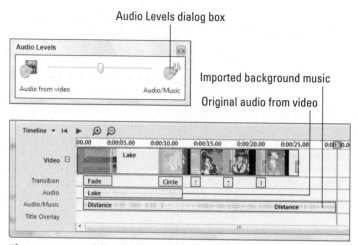

Figure 18-13: Adding background music to a movie

If the song runs much longer than the movie, drag its right edge in the Audio/Music bar to line up with the end of the movie, as shown in Figure 18-3. To prevent a song from ending too abruptly, right-click the Audio/Music bar and choose Fade Out. (You can also right-click and choose Fade In to have the music fade in gradually.)

Video cameras record sound as well as video. So both the original sound from the video and the background music you add will play when you play the movie. To adjust the relative volume of the original audio and background music, right click on the audio track and select Volume from the menu, or choose Tools ➪ Audio Levels from the Movie Maker menu bar. In the Audio Levels dialog box that opens (also shown in Figure 18-13), drag the slider bar to the left to make the original audio louder or to the right to make the imported music louder.

You can also add narration to a movie. You'll need a microphone or headset plugged into your sound card to do this. Also, you might want to write up a quick script and practice delivering it, so you're not constantly stumbling over words while you're trying to narrate. Aside from that, adding narration is pretty easy. The narrative will actually be stored in a clip, which you can then add to the movie as you would background music.

To get started on narration, get your microphone into position or your headset on. If you're in Storyboard view, click the Show Timeline button to switch to Timeline view. In the Timeline view, drag the Play Indicator to where you want to start the narration (or just click the Rewind button to get to the beginning of the movie to narrate the whole thing).

Next, choose Tools ➪ Narrate Timeline from the Movie Maker menu bar. In the Narrate Timeline pane that opens (see Figure 18-14), talk into your microphone to test it. Adjust the slider as you're talking to make sure your voice reaches up to near the yellow part of the spectrum, but isn't so loud as to keep you in the red part of the spectrum.

It helps a lot to see the movie as you're talking. So when you're ready to go, click the Start Narration button in the pane. Start talking, synchronizing your narration to whatever scene is currently playing in the movie.

To stop narrating, click the Stop Narration button. The Save Windows Media File dialog box opens. If you made a mess of things (as is often the case on the first few tries), you can click the Cancel button in that dialog box to start over. Otherwise, if you're happy with the narration, type a file name (perhaps one that matches the title of your movie), and click the Save button. Then click the Close button under the Stop Narration button.

The icon for the narration sports a musical note, like an imported song. The narration is also added to the Audio/Music bar, just like an imported song. You can also use the Audio Levels dialog box described earlier to adjust the relative volume of the original video and your narration.

Figure 18-14: The Narration Timeline pane

To remove an imported song or narration from the movie, click its name in the Audio/Music bar in the timeline; then press Delete (Del), or right-click it and choose Remove.

Saving a Project (Work in Progress)

As you may recall, a movie that's still a work in progress is referred to as a *project*. It's not always possible to create a movie in one sitting. So you may want to save the work you've accomplished so far at any given time. In fact, it would be a good idea to save your work often, so a power outage or some other mishap doesn't cause you to lose all that work. Saving a project is easy. Follow these steps:

1. Choose File ➪ Save Project from the Movie Maker menu bar. The Save Project As dialog box opens.

2. Navigate to the folder in which you want to store the movie (for example, the Videos).

3. Type a file name for your movie.

4. Click the Save button.

That's all there is to it. To save your work from time to time as you're working on your movie, click the Save button on the toolbar, choose File ➪ Save Project from the Movie Maker menu bar again, or press Ctrl+S. You won't need to enter a file name or anything. The current project will be saved to the file name you provided the first time you saved it.

To resume work on your movie at any time, open Windows Movie Maker normally. Then choose File ➪ Open Project from the Movie Maker menu bar. Double-click the icon for the project you want to reopen. The project will be placed in the storyboard/timeline. Of course, if Movie Maker isn't already open, you can double-click the project file's icon to open both the project and Movie Maker.

Tip   To make Movie Maker automatically open with your latest project already loaded, choose Tools ➪ Options from the Movie Maker menu bar. Click the General tab, select Open last project on startup, and click OK. You can also set a time frame to have Movie Maker do an AutoRecover backup in case your system does crash. This time frame is also set in the General tab and is defaulted to every 10 minutes.

Creating the Final Movie

At some point, your movie will be complete and you'll be ready to take the final step of converting your project into a finished *movie file*. The file you create will have a .wmv (Windows Movie) extension, which can be played by anyone who has Windows Media Player on his or her computer. Creating the final movie is easy.

STEPS: Create the Movie File

1. Choose File ➪ Publish Movie from the Movie Maker menu bar. The first page of the Save Movie wizard opens.

2. Select where you want to publish the movie to. You can choose to publish to your computer, to a DVD, to a recordable CD, to a file attached to an email, or to a tape on a digital camera. Click This Computer to save the movie to a file; then click Next. You can always copy the file to one of the other locations later.

   Note   You can go straight to Step 2 by selection one of the options in the Publish to section of the Tasks pane.

3. On the second wizard page, type a file name for the movie (this can be the movie's title). Then use the Browse button to choose a folder in which to save the movie (for example, Videos). Click Next.

4. On the third wizard page (shown in Figure 18-15), choose a Quality setting for your movie. For your first go-around, your best bet is to just choose the first option: Best quality for playback on my computer (recommended); then click Publish.

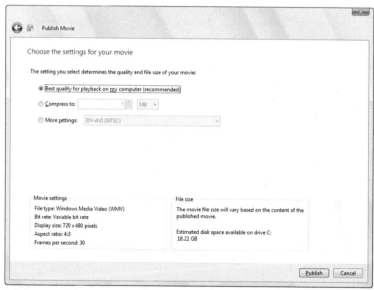

Figure 18-15: Choosing quality settings for your movie

5. The next page of the wizard opens, and Movie Maker starts making your movie. How long that takes depends on the length of the movie. The wizard will let you know when the movie has been generated.

6. Optionally, you can choose Play movie when I click finish to watch the movie in Windows Media Player.

7. Click the Finish button.

If you opted to watch the movie after clicking Finish, the movie will open and play in Windows Media Player. The movie file itself will be stored in whatever folder you chose in Step 3. For example, if you chose the Videos folder, the movie will be in that folder.

If you gave the movie file the same name as the project, you'll be able to tell them apart by their icons and file name extensions. The project — the stuff that appears in the Movie Maker storyboard/timeline — has a Movie Maker icon and the .mswmm (Microsoft Windows Movie Maker) file name extension, as on the left of Figure 18-16. The finished movie will have a Media Player icon and a .wmv extension, as on the right side of Figure 18-16. If you plan to distribute copies of the movie, distribute only the WMV file.

Figure 18-16: Icons for a saved project (right) and a completed movie (left)

Tip   File name extensions are visible only if *the* Hide extensions for know file types option in Folder Options is turned off. See "Showing/Hiding File Name Extensions" in Chapter 6.

Trying Other Quality Settings

You can choose a quality setting for your movies. Here's the trade-off: The higher the quality of the movie, the larger the resulting file. Disk-storage space is cheap, so we always make a super-high-quality copy of our movies and use that to make videotapes and DVDs. If you need a small version of the movie for e-mailing to people, you may want to make a lower-quality copy of the movie that can fit within the allowable limits.

Tip   Most ISPs limit the size of e-mail attachments to 1 or 1.5MB, which isn't much video.

To really experience what *quality* means in terms of file size, and how the video looks, you can make extra copies of a movie from a single project. For example, in the same project you just created a movie from, you can choose File ➪ Publish Movie again. This time, when you get to the wizard page that asks for a file name, give this copy of the movie the same name as the first movie, but add some text that will help you identify this as the high-quality version of the movie. For example, you might name the movie something like *My first movie (Max Quality)*. When you get to the Quality Settings page of the wizard (that was shown in Figure 18-15), click More settings. Then click the drop-down list button and choose the highest-quality setting available, DV-AVI (NTSC), as in Figure 18-17.

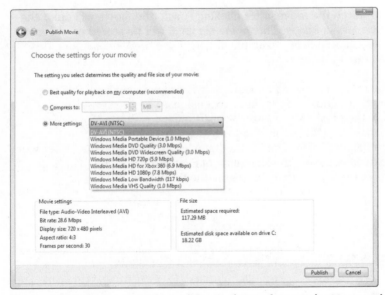

Figure 18-17: There are many qualities to choose from under More settings.

Tip The quality of a movie is measured in *bits per second* (bps). *Kbps* stands for *kilobits per second* or roughly 1,000 bits per second. *Mbps* stands for *Megabits per second* or roughly a million bits per second. Hence, 1 Mbps is of slightly higher quality than 999 Kbps.

When the ultra-high-quality copy of the movie is finished, you can create a low-quality version for comparison. Again, choose File ➪ Publish Movie from Movie Maker's menu bar. When you get to the page where you name the file, add something to the file name to make this copy stand out as the low-quality version of the movie. For example, you might name it *My First Movie (Low Quality)*. On the Movie Setting page of the wizard, choose More settings; then choose Compress to, and try setting the size to 1MB (one megabyte, the maximum attachment size for many ISPs). Click Next, and let Movie Maker create the movie.

Caution It may not even be possible to squeeze a large movie down to a 1MB file. If you plan to e-mail movies to people, you should think in terms of making small movies that are just a couple of minutes in length.

If you then open the folder in which you saved all the movies, you'll see an icon for each one. If you Tiles or Details view, you'll be able to see their file sizes as well (see Figure 18-18). To see how the movie looks, just double-click its icon to play it in Windows Media Player.

Figure 18-18: A saved project (MSWMM file) and several finished movies at different-quality settings (WMV files)

Note It is worth pointing out that Windows Movie Maker supports HD movies. You can generate HD 720p, 1080p, and HD for Xbox 360.

Copying Movies to Tape and DVD

Recall that when you choose File ➪ Publish Movie, the first page of the Publish Movie wizard asks where you want to publish the movie. Additionally, the Tasks pane lists a number of additional targets under the Publish to section.

The This Computer option lets you choose any folder on your hard disk. The other options on the first wizard page provide these options:

✦ **DVD:** If you use a blank DVD-R or DVD-RW disk, you can choose the DVD option to write the movie to a DVD rather than your hard disk. (As you'll learn in Chapter 22, however, you can just as easily copy the completed movie from your hard disk to a blank DVD.)

✦ **Recordable CD:** If you use a blank CD-R or CD-RW disk, you can choose the Recordable CD option to write the movie to a CD rather than to your hard disk. (As you'll also learn in Chapter 22, however, you can just as easily copy the completed movie from your hard disk to a blank CD.)

✦ **E-mail:** The E-mail option on the wizard will prepare a low-quality copy of the movie, small enough to e-mail. (This might not work with all e-mail systems, though.) As an alternative to going this route, you can also just attach a finished movie to an e-mail message.

> **Tip**   E-mail a copy of the movie to yourself first to see how it will look to the intended recipients.

✦ **Digital Video camera:** If you have a digital video camera that connects through a FireWire port, you can choose this option to copy the movie to a blank Mini-DV tape. Make sure you put a blank tape in the camera first, so you don't overwrite any existing footage.

> **Tip**   A DVD can hold 4.7GB of data, which is enough for a couple hours of ultra-high-quality video. A CD only holds about ½GB (650–700MB), which is still a fair amount of disk space. See Chapter 22 for more information about DVDs and CDs.

Getting movies from the computer to VHS tape is a tougher nut to crack, because you have to get video and audio out from the computer and into the VCR. Few computers have Video Out and Audio Out jacks. So you're likely to need a bridge. Once again, the Dazzle DVC 150 can be that bridge. (The DVC 80 won't allow you to copy from the computer to tape.) The bridge setup with the DVC 150 looks something like Figure 18-19.

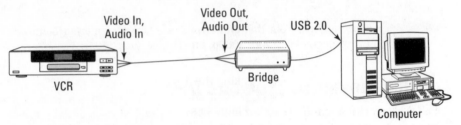

Figure 18-19: Using a bridge to copy a finished movie to VHS videotape

Things get weirder still, because you want to capture the movie to tape as it's playing on the computer. To do that, open your Videos folder (or whatever folder you put the finished movie in), right-click the finished movie (WMV file) that you want to copy to tape, and choose Open With ➪ Windows Media Player. In Media Player, click the Play button to start the movie playing; then click the Full Screen button in the Media Player program window, shown at left. When you're in Full Screen mode, press Ctrl+P to pause playback; then press Ctrl+Shift+B to rewind to the beginning.

Put a blank tape into the VCR. Hit the Record button on the VCR (or the Play and Record buttons, if that's what your VCR requires) to start taping. On the computer, press Ctrl+P to start the movie playing. The movie should copy to the VHS tape as it's playing. You'll need to watch the entire movie. When copying is complete, stop the VHS tape, and close Windows Media Player. To test the results, just rewind and play the VHS tape normally in any VCR.

Closing Windows Movie Maker

You can close Windows Movie Maker using the same techniques you use to close any other program window. That is, click the Close button in its upper-right corner, or choose File ➪ Exit from the Movie Maker menu bar. If you made any changes to the current project, you'll be asked if you want to save those changes. Assuming you don't want to lose your work, choose Yes.

Letting Movie Maker Do It for You: AutoMovie

In this chapter, you have seen how to use the timeline and the storyboard. Windows Movie Maker has a feature that allows you to save some time by letting it do all the work. This is the AutoMovie feature.

The AutoMovie wizard will create a movie for you based on the items you currently have selected in the open collection or using all the items if nothing is selected. To use AutoMovie, do the following steps.

STEPS: Using AutoMovie

1. Select the items you want included in your movie. Do this by holding down the Ctrl key and then clicking on each picture, video, or other media file.

2. Start AutoMovie by either clicking the AutoMovie button in the taskbar or by selecting Tools ➪ AutoMovie from the Movie Maker menu. The AutoMovie wizard launches.

3. On the first page, select the editing style you want AutoMovie to use for the movie it will generate. These are listed along with descriptions of the editing style as shown in Figure 18-20.

4. Optionally, you can click the links to add a title. If you choose to add a title, you can get back to the editing style page by clicking the link under More options.

5. Optionally, you can also click the link to select audio or background music. You can pick an audio file to include as well as adjust the audio levels.

6. Click the Create AutoMovie button to generate the movie.

The AutoMovie wizard generates the movie based on your selected settings. The final project will be placed into the storyboard/timeline. You can then play, save, publish, or otherwise edit the movie that was generated.

Tip If you have a bunch of photos, you can select them all and let AutoMovie link them together into a movie with transitions. You can then burn this to DVD and give it to friends and family!

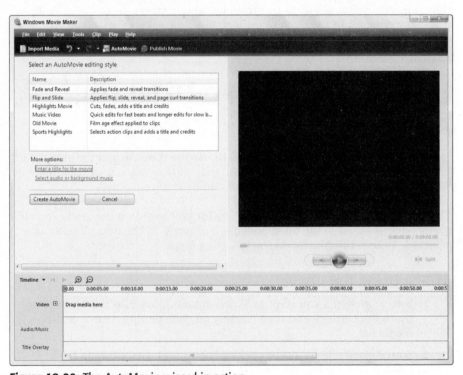

Figure 18-20: The AutoMovie wizard in action

Managing Collections

We stuck this section near the end of this chapter, because everything in this chapter is entirely optional. You don't really *need* to manage your clips to create a movie—you just have to add clips to the storyboard/timeline to make a movie. But if you import lots of videos, stills, and music into Movie Maker, you're likely to end up with a lot of collections and a lot of clips—so many that it becomes difficult to find specific clips when you're trying to make a movie.

Managing clips involves tasks such as renaming clips and deleting junk clips you'll never use in any movie, perhaps combining multiple small collections into one larger collection. You can also split one clip into two or, in some cases, combine multiple short clips. We'll look at the latter techniques first.

Splitting a Clip

Let's say you have a rather lengthy clip in one of your collections that you prefer to treat as two separate clips. Perhaps you just want to get rid of some stuff in the clip, or maybe you want to show part of the clip at the beginning of the movie and part of the clip at the end of the movie.

To split one clip into two, follow these steps:

1. In the Collections pane, click the collection that contains the clip you want to split.

2. In the Contents pane, click the clip you want to split into two clips. The first frame of that clip appears in the Monitor.

3. Click the Play button under the monitor, and watch it play. When you get near the place where you want to split the clip, click the Pause button.

4. Optionally, use the Previous Frame and Next Frame buttons in the Monitor to zero-in on the exact frame where you want to make the split.

5. Click the Split button under the monitor (see Figure 18-21).

The one clip will now be two. The first half of the clip will retain the original name. The second half of the clip will have that same name followed by (1). Click either clip; then click the Play button to see the clip play.

Tip To rename one of the clips, right-click and choose Rename. If one of the clips is just trash you'd never use in any movie and you just want to get rid of it, right-click the useless clip and choose Remove. Only remove a clip if you're certain you'll never use it in any movie you create.

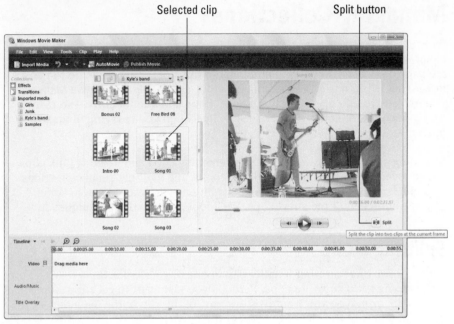

Selected clip   Split button

Figure 18-21: About to split one clip into two

Combining Clips

Sometimes when you import video, Movie Maker might split clips in a manner that doesn't reflect how you intend to use the clips. For example, I imported a music video that really needs to be played as one long scene, because there's music that goes along with that video. Rearranging the clips would also rearrange the music, which just wouldn't make sense. So rather than deal with the piece as multiple separate clips, I'm more inclined to combine them into a single clip that I can treat as a unit.

You should only combine clips that are adjacent to one another in the Contents pane. If in doubt, switch to Details view and click the Name column heading until the triangle in that heading is pointing up. That way, the clips will be listed in the order in which they were captured or imported. Then, in the Contents pane, click the first clip to be combined. Hold down the Ctrl key, and click adjacent clips to combine with it. Figure 18-22 shows three adjacent clips selected in a collection.

To combine the clips, choose Clip ➪ Combine from the Movie Maker menu bar, or right-click any selected clip and choose Combine. The selected clips will be combined into a single clip that has the same name as the first clip you selected. To verify, just click the clip's name in the Contents pane, and click the Play button in the Monitor.

Selected collection   Selected clips

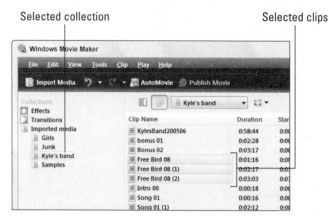

Figure 18-22: Three adjacent clips selected in the Contents pane

Moving, Renaming, and Deleting Clips and Collections

The collection and clip names that appear in Movie Maker aren't set in stone. You can change the name of any clip, or any collection, to something more meaningful for you. To do so, just right-click the collection or clip name you want to change and choose Rename. Type the new name and press Enter.

If you have any junk clips that you wouldn't use in any movie and therefore just want to get rid of, you can do that. But be careful not to accidentally delete anything you might need in the future. Once you delete an item, that's the last you might ever see of it. Anyway, to delete a clip or collection, right-click it and choose Remove.

If you do remove a clip or collection accidentally, you can undo the deletion, but you need to do so before you do anything else (and definitely before you close Windows Movie Maker). To undo the deletion, choose Edit ➪ Undo Remove Clip or press Ctrl+Z.

 Tip   Ctrl+Z is sort of the universal undo keystroke in Windows Vista. Try using it right after you've accidentally done anything, in any program. But don't count on it always being available.

To move a clip from one collection to another, first open the collection that the clip is currently contained within. If you just want to move one clip, point to its name in the Contents pane, hold down the left mouse button, drag the clip so that it's right on top of the collection into which you want to move the clip (over in the Collections pane), and release the mouse button. The clip will disappear from its current collection. But when you click the name of the collection into which you moved the clip, you'll see it listed in the Contents pane of that collection.

To move multiple clips, you can use the Ctrl+Click or Shift+Click method to select multiple clips first. Or, to move all the clips within a collection, right-click some empty space within the Contents pane and choose Select All (or press Ctrl+A or choose Edit ➪ Select all). Then drag any selected clip and drop it onto the name of the collection to which you want to move the clips. All those clips will disappear from the current collection and land in the collection to which you just dropped them.

Summary

Movie Maker is one of those huge, built-in programs one could easily write an entire book about. But what you've learned in this chapter will certainly let you create just about any movie imaginable. There's plenty of additional information available to you at all times. For starters, you can choose Help ➪ Help Topics from the Movie Maker menu bar at any time for help. And there are lots of videos, demos, tutorials, FAQs (Frequently Asked Questions), and freebies at the Movie Maker web site (choose Help ➪ Windows Movie Maker on the Web from the Movie Maker menu bar. Now let's get back to the main points you've learned in this chapter:

✦ Windows Movie Maker is a program for creating your own custom movies from video, photos, and music.

✦ To get video from a videotape into the computer, use Movie Maker to *capture* the video as it's playing on your computer screen.

✦ To get video, music, or photos from files already on your hard disk, choose File ➪ Import Media Items from the Movie Maker menu bar.

✦ To view the clips in a collection, choose the collection's name from the drop-down list, or click the collection name in the Collections pane. Clips within that collection appear in the Contents pane.

✦ To watch a clip, click its icon in the Contents pane; then click the Play button in the Monitor.

✦ To add a clip to your movie, drag the clip to the storyboard or timeline.

✦ Use the Video Effects and Video Transitions collections to add special effects to your movie.

✦ When you've finished creating your movie, save it to a movie (WMV) file by choose File ➪ Publish Movie from the Movie Maker menu bar or taskbar.

✦ Use AutoMovie if you want Movie Maker to create a movie for you based on one of several predetermined editing styles.

✦ You can use Movie Maker to create movies in a number of different levels of quality ranging from low quality for e-mailing to HD quality for 720p, 1080p, and HD for Xbox.

Getting Organized, Staying Organized

✦   ✦   ✦   ✦

Look at the title of this part, "Getting Organized, Staying Organized." Maybe we should have just titled it "Borrrrr – ing." Really, who *isn't* going to read that title and wonder, "What on earth does being organized have to do with computers? And why would I want to waste one precious moment of time finding out?" Answer to Question 2: So you don't spend all your precious time with a fishlike stare, hoping whatever it is you're thinking about will suddenly appear on your computer screen all by itself.

Which brings up the question, "Why can't the computer just keep stuff organized for me?" As we say back in Part I, your computer is kind of like a file cabinet with muscle. We don't say anything about brains. As a nonliving object, your computer's IQ is equal to that of all other nonliving things. You know, like rocks, fence posts, and car tires: IQ = 0. If you hope to find things you've saved on your computer, you'll have to be the brains of the operation. The only way to do that is to face the drop-dead boring concepts set forth in Part V's title.

Windows Vista isn't all boring. In fact, new in Vista is the ability to work with calendars to organize time, tasks, and appointments. The result is that in this part, you'll not only learn to organize things on your computer, you'll also learn how to organize a part of your life as well!

✦   ✦   ✦   ✦

Managing Files and Folders

Although all the technical stuff about computers is daunting enough, that's not all there is to it. Many problems stem from just being plain disorganized. Being disorganized, in turn, boils down to not being able to find the document you want, when you want it.

In Chapter 5, you learned that *documents* are things such as pictures, text, songs, and movies stored in files and that you use *folders* to store and organize files in much the same way you use folders in a filing cabinet. You open and navigate through folders using a program named Windows Explorer (commonly referred to as *Explorer*, for short).

The simplest way to get to the Windows Explorer program is to just open your Documents folder by clicking the Start button and choosing Documents (or by double-clicking the Documents icon on your desktop, if you have one). When you open your Documents folder, you see the title bar, navigation pane, and toolbar for Windows Explorer, along with the contents of your Documents folder. The navigation box in Windows Explorer always shows the name of the folder whose contents you're currently viewing.

Tip

Windows Explorer is the program for exploring *local resources* — stuff on your computer. *Internet Explorer* is the program for exploring *remote resources* — stuff outside your computer that you can access through the Internet.

Unlike a file cabinet, where each folder contains only documents, a computer folder can contain documents, more folders, or both. For example, if you go to your personalized folder, you see that it contains several others. As you learned in Chapter 5, your personalized folder is the one above the Documents folder that has your login name. You can get to it from the Documents folder by clicking its name in the address bar of Windows Explorer as shown in Figure 19-1. You can also get to your personalized folder by selecting the start button and choosing the top item of the right column, which should be the name of your personalized folder. Figure 19-1 shows the personal folder called Brad!

When you are viewing your personalized folder in Windows Explorer, you will probably see at least four folders: the previously mentioned Documents folder as well as Music, Pictures, and Videos folders. You might also have some documents and other folders. It's easy to tell folders and documents apart—icons that represent folders always sport a little manila file folder, as is also pointed out in Figure 19-1. Before we go any further here, let's review some basic facts about program windows in general and Windows Explorer:

✦ Unlike most programs, Windows Explorer never shows its name in its title bar. It contains an address bar that shows the name of the folder whose contents you're currently viewing.

✦ To change the appearance of icons in the folder, click the Views button in the toolbar to go to the next view. You can also click the down arrow next to the Views button and then select a view from the pop-up menu (for example, Extra Large Icons, Medium Icons, Small Icons, List, Details, Tiles).

✦ To rearrange icons, choose View ➪ Sort By on the Explorer menu (or right-click an empty space within the folder and choose Sort By); then choose an order. If the menu isn't displayed, you can display it by clicking the Organize toolbar button then choosing Layout ➪ Menu Bar.

✦ To hide or show toolbars and panes in Explorer, click the Organize toolbar, then choose Layout from the menu. Click the name of the toolbar or pane that you want to show or hide.

✦ To move the Explorer window (when it's not maximized), drag it by its title bar (the area above the address box).

✦ To size the Explorer window (when it's not maximized), drag any corner or edge.

✦ If you size the window down too much, the Details pane and Navigation pane will disappear. Enlarge the window to make them reappear.

✦ If the Details pane or Navigation pane never appear, click the Options button, then select Layout ➪ Details Pane and Layout ➪ Navigation Pane to display them.

✦ You can view both, Favorite Links and Folders in the Navigation pane.

✦ To open a folder whose icon appears in the navigation pane, double-click that folder's icon. To return to the folder you just left, click the Back button in Explorer's toolbar.

✦ To go to the parent of the current folder, click its name in the address box or from the menu bar select View ⇨ Go to ⇨ Up One Level. You can also press Alt+↑.

As you may recall from Chapter 5, a folder that contains other folders is referred to as the *parent* of the folders it contains. For example, Figure 19-1 shows you the contents of a folder named Brad! Within Brad! are several other folders including: Documents, Music, Pictures, Videos, and Downloads. Because those folders are contained within the personal folder called Brad!, you can refer to them as *subfolders* or *children* of the Brad! folder.

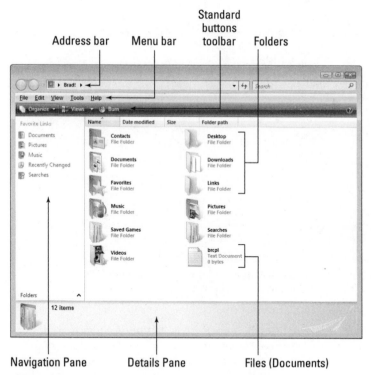

Figure 19-1: A sample folder containing subfolders

Creating Folders

Given that Windows already has folders for storing documents, why would you want to create your own folder? The answer is simple: for the same reason you probably have more than four or five folders in your filing cabinet — you just need more folders to organize your stuff. For example, suppose you have 1,000 photos. Do you really want to open your Pictures folder and have to scan through 1,000 file names every time you want to find a particular photo? How will you remember all those file names?

Creating new folders within Pictures lets you group your photos however you want. For example, you can create a folder for each major photo event, as in the example shown in Figure 19-2. (If you import photos from a digital camera, it might do that for you.) Each folder can contain any number of photos.

Figure 19-2: Contents of a sample Pictures folder with subfolders of photos

You don't have to stop there, though, because you can put folders in folders. For example, you can create a folder for each year, moving all the folders for each year into the appropriate Year folder. So, when you're thinking, "I need a photo," you open your Pictures folder. There, you see a folder for each year. Then you might think, "I'm looking for photos from Christmas 2005." So you open the 2005 folder, and there's the folder for all your 2005 Christmas photos (see Figure 19-3).

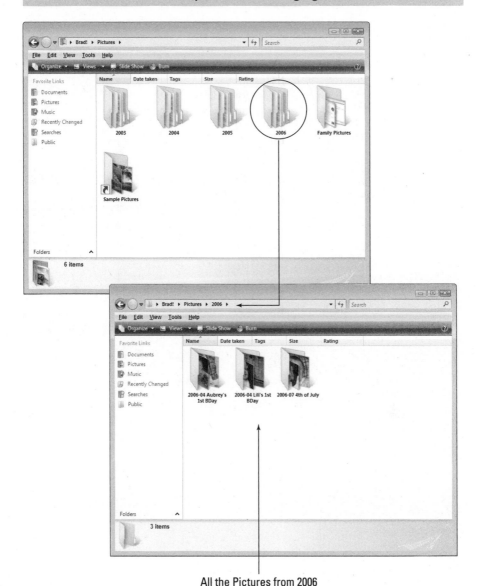

All the Pictures from 2006

Figure 19-3: Groups of photos further broken down by year

Then again, maybe organizing photos by year might not do the trick for you. Perhaps you'd rather organize by event. For example, you might have a folder for birthday photos, Christmas photos, vacations, and so forth, as in the top wof Figure 19-4. So when you're thinking, "I need a photo," you open Pictures. Then you think, "I'm looking for photos from a vacation." So you open your Vacations folder, and there you find folders for different vacations, as shown at the bottom of the same figure.

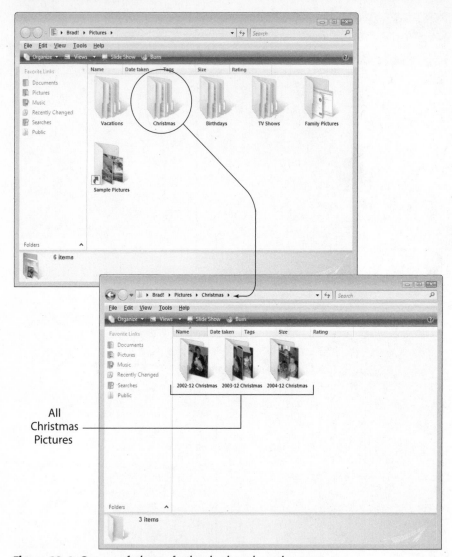

All
Christmas
Pictures

Figure 19-4: Groups of photos further broken down by event

Exactly how you organize your files and folder is entirely up to you, just like creating manila file folders in your filing cabinet. There's no right way or wrong way doing it. The one good and right way is whatever organization method makes it easy for you to find the files you need, when you need them. The goal is simply to get organized, and stay organized, so you don't waste all your time searching around for files.

Cross-Reference In Chapter 20 you will learn how to tag your folders and files so that you can easily find them.

Why Do I Always Lose My Files?

Arranging your existing documents into folders is a good start to getting organized. But staying organized requires that you use those folders whenever you save or download a document. As discussed in Chapter 5, that means never ignoring the address of the folder to save the file and the File Name options that appear in the Save As and File Download dialog boxes that appear whenever you're about to save something. You need to pay attention to those options (shown in the example that follows) whenever they appear on your screen.

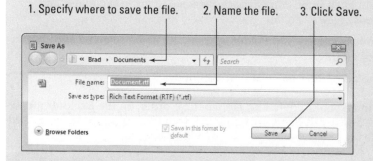

1. Specify where to save the file. 2. Name the file. 3. Click Save.

If none of what we just said seems familiar, you'll do well to review the section titled "Saving a Document" in Chapter 6. *Staying* organized starts in the Save As (or File Download) dialog box.

Creating Your Own Folders

Creating a folder is simple. But you need to think about where you want to put the folder. For example, it wouldn't make much sense to put a folder full of photos in your Music folder or in some random folder. The only place that makes sense for a folder full of photos is within your Pictures folder or some subfolder within Pictures.

 Tip   The term *directory* means the same thing as *folder*. But *directory* is kind of an old, outdated term.

To tell Windows where to put the folder, navigate to that folder before you create the folder. For example, if you're going to put the folder in your Pictures folder, open your Pictures folder. If you want to put the folder inside some folder in Pictures, open that folder. In other words, you need to open the folder that will be the parent to the new folder you're about to create. Here are the exact steps for creating a folder.

STEPS: Create a New Folder

1. Open your personal folder. Then navigate to the folder that will be the new folder's parent. It is recommended that you use one of the sub-folders within your personalized folder to save documents.

2. Do whichever is most convenient at the moment:

   • Click the Organize button on the Explorer toolbar, then select New Folder from the menu.

   • Choose File ➪ New ➪ Folder from the Explorer menu bar.

   • Right-click some empty space between icons in the folder and choose New ➪ Folder.

3. A new folder named New Folder appears, its name selected and ready for editing.

4. Type the new folder name and press Enter.

To quickly whip all your folders into alphabetical order, on the Explorer menu, choose View ➪ Sort By ➪ Name, or right-click some empty space between folders and choose Sort By ➪ Name.

If you need to move some existing files into a folder, you can use any of the techniques described in the section "Moving and Copying Files," later in this chapter, to do so.

Creating a Folder on-the-Fly

As you know, whenever you create and save a document or download one, the Save As dialog box opens. There, you tell Windows where to put the file and what to name it. Suppose that you're already in the Save As dialog box, when you think, "Darn, I should have created a new folder for this, because I'm going to have more documents like this one." It's not too late, though, to create a new folder. You can create the new folder on the spot, right there in the Save As (or File Download) dialog box. Here's how:

1. In the Save As dialog box, click Browse Folders in the lower left. This expands the Save As dialog box to show Explorer as in Figure 19-5.

2. At this point, you can create a new folder as described before:

   • Click the Organize button on the Explorer toolbar, then select New Folder from the menu.

   • Right-click some empty space between icons in the folder and choose New ➪ Folder.

3. A new folder named New Folder appears in the main pane. Type a new name, and press Enter. The folder will be automatically opened, and its name will appear in the address box, indicating that this is where your file will be saved.

4. Type a file name in the usual manner; then click the Save button.

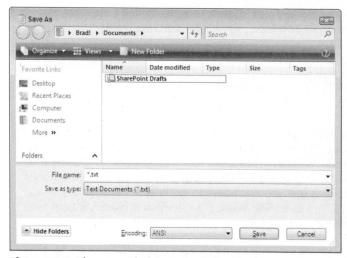

Figure 19-5: The expanded Save As dialog box

When you get back to Windows Explorer and navigate to the parent folder you selected in step 1, you'll see that it contains the folder you created in Step 3. Opening that folder will reveal the file you saved in Step 4.

Renaming Files and Folders

The name you give to a file or folder isn't set in stone. You can change the name of a file or folder at any time. However, it's important to understand that you never want to change the extension on a document file, as doing so will make it impossible to open the document in the future. We'll show you an easy way to change only the file name, not the extension, in the steps that follow.

 Caution You can't rename a file on a CD-ROM or DVD, unless it is a Read/Write CD set up to be modified, or unless you have special software installed. See Chapter 21 for more information.

STEPS: Rename a File or Folder

1. Right-click the icon of the folder or file you want to rename and choose Rename from the shortcut menu that opens.

2. The name is selected.

3. If you're renaming a document, and file name extensions are visible, make sure you don't change the extension. To play it safe, you can put the mouse pointer just to the left of the period that starts the extension and drag the mouse pointer through everything to the left, so that the extension is no longer selected, as in Figure 19-6. When you select Rename, the selection will be the default.

It's OK to change the filename...
...but never change the extension

Figure 19-6: Renaming a file when file name extensions are visible

 Tip   File name extensions are visible only if the Hide extensions for known file types option in Folder Options is turned off. See the section "Showing/Hiding File Name Extensions" in Chapter 6 for details. One of the advantages of keeping file name extensions hidden is that you don't have to worry about accidentally changing a file's extension. When the extension is hidden, it's not even possible to change it!

4. Type a new name, or use any of the standard text-editing techniques to change the name.

 Cross-Reference   See the section "Changing Text in a Text Box" in Chapter 2 for a refresher on standard text-editing techniques for small amounts of text.

5. Press Enter.

If you have chosen to sort the directory, then, when you rename the file, it will be automatically sorted into the correct location in the folder. If this doesn't happen, you can always force the sort — just right-click some empty space between icons and choose Sort By ➪ Name.

 Tip   If you change your mind right after renaming a folder, press Ctrl+Z to undo the change.

Working with Multiple Files and Folders

In a moment, we'll talk about deleting, moving, and copying files and folders. But before we do, be aware that it's not necessary to work with only one file, or one folder, at a time. You can *select* multiple files (or folders), then move, copy, or delete them all in one fell swoop. There are lots of ways to select multiple files. Choosing one method or the other is generally a matter of whatever method is most convenient at the moment.

If you're selecting multiple icons from a folder that contains many icons, it might help to start by choosing a view and sort order that makes it easy to see all the icons you want to select. You can use any view and sort order you want.

For example, if you choose List from the Explorer View options (click the Views button in the toolbar and choose List), you'll be able to see many icons at a time. If you choose View ➪ Sort By ➪ Type, all the files of a certain time (for example, all pictures) will be clumped together within the folder (or right-click on an open area within the Explorer content area and choose Sort By ➪ Type from the pop-up menu).

Selecting Multiple Icons by Dragging

If the icons you want to select are adjacent to one another within the folder, perhaps the easiest way to select them will be to drag the mouse pointer through them. It's a little tricky, though, so pay close attention to these steps.

STEPS: Select Multiple Icons by Dragging

1. Position the mouse pointer so it's near the first icon you want to select, but not actually touching that icon, or any other icon, as in the top of Figure 19-7.

2. Hold down the left mouse button, and drag the mouse pointer through the name or icon of each item you want to select.

3. When all the items you want to select are highlighted, as in the bottom of Figure 19-7, release the mouse button.

The selected items are highlighted. If you need to remove one or more items from your selection, hold down the Ctrl key and click the items you want to remove. Or, to start over, just click some empty space between icons to get back to your starting point.

 Caution When using single-click navigation as discussed in the following section, it's important to move the mouse pointer to some neutral place between icons after selecting icons. If you leave the mouse pointer resting on an icon, doing so will be taken as a new select, thereby unselecting the currently selected icons and selecting only the one the mouse pointer happens to be resting on. Also, when using single-click navigation, it's important to move the mouse pointer to some neutral place between icons before selecting the icons. If you start your selection by clicking an icon, then you might drag it to a new location rather then select multiple items.

1. Start with the mouse pointer near, but not touching, the first item you want to select.

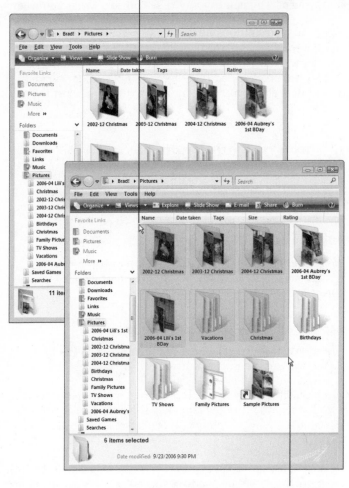

2. Drag the mouse pointer through the items you want to select, then release the mouse button.

Figure 19-7: Selecting multiple icons by dragging the mouse pointer through them

Selecting All Icons in a Folder

If you want to select all the icons within the current folder, that's easy. In addition to the other selection methods you learn in this chapter, you can more easily use one of the following methods:

✦ Click the Organize button and then choose Select All from the menu.

✦ Choose Edit ⇨ Select All from the Explorer menu bar.

✦ Press Ctrl+A.

All the icons will be selected. You can remove individual icons from your selection using Ctrl+*select* or Shift+*select*, described as follows. To unselect all icons, click any empty space between icons.

Selecting Multiple Icons Using Ctrl and Shift keys

If you want to select multiple icons that aren't near each other, you can use the Ctrl and Shift keys in combination with the mouse. Exactly how you do it depends on the navigation method you're currently using. To see (and optionally change) your current navigation method, follow these steps:

1. Open your Documents folder or any other folder (it doesn't really matter, because the setting you choose will applies to all folders and all document icons).

2. Choose Tools ➪ Folder Options from the Explorer menu bar.

3. Under Click items as follows on the General tab (see Figure 19-8), choose one of the following options:

Figure 19-8: The General tab of the Folder Options dialog box

- **Single-click to open an item (point to select):** Lets you open a folder or document by clicking its icon once. To select an icon, point to it (rest the mouse pointer on it for a second). If you choose this option, you can also choose to show all icon titles with or without underlines.

- **Double-click to open an item (single-click to select):** Requires that you double-click a folder or document icon to open it. To select an icon, click it once.

Caution The single-click option requires split-second timing on selecting icons. If you're a beginner, or have trouble selecting icons using that method, you would probably be better off using the double-click method.

4. Click the OK button to close the dialog box.

I'll use the terms *Ctrl+select* and *Shift+select* in the sections that follow. It's important to understand, though, that the definition of *select* depends on which option you chose previously. Here are specific definitions for the two navigation methods:

✦ **Single-click to open method:**

- **Select:** Point to the icon (rest the mouse pointer on it for a second).

- **Ctrl+select:** Hold down the Ctrl key, and point to the icon for a second.

- **Shift+select:** Hold down the Shift key, and point to the icon for a second.

✦ **Double-click to open method:**

- **Select:** Click the icon you want to select.

- **Ctrl+select:** Hold down the Ctrl key; then click the item you want to select.

- **Shift+select:** Hold down the Shift key; then click the item you want to select.

Selecting Multiple Icons with Ctrl+Select

To select multiple icons that aren't adjacent to one another within a folder, follow these steps:

1. Select the first icon you want to select.

2. Hold down the Ctrl key while selecting additional icons.

3. Release the Ctrl key when you're done selecting.

Figure 19-9 shows an example of multiple icons selected using Ctrl+select. Note that you always select the first icon without holding down the Ctrl key. You hold down the Ctrl key only when you want to start selecting more icons without unselecting the first one.

You can also use Ctrl+select to deselect a single selected icon without deselecting them all. Just Ctrl+select any selected icon a second time.

Select

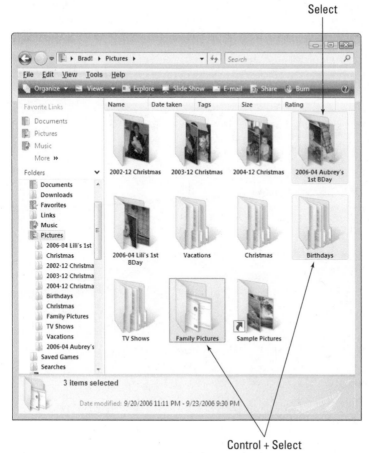

Control + Select

Figure 19-9: Selecting multiple icons with Ctrl+select

Selecting Multiple Icons with Shift+Select

You can also use the Shift key to select multiple icons. Unlike the Ctrl key, which selects one icon at a time, the Shift key enables you select a range of icons. The steps are fairly straightforward:

1. Select the first item without holding down any keys.

2. Hold down the Shift key, and select the last item you want to select.

3. Release the Shift key.

For example, in Figure 19-10, the first icon is selected without holding down any keys. Then the last item is selected using Shift+select. Because the Shift key is used, both icons — and all the icons in between — are selected.

Shift + Select

Figure 19-10: Selecting multiple icons with Shift+select

If you need to unselect a few of the selected icons, Ctrl+select those you want to unselect. To unselect all selected files and start over, click an empty space between icons.

Inverting a Selection

You can invert the current selection in a folder, thereby unselecting icons that were selected and selecting the icons that weren't selected. This can be handy when you want to select most, but not all, of the icons in the folder.

For example, suppose you want to select all the pictures in a folder, but none of the folders or documents. Rather than painstakingly selecting each picture, you can first select the items you *don't* plan to select, as at the top of Figure 19-11. Then choose Edit ➪ Invert Selection from the Explorer menu bar. All icons except the one(s) you originally selected will be selected, as at the bottom of Figure 19-11.

Three icons
selected

After inverting, all but the
original three are selected

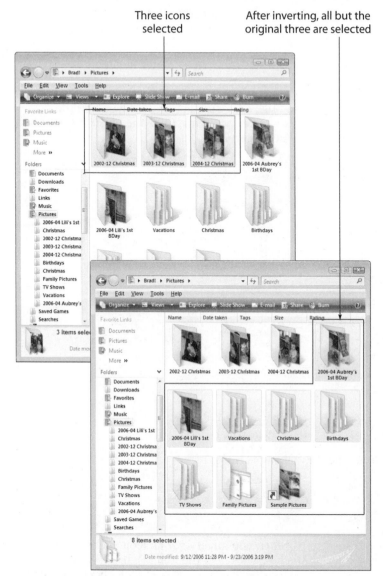

Figure 19-11: Selecting multiple icons with Shift+select

Selecting Multiple Icons Without Using the Keyboard

So far, most of the procedures for selecting multiple icons that have been pre-sented require that you press the Shift or Ctrl keys on the keyboard. You can also select multiple files without ever touching the keyboard. To accomplish this, follow these steps:

1. Open your Documents folder or any other folder (it doesn't really matter, because the setting you choose will apply to all folders and all document icons).

2. Choose Tools ⇨ Folder Options from the Explorer menu bar.

3. Select the View tab.

4. Within the Advanced settings area, scroll down until you find the option for Use check boxes to select items. Click the check box next to this item to select it (see Figure 19-12).

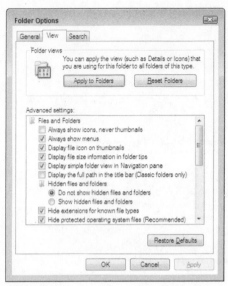

Figure 19-12: The View tab in the Folder Options dialog box

5. Click OK.

After you've done these steps, when you hover over an icon, a check box will be displayed by it. Clicking the box will select the item. Figure 19-13 shows a couple of items selected using the check boxes. Selecting the check box again will remove the icon and thus remove the selection.

Tip
A check box may also appear by the Name column heading in the content area of Explorer. You can see this check box in Figure 19-13. By clicking it, you will select all items in the folder.

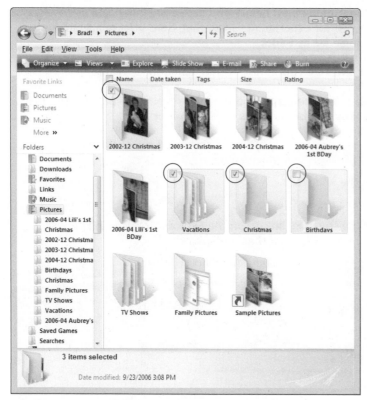

Figure 19-13: The display of check boxes for selecting items

Deleting Files and Folders

There's no rule that says you have to keep a file or folder forever. You can delete a file or folder at any time. But deleting can be dangerous and isn't something you want to experiment with. You need to be aware of some facts first:

✦ The term *delete* means get rid of it forever. It's not the same as closing something, which merely takes it off your screen.

✦ You should delete an item only if you know exactly what it is and you're absolutely certain you will never need it again for the rest of your life.

✦ When you delete a folder, you also delete *all* the files and subfolders within that folder. Don't delete a folder unless you're sure you won't need anything in the folder for the rest of your life.

So the bottom line is, think hard before you delete anything, and never, ever delete something just for experiment. Given that, here's the quick-and-easy way to delete a single file or folder:

✦ Right-click the item you want to delete and choose Delete.

You don't have to delete icons one at a time, however. You can also use this method to delete any number of items within a folder:

1. Select the icon(s) you want to delete by using any of the methods described previously in this chapter.

2. Do one of the following:

   • Press the Delete (Del) key.

   • Click the Organize button on the Explorer toolbar and choose Delete from the menu that is displayed.

   • Select File ⇨ Delete from the Explorer menu bar.

   • Right-click any selected icon and choose Delete.

3. You'll see one of the dialog boxes shown in Figure 19-14.

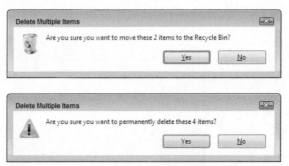

Figure 19-14: One of these confirmation dialog boxes will appear when you delete files or folders.

4. If you're sure you want to delete the files, go ahead and click Yes.

The selected items disappear.

Using the Recycle Bin

Notice that the top dialog box in Figure 19-14 is asking "Are you sure you want to send these items to the Recycle Bin?" That dialog box appears when you delete a file or folder from your computer's hard disk. When you delete a file or folder from your hard disk, it isn't truly deleted right away. Instead, it's moved to a special folder called the Recycle Bin. The Recycle Bin, in turn, is a safety net that allows you to recover any files you deleted by accident.

Tip Actually, if you realize your mistake right after deleting a file or folder on your hard disk, you can press Ctrl+Z to undo the deletion and bring the files back, without going through the Recycle Bin.

However, the Recycle Bin only stores files that you delete from your hard disk — not files you delete from floppies or any other removable media. Files from removable media are permanently deleted right on the spot, and there's no way to change your mind. When a file is about to be permanently deleted, you see a dialog box that appears at the bottom of Figure 19-14. As soon as you click Yes in that dialog box, the deleted files and folders are gone forever!

Tip Another name for a hard disk is a *fixed disk*. That's *fixed* as in *can't be removed*, not *fixed* as in *previously broken*. The opposite of that is a *removable disk*, such as a floppy disk, CD, DVD, or Zip disk, which you can remove from the drive and replace with another disk.

Leaving deleted files and folders in the Recycle Bin has only one drawback — the files and folders there take up just as much space on your hard disk as they did before you deleted them. So if you're looking to get back some disk space, you'll have to *empty* the Recycle Bin, which is roughly equivalent to emptying your real trashcan into an incinerator, from which there's no hope of ever getting the trash back. Keep in mind that when you empty the Recycle Bin, that's it; there's no way (in Windows Vista) to get those files back.

 To see which files and folders are currently in your Recycle Bin, double-click the Recycle Bin icon (shown at left) on your Windows desktop. When the Recycle Bin opens, it really won't look much different from any other folder you see in Explorer (see Figure 19-15). The icons in the main pane represent files and folders you've deleted from your hard disk.

Undeleting Files and Folders

Even though there's no way to recover a permanently deleted file in Windows Vista, that doesn't mean it's entirely impossible. You can purchase and install a third-party undelete program that provides one last, slim hope of restoring deleted files from removable media and even files that have been emptied from the Recycle Bin. But those deleted files won't hang around forever. Eventually, new files you save will replace the deleted ones. And when that happens, the deleted files no longer exist and nothing can bring them back.

Still, if you can jump on the problem shortly after an accidental deletion, there's a good chance you'll be able to undelete. As an example of a third-party undelete program, check out the RecoverMyFiles program at www.recovermyfiles.com. Or try out the free trial version by going to www.tucows.com and searching for RecoverMyFiles.

Restoring Accidentally Deleted Files and Folders

Before you do anything else in the Recycle Bin, you should look through every single item in the bin. If you come across any file that really shouldn't be deleted, right-click that item and choose Restore to put it back into its original folder (see Figure 19-15). Optionally, you can select multiple icons using any of the techniques described earlier; then right-click any one of the selected icons and choose Restore to restore them all (or click Restore the selected Items on the Explorer toolbar).

Figure 19-15: Restoring an accidentally deleted file from the Recycle Bin

Giving Files and Folders the Axe

When you feel confident that the Recycle Bin contains only folders and files that you'll never need again, for the rest of your life, empty the Recycle Bin. To empty the Recycle Bin:

✦ Click Empty the Recycle Bin on the Recycle Bin's toolbar.

✦ Or choose File ➪ Empty Recycle Bin from the Recycle Bin menu bar.

Everything within the Recycle Bin will disappear and head up to software heaven, from which there is no return. The disk space that was consumed by those files will be recovered, making room for new files.

 Caution Never use the Recycle Bin as temporary storage for a file or folder you don't plan to delete. That would be like storing important paper documents in your trash can. Just too darn risky!

When you've finished with the Recycle Bin, you can close it as you would any other window — by clicking the Close (X) button in its upper-right corner. And

that about covers it for deleting files. If there's one point that I must stress one more time, it's that you never want to delete a file just because you don't know what it is. The only time you want to delete a file is when you know exactly what it is and are 100 percent sure you'll never need the file again.

Tip   You can also delete a file by dragging its icon and dropping it right onto the Recycle Bin's icon. And you can empty the Recycle Bin without opening it. Just right-click its icon and choose Empty Recycle Bin. (Yes, those are two tips, although the second one is dangerous if you don't know what's in the Recycle Bin!)

Moving and Copying Files

Keeping files organized often requires moving and copying files. Whenever you move or copy a file, there's a *source* and a *destination* involved. The difference is as follows:

- ✦ **Source:** Where the file or folder is currently located.
- ✦ **Destination:** Where you want to put the file or folder.

The source can be any folder on your hard disk, a floppy disk, or a CD. (Likewise for the destination.) But techniques for copying files to CDs and DVDs are somewhat different from the general techniques we'll describe in this chapter. Chapter 21 talks about how you get files from your hard disk to CDs and DVDs.

Move versus Copy

The terms *move* and *copy* in the computer sense have the same meanings that they do in regular English. When you *move* a file from one location to another, you remove it from its current location and place it in a new location. For example, if you move a file from your Documents folder to your Pictures folder, you still have only one copy of that photo — the one now in your Pictures folder.

When you *copy* a file, you end up with two exact copies of the file. For example, if you copy a file from your Documents folder to a floppy disk, you'll have two copies of the file: the one still in your Documents folder and the one on the floppy. You can say that the copy on the floppy is a *backup* of the one in the Documents folder. If you somehow mess up the copy in your Documents folder, it's no big deal. You can just grab a copy of the original from the floppy disk.

Here's another way to think about it, using a real-world example. If you remove a paper document from one folder in your file cabinet and put it in another folder, you *move* the document to a new location. If you take a paper document out of the file cabinet and make a photocopy of it, you make a *copy*, in that you have two versions of the same document.

There are lots of ways to move and copy files. As usual, there isn't a right way or a wrong way of doing it. The result is always the same. Choosing one method over another is simply a matter of deciding what's most convenient at the moment or what's easiest for you to remember.

Moving Files to a Subfolder

One of the most common reasons to move files is when you create a new, empty subfolder within some existing folder. Then you want to move some files into that new subfolder. For example, let's say you have songs by various artists in your Music folder. Several of the songs are by the group Newsboys. You'd like to create a subfolder named Newsboys and move all of their songs into the Newsboys folder.

The first step, of course, is to create the new, empty Newsboys folder. You can use any technique described earlier in this chapter to create the new folder. Next, you need to select all the songs that you want to move. In this case, select all the songs by Newsboys, as in Figure 19-16. (Use the Ctrl and Select methods described earlier in this chapter to select multiple nonadjacent files.)

New, empty folder named Newsboys

Songs by Newsboys selected

Figure 19-16: About to move Newsboys songs to the new Newsboys folder

When the files you want to move are selected, just drag any selected icon so that it's covering the destination folder's icon. That is, point to a selected file, hold down the left mouse button, drag the ghost image (semitransparent image) of the selected icon that appears when you start dragging, so that the mouse pointer is right smack on top of the destination folder and the destination folder looks highlighted, as in Figure 19-17. Then release the mouse button.

Tip　If you just want to move a single file into a subfolder, there's no need to select anything. Just drag the file's icon so it's right on top of the destination folder's icon, and release the mouse button.

Drag any selected file so the mouse pointer
is right on top of the destination folder,
then release the mouse button.

Figure 19-17: About to drop selected file onto the Newsboys folder

As soon as you release the mouse button, all the selected icons disappear, as in Figure 19-18. That's because the files are no longer in the Music folder; you *moved* them to the Newsboys folder. If you open (double-click) the Newsboys folder, you'll see the files inside that folder.

Tip　If you wanted to *copy* (rather than *move*) the files to the subfolder, you could drag using the right mouse button rather than the left mouse button. Once the mouse pointer is smack on top of the destination folder, release the right mouse button and click Copy Here in the little menu that appears.

Moved files are no longer in the open folder. They're in the destination folder now. Open (double-click) the destination folder to see the contents.

Figure 19-18: Moved files have disappeared; they're in the Newsboys folder.

Moving and Copying Across Any Folders

The whole business of dragging a file to a subfolder works fine when you can see both the destination folder and the files to be moved in the same Explorer window. But what about when you want to move or copy files when you can't see the files and folders at the same time? There are a couple of ways to deal with that. One is the drag-and-drop method, which we'll discuss next.

Moving and Copying by Dragging

When you can't see the source folders and destination folders at the same time, you can just open both folders. Then select and drag files from one folder to the other. This is best illustrated by an example. An easy way to move or copy files from the Pictures folder to the Public Pictures folder is by right-dragging the items to the destination folder (where *right-dragging* means holding down the right mouse button, rather than the usual left mouse button, while moving the mouse). Here are the steps.

STEPS: Move or Copy Folders by Dragging

1. Open Windows Explorer (or your Documents folder); then navigate to the destination folder.

2. Open Windows Explorer (or your Documents folder) again; then navigate to the source folder.

3. Size and position the two open windows so you can see the main pane of each one. For example, in Figure 19-19, the Pictures folder will be the source folder (upper left), and Public Pictures will be the destination folder (lower right).

Tip
The address bar at the top of Windows explorer can be used to navigate to any folder on your computer. If you type `public` into the address bar and press the enter key, you will be taken directly to the public folder. You can then select the Public Music folder within it.

4. If you want to move or copy multiple items from the source to the destination, select the items using any technique described earlier in this chapter.

5. Point to the item you want to move (or any selected item) and hold down the right (secondary) mouse button.

Source folder

Destination folder

Figure 19-19: The Pictures folder is the source folder; Public Pictures is the destination folder.

6. Keep the right mouse button held down while moving the mouse pointer into some empty area within the destination folder; then release the right mouse button. Then:

- To move the files to the destination click, click Copy Here in the little menu that appears (see Figure 19-20).

- To copy the items to the destination folder, click Move Here in the little menu that appears (see also Figure 19-20).

The icons will be copied or moved to the destination folder.

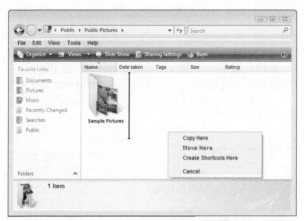

Figure 19-20: The menu that appears after right-dragging items

Tip To quickly size your open windows, right-click the current time in the lower-right corner of your screen and choose Cascade Windows. Then move one of the folders down, and to the right, by dragging its title bar. You can also set your windows side-by-side or stack them.

Dragging with the right mouse button, as in the preceding steps, is actually optional. But if you drag using the left mouse button, you won't get the choice to move or copy. Windows will just decide for itself what to do as follows:

✦ If you drag the files to a new folder on the same drive (for example, from the Pictures folder to Public Pictures, both of which are on your hard disk), the files will be moved, on the assumption that you're reorganizing the files.

✦ If you drag files to a window for a different drive (for example, floppy disk, Zip disk, or CD), the files will be copied, on the assumption that you're making backup copies.

Caution If you start dragging icons, but change your mind, just press and release the Esc key (before you release the mouse button) to cancel the operation.

If you do drag using the left mouse button, the mouse pointer will show a little + sign in the destination folder if Windows intends to copy the file. If Windows intends to move the file, there will be a little arrow instead of the + sign. But you can still choose whether to move or copy the file, though, so long as you do so before you release the mouse button. Here's how:

✦ To copy the files, hold down the Ctrl key, release the mouse button, and release the Ctrl key.

✦ To move the files, hold down the Alt key, release the mouse button, and release the Alt key.

Then again, you can move and copy files and folders without any dragging at all. You can use cut and paste, or copy and paste instead, discussed next, if those techniques are easier for you.

Tip

The terms create, rename, select, delete, restore, move, **and** copy are all official buzzwords that you can locate in Windows Help and Support Center when you need a quick reminder or reinforcements on techniques described in this chapter.

Using Cut and Paste to Move or Copy Files

As an alternative to dragging things around to move or copy them, you can use simple cut and paste (to move) or copy and paste (to copy) the files.

STEPS: Move/Copy Files with Cut and Paste

1. Open Windows Explorer (or the Documents folder), and navigate to the folder that contains the items you want to move or copy.

2. If you intend to move or copy multiple items, select those items using any technique described earlier in this chapter. Then do one of the following:

   • To move the items, do any one of the following:

   • Press Ctrl+X.

   • Select Edit ⇨ Cut from the menu bar.

   • Click Organize on the toolbar and then select Cut.

   • Right click one of the selected items and choose Cut on the menu that pops up.

   To copy the items do any one of the following:

   • Press Ctrl+C.

   • Select Edit ⇨ Copy from the menu bar.

   • Click Organize on the toolbar and then select Copy.

   • Right-click one of the selected items and choose Copy on the menu that pops up.

3. Navigate to the destination folder (wherever you want to put the files).

4. To paste the items, do any one of the following:

   - Press Ctrl+V.

   - Choose Edit ➪ Paste from that folder's menu bar.

   - Click Organize on the toolbar and then select Paste.

   - Right-click some empty space within the destination folder and choose Paste.

Making a Copy in the Same Folder

Sometimes it's helpful to have two copies of the same file in a single folder. For example, let's say you have a file named *January Newsletter*. When February rolls around, you want to use January's newsletter as the starting point for your new newsletter. Rather than altering January's newsletter directly, you can keep that one and use a copy as the starting point for the new newsletter.

To do so, right-click the file you want to copy (*January Newsletter* in this example) and choose Copy. Then right-click any empty space between icons and choose Paste. Or, using the keyboard, select the item(s) you want to copy and press Ctrl+C. Then click some empty space within the same folder so that no items are selected, and press Ctrl+V.

You can also make a copy of a file within the same folder by dragging. Point to the item you want to copy, hold down the Ctrl key, drag (using the left mouse button) to some empty space within the same folder, and release the mouse button.

Either way, a copy of the file will appear. Its name will be the original name followed by - *Copy*. If you don't see the copied file, choose View ➪ Arrange Icons By ➪ Name. This should put the copied file next to or near the original file. To rename the copied file (for example, to change its name from *January Newsletter - Copy* to *February Newsletter*, right-click its name and choose Rename, as described earlier in this chapter).

File Clashes with Copies and Moves

What happens if you copy or move a file to a folder and a file already exists in that folder with the same name? Never fear, Windows Vista has you covered. When a name clash occurs, you will be asked what should be done. Figure 19-21 shows the prompt when a file is copied from a source file called Guidelines.pdf that already exists in the destination folder.

Figure 19-21: Copy a file when one already exists.

As you can see in the dialog box in Figure 19-21, you have a couple of options:

✦ The file being copied can replace the existing file in the destination folder

✦ You can choose to cancel the copy by selecting Don't Copy in the dialog box

✦ You can choose to do the copy, but give the new file a new name.

If you select the option to give the file a new name, Windows Vista will create a name automatically. The original name will be used followed by a number in parenthesis.

Undoing a Move or Copy

If you complete a move or copy operation and then change your mind, you can undo the action as long as you don't do any more moving or copying.

To undo a move or copy, press the universal Undo key, Ctrl+Z. Or right-click within the source folder or destination folder (or Desktop, if that was your source or destination), and choose Undo Move or Undo Copy. Or choose Edit ➪ Undo from the source or destination window's menu bar. You may see a prompt asking if it's OK to delete the files. Choosing Yes will delete only the copied file(s), which is OK, since that's what's actually required to undo the copy.

Summary

We've covered a lot of ground in this chapter, and the things described here are the most common things people do to manage files. There's a whole lot more coming up, though, including tasks such as copying files to CDs and floppies, finding lost files, combining files from multiple folders into one folder, and more. But first, here's a quick recap of the most important points covered in this chapter:

✦ To create a new folder, go the folder that will be the new folder's parent. Then choose Organize from the Explorer toolbar and select New Folder, or choose File ➪ New Folder from the menu bar, or right-click some empty space between icons and choose New ➪ Folder.

✦ To rename a file or folder, right-click its icon and choose Rename.

✦ To perform the same operation on multiple items within a folder, first select the items you want to delete/move/copy by using any of the techniques described earlier in this chapter.

✦ To delete an item, right-click it and choose Delete.

✦ To delete multiple items, first select the items you want to delete. Then press Delete (Del), or click Organize on the Explorer toolbar and select Delete, or right-click any selected item and choose Delete.

✦ Files and folders that you delete from your hard disk are initially just moved to the Recycle Bin.

✦ To restore an accidentally deleted file, open the Recycle Bin on your Windows desktop. Then right-click the item you want to restore and choose Restore.

✦ To permanently delete files in the Recycle Bin and reclaim the hard-disk space they're using, choose Empty the Recycle Bin from the Explorer bar in Recycle Bin.

✦ To *move* a file or folder means what the name implies — to take it from one place and put it in some other place instead.

✦ To *copy* a file or folder means to make an exact duplicate of it, as you can with a photocopy machine.

✦ The *source folder* in a move or copy operation is the folder in which the files are currently stored. The *destination folder* is the folder to which you want to move or copy the files.

✦ To move a file to a new folder, just drag its icon to the destination folder's icon or to an open copy of the folder.

✦ To copy a file to a new folder, hold down the Ctrl key and drag the file to the destination folder's icon or to an open copy of the folder.

✦ You can also move files using cut (Ctrl+X) and paste (Ctrl+V) key combinations. You can copy files using copy (Ctrl+C) and paste (Ctrl+V) key combinations.

Finding Things on Your Computer

Everything on your computer is actually stored on your computer's hard disk. That includes Windows Vista, all your installed programs, every document you create or download, and all the built-in folders Windows provides for storing your documents, such as Documents, Public Documents, and Music folders.

Although few people realize it, a hard disk is home to hundreds of folders and tens of thousands of files, even on a brand-new computer. If you lose something in all of that, finding it again in the future is no small feat. In this chapter, you'll learn how to go looking for lost items. What you will find — in addition to your files and documents — is that Windows Vista has greatly improved search features over prior versions of Windows.

Caution   If you've used Windows Companion in the past for searching, you may be shocked to learn it is gone in Vista. While the search companion is gone, searching features are still available, and they are more powerful than ever before!

Searching for Lost Files

Contrary to popular belief, computers don't eat files. Windows will never rename your files, delete your files, or move your files on its own. But that doesn't mean you won't ever lose track of a file. As mentioned a few times in this book, whenever you save a file—be it one you created yourself or one you downloaded—you have to tell Windows where to save the file and what name to give it.

Even if you do remember to do all that, there's no guarantee that you'll remember where you put a file six months from now. Sometimes, you just forget where you put things. When things get lost on your computer, it's time to enlist the help of the Windows Vista search features.

Using the Windows Vista Search

In prior versions of Windows, you often relied upon the Search Companion tool offered by Windows Explorer to help you find lost files. In Windows Vista, basic searching has been simplified. Additionally, because it is very common to need to find a file, the ability to search is available in several areas and with several levels of detail. The primary three areas that you will learn about first are:

✦ Searching from the Start menu

✦ Searching from Windows Explorer

✦ Searching from the Search Folder

Which of these three you are likely to use depends on what you are looking for and what information you have readily available regarding the file you want to find.

Searching for Programs from the Start Menu

If you're primarily interested in finding a program that you know is on your computer, then the best place to start is with the search that is available on the Start menu. When you click the Start menu, you will notice a Search box just below the All Programs option as shown in Figure 20-1.

You can use this search at any time to find programs as well as your favorites and history. This search works as a filter, so after you start typing, Windows Vista will look for any results that match what you enter and only display them. The more you type, the more will be filtered out of the selection. The right side of Figure 20-2 shows the results of typing S into the search box. On the right side, you see what is displayed when Sol is entered.

At any time you can stop entering text and select form the list of items shown. If you want to clear the selection, you can press the Esc key to return to the standard Start menu, or you can backspace over what you've entered. Either way, if the search box is blank, you will see the standard Start menu displayed.

Figure 20-1: The Start Search option on the Start menu

The display is filtered as the search value is entered

Figure 20-2: Filtered search results in the Start menu

In Figure 20-2, you should also notice that two additional links are at the bottom of the search results. The first link, See all results, will not show you additional results. Rather, it will give you additional information about the results that match your search criteria. Clicking the See all results option will take you into the Search Folder with the results of your current search shown (see Figure 20-3). We'll cover the details of the search folder in one of the sections that follow.

The other option is Search the Internet. If you are connected to the Internet, then you can click this option to open Internet Explorer and display the results of using Windows Live Search with the value you had entered into the search box. Figure 20-4 shows the result of clicking Search the Internet with the Sol value entered into the search box.

Be aware that the results of the Internet search will be more than just program files. It will contain nearly any information that can be found on the Internet using the search information you entered. You can learn more about using Windows Live and Internet Explorer in Chapter 10.

 Note The results displayed using the Internet may change over time. This is because the information on the Internet changes.

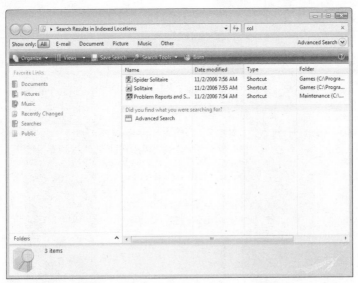

Figure 20-3: The Search folder display after coming from the Start Search

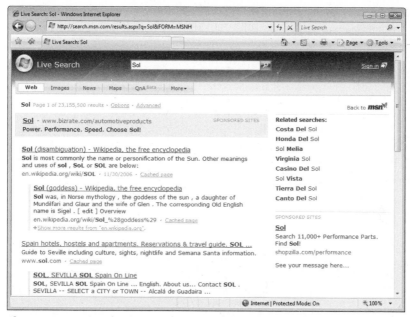

Figure 20-4: Using the Start menu's Search the Internet option

Searching Within a Specific Folder

In Chapter 19, you learned how to use the Windows Explorer program to navigate to a specific folder to display its contents. Explorer also enables you to search and filter the contents of the folder you are currently viewing.

Just like with the Start menu search box, as you enter information in the search box in Windows Explorer, the files and folders will be filtered to only those that match. In Figure 20-5 you see an example of a search being done in the Music folder. In this example, the search is for the song called *My Sacrifice*. Figure 20-5 shows Explorer after Sa is entered into the search box.

By entering just a few characters, a relatively cluttered list of files and is filtered down to just a few. The target file you want is easily found with the shorter list of results from the search.

You should notice that the search only applies to files in this folder. If you want to search more than just the current file, you should use the Search folder.

You might notice in Figure 20-5 that Sa is the search term, but that the search results don't all show Sa in their file names. This is not an error — rather it has to do with what search is looking at. For now, know that a search index has been created by Windows Vista that contains key information about a file. This information includes the title, content, properties, and more. Later in this chapter, in the section "What's Searched," we will describe more exactly what is being searched.

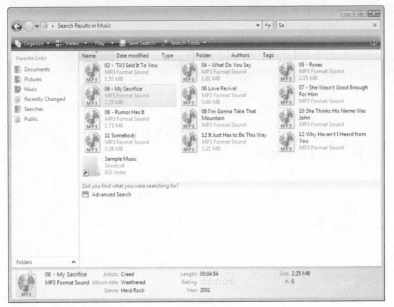

Figure 20-5: Searching with Windows Explorer

Searching with the Search Folder

If you need to do more than look for a file in a single folder, or find a program from the Start menu, then you will want to use the Search Folder. The Search Folder allows you to search a larger portion of your computer. Additionally, it gives you more criteria to use for filtering down your search.

You can access the Search Folder by selecting Search from the right side of the menu. This presents the standard Search Folder as shown in Figure 20-6.

As you can see, the Search Folder looks similar to Windows Explorer but has a different toolbar. Additionally, some of the panes are initially missing. If, however, you enter a search term into the Search box in the upper-right corner, you will quickly see that the Search Folder looks even more like Windows Explorer. Figure 20-7 shows the results after Sa is entered into the search box.

Figure 20-7 shows a lot more results than just those that were seen earlier in Figure 20-5 when searching in the Music folder for the save value. This is because the Search Folder is not limited to just one folder, but rather looks in all the common locations on my machine.

You should also notice that after information is entered into the search field, the Search Folder changes to look just like Windows Explorer. This makes sense because the result of the search is a list of files, and Windows Explorer is perfect for browsing files. What you will also find is that you can manipulate the search results just as you would manipulate files in Windows Explorer. What you learned in Chapter 19 applies here as well.

One thing that you will see that is different is the new toolbar labeled *show only*. This tool bar adds an extra level of filtering to your searches. The default is All, which displays all file types. If you want to look for a specific type of file, you can select an item on this toolbar. You can also select Other, which shows results that are not e-mails, pictures, documents, or music.

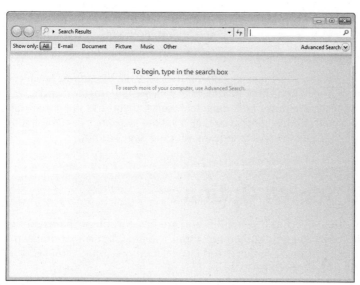

Figure 20-6: The Search Folder

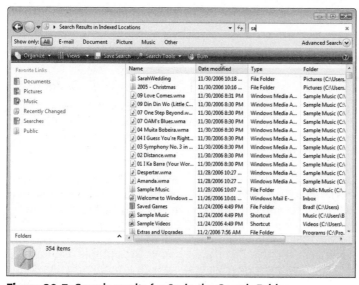

Figure 20-7: Search results for Sa in the Search Folder

For example, when searching for a song, you can select Music on the show results for toolbar to eliminate any non-music items from my list. You can do the same for any file type.

Narrowing your search to the fewest possible matching files is an important part of performing a search. Too broad a search results in hundreds, if not thousands, of files, which doesn't do you much good when you're trying to locate one file. If you can narrow the type of file that will reduce the number of results you will get and increase your chance of finding the file you are trying to find.

Caution   E-mail messages aren't files or folders. They're, well, *messages*. Advanced Search can only find e-mail messages if your e-mail program works with Windows Vista. Windows Mail definitely works. If you use any other mail package, you'll need to confirm by looking at the program's documentation as to whether Windows Vista indexes your messages or not.

Advanced Search Options

If you don't know the name of the file and if you are not certain of the exact file type, then you still need to know *something* about the file. That *something* can be any combination of characteristics listed here. The more things you know, the easier it will be to find the file:

✦ When you saved or downloaded the file

✦ All, or part, of the file name

✦ Some word or phrase in the document (if it's a document that contains text)

✦ The name of the person that created the file originally

✦ The size of the file

After you think of something unique about the file that will help Windows find it, you can then search for it. You've seen how some of this information can be used directly in the primary search box. Some of the other types of information are easier to use from the Advanced Search options.

Within Windows Explorer and within the Search Folder you might have noticed a link for Advanced Options. In Windows Explorer, the link to Advanced Search options is shown below the results of your search (see Figure 20-3 earlier in this chapter). In the Search Folder, the link to the advanced options is below the search box. Clicking this link in either place will add the Advanced Search options to the window near the top. Figure 20-8 shows the options displayed in the Search Folder. The display is nearly identical with Windows Explorer as well.

A number of options get displayed when you select Advanced Search. Let's look at the various options that appear and at how you can use them.

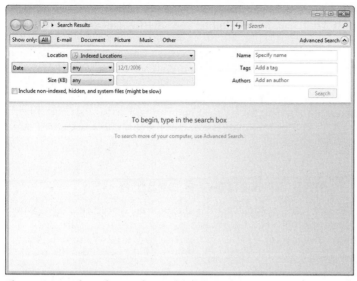

Figure 20-8: The advanced search options

 Caution   Entering text into the search box causes the search to happen immediately. In some cases, the Advanced Search options might not be applied to your search until you click the Search button. Clicking the Search button will apply them.

Setting Where to Look

The Location drop-down list, shown in Figure 20-8, tells the Search how much area to search. If you select the drop-down list, you will see a list of choices. Figure 20-9 shows the locations listed on Brad's machine. You can see that the list allows you to select your Indexed Locations, as well as the individual drives. You can even search the entire computer.

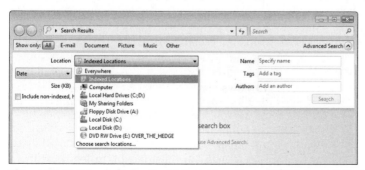

Figure 20-9: Search first using Indexed Locations. If that doesn't find the file, then search Local Hard Drives (C:) unless you happen to know the file is in a specific file or removable disk.

Most likely, if the file is lost, you should start by searching the Index Locations. If that doesn't return what you are looking to find, then you'll want to choose the Local Hard Drives option. That will be your entire hard disk or even all your hard disks in the event that you have more than one. That choice will certainly cover the most ground and, therefore, increase your chances of finding the file.

If you think the file is in a specific folder, you can replace Local Hard Drives. But don't do this unless you're really sure you can narrow the search to a specific folder on your hard drive.

Using a File Name to Narrow a Search

If you can remember anything about the file's name, that would be great. You can fill in the Name option with the information you know (see Figure 20-8). For example, if you're looking for a letter you wrote to Wilma Wannabee six months ago, there's a good chance the name Wilma might be in the file name. So you could type that under Name.

If you're searching for a song, entering any word from the song title, or even the artist's name, here might help, too.

If, by chance, you happen to know the file's type and extension, you can enter that, although you'll have to use the following format: *.*ext* where *ext* is the extension you're looking for. For example, if you're looking for a JPEG image (or all JPEG images), you could enter *.jpg. If you're looking for a document you created in WordPad or Microsoft Word, you could enter *.doc. Of course, if you are not exactly sure of the extension, then you might want to use the Show only option to narrow down the results first.

If you don't have a clue what the file name is, or what the extension is, leave this option blank. Guessing here isn't likely to help.

Stating When You Created, Last Used, or Last Modified the File

If the file is one you saved or downloaded recently, you can greatly increase your chances of finding it by entering into the Advanced Search options some clue as to the age of the file. If you recently modified, accessed, or created the file, then you can also indicate this within the Advanced search options. By isolating a date associated with the file, you can once again narrow the number of results that may be returned in a search and thus have a better chance of finding your file.

Within the advanced options there is a drop-down list button called Date. If you select this button, you will see (as shown in Figure 20-10) that you can select either Date modified (the last time you changed and saved the file) or the Date created (the date you created the file).

Figure 20-10: Even knowing when you created or last modified the file can help.

Nobody expects you to remember the exact date for any of these events. Because of this, the option to the right of the Date list button allows you to set the relativity of the date. Specifically, the option enables you to set whether the event (modified, created, or accessed) happened before a certain date (*is before*) or after a certain date (*is after*). Of course, if you remember a certain date, you can set the relativity of the date to *is*.

When you've set the type of date and whether it was before, after or is a specific date, you will then be able to enter a date to work from. You can either type the date into the date field as shown in Figure 20-10, or you can click the small calendar icon and select the date from a calendar as shown in Figure 20-11.

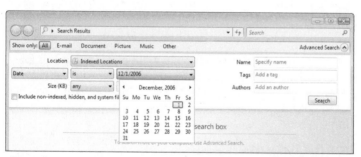

Figure 20-11: Selecting a specific date to search based upon

If you really don't have a clue as to when the file was last saved, last opened, or created, then don't set this option.

Stating the Size of the File to Narrow a Search

It's unlikely that you'll ever know, offhand, what the size of the file was. So the options shown in Figure 20-12 are of dubious value. You don't have to know the exact size, however. If you know the file was bigger (*is greater than*) or smaller (*is less than*) than a certain size, then you can use this information to try to narrow the search based on those factors.

Figure 20-12: If you can estimate the size of the file, you can use the Size option.

In addition to selecting equals, is less than, or is greater than, you will also need to enter a value into the box on the right. This is a size in kilobytes (KBs). If you are not using *equals,* then you can round this number.

If you really have no clue about the file's size, it would be best to leave this option set to any.

Providing the Author's Name to Narrow a Search

Some file types enable you to associate an author to them. For example, Microsoft Office applications associate a name with a document. If you know such a name was used to create the document that you are searching for, then you can enter all or part of this name into the Name field of the Advanced Search Options. Of course, if you are unsure whose name is being used, then you should leave this option blank.

Using Tags to Narrow a Search

The only major item that hasn't been discussed in the Advanced search options is the Tags option. With Windows Vista, you have the ability to associate tags to certain file types such as some image files and music files. Tags are simply words.

If you have added tags to some of your files, then you'll be able to search for them by using the Tag option in the Advanced Search options. You can enter more than one tag word; however, you need to separate them with semicolons. Tags will be covered in more detail later in this chapter.

More Advanced Options

You might see other search options displayed depending on your computer's settings. For example, you might see a check box option as shown in Figure 20-13. You should only select such additional options if you know what is specifically being asked. If in doubt, leave it out!

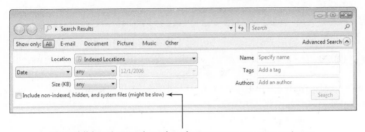

An additional search option that you may or may not see

Figure 20-13: An additional search option you might see

Starting the Search

After you've answered as many questions as you can, you're ready to begin the search. If the search hasn't happened automatically, then just click the Search button at the bottom of the Advanced Search options. Any files that match your search criteria will start to appear in the main pane. When the search is complete, you'll see the files (if any) that matched your search, as the options shown in Figure 20-14.

What you do from here depends on what you've got:

✦ If you've found what you're looking for, then you can use the file just as you would from Windows Explorer.

✦ If you haven't found what you're looking for, you can click one of the options to change your search criteria and try again.

Even though the window is titled "Search Results," you're actually in Windows Explorer. As such, you can choose a View, such as Icons, List, or Details, using the Views button in the toolbar or the View option on the menu bar.

In Details view, you can sort the results on any column heading. For example, to put the files in alphabetical order by name, click the Name column heading until its little triangle is pointing up. To change the width of a column, drag the bar at the right edge of the column heading. Or scroll over to the right and click the Date modified heading to order files by the date they were last modified. To add columns to the Details view, select View ➪ Choose Details from the menu bar — you can press the Alt key to temporarily show the menu.

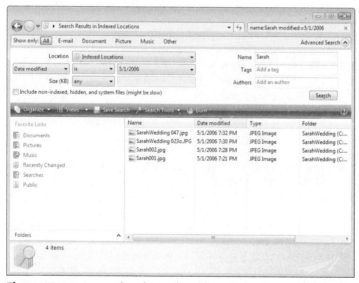

Figure 20-14: A completed search, with options above and found items below

Cross-Reference For a reminder on working with columns, see the section "Working with Columns" in Chapter 5.

At this point, you can do anything you want with any of the files you found. For example:

✦ If scroll bars are visible in the search results window, use them to scroll up and down, left and right.

✦ To open the folder that the file is contained within, right-click a file name and select Open file location from the pop-up menu.

✦ To move the file to a different folder, use any technique described in Chapter 19.

✦ To open a file, double-click its name. Or right-click the file name and choose Open With ⇨ and the name of the program you want to use to open the file.

Exactly what you do with the found files is entirely up to you. However, having to go searching for a file in the first place implies that you didn't know where it was. So you might want to move it to a folder that makes sense. For example, if it's a song, move it to your Music folder. If it's a video, move it to your Videos folder. When you've finished working with the Search Results window, just close it as you would any other program window, by clicking the Close button in its upper-right corner.

Using Search to Gather Like Files

Search is good for more than just finding lost files. It's also a good way to organize your stuff. For example, let's say you've downloaded a bunch of songs or videos from the Internet, but they're in some weird folder other than the simple Music or Videos folder. Or maybe you just want to gather all your ZIP files (compressed files) and put them all together in one folder. Whatever it is you want to gather up, just start a new search and specify what you're looking for.

After specifying the criteria that define the files you're looking for and clicking the Search button, the main pane will show all the files. Browse through all the files to make sure you know what you got. If you want to move all those files into one folder, click the Organize button and choose Select All from the menu or press Ctrl+A. You can then copy or move the files in any of the ways described in Chapter 19.

So how would you create a search that would find all the Music files or all the files of a single type? Simply set two things — click the item type you want to find in the Show only list and select the Location you want (the Local Hard Drive (C:)). Click the Search button with all of the other advanced search options left open and nothing in the search text box. This search will go find all files that are of the type you selected.

Saving Searches

Sometimes you do a search that gives you great results. At other times, you may find that there is a search you need to do more than one time. In these cases, and in any other cases, you can save a search.

When you save a search, you actually save the options that you entered for the search to filter down the results. For example, in the previous section you learned how to find all music files by selecting a show results for value of Music and by setting the location to your local hard drive. This is a search you might want to do more than once, so it is worthy of being saved.

In Figure 20-15, you can see the results of this Music search on my machine.

After you do a search, a new item is added to the toolbar called Save Search. You can see this in Figure 20-15. Clicking this button opens the Save As dialog box shown in Figure 20-16.

The Save As dialog enables you to save the search you just did. Just as other Save As dialog boxes you've seen, you can enter a name for the search. You can also change the location where the search is saved by selecting Browse Folders or changing the location in the address bar. The search will be saved as a Search Folder and by default it will be saved in the Searches folder.

Figure 20-15: The results of the search for all music on my machine

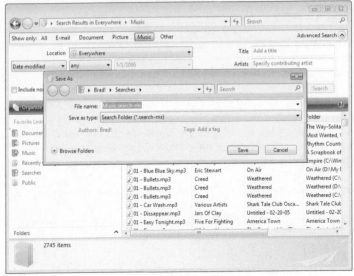

Figure 20-16: The Save As dialog box for saving searches

You should also notice two other items in the Save As box for searches. The first is the Authors item. In Figure 20-16, you can see that Brad is listed as the author. This is defaulted to the name of the user account that is being used on Windows Vista. You can click the name and add additional authors, or you can change the one that is there. Later, you can then search on the author to find this search again!

The second item you should notice is the Tags item. If you click the Add a tag text, you will be able to add tags to this search. Tags are simply keywords that you can then use to find this search again later. Tags are covered in more detail later in this chapter.

After you've entered a name for your search and saved it, you will then be able to navigate to it later and execute it quickly. If you save the search to the default location, then it will be available in the Searches option under Favorite Links within Windows Explorer. Searches in Favorite Links is simply a folder that contains saved search files. If you select it, you will see a few searches that Windows Vista provides for you by default. Figure 20-17 shows the default searches that are on Brad's machine along with the saved All My Music search.

The saved searches are all simply folders. As such, you can use them and treat them like any other folder. You can double-click (or right-click them and select open) any of the saved searches to cause them to be executed again.

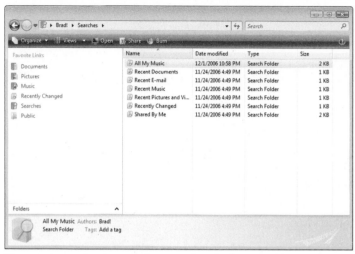

Figure 20-17: Viewing existing searches in the Searches folder

What's Searched

You should always know what is being searched. For example, if you use the search in the Start menu, you are primarily looking for applications on your computer. If you are looking for a music file, you are unlikely to find it using the Start menu search.

If you are using the Search Folder or the search in Windows Explorer, then by default you are searching an index that has been created based on index locations. These locations are defaulted to the common areas where you keep files such as your Documents folder as well as your Pictures, Music, and Videos folders. If you are using Windows Mail or a Vista-friendly mail program, then they may also be indexed. Offline content from the Internet (See Chapter 10 for more on Offline content) can also be included. In general, the most frequently used files and folders will be indexed. Those that are less likely to be searched won't be.

 You can, however, change what files are included in the index. You can do this in the Indexing Options dialog box. To go to the Indexing Options dialog box, open the Start Menu and select Control Panel. In the Control Panel Home screen, select System and Maintenance. This displays a list of options you can use to customize your system. Within this list are Indexing Options. Selecting it displays the dialog box shown in Figure 20-18.

Tip   A quicker way to get to the Indexing Options dialog box is to use search! In the Start Menu search box, enter **Index**. You can then select Indexing Options from the results that are displayed.

Figure 20-18: The Indexing Options dialog box

The Indexing Options dialog box shows you what locations are already indexed. You can add additional locations as well as remove existing locations. Click the Modify button to modify the locations that will be included in the index. If nothing is shown in the Indexed Location dialog that is displayed as a result of clicking the Modify button (see Figure 20-19), then click the Show all locations button at the bottom of the dialog box. This adds the locations to the dialog box (you may have to select Continue in a User Access Control dialog). Figure 20-19 shows what your selected Index locations might look like if they've never been changed (bottom part of the dialog box).

The top portion of the Index Location dialog box allows you to select additional locations — or remove existing locations. This is done by using the check boxes on the left side of the dialog box. Selecting a check box includes the folder and any subfolders. Clearing a check box removes the item from the selected indexed locations.

The folders within the Change selected locations area can be expanded to show subfolders. This allows you to pick any areas you want. Additionally, if your computer has additional drives other than a primary Local Drive (C:), then these will be shown as well. In Figure 20-19, you can see that a secondary local drive (D:), as well as a Removable Disk. These drives or folders within these drives can be added to the search index as well.

As you select or clear items, you will notice that a summary of them is listed in the bottom section of the Index Locations dialog box. This allows you to keep track of what you are indexing. When you are happy with your selections, click the Ok button to save the changes. If you want to leave without saving the changes, click the Cancel button. When you return to the Indexing Options dialog box, you should notice that the number of items indexed will either go up or down based on whether you added more areas to index or removed them.

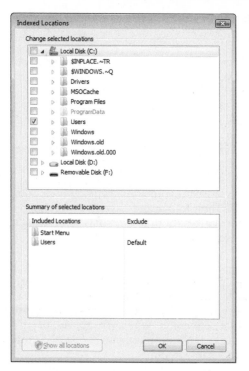

Figure 20-19: The Index Location dialog box with a couple of locations shown

You might be tempted to simply select all your drives and let Windows Vista index everything. This is not wise. Rather, you will end up with a huge index file that contains a lot of index information for files you'll not need to actually search — files such as temporary junk files and system files. You are better to only index folders that contain information you might actually need to search or find items within.

You have the ability to search for files that are outside of the search index. Searching within these areas simply takes a little longer than the initial search. Just because a file is outside of the index does not mean it cannot be found.

Tip   You can restore your index to its original settings. Do this by first selecting the Advanced button on the Indexing Options dialog box. This displays an Advanced Options dialog box. On the Indexing Settings tab, click the Restore Defaults button. This removes your current index and rebuilds a new one with the default settings.

Tagging Files and Folders

Another feature that will make searching more effective is the concept of tagging. Tagging is associating tags — simple words — to documents. For example, if you have a picture, it might contain the date and time it was taken in the properties associated with it; however, it will have little other information that is useful for finding it.

If you want to find all your Christmas pictures, then you need something more. For example, when you put pictures on your computer, you could tag them with the word *Christmas*. You could also tag them with any other descriptive words. These tags will then be added to the search index. You can use tags in the advanced search options to help find them as well.

 Note You can also use tags to sort, group, and stack documents in Windows Explorer.

Adding tags can be done via Windows Explorer. If your Preview Pane is not displayed, then click the Organize button on the toolbar and Layout ➪ Preview Pane. When you select a document, information about it is displayed in the preview pane at the bottom of Internet Explorer as shown in Figure 20-20.

In Figure 20-20, you see a picture has been selected. You can see when it was taken, its rating, if it has one, and more. In this example, there are no tags. To add a tag, click the Add a tag text, next to Tags. You can then enter the word you would like associated with the shown image. If you want to associate more than one word, then separate them with a semicolon. When you are done, press the Enter key or click outside the tag area and the tag will be added. You can also change or remove the tags in this same manner.

Figure 20-20: Preview Pane with document information displayed

Customizing Windows Explorer Search Tools

When you start entering a search in a folder using Windows Explorer, the toolbar changes to include two additional options. These are Save Search and Search Tools. You can see these options in the toolbar in Figure 20-3. As you learned earlier in this chapter, *Save Search* enables you to save the search that you just entered. This places it within the Searches Favorites Link in the navigation pane of Windows Explorer. Search Tools presents you with additional items:

✦ Search Options

✦ Index File Location

✦ Search Pane

Setting Search Options for Windows Explorer

Selecting Search options form the Search Tools button displays the Folder Options dialog box with the Search tab selected as shown in Figure 20-21. You will see several options that enable you to select what to search, how to search, and when to search non-indexed locations. You can also select to avoid using the index file, which is not recommended, as well as select to use partial matches, which is recommended.

Figure 20-21: Setting options in the Search Folder Options dialog box

Most of the options in this dialog box should be obvious. One that is unique is the Use Natural language search. This option enables you to be more natural in how you enter your searches. For example, to find all the Christmas pictures on your computer you could use the advanced search and enter **Christmas** in the tags and set the Show only: value to be Picture. If you were to turn natural language search on, then you could simply enter **Christmas pictures** into the search box and it would find all the Christmas pictures. Other natural language searches that I could do include:

✦ **Pictures created this month**

✦ **Documents created by Brad**

✦ **E-mail from Alan**

✦ **Vista or Flower Pictures**

 Caution   Not all natural language searches work as expected. If something doesn't work at first, then try wording it differently. For example, **Pictures of Vista and Flowers** may not work, whereas **Vista and Flower Pictures** might.

Setting the Index Locations in Windows Explorer

The Search Tools options button also contains a link for modifying the Index Location. Selecting this option opens the Indexing Options dialog box that was discussed earlier in the "What's Searched" section.

Activating the Search Pane in Windows Explorer

The third option in the Search Tools is the Search Pane option. This option determines whether the search pane is displayed or hidden in Windows Explorer. The search pane is shown in Figure 20-22.

Figure 20-22: The Search pane that can be displayed or hidden

Condensed Searches

You've seen a lot about searching in this chapter. Windows Vista has been greatly improved to help make it easy to find, sort, and use documents. Although you've learned a lot about searching, there are still a couple of tricks you can learn.

One trick is to use advanced search features without opening the advanced Search options. You can do this by using a condensed search. You can enter the advanced options directly into the search box. In fact, if you watch when you select advanced search options, a condensed search is entered into the search box for you.

The format of a condensed search is **Properties:value**, where Property is any property type you can find in a folder, and where value is the value you want to find for that property. The property and value are separated by a colon. Examples of common properties are Name, Type, Tags, Authors, and Title. You can determine other valid property types by right-clicking any of the column headings in the content area of Windows Explorer.

Using Conditions on Your Searches

Another trick in searching is using conditions with your search criteria. For example, what you want to find might be based on complex criteria. You might want all pictures that are tagged Halloween or Christmas. If you enter both Halloween and Christmas into the search box, you will only get pictures that have both words. To get around this, you can use an option called a Boolean condition. Boolean conditions that you can use are shown in Table 20-1.

Table 20-1
Boolean Search Conditions

Boolean Filter	What It Does
AND	Finds documents containing the word to the left and right of the AND. These words both simply need to be in the document. For example, **Christmas AND Halloween** returns all documents that had both Christmas and Halloween associated with them.
OR	Finds documents containing either of the word to the left and right of the OR. If either word is associated to a file, it is included in the search results. For example, **Christmas OR Halloween** returns all documents with either Christmas or Halloween associated with them.
NOT	Would find all documents that didn't have the word following NOT associated with them. For example, **NOT Christmas** returns all documents that didn't have Christmas associated with them. **Not Picture** returns all document files that were not pictures.
Quotes	Putting quotes around text will search for the exact text rather than the individual words. For example, **"Bradley L. Jones"** searches for *the* exact text between the quotes, not for the two individual names. Bradley Jones would be found where as Bradley L. Jones would not.
Parenthesis	Putting parenthesis around words allows you to find word groups in any order. For example, **(Bradley Jones)** finds **Bradley Jones** and **Jones Bradley**. It still would not find Bradley L. Jones.
< or >	The less than and greater than signs can be used to find things relative to others. For example, size: > 4 MB finds all files bigger than 4 megabytes.

Note   You can use MB for megabytes, KB for kilobytes, and GB for gigabytes.

 Caution   The above Boolean conditions must be used in all capital letters. You should use **AND**, not **And** or **and**.

Summary

That should be enough information about searching for things on your computer to hold you over for quite some time. Here's the standard recap of the main points covered in this chapter:

✦ When you lose a file or folder on your hard drive, you can search for it.

✦ There are at least three primary ways to search. Use the Start menu search to quickly find a program, use Windows Explorer to find files and folders, or use the Search Folder to do more advanced searches.

✦ Search filters files and folders that don't match the criteria you enter. If you don't remember the name or basic information that you are searching for, then you can use the advanced search options to find a file or folder based on its size, a date, its author, or tags.

✦ By adding tags to your files, you can make them easier to find later.

✦ By adjusting the Index File, you can change what folders get searched by default.

✦ Advanced search features enable you to set natural language querying. This lets you use regular sentence structures when entering search information.

✦ Boolean conditions enable you to create more complex searches.

Using Your Hard Drive

Everything in your computer, so to speak, is actually stored on your computer's hard disk drive (or hard drive). That includes Windows Vista, all your installed programs, every document you create or download, and all the built-in folders Windows provides for storing your documents, such as the Documents, Public Documents, Music, and Pictures folders.

Although few people realize it, a hard drive is home to hundreds of folders and tens of thousands of files, even on a brand-new computer. In the prior chapter you learned about searching through this magnitude of files. In this chapter, you'll learn techniques for exploring and maintaining your computer's hard disk and the files that are on it.

> **Note** Most of the tasks for managing your hard drive require that you are an administrator. If you are not an administrator, then you may be asked to enter an administrator password before you are allowed to perform the task. Additionally, if User Access Controls are turned on, then you may be asked for permission to continue when performing many of the following tasks.

Managing Your Hard Drive

OK, it's time to get into some technical stuff regarding what's really going on behind the scenes on your computer's hard drive. First, your computer's hard drive (also called a *fixed disk* or *primary drive*) lives inside the

---

♦ ♦ ♦ ♦

In This Chapter

Managing your hard drive

Exploring your hard drive

Instructions on cleaning up and organizing your hard drive

Windows Explorer tips and tricks with your hard drive

♦ ♦ ♦ ♦

system unit, so you never actually see it. All drives on your computer have a short, one-letter name followed by a colon (:). The name of your hard disk is C:. If your computer has multiple hard drives, they may be named D:, E:, F:, or anything up to Z:.

Although you can't see your hard drive directly, you can see its icon in the Computer folder. To open the Computer folder:

✦ Click the Start button and choose Computer.

✦ Or double-click the Computer icon on your desktop.

Your Computer folder will open. The contents of this folder depend on the disk drives you have in your computer, among other things. But if you scroll down, you'll see an icon for every disk drive in your system, perhaps looking something like the example shown in Figure 21-1. In that example, the hard drive is named Local Disk (C:). (The other icons represent other disk drives, which you'll learn about in Chapter 22.)

> **Tip** If you don't see the Hard Disk Drives and Devices with Removable Storage headings in your Computer folder, choose View ⇨ Group By ⇨ Types from the menu bar in Windows Explorer. You can display the menu by clicking the Organize button in the toolbar and then selecting Layout ⇨ Menu Bar.

Figure 21-1: Examples of icons for disk drives in the Computer folder

Discovering How Much Hard-Disk Space You Have

One thing that you definitely want to know about your computer is how much space is available on your hard disk. Beginners often waste a lot of time and money by constantly moving files to floppy disks and other removable media, in an effort to conserve hard-disk space. You really don't need to worry about that until you really understand how much storage space you have.

For starters, you need to understand that the storage capacity of a drive is measured in bytes, where 1 byte equals roughly the amount of space needed to store a single character of text, like the letter x. For example, it takes 3 bytes to store the word *cat* and 6 bytes to store the word *banana*. Most drives can store billions of bytes.

Because most disks store huge numbers of bytes, nobody ever bothers with saying things like "I have 20,545,642,321 bytes of hard disk space available." It's much easier to round these big numbers off to the nearest thousand, million, or billion. And we use some short names and abbreviations for those words, too, as shown in Table 21-1.

Table 21-1
Computer Names and Abbreviations for Large Numbers

Bytes	Name	Abbreviation	Word	Spoken Slang
1,000	Thousand	KB or K	Kilobyte	*kay*
1,000,000	Million	MB or M	Megabyte	*meg*
1,000,000,000	Billion	GB or G	Gigabyte	*gig*
1,000,000,000,000	Trillion	TB or T	Terabyte	*tee*

Note   The numbers in Table 20-1 are rough. A kilobyte is actually 1,024 bytes. A megabyte is 1,048,576 bytes (1,024×1,024). But if you just remember that each new word adds another *,000* to the previous number, that's close enough.

Every disk has an overall *capacity*, which is the number that describes how many bytes the disk can hold. Your hard drive already has lots of files on it — most of the files that make up Windows Vista and your installed programs. Each of those files takes up space. Every document on your hard drive also takes up space, *used space*. Any space that isn't already used is yours to do with as you please. We call that *free space* or *available space*. To find out the capacity of your hard drive, and how much hard disk space you have available (free space), follow these steps.

STEPS: Find Out How Much Hard Disk Space You Have

1. If you haven't already done so, open your Computer folder (click the Start button and choose Computer).

2. Right-click the icon for your hard disk and choose Properties.

3. If the General tab isn't visible automatically, click the General tab.

Granted, you might be able to see how much space is available after the first step. When you open the Computer folder in Windows Explorer, by default it is in the tile view. This View shows you the amount of free space as well as the full space. By doing all three steps, however, you will see the pie chart that appears (see Figure 21-2). It shows you, at a glance, how much hard disk space is currently being used and how much is still available. Most likely, you'll have billions of bytes (gigabytes) of each. What that works out to in terms of things in the real world is something you really have to be flexible in estimating. Table 21-2 shows some examples of what 1 gigabyte (1GB) represents in terms of what you can store, with some empty columns you can fill in for yourself if you like.

Table 21-2 How Many Things You Can Store in 1 Gigabyte of Disk Space					
Familiar Thing	*How Many Fit in 1GB*	*Times*	*Your Free Space*	*Equals*	*How Many You Can Store*
Type, double-spaced pages	500,000	x		=	
Photos	2,500	x		=	
CD-Quality songs	200	x		=	

For example, if you fill in the Free Space in the third column with the amount of gigabytes available on your hard disk, and multiply that by the number in the second column, that'll give you a rough estimate. For example, if you have 30GB of space left, that comes out to 200×30, or enough space for about 6,000 CD-quality songs.

 Tip If you need a calculator to do the math, click the Start button and choose All Programs ➪ Accessories ➪ Calculator.

If you did need more hard disk space, adding a second hard drive is usually inexpensive. In fact, hard disk space is one of the least expensive things on Earth. A 200GB hard drive would probably cost you about $90 to $100. Ain't nothing else you can buy 200 billion of for that kind of money. I'll bet 200 billion grains of dirt cost more than $100. Two hundred gigabytes worth of floppy disks would probably cost you about $100,000 and fill a two-car garage.

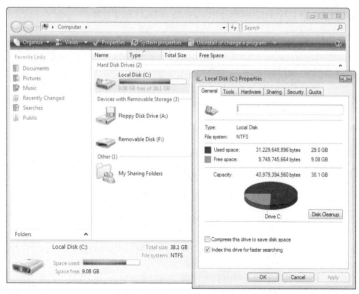

Figure 21-2: The General tab of a hard drive's Properties dialog box

When you've finished viewing your available disk space, click OK or Cancel in
the dialog box.

 Note In some of the steps within this chapter, the User Access Control dialog box
may be displayed, making sure that you are providing the permission for
the steps to happen.

Maintaining Your Hard Drive

Besides being cheap, your computer's hard drive is virtually maintenance free.
You don't ever have to touch the actual disk or do anything to it. But there are
some things you can do in Windows Vista to avoid wasting disk space and
keep your hard drive working at its highest possible speed and efficiency. We'll
take a look at those things in this section.

Recovering Wasted Hard Disk Space

Because hard disk space is cheap and plentiful, some programs take liberties
in creating temporary files that aren't really essential to the proper functioning
of your computer. Your web browser is a good example, because it keeps
copies of every web page you've visited recently (and even not so recently) sitting around in a folder known as your *temporary Internet cache*. Other programs may occasionally create temporary files of their own and let them hang
around the hard disk longer than is really necessary.

Over time, these copies can build up and start using up a fairly significant
amount of disk space. Plus, they all add up to just more files for Windows to

keep track of behind the scenes, which means slightly less performance (speed-wise) from your hard disk.

Even if you're not running low on hard disk space, it can't hurt to do some occasional spring cleaning and unload some unnecessary junk, say maybe once a month at most. You can do your spring cleaning, or let Windows Vista do the cleaning. It's easy to do and usually takes only a few minutes. Here's the procedure.

STEPS: Clean Up Your Hard Drive

1. Click the Start button and choose Computer.

2. Right-click the icon for your hard drive and choose Properties.

3. On the General tab, click the Disk Cleanup button.

If you are an administrator on the computer, then you will be asked if you want to clean up your files or files from everyone that uses your computer (see Figure 21-3). After you've made this selection, processing will be basically the same, except that you will be cleaning up just your files or everyone else's files.

After choosing, wait while Windows analyzes the disk and figures out how much space it will be able to free up. When the Disk Cleanup dialog box shown in Figure 21-4 opens, you can scroll through the list of files to delete to see the temporary files that are available to delete. There's absolutely nothing in the list that's required to make your computer work properly. And none of the documents you created or downloaded will be included in the list. Basically, the list only shows junk you can get rid of.

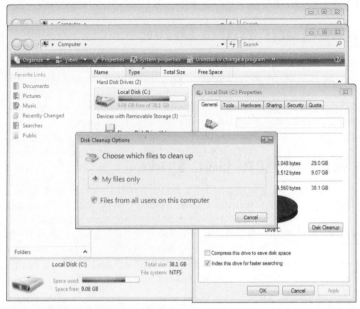

Figure 21-3: Disk cleanup option

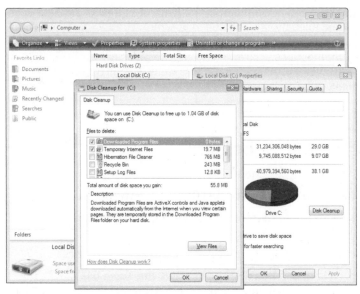

Figure 21-4: The Disk Cleanup dialog box for a hard drive

Recycle Bin will be one of the items in the list. If you haven't looked in the Recycle Bin option, you can click that option; then click View Files to see what's in there. If you find any files you might have deleted accidentally, you'll want to restore them (as described in Chapter 22) before allowing Disk Cleanup to delete them permanently.

Anyway, if you want to clean up all the junk, you can select any of the options. If you want to know more about each option, select it to show a description in the lower half of the dialog window.

After you've selected the items you want to delete, click the OK button. You'll see an *Are you sure?* prompt. Click Delete Files and wait a while as Windows does its cleaning. The dialog box closes automatically when the job is complete.

Because the temporary files are eating up so little disk space, percentage-wise, you probably won't notice any dramatic change in the amount of free space available after you clean the drive. Still, it's better not to have too much extra junk hanging around for no reason. Running Disk Cleanup once a month or every couple months is probably sufficient for keeping any significant amount of junk from accumulating on your hard drive.

Scanning the Disk for Errors

Your hard disk spins at a walloping 5,400 to 10,000 RPM, all the while the head that reads and writes data to the drive is zipping across its surface not more than a few molecules' distance away from its surface. With so much activity, it's not unusual for an occasional little hiccup to occur. These usually go by unnoticed. But they, too, can accumulate in the form of bad links and bad sectors. If enough of them accumulate, the speed at which you're able to move data to and from the disk can diminish.

If you scan your hard disk for errors two to four times a year (or whenever your hard disk seems to be running slowly), you can clean up the little blemishes and get the disk back to running at peak performance. Scanning the disk takes a few minutes, and you can't use the computer for anything else while the program is running. So you might want to plan on doing a scan when you can leave the computer unattended, but running, for a while. Doing the scan is easy.

STEPS: Scan Your Hard Disk for Errors

1. Open your Computer folder if it isn't already open (click the Start button and choose Computer).

2. Right-click the icon for your hard drive and choose Properties.

3. In the Properties dialog box that opens, click the Tools bar.

4. Under Error checking, click Check Now. The dialog box in Figure 21-5 is displayed.

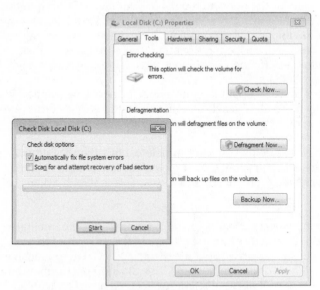

Figure 21-5: The dialog box for checking a disk.

5. For maximum cleanup, select both check boxes.

6. Close all open programs and save any unsaved work.

7. Click the Start button.

When you click the Start button, one of two things is likely to happen. You will either get a message saying that the disk is in use and you'll need to schedule the disk scan, or the scan will begin. When the scan begins, you will see the status bar in the dialog box shown in Figure 21-5 progress as the disk is scanned.

If your disk was in use, then you will see a dialog box like the one in Figure 21-6.

Figure 21-6: Warning message that disk is in use

When the disk is in use, then things on it might be changing. This makes it hard to ensure everything is okay. As such, if you get the dialog box in Figure 21-6, you'll want to either close all programs or you'll want to select to schedule the scan to occur the next time you start your computer. If you select to schedule the scan, then the next time you start the computer, the scan will happen and Windows will start as normal.

If your disk isn't being used, then the scan will start, and the progress will be shown as the disk is being checked. You can go catch up on your phone messages and paper mail or anything else you've been neglecting since you got your computer. This is likely to take some time depending on the size of your disk.

After the scan has completed, if everything goes smoothly, you will see a dialog box similar to Figure 21-7.

Figure 21-7: The Successful scan message

This message lets you know that the disk was successfully scanned. You can click the Close button to end the scan processes and return to doing other things. You may also choose to click on See details to get addition information about the scan that just completed. Figure 21-8 shows the additional information provided by a successful scan of a secondary hard drive on my machine.

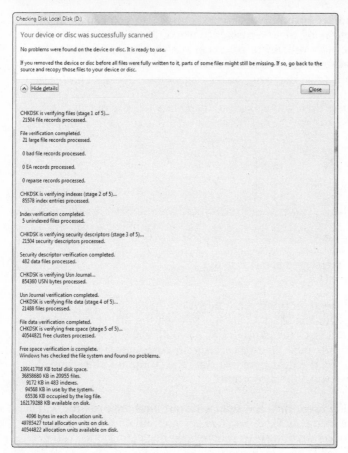

Figure 21-8: Detailed information about a successful disk scan

You can skim through the details, and you'll see there is a lot of information. If there had been any errors fixed, then information on this would also be listed in the details. For the most part, however, you don't need to worry about the details as long as the scan was successful.

Defragmenting Your Hard Drive

Whenever you delete a file, Windows makes the space it was using available to new files you save. If a file you're about to save is too big for one of the empty spaces available, Windows might divide up the file into several different old deleted files' old space. While this is not problem, it can get to a point where you have a lot of little chunks of files spread all over the disk.

When that happens, the drive head has to move around a lot more to read and write files. You might even be able to hear the drive chattering when things get really *fragmented* (spread out). This puts some extra stress on the mechanics of the drive and also slows things down a bit.

To really get things back together and running smoothly, you can *defragment* (or *defrag* for short) the drive. When you do, Windows takes all the files that are split up into little chunks and brings them together into single files again. It also moves most files to the beginning of the drive, where they're easiest to get to. The result is a drive that's no longer fragmented, doesn't chatter, and runs faster.

Defragmenting is one of those things you don't really have to do too often. Two to four times a year is probably plenty. It could take an hour or more, during which time you don't want to use the computer. So you have to plan ahead a little on this one.

Tip For the ultimate in hard drive performance tuning, do the maintenance tasks in the order described in this section. First, clean up the hard disk to get rid of any unnecessary junk. Then do your error-checking to fix any little blemishes. Then defragment what's left so everything is perfectly arranged for quick and easy access by your computer.

STEPS: Defragment Your Hard Disk

1. Open the Computer folder if it isn't already open (click the Start button and choose Computer).

2. Right-click the icon for your hard drive (for example, C:) and choose Properties.

3. In the Properties dialog box that opens, click the Tools tab.

4. Click the Defragment Now button. The Disk Defragmenter dialog window shown in Figure 21-9 opens.

5. Click the Defragment Now button on this new dialog box. The dialog box changes to show that the defragmentation is happening.

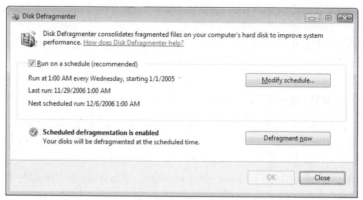

Figure 21-9: The Disk Defragmentation prompt for when to defrag your hard drive

This is the part that could take as little as a few minutes or as much as several hours, during which time you shouldn't use the computer. You may hear a lot of disk chatter as defrag is doing its things. That's because the drive head is moving things around to get everything into a better position. Defrag will defragment all the fragmented files and move a lot of files to the beginning of the disk, where they can be accessed in the least time with the least effort. Some files won't be moved. That's normal. If Windows decides to leave them where they are, it's for good reason. When defrag is finished, you can just close any open dialog boxes and the Disk Defragmenter program window.

Scheduling Disk Defragmenter

You can choose to defragment your disk any time you want following the steps in the prior section. Alternatively, you can schedule the defragmentation to happen on a regular basis. After you see how long it can take, you're likely to decide that having it happen automatically during the time you are not using the computer is a better option because a defrag can take quite a bit of time.

 Note   By default, Windows Vista sets the Disk Defragmenter to run weekly.

STEPS: Scheduling Disk Defragmentations

1. Open the Computer folder if it isn't already open (click the Start button and choose Computer).

2. Right-click the icon for your hard drive (such as C:) and choose Properties.

3. In the Properties dialog box that opens, click the Tools tab.

4. Click the Defragment Now button. The Disk Defragmenter dialog window shown in Figure 21-9 opens.

5. If it isn't already selected, click the Run on a schedule check box to use a schedule (see Figure 21-9).

6. Click the Modify Schedule button. This displays the dialog box in Figure 21-10.

7. On the Modify Schedule dialog box, fill in the frequency, day of week, and time you want the defragmenter to run. I recommend Monthly for the frequency (How often). If you are saving a lot of files on your computer and moving things around, or if you have very little free space on your hard drive, then you might want to schedule more frequently. In general, monthly is more than often enough.

8. Click the OK button to save your changes. You will see the date and time for the next scheduled defragmentation in the Disk Defragmentation dialog window.

9. Click OK to close the Disk Defragmentation dialog window.

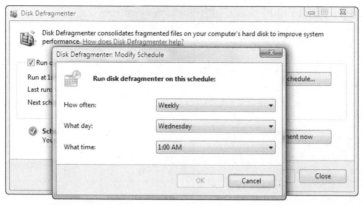

Figure 21-10: Scheduling when a disk defragmentation should occur

The disk defragmenter will automatically run if needed at the date and time you scheduled.

Caution   If you schedule the defragmenter to run when you are not at the computer, then that is good. You do, however, need to make sure you leave the computer on so that the program can actually run!

Exploring Your Hard Drive

You've seen several examples of folders on your hard disk in previous chapters. Documents, Pictures, Music, and Videos are all examples of such folders. Windows automatically creates those folders for you so you have places to store your documents. But those aren't the only folders on your hard disk, not by a long shot. There are lots more.

Like all disks, folders on your hard disk are organized in a hierarchical manner, with folders inside of folders. The hierarchical organization enables you to find things by drilling down from the general to the specific. The highest-level folder is called the *root folder* (or *root directory*), and its name is simply a back-slash (\). For example, C:\ refers to the root folder of drive C:.

The root folder contains several folders. Each of those folders, in turn, contains more folders. And so it can continue, many folders deep. Although no two hard drives will be exactly alike, the typical arrangement of folders on a new installation of Windows Vista will likely look similar to Figure 20-11.

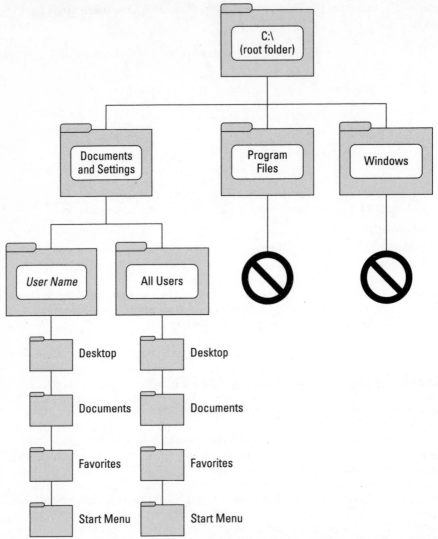

Figure 21-11: Sample hierarchical arrangement of top-level folders on a hard disk

The diagram shown in Figure 21-11 is just a representation of how the folders are arranged. You won't actually see a folder arrangement like that on your screen. And your folders probably won't match those exactly. But you can use the *folder list* in Windows Explorer to browse and see what's available on your hard drive. You can expand, or close, the folder list in Explorer at any time by clicking the Folders button in the Explorer navigation pane on the left side. If the Navigation pane is not showing, you can click the Organize toolbar button and then select Layout ➪ Navigation Pane to display it.

If you're starting from the Windows desktop, you can follow these steps to start exploring your hard disk:

1. Open Computer in Windows Explorer (click the Start button and choose Computer).

2. Double-click the icon for your hard drive, usually Local Disk (C:).

3. Click the Folders button in the navigation pane to expand the Folders view.

> **Tip** To change the width of the Navigation pane, drag to the left or right the bar that separates the folder list from the main pane on its right. You can use the small triangles that appear next to a folder name to show or hide subfolders within the folder.

4. In the folder list, click the icon for your hard drive (usually Local Disk C:).

5. If you see a small, black triangle sign next to a folder icon, click it to expand the folder in order to see the subfolders contained within it.

> **Tip** You can right-click any folder name in the Folders list to get to the usual options (Rename, Delete, Copy, and so on).

The pane on the right always shows the contents of whatever icon you click in the Folders list. When you click the icon for your hard disk, you actually see folders in C:\, the root folder of drive C:. If you click the triangle next to the drive's icon, you'll see those same folders listed beneath the drive's icon, as in Figure 21-12.

To view the contents of any folder or drive, click its name in the Folders list. The contents appear in the main pane on the right. As always, you can choose a view for the main pane by using the Views button on the toolbar or the View menu. To arrange icons in the main pane, choose View ⇨ Sort by from the menu bar, or right-click any space between icons, or click any column heading in Details view.

> **Tip** You can use the Folders list to move and copy files. Click the name of the source folder in the Folders list to view its contents in the main pane. Then right-drag any item from the right pane to the destination folder's icon in the Folders list. Release the mouse button and choose Move Here or Copy Here from the menu that appears.

Navigation Pane

Address bar

Selected icon

Folders "button"

Folders in C:\

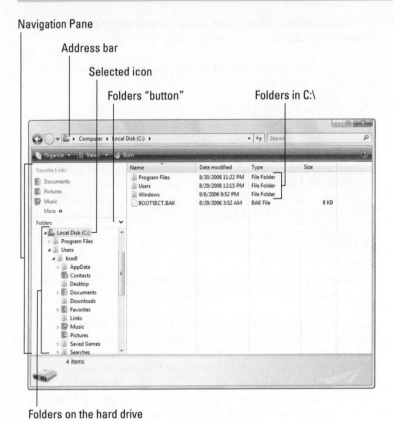

Folders on the hard drive

Figure 21-12: Viewing contents of C:\ in Windows Explorer

A Note on User Accounts, Documents, and Settings

Before we dig any deeper into the folders on your hard disk, you first need to understand a little about *user accounts*. We cover those in depth in Chapter 25. For now, it's sufficient to know that your computer currently has at least one user account on it as well as a public area. The public area is named Public, and the items within that area are accessible to all other user accounts on the computer.

The primary user account has the same name as your *user name*. To see what your user name is, click the Start button and look at the top of your Start menu. If Windows came preinstalled on your computer, your user name is probably something generic, like Owner or Administrator. If someone set up a user account for you, your user name might be the same as your first name.

A document, as you know, is something you create or download from the Internet. Examples include things such as typed text documents, pictures, photos, songs, and video clips. A *setting* is a personal preference, like the picture that covers your Windows desktop or the specific screen saver that pops up when your computer has been idle for a while.

So now, given all of that, here's what the three highest-level folders in the root folder of your hard drive represent:

✦ **Users:** Contains a subfolder for the Public items, another subfolder for your user account, plus another folder for each additional user account you create. In Figures 21-11 and 21-12, the subfolder named Brad! contains documents and settings for the main computer user. The subfolder named Public contains documents available to everyone who has a user account on the computer.

✦ **Program Files:** Most programs you installed will automatically be put in your Program Files folders. Each program will usually be placed in its own subfolder within the Program Files folder. Windows and your programs manage all files and subfolders within Program Files automatically. There's really nothing in there for normal humans. And unless you have some specific need to go in there, it's best just to stay out of the folder.

 Caution   Never move, copy, delete, or rename a folder or file within the Program Files or Windows subfolders. Doing so could have disastrous consequences that would require reinstalling Windows or whatever program(s) you damage.

✦ **Windows:** The Windows folder contains many of the files and subfolders that make up your Windows Vista operating system. These are sometimes called system folders and system files, because they contain the computer's *operating system* (Windows Vista). Windows manages these subfolders and files on its own—there's no reason for you to get involved in that at all. Just stay out of this folder, unless you really know what you're doing and have some reason to go in there.

Simple Names and Paths

Every folder and file has a *path* that describes its exact location within the computer. Most of the time, Windows hides the lengthy, technical-looking path from you and instead shows only the *simple name* of the folder. For example, Documents, Public Documents, Pictures, and Public Pictures are all examples of simple names.

A path is much longer than a simple name. The path tells the *processor* exactly how to get to a given file or folder, starting with the drive and working down through folders and subfolders. For example, the path to a file named MyStuff.doc currently stored in your Public Documents folder would look like this:

```
C:\Users\Public\Public Documents\MyStuff.doc
```

When the processor receives the instruction to open the file at that location, it can follow the path to the file without even the slightest chance of a mistake. The path tells the processor, "Go to the hard drive (C:), and look in its root folder (\). From the root folder, drill down through the folders named Users, Public, and Public Documents. In that last folder, you'll find a folder named MyStuff.doc. Open that folder up and put it on my screen."

We humans don't need quite so much detail. It's just easier for us to think of MyStuff.doc in Public Documents than it is to think of C:\Users\Public\Public Documents. So Windows just shows us the simple names for folders. You can see their names in the Folders list even when your hard disk's subfolders are hidden, as on the left side of Figure 21-13. So there's really no need to go digging around through the hard drive to get to those folders. But if you do expand subfolders under your hard drive's icon, the folders will be visible there as well, as on the right side of Figure 21-13.

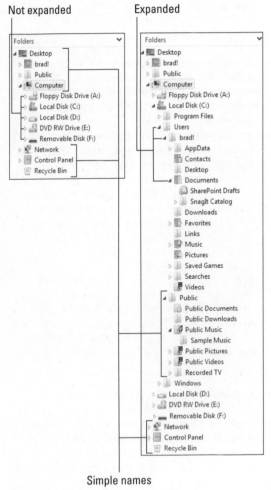

Not expanded

Expanded

Simple names

Figure 21-13: Hard drive subfolders hidden (left) and expanded (right)

What the Heck Is a Processor?

Every computer has a *microprocessor* (or processor, for short) that is, in essence, the actual computer. The processor isn't in or on any disk drive. It's a separate piece of hardware. If you looked at it, you wouldn't see much, because it's small enough to easily fit on your thumbnail. But if you looked at it with a really powerful microscope, you'd see that it contains millions of microscopically small switches and wires.

It's called the processor because it's the thing that actually processes (performs) your every request. When you tell the computer to do something, via your mouse or keyboard, it's the processor that first gets that command and carries out your wishes. Examples of processors include the Intel Centrino, the Intel Xeon, and the AMD Turion.

The speed of a processor is measured in how many instructions it can perform in one second. That's usually expressed in megahertz (MHz) or gigahertz (GHz). 1 MHz equals one million (1,000,000) instructions per second. One gigahertz equals one billion (1,000,000,000) instructions per second.

Caution   If you don't see simple folder names in your Folder list, you need to change one little setting. Choose Tools ➪ Folder Options from the Explorer menu bar. In the Folder Options dialog box, click the View tab. Make sure the Display simple folder view in Navigation pane check box is selected; then click OK.

So I guess the next question is, "What's the advantage of digging down through folder names on the hard drive to get to those folders?" The answer is, "There is none." The simple names are always displayed in the Folders list as a convenience to you — so you don't have to go digging. If you want to go digging, you can. But there really is no need to, unless you plan to go digging through some other user's documents. But let's hold off on that tidbit of info until we get to Chapter 25, where we'll discuss user accounts in depth.

A good general advantage to the Folders list is this: You can view the contents of any folder with minimal digging around. You just click the name of the folder, or even disk drive, whose contents you want to view in the Folders list. The contents appear in the main pane right away. (You may have to click the triangle icon next to some folders that aren't expanded just to see the names.)

Entering the Path in the Address Bar

You can actually type the expanded path to a folder into the address bar of Windows Explorer to get there. For example, you can get to the public music folder by entering C:\Users\Public\Public Music into the Windows Explorer address bar. After this is entered, the address bar changes to show the friendlier folder names.

Windows hides paths from you because the average computer user really never needs to see them. The average computer user can get by with only knowing about Documents, Pictures, and so forth. But there's no rule that says you're not allowed to view the paths to files and folders. In fact, there are a couple settings in Windows Explorer that you can use to make the current folder's path visible in the Explorer address bar. Personally, I prefer to always see the simple name in the title bar. To do this, you must be using the Classic Start menu. Chapter 25 shows you how to change to the Classic menu if you want to use this.

To make the address bar in Windows Explorer display the path to the current folder, follow these steps:

1. From the Explorer menu bar (in any folder), choose Tools ⇨ Folder Options.

2. In the Folder Options dialog box, click the View tab.

3. Select the Display the full path in the title bar check box.

4. Click OK.

Folder and File Tips and Tricks

You've hopefully learned quite a bit in this chapter already. Now, however, is the time to step back from discussing just the hard drive and learn a few tips and tricks you can do with files and folders. This includes learning how to change a folder's icon and how to apply a view style to all your folders.

Choosing Your Own Folder Icon

The *default icon* for a folder (the icon that appears automatically when you create a folder) isn't set in stone. Additionally, you can change whether snapshots of items within a folder are shown in the icon, or if a set image is shown. Figure 21-14 shows the default icon for a folder called Pictures of Aubrey & Lili. This is a subfolder of Pictures and contains pictures. The view in Windows Explorer is set to Extra Large so you can see the icon clearly.

Although this default is very effective at showing that this is a folder and that it contains images — some of which you can see previews of in the icon, you can replace it with something of your own icon if you want. This can be handy when you want a particular folder to stand out, visually, from the crowd. For example, if there's a folder you use often, and you want its icon to stand out from other folders, you might give it a different icon. To change a folder's icon, follow these steps:

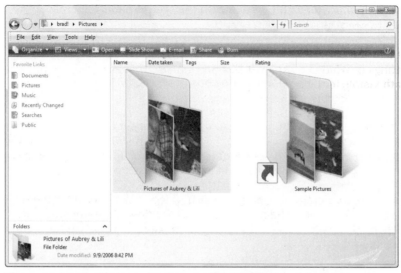

Figure 21-14: The Picture of Aubrey & Lili folder that contains pictures

1. Right-click the icon of the folder you want to change and choose Properties from the menu that pops up.

2. In the Properties dialog box that opens, click the Customize tab.

3. At the bottom of the Customize tab, click Change Icon. The Change Icon dialog box, shown in Figure 21-15, opens.

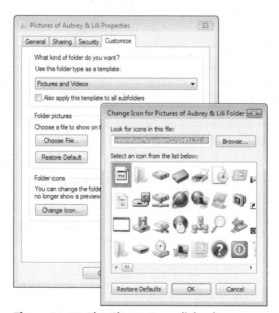

Figure 21-15: The Change Icon dialog box

4. Use the horizontal scroll bar beneath the sample icons to scroll through all your options.

5. When you find an icon you like, click it. For example, choose a camera icon.

6. Click OK in the Change Icon dialog box; then click OK in the Properties dialog box.

Tip Near the top of the Change Icon dialog box, under Look for icons in this file, you're likely to see %SystemRoot%\system32\SHELL32.dll. If you change that to %SystemRoot%\system32\moricons.dll and press Enter, you'll see a different set of icons to choose from.

When you have completed these steps, your new icon will be used for the folder. It will also be seen in the preview pane of Windows Explorer when the folder is selected. It will also be in the Navigation pane. You can see the camera icon in Figure 21-16.

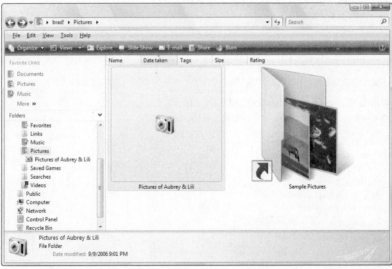

Figure 21-16: A custom folder icon in use

You can also create your own custom icons, but there's nothing in Windows Vista that will allow you to do that. You'll need a third-party *icon editor* for that. Some examples include IconCool Editor (www.iconcool.com), Icon Maker (www.icon-maker.com), IconXP (www.aha-soft.com), or Buddy Icon Grabber (www.icongrabber.com). Or you can go to www.tucows.com and search for *icon* to view a larger selection of programs.

The steps above change the complete icon and eliminate the preview that you see when looking at the icon. If you find you want the preview back, then you can reset the default icon. To do this, follow Steps 1 through 3 above to display the Change Icon dialog box. Then select the Restore Defaults button. Click Ok in the Properties dialog to close it. The default icon should be restored.

Replacing the Icon Preview with Your Own Picture

You can also continue to use the folder icon and change it so that the preview is replaced with a single image. This image would be shown instead of showing the preview of the icons. To accomplish this, follow these steps:

1. Right-click the icon of the folder you want to change and choose Properties from the menu that pops up.

2. In the Properties dialog box that opens, click the Customize tab.

3. In the Customize tab, click Choose File within the Folder pictures section. A Browse dialog box will be displayed.

4. Use the Browse dialog box to navigate to the icon you'd like to use.

5. When you find an icon you like, click it.

6. Click Open in the Change Icon dialog box; then click OK in the Properties dialog box.

The picture will now be used within your folder instead of the preview images. In Figure 21-17, the image is of a girl wearing sun glasses.

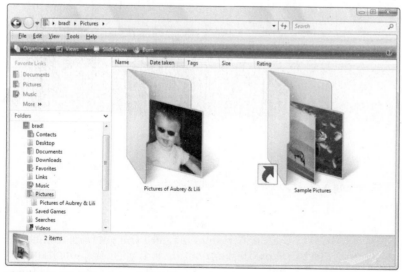

Figure 21-17: Using a set image instead of the preview images on a folder icon

You can go back to displaying the preview items by selecting Restore Defaults within the Folder pictures section on the Customize tab of the Folder properties dialog window.

Creating Shortcuts to Favorite Files and Folders

If you have a folder or file that you use frequently, but it's buried deep within some other folders, you're likely to get tired of navigating to it over and over again. In that case, you can create a *desktop shortcut* to the file or folder. The desktop shortcut will be an icon on your Windows desktop. Double-clicking that icon on the desktop will open the folder or file straightaway, without your having to dig through folders.

To create a desktop shortcut to a favorite file or folder, follow these steps:

1. Navigate to the folder that currently contains the item to which you want to create a shortcut.

2. Right-click the item to which you want to create a shortcut and choose Send To ➪ Desktop (create shortcut) as in Figure 21-18.

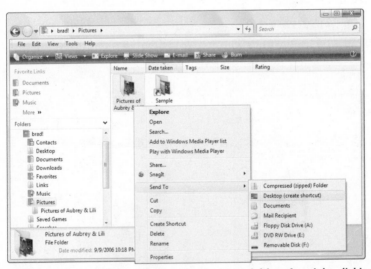

Figure 21-18: Creating a desktop shortcut to a folder after right-clicking its icon

That's all there is to it. You won't notice anything until you get back to the Windows desktop. (Click the Show Desktop button in the Quick Launch toolbar, or right-click the current time and choose Show the Desktop.) The shortcut icon will look like the original icon but will have a little curved arrow on it, indicating that it's just a shortcut to the item.

Cross-Reference See "Creating Your Own Shortcuts" in Chapter 26 for more information on creating shortcuts.

Making Views Stick

As you know by now, you can use the View button on the Explorer menu bar, or its View menu, to change how icons look within the folder. Normally, the view you chose only lasts while the folder is open. If you close the folder, and reopen it later, it opens in its *default view* (that is, the view that Windows thinks is best for that folder). If you want to make the views you choose stick, you need to tell Windows to remember each folder's previous view. Here's how:

1. Open your Documents folder (or any folder, for that matter).

2. Choose Tools ⇨ Folder Options from the Explorer menu bar. The Folder Options dialog box opens.

3. In the Folder Options dialog box, click the View tab.

4. Scroll down to and select the Remember each folder's view settings check box, as in Figure 21-19.

5. Click OK.

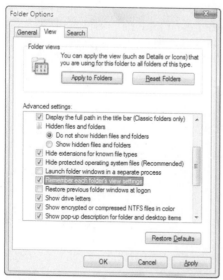

Figure 21-19: The View tab of the Folder Options dialog box

Summary

That should be enough information about your computer's hard disk to hold you over for quite some time. Here's the standard recap of the main points covered in this chapter:

+ To view the icons that represent disk drives in your computer, click the Start button and choose Computer.

+ To clean up, scan, or defragment your computer's hard drive, right-click the drive's icon in your Computer folder and choose Properties. Use buttons on the General and Tools tab for hard disk maintenance.

+ To keep your hard drive operating effectively when working with files, it is beneficial to defragment the drive on a regular basis. You can configure Windows Vista to do disk defragmenting automatically.

+ A folder or file's *path* describes the item's exact location.

+ To change the icon for a folder, right-click the folder's icon and choose Properties. Then click the Customize button in the Properties dialog box that opens.

+ To create a desktop shortcut to a folder, right-click the folder's icon and choose Send To ➪ Desktop (Create Shortcut). The same technique works for documents and programs on the All Programs menu.

+ To make Windows Explorer remember each folder's previous view, choose Tools ➪ Folder Options from its menu bar. Click the View tab and select the Remember each folder's view settings check box.

Using Floppies, Thumb Drives, CDs, and DVDs

In addition to your computer's hard disk, you can use files stored on *removable media*. Most removable media types use disk drives that are plainly visible on the front of your computer (or perhaps the sides, if it's a notebook computer). These are called removable media because you can put disks into the drives and remove them from the drives.

A newer type of removable media is called a thumb drive or USB drive. These devices plug into a USB connection on your machine.

You may already be familiar with some types of removable media, such as floppy disks, CDs, and DVDs. If not, don't worry about it. You will be by the time you finish this chapter.

One of the first things you need to understand about removable media is that it's virtually impossible to copy your entire hard disk to a single floppy disk or CD. That's because the capacity of removable disks is generally much less than the capacity of your computer's hard drive.

For example, if you envision various types of disks as filing cabinets, your hard drive would be several rows of filing cabinets, as in Figure 22-1. A DVD would be a good-sized filing cabinet. A CD would be a decent-sized cabinet. A floppy disk, whose capacity is so limited, wouldn't even count as a whole filing cabinet. Its capacity is more along the lines of one manila-file folder inside a cabinet. Hence, the floppy in Figure 22-1 doesn't even get a whole filing cabinet as its picture.

It is interesting to note that even as newer types of removable media are developed that can hold more information, the size of hard drives also increases so that the hard drives are almost always larger than what can be put onto removable storage. For example, the new HD-DVD and Blue-Ray DVDs can hold substantially more than a regular DVD; however, they are still not large enough to hold all the information that could be stored on a hard drive.

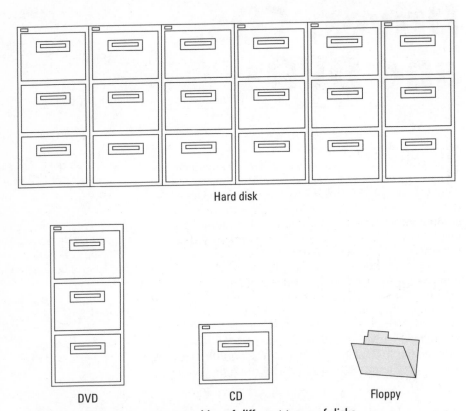

Figure 22-1: Relative storage capacities of different types of disks

Table 22-1 lists the capacities of various types of removable media in terms of bytes, the usual method for specifying how much information a disk can hold. (Recall that a byte is the amount of storage space required to store one character, like the letter *a* or the letter *q*.)

Table 22-1
Capacities of Various Types of Removable Disks

Name	Capacity	Bytes (approx)	Bytes (English)
Floppy	1.4MB	1,400,000	1.4 million
Zip/Jaz	100MB to 1,000MB	100,000,000 to 1,000,000,000	100 million to 1 billion
CD	650MB to 700MB	650,000,000 to 700,000,000	650 million to 700 million
DVD	4.7GB to 8.5GB	4,700,000,000 to 8,500,000,000	4.7 billion to 8.5 billion
Blu-Ray DVD*	25GB to 100GB	25,000,000,000 to 100,000,000,000	25 billion to 100 billion
HD-DVD	15GB to 90GB	15,000,000,000 to 90,000,000,000	15 billion to 90 billion

*Blu-Ray and HD-DVD were new at the time this book was written. As such, the amount of storage space could increase. For example, TDK announced that they had a working 200GB Blu-Ray disk.

Why Use Removable Disks?

When it comes to using a computer, in general, the idea is to use your hard drive to store Windows, all your installed programs, and all your documents — *everything*. This might lead one to wonder why there's a need to have removable disks. In general, you use removable disks for distribution and backups only, as summarized here:

✦ **Distribution:** To copy files to send to someone through regular mail or to copy files from one computer to another when e-mail or a network transfer isn't possible. CD and DVD disks can be used to make disks that play in regular (non-computer) stereos and DVD players.

✦ **Backup:** To make extra copies of important files on your hard drive, in case a serious hard drive crash (or incompetent file deleting) destroys the original files.

Exactly how you use removable disks depends on what type of disk you're using. But we can break it down into three basic categories:

✦ **Magnetic media:** Floppy disks, Zip disks, Jaz disks (and even your hard drive) are examples of magnetic media, in that they use magnetism as the means of storing data. (You hard disk is a magnetic disk, too.)

✦ **Laser media:** CDs and DVDs are laser media, in that they use laser light as the means of storing and retrieving data.

✦ **Flash media:** USB flash drives and memory cards use flash memory to store information. Flash media generally have no moving parts and stand up to wear and tear better than laser and magnetic media.

The techniques for using three different media types are the same in some ways but different in other ways. So we'll look at each type of media in the sections that follow.

Note Since Zip disks and Jaz disks are virtually the same thing, we'll lump them together for the rest of this chapter and just refer to both types as Zip disks.

Each disk drive in your computer has an icon in the Computer folder. In your Computer folder, drives that support removable disks are listed under Devices with removable storage, as in the example shown in Figure 22-2. When it comes to disk drives, not all computers are created equally. If your computer happens to have two hard drives, a DVD drive, a floppy drive, and a USB thumb drive, your Computer folder might show icons similar to those shown in Figure 22-2. (You can open the Computer folder by clicking the Start button and choosing Computer on the right side.)

Figure 22-2: Some examples of icons that represent disk drives that support removable media (under the second heading)

Like your hard disk, which is named C:, disk drives that support removable media have one-letter names. For example, if you have a floppy disk drive, it will likely be named A:; a second floppy (which is rare) would be B:; additional drives could be named D:, E:, F:, and so forth, up to Z:.

If you double-click the icon for a drive that supports removable disk media, and no disk is in that drive at the moment, you'll just get an error message similar to the one shown in Figure 22-3. There's nothing to do there but click the Cancel button or get some additional help. However, if you insert a disk into the drive and double-click the drive's icon, Windows Explorer will show you the contents of that disk. As always, folders on the disk (if any) will be represented by icons that look like manila file folders. Files on the disk will be represented by other icons.

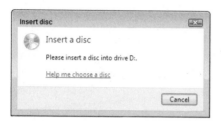

Figure 22-3: Error message that appears when you attempt to read the contents of an empty disk drive

Using Floppy Disks and Zip Disks

Just about every desktop PC has a floppy disk drive Relatively few have Zip drives (although anybody can purchase a Zip drive and connect it to a computer). Floppies and Zip disks are similar in that they're both *magnetic media*. That is, they use magnetism to store data. The only real difference between a floppy disk and a Zip disk is in the capacity of the disks. Floppies can hold very little information. A single Zip disk can store the equivalent of anywhere from 100 to 1,000 floppy disks.

Viewing the Contents of Floppy and Zip Disks

To use a floppy disk or Zip disk, you first need to insert one into the floppy or Zip drive, respectively, of your computer. Make sure that you insert the disk correctly, as indicated by the arrow in Figure 22-4.

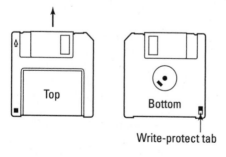

Figure 22-4: Always insert floppy and Zip disks top-side up, with the sliding door first.

After you've inserted the disk into its drive, wait a moment to see if a window opens on your screen automatically. If such a window does open, it will be Windows Explorer. If that happens, skip the paragraph and steps that follow.

If nothing happens after you insert the disk (as is usually the case with floppy disks), follow these steps to view the contents of the floppy disk:

1. Open your Computer folder (click the Start button and choose Computer on the right side).

2. Double-click the icon that represents the drive into which you just inserted the disk.

Windows Explorer will open and show you the contents of the disk. Folders and files will be displayed using the standard icons — manila file folder icons for folders, other icons for files. If the disk is empty, the main pane in Windows Explorer will be empty. If the disk hasn't been *formatted* yet, you'll need to format it before you can use it at all.

Formatting a Disk

Magnetic disks often need to be formatted before you can use them for the first time. That's not to say you need to format every disk. Nor do you need to format a disk each time you intend to use it. On the contrary, you format *unformatted* disks only (not preformatted disks, nor disks that already contain files). And even if you do need to format a disk, you need only do that once.

Caution *Never* format your hard drive. Never format a floppy or Zip disk that already has information on it. If you do format such a disk, the information on the disk will be permanently erased, and there will be no way to undo that mistake.

It's easy to tell if a magnetic disk is already formatted or not. When you attempt to view the contents of a disk that hasn't been formatted, you'll see an error message asking if you want to format the disk.

Note Depending on how your computer is set up, you may need to enter an administrative password in order to be able to format a disk. If this is the case, you will be asked to enter the administrator password before you will be allowed to continue.

If you do not want to format the disk, then select No. If the disk had not been formatted before, then you most likely want to format it, so you should click the Yes button to continue with the format procedure. Before the formatting process begins, you will be asked for permission to continue by the Windows User Account Control. When you click Continue, the formatting process begins.

You are allowed to set a few options when formatting a floppy. If in doubt, leave the options alone. The Volume Label option is yours to do with as you please. You can type a brief label there (up to 11 characters). That label will appear next to the drive's icon in the Computer folder whenever you insert the disk into the drive.

Select the Quick Format option only if you're reformatting (erasing) a disk that already contains data. The Create an MS-DOS startup disk option creates an

Emergency boot disk. Such a disk enables an expert to start the computer from the floppy disk drive even if the hard drive is damaged. If you select that option, you won't be able to put anything else on the floppy disk.

After choosing your options (or leaving them all alone, as is the more likely scenario), click the Start button. You may see a repeat of the warnings we've already mentioned (that the entire disk will be erased). Assuming that and are ready to proceed, click the OK button. Then just wait as Windows formats the disk. When formatting is done, you'll see a message to that effect. Click the OK button in that message box. Then click the Close button in the Format dialog box. This time, when you double-click the drive's icon, you'll see an empty Explorer window on your screen. (It's empty because the disk is formatted but still blank.) You can copy a file (or files) to the disk by using the techniques described in following section.

Copying Files to Floppy and Zip Disks

Copying files to Zip and floppy disks is virtually identical to copying files from one folder to another. You just have to know how much stuff you're about to copy to the disk, because the capacity of the disk will be limited (*very* limited, in the case of a floppy). To see exactly how much space is currently available on a Zip or floppy disk, follow these steps:

STEPS: Copy Files to a Floppy or Zip Disk

1. If you haven't already done so, insert the disk you want to copy files to and open the Computer folder.

2. Right-click the icon that represents the drive into which you just inserted the disk and choose Properties.

3. In the Properties dialog box that opens, the numbers next to Free space show you how much space is available on the disk. For example, a brand new floppy disk with no files on it yet will offer about 1,457,664 bytes, or roughly 1.38MB, of space.

4. Click OK in the Properties dialog box to close the dialog box.

The next step is to open the *source folder* — the folder that currently contains the files you want to copy to the disk. Presumably, this will just be some folder on your hard disk that you can navigate to by opening your Documents folder and by using the standard Windows Explorer techniques to navigate to the folder.

Finding the Combined Sizes of Multiple Files

When you can see the icons for the items you intend to copy to the disk, you need to select those icons. Use any technique described in the section "Working with Multiple Files and Folders" in Chapter 19 to select the files and folders you want to copy. To see how many bytes it's going to take to store those files, follow these steps:

1. Right-click any selected icon and choose Properties.

2. In the Properties dialog box that opens, look at the number next to Size on Disk.

3. Click the Cancel button in the dialog box.

Figure 22-5 shows an example of the combine4d size of two pictures selected in the Pictures folder. Since the total is less than 1.4MB, these files can fit on a single floppy.

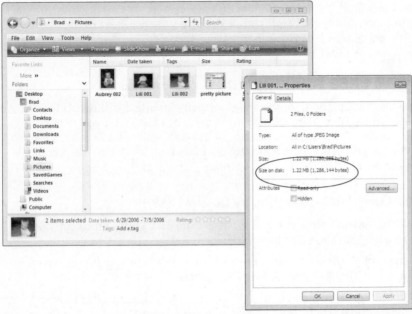

Figure 22-5: Viewing the combined sizes of multiple selected files in a folder

If you selected more files than there is room for on the disk, you should select fewer files and try again. After you've selected the files you want to copy (but not more than can fit on the disk), use whichever technique given here is most convenient to copy the files to the disk:

✦ Select Edit ➪ Copy To Folder from the Explorer menu bar; then click the icon of the drive in which the floppy or Zip disk is located (see Figure 22-6).

✦ Select Organize ➪ Copy. This copies the selected items. You can also right-click one of the selected items and choose Copy from the pop-up menu. Once copied, you should use Windows Explorer to navigate to the floppy or Zip drive. When that drive is displayed in the Windows Explorer, select Organize ➪ Paste to copy the files. You can also right-click within the Windows Explorer content pane and choose Paste from the pop-up menu that is displayed.

Figure 22-6: About to copy files to the floppy disk currently in drive A:

✦ Right-click any selected icon and choose Send To. Then click the name of the disk drive to which you want to copy the files.

✦ Drag any selected item to the drive's icon in the Folders list.

✦ Drag any selected icon to the drive's icon in your Computer folder.

✦ In the Computer folder, open the icon that represents the floppy or Zip drive; then drag any selected icon into the Explorer window that opens.

Tip

Here we're assuming that you want to *copy* the files to the floppy or Zip disk, because that's usually the case. The only time you need to *move* files to a floppy or Zip disk is when you're running seriously low on disk space (have less than 1GB of hard disk space left). If you do want to move the files to the disk, you can select Cut instead of Copy from the menus, or you can drag the items to the drive's icon using the right mouse button rather than the left.

Copy Files from a Floppy or Zip Disk

To copy files from a floppy or Zip disk to a folder on your hard disk, follow these steps:

1. Insert the disk that contains the files you want to copy into the floppy or Zip drive of your computer.

2. If the disk's contents don't appear automatically, click the Start button and choose Computer. Then double-click the icon that represents the drive into which you just inserted the disk.

3. In the Explorer window that displays the contents of the disk, select the files or folders you want to copy using any of the standard selection techniques (as discussed in the section "Working with Multiple Files and Folders" in Chapter 19).

4. Do one of the following:

- Select Edit ➪ Copy To Folder from the menu bar in Windows Explorer. Then click the name of the folder to which you want to copy the items. For example, Figure 22-7 shows some files that are about to be copied to the Pictures folder.

Figure 22-7: About to copy files from a floppy or Zip disk to the Pictures folder

- Right-click any of the selected items and choose Copy from the menu that pops up. Then navigate to the folder where you want to copy the items. Within that folder, right-click and select Paste. You can also copy and paste using the options on the Organize menu of Windows Explorer.

- If you want to copy the files to your Documents folder, right-click any selected icon and choose Send To ➪ Documents.

- Navigate to and then open the folder to which you want to copy the files. Then drag any selected file into that folder.

When the files are copied, you can remove the disk from its drive and store it as a backup. When you open the folder to which you copied the items, you'll see their icons. If you don't see the icons, choose View ➪ Refresh from that folder's menu bar to bring Explorer up-to-date with the folder's current contents. If the items are out of order, choose View ➪ Sort By ➪ Name from the menu bar, or right-click any empty space between icons and choose Arrange Icons By ➪ Name.

Write-Protect a Floppy

If you copy files to a floppy disk, and want to protect that floppy disk from accidentally being erased or reformatted, you can *write-protect* the disk. When the disk is write-protected, you can still open and view the files on the disk. You can still copy the disk, but you cannot change or delete the files on the disk.

To write-protect a disk, just slide the little write-protect tab, shown in Figure 22-4, to the opposite side, so you can see through the little hole that appears.

If you change your mind and do want to change the contents of the disk, just slide the tab back to the previous position, where the hole is covered.

Cloning a Floppy Disk

You can make an exact copy of any floppy disk that already contains data. You'll need the original disk and a blank, formatted floppy disk. Then you need to follow these steps:

1. Insert the original disk (the one you want to copy) into your computer's floppy disk drive.

2. Open your Computer folder.

3. Right-click the icon that represents your floppy disk drive and choose Copy Disk. This displays the Copy Disk dialog box shown in Figure 22-8.

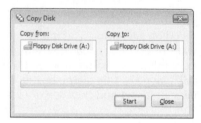

Figure 22-8: The Copy Disk dialog box for copying a floppy or Zip disk

4. Click the Start button in the Copy Disk dialog box; then follow the instructions on the screen.

Using CDs and DVDs

CDs and DVDs have grown rapidly as *distribution media* and are used to distribute all kinds of media. Most programs you buy these days are delivered on CDs or DVDs. When you buy a CD or DVD with information already on it, you're really getting a CD-ROM or DVD-ROM disk. The *ROM* stands for *Read-Only Memory*, which means that a computer (or CD player or DVD player) can read (or play or copy the contents of) the disk. But nothing can *change* the contents of a CD-ROM or DVD-ROM disk.

Using Prerecorded CDs and DVDs

To use a CD that already contains data, your computer needs to have a CD drive installed. Most computers do have a CD drive installed. If your computer has a DVD drive installed, you can also play DVDs. Most DVD drives are *downwardly compatible* with CD drives, meaning if your computer has a DVD drive, you can most likely use that drive to play both CDs and DVDs.

To insert a CD or DVD disk into the drive, click the little button on the front of the drive. Then place the CD or DVD, label-side up, in the little tray that opens. Press the same button on the drive or gently push the disk tray. The disk will disappear into the drive. Now wait a few seconds. What happens next depends on what's on the disk and how your computer is currently configured to deal with that type of disk. But the most likely scenarios are as follows:

✦ If you inserted a music CD, Windows Media Player (or some other multimedia program) will open and start playing the music.

✦ If you inserted a DVD that has a movie on it, Windows Media Player (or some other multimedia program) will open and display the DVD's main menu.

 See Chapter 16 for information on playing CDs and DVDs in Windows Media Player.

✦ If the CD you inserted contains a program, an installation program will start. You need to follow the instructions on the screen to install the program.

✦ As an alternative to one of the preceding scenarios, you might see a dialog box asking you what you want to do next, as in the example shown in Figure 22-9. Your job is to click the option you want; then click the OK button. The options displayed in this dialog box will vary depending on the type of disk you insert and the type of content on it.

Figure 22-9: The AutoPlay dialog box asking you what to do with an inserted disk

✦ Then again, absolutely nothing might happen.

What you do next is really up to you. If some program opened to play the CD, and it's the program you were expecting, there's really nothing else to do, other than maybe change the volume of the music or expand the program that's playing a movie to show full-screen. How you do that depends on what program is playing the CD. If it's Windows Media Player, you can use the techniques described in Chapter 17 to do all of that.

Tip
To eject a CD or DVD from its drive, push the little button on the drive door again. Or right-click the drive's icon in your Computer folder and choose Eject.

If some unexpected program opened and started playing the CD, you can close that program by clicking its Close button. Then you can view the contents of the disk as described in the "Exploring the Contents of a CD or DVD" section that follows. If nothing happened after you inserted the CD or DVD, you can also use the techniques that follow to view the contents of the CD or DVD.

Exploring the Contents of a CD or DVD

CDs and DVDs are disks. As such, they store their information in files and folders — just like any other disk. Each file and folder will be represented by an icon. If you chose the Open folder to view files option in Figure 22-9, you will see the files and folders on that disk in an open Explorer window. If you don't want to take any action, you can click the Close button (the "X" in the top-right corner) to close the AutoPlay dialog box. If you choose to close the AutoPlay dialog box, or if nothing happens after you insert the disk into the drive, you can still view the contents of the disk in Windows Explorer. Here's how.STEPS: View Files on a CD or DVD

1. Open your Computer folder.

2. Right-click the icon that represents the drive into which you inserted the disk and choose Open. Alternatively, you can double-click the icon representing the drive.

CD and DVD Speeds

Many CD and DVD drives, as well as blank disks, have *speed ratings* described as some number followed by an *X*. The number is some multiple of the standard speed of a CD or DVD. To understand what that means, consider a vinyl phonograph record. To make it sound right, you have to play it at a certain speed, like 33 1/3rd RPM. If you play it faster than that, at 78 RPM, for instance, it will indeed take less time to listen to the whole album. But it will sound like The Chipmunks.

When you listen to an audio CD, or watch a DVD using your computer, you want it to play at normal speed — the speed we refer to as 1X. If it plays any faster, you'll get The Chipmunks or a fast-motion version of your movie. But when you're just copying files to or from a disk, there's no music to hear, no movie to watch. You don't care if copying happens faster than normal 1X speed. In fact, the faster the better on those; it means less waiting.

The *numberX* rating describes how quickly the drive can copy files and create CDs. For example, if the drive has a 1X speed, it will take 75 minutes to create a 75-minute audio CD. A drive of 2X can create a 75-minute CD at twice the normal speed. Hence, it will take half as long or about 37.5 minutes. A 24X drive can create the CD in 1/24th the amount of time — about 3 minutes rather than 75 minutes.

The contents of the CD appear in a standard Windows Explorer folder. You can do all the things you'd expect in Windows Explorer. For example, you can choose a view (such as Large Icons or Details) from the View menu or Views button. You can arrange the icons by choosing View ➪ Sort By. You can move and size the Explorer window. You can open any file or folder on the disk by double-clicking its icon (or by right-clicking a document icon and choosing Open With).

Copying Files from CDs and DVDs

You can copy files and folders from CDs using any of the techniques described in Chapter 19. For example, let's suppose someone sends you a CD containing a bunch of pictures he or she took. If you just want to look at the pictures, you can leave them in the CD drive and just browse through them using the Icon view in Windows Explorer. But if you want to touch them up in a graphics program, you'll want to copy them to your hard drive first — perhaps to your Pictures folder or to a new subfolder you create within the Pictures folder. To copy files from a CD or DVD:

Caution   If you're trying to install a program from a CD, copying files in this manner won't help. Programs need to be *installed* on your computer, not *copied to* your computer. See Chapter 29 to learn about installing programs.

If you want to copy songs from an audio CD (the type you buy in a music store), don't use this method. Instead, use Windows Media Player, as described in Chapter 17.

Copying movies from DVDs usually doesn't work. Most movies are copy-protected, so that the copies don't play correctly. Also, there's nothing to be gained by copying a movie from a DVD to your hard disk (only a few gigabytes of storage to be lost).

STEPS: Copy Files from a CD or DVD

1. Insert the CD or DVD disk into the appropriate drive and wait a few seconds. What you do next depends on what happens after a few seconds:

    • If some program opens to play the disk, close that program.

    • If a dialog box appears on the screen asking what you want to do, click Open folder to view files using Windows Explorer. Click OK.

    • If nothing happens, open your Computer folder, right-click the drive's icon, and choose Open.

2. Select the files or folders you want to copy using any technique described in the section "Working with Multiple Files and Folders" in Chapter 19. Then do one of the following:

    • Click Copy to Folder from the Edit menu in Windows Explorer. Then navigate to and click the icon that represents the destination folder.

- If you want to copy the selected items to your Documents folder, right-click any selected icon and choose Send To ➪ Documents.

- Right-click any selected item and choose Copy. Then navigate to the destination folder and choose Edit ➪ Paste from its menu bar.

- Open your Documents folder, and navigate to and open the destination folder. Drag any selected item to the open destination folder.

Tip You can't move files from a CD-ROM or DVD-ROM, because that would require removing the files from their current location on the disk. That would require changing the disk, and you can't change the contents of a Read-Only Memory (ROM) disk.

In short, copying files from a CD or DVD is much like copying files from a folder or magnetic disk. You select the items you want to copy and use whichever copy method is most convenient for you. Copying files *to* CDs and DVDs is an entirely different matter.

Copying Files to CDs

You can't copy files to a CD using just any CD-ROM or DVD drive. Your computer needs to have a *CD burner* installed. You also need appropriate *blank media* (blank disks) for the drive. Copying files to a CD is often referred to as *burning* the CD, because a laser actually burns the information onto the disk.

Tip Many DVD burners can also burn CD-R and CD-RW disks.

There are two types of CD burners, and two types of blank CD disks, on the market:

✦ **CD-R:** These burners enable you to burn data to blank CD-R disks. You can use the resultant disk in any computer that has a CD drive installed. If you create an audio CD using a CD-R disk, you can also play that audio CD in most standard stereos.

✦ **CD-RW:** These burners enable you to burn data to a blank CD-R or CD-RW disk. The resulting disk will work only in computers that have a CD-RW disk drive installed. The disk will not play in a stereo, unless it happens to be one of the rare stereos specifically designed to read CD-RW disks.

Tip CD-R disks are Write Once, Read Many (WORM), meaning you get only one shot at burning the CD. When you copy anything to a CD-R disk, it is on the disk to stay. You can't update it or rewrite the file with a newer version. This is true even if you use a CD-RW drive to burn the CD-R disk.

As is often the case, there are several ways to copy files to blank CD disks.

Using a Blank CD

The first time you insert a blank CD into your computer, you may see a slightly different AutoPlay menu than what is shown in Figure 22-9. This menu will give you options related to using a blank CD as shown in Figure 22-10.

Figure 22-10: AutoPlay for a blank CD-R

You should make your selection from the AutoPlay menu based on what you want to do. In you are unsure, then select Burn files to Disc using Windows. When you do this, you will be asked to prepare your CD for use. This may include formatting it or simply stating what you plan to do with the CD. If preparation is needed, a basic Burn a Disc dialog box will be displayed (see Figure 22-11).

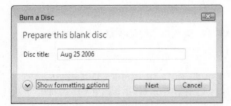

Figure 22-11: The basic Burn a Disc dialog box

You can give the disk a title of up to 11 characters and then press Next to prepare the disk. If you want more say in how files will be put onto the disk, then you can select Show formatting options in the dialog box. This will present the two options in Figure 22-12.

In general, you will want to select the default of File System. By using this option, you can read and write files to the CD just as you would any other drive or disk. When a file is copied to the CD, it is immediately copied. Remember, however, that once a file is written to a regular CD-R, it cannot be updated or changed.

Figure 22-12: The formatting options for a CD

The Mastered option does not write files immediately to the CD. Rather, it uses a staging area to place files. You can then write all of the files at once to the CD. This enables you to update and change files in the staging area before they are actually written to the CD.

Once you have selected either method, the dialog window in Figure 22-13 will be displayed and the CD will be formatted. You will then be able to copy files to it.

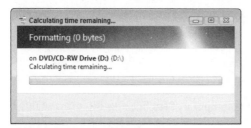

Figure 22-13: Formatting a CD

General Method for Copying to CDs

The general methods for copying files to CDs described here will work with any CD burner.

1. Insert a blank CD-R or CD-RW disk into your CD drive and wait a few seconds. Then:

   • If you see the Burn a Disc dialog window shown in Figure 22-10, prepare your disk for use.

   • If you see a dialog box asking what you want to do with the disk, click *Burn files to Disc using Windows Explorer* and click OK. Then skip to Step 2.

- If nothing happens within a few seconds of inserting the blank disk, open your Computer folder. Then right-click the drive's icon and choose Open.

2. Navigate to the source folder (the folder that contains the files you want to copy) using Windows Explorer.

Tip   If you want to copy files across several folders to a CD, you can use Search to find all the files. See Chapter 19 for more information on using Search.

3. Select the items you want to copy using any method described in the section "Working with Multiple Files and Folders" in Chapter 19. Then do one of the following:

- Right-click any selected item and choose Send To and then the name of the CD drive you want to copy the files to.

- Right-click any selected icon and choose Copy. Then click in the Explorer window that represents the blank CD and choose Edit ⇨ Paste from its menu bar.

- Drag any selected icons to the folder window that represents the blank CD and drop them in there.

- Select the Burn button from the Explorer toolbar.

4. If you selected the File System option when preparing your disk, then the files should now be copied to your CD. You can skip to Step 8.

If you selected the Mastered option when you prepared your disk, then each item to be copied will appear as a *temporary file* — the icon will be grayed as shown in the example in Figure 22-14 where four files have been added to the temporary folder. The icons indicate that the file is waiting to be copied (it hasn't actually been copied to the CD yet).

Tip   You can also tell that these are temporary files because the CD contains 0 items as shown in the details area at the bottom of the Windows Explorer (see Figure 22-14).

5. Optionally, if you want to see how much data you've selected so far, right-click any selected file and choose Properties, as described in the section "Finding the Combined Sizes of Multiple Files," earlier in this chapter.

Caution   The Free Space measurement under Details in the Explorer bar is the amount of space available on the disk now, *before* you copy the temporary files to the disk.

6. Optionally, if you have room and want to copy more items to the CD, you can repeat Steps 2 to 5 until you've reached the capacity of the CD.

Figure 22-14: Windows Explorer folder containing temporary files waiting to be copied to a CD

7. When icons representing all the folders and files you want to copy are visible in the CD's Explore window, click the Burn to Disc button from the toolbar in the Explorer bar of the CD's folder window. Alternatively, you can select File ➪ Burn to Disc to start the process of writing the files to the CD.

8. In the first page of the CD Writing Wizard that opens, you can type a new name for the CD, as opposed to using the date that appears. This should be a brief label, as it will appear next to the CDs icon in Computer in the future, when you looking at the CD.

9. Optionally, you can select the recording speed. You should pick a speed that fits with the disk you are using. Most disks indicate their maximum speed. Writing faster than that speed can cause errors to be introduced when the information is copied to the disk. However, choosing a slower speed means that it will take longer to write the CD (as discussed in "CD and DVD Speeds" earlier in this chapter. When the title and speed have been selected, click Next.

10. Wait while the wizard burns the data to the CD. If you used the Mastered option for selecting and writing your CD, then you will be prompted to write the file to another disk. Alternatively, you can click the Finish button on the last page of the CD Burning wizard.

To view the contents of the disk, use the same technique you use to view the contents of any CD or DVD, as described earlier in this chapter. Close the window containing the icons that were waiting to be burned to the CD.

Tip You may need to select View ➪ Refresh from the Windows Explorer menu to see them. At this point you have completed the copying process.

Deleting All the Files on a CD-RW Disk

You can wipe clean a CD-RW disk to which you've already copied data. This is often useful for making backups of files. For example, suppose you copied your entire Documents folder to a CD-RW disk last month. You've added and changed a lot of files since then and would like to make a new backup. You can delete the old Documents folder on the CD-RW first. Then you can copy your current Documents folder to the disk. To wipe clean a CD-RW disks, follow these steps:

Caution Files you delete from CD-RW disks are not copied to the Recycle Bin. When you erase a CD-RW disk, there's no way (in Windows) to recover the deleted files.

1. Insert the CD-RW disk into your CD-RW drive. Then:
   - If a dialog box appears asking what you want to do, choose Open folder to view files using Windows Explorer; then go to Step 2.
   - If a program opens and starts playing the CD, close that program and complete the next item.
   - If nothing happens after you insert the CD, open your Computer folder, right-click the icon for the CD-RW drive, and choose Open.
2. Navigate to the Computer folder in the Explorer window.
3. Right-click the icon representing the drive containing the CD you want to erase. This displays a pop-up menu.
4. Click the Quick Format check box under the Format options. Note that you might be prompted to enter an administrative password or confirm that you actually want to format a disk. You'll need to respond to this prompt in order to erase the files from the CD.
5. Click the Start button. The files on the CD-RW will be erased.

Using Third-Party Programs to Burn CDs

The techniques for burning CDs, and erasing CD-RW disks, you've learned so far can be used by all Windows Vista owners. That's because they're capabilities built into Windows Vista. Many computers that have CD-R and CD-RW drives also have preinstalled, specialized CD-burning software, such as Roxio Easy CD Creator (www.roxio.com) or Nero (www.nero.com).

Many of these third-party programs support a technology referred to as *packet-writing*, which lets you copy files to CD-RW disks freely, as though the disk were a Zip disk or giant floppy disk. Packet-writing also lets you delete files from a CD-RW individually as on a magnetic disk (by right-clicking the file's icon and choosing Delete). Some may require that you *format* a blank CD, much like formatting a floppy disk, before using packet-writing capabilities.

If you have third-party CD-burning software installed on your computer, you can certainly use it as an alternative to the techniques described here. You'll have to learn to use that software first, of course, if you don't already know how. You can get information from the manual that came with that software, or from the Help within the program. Also, you can visit the program manufacturer's web site.

Copying Files to DVDs

Windows Vista also has built-in capabilities for copying files to DVDs. These capabilities work just like copying files to a CD, except that you can copy more files because the capacity of a DVD is greater. You can also erase and otherwise work with files on DVDs just as you would with files on CDs.

 Note Most DVD burners come with their own built-in software for creating DVDs. For example, some Sony DVD burners come with a program called My DVD that makes it easy to burn DVDs. Your DVD burner may have come with the same, or similar, software. You'll need to refer to the manual that came with your DVD burner or computer for specifics on using any included software.

You really need to be aware that there are several different types of DVD drives and different types of blank DVD disks. The type of blank DVD you purchase needs to match the capabilities of your DVD burner. For example, if you have a DVD±RW/DVD±R/CD burner, it can read and copy to CDs as well as all of the DVD disk types summarized in Table 22-2. (As with CDs, *WORM* stands for *Write Once, Read Many*.)

Table 22-2
Different Types of DVD Burners and Blank Disks

Type	Storage Type	Can Be Read By[1]
DVD-R	WORM	Any DVD player
DVD+R	WORM	Any DVD player
DVD-RW	Read/Write	Computer DVD-RW drives only
DVD+RW	Read/Write	Most DVD players
Blu-Ray	WORM[2] Read/Write	Blu-Ray drives only
HD-DVD	WORM Read/Write	HD-DVD drives only

[1] "Any DVD player" includes non-computer DVD players that connect to a television.

[2] Note that Blu-Ray and HD-DVD players should be able to use standard DVDs (those mentioned in this table); however, the Blu-Ray and HD-DVD disks will only be usable in their respective players. A Blu-Ray disk cannot be played in an HD-DVD player and vice versa. Additionally, Blu-Ray and HD-DVDs come in both a WORM version and a Read/Write version.

Copying Files with DVD Maker

Windows Vista includes a program called Windows DVD Maker that is used to copy pictures and videos to DVDs. This program is only available in Windows Vista Home Premium and Windows Vista Ultimate. If you have one of the other editions of Vista, then Windows DVD Maker was not included.

Windows DVD Maker can be run by clicking the Start menu then selecting All Programs ➪ Windows DVD Maker. You can then simply follow the wizard to create a DVD containing pictures and videos. Figure 22-15 shows the initial window for Windows DVD Maker.

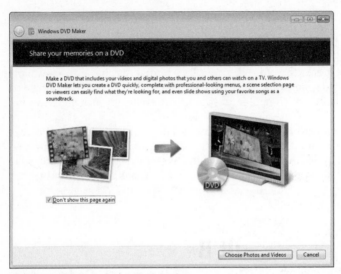

Figure 22-15: Windows DVD Maker

Click the Choose Photos and Videos button to start the process of creating a DVD. This will present a window that contains a list of items to burn to your DVD. Initially it will be blank as shown in Figure 22-16.

To add items, click the Add items button. This opens a copy of Windows Explorer. You can then navigate and select the items you want to add to your DVD. When selected in Explorer, click the Add button and the files will be copied into Windows DVD Maker. You can then repeat this process until you've added everything you want on your DVD.

Figure 22-16: Adding items to Windows DVD Maker

As you add items, the Windows DVD Maker will indicate in the bottom-left corner how much time (space) you have left on your DVD. When you've used all the space, or when you are done adding, you can click the Next button to continue the process of building your DVD. When you've completed the wizard, you can select the Burn button to create the DVD.

Changing the Default Behavior of CDs and DVDs

When it comes to CDs and DVDs, the phrase *default behavior* or *default action* refers to whatever happens on your screen, automatically, after you insert a CD or DVD disk into its drive. Since there are many different types of CDs and DVDs, there are many possible default actions. For example, when you insert an audio CD into your CD-ROM drive, the CD might just start playing in Windows Media Player. In that case, we'd say that playing songs in Windows Media Player is the default action for audio CDs.

You can override the default action, so nothing happens after you insert a CD or DVD disk, by holding down the Shift key as you insert the disk into the drive. Optionally, you can change the default action of any disk type, so that you don't have to override that action or put up with some undesired program opening every time you insert a particular type of CD or DVD.

You can set different default behaviors for different disks based on the contents of the disk you insert. That is, you can set a different default behavior for disks that contain mostly music, mostly pictures, or even nothing (blank disks), as follows:

✦ **Music files:** Defines what happens when you insert a disk that contains mostly music in WMA, MP3, and other popular formats.

✦ **Pictures:** Defines what happens when you insert a disk that contains mostly pictures.

✦ **Video files:** Defines what happens when you insert a disk that contains mostly video files in the popular MPEG and WMV formats.

✦ **Mixed content:** Defines the default behavior of disks that contain many different types of files.

✦ **Music CD:** Defines what happens when you insert an audio CD—the kind you can play in a stereo.

✦ **DVD movie:** Defines what happens when you put a movie stored on DVD into the drive.

✦ **Blank CD:** Defines what happens when you insert a blank CD into your CD or DVD drive.

After you've told Windows what type of CD you're referring to, you can choose an action for that type of CD. For example, you might tell Windows that whenever you insert a music CD, you want Windows to start copying songs from the CD using Windows Media Player. Or you might tell Windows to open the folder and display its contents in a folder. Or you might tell Windows not to take any action when you insert that type of CD.

You can even tell Windows to prompt you for an action. For example, you can tell Windows to "Ask me what I want to do each time I insert a . . ." certain type of disk. That's a lot of options. But since they are options, you can change them at any time. So it's not like you're making any lifelong commitments here. Here are the general steps for choosing a default action for a newly inserted CD or DVD disk.

STEPS: Change the Default Action for CDs and DVDs

1. Open your Computer folder (click the Start button and choose Computer).

2. Right-click the icon that represents your CD or DVD drive and choose Open AutoPlay. This displays the AutoPlay menu similar to what you saw in Figure 22-10.

3. In the AutoPlay dialog box, click the text at the bottom: Set AutoPlay defaults in Control Panel. This opens the AutoPlay dialog window shown in Figure 22-17.

4. You can use the drop-down lists next to each type of media to determine what action is taken. You can also clear the Use AutoPlay for all media and devices check box to turn AutoPlay off. You'll see that there are a lot of settings that range from Audio CDs to HD DVD movies and Blu-ray Disc movies. You don't have to set all of these. Rather you can select and set the ones you want.

5. Click Save in the dialog window to save your changes.

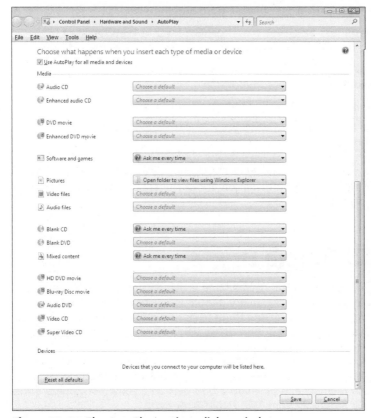

Figure 22-17: The AutoPlay settings dialog window

The next time you insert a CD or DVD of the appropriate type into the drive, you'll see the default action take place within a few seconds. It always takes a few seconds for the drive to get up to speed and for Windows to analyze the contents of the disk.

Troubleshooting CDs and DVDs

Using CDs and DVDs is generally trouble-free if you use the techniques and methods described in this chapter. But things can go wrong, of course. Often, fixing a problem is a simple matter of changing some setting in the drive's Properties dialog box. If problems do arise, you can use the Windows CD or DVD troubleshooter to step through the problem and find a quick solution, if possible.

To get to the Troubleshooters on most computers, click the Start button and choose Help and Support. Then click Fixing a Problem. If you can't find the Fix a Problem option in your Help and Support Center, follow these steps instead:

1. Click the Start button and choose Help and Support.

2. In the Search text box, type **troubleshoot DVD** or **troubleshoot CD,**
   depending on which you are having trouble with. Then press Enter.

3. Under Suggested Topics, scroll down to and click List of
   Troubleshooters and other help items.

4. Select the item that best corresponds to your issue.

5. Follow the instructions to work your way through the
   Troubleshooter.

The manual that comes with your CD or DVD drive, or with your computer,
also can be good resource for information about the specific make and model
of drive in your computer.

Using USB Thumb Drives

In the past few years, USB thumb drives have grown in popularity as a cheap
form of removable storage. In fact, many people now use USB thumb drives as
a means of sharing files or of copying them from one machine to another when
a network isn't available. A USB thumb drive also makes a good backup device.

 Note USB thumb drives are also called jump drives, pocket drives, keychain drive,
and any of a variety of other names. Regardless of what you call them, all
use flash memory and plug into a USB port on a computer. Thumb drives
can have a capacity from 8MB to 64GB, or more.

Thumb drives operate just like any other removable storage. When plugged
into a USB connection on your computer, a thumb drive will be shown just like
any other removable storage. If you look in Figure 22-2, you will see that drive
F: is a removable storage device. It is actually a thumb drive plugged into the
computer.

When plugged into the computer, you can copy files just as you could to a
floppy disk or a CD. Rather than repeat the same material here, you can review
the procedures in the sections earlier in this chapter for copying, moving, and
deleting files.

The benefits of a thumb drives over floppy disks and CDS are its small size and
its lack of moving parts. In addition to its limited size, a floppy disk has moving
parts. CD and DVD players also have moving parts. A USB thumb drive does
not. This helps it stand up to wear and tear better than other devices.
Additionally, because a thumb drive plugs into a USB port, almost all computers will recognize them.

Using a USB Drive to Speed Up Your Computer

USB thumb drives can be used by Windows Vista to help increase your computer's performance. The more RAM you have in your computer, the faster it

might be able to run programs. If your computer doesn't have enough RAM to do what needs to be done, then it will use the hard drive as an extra area of storage. This use of the hard drive, unfortunately, is very slow.

Although USB thumb drives are not the same as RAM installed within your computer, with Windows Vista, USB flash memory can be used to supplement your computer's RAM. More importantly, they can do it much faster than using the hard drive. Because USB drives are generally cheaper than standard RAM for your computer, this is a relatively inexpensive way to give your computer a boost. This feature is called ReadyBoost.

Using Windows Vista ReadyBoost

If a USB drive contains memory that is usable for ReadyBoost, then, when you insert the drive into the computer, the AutoPlay dialog window will include an option for enabling it. Additionally, you can go to the Properties dialog window for the USB drive and set up ReadyBoost.

To display the drive's Properties dialog window, select Computer from the Start menu. This displays your computer information within Windows Explorer. Click the icon showing your USB drive to select it. You can then right-click the same icon to display a pop-up menu. Select Properties from the menu. This displays the Properties dialog window for the USB drive as shown in Figure 22-18

Figure 22-18: The Properties dialog window for a USB drive

In the Properties dialog window, select the ReadyBoost tab. This tab is where you can first determine if your USB drive will work for ReadyBoost, and if so, then you can set aside the amount of the USB drive's fast memory you would like to use. It is recommended that you use from one to three times the amount that you have of RAM in your computer. If you have 1GB of RAM, then it is recommended that you use between 1 and 3GB on a USB drive for the optimal performance boost.

In order for a USB drive to be useable for ReadyBoost, it needs to have at least 256MB of memory. If you don't have at least that much on the drive, then there really isn't enough to help the system improve performance. Additionally, your USB drive needs to be USB 2.0 compliant and plugged into a USB 2.0 connection. The older, slower USB connections won't run fast enough to give you the added performance, so ReadyBoost won't let you use these. Figure 22-19 shows you some of the information you might see in the ReadyBoost options if your USB drive isn't compatible for ReadyBoost.

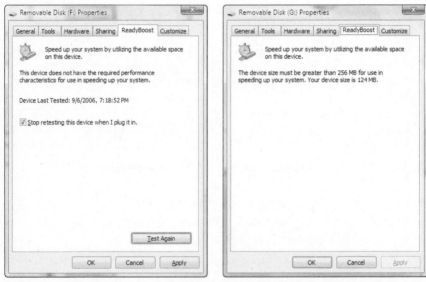

Figure 22-19: USB drives that won't work for ReadyBoost. The left drive is big enough but plugged into a USB 1.1 connection. The right drive is too small.

Using Other Storage Devices

Up to this point, we've ignored another type of removable media that you can use with your computer. Many computers now come with a memory card reader that can read a number of different media types such as ScanDisks, SD cards, XD cards, and Sony memory sticks.

These cards are generally used to store pictures or music files. Additionally, they were made to primarily work with digital cameras, MP3 players, and cellular phones.

Like a CD or DVD, memory cards have no moving parts. Rather they plug into a card reader or are attached along with a digital device. Files and folders can then be added and removed in exactly the same way as files and folders on any other drive.

Cross-Reference You'll learn a little about these cards in Chapter 14 and Chapter 17.

Summary

Floppy disks, Zip disks, CDs, DVDs, thumb drives, and memory cards are examples of removable media. These media are often used for distribution (such as music and programs you buy on CDs). They can also be used to copy files from one computer to another when e-mail or some other type of network transfer isn't possible. You can also use removable disks to make backup copies of important files on your hard disk. The main points to know about removable media are as follows:

✦ Floppy, Zip, and Jaz disks are examples of magnetic removable media.

✦ To see the contents of a removable disk, insert the disk into the appropriate drive in your computer. Then double-click the drive's icon in your Computer folder.

✦ You can move and copy files to and from magnetic removable disks using the same techniques you use to move and copy files between folders on your hard disk.

✦ You can delete files from a magnetic disk by right-clicking any icon and choosing Delete.

✦ CDs and DVDs are examples of laser media.

✦ You can copy files from a CD or DVD using the same techniques you use to copy files from floppies and Zip disks.

✦ Copying files to a CD or DVD usually involves burning the files to the disk.

✦ After you've burned a CD-R or DVD-R disk you cannot change its contents; you cannot add more files to it.

✦ Windows Vista Home Premium Edition and Ultimate Edition come with Windows DVD Maker that helps you create DVDs from your pictures, videos, and other files.

✦ USB thumb drives and memory cards are examples of flash media.

✦ You can use a USB 2.0 flash drive to supplement your computer's RAM memory and thus improve your computer's performance using Windows Vista ReadyBoost.

✦ You can copy files to and from thumb drives and memory cards in the same way you copy files from floppies and Zip disks.

Working with Compressed (Zip) Files

CHAPTER

23

A *Zip file* — also called a *compressed folder* — is a means of packing one or more files into a single, smaller, compressed file. Zip files are a common means of sending files via e-mail, because the compressed file is smaller than the original (in terms of bytes) and, therefore, transfers more quickly over the Internet. Some files you can download from the Internet might also be delivered to you as Zip files, again to make the file smaller and quicker to download.

Beyond compression, though, Zip files can just make multiple files more convenient to work with. For example, when we write a chapter like this one, the resulting chapter ends up being quite a few files. All the text is in one file, and each picture is in its own separate file.

When it comes time to submit a chapter to the publisher, we could send in each file individually. But what a pain! It's much easier to zip up all the files into one file named *Chapter 23* and send just that one Zip file as an e-mail attachment. The acquisitions editor who receives that chapter can then easily forward the single Chapter 23 file to the copy editor, tech editor, and whoever else needs to see the chapter. There's no need for anyone to fumble around with a bunch of separate files along the way.

Programs for Managing Zip Files

There are basically two ways to work with Zip files. One way is to use the capabilities built into Windows Vista. Those are the methods we'll be describing in this chapter. As an alternative, you can use a third-party Zip program, such as the ever-popular WinZip. If you're already

Zip Files, Zip Disks, Compressed Folders

In Chapter 21, we talk about Zip disks, which are sort of like floppy disks but are able to hold as much information as 10 to 1,000 floppies. There's no connection, however, between Zip disks and Zip files. The matching names are purely coincidental. Nothing in this chapter has anything to do with Zip disks.

Microsoft uses the name *compressed (zipped) folders* rather than just Zip file. But the name *compressed folder* is a little misleading too. The Zip file truly is a file, not a folder. For example, when you arrange icons in a folder, subfolders are listed first, followed by files. The *compressed folder* won't be listed with the *real folders*, though. The icon for the Zip file will be mixed with the other regular files.

familiar with such a third-party program and are happy with it, you can continue using that program.

But you have to realize that it's one method or the other — not both. As soon as you install a third-party Zip program on your computer, Windows' built-in capabilities vanish! If you want to try out the built-in capabilities, you need to uninstall your third-party program. The term *uninstall* means to remove from your computer. So it's not something you want to take lightly. Make sure that you understand what uninstall means (as discussed in Chapter 29) before you actually uninstall any program.

Having two or more programs for managing Zip files on your computer could cause compatibility issues that render some zipped files useless. So Microsoft was wise to ensure that its own built-in zip capabilities go into hiding when some other Zip program is on the system.

Generating Zip Files in Windows Vista

Like so many things in Windows, compressing files is one of those *select, then do things*. You select the files you want to compress, using any of the techniques described in the section "Working with Multiple Files and Folders" in Chapter 19. Then you right-click any one of them and send them to a compressed folder.

Windows doesn't *move* the selected files into the compressed file. The files you compress don't disappear into the compressed file. Rather, the compressed file contains *copies* of the selected files. It works that way because the usual reason to create a Zip file is to send the files to someone via a network — usually as an e-mail attachment, since that's an easy way to do it. You rarely want to send people your one-and-only original file. You usually want to send them copies and retain your originals.

Let's work though the specific steps for selecting some files and compressing them into a single Zip file. We'll use an example of sending a chapter that consists of one Microsoft Word document and several pictures.

STEPS: Create a Zip File

1. Open your Documents folder and navigate to the folder that contains the files you want to compress into a Zip file.

 Tip To select files from multiple folders, use the Search option within Windows Explorer (as covered in Chapter 21) to locate the files you want to copy. Then select the appropriate files in the Windows Explorer content area. If you use search, you may be asked to save your compressed folder to the desktop.

2. Select the files you want to compress. For example, Figure 23-1 three picture files and a document file selected.

3. Right-click any selected icon and choose Send To ⇨ Compressed (zipped) Folder, as is also shown in Figure 23-1.

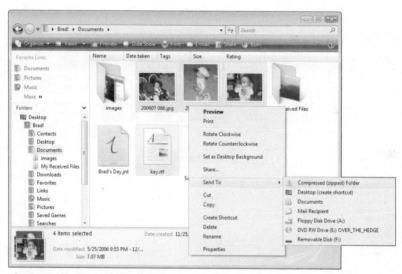

Figure 23-1: Several files selected and about to be zipped

Tip As usual, the combined sizes of all the selected items appear under Details in the Explorer bar (7.07MB in Figure 23-1).

4. After a brief delay, an icon representing the Zip file will appear in the folder (usually below the existing file names).

 The icon for a Zip file looks like a manila file folder with a zipper on it, like the example shown at left. The file name of the Zip file will be the same as the name of the file you right-click in Step 3. But you can easily change that by right-clicking the Zip file's icon, choosing Rename, and typing your own name or editing the existing name. Whether or not the .Zip file name extension is visible depends on the Hide extension . . . setting in your Folder Options dialog box.

To view the size of the resulting Zip file, do any of the following:

✦ Point to the file and look at its tooltip.

✦ Switch to Details view or Tiles view in Explorer.

✦ Click the Zip file's icon in Windows Explorer and look in the Details area.

✦ Right-click the file and chose Properties.

Zipping the files provides no guarantee that the resulting file will be small enough to send as an e-mail attachment. The size limit of an e-mail attachment varies from one Internet Service Provider (ISP) to the next. And the only way to determine your attachment-size limit is by checking with your ISP. For example, the 7.07MB of selected files in Figure 23-1 compress to a single Zip file that's 1.68MB (see Figure 23-2). That's still too big for an e-mail service that allows only attachments of 1.0MB.

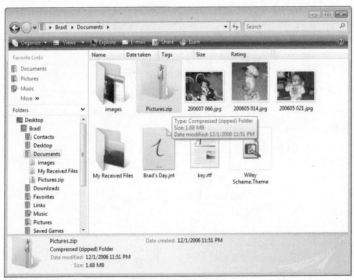

Figure 23-2: The compressed (zipped) file.

 Tip If you can't compress your files into a single Zip file that's small enough, consider creating two or more Zip files, each containing fewer files.

E-Mailing a Zip File

To e-mail a Zip file, you need to attach the Zip file to an e-mail message. However, before you can do that, you have to know how to send e-mail messages in general. Unfortunately, exactly how you go about doing that depends on your e-mail client (the program you use to send and receive e-mail). When it comes to e-mail and attaching files, no one rule fits all. You really have to learn how to e-mail from the company that provides your e-mail service (most likely your ISP).

Even though we can't tell you exactly how to attach files to e-mail messages in your particular e-mail program, we can point out some general techniques that *might* work, as they apply to particular types of e-mail. The only people who can tell you how *your* e-mail works are the people from whom you got your e-mail account.

Tip If you can send and receive mail, you can probably learn how to attach files by searching your e-mail client's Help for **attach**.

Shortcut for Attaching Files to E-mail

If you use standard POP3 e-mail, and Windows Mail as your e-mail client, you can use the shortcut described here to send an e-mail attachment to someone. This actually works with some other e-mail clients as well. It's worth a try. There's a point at which you should bail out if it doesn't work, as I point out under Step 2.

STEPS: Attach a File to an E-mail Message

1. Right-click the icon that represents the Zip file (or any other file) you want to send and choose Send To ➪ Mail Recipient. Then:

   - If a Choose Profile dialog box opens, choose the name of the program you want to use to send the e-mail; click OK.

   - If a dialog box appears asking you to enter your Display Name, click the Cancel button and don't proceed with this process. This dialog is the first step to setting up Windows Mail as your e-mail client. Refer to Chapter 11 to learn how to set up Windows Mail before proceeding.

Caution Don't attempt to guess your way through setting up Windows Mail. You cannot provide the information required by the set-up wizard by guessing. You stand about as much chance of guessing correctly as you do at guessing to complete a stranger's phone number!

2. An e-mail message, similar to the one in Figure 23-3, appears. As you can see in the Attach line, the file you right-click in Step 1 is already attached to the message.

3. Fill in the To: box with the recipient(s) e-mail address(es).

4. Optionally, change the Subject line and main body of the message to something more meaningful to the reader.

5. Click the Send button.

6. If your e-mail client isn't configured to send messages immediately, click the Send/Receive button or whatever button you usually click to send and receive messages.

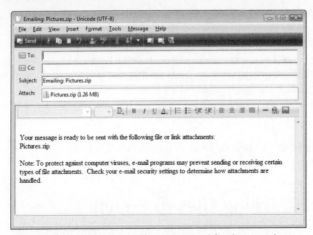

Figure 23-3: A new e-mail message with Pictures.zip already attached

That's all there is to it. The message and file are on their way to the recipient(s).

Attaching Files Without the Shortcut

As mentioned, the shortcut doesn't work with all e-mail clients, and there are no hard-and-fast rules that apply to e-mail attachments. As a general rule of thumb, the standard method is to create a new, regular e-mail message. Then look around the program for an Attach, Attach files, or Insert Attachment option, as in the examples shown in Figure 23-4.

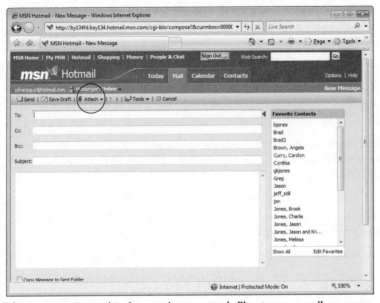

Figure 23-4: Example of an option to attach files to an e-mail message

If all else fails, and you can't figure out how to attach a file to an e-mail message with your e-mail account, you'll have to (dare I say it?) read the instructions. Look for the word *Help* where you're typing your e-mail message and click it. Or open the Help menu for your e-mail program and search the word attach. Or ask your ISP for information on using the e-mail service that came with your account.

Using Zip Files

When someone sends you a Zip file as an e-mail attachment, or you download a Zip file from the Internet, you first need to save the file to your hard disk. Then you need to *decompress* the file to get at the real files and folders inside it. If someone sent you a Zip file as a file attachment, you'll see the attachment's file name in the Attach line or box of the e-mail message. Figure 23-5 shows an example where the attached file is clearly a Zip file, as indicated by the zippered folder icon and .zip file name extension.

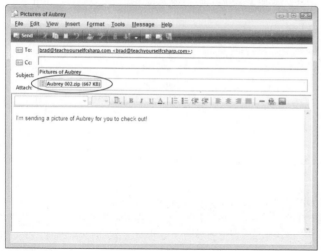

Figure 23-5: A Zip file attached to an e-mail message

 Tip File name extensions are visible only if the Hide extensions check box in the Folder Options dialog box is not selected. See "Showing/Hiding File Name Extensions" in Chapter 6 for details.

When you download a Zip file, you'll see a similar icon and a .zip file name extension on the file you're downloading. The file's type will be Compressed (zipped) Folder.

Your first step is to get the Zip file to your hard disk. If it's an e-mail attachment, you need to Save (not Open) the attachment. In Windows Mail, you can right-click the file name and choose Save As. You can also select File ➪ Save Attachments.

When the Save As dialog box appears, navigate to the folder in which you want to save the Zip file. If you created a Recent Downloads folder, you can put the file in that folder, as in Figure 23-6. (Don't forget that most viruses are spread by e-mail attachments and file downloads. If in doubt, scan the file for viruses.) Take a look at the file name, or change it if you like, so you know what to look for when you want to decompress the file. Then click the Save button.

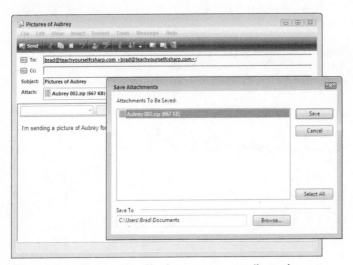

Figure 23-6: Saving a Zip file that was an e-mail attachment

Before you use the files within the Zip files, you should *extract* them. That means to take the compressed files (or file) from the Zip file and to make them normal, uncompressed files. Here are the steps.

STEPS: Extract Usable Files from a Zip File

1. Open your Documents folder and navigate to the folder in which the Zip file is stored.

2. Right-click the Zip file's icon and choose Extract All as in Figure 23-7.

3. A dialog box is displayed as shown in Figure 23-8. To place the extracted files in a folder within the same folder as the Zip file, click the Next button. Or, if you prefer, you can click the Browse button and choose a different folder for the extracted files. Then click the Extract button.

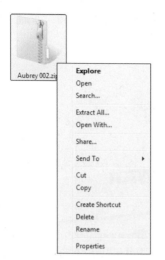

Figure 23-7: About to decompress a Zip file (extract the files from it)

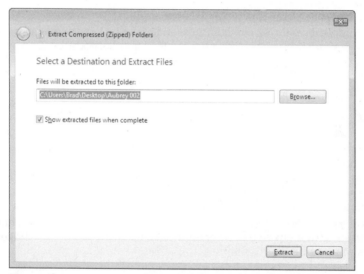

Figure 23-8: Extract Compressed (Zipped) Folder dialog window

The extracted file(s) open in Windows Explorer on your screen. Those are normal files that you can open by double-clicking. If you press Alt+↑, or choose View ➪ Go To ➪ Up One Level from Explorer's menu bar, you'll be taken to the parent of the files, where you'll see the icon for the uncompressed file. Its icon will be a normal folder icon, as in Figure 23-9. You can delete the Zip file once you have the extracted files on hand. You won't really need the Zip file anymore, unless you just want to keep it as a backup.

Folder containing extracted files

Original compressed (zipped) folder

Figure 23-9: Use the extracted files in the regular folder. You can delete the Zip file if you like.

Dragging and Dropping with Compressed Folders

In most ways, a compressed folder will operate like a regular folder. In fact, you can use the mouse to drag and drop files into a compressed file. This makes it an easy task to add new files from files in Windows Explorer.

You can also view the contents of a compressed folder within Windows Explorer. When you have the contents of a compressed file displayed, you can use the mouse to drag and drop a copy of a file from it to another location. In doing this, the file will not only be copied, but it will also be uncompressed.

Weird Compression Facts

Zip files aren't the only way to shrink large files. They're not even the best way. Sometimes, you can get a lot more compression just by changing the file type. For example, Brad recently downloaded some pictures from the Hubble Telescope site (www.hubblesite.org). They were mostly huge bitmap (BMP) files. The largest one came in at a hefty 55,000K, a trivial amount of disk space but definitely on the large size for one photograph. Out of curiosity, Brad packed it into a Zip file. The Zip file ended up being about 18,000K, a considerable amount of compression.

Next, Brad opened the original bitmap file in a graphics program and saved it as a JPEG file. (Choose File ➪ Save As from the graphics program's file menu. Choose JPEG form the Save As Type drop-down list in the Save As dialog box.) When he looked at the JPEG image, it was about 1,200KB — much smaller than the compressed bitmap image.

 Caution   Never attempt to change a file's type just by changing its file name extension. It won't work, and you'll make the file unreadable. To make the file readable again, you'll need to rename it, giving it back its original extension.

Realize that we're talking strictly about the sizes of the files, in bytes, here, not the size of the picture as it appears on the screen. If you look at the BMP and JPEG images side by side on the screen, they're virtually identical. Yet in terms of disk storage, the bitmap image is 55 times larger than the JPEG.

This brings me to another point. Many file types are already compressed. And adding them to a Zip file does little to shrink them further. Some examples of file types that are already compressed include MP3 and WMA music files, MPEG and WMV movies, and, of course, the aforementioned JPEG images. None of these files need to be decompressed for use. They're already small because the compression is built in.

Compressing files that are already in a compressed format won't buy you much. For example, the bitmap format used in my previous example isn't compressed at all. Recall that compressing a bitmap image reduced it from 55,000KB to 18,000KB—a difference of 37,000KB. When we compress the JPEG version of that same picture, the JPEG shrinks from 1,200KB to 1,100KB—a mere 100KB difference. The moral of the story is that it's better to know the file types and actual sizes of your files than it is to ignore actual sizes and just assume that zipping a file is the only way to make it smaller.

Of course, when it comes to e-mailing multiple files to people, Zip files still offer the benefit of combining multiple files into one file (kind of like ordering a bunch of products and having them all shipped to you in one box rather than in many little boxes). And that's convenient whether the files shrink a lot, or a little, in the process.

Summary

Alrighty then; let's do a quick recap of the main points in this chapter:

✦ Zip files, also called compressed folders, are a means of combining and compressing one or more files into a single, smaller file.

✦ You can compress files using Windows Vista or a third-party Zip program, but not both.

✦ To compress files, select their icons in Windows Explorer, right-click, and choose Send To ➪ Compressed (zipped) folder.

✦ When you receive a Zip file as an e-mail attachment, or download one from the Internet, you'll probably find it easiest to save it to your hard disk first.

✦ To extract the files from a Zip file, right-click the Zip file's icon and choose Extract All.

Managing Your Time, Tasks, and Appointments

Windows Vista includes a calendar program that enables you to keep track of appointments, tasks, and other events. This program is rightfully named Windows Calendar.

Using Windows Calendar, you can keep track of personal events and tasks. You can schedule reoccurring events; you can add reminders; you can even use color coding and more. You can set up multiple calendars as well as share your calendars with other people. You can even publish your calendar to the Internet where others can retrieve it.

Viewing a Calendar

To use Windows Calendar, open the Start menu and select All Programs ➪ Windows Calendar. The Windows Calendar program starts with the current date selected. Additionally, the name of the calendar is selected on the left side as shown in Figure 24-1.

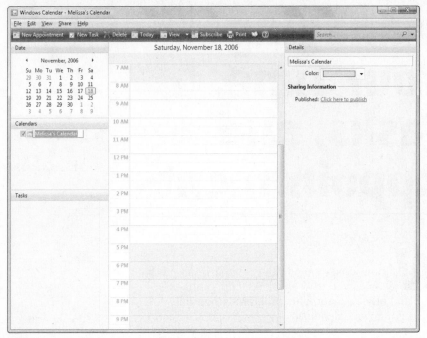

Figure 24-1: Windows Calendar the first time it is opened

When you open a calendar for the first time, a default calendar is created using your Windows Vista Account ID. This default name is highlighted so that you can simply type in a new name for your calendar. In Figure 24-1, you can see that the user account called Melissa is being used. The default name for her calendar is Melissa's Calendar. This name can be changed by typing in a new name. If you decide later that you want to change the name again, you can right-click the name of the calendar within the Calendars section and select Rename from the menu that is displayed.

Setting Different Calendar Views

The default view for the calendar shows the current day in the primary pane with time broken out by hours as seen in Figure 24-1. You can change this to show different views by clicking the View button in the task bar or by selecting an option in the View menu. The different views you can select are:

Day: The default view that shows a single day broken down by hours. You can go directly to this view by selecting Ctrl+Shift+1.

Work Week: This view shows the work week, generally Monday through Friday, in columns. Within each column, the days are broken into hours. You can go directly to this view by selecting Ctrl+Shift+2.

Week: This view is like the Work Week view, except that all of the days of the week are included. You can go directly to this view by selecting Ctrl+Shift+3.

Month: This view shows the current month. Unlike the other views, there is not a display of individual hours per day. Rather, you will see only links to any appointments on the calendar based on the day they occur. You can go directly to this view by selecting Ctrl+Shift+4.

Viewing the Windows Calendar Panes

In addition to the view within the main pane, a number of other items in Windows Calendar provide feedback. In Figure 24-2, you see a calendar that has a number of appointments and tasks. On the left side, you can see the Navigation pane. On the right side, you can see the Details pane.

If you don't see the Navigation pane, you can display it by selecting View ⇨ Navigation pane from the menu bar, by pressing Ctrl+I, or by clicking the down arrow next to the View button and then selecting Navigation pane from the list. After you have the Navigation pane displayed, you'll be able to see a calendar for the current month, a list of calendars that you have access to, and your list of tasks.

Figure 24-2: A calendar that has appointments and tasks

On the small calendar (see Figure 24-3), dates that have task or appointments associated to them will be in bold. Today's date will also be noticeable because it will be in a small, solid box. The currently selected date will be in a shaded dashed box. The selected date within the small calendar will also be what is selected and displayed in the main pane of Windows Calendar.

Previous month

Next month

No bold indicates no activities

Bold indicates activities

Today

Selected Date

Figure 24-3: The Date section of the Navigation pane

The Details pane is shown to the right of the main pane as you can see in Figure 24-2. If you don't see the Details pane, then you can display it by selecting View ⇨ Details pane from the menu, by pressing Ctrl+D, or by clicking the down arrow next to the View button and then selecting Details pane from the list. What you see in the Details pane will depend on what is currently selected. As you will see throughout this chapter, the Details pane provides additional details on calendars, appointments, and tasks.

Creating a New Calendar

A default calendar is created when you first open Windows Calendar. In addition to the default calendar, you have the ability to create new calendars as well as share calendars from others.

Each calendar you create or share will be listed in the Calendars section of the Navigation pane. In Figure 24-2, you could see that two calendars were being used. One is Brad!'s Calendar, which was the default calendar that was created for the Brad! account. The second calendar is called Work Items.

You might wonder why you would want more than one calendar. One reason to have multiple calendars is to separate different types of appointments and tasks. In the example of Figure 24-2, worked-related items were separated from personal items. A second reason to create multiple calendars is when you might want to share some appointments or tasks, but not everything on your calendar. By separating out the items you want to share, you keep them independent of those items you don't want to share.

This makes even more sense when you realize that you can display one or more of your calendars at the same time. In Figure 24-2, you can see a check box next to the two different calendars. Only the selected calendar will have its information displayed. In the case of Figure 24-2, only the items in the Brad!'s Calendar are being displayed. If Work Items is also selected as shown in Figure 24-4, then all items in the Work calendar will also be displayed.

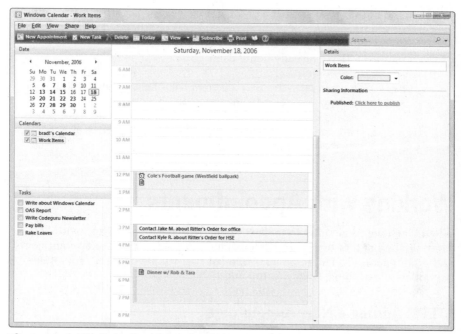

Figure 24-4: Displaying multiple calendars

Clicking Brad!'s Calendar again would cause only the work items to show. You should also note that the task list on the left side within the Navigation pane also reflects different items, depending on what calendars are selected. In Figure 24-2, only personal tasks are shown.

You can quickly tell which calendar an item belongs to based on its background color. Although you can't easily tell this in black and white pictures in a book, in Windows Calendar it is easy to tell one calendar's items from another. For the calendar in Figure 24-4, the personal items are in blue and the work items are colored brown.

Knowing that multiple calendars can be used is great, but what is more important to know is how to create a new calendar. To create a new calendar, do the following steps.

STEPS: Creating a New Calendar

1. Select File ➪ New Calendar from the Windows Calendar menu. This displays a new item called *New Calendar* in the Calendars section of the Navigation pane. This new item is highlighted.

2. Enter a new name for your calendar. This replaces the highlighted New Calendar text. Press Enter to save the change.

3. In the Details pane, select a color from the color list. This is the color that will be used for appointments and tasks associated with your new calendar. You will most likely want to choose a color that is different from those already being used.

 Note You can later choose a different color for a calendar. Do this by clicking the calendar name in the Calendar's section of the Navigation pane and then selecting the new color from the Details pane area. The newly selected color will be applied to all appointments and tasks associated with that calendar.

Working with Appointments

When you have a calendar, to make it useful, you need to add appointments. After all, the point of working with a calendar is to keep track of appointments and other events. To create an appointment that will be listed on your calendar, follow these steps.

STEPS: Adding a New Appointment

1. If you have more than one calendar, then select the calendar you want to use from the Calendar section within the Navigation pane. If you only have one calendar, then it will be selected by default.

2. Optionally, click the day or calendar view in the date or time slot where you want the new appointment to appear.

3. Do one of the following:

    • Click the New Appointment button in the taskbar.

    • Select File ➪ New Appointment.

    • Press Ctrl+N.

    • Right-click the calendar in the main area and select New Appointment from the menu that is displayed.

4. In the New Appointment box that appears (or in the top box in the Details pane), enter a name for your appointment.

At this point, you have added the new appointment. You can continue to customize the information about the appointment. The following information can be customized in the Details pane. This information can be added at the same time as you enter the appointment, or you can come back at any other time, select the event, and add the information.

Location: This is information on where the appointment is. This information appears after the appointment name in the main view. In Figure 24-2, you can see that the location of the selected appointment is Westfield ballpark. You can see this in both the Details pane and in the main view in parenthesis.

Calendar: This is the calendar that the appointment is associated. If you have more than one calendar, you select which calendar to use.

URL: This is a web address that you can associate to the appointment.

Appointment Information: If the appointment is an all-day event, you can select the All-day option to list the appointment at the top of the given day. Otherwise, you can select a start date and time as well as an ending date and time. The appointment will be adjusted on the calendar based on what you select here.

Recurrence: If an appointment is a regular event, then you can enter it once and then set the recurrence field to list it on subsequent date. More will be said about Recurrence in the following section, "Creating Reoccurring Appointments or Events."

Reminder: Windows Calendar can provide a prompt to remind you of an appointment. Set the amount of time before the appointment that you would like to be reminded of it. This can be anywhere from 0 minutes (meaning at the appointment start time) to 2 weeks. You can also select On Date and pick a specific date to be used to remind you of the appointment. More will be said on Reminders in the section, "Reminding Yourself" later in this chapter.

Participants: If others are also involved in an event, you can list them in the Attendees section. When you click on Attendees, you will be given a list of your Windows Contacts that you can select to add to the Attendees list. After the contacts are added, you can click the Invite button to open up Windows Mail to send an invitation to each person in your list. The invitation e-mail will include an attachment that the recipient can click to add the event to their own calendar.

 Cross-Reference For more on Windows Contacts, see "Managing Your Contacts" in Chapter 12. For more on e-mailing, see Chapter 11.

Notes: The notes field is an area for you to enter any additional information related to the appointment.

Creating Reoccurring Appointments or Events

One of the options you are able to set for an appointment is Recurrence. The recurrence frequency can be daily (every day), weekly, monthly, or yearly. For example, you can set an appointment such as a play date for every Monday by setting up the first appointment on the first Monday it occurs and then selecting weekly for Recurrence. The appointment would then be listed from that Monday forward.

Not all reoccurring appointments or events go forever. If this is the case, then you can also select Advanced from the list of options. This presents you with the dialog box on the far left in Figure 24-5.

A daily event that happens every day, forever. (Default screen for Advanced Recurrence options)

A weekly appointment that occurs every Monday and Friday until 12/31/2007

A monthly appointment that occurs on the last Monday of every month, forever

Figure 24-5: Advanced options for reoccurring events and appointments

The advanced options enable you to set how often to repeat an event. This can be a given number of days, weeks, months or years. It also enables you to state how often to list the event. You can select to go forever or you can choose to set a specific number of times or until a specific date.

If your event is weekly or monthly, then you can set additional options as also shown in Figure 24-5. For weekly events, you can choose what days during the week you want the appointment to appear. You can select as many days as you'd like as shown in the middle of Figure 24-5.

For monthly events, you are given a number of options based on the initial date of the appointment. If you select Monthly from the main Recurrence list rather than Advanced, then the appointment would happen on the same date each month. If, however, you want a monthly event based on a different criterion such as the second Monday of the month, then you can use the Advanced options. For example, in Figure 24-5 on the right, a monthly appointment has been set that will occur on the last Monday of every month.

Reminding Yourself

As mentioned earlier, you can set a reminder on an appointment. When the time for the reminder occurs, you will get a pop-up window similar to the one in Figure 24-6.

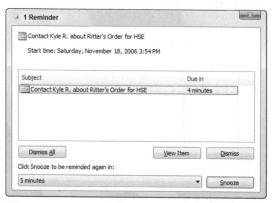

Figure 24-6: A reminder from Windows Calendar

The window is displayed based on the time you set in the Details pane for the given appointment. At that time, regardless of what you are doing, Windows Calendar displays the reminder notice. In fact, you don't even have to be running Windows Calendar at the time.

When you get this notice, you have a couple of options. You can choose to dismiss the notice by clicking the Dismiss button. This will cancel any additional reminders for the selected item.

You can also choose to have Windows Calendar remind you again a little later. To do this, select a time from the drop-down list at the bottom of the dialog box. This can generally be anywhere from in five minutes to in two weeks. After you've selected the time, click the Snooze button. A reminder will be displayed again at that time.

You can also select the View Item button. When this button is clicked, the item that is highlighted in the reminder section will be found and displayed in Windows Calendar. You will then be able to see the specific information on the appointment in the Details pane. With the item opened in Windows Calendar, in the Reminder dialog box, you can then choose to dismiss the item or set a Snooze time.

If you have more than one reminder that has popped up or has not been responded to, then they will be listed in the center of the Reminder dialog box. In Figure 24-7, you can see that there are two appointments that are now overdue. Each of these can be addressed individually as described above, or they can all be dismissed by clicking on the Dismiss All button. When dismissed, however, no more reminders will be given for these specific appointments.

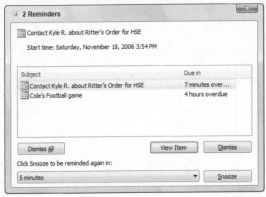

Figure 24-7: Multiple reminders from Windows Calendar

Finding Appointments

With Windows Vista, searching is made easy in a lot of ways. The same is true for finding an appointment or task. If you are in Windows Calendar, you can find items by using the Search box near the top of the Window. As you enter an item into the box, Windows Calendar will show search results (see Figure 24-8).

Figure 24-8: Finding appointments and tasks in Windows Calendar

If you double-click any of the items that have been found, then the calendar will be moved to the date of the item, and it will be displayed in the window below. If you have the Details pane open, then the details will be displayed as well.

You can change the order that the search results are displayed in by clicking the column headings. Clicking a heading once sorts the list by that column. Clicking the column heading again reverses the sort order for that column. You can sort by any of the displayed columns. When you are done with the search results, you can close the search window by clicking the red close button in the right corner of the search results area.

But wait, there's more! In addition to the search within Windows Calendar, you can use the other Windows Vista searches as well. For example, the search box on the Start menu also searches within your tasks and appointments to find matches. If there is a match, then the result will be the calendar in which the matches are found.

 Cross-Reference For more on using Windows Vista searches, see Chapter 20.

Working with Tasks

In addition to creating appointments, you can also create Tasks. Tasks tend to be to-do items that are not necessarily associated with a specific time on a given date, but rather are items you simply need to get done. Tasks can, however, have deadlines and be focused on a given date.

Windows Calendar gives you the tools to manage your To-do (tasks) lists as well. Just like with appointments, you can assign tasks to specific calendars, thus grouping them. To create a new task, do the following steps.

STEPS: Creating a Task

1. Choose the calendar that you want to associate the task to. Do this by clicking the calendar name in the Calendars section of the Navigation pane.

2. Do one of the following:

   • Click the New Task button on the taskbar.

   • Select File ➪ New Task from the Windows Calendar menus.

   • Press Ctrl+T.

   • Right-click within the Tasks area of the Navigation pane and select New Task from the menu that appears.

3. The new task is created with the name of New Task. Type in the name of your task and press Enter.

At this point, your new Task has been created and named. It will show in the Tasks area of the Navigation pane with the name you've given it. You can change additional settings for your task by making sure it is selected (click it), and then entering the information in the Details pane as shown in Figure 24-9.

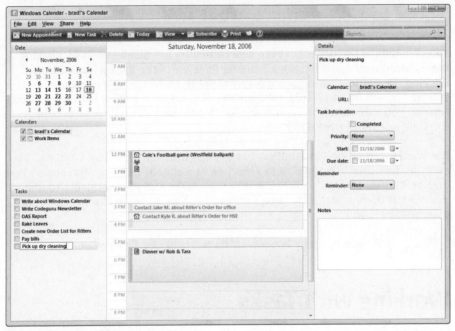

Figure 24-9: Entering a new task

Within the Details pane, you can modify a number of different items for a Task. Some of these are going to be similar to what you saw for Appointments earlier.

Calendar: This is the calendar that the task is associated with. If you have more than one calendar, you select which calendar to use.

URL: This is a web address that you can associate with the task.

Completed: Check this box when you have completed the task. Note also the box next to the task listed in the Tasks area of the Navigation pane. When you check the Completed check box in the Navigation pane, it will also check this box.

Priority: This is an indicator of the importance of this task item. You can select None (default), Low, Medium, or High. You can use this information to sort your tasks later.

Start: This is the date you associate to the start of the task.

Due date: This is the date when the task needs to be completed.

Reminder: Windows Calendar can provide a prompt to you reminding you of a task. Set the amount of time before the task start date that you would like to be reminded of. This can be set to None or to any date and time you'd like. To set a specific date and time, choose On date from the drop-down and then enter the date and time.

Notes: The Notes field is an area for you to enter any additional information related to the task.

Sorting and Prioritizing Your Tasks

You can sort the order in which your tasks are displayed in the Tasks section of the Navigation pane. You do this by right-clicking in the Tasks area of the Navigation pane and then selecting Sort by from the menu that is displayed. You can then select to sort by the Due Date, the Priority, the Title, or the Calendar in which the task is associated.

Changing and Resolving Tasks

Your task list can get bigger and bigger unless you complete tasks, or at least mark them as completed, and then have them removed from the task list. Earlier it was stated that you could select the check box next to the word Completed in the Details pane to mark a task as completed. Additionally, you can select the box next to the task item in the Tasks area of the Navigation pane. Either way, the task will be marked as completed. The task will, however, still be in your Tasks list.

By default, Windows Calendar never hides completed tasks. You can change this behavior so that when a task is completed, it can be hidden from the Tasks list. To do this, you need to make a change to the Windows Calendar options.

Start by selecting File ➪ Options from the Windows Calendar menu. This opens the Options dialog box shown in Figure 24-10.

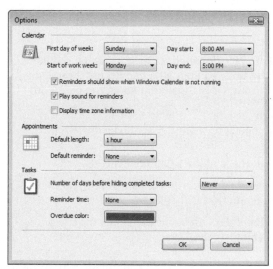

Figure 24-10: The Windows Calendar Options dialog box

The lower section of this dialog box contains options specific to Tasks. To change how long completed tasks are displayed, click the list button next to Number of days before hiding completed tasks. You can change the defaulted value of Never to one of several settings listed that range from one day to two weeks.

You'll also notice two other settings for Tasks in the Options dialog box. Tasks are generally associated with a given date rather than a specific time. You can, however, set a time that will be used for task reminders. If you don't set a time, 12:00 am is set as the default. You can also set an Overdue color. This color is used for the font in the Tasks list in the Navigation pane when the task becomes overdue. The default color of Red is very good for making overdue tasks stand out!

Sharing Calendars

Although a Windows Calendar can be a private thing, it doesn't have to be. You can actually share your calendar with others as well as add other people's calendars into Windows Calendar. As you saw earlier, you can simply check to select or unselect any calendars in the Calendars area of the Navigation pane.

This ability to get to other people's calendars can be beneficial for synchronizing appointments across people in your family who are using the same computer with separate accounts. It is also good for sharing in a work setting. Even more interesting is the ability to pull in (subscribe to) a calendar from someone on the Internet. This could be a sports team calendar showing games or a school calendar showing school events.

Publishing Calendars

To share a calendar, it first needs to be published. After it has been published, others can access it by subscribing to it. To limit who can access a published calendar, you can add a password to it. Only those that know the password will be able to gain access to it.

To publish your calendar, start by doing one of the following:

✦ Select Share ➪ Publish from the Windows Calendar menus.

✦ Select a calendar in the Calendars area, right-clicking on it and then selecting Publish from the menu that is displayed.

✦ Select the calendar in the Calendars area and then click the Click here to publish link in the Details pane.

Regardless of which way you start the process, the Publish dialog window is displayed (see Figure 24-11).

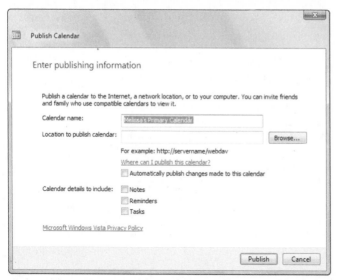

Figure 24-11: The first step toward publishing a calendar

As you can see in the Publish Calendar dialog window, Melissa's Primary Calendar is being published. In the Location to publish calendar box, you can choose a location that is on your local computer, network, or on a web server that you have the right to post a file to. If this is on your computer or network, you can click the Browse button and navigate to the location. For example, you can publish to the Public folder to share the calendar with anyone else on the current computer or network.

You can also select whether or not the published calendar should stay as it is currently or whether it should be updated as changes are made to the original calendar. If you select the box next to Automatically publish changes made to this calendar, then the published calendar will be updated.

The last option on the page enables you to determine whether Notes, reminders, and tasks are included in what is published. If you don't click the corresponding boxes to select these items, then they will not be included on the published calendar information.

After you've entered the location and made your selections, you can click the Publish button. You will then see a dialog box showing the status of the calendar being published. When the publishing is completed, a dialog box similar to Figure 24-12 is displayed confirming that the calendar has been published.

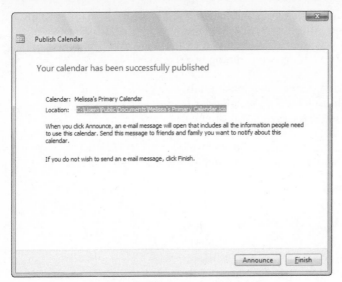

Figure 24-12: Confirmation that a calendar has been successfully published

The confirmation includes the location where the calendar was published. In Figure 24-12, you can see that Melissa's Primary Calendar was published to C:\Users\Public\Documents\Melissa's Primary Calendar.ics. This is the location on the hard drive that corresponds to Public Folder. Melissa's Primary Calendar.ics is the name of the file for the published calendar. From this dialog box, you can choose to inform others that the calendar has been published. If you click the Announce button, you will be able to send an e-mail to people you want to inform that you have published your calendar. Clicking the button opens Windows Mail (or your default e-mail program) and creates an e-mail (see Figure 24-13). You can then add people to the e-mail and send it.

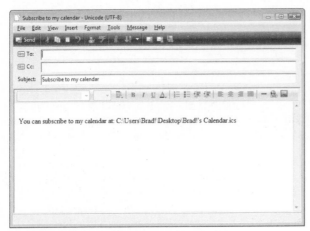

Figure 24-13: The Announcement e-mail for a published calendar

If you don't want to announce your published calendar, you can simply skip clicking the Announce button and click the Finish button instead. If you do choose to announce your calendar, then you will still need to click the Finish button to close the Publish Calendar dialog box.

After publishing a calendar, you can make changes to your sharing options. When you select a shared, published calendar from the Calendars section of the Navigation pane, the sharing information will be shown in the Details pane.

 Caution If the Automatically published changes check box is not selected, then changing the other options won't impact the calendar that has already been published.

Subscribing to Calendars

To add a shared calendar to your list of calendars, you need to subscribe to it. You can subscribe only to calendars that have been published. To start the subscription process, either select Share ➪ Subscribe from the Windows calendar menu or right-click within the Calendars section of the Windows Calendar Navigation pane and select Subscribe from the menu that is displayed. The Subscribe to a Calendar dialog box is displayed similar to what is shown in Figure 24-14.

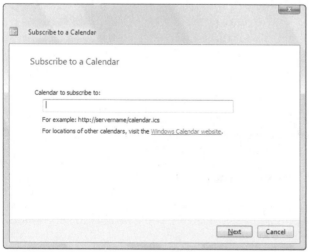

Figure 24-14: Subscribing to a published calendar

Within this dialog box you need to enter the address of a calendar file that has been shared. This can be a location on the Internet, on your network, or on your local computer. The calendar file is the ICS file that was listed in Figure 24-12 as well as in the Announcement e-mail that could be sent (Figure 24-13). In the case of Melissa's Primary Calendar, this is the file

C:\Users\Public\Documents\Melissa's Primary Calendar.ics. Entering this into the dialog box in Figure 24-14 subscribes you to Melissa's Primary Calendar.

 Note You should subscribe to a calendar from a different user account than the one that is using the calendar. If you enter the location incorrectly, you will get an error message. You will be able to go back to enter the location again.

After you enter a valid location, you will see the status of the Calendar being loaded. When the load has completed, you will be presented with subscription settings as shown in Figure 24-15. Within these settings, you can choose the name you want to display for the calendar, how often you want it updated — if at all, and whether you want to include reminders and tasks. Obviously if the publisher isn't providing updates, reminders, or tasks, then these options won't be of value.

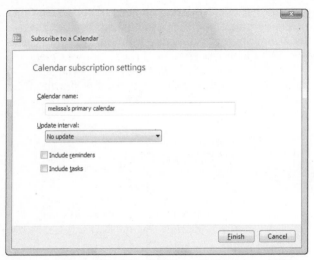

Figure 24-15: Configuring calendar subscription settings

When you click the Finish button, the subscribed calendar will be added to your Calendars list within the Navigation pane. The icon for the calendar will be slightly different to indicate that it is a subscribed calendar rather than one of your own. Like other calendars, when selected, you'll be able to set a color and change settings in the Details pane.

 Tip If you receive an e-mail announcement for a published calendar, then you can click the file name in the e-mail. This should automatically open the Subscribe dialog window. If not, you can follow the process mentioned earlier instead.

Printing Your Calendars

Many people use paper day-timers and other schedule systems. Windows Calendar enables you to print information from your calendars so that you can take it with you. To print information from your calendar, select File ➪ Print from the Windows Calendar menu or click the Print button in the taskbar. This opens the calendar Print dialog box (see Figure 24-16).

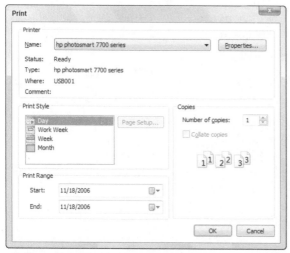

Figure 24-16: The dialog box for printing calendar information

This Windows Calendar print dialog box includes a number of additional options for printing calendar information. This includes the print style settings and the date range.

In the Print Style section, you can select whether information should be printed using a day, work week, week, or monthly view. The amount of information printed will be similar to what you see in the displayed views. In Figure 24-17, you can see a printout for the Day style as well as for the Week style.

You can also select the Print Range, which is a Start and End date. The information between these dates will be printed. If you select a date range larger than the view selection (such as selecting a date range with more than one day) and the day style, then multiple pages will be printed.

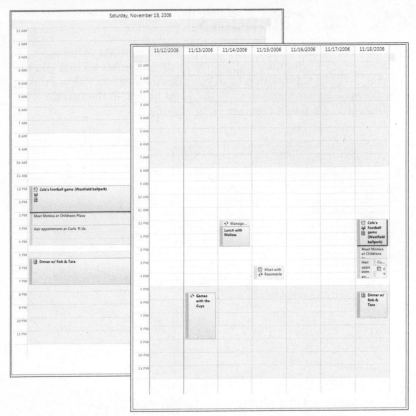

Figure 24-17: Printouts showing the calendar day style on the left and the week style on the right

Modifying Other Windows Calendar Settings

Earlier in this chapter, you learned how to adjust task settings by using the Windows Calendar Options dialog box. You can also use this dialog box to adjust a few other settings for your calendars and appointments. You can open the Options dialog box by selecting File ➪ Options from the Windows Calendar menu (see Figure 24-10).

Changing Calendar Options

At the top of the dialog box, you have the ability to change Calendar settings. These options enable you to customize the look of your calendar and more. Several of the options are obvious. The importance of others may not be.

The Day start and Day end settings determine the key time during the day. If you look in some of the earlier figures within this chapter, you will see that part of the day is slightly shaded, while the main hours of the day are not. You could also see this in the printouts in Figure 24-17. The areas that are not shaded are those between the Day start and Day end time. If your primary day starts earlier or later, then you can adjust these settings. For example, many people work from 9:00 A.M. to 6:00 P.M. instead of from 8:00 A.M. to 5:00 P.M.

There are several options for the calendar that you can select (check) to turn on or off. By default the Reminders should show when Windows Calendar is not running check box is selected. If you clear this check box, then you won't get the pop-up window reminders for appointments and tasks if you don't have Windows Calendar running. This can be beneficial if you don't want pop-ups interfering with other programs, but it also means you may not get timely reminders. The Play sound for reminders option is similar in that you will have a sound notification when a reminder is displayed. This can help draw your attention to the reminders when they happen. Of course, if your computer is muted, then this sound won't happen!

The other option you can select for the calendar is Display time zone information. When you select this option, then Time Zone information will be added into the Details pane for appointments. You'll be able to set a time zone for the Start and End times on your appointments.

Changing Appointment Options

In addition to options for Tasks and the Calendar as a whole, you can also set options for appointments. These options are default values for the length of an appointment and for the length of a reminder. These values are the default that will be used when an appointment is created or a reminder added. They can be changed for each appointment individually, but by setting the defaults to the most frequent values, it will save you a few seconds of time later.

Importing and Exporting

One additional topic deserves mention regarding calendars. You have the ability to share individual tasks and appointments with others. This can be done by selecting the task and exporting it to a calendar file (an ICS file). You can then send this file to others and they can choose to import it. This import will add it to their calendars as if they had added it themselves.

To export an item, first select it by clicking it. Then select File ➪ Export from the Windows Calendar menu. You will then be prompted to enter a file name for the exported item. You can use the default or add your own. The file will then be exported to this file.

You can then send this file to someone else through the Internet or by copying it to a disk. When they get the file, they can import it into their copy of Windows Calendar by selecting File ➪ Import from the menu. They will then be prompted to enter the imported file name (see Figure 24-18). They can enter the file name or chose the Browse button and navigate to it. They can also choose to add the item to an existing calendar or to add it to a new calendar by selecting Create new calendar. After the Import button is clicked, the item will be pulled in and added to the selected calendar — or a new calendar if that was selected.

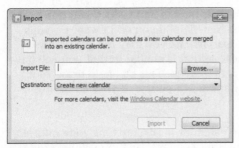

Figure 24-18: Importing a task or appointment

An alternative to importing and exporting is to simply right-click a task or appointment and select Send via E-mail. This does the same as exporting the item and adding it to an e-mail. When the person receives the e-mail, they should be able to double-click the attached file to start the import process.

Summary

Windows Calendar is a detailed program that can help you organize your life. By using color coding, multiple calendars, and some of the settings, you can quickly organize the events in your life. You can also set up calendars and share them to make it easy to coordinate between several people.

You learned several key points in this chapter:

✦ Windows Calendar is a program for organizing your tasks and appointments.

✦ Windows Calendar enables you to set up multiple calendars of your own as well as enables you to subscribe to other calendars. You can then decide which to display with a simple click of the mouse.

✦ You can set reminders to let you know when a task needs to be done or when an appointment is getting near. When a reminder happens, you can dismiss it or have it snooze until a later time when it can remind you again.

✦ You can view your calendars in a variety of ways. This includes daily, weekly (work or regular), and monthly.

✦ You can print your calendar in a variety of views as well. This also includes a daily, weekly (work or regular), and monthly view.

✦ Where to set options for your calendars, appointments, and tasks.

Have It Your Way

✦　✦　✦　✦

Here's a part title that really scores big in the originality department; We'll probably get sued or something. Other phrases like "personalizing your computer" or "customizing your computer" are just too many syllables. Besides, people have been using that expression for ages. Like at the end of an argument: "Fine, have it your way." (Followed by the unspoken "ya moron" or worse.)

Anyway, after you get the hang of how to work a PC and can actually get it to do what you want, tweaking it out can be fun—maybe give the screen a little personality, so it doesn't look exactly like everyone else's; add some new programs; maybe even let other people use the PC (as long as they stay away from your stuff). Most of these things are easy to do. So, what the heck, go ahead and have it your way.*

*Not spoken in aforementioned argumentative tone.

✦　✦　✦　✦

Creating and Managing User Accounts

The whole idea behind a personal computer (or PC for short) is that it's supposed to be personal. Unlike a terminal on some large corporate network, where you're just one of many users on a network, you are in complete control of your PC; you get to decide how things look on the screen. You get to decide how you want to organize your documents. You get to decide what programs you do and don't want on your computer.

When two or more people use the same PC, some of the personal parts of PC get lost in the shuffle. For example, let's say Melissa is one user, and she has everything on her screen set up just the way she likes. She has her own Documents folder that she keeps organized and so forth. Then user Alan comes along, plops down at the same computer, and starts changing things the way he wants them. Melissa gets back on the computer and finds that Alan has totally messed things up for her. Melissa is not happy with Alan. Melissa wants to keep things her way.

One solution is to give each user his or her own separate PC. That way, nobody steps on anybody else's toes. You can, however, see the downside to that approach right away—it costs a lot of money to give each person a separate PC. The other solution is to give each person one *user account* on the same PC. When you do that, each user has his or her own desktop, Documents folder, and so forth. It's the next best thing to each person having a PC. Best of all, it doesn't cost a penny.

What's a User Account?

Windows Vista will know who is using the computer because you have to select a user account when you start up the computer. When Windows Vista is originally installed, at least one account also had to be set up. When the computer first starts up, you are taken to a Welcome screen, like the example shown in Figure 25-1.

Figure 25-1: The Windows Vista Welcome screen

Each one of those user names on the Welcome screen represents a user account. As mentioned, each user account will have its own desktop and its own Documents folder (and subfolders). You could also set up each user account to have its own separate e-mail and .NET Passport, as if each user account were an entirely separate PC.

However, unlike having separate PCs, all of the user accounts will have access to the Public folders. For example, if you put a bunch of songs in the Public Music folder, anybody who logs onto the computer can play the songs, create CDs from the songs, and so on. But that wouldn't be true if you put those songs in your Music folder. Anything in your personal folders will be invisible and inaccessible to other users. Figure 25-2 illustrates the concept.

When you start creating user accounts, Windows will ask whether you want the user to be an administrator or standard user.

Figure 25-2: Each user account has its own desktop and personal folders, but everyone has access to Public folders.

Administrators versus Standard Users

When two or more people share a computer, and each person has a user account, one or more persons usually play the role of *administrator*. The administrator has limitless power over the computer, in that she can look at other peoples' stuff (as in spying on what kinds of things the kids are up to), create (and take away) user accounts, install new hardware and software, make system-wide changes (things that affect all user accounts), and more.

Note   Microsoft recommends that you don't use an Administrator account unless you need to do administrative tasks. As such, they recommend you give everyone, including yourself, a standard account. If you happen to try to do something that requires administrative rights, you will be prompted to enter the administrator password. Enter it correctly and you'll be allowed to continue.

A *standard* user can still use the computer normally. However, a standard user can't do certain things. For example, a standard user can't see other peoples' documents and can't make big changes to the computer that might affect other users. Only the administrator can do the big things. That's because the administrator is (presumably) the most knowledgeable user and, therefore, gets to be the person in control. Table 25-1 summarizes the differences between administrator and standard-user capabilities.

Table 25-1
Differences Between Administrators and Standard Users

Capability	Administrator	Standard User
Install programs and hardware	Yes	No
Create and delete user accounts	Yes	No
Change other peoples' user accounts	Yes	No
Change your own user account type	Yes	No
Change your own user account picture	Yes	Yes
Create, change, or remove your own password	Yes	Yes
See other people's documents	Maybe	No

Private Documents versus Public Documents

Notice that we write *maybe* as to whether or not an administrator can see other peoples' documents. That's because there's no rule that says there can be only one administrator user account on the computer. You can have any number of administrator accounts and standard accounts. How you set up your user accounts is entirely up to you.

An administrator can always look at the documents created and stored by standard users. That is, there's no way standard users can keep an administrator from peeking at their files. So what about two different administrator accounts? If you create an administrator account for yourself, you can make its documents *private*, which means nobody else on the computer can see your documents — not even other administrators.

Password-Protecting a User Account

Recall that the Welcome screen, shown in Figure 23-1, displays an icon for each person who has a user account on the computer. Now imagine that you're the user named Owner, and you're also the only administrator of the computer. All other users have user accounts. Suppose that the user named Wilbur is sitting alone at the computer, looking at the Welcome screen. Wilbur decides he wants to be administrator for a while. So, rather than clicking his own user account icon, he clicks yours.

Can the computer *see* that it's really Wilbur sitting at the computer and keep him from logging into your account? Of course not, because computers don't have eyes or brains. They're just machines that wouldn't know a human being from a golf ball. So the computer assumes you are logging in, displays your desktop, and grants all administrative powers. Wilbur then has free reign over your user account and all your administrative privileges. As far as the computer is concerned, Owner, not Wilbur, is controlling the keyboard.

To prevent this from happening, you need to *password-protect* your user account. That is, you need to think of a password and write it down. After you password-protect your account, only you can get into your user account. Clicking your user account icon in the Welcome screen won't take you, or anybody else, to the desktop or into your account. Instead, a prompt will appear, asking for the password. Only a person who knows that password can type it and get to the desktop. Anybody taking a wild guess will be rejected and locked out of your account.

 Caution   You never want to forget your own password; presumably, you're the only person on the planet who knows it. If *you* forget the password, there's nobody else to ask!

So those are some things to consider when planning user accounts for a personal computer. It boils down to how much power you want to allow each user (person) and how much privacy you want for your own account. To keep everyone — even other administrators — out of your account, you can make your account private and password-protected. You'll get to choose your options as you create the account. Optionally, you can go in and change those choices at any time.

The Guest Account

Windows Vista has a built-in *Guest account*, which you can activate while you're setting up accounts. That account isn't ascribed to any one person. Rather, it's a catch-all account for anyone who doesn't have a user account.

For example, let's say you're having a houseguest who wants to be able to use the computer once in a while. You don't want to create a user account for your guest, so you just let the person use the Guest account. Like a standard user, a guest won't be able to make any substantial changes to the overall computer system but will be able to do the day-to-day things that a regular computer user needs to do. As described in the section "Activating/Deactivating the Guest Account," later in this chapter, whether or not you even have a Guest account is entirely up to you.

How to Create a User Account

Creating a user account is simple — a wizard will take you through the whole procedure. Think of the name you want to give the account first (just the person's first name will do), and think about whether or not you want to make this person an administrator or standard user. Then follow these steps.

STEPS: Create a New User Account

1. Click the Start button and choose Control Panel.

2. In Control Panel, under the User Accounts and Family Safety section, click the Add or remove user accounts link. Icons for user accounts currently defined on your computer appear in the User Accounts window, as in Figure 25-3.

Figure 25-3: The User Accounts window

3. Click Create a new account. This displays a dialog box for creating a new user as shown in Figure 25-4.

4. As instructed, type the new user's name.

5. Choose whether you want to make this new user an Administrator or Standard user; click Create Account. The new user account name and picture appear in the User Accounts window.

6. Close the User Accounts window by clicking the Close (X) button in its upper-right corner.

Don't worry about the account picture, password, or privacy settings. You will learn how to change those later in this chapter, so that you'll be able to change those at any time. If this is your first experience with user accounts, take a moment to get familiar with the new account.

Figure 25-4: The User Accounts window

Logging on to a New Account

When you first create a new user account, it's really little more than a place-holder. Windows doesn't actually create that user's personal folders until the user (or you) logs into the account. To really get the job done and to make it easier to configure the account additionally, you should log into the account. Here's a quick and easy way to do that:

1. Click the Start button and then click the arrow button next to the lock in the bottom-right corner of the start menu. This displays a pop-up menu (see Figure 25-5).

2. Choose Switch User from the menu. You will be taken to the Windows Vista Welcome screen.

3. Click the name or picture of the new user account you just created; then wait.

It takes a minute or two to get a new account all squared away. You don't have to do anything except be patient. Eventually, you'll be taken to the Windows desktop. Right off the bat, you'll notice something about this desktop — it might not look exactly like yours.

When you create a new user account, the new user's desktop is a clone of what a desktop looks like when you first install Windows or when you buy a new computer with Windows Vista preinstalled. That's because every user account has its own desktop. Since this is a new user account, it gets a fresh desktop.

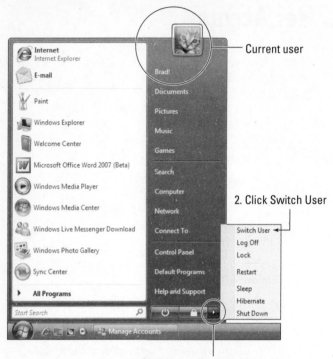

Current user

2. Click Switch User

1. Click the arrow to display options

Figure 25-5: Menu options for shutting down or switching users

If you peek into the Documents, Pictures, or Music folders in this new user account, you won't see any of your documents either. The new user has his or her own personal folders, separate from yours. If you click the Start button, you'll notice some differences there, too. This user will have access to all the programs you do. But any customizing you've done on your Start menu won't be visible in the new user account.

Getting Back to Your Own User Account

To get back to your own user account, and perhaps do more work on this new account, or create more accounts, follow these steps:

1. Click the Start button; click the arrow next to the lock icon to display the options for shutting down or switching users (see Figure 25-5 again).

2. Select the Log Off option. This takes you back to the Windows Vista Welcome screen.

3. Click your own user account name or picture.

You'll be taken back to your own user account, where things will be just as you left them.

Changing a User Account

From this point on, each user can actually manage his or her own account. But as the all-powerful administrator, you're free to manage their accounts for them. For starters, you might want to change the picture that Windows gave to the account. Like everything else that has to do with managing user accounts, you'll make changes in the User Accounts window. Follow these steps to change an existing user account.

STEPS: Change an Existing User Account

1. Click the Start button and choose Control Panel.

2. Open the User Accounts icon.

3. Click the name or picture of the account you want to change. You'll see options like those in Figure 25-6.

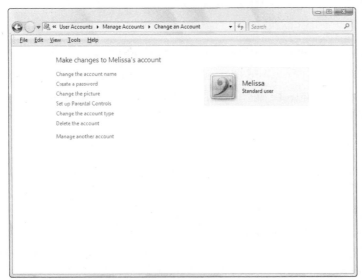

Figure 25-6: Options for changing some other person's user account

What happens from here depends on which option you choose. You'll find them all self-explanatory. For example, if you click Change the Picture, you'll be taken to a page of pictures to choose from (see Figure 25-7). Use the scroll bar to the right of the pictures to scroll through them all. Then click the picture you want to use, and click the Change Picture button.

Figure 25-7: Choosing a picture to represent a user account

Other options that an administrator can change for any user account include:

✦ **Change the account name:** Change the user's name.

✦ **Create a password:** Password-protect the user account.

✦ **Set up Parental Controls:** Set up parental controls for the account. This is covered in detail in Chapter 27.

✦ **Change the account type:** Change the account from administrator to standard, or vice versa.

✦ **Delete the account:** Delete the user account. Do not take this lightly; read the following section first.

Deleting a User Account

When you delete a user account, you delete all the documents, e-mail messages, and settings within the account. If your computer came with a generic Administrator or Owner account, and you want an account with your own name, it would be better to change the name on that existing account. You won't lose any files or settings that way.

If you really want to delete an account, you can click the Delete the account option. You'll be given the option to Keep Files or Delete Files. The Keep Files option will move the personal files from the old account to a new folder on your own desktop. Although you'll still lose e-mail messages and settings from the previous account, at least you won't lose the documents! Specifically, Windows will copy content from the deleted accounts desktop, and from the Documents, Favorites, Pictures, and Video folders.

Using Your Own Pictures for User Accounts

The pictures that you see in Figure 25-7 are just some freebies from which you can choose. You can actually use any picture you like. But it has to be something that looks OK at a tiny size. If you just pull in any old photo you have sitting around, it might look like little more than a random blob when reduced to that tiny size.

If you really want to use a personal picture for your user account, you should prepare a picture ahead of time. You'll need a graphics program and the ability to use it. Open a photo, as in the example that follows, and crop out a perfect square. Then shrink the perfect square to about 50×50 pixels, as in the tiny photo to the right that follows. Save that tiny photo as a JPEG image.

Go back to the User Accounts window, and click the user account you want to change; then click Change the picture. Rather than choosing one of the little freebie sample pictures, click the Browse for more pictures link. Navigate to the folder in which you placed the picture, double-click the picture's icon, and you're done.

You can't delete your own account. If there is only one administrator account on the computer, you cannot delete it because at least one account on the computer must be an administrator account. In that case, you'll be forced to create a new administrator account or change a standard account to an administrator account and then log into that other administrator account. From this other administrator account, you can delete the original administrator account.

Activating/Deactivating the Guest Account

The Guest user account, as mentioned, is sort of a catch-all account for guests, people who want to borrow the computer for a short time. Allowing such people to use the Guest account prevents them from accessing any other user accounts.

The Guest account is built into Windows Vista, so you don't need to create it. Instead, you can just activate it, thereby making it an option on the Welcome screen, or deactivate it so it's not accessible at all. To activate or deactivate the Guest account.

STEPS: Activating or Deactivating the Guest Account

1. Click the Start button and choose Control Panel.

2. In Control Panel, in the User Accounts and Family Safety section, click the *Add or remove user accounts* link to open the User Accounts window.

3. Click the picture that represents the Guest account.

4. If the account is not activated, you will be presented with a dialog box asking if you want to activate the account. If so, click the Turn On button.

5. When the account is active, then clicking the Guest account picture will take you to a dialog box that gives you the option to change the picture used with the account or to turn off the account. Click the Turn off guest account link to deactivate the account.

You won't see any change on your screen, and you won't be logged into the account. But when you activate the account, the next time you see the Welcome screen, an icon for the Guest account will be available.

Keeping Your Documents Private

As mentioned earlier, standard users can see only their own documents and shared documents. Administrators, by contrast, can see everything. That means when there are two or more administrator accounts on a computer, each administrator can see the other's folders. If you want to hide the contents of your personal folders from other users, follow these steps:

1. Open the Computer folder; click the Start button, and choose Computer.

2. Double-click the icon that represents your hard disk (typically Local Disk C:).

3. Double-click the Users folder.

4. Double-click the folder icon whose name matches the name of your own user account. This displays the primary folders in your account.

5. Right-click the folder icon that you don't want to share and choose Share. This displays the dialog box shown in Figure 25-8.

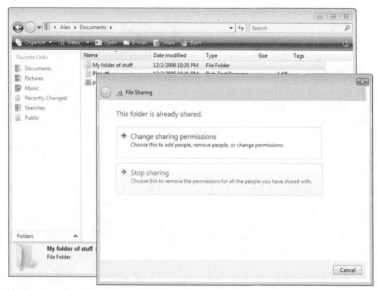

Figure 25-8: Hiding an administrator's documents from other administrators

6. Click Stop Sharing. The files will be marked to prevent them from being shared. While this is being done, you will see a message indicating work is happening. If an issue arises, you will be informed of the issue.

Caution You need to have a password on your account in order to be able to stop sharing files.

Signing into and out of User Accounts

As mentioned near the start of this chapter, you'll see the Welcome screen each time you start your computer. You just have to click your own user-account picture (and possibly enter a password, if you password-protected your account). Then you'll be taken to your own desktop.

When you've finished using the computer, you can either shut it down, as usual, or just *log off* so that you're no longer signed in to your account but the computer is still running. Logging off is similar to shutting down, in that you'll want to save any unsaved work, and close any open programs, before you log off. If you forget to save your work, Windows will prompt you to save it before it logs you off. To log off from your account, follow these steps.

STEPS: Log off from Your Account

1. Click the Start button; click (or hover the mouse pointer over) the arrow button next to the lock icon near the bottom of the Start menu (as was shown in Figure 25-5).

2. In the pop-up menu that appears (as was also shown in Figure 25-5), click the Log Off option.

It will take Windows a few seconds to get everything closed and squared away. Then your desktop will disappear, and you'll be taken to the Welcome screen. At that point, anybody else who has an account on this computer can click his or her user-account picture and log in.

Switching Users

It's always best to log off from your account if you won't be using the computer for a while. Leaving your account open and a bunch of programs and documents on the screen while you're away from the computer is just a bad policy. You greatly increase the likelihood of losing some work when you leave things lying around on the desktop.

If, however, some other user comes along and just wants to borrow the computer for a few minutes—to check e-mail, for example—you probably won't want to go through the hassle of closing everything, logging out, and logging back in when the other user is done. In that case, you can click Switch User in the pop-up menu instead of Log Off as shown at the right side of Figure 25-5. Clicking the Switch User option will take you back to the Welcome screen, where the other user can sign in and do whatever needs to be done.

When that person is done using the computer, he or she should log off, using the Log Off option (not Switch User). When he or she does, the Welcome screen will appear, and you can click your own account picture to get back to where you were before you switched user accounts.

You really don't want to use Switch User for any situation other than the preceding one, where you'll be leaving your account only for a few minutes, then coming right back. There are a couple reasons for this:

✦ Each open user account needs to store data in RAM (random access memory). The more stuff you cram into RAM, the slower your computer runs.

✦ Leaving user accounts open by using Switch User rather than Log Off complicates things immensely for the computer. The more complicated things are at any given moment, the more likely the computer is to hang (freeze up) or to generate some *fatal error* (a problem that requires restarting the computer without even getting a chance to save any unsaved work you left behind).

So the bottom line is: If you want to keep things running fast, and running safely, don't use the Switch User button. Always log off from your account (or shut down the computer) whenever you plan to be away from your account for more than a few minutes.

Snooping Through User Accounts

If you have an administrator account, you have access to all standard users' documents, as well as the documents of other administrators who haven't made their folders private. The quickest way to get to those other peoples' documents is though the Computer folder. That is, click the Start button and choose Computer. When displayed, double-click your primary hard drive — most likely called Local Disk (C:). Double-click the folder called Users that is displayed. Within the Users folder will be a folder for each user account, as well as one for the Public folder (see Figure 25-9).

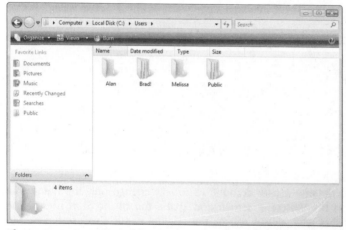

Figure 25-9: Icons for Public Documents and multiple users' folders

Each of those folders represents a single user's folders. Within each one will be a Documents folder, a Music folder, a Videos folder, and so on. You can open these folders as you would any others. For example, double-clicking Melissa's folder displays her Documents folder as well as her Music, Pictures, and other folders.

If you double-click the folder icon for another administrator who has made his or her documents private, you won't see anything but the ever-famous Access Denied message used in movies and TV shows. You can't view, change, move, copy, or rename documents in another administrator's private folders.

You can also use the Folders list within the Windows Explorer navigation pane to navigate through all users' folders (excluding, of course, other administrators' private folders). Open your Computer folder; then expand the Folders in the navigation pane by clicking the Folders bar. Click the triangle next to the Computer icon if it isn't already expanded; then click the icon for your hard drive, usually labeled Local Disk (C:). Next, click the triangle sign next to the Users folder. When expanded, you will see a subfolder under Users for each account on the computer, as in the example shown in Figure 25-10.

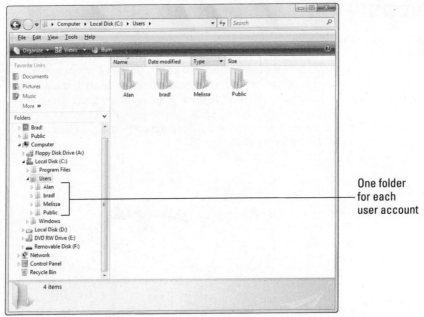

Figure 25-10: The Users folder contains a subfolder for each user account.

 Caution When you rename a user account, you really change only the name that appears on the Welcome screen and at the top of the Start menu. The folder for that user always retains the original name. Confusing, yes. But changing folder names after the user has already created documents can cause a lot of problems. So at the folder level, Windows locks in whatever name you originally gave the account.

Expanding a single user's folder displays all folders for that particular user. For example, Figure 25-11 shows the result of clicking the triangle next to Melissa's folder. Here's what each subfolder within a user account represents:

 Tip As always, you can click any folder name in the Folders list to see that folder's contents in the main pane to the right.

✦ **Contacts:** Contains that user's personal contacts.

✦ **Desktop:** Contains the user's unique, personal desktop shortcut icons.

✦ **Documents:** Is the user's Documents folder.

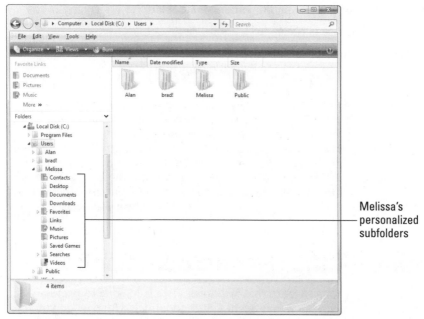

Figure 25-11: Each user's subfolders contain folders and settings unique to that user.

✦ **Downloads:** Contains any downloads the user has saved from the Internet. You can learn more about this folder and downloading in Chapter 10.

✦ **Favorites:** Contains the user's Internet favorites links.

✦ **Links:** Contains shortcuts to the items that appear in the Favorite Links area of the Windows Explorer Navigation pane.

✦ **Music:** Is the user's personal Music folder.

✦ **Pictures:** Is the user's personal Pictures folder.

✦ **Saved Games:** Is the user's personal game information such as high scores.

✦ **Searches:** Contains folders of search results for common searches (but with results specific to this user) as well as custom searches saved by the user.

✦ **Videos:** Is the user's personal Videos folder.

You'll also see a subfolder named Public within the Users folder. That folder contains shared, public folders and files — the things that all user accounts can access. If you click the triangle next to the Public folder, you'll see icons for these folders:

✦ **Public Documents:** Contains documents accessible to all users.

✦ **Public Downloads:** Contains downloaded files accessible to all users.

✦ **Public Music:** Is the shared, public Music folder.

✦ **Public Pictures:** Is the shared, public Pictures folder.

✦ **Public Videos:** Is the shared, public Videos folder.

✦ **Recorded TV:** Is the shared, public folder for recorded television files.

You can freely move and copy files among user accounts using all the standard techniques described in Chapter 19 (except, of course, any private administrator folders, which you can't even get to). For example, you can open Melissa's Pictures folder, select all the icons in that folder, and press Ctrl+C to copy them. Then navigate to some other user's Pictures folders, or the Public Pictures folder, and press Ctrl+V to copy the selected pictures into the Public Pictures folder. The fact that the folders and files all belong to different user accounts is irrelevant. As an administrator, you have the power to do as you please!

Turning off the User Account Control

It doesn't take very long to learn that Windows Vista is looking to protect you. In some cases, the protection may seem a little too much. Often when you try to run a program or change a setting, you will be asked to confirm that it is really you asking to do the task. This request is done via the User Account Control (UAC) dialog box.

The UAC is on by default for your protection. This pop-up will occur with one of several messages including:

✦ **Windows needs your permission to continue.** This generally happens when a program tries to do something that could impact more than one user. This is to confirm that you really want to impact users.

✦ **A program needs your permission to continue.** This generally happens when a program that isn't a part of Windows Vista needs to start. This is to confirm that it was you that started the program.

✦ **An unidentified program wants to access your computer.** This generally happens when a program wants to run that isn't a part of Windows and isn't registered as an official signed program. When you get this message, you should confirm not only that it was you who started the program, but that it is a program that you trust.

✦ **This program has been blocked.** This message occurs when you try to start a program that an administrator has blocked on the computer.

As you can see, these messages can come up quite often. This is for your protection as it helps prevent viruses and other malicious programs from doing anything on your computer. If, however, you find it too annoying, you can turn it off. Let me mention again that this is not recommended.

Steps to Turning off (or on) the User Account Control

1. Open your user account. You can do this through the Control Panel as described earlier in this chapter, or you can simply click the Start button and click your personal icon at the top of the right column.

2. In the User Account dialog window that is displayed, select the last option, which is Turn User Account Control on or off. You will likely get a User Access Control pop-up at this point stating that Windows needs your permission to continue!

3. The dialog box shown in Figure 25-12 is displayed. If you want to turn on UAC, then select *Use User Account Control (UAC) to help protect your computer* check box. If you want to turn it off, clear this check box by clicking it.

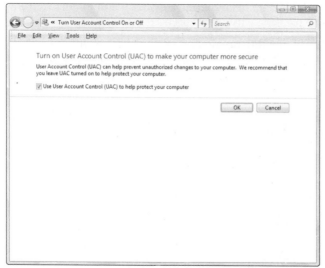

Figure 25-12: The User Account Control (UAC) dialog box

4. Click the OK button. You will see an additional dialog box letting you know you need to restart your computer before the change will take affect (see Figure 12-13).

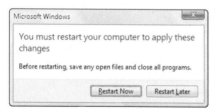

Figure 25-13: The computer restart prompt

After your computer is restarted, the changes will take affect. Let me reiterate one last time that although it can be annoying, the UAC is there to help protect you.

Summary

User accounts are one of those computer things that many computer users find totally perplexing. I hope this chapter has shed some light on why a person might want to create user accounts and how to go about creating them. The main points are summarized as follows:

✦ User accounts are the next best thing to giving each family member a personal PC.

✦ Each user who has an account has a desktop and folders to do with as he or she pleases, without stepping on anyone else's toes.

✦ Everything you need to create and manage user accounts is in the User Accounts window, which you can open from the Control Panel.

✦ As an administrator, you have access to all users' documents and settings.

✦ An administrator can use all the standard techniques to move and copy files among separate user accounts.

✦ User Access Control is on by default for your protection. You can turn it off if the pop-ups annoy you too much; however, you lose its protection if it is off.

Personalizing Your Desktop

T he Windows desktop is like your real, wooden desktop, in that it's the place where you do all your work. As you learned in Chapter 4, you control what's visible on your Windows desktop by moving and sizing open program windows. No matter how many open program windows are piled up on the desktop, you can quickly get to the desktop by clicking the Show Desktop button in the Quick Launch toolbar, by right-clicking the current time in the lower-right corner of your screen and choosing Show Desktop, or by pressing ⊞+D.

In addition to those all-important basic skills for managing open program windows, you can customize the appearance of the desktop itself. For example, you can change the picture that covers the desktop, change the size or appearance of the taskbar, create your own desktop shortcut icons, place gadgets on the sidebar, and more. Figure 26-1 points out the names of the major components of the Windows desktop—the things you'll learn to customize in this chapter.

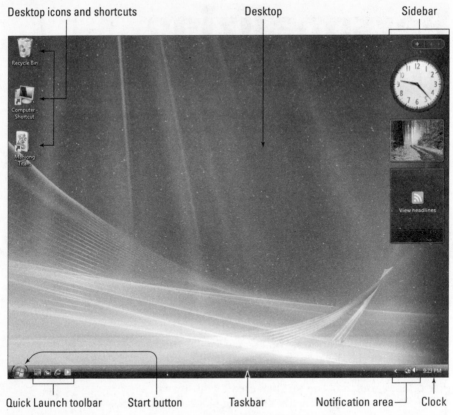

Desktop icons and shortcuts   Desktop   Sidebar

Quick Launch toolbar   Start button   Taskbar   Notification area   Clock

Figure 26-1: The Windows desktop and its various components

Creating Your Own Desktop

Personalizing (or customizing) your screen involves changing settings in dialog boxes. Most of these settings can be adjusted by starting with the personalization dialog box shown in Figure 26-2.

There are two ways to get to the Personalization dialog box:

✦ Right-click the Windows desktop and choose Personalize.

✦ Click the Start button and choose Control Panel. From the Control Panel home page click Appearance and Personalization ➪ Personalize.

From this dialog box you will be able to customize many of the settings for your computer. In the following sections, you will delve into several customizations you can do.

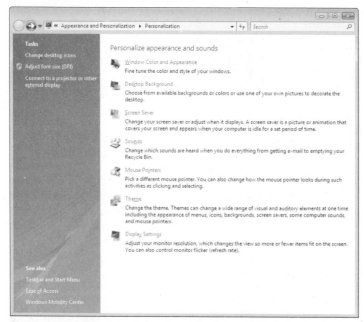

Figure 26-2: The main dialog box for personalizing your desktop

As a general note, when working with the various settings within this chapter, you will often see three buttons: OK, Cancel, and Apply. OK generally accepts the current settings and exits the dialog box. Apply accepts the current settings but leaves the dialog box open. Cancel closes the dialog without saving any unapplied settings.

Choosing a Theme

A Themes tab in Control Panel enables you to choose a color scheme and overall look and feel for your desktop. More specifically, themes enable you to personalize a number of different features within Windows all at once. This includes what menus look like as well as icons, the background, the screen saver, computer sounds, and the mouse pointer. Selecting Theme from the personalization menu (shown in Figure 26-2) presents the dialog box shown in Figure 26-3.

When you choose an option from the Themes drop-down list, the preview (under the heading Sample) gives you a sneak peek at how that theme will look if you apply it to your desktop.

You can also use any theme in the list as the starting point for creating your own theme. Just choose the theme you want to use as your starting point and change other settings as shown in the following sections. When you find a combination of settings you like, come back to the Themes tab and click the Save As button. Give your theme a file name and click OK.

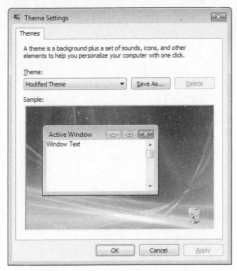

Figure 26-3: The Theme Settings dialog box

Tip   The Brightness and Contrast controls on your monitor work like those on a TV. You can't work those with the mouse or keyboard, though. You have to use controls that are right on the monitor, according to the instructions that came with your particular make and model of monitor or notebook computer.

Changing the Picture on Your Desktop

You can have your desktop display any picture in your Pictures folder, no picture at all, or a picture from another location on your computer. Alternatively, you can choose to set your background to a solid color.

To choose a picture, start by selecting Desktop Background from the Personalization dialog box shown in Figure 26-2. This displays the desktop background dialog box shown in Figure 26-4.

The Picture Location option enables you to select from a variety of image groups. This includes Windows Wallpapers, Pictures, Sample Pictures, Public Pictures, and Solid Colors. When you select one of these options, the middle section changes to show any images that are within the category. Alternatively, you can select the Browse button to pull up an Explorer window that can be used to search for a specific image on your computer to use for the background.

The Windows Wallpapers includes a number of images Microsoft created to be used as backgrounds for Windows. These images are categorized to make it easier to find one you like. It is worth scrolling through the middle section to see the various images. You will find categories including Black and White, Vistas, Wide screen shots, and more.

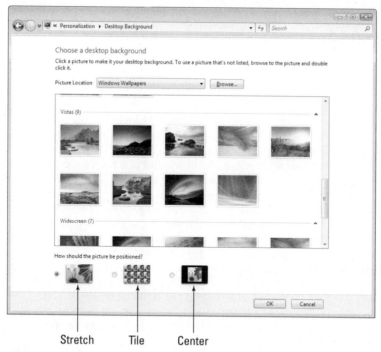

Stretch   Tile   Center

Figure 26-4: The Desktop Background dialog box for selecting a background

You can do this using the scroll bar to the right of the images, or you can click on an image and then use the arrow keys to go from one to the other. When you click one of the icons, you will see the current background change to show what is highlighted. If you decide you don't want to change your background, you can click the Cancel button at any time. Otherwise, you can select OK to make the current background stay.

The Sample Pictures and Public Pictures options under Picture Location can also be selected. These show pictures in the corresponding folders on your hard drive. Selecting Solid Colors from the Picture Locations presents a number of solid icons you can choose from. You can also click the More button if you want to pick a custom solid color.

To use a picture not listed under Background, click the Browse button. Then navigate to the folder in which the picture is contained, click its icon, and double-click the picture you want to use. If the picture you chose is smaller than your desktop, you can choose one of the options from the bottom of the Desktop Background dialog box to determine how the picture should be positioned. Your choices are:

✦ **Center:** The picture is centered on the desktop, surrounded by a solid color.

✦ **Tile:** The picture is repeated like tiles to fill the entire screen.

✦ **Stretch:** The picture is stretched to cover the entire desktop.

Caution If the picture you're displaying on your desktop is as large as, or larger than, the desktop, the Center and Tile options will have no effect.

Choosing a Screen Saver

A *screen saver* is a moving image that automatically appears on your screen after the computer has been sitting idle for a while. Originally, screen savers were created to prevent monitor *burn-in*, a condition caused by leaving an unchanging display on the screen for a long period of time (many hours). Burn-in isn't really a problem on modern monitors. But a screen saver can still be a fun thing to have and certainly can't hurt anything.

To choose a screen saver, first click the Screen Saver option in the Personalization dialog box (shown earlier in Figure 26-2). Then within the Screen Saver section of the dialog box, choose any of the options. Each option ranging from 3D Text to Windows Logo is a different screen saver. When you click the item, a preview is displayed in the small screen on the dialog box. Some screensavers require that you have a good graphics card in your system and support for Direct3D. If you are able to run the Aero interface in Vista, then you will be able to run these screen savers. If you are not able to run the Aero Interface (which is the case if your dialog boxes do not have transparent title bars), then you will get a message in the preview screen similar to the one in Figure 26-5.

Figure 26-5: The Screen Saver dialog box with a preview message saying the selected screen saver is not supported

To see what the screen saver will look like in real life, where it covers most or all of the screen, click the Preview button and let go of the mouse. After watching the screen saver, just move the mouse to return to the dialog box. After you've chosen a screen saver, you can click the Settings button to refine how the screen saver behaves.

The Wait option specifies how long the computer must sit idle (with no mouse or keyboard activity) before the screen saver kicks in. If you select the On resume, display logon screen check box, turning off the screen saver will take you to the logon screen described in Chapter 25, rather than to your desktop. When the actual screen saver does kick in on your computer, simply moving the mouse or pressing a key will turn the screen saver off and bring back your regular screen.

Caution　If the time delay for the Turn Off Monitor power option is less than the time delay for the screen saver, you'll never see the screen saver. That's because the monitor will turn off before the screen saver can appear!

You also have the ability to adjust the power settings on your computer from this dialog box. You can do this by selecting the Change power settings link near the bottom of the dialog box. This opens the Power Options dialog box. This dialog box is used mainly to conserve battery power on laptop computers running on batteries but is also good for conserving energy on a desktop computer, too. Within the different power option plans, you can change the plan settings. One of the settings you can adjust is when to turn off the display. The turn off the display option specifies the amount of idle time required before the monitor shuts itself off. If you want your screen saver to play without the monitor going blank, set the option to Never. Figure 26-6 shows the power options in the Settings dialog box on a notebook computer; on a desktop computer, the settings will be slightly different.

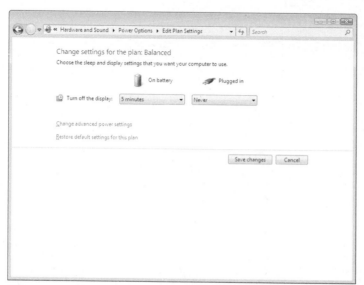

Figure 26-6: The power options dialog box on a notebook computer

Note that the Photos screen saver actually shows all the pictures in your Picture folder in a slideshow fashion. If you want to display pictures from some other folder, first choose Photos as your screen saver. Then click the Settings button. In the dialog box that appears, use the Browse button to navigate to the folder that contains the pictures you want to display. Use other options in that dialog box to refine how the pictures are displayed. Then click OK.

Fine-Tuning Your Color Scheme

As mentioned earlier, you can choose an overall color scheme for your screen using the Theme link within the Personalization dialog box. You can further refine the general appearance of program windows and buttons, colors, and the size of text on the screen by setting additional options in the Appearance Settings dialog box. You can access this dialog box by selecting the Window Color and Appearance link from the Personalization dialog box.

It is worth noting that when you select the Windows Color and Appearance link, you will get one of two dialog boxes. If your computer supports the Aero interface, then you will see the dialog box in Figure 26-7. If your computer does not support the Aero interface (if you are using Vista Home Basic, or if you don't have a powerful enough graphics card), then you will see the classic appearance properties as shown in Figure 26-8.

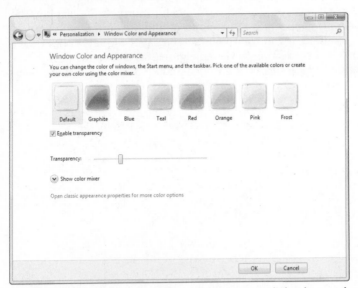

Figure 26-7: The Windows Color and Appearance dialog box under Windows Vista Aero

When running Aero, you are able to select a color to use with Windows in the Windows Color and Appearance box. You can also turn on or off transparency by selecting or clearing the Enable transparency check box. Finally, you can set the degree of transparency by adjusting the Transparency slider. If you select the Open classic appearance properties for more color options text near the bottom, you will be taken to the classic appearance dialog box — the same box that those not using the Aero interface will see by default.

If you are using the classic appearance dialog box, then when you make a selection from the Color scheme list, the preview area on the Appearance tab will show you what to expect if you apply the new settings (see Figure 26-8).

Figure 26-8: The Appearance settings

Clicking the Effects button on the Appearance Settings dialog box takes you to the Effects dialog box, where you can pick and choose special effects. If you use a notebook computer, or some other flat screen, and the text on your screen looks blocky, the Effects tab can help. Click the Effects button and select the Use the following method to smooth edges of screen fonts check box. Then choose Clear Type as the method. If, after reviewing the fonts on your screen, you don't like the result, you can return to the Effects dialog box and try the Standard method of smoothing screen fonts.

Clicking the Advanced button on the Appearance tab takes you to the Advanced Appearance dialog box. There you can control colors and sizes of individual items such as icons, menus, and scroll bars. As you try out different options in the Advanced Appearance dialog box, the preview will show how the current selections will look on your actual desktop. Click OK in the Advanced Appearance dialog box after making your selections.

Tip If you want to turn Aero off, then select Windows Vista Basic in the Color scheme list on the classic Appearance Settings dialog window.

Choosing a Screen Resolution and Color Depth

While your screen looks like a smooth picture from where you're sitting, it's actually a collection of tiny lighted dots called *pixels*. The resolution of your screen determines how many pixels are visible, expressed as the number of pixels across the screen, and the number of pixels down. You can also choose a *color depth*, which determines the number of colors your screen can show.

To choose a screen resolution or color depth, click the Display Settings link in the Personalization dialog box (shown in Figure 26-2). Use the Resolution slider (shown in Figure 26-9) to adjust the resolution. With Windows Vista, a minimum of 800×600 pixels is recommended, although you'll be able to get more stuff on the screen at a higher resolution, such as 1024×768. Be aware, however, that the higher the resolution, the smaller everything will look on your screen. Your best bet is to try both 800×600 and 1024×768 and to stick with whichever is most comfortable for your eyes. The specific options screen resolutions you will have available depend on your computer's graphics card. If you have a larger screen and if your computer's graphics card will support it, then you may want to select a higher resolution. Additionally, many computers come with wide screens. A setting such as 1200×800 works well for a large, wide screen monitor.

 Caution Some notebook computers and flat monitors have their own separate dialog boxes for screen resolution and color depth. If changing those settings in the Display Settings dialog box has no effect on your screen, refer to the manual that came with your computer or monitor for instructions on changing its settings.

The color depth is set with the Colors drop-down list. With color depth, bigger is generally better. The full range of options available to you depends on your computer's video card and monitor. As a rule, you want to choose Highest (32 bit) for the best display. However, 24 bit and 16 bit are also acceptable.

Figure 26-9: The Display Settings dialog box from two different computers. The computer on the right can support two monitors.

Why Is My Screen All Whacky?

The first time you switch from one screen resolution to another, the image on your monitor might be off center, as in the example at left below. Or the image might be too tall, too wide, too short, or too narrow, like in the center example. To fix that, you need to adjust the Width, Height, Horizontal Center, and Vertical Center adjustments on your monitor.

You can't adjust the previously mentioned monitor settings using either mouse or keyboard. You must use the controls that are right on the monitor itself or on your notebook computer. The only place to get information on using those controls is in the manual that comes with your monitor or computer. When you find the right controls, you should have no problem sizing the desktop so that it fills the screen as in the example above on the right.

Using the bit number as an exponent of 2 tells you the number of different colors the screen can display. For example, 32 bits of color (2^{32}) gives you 4,294,967,296 different colors, ideal for viewing photographs and video. A lower resolution such as 2^{24} (16,777,216 colors) or 2^{16} (65,536 colors) can make photos look blotchy.

Saving Display Properties Settings

If you make any changes to the settings in any of the Personalization areas mentioned so far in this chapter, then remember that you can save those settings under any name of your choosing. Just click the Theme link from the Personalization dialog window; then click the Save As button. You can accept the default file name, My Favorite Theme, or enter a new name. After you've saved a theme, its name will be visible in the Theme drop-down list on the Themes tab, so you can easily apply the entire theme just by selecting its name.

When you've finished changing settings, click OK. All your settings will be applied, and the dialog box will close. If you want to make further changes, just reopen the Theme dialog box again.

Customizing Mouse Pointers

Windows Vista also gives you the ability to customize the images used for your mouse pointer. Like the other settings you've seen so far, you can customize your mouse pointer by selecting the Mouse Pointers link in the Personalization dialog window. This displays the Mouse Properties dialog window shown in Figure 26-10.

Figure 26-10: The Mouse Properties dialog window

On the Pointer tab, you can select an overall scheme to use for your mouse pointers. When you select a scheme, the different pointers will be displayed in the Customize area. You can scroll through the list to verify that you like the scheme that is selected. You can also select an item in the Customize section and click the Browse button to change an individual pointer graphic. When you are happy with your choices, click the OK button to save the changes and exit the dialog box.

Note   There are a variety of mouse pointer schemes. Younger kids may like the Dinosaur theme. If you are feeling nostalgic, you can select the Old-Fashioned theme. If you are feeling musical, there is a conductor theme!

Choosing Icons to Display on the Desktop

To choose some icons for your Windows desktop, click the Change Desktop Icons link on the left side of the Personalization dialog box (see Figure 26-2). A new dialog box titled Desktop Icon Settings opens. Select the name of any icons you want to place on your desktop.

If you want to change the image displayed for the Computer, your personal folder, Network, or Recycle Bin icons, first click the icon you want to change in the middle of the Desktop Icons Settings dialog box. Then click the Change Icon button and choose a different icon. To return to the original default icon, click the Restore Default button.

Click OK after making your selections to save them and close the dialog box.

Arranging Icons on Your Desktop

You can move icons around the desktop just by dragging them. You can delete any icon on your desktop by right-clicking the icon and choosing Delete. If your icons get all out of order and difficult to find, you can quickly rearrange them. Just right-click the Windows desktop and choose Sort By ➪ Name. Built-in icons that you've chosen to display — such as Documents, Computer, and Recycle Bin — are always listed first near the upper-left corner of the screen. Remaining icons will be listed in the order you select.

Personalizing Your Start Menu

The Start button, as you know, is the gateway to every program currently installed on your computer. The Start menu also provides easy access to commonly used folders such as Documents, Computer, Control Panel, and any others you care to add. As a rule, you want the Start menu to contain items you use frequently, so you can get to those items without navigating through too many submenus.

The Windows Vista menu is split into two columns (see Figure 26-11), with icons for programs on the left and icons for folders on the right. The left side of the menu is split into two groups. Icons above the horizontal line are *pinned* to the menu, meaning that they never change unless you change them. Beneath the horizontal line are icons that represent programs you use frequently. These icons might change at any time to reflect programs you've been using frequently in the last few days.

 Note   The layout of your Start menu may be slightly different from that in Figure 26-11 if you are using the Windows Vista Aero Interface.

You can customize your Start menu in many ways, by choosing which folders are accessible from the menu, which programs are pinned to the Start menu, and even the size and number of icons on the menu. The dialog box you use to adjust those settings is named Taskbar and Start Menu Properties.

Pinned items   Programs   Folders

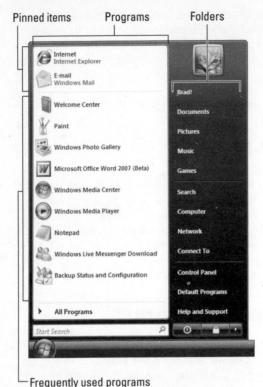

Frequently used programs

Figure 26-11: Areas on the Windows Vista Start menu

Controlling What You See on the Start Menu

Earlier, we mentioned that you can usually get to an object's properties just by right-clicking the object and choosing Properties. Or you can take the longer route through Control Panel. In this case, however, you don't actually right-click the Start menu itself. Rather, you can use whichever of the following techniques is easiest for you:

✦ Right-click the Start button and choose Properties.

✦ Click the Start button and choose Control Panel. From the Control Panel Home screen, click Appearance and Themes. Then select the Taskbar and Start Menu option.

Options for customizing the taskbar and options for customizing the Start menu share the Taskbar and Start Menu Properties dialog box. After you've opened that dialog box (using either of the preceding techniques), you need to click the Start Menu tab to get to options for personalizing your Start menu.

Initially, you'll be presented with two options: Start menu (which displays the two-column Windows Vista Start menu) and Classic Start menu (which displays an old-fashioned Windows 98–style menu). To access the settings described here, select the first option, Start menu. Then click the Customize button just to the right of that option. The Customize Start Menu dialog box will open as shown in Figure 26-12.

Figure 26-12: The Customize Start Menu dialog box

The Customize Start Menu dialog box provides a lot of options. Ignoring the list box of options at the top of the dialog box for a moment, your options are:

✦ **Number of recent programs to display:** This option is within the Start menu size area. It enables you to specify the maximum number of items displayed on the left side of the menu. This number can be from 0 to 30. If you set this too high for your screen resolution and icon size, Windows will display a Some items will not fit message each time you open the Start menu. To get rid of that message, you need to decrease the number of items selected here.

✦ **Internet link:** This option is within the Show on Start menu area. If you want to pin the icon for your web browser to the top of the Start menu, choose this option. Then choose your favorite web browser from the drop-down list to the right.

✦ **E-mail link:** This option is also within the Show on Start menu section. If you want to pin the icon for your e-mail client to the Start menu, choose this option. Then choose the name of your e-mail client or service from the drop-down list to the right.

The scroll list of options at the top of the Customize Start Menu dialog box provides options that define the general behavior of the Start menu and the items visible on the right side of the menu. Many of these items enable you to choose which folder names you want to make available on the right side of the . menu. For most items, you'll be given three options:

✦ **Display as a link:** Choosing this option tells Windows to open the corresponding folder when you click the menu option. This is the most natural method, once you're familiar with working in folders.

✦ **Display as a menu:** Choosing this option tells Windows to show items within the folder as options on a menu, without opening the folder. This option is a reasonable alternative for folders that contain few icons but is unwieldy for folders that contain many icons.

✦ **Don't display this item:** As it says, choosing this option will prevent the option from being displayed at all on the right side of the Start menu.

The Start Menu Items list contains mostly specific items you can choose to show, or hide, on the Start menu. But as you scroll through the list, you'll also find some options that define the overall behavior of the Start menu rather than specific items. Those items are summarized as follows:

✦ **Use Large Icons:** Choosing Large Icons displays icons at the size you've seen throughout this book. Choosing Small Icons displays smaller icons that are harder to see. But you can get more icons on the menu at the smaller size.

✦ **Open submenus when I pause on them with my mouse:** If you select this option, you can open any submenu simply by pointing to the option on the menu rather than clicking it. Items on the menu that have a ▶ to the right, such as All Programs and Recent Items, have submenus.

✦ **Highlight newly installed programs:** Selecting this option for starting any new program you install will be highlighted on the All Programs menu. That makes it much easier to find the appropriate icon after you've installed a new program.

✦ **Enable context menus and dragging and dropping:** If selected, this enables you to rearrange icons on the Start and All Programs menus simply by dragging them into position. You also need to select this option if you want to be able to create desktop shortcuts by right-clicking options on the Start and All Programs menus. We recommend that you select (check) this option.

✦ **Sort All Programs menu by name:** If you select this option, the items on your All Programs menus will be sorted. This will make them easier to find, especially as your menus get longer as you add programs and other files to your computer.

After making your selections from the Customize Start Menu dialog box, click its OK button, and click the OK button in the Taskbar and Start Menu Properties dialog box. Click the Start button to see the effects of your changes on the Start menu.

Pinning Items to the Start Menu

As mentioned, some items on the left side of the Start menu tend to change to reflect the programs you've run the most in recent days. That can be a good thing or a bad thing, depending on how you use your computer. If there are any items that you want to appear on the left side of the menu at all times, you can pin those items to the menu. To do so, right-click the item you want to pin and choose Pin to Start Menu.

You can also pin any program name from the All Programs menu to the Start menu. Click the Start button, choose All Programs, and work your way to the icon you want to pin. But don't click that icon to open the program. Instead, right-click the program's icon and choose Pin to Start Menu.

You're not limited to pinning program icons either. If you have a folder you're using often, you can pin its icon to the Start menu as well. To pin a folder's icon to the Start menu, navigate to the parent of the folder using Windows Explorer. Then, when you see the icon for the folder you want to add to the Start menu, drag its icon to the Start button and drop it. You won't notice any immediate change. But the next time you click the Start button, you'll see an icon for the folder pinned near the top of the Start menu.

Unpinning, Renaming, and Removing Start Menu Items

The left side of the Start menu is very flexible. For example, if you pin an item to the Start menu, but later decide you don't need it there, you can unpin it. Just right-click the icon you want to unpin and choose Unpin from this list. To get rid of an icon that isn't pinned to the Start menu, you can do the same thing — right-click the item and choose Remove from this list.

Removing a program's icon from the Start menu doesn't delete the actual underlying program. It only removes the program's icon from the menu. To uninstall a program, see the section "Uninstalling Programs" in Chapter 29.

 Tip To add or remove icons from the right side to the Start menu, use the Start Menu Items list described in the section "Controlling What You See on the Start Menu," earlier in this chapter.

If you want to change the name of an item on the Start menu, right-click the item and choose Rename. Then edit the existing name or type a new name, and press Enter. Some pinned items such as E-mail and Internet can't be renamed.

Rearranging Start and All Programs Menu Items

In the previous section, you learned that you can select the Sort All Programs menu by name check box. This option keeps your All Programs menu sorted by the names of the items on it. If you clear this check box, you can rearrange icons on All Programs menu just by dragging any item up or down and dropping it wherever you want to place it.

 Caution If you can't move items around on the Start or All Programs menus, make sure the Enable context menus and dragging and dropping check box is selected in the Customize Start Menu dialog box as described in the section "Controlling What You See on the Start Menu" earlier in this chapter. If they still can't be moved, then make sure you cleared the Sort All Programs menu by name check box.

After you've turned off the sort option, you can still sort the All Programs menu by name by following these steps:

1. Click the Start button and choose All Programs.

2. Right-click any icon on the All Programs menu (or a submenu that you can get to from All Programs) and choose Sort By Name from the shortcut menu that opens.

On the All Programs menu, program folders (groups) are always listed first. Program groups all have a similar icon and an arrow pointing to the right. Icons that represent programs have the program's logo as their icon and no arrow character to the right.

Displaying Recently Opened Files and Programs

We discussed the Customize option on the Taskbar and Start Menu Properties dialog window earlier in this chapter. On that same dialog box you have two privacy options:

✦ Store and display a list of recently opened files

✦ Save and display a list of recently opened programs

If you unselect these, they will change what is displayed on your Start menu. Selecting to display recently opened files will add an option to the right side of your Start menu called Recent Items. This lists document files you've recently opened.

Selecting to save and display recently opened programs is what controls the display of program items on the left side of the start menu. If you clear this item, then only pinned programs will be displayed.

Personalizing Your Taskbar

The taskbar at the bottom of your screen provides many useful items, including the Start button, the Quick Launch toolbar, the general taskbar area, which contains a button for each open program window, and the notification area. Options for personalizing your taskbar are in the Taskbar and Start Menu

Properties dialog box, which you can get to by using whichever of the following techniques is most convenient:

✦ Right-click the Start button and choose Properties.

✦ Click the Start button and choose Control Panel. Then select Appearance and Personalization followed by Taskbar and Start Menu.

The Taskbar and Start Menu Properties dialog box opens on your screen. Click the Taskbar tab to reveal the options shown in Figure 26-13. The two preview taskbars let you see how the options you choose will affect the real taskbar. Your options are:

Figure 26-13: The Taskbar tab of the Taskbar and Start Menu Properties dialog box

✦ **Lock the taskbar:** When you select this option, you'll lock the taskbar, which will prevent you from accidentally moving or resizing it. If you want to move or resize the taskbar, you first need to clear this option to unlock the taskbar.

✦ **Auto-hide the taskbar:** When you select this icon, the taskbar will automatically slide out of view when you're not using it, to free up the little bit of screen space it takes up. After the taskbar hides itself, you can rest the tip of the mouse button on the thin line at the bottom of the screen to bring the taskbar out of hiding.

✦ **Keep the taskbar on top of other windows:** Selecting this option ensures that the taskbar is always visible and can't be covered up by open program windows. To ensure that the taskbar is always visible, select this option, and clear the Auto-hide the taskbar check box.

✦ **Group similar taskbar buttons:** Choosing this option allows the taskbar to combine multiple open documents or pages for a program into a single taskbar button. Taskbar buttons that represent multiple documents display a number next to the program name on the button. You can open any document by clicking the taskbar button and clicking a document name. To close all open documents or pages in one fell swoop, right-click the button and choose Close Group. Figure 26-14 shows an example where four web pages are currently open in four different Internet Explorer windows.

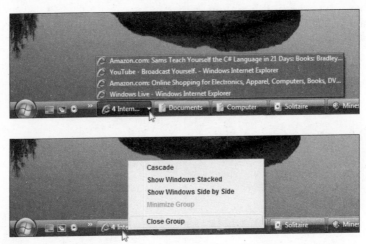

Figure 26-14: Click or right-click a taskbar button that represents two or more open documents or pages.

✦ **Show Quick Launch:** Select this option to make the Quick Launch toolbar visible on the taskbar. Clear this option to hide the Quick Launch toolbar. (More on the Quick Launch toolbar later.)

✦ **Show window previews (thumbnails):** Choose this option to have small previews display when you hover over a button on the Taskbar as shown in Figure 26-15. If your system does not support the Windows Vista Aero interface, then this option will not be available to set.

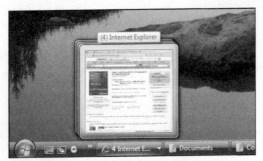

Figure 26-15: Window thumbnail previews on the Taskbar (using the Aero Interface)

Moving and Sizing Taskbar Items

When the taskbar is unlocked, you can move and size the taskbar and size the Quick Launch toolbar as well. A quick way to lock or unlock the toolbar is to right-click the current time and choose Lock the Taskbar. The option works as a toggle, locking the taskbar if it's unlocked or unlocking it when it's locked.

You can tell if the taskbar is currently unlocked by the dragging handles at the top of the bar and within the bar. Also, the Lock the Taskbar option won't be checked if the taskbar is unlocked, as in the top of Figure 26-16. When the taskbar is locked, no dragging handles are visible and the Lock the Taskbar option on the shortcut menu has a check mark next to it, as in Figure 26-16.

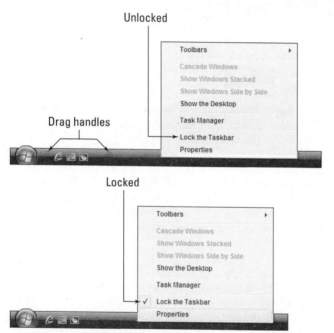

Figure 26-16: An unlocked taskbar (top) shows dragging handles.

Tip

You may find it easiest to close all open program windows before fiddling with the taskbar. That way, you won't have any taskbar buttons in the way to confuse matters.

When the taskbar is unlocked, you can do any of the following:

✦ To move the entire taskbar, point to an empty portion of the bar and drag the entire bar to any edge of the screen.

✦ To size the taskbar, point to the thin bar at the top of the taskbar until the mouse pointer turns to a two-headed arrow. Then hold down the left mouse button and drag that edge up or down (see Figure 26-17).

✦ To change the width of the Quick Launch toolbar, drag the handle to the right of the bar left or right (also shown in Figure 26-17).

✦ If you drag one of the dotted handles up or down, the taskbar will split into two rows (as at the bottom of Figure 26-17).

Drag left or right   Drag up or down

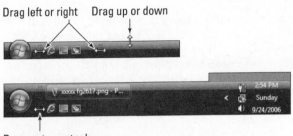

Drag up to unstack

Figure 26-17: A two-headed arrow appears when you point to a dragging handle.

 Caution   If you accidentally drag a dotted dragging handle up or down and want to get back to a single-row taskbar, drag the same dotted handle up a notch. Then drag the very top of the taskbar down a notch.

If you drag the top of the taskbar right off the bottom of the screen, the taskbar seems to disappear. But if you look closely, you'll see that the thin, gray bar is still visible along the bottom edge of the screen. If you rest the tip of the mouse pointer right on that bar, you'll see the two-headed arrow again, indicating that you can drag the top of the taskbar straight up to make the taskbar wider again.

When you have the taskbar arranged the way you like, you'll be wise to lock it. That way, you don't have to worry about inadvertently rearranging it just by being a little klutzy with the mouse.

Using the Quick Launch Toolbar

The Quick Launch toolbar is a handy place to store icons for programs and folders you use often. If there are more buttons on the taskbar than will fit in the size allotted, you'll see a little >> symbol on the Quick Launch toolbar. You can click the >> symbol to see other icons on a menu. Then click any icon on the menu that opens to open the program.

To add an icon to the Quick Launch toolbar, right-drag any shortcut icon from the desktop, All Programs menu, or a folder right onto the Quick Launch toolbar. Then release the mouse button and choose Create Shortcuts Here.

 Tip   The term *right-drag* means to drag using the right mouse button rather than the left mouse button.

To move an icon on the Quick Launch toolbar left or right, point to the icon you want to move and drag it left or right. The mouse pointer will turn to an I-beam, like the example at left. When the I-beam is where you want to place the icon, release the mouse button.

To delete an icon from the Quick Launch toolbar, right-click the icon and choose Delete.

Personalizing the Notification Area

At the right side of the taskbar, you'll see icons for running processes. A process is slightly different from a regular program, in that a process runs in the background, meaning it has no program window or taskbar button. Examples of programs that run as processes include anti-virus software and Windows Live Messenger among other programs.

To see what program any icon in the notification area represents, point to the icon and look for the tooltip. If that doesn't help, try double-clicking the icon or right-clicking it to see what other options are available to you. For example, you can often close a program running as a process by right-clicking its icon in the notification area and choosing Close or Exit.

By default, Windows Vista hides most inactive icons to prevent them from hogging up space on the taskbar. To view the icons currently hidden, just click the < button at the left side of the notification area.

If you want Windows Vista to stop hiding notification area icons, you can modify a setting the Taskbar and Startup Menu properties dialog box that you've seen before in this chapter. You can also use this dialog box to set a few common system processes on (or off) the notification area. To get to the notification area settings, do one of the following:

✦ Right-click the Start button and choose Properties.

✦ Click the Start button and choose Control Panel. Then select Appearance and Personalization followed by Taskbar and Start Menu.

The Taskbar and Start Menu Properties dialog box opens on your screen. Click the notification area tab to reveal the options shown in Figure 26-18.

Within the notification area tab, your first option is to determine whether inactive icons are displayed. If Hide inactive icons is selected, then notification icons that have not been clicked in a while will be hidden to conserve space on the taskbar. An exception to hidden icons are the System icons. These will not be hidden if inactive. Rather if you want to hide them, you can do this by unselecting them in the System icons area.

Figure 26-18: The notification area settings

There are four common system icons you can turn on or off. These are on by default:

✦ **Clock:** This is the clock that displays on the far right of the notification area.

✦ **Volume:** This is the volume control for your Windows to control your computer's volume.

✦ **Network:** This icon allows you quick access to network features. Hovering over the icon shows you information on your network (or Internet) connection.

✦ **Power:** This icon gives you information on your computer's power set up. When using a battery for power, such as in a notebook computer, it gives you information on remaining battery time.

In addition to the common icons, you can set other icons in the notification area to always be visible. To choose which icons are visible, either click the Customize button in the notification area dialog box shown in Figure 26-18, or simply right-click the current time and choose Customize Notifications. In the Customize Notifications dialog box that opens, you can click any icon's name; then choose one of the following options (shown in Figure 26-19) to decide how to show the icon:

✦ **Hide when inactive:** This is the normal behavior for notification area icons, where they're visible only when the process the icon represents is running.

✦ **Always hide:** Keeps the icon from ever showing, even when the process is running.

✦ **Always show:** Ensures that the icon is always visible, whether its corresponding process is running or not.

The Default Settings button changes all icons in the list to their original default settings, as shipped with Windows Vista.

Figure 26-19: The Customize Notification Icons dialog box

Optional Taskbar Toolbars

Windows Vista comes with extra, optional toolbars you can add to the taskbar or allow to float freely on the desktop. To view their names, and show one, right-click the current time in the lower-right corner of your screen, choose Toolbars; then click the name of the toolbar you want to display. Your options are:

✦ **Address:** Displays an address bar like the one in your web browser. Typing a URL into the bar opens your web browser to the page that belongs to the URL.

✦ **Windows Media Player:** Adds a set of Play Controls to the taskbar. However, this toolbar is visible only when you open, then minimize, Windows Media Player.

✦ **Links:** Displays the Links toolbar from Microsoft Internet Explorer.

✦ **Tablet PC Input Panel:** If your edition of Windows Vista supports Tablet PC input, then this option places an Input Panel icon onto the toolbar that can be used to activate the Input Panel which can be used to simulate a keyboard or accept written information.

Note Even if your computer isn't a Tablet PC, you can use the Input Panel. It works with the mouse. It is much easier to use with a Tablet PC stylus.

✦ **Desktop:** Shows all desktop shortcut icons from your Windows desktop in a condensed toolbar format.

✦ **Quick Launch:** Shows (or hides) the Quick Launch toolbar described earlier in this chapter.

✦ **Language bar:** Displays the optional language bar, but only if your computer has voice recognition or some similar software installed to activate voice recognition.

When you first open one of these optional toolbars, you might see only its label in the taskbar. If the taskbar is unlocked, you can drag the handle to the left of that label toward the left to increase the size of the toolbar.

Creating Your Own Shortcuts

You can create a desktop shortcut to any program, document, or folder you want. Doing so makes it easy to find the icon when you need it. The easiest way to create a desktop shortcut icon is as follows:

1. Get to the icon to which you want to create a shortcut. This can be any program icon on the All Programs menu or any folder or document icon in Windows Explorer.

2. Right-click the icon to which you want to create a shortcut and choose Send To ➪ Desktop (create shortcut).

Tip   As an alternative to Steps 1 and 2 above, you can right-drag any selected icon(s) to the desktop and choose Create Shortcut(s) Here. To create a shortcut to the web page you're currently viewing in Internet Explorer, choose File ➪ Send ➪ Shortcut to Desktop from Internet Explorer's menu bar.

You'll see the icon on the desktop when the desktop is visible. The shortcut will likely be named Shortcut to... followed by the name of the original icon. But you can rename the shortcut, if you want, by right-clicking its icon and choosing Rename. Of course, you can just double-click the shortcut item to open the object that the shortcut represents.

Handy Folder Shortcuts

If you create desktop shortcuts to your favorite folders, you can use those to quickly jump to a folder from the Open or Save As dialog box. When the dialog box opens, you can choose Desktop from the Favorite Links. Then double-click the shortcut icon for the folder you want to open.

You can copy shortcut icons from the desktop into your personal Documents folder as well. Since Documents is often the folder selected automatically in the Open and Save As dialog boxes, you won't even have to switch to the desktop. Just double-click the shortcut icon in the Documents folder.

Shortcut icons look almost exactly like the original icon, except that shortcuts have a little curved arrow on them, as in the examples shown in Figure 26-20. The curved arrow is important, because it enables you to discriminate between a shortcut icon and the real thing. For example, you wouldn't want to delete your Public Pictures folder, as doing so would delete all the pictures within that folder. But when you delete a shortcut icon, you delete only the shortcut. The folder, document, or program that the shortcut icon represents will not be deleted.

Original   Shortcut   **Figure 26-20:** Examples of an original icon at left and its shortcut
icon   icon   icon on the right

When the shortcut icon is on the desktop, you can copy it to the Quick Launch toolbar or Start menu or both using the familiar drag-and-drop approach.

You can also right-click just about any icon and choose Copy. Then navigate to wherever you want to create a shortcut to that item and choose Edit ⇨ Paste. Or right-click an empty spot and choose Paste Shortcut. The icon will be pasted and will also remain in the Clipboard. You can paste the same icon to as many locations as you want.

Using the Sidebar

Windows Vista adds a new feature called the Windows Sidebar. This feature enables you to run gadgets on your desktop. Gadgets are simply small programs that can provide useful, fun, or interesting information. In Figure 26-1 you can see the default Sidebar running on Windows Vista.

If you don't see the Sidebar, you can display it by double-clicking the Sidebar icon in the notification area (or you can right-click the icon and select Open). When displayed, you can customize your settings for the Sidebar, you can use gadgets that were included with Windows, or you can add new gadgets.

Customizing the Sidebar

There are several settings that can be customized for the Sidebar by using the Sidebar Properties dialog box. You can open this dialog box in one of two ways:

✦ Right-click an open area within the displayed Sidebar. Choose Properties from the pop-up menu.

✦ Open the Control Panel from the Start Menu. Within the Control Panel, select Appearance and Personalization. Then select Windows Sidebar Properties.

The Windows Sidebar Properties dialog box (shown in Figure 26-21) enables you to modify several settings:

✦ **Start Sidebar when Windows starts:** Selecting this option will cause the Sidebar to automatically run (thus be displayed) when Windows Vista starts. If you are always going to use the Sidebar, then you should select this.

✦ **Sidebar is always on top of other windows:** Selecting this option will prevent other windows from displaying on top of the Sidebar. If you are using a wide screen, then you will likely want to always have the Sidebar on top. If you are using a more normally sized screen, then you may not want the Sidebar to be on top, and thus use up valuable screen space.

✦ **Display Sidebar on this side of screen:** You can choose to have the Sidebar on the right or left side of your screen.

✦ **Display Sidebar on Monitor:** If you are using more than one monitor, then you can determine which monitor you want the Sidebar displayed on.

Figure 26-21: The Windows Sidebar Properties dialog window

Using Included Gadgets

The Sidebar displays with a couple of gadgets already on it. You can add new gadgets to the sidebar by using the Gadgets Gallery. You can display the gallery doing any of the following:

✦ Click the plus sign (+) near the top of the Sidebar. When you hover over the plus sign, the word *Gallery* will appear to the left of it.

✦ Right-click within an open area of the Sidebar and select Add Gadgets.

✦ Select the Control Panel on the Start Menu. Within the Control Panel select Appearance and Personalization to display the Appearance and Personalization dialog box that you have seen before in this chapter. From that dialog box, select Add gadgets to Sidebar from below the Windows Sidebar Properties option.

The Gadgets Gallery shows the current gadgets installed on your computer that you can select to display on your Sidebar (see Figure 26-22). If you want to add a gadget to your Sidebar either double-click its picture or right-click the picture and select Add. If you want to remove the gadget from your gallery, right-click it and select Uninstall. If you'd like to get more information on a gadget, click the gadget's picture, then click Show details at the bottom of the dialog window.

Figure 26-22: The Gadget Gallery with some of the default gadgets in Windows Vista

Common Gadget Controls

Each gadget can have its own controls that customize it or manipulate its settings. A stock gadget will have a method for adding new stocks. A clock may have options for setting its face style and its time zone. There will be a couple of options with each gadget on the Sidebar that should be standard.

Figure 26-23 shows the Sidebar with the mouse currently over the clock gadget. When the mouse hovers over a gadget, the controls for that gadget will be shown as can be seen in Figure 26-23. You can use these controls to close the gadget, modify the gadgets settings, or move the gadget. To move the gadget, click and drag the handle control from its current location to a new location on the Sidebar. If the handle is not displayed, then it means the gadget cannot be moved.

Click to open Gadget Gallery

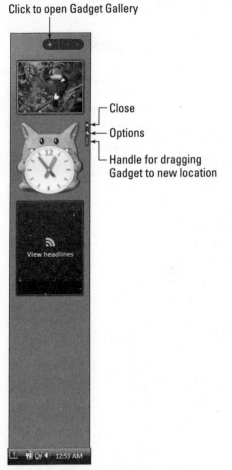

Close

Options

Handle for dragging
Gadget to new location

Figure 26-23: The standard controls
on a gadget

Detaching a Gadget from the Sidebar

Gadgets don't have to be on the Sidebar. You can actually drag a gadget onto your desktop. This detaches the gadget from the Sidebar and lets it operate independently—meaning it will stay open even if you close the Sidebar. When on the desktop it will continue to operate normally. Remember, gadgets are just simple programs similar to other programs on your computer.

You can also detach a gadget from the Sidebar by right-clicking it and selecting Detach from Sidebar. This also places the gadget onto the desktop.

Adding New Gadgets

In Figure 26-22 you may have noticed the link at the bottom of the dialog box for getting more gadgets. Microsoft and others will create and offer new gadgets over time. Clicking the Get more gadgets online link at the bottom of the Gadget Gallery will take you to the Microsoft web site where you will find a more robust gallery of gadgets that you can download and install.

To install a gadget, click the download button for it. You will then want to open the gadget file that is downloaded and follow any prompts. It is most likely that the gadget will simply be installed with no further information.

 Caution Gadgets are programs, and some programs are evil. As such, you should only download and install gadgets from sites and people you trust.

Summary

Everyone who uses Windows Vista gets to design a unique work environment by customizing his or her desktop, Start menu, taskbar, and other areas. Here's a quick summary of the major points covered in this chapter:

✦ To customize the desktop, right-click the Windows desktop and choose Properties. Or open the Personalization Properties dialog box via Control Panel.

✦ The Personalization dialog box enables you to work with Window Vista colors, background, screen saver, mouse pointer, sound, theme, and display settings.

✦ To personalize your Start Menu, taskbar, or notification area, right-click the Start button and choose Properties. Or access this same dialog box via the Control Panel.

✦ To create a desktop shortcut to a frequently used program, folder, or document, right-click that item's icon and choose Send To ➪ Desktop (Create Shortcut).

✦ Windows comes with a number of gadgets. Gadgets are small programs that can be placed on the Sidebar or on your desktop.

Using Parental Controls

Unfortunately, neither everything nor everyone in the world is good. If you are a parent, then there are likely games and programs you would like to prevent your children from playing and programs you'd like to avoid them running or seeing. As a parent, you have the right to control what your kids do or don't do on the computer. Windows Vista has included a number of features that help you.

One way to provide parental controls is to limit when and for how long your kids can use the computer. Although playing solitaire is probably not an issue, you might like to avoid having them play first-person shooter games. Letting your kids run WordPad and other programs is also likely to be okay, but keeping them out of your home financial programs is something you'd probably want to do.

When you add the Internet and e-mail to the mix, you open up a whole new realm of threads and dangers to your children. Being able to restrict what web sites your kids can go to as well as whether they can download files can help protect kids.

Of course, the first step of parental control is letting children know what they can and can't do with the computer. When that doesn't work, Vista offers many settings to help otherwise—with parental controls.

Windows Vista parental controls can be personalized for each individual on the computer. You can do this by setting up individual accounts for each member of your family. Setting up user accounts is covered in Chapter 25. You'll want to make sure that you set up the kids as standard accounts.

Accessing Parental Control Features

The parental control features are located near the User Account settings area. Chances are that you will want to set up the parental controls at the same time you create an account. To get to the user account area, select Control Panel from the Start menu. Then select User Accounts and Family Safety, followed by Parental Controls. You'll see a dialog box that lists the accounts on your computer (see Figure 27-1).

Note As with many things you do on your computer, if it is not turned off, you are likely to get the User Account Control pop-up window. Since you are the one accessing the parental controls, you'll want to continue.

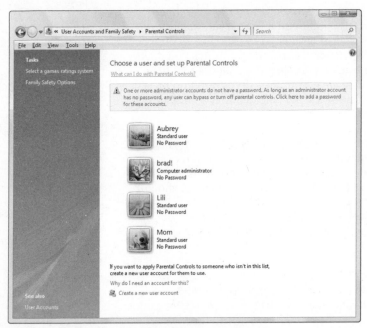

Figure 27-1: The starting point for parental control

The Use of Passwords

In order for parental controls to be effective, you need to have separate accounts for those that will be controlled and those that won't. If you don't put a password on your administrator account, then kids can simply use it to get to anything they want — including the parental control settings!

As such, the first step for achieving parental control is to make sure that you set passwords on any administrator accounts on the computer. More importantly, you should make sure that there is a password on any account that has less controls — and therefore more access — than any other account. If you don't do this, then there is nothing preventing a child from using that account instead of their own.

Remember, as the administrator of the system, you have access to nearly everything. As such, you can set up an account for your kids and let them pick the password. They don't have to tell you what it is — it can be their secret. As the admin, you can get to their account anyway — but that is your little secret!

If your system has an administrator account that does not have a password, then you will get a warning when you go to the Parental Control windows. You can see this warning in Figure 27-1. Clicking the warning will take you to a dialog box where you can enter a password for your accounts (see Figure 27-2).

Figure 27-2: Setting up an administrator password from the Parental Control dialog box

 Caution   You cannot place parental controls on an administrator account. You can place them on standard accounts and the guest account.

Tips on Passwords

When creating your own passwords, it is best to not use the obvious. It is also a good practice to use a few guidelines to make your passwords a little harder to guess:

✦ Don't use the names of family members and pets. These are easy to guess.

✦ Don't use common dates like anniversaries or birthdates. These are easy to guess, too.

✦ Do use at least eight characters. The longer the password, the harder it is to guess.

✦ Do use a mixture of upper- and lowercase letters. Most passwords are case sensitive, so **Mom12345** is different from **mom12345**.

✦ Do use both regular characters (the letters from a to z) as well as special characters or numbers. This makes guessing a password much harder.

✦ Don't write the password down and leave it by the computer. Obviously, this negates the entire point of having a password, if it is right there.

✦ When using a password on a web site or on a location where Windows Vista asks whether you want it to remember it for you, click No. If you have the password automatically filled in, then if someone gets on the computer with your account, they won't need to know your password to do other things!

Other Steps for Effective Parental Control

You should do a few other things in order to avoid negating the effects of parental control. As long as you have your computer set up to where your kids can only use their own account, then the parental control features are in the best position to be effective. As such, you need to make sure that you make it less likely that they can get into other accounts.

Passwords on the other accounts are the best defense to keeping unwanted people out of accounts they don't belong. Like a house, if the door is open, then even if the lock is turned, someone can still simply step in. An account is the same way. If Windows Vista is running and you're logged into your account, then someone simply can sit down and start using the computer to gain the same access you have. It is not likely that this is what you want your children to be able to do.

To help prevent this, in addition to passwords, you should also set up your system to require a password if you've been away from the computer for a period of time. To require a password you should do the following:

✦ Put a password on all accounts if they don't already have one. This is covered in Chapter 25.

✦ Add a Screen Saver to your account:

1. Right-click an open spot on the desktop. This displays a pop-up menu.

2. Select Personalize from the menu. This displays the Personalization dialog box within the Control Panel.

3. Select Screen Saver to display the Screen Saver Settings dialog window as shown in Figure 27-3.

4. Select a screen saver from the drop-down button list in the Screen saver section.

5. Set a Wait time. This time determines how long the computer will wait with nothing happening before turning on the screen saver. You should set this to the smallest amount of time that will work for you. In Figure 27-3, the wait time is set to 75 minutes. That is a long time to potentially leave your account open for others to access and use. A time of 10 to 15 minutes is much more secure.

Cross-Reference For more on working with screen savers, see Chapter 26.

6. You can adjust any additional settings for your screen saver.

✦ Within the Screen Saver Settings dialog box, select the On resume, display logon screen check box.

Figure 27-3: The Screen Saver Settings dialog window

By setting a password on your account, then setting up a screen saver and forcing the result to go to the logon screen, you help secure your account and your computer. By doing these steps, you will force Windows Vista to go to the sign-on screen instead of going back into your account. If you have a password on your account, then it will be required before you — or anyone else — can return to your account.

With your accounts securely configured, you should now be ready to start applying parental controls. Each of the parental control features should be added to the accounts that you want controlled.

Turning on Parental Controls

With passwords on your key accounts, you are ready to turn on parental controls and configure any accounts that you want to restrict. You should return to the Parental Control dialog box as shown earlier (see Figure 27-1). Once there, you should select the account that you want to add parental controls.

Select the account by clicking the icon. This displays the User Controls window as shown in Figure 27-4. You should see this dialog box regardless of which of the accounts you select from the Parental Controls dialog box.

You will use this window to turn on parental controls. To turn on parental control for this account, click the On, enforce current settings text. This activates the rest of the items on the window so you can set specific parental control settings. When you turn parental controls on, the window will also display additional information that tells you the status of different parental controls.

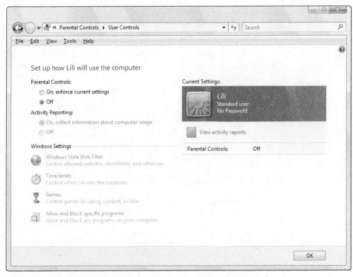

Figure 27-4: The User Controls for parental control

In Figure 27-5, you can see that the account for Lili has been turned on. You can also see that her account is defaulted to standard settings. Her Web Restrictions are set to Medium. Her Time Limits, Game Ratings, and Program Links are turned off. In the following sections, you'll learn about each of these settings and how to adjust them.

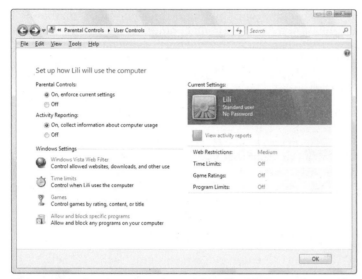

Figure 27-5: The User Controls page for Lili with parental controls turned on

You can select OK to save and close the dialog box. You can then click other accounts to turn their parental controls on as well.

 Caution   If you select an administrator account, you will get an error message saying you can't add parental controls to an administrator account.

Reviewing Others' Activity on the Computer

An activity report is, well, a report of activity that has occurred on the computer. By viewing an activity report for an account on Windows Vista, you can see what has been done on the computer. Before a report will contain interesting information, you first need to turn on activity tracking.

Turning on activity report tracking will enable you to get the full details of what a user such as your child is doing. You can turn on the tracking by going to the User Controls window (shown in Figure 27-5). Within the Activity Reporting option, make sure that On is selected. This will cause the computer to start tracking activities for this account. You should do the same for any other accounts for which you want to track activity.

Obviously, if you just turned tracking on, then there are not going to be many details to see on an account. Later, however, you will be able to review many of the things that have been done by this account on the computer. To see what was done, you can click the View activity reports text on the right side of the User Controls window. This displays the account's activity report similar to what is shown in Figure 27-6.

As your children use the accounts with the report tracking turned on, the information in the Account Activity report will continue to fill. You'll be able to review this at any time. When on the Activity Report page, you can switch to the report for another user quickly by clicking on their account name on the left side of the window.

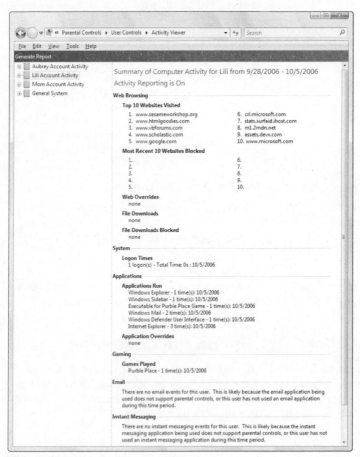

Figure 27-6: The Account Activity report

Note Some programs and web sites may seem a little unusual. For example, in the report in Figure 27-6, you can see that Lili has gone to sites called `stats.surfaid.ihost.com` and `ml.2mdn.net`. I know that Lili didn't go to those web sites. Rather, these are links that were loaded by her having gone to the other sites. Additionally, in the Applications section of the report, she did not actually run the Defender program. Rather, it was run automatically by Windows Vista when she logged into her account. The web pages and the applications were, however, run from her account. In the following sections, you'll learn more about blocking web pages and applications.

Seeing Specific Details on an Activity Report

In Figure 27-6, you can see each of the trackable accounts on your computer. If you click the little plus sign or triangle to the left of an account name, you will expand the menu to show sections of the Activity report. Some of these sections can also be expanded by clicking the triangle next to them.

Each of the primary sections is on the main report you saw in Figure 27-6. If you click one of the sections in the expanded menu, the report will change to only show this section. If you select a subsection, then the subsection will be shown. When these subsections are shown, you may actually see additional details. For example, Figure 27-7 shows the Websites Visited subsection shown on Lili's Activity report. You can see that the level of detail is much greater than what was shown in the primary report

You can click on other sections of the activity report and see specific details for those sections as well. In general, the level of detail will be enough to let you know what and where your child has been. It is worth expanding the subsections of the activity report. You'll find that you can see a number of interesting items, including:

✦ Web sites that were visited

✦ Web sites that were blocked

✦ Files that were downloaded from the Web

✦ Applications that were run

✦ When the child logged into the system

✦ What games were played

✦ What media was played

✦ What e-mails were received or sent

✦ What instant message conversations occurred

✦ What files were exchanged

✦ And much more

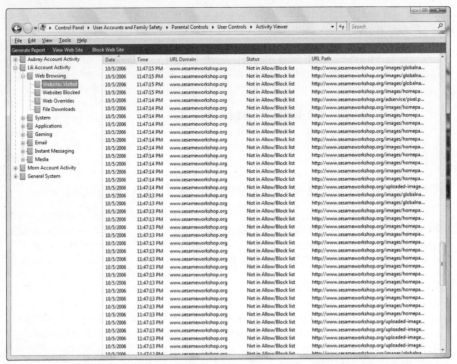

Figure 27-7: A subsection of an Activity Report

For some of the features to be effective you need to turn them on. For example, to have blocked web sites listed, you first have to set up the computer to block them. You'll see how to set several such settings later in this chapter.

Note   In Figure 27-7 you might think that Lili went to the Sesame Street web site a lot. Actually, when a web site is displayed, it is composed of a lot of images and other items. Each separate item that is a part of the web page is listed in the activity report. You might think this is bad; however, the extra details give you added information on the pages such as specifics on some of the ads that may have been displayed and more.

Seeing General Activity

The last report in the Activity Viewer is not a personal account, but rather is called General System. This Activity Report provides you with general information about the activity on your system. The subcategories for General System activity include:

✦ Changes to settings

✦ Account changes

✦ System clock changes

✦ Failed logon attempts

This information is beneficial in case someone is trying to get around some of the other settings. For example, if a child is restricted on when they can use the computer, then knowing if they managed to change the clock is worth noting. These options will let you know if such a change occurred!

Limiting Time on the Computer

Knowing what someone is doing on the computer is great, but there are times when you will want to place limits on what they can do. One limit you can set is when a child or other user can actually use the computer. By limiting the time, you can prevent them from sneaking onto the computer for late-night chats or at times other than what you dictate.

To set up time limits for an account, go to the User Controls window as shown earlier in the section called Turning On Parental Controls (see Figure 27-4). When there, select *Time limits* under the Windows Settings section on the left side of the window. This takes you to the Time Restrictions window that will enable you to control when the account can use the computer.

On this window is a grid that displays the days of the week down the left side and the time of day across the top. An entire week is displayed within the grid. By clicking a square in the grid, you either fill it or clear it. The filling and clearing works as a toggle, so if the box had been filled, then clicking it will clear it. If it had been clear, then clicking will fill the box. In addition to clicking a box, you can select multiple boxes by clicking the mouse button, holding it, then dragging to another box, then releasing. All of the boxes within that area will be either selected or cleared.

Each box represents a given hour on a given day. Selected boxes — those filled — will be times when the account will be blocked and, thus, cannot be used. Cleared boxes will be times when the user is allowed on the computer. Figure 27-8 shows the grid for Lili's account. You can see that most of the grid is filled in.

The cleared boxes are the times when the account called Lili can be used. During the filled boxes, the account will not be able to sign in. In the case of Lili's account, she can log onto the computer between one and seven on Sunday, between three and seven on Tuesday through Thursday, from three until nine on Friday, and from noon until seven on Saturday.

Each account can be set up with its own time restrictions. If someone tries to log onto an account during a blocked time, they will be told that the account is unavailable at that time. If they are logged onto an account, then when a blocked time is reached, they will be automatically logged out of the account.

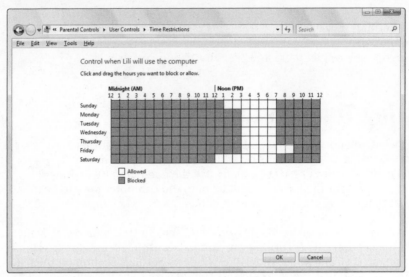

Figure 27-8: The Time Restrictions placed on Lili's account

Restricting What Games Can Be Played

Most kids like to play games. Unfortunately, not all games are appropriate for kids. As such, you might find that you want to restrict the games that your kids play on the computer. Although *Purble Puzzle* is kid friendly, if you've installed a game like *Halo*, you may not want a young child playing it.

Note Purble Puzzle is a game that comes with most versions of Windows Vista. You'll find it by going to the Start menu and selecting All Programs ➪ Games ➪ Purble Place. Of course, if you don't like alien-looking characters, then you might want to block this game as well!

Windows Vista actually provides a number of different options for choosing how to block games. In addition to blocking specific games, you can also block games based on:

✦ The fact that it is a game (you can block all games)

✦ An age rating for the game

✦ The type of content within the game

Just like blocking out times, you also start at the User Controls window for blocking games. On the User Control page for the account you are setting restrictions on, select the Games option under the Windows Settings section on the left of the window. This displays the Game Controls window as shown in Figure 27-9 where you can decide on the settings.

Figure 27-9: The Game Controls window for configuring parental controls on games

The first setting you'll see on the Game Controls window determines whether the account can be used to play games. This is a simple yes or no question. If you select No, then no other game settings matter since games will be turned off. If you are willing to allow games to be played, then keep Yes. You can then set other restrictions.

Caution   Some games may not be recognized as a game. If this happens, then you may still be able to get to the game even if you select that an account cannot play games. If this happens, then you should treat the game as a regular application and block it as such. This is covered later in this chapter in the section titled "Restricting Access to Applications."

Blocking Games Based on Ratings and Content

The Motion Picture Association of America (MPAA) provides ratings for movies that appear in the theaters. To some extent, you can use these ratings to determine if a movie is appropriate for your child. A movie rated R is aimed at people over the age of 17. You know the movie will have some content that is not appropriate for those that are 17 or younger.

Just like movies, most retail games today are also given ratings. These ratings come from the Entertainment Software Rating Board (ESRB) and are similar to what you see for motion pictures. You can use these ratings in many cases to determine if a game is appropriate for your child. For example, if you have a young child, you may only want them to use games that are rated E for Everyone.

In addition to game ratings, many games now indicate type of content they contain that may be questionable. Such questionable content may be violence, blood and gore, drug references, language, crude humor, nudity, or any of a number of other questionable types of content. You may be willing to allow partial nudity, but want to restrict your child from full nudity or violence. You may find mild violence okay, but blood and gore to be too much.

With the Windows Vista parental controls for games, you can decide. From the Game Controls window you saw in Figure 27-9, select Set game ratings. This takes you to the Game Restrictions dialog window, partially shown in Figure 27-10.

Not all games provide ratings. Your first decision is to determine if you only want to allow games that do provide ratings. If you want to be safe, then you will block games with no ratings. You can always unblock specific games if you find they don't have ratings and you want to allow them.

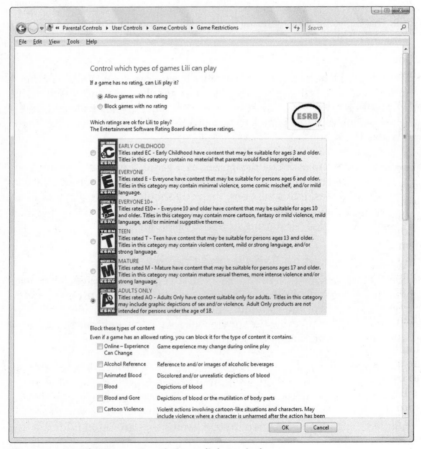

Figure 27-10: The Game Restrictions dialog window

You can restrict a game by its ESRB rating. In the Game Restrictions dialog window, you will see that the different ESRB ratings are listed. Each rating listed is progressively more mature than the prior rating listed. By default, ADULT ONLY is selected which allows all rated games. If you select E for Everyone, then that will allow games that are EC for early childhood to be played as well as games that are E for everyone. Anything with a higher rating will not be allowed.

You can also block games by content types. After the ratings, there is a list of content types. Regardless of what rating you select, if you select any of the content types, then any games that are listed to contain that type of content will be blocked. For example, you can leave the ESRB at ADULT and select that violence cannot be shown. This still blocks games such as *Halo* — although it would pass the rating; it would fail the content check.

There are a large number of content ratings. This enables you to filter out exactly what you don't want your kids seeing. After you've selected the settings for the account, you should click the OK button to save them. This returns you to the Game Controls window, which will list the settings you selected.

It is important to note once again, however, that games will only be blocked from these settings if the game has been rated. Most major games should be rated; however, some games you download from the Internet or that are not well known, may not have a rating. In that case, if you didn't choose to block non-rated games, then they may still be accessible. You can, of course, block them individually.

Blocking (or Unblocking) Specific Games

Settings for blocking games based on ratings and content are not perfect. As such, you may still need to block a specific game — or unblock a game. You can do this by first selecting the Block or Allow specific games link on the Game Controls window. This will present you with the Game Overrides window as shown in Figure 27-11.

The game overrides window will list all the programs that Windows Vista recognizes as games. It also shows each games rating if known and whether the account can currently play it. If you've set restrictions based on rating or content, then some games may not be allowed.

By default each games permission is set to User Rating Setting, which means that the status is based on the settings you've made up to this point. If you want to override those settings, you can select to either Always Allow or Always Block. Simply click the indicator to the right of the game name within the appropriate column. You will see that if you set the Always Block option, then the Status will change from Can play to Cannot play. After you've made your changes, click the OK button to save them.

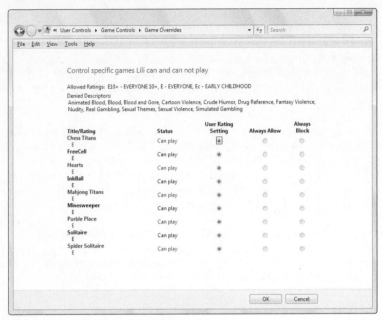

Figure 27-11: The Game Overrides window

Caution   As mentioned earlier, not all games on your computer may be recognized. I installed Toyland Racer (by IncaGold/Blimb Entertainment) and it did not show up on the list of games even though it was placed in the Games folder. As such, if I want to block this game, I'd have to block it in the same manner as a regular application rather than as a game.

Restricting Access to Applications

As mentioned above, not all games may be recognized and thus you may need to block them on your own. Additionally, you may have other programs on your computer that you want to block from certain accounts. You may want to block your financial program from the kids' accounts, yet leave it open on your spouse's account. If there is a specific program you want to block, this, too, can be done through the parental controls.

From the User Controls window shown earlier in Figure 27-4, select the Allow and block specific programs check box in Windows Settings. This option may take a minute while Windows Vista determines what programs are on the machine. When completed, the Application Restrictions window will be displayed. When this window initially displays, it will have just the question at the top of the dialog box that asks if the user can use all programs or only the ones you want to allow. If you change this to say that the user can only use the programs allowed, then the dialog box will be expanded as shown in Figure 27-12.

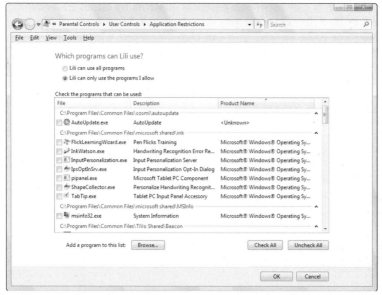

Figure 27-12: The Application Restrictions for Lili's account with *Lili can only use programs I allow* selected

What is displayed in the middle section of the Application Restrictions dialog box will depend on the applications on your computer. Even with a brand-new computer, you will see a lot of items listed. That is because Windows Vista includes a large number of applications itself.

You can restrict any program in the list by simply selecting the check box to the left of its name. If you want to lock the person out of the computer, you can click the Check All button to restrict all the applications. You can then clear the ones you really want to allow. If you want to restrict the user from files that are not listed or from files that are not executable (such as files and documents) you can click the Browse button and select the item using the Open dialog box. This adds the item to the end of the list and selects it to be restricted.

After you've decided what to allow, or not to allow, click the OK button. This saves your settings and returns you to the User Controls window.

Tip If a program was included with Windows Vista, then it will generally have Microsoft Windows listed as the Product Name.

Restricting Access to Web Sites

The Internet and the Web are great places to learn and interact with others. Unfortunately, there are places on the Web that are bad for children. As such, if you are going to implement parental controls, then the Web is the most important place to watch.

With Windows Vista you can approach parental controls by either determining what is allowed or by selecting what you want to block. In addition to blocking or allowing web sites to be viewed, you can also determine whether an account is allowed to download files from the Web.

To set these controls, you once again start at the User Controls window. For the web settings, you should select Windows Vista Web Filter in the Windows Settings section. This displays the Web Restrictions window shown in Figure 27-13.

Figure 27-13: The Web Restrictions window

If you plan to block any web content or downloads, then you need to select the Block some web sites or content check box. After you select this check box, you will be able to make selections within the rest of the Web Restrictions window.

If you want to block all content except for sites you choose to allow, then you'll want to select the *Only allow websites which are on the allow list* check box. You'll then need to state which web sites you want to allow.

Blocking or Allowing Specific Web Sites

You can block or allow specific web sites by modifying the Allowed or Blocked lists. From the Web Restrictions page, select the Edit the Allow and block list link to open the Allow Block Webpages window as shown in Figure 27-14.

Figure 27-14: The Allow Block Webpages window for restricting or allowing specific web pages

On this page, you can enter addresses for web pages and then choose to either allow or block them. For example, you can enter **www.sesamestreet.com**, which is the address for the Sesame Street site. You can then click the Allow button to add this address to the Allowed websites list. In the same way, you can enter a site name such as **www.Smallsins.com** and choose the Block button to add it to the Blocked site.

Based on the settings you select, you can control the web sites that are accessible on the account. When the user tries to access a blocked web site, they will get a parental control message instead of the page. For example, Figure 27-15 shows what Lili will see if she tries to go to www.SmallSins.com.

Note   The www.Smallsins.com site does not currently contain anything bad for younger children.

If you are going to set up blocked or allowed lists of sites for more than one account, you don't need to enter each web address again. Rather, you can click the Export button to save the list of allowed and blocked web sites. On the additional accounts, you can select Import and select the file you saved with the Export button. You can then add additional sites specific to the new account, or you can select sites in the lists and click the Remove button to remove sites from the list.

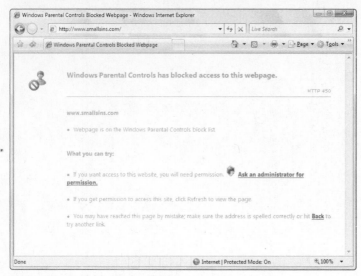

Figure 27-15: A blocked web site

When you have completed your lists, you can click the OK button to save everything and return to the Web Restrictions window. You can then click OK on that window to save those changes as well.

Blocking Web Content Automatically

If you'd prefer to avoid entering a lot of specific web site addresses, you can let Windows Vista choose to block web sites automatically. You can do this on the Web Restrictions page by selecting a web restriction level. The options are:

✦ **High** — This setting will restrict content to web sites that are believed to be aimed at children aged 12 or lower.

✦ **Medium** — This setting will prevent sites believed to contain mature content, pornography, drugs, hate speech, and weapons.

✦ **None** — This setting will not block any content.

✦ **Custom** — This setting enables you to select specific types of content to block. When you click this option, the available filters will be displayed for you to select. The options are:

  • Pornography

  • Mature content

  • Sex education

  • Hate speech

- Bomb making

- Weapons

- Drugs

- Alcohol

- Tobacco

- Gambling

- Unratable content

You can select any or all of the categories for filter. Be aware that filtering is not a perfect science. As such, there will still be sites that can get past the filters unless you specify specifically which sites to allow as shown in the previous section.

Blocking Downloads

The final option on the Web Restrictions page may be one of the most important to set. This is the Block file downloads option. By selecting this option you prevent the account from downloading files. Downloads can include executable programs, pictures, music files, and more. By blocking downloads, you help prevent your child from installing programs that could be harmful to the computer as well as prevent them from illegally downloading music and other copyrighted files.

Setting up a Parental Control Plan

The amount of parental control that Windows Vista provides can be overwhelming. Before jumping into the settings, you may want to decide what you want your child or other users to be able to do, or not do. You'll also want to have an idea of what is on your computer.

The User Controls window is the central location for setting an account's parental control settings. As you set features, the User Controls window will indicate an overview of whether a feature is on or off. If you find the settings are not quite what you want, you can always come back and adjust them. Additionally, as your child gets older, you may find that you want to change some of the settings.

Note   Unless you completely lock down the computer making it unusable, there is always a chance that something will slip through the parental controls. As such, it is always good to use the non-computer parental control of talking with your kids about what is good and bad so they can control some of it on their own.

Summary

Windows Vista added a number of parental controls that help you protect what your children, or others, can see or access when using your computer. In this chapter, you specifically learned how to use the Parental Control features. To summarize:

✦ You learned how to get to the Parental Controls window with the User Accounts and Family Safety section of the Control Panel. From this window you can select an account for setting parental controls.

✦ You discovered the User Controls window that not only summarizes the settings for an account, but also enables you to change settings for various types of parental control.

✦ Activity reports can be viewed that will tell you what a child or other user has been doing on the computer. You need to turn on tracking in order to collect the information.

✦ Time restrictions can be placed on an account to prevent it from being used at times other than what you designate. The user will be logged out if they are on the computer when a blocked time begins.

✦ Games that have ESRB game ratings can be restricted based on their rating or the type of content they contain.

✦ You can specifically allow or block any applications on your computer.

✦ Web pages can be filtered to allow you to control the web pages that can be seen or not seen.

✦ You can determine whether an account can or cannot download files from the Internet.

✦ Combining all the items in this chapter you can build an effective plan to add parental controls to what your kids do on their computer.

Speech, Writing, and Other Accessibility Features

✦ ✦ ✦ ✦

In This Chapter

The Ease of Access Center

Accessibility for sensory and motor impairments

Letting Windows Vista narrate

Magnifying what is on the screen

Talking to Windows Vista

✦ ✦ ✦ ✦

The Windows desktop is like your real, wooden desktop, in that it's the place where you do all your work. As you learned in Chapter 4, you control what's visible on your Windows desktop by moving and sizing open program windows. In Chapter 26, you expanded on this by learning how to customize your desktop to your own personal preferences.

If you have a sensory or motor impairment that makes it difficult to see the screen, hear computer sounds, or operate the mouse and keyboard, you can further customize your desktop to better suit your needs. The Windows Vista Ease of Use feature provides tools for configuring your desktop in this manner. In this chapter, you learn how to turn on and use these accessibility features. Although these features are often associated with disabilities, you don't have to have a disability to use them. For example, the Windows Vista speech features are valuable for those that have trouble with viewing the screen, but the speech features may also be valuable to others.

Tip   If several people share your computer, be sure to set up a separate user account for the person with disabilities. That way, those settings will be turned on automatically each time that user logs in to Windows.

The Ease of Access Center is the central location for modifying accessibility settings. If you used Windows XP, then you may have used the Utility manager or the Accessibility wizard. You won't find these in Windows Vista. Rather, the Ease of Access Center will take care of your needs.

To access the Ease of Access Center, go to the Start menu and select All Programs ➪ Accessories ➪ Ease of Access ➪ Ease of Access Center. This displays the Ease of Access Center as shown in Figure 28-1.

You will quickly notice that the Ease of Access Center operates differently than other dialog windows that open. It will automatically cycle through options and let you select them by using the keyboard. It will also read the options out load for you to know what they are.

The Ease of Access Center has a number of options you can select to help set up different settings for your computer. Additionally, you can activate several programs such as the Magnifier, On-Screen keyboard, and Narrator. Each of these programs will be covered later in this chapter. You'll also explore some of the settings you can select in the bottom half of the dialog. First, however, you should use the Ease of Access questionnaire.

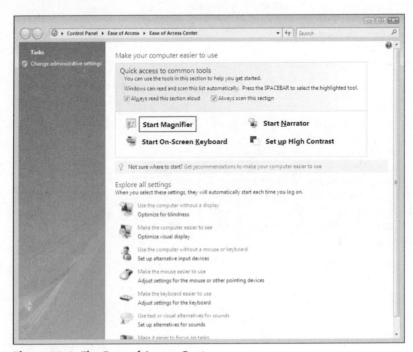

Figure 28-1: The Ease of Access Center

Ease of Access Questionnaire

The best starting place in the Ease of Access Center is the questionnaire. The questionnaire can be started by clicking Get recommendations to make your computer to use. By stepping through this wizard, you will be able to customize your computer settings to make it visibly and audibly easier to use. Figure 28-2 shows the first dialog window of the wizard.

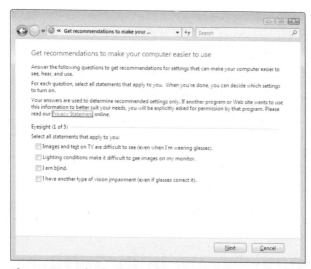

Figure 28-2: The first step of the Ease of Access questionnaire

The questionnaire is relatively self-explanatory. The key to getting the best results is to simply check the options that fit your situation. The options are relatively clear. After selecting the check boxes you want, click the Next button to continue. On the fifth page, you will need to click the Done button to complete the questionnaire. The result will be recommendations from Windows Vista on settings you should consider. Figure 28-3 contains the recommendations based on having selected a vision issue on the first page.

As you can see, nothing has been changed. Rather, only recommendations are being suggested. You can select any of the recommendations you want to have implemented and then click either Apply or Save. Apply will save your selections and leave the recommendations displayed. Save will save your selections and return you to the Ease of Access Center. Cancel will close the dialog without making any additional changes and return you to the Ease of Access center.

You can always run the questionnaire again to make additional changes. If you want to reset something you set, you should select the same settings as before. If you run the questionnaire and don't select anything, there won't be any recommendations.

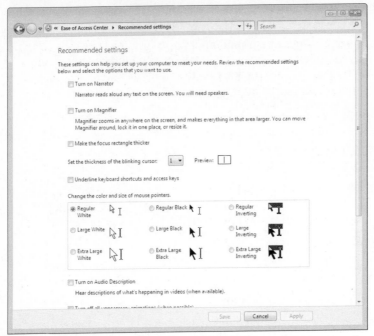

Figure 28-3: Recommended settings from the Ease of Access questionnaire

Modifying General Accessibility Settings

The Explore all settings section of the Ease of Access Center enables you to modify a number of general settings on your computer. This includes general display, mouse, keyboard, and sound settings. You can use the information you learned in Chapter 26 to modify these settings as well. The difference with these options is that they provide dialog windows containing a number of settings specific to given accessibility issues. For example, if you select the check box Use the computer without a display, you will see a dialog box similar to Figure 28-4.

As you can see in the dialog box, the options enable you to turn on audio features as well as to turn off unnecessary animations. Equally important, if you need extra time to see notification dialog boxes, then you can set the minimum time that they stay displayed.

In addition to the Use the computer without a display option, you also have several others you can select as well:

✦ **Use the computer without a display**

Select this for settings to optimize the computer for blindness and for not using a monitor. You'll be able to set text to be read aloud and to set how long notification dialogs are displayed.

✦ **Make the computer easier to see**

Select this for settings to adjust the contrast and color scheme as well as to turn on the narrator and audio prompts. You can also adjust a variety of other settings that will help to increase the contrast and decrease the distractions on the windows.

✦ **Use the computer without a mouse or keyboard**

Select this for settings to enable you to turn on the On-Screen Keyboard as well as to turn on speech recognition. These are both covered later in this chapter.

✦ **Make the mouse easier to use**

Select this for settings to adjust the look of the mouse pointer as well as to control the mouse with the keyboard. There is also a setting that enables you to select windows by simply hovering over them.

✦ **Make the keyboard easier to use**

Select this for settings that impact the use of the keyboard. This includes controlling the mouse with the keyboard.

✦ **Use text or visual alternatives for sound**

Select this for settings that enable you to use visual cues instead of sounds. You can also turn on spoken text captions.

✦ **Make it easier to focus on tasks**

Select this for settings such as turning on narrator, removing background images, and adjusting the length of time for notifications to display. You can also adjust settings to make it easier to type.

Figure 28-4: The settings for using the computer without a display

Each option has different settings that you can review. One that you might find useful is the option for making it easier to focus on tasks (see Figure 28-5). This dialog box operates like the others in that you can make your selections and then click Save. You can always come back and reset your settings as well.

Figure 28-5: The Make it easier to focus on task options

General Accessibility Features

The following list summarizes several features that the dialog boxes might or might not activate (according to how you select items).

✦ **High Contrast:** Improves screen contrast using alternative colors and font sizes. You can activate via the Ease of Access Center, or by holding down the left Alt and Shift keys, and tap the Print Screen (PrtScn) key; then release all keys.

✦ **Toggle Keys:** Emits a sound when you press an on/off key, such as Caps Lock, Num Lock, or Scroll Lock, so you can hear when these keys are pressed. You can activate via the dialogs or by holding down the Num Lock key for five seconds.

✦ **Sticky Keys:** Enables you to type combination keystrokes such as Ctrl+P by pressing one key at a time (for example, to press Ctrl+P, press the Ctrl key twice; then press the P key). You can activate via the dialogs or by tapping the Shift keys five times in a row.

✦ **Filter Keys:** Delays or prevents autotype, whereby a character is typed repeatedly when you hold the key down for a brief time. You can activate through the dialog boxes or by holding down the Shift key on the right for eight seconds.

✦ **Mouse Keys:** Enables you to perform mouse functions using the keyboard. You can activate via the dialogs or by holding down the left Alt and Shift keys; tap the Num Lock key.

✦ **Serial Keys:** Enables you to use alternative input devices rather than a keyboard or mouse. Serial Keys doesn't do anything on its own. It simply enables you to connect an alternative input device to Windows.

Accessibility Utilities for Everyone

There's more to accessibility than the features offered by the Ease of Access Center setting options. Windows also offers several utility programs that could be useful to anyone but are likely to be especially useful in the case of visual or motor impairments. Those programs can be accessed from the Start menu by selecting All Programs ⇨ Accessories ⇨ Ease of Use. They are:

✦ Magnifier

✦ Narrator

✦ On-Screen Keyboard

✦ Windows Speech Recognition

Using the Windows Vista Magnifier

The Magnifier is a utility that shows the screen area around the mouse pointer magnified at the top of the screen as shown in Figure 28-6.

Click Start and choose All Programs ⇨ Accessories ⇨ Ease of Access ⇨ Magnifier to turn this feature on. The Magnifier can be configured to the dialog box that is displayed as shown in Figure 28-7. You can determine the level of magnification as well as the location on the screen where the magnified region should be displayed. Figure 28-7 shows all of the various settings.

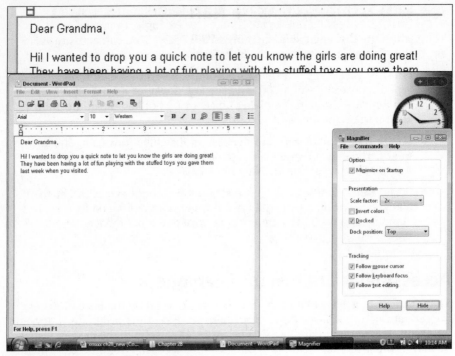

Figure 28-6: The Magnifier in action

Figure 28-7: The Magnifier settings

Using the Windows Vista Narrator

The Vista Narrator reads text from the screen aloud and narrates what you are doing. To turn this feature on, Click the Start button and choose All Programs ➪ Accessories ➪ Ease of Access ➪ Narrator. You can also turn it on from the Ease of Access dialog. When activated, the Microsoft Narrator dialog window will be displayed as shown in Figure 28-8.

Figure 28-8: The Microsoft Narrator dialog window

Within this dialog box, you can control some of the Narrator's settings. Specifically, you can determine whether keystrokes are echoed, messages announced, and more. You can also set the dialog box to start minimized so that it is out of the way. You can select a few additional settings in the Preferences menu.

After you start the Narrator, you will quickly realize that it can become annoying if you don't need it. For example, if you turn on Echo User's Keystrokes (which is on by default), then the Narrator will try to say everything you type. When you type fast, this makes for a lot of stuttering. You can, however, adjust the voice settings to speed up a little bit. Do this by selecting the Voice Settings button. These settings also enable you to set the volume, pitch, and specific voice you want to use—Anna by default.

To turn it off, click the Exit button in the Narrator dialog box, or right-click the Narrator taskbar button and choose Close. If you don't want the Narration to stop, then just minimize the dialog box.

Using the Windows Vista On-Screen Keyboard

The On-Screen Keyboard enables you to type text by clicking keyboard buttons in the screen. To turn this feature on, click the Start button and choose All Programs ➪ Accessories ➪ Ease of Access ➪ On-Screen Keyboard. The keyboard will be shown on your screen similar to Figure 28-9. You can use this keyboard by clicking with the mouse or any other pointer device you have connected to your computer.

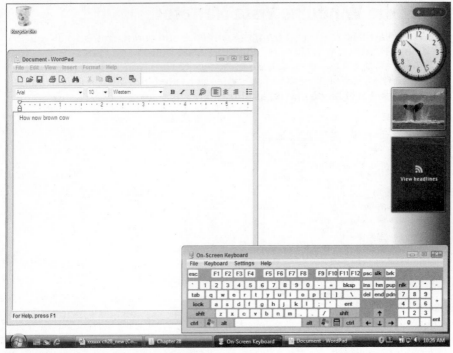

Figure 28-9: The On-Screen keyboard

You can also change the layout of the keyboard as well as a few other settings. You can see the various layouts by clicking the Keyboard menu item. Using the Settings menu option, you can turn on or off clicking sounds, you can set a typing mode, and you can select a font for the keyboard. The typing mode enables you to set the keyboard to select a character by hovering over it rather than by clicking.

You also have the option in the Settings menu to keep the keyboard on top of all other windows. When you are done with the On-Screen keyboard, you can click its Close button or right-click its Taskbar button and choose Close to shut it down.

Using the Windows Vista Speech Recognition

Speech recognition is the opposite of the Narration feature. Whereas the Narration feature reads what is on the screen to you, Vista speech recognition listens for what you say.

In order to use Windows Speech Recognition, you need to have a microphone. You also need to set up speech recognition so that it recognizes that someone is talking. Everyone talks slightly different, so letting the speech software know how you sound is important for getting the best results. To set up speech recognition, open the Speech Recognition Options page shown in Figure 28-10.

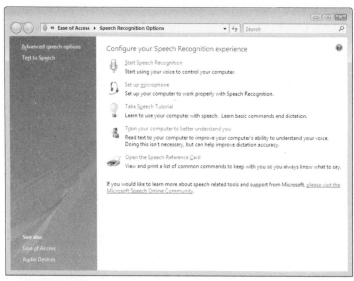

Figure 28-10: The Windows Speech Recognition Options page

You can open this dialog box by selecting Start ⇨ Control Panel ⇨ Ease of Access ⇨ Speech Recognition Options. You can then use the options in this dialog box to get ready to use speech on your computer.

Note If you want to see whether your computer is able to do speech recognition, you can click the Start Speech Recognition link on the Speech Recognition Options dialog box (or on the Start menu select All Programs ⇨ Accessories ⇨ Ease of Access ⇨ Windows Speech Recognition). If your microphone isn't set up or your computer won't support speech recognition, then you will get an error message.

Setting up Speech Recognition

The first time you access a Speech Recognition page, you will start the Speech Recognition setup wizard as shown in Figure 28-11.

You can click Next and follow the instructions to set up your microphone as well as the speech recognition program.

We recommend you start by clicking the Set up microphone option. This walks you through a set of screens that will ensure your microphone is configured and working for speech recognition. The dialog boxes, such as the first one in Figure 28-12, are relatively self-explanatory.

After selecting your microphone type, you can continue to the next step where you will see proper placement for your device. Clicking Next to go to the third dialog box brings you to where Windows Vista will listen to your Microphone. You'll read a goofy sentence and then be able to continue to the next page, which will confirm that your microphone is set up correctly if all went well.

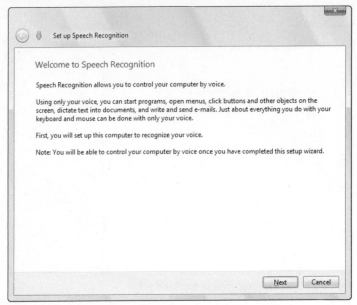

Figure 28-11: The Setup Speech Recognition wizard

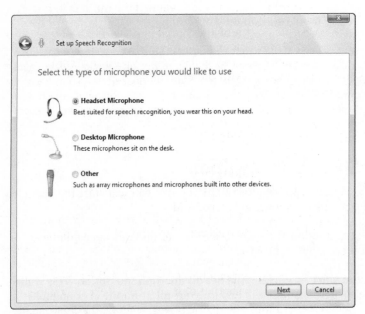

Figure 28-12: Setting up a microphone

If you are running the microphone setup wizard, you will see a Finish button that you can click to finalize the wizard. If you are running the Speech Recognition wizard, then you will be taken to a page to set up speech recognition as shown in Figure 28-13.

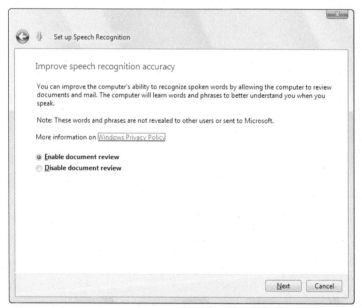

Figure 28-13: Setting up Speech Recognition

The dialog box in Figure 28-13 is asking for permission to review documents and e-mails on your computer that can be used to help improve speech recognition accuracy. Selecting the Enable document review check box will help the accuracy, so if you plan to use speech recognition you should select this option and then click Next. Continue with the wizard to finish setting up speech recognition.

Training the Speech Software

When your microphone and speech recognition are set up, then the best starting point is a bit of training. You should train your software, and you should train yourself to use the software. Start by training your software.

On the Speech Recognition Options dialog box, select Train your computer to better understand you. This starts the training program for your computer. What this program will do is step you through reading a number of items. The computer will use these items to associate your voice and accent to specific words. It will learn how you speak so it can better understand you. The first page of the wizard provides instructions that overview the process that takes place. Read those instructions and then click the Next button to proceed.

The trainer will have you read sentences. It will let you pause and restart should you get interrupted. Go through each of the sentences, reading them as you would in a normal voice. As you progress through the trainer, you will see a progress bar at the bottom of the screen indicating how far along you are (see Figure 28-14). When you have completed reading all the sentences, you can click Finish to end the trainer, or you can choose to do More Training.

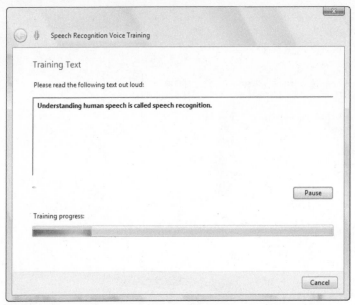

Figure 28-14: Teaching the Speech Recognition software how you talk

Training You

The speech recognition training will give you lots of tips and tricks. Although you might believe this to be enough to jump right into using speech recognition, we suggest you get a little training first. Rather than write pages and pages on how to use the software, you are better off to take the speech tutorial.

To use the tutorial, select Take Speech Tutorial on the Speech Recognition Options page. This starts the tutorial as shown in Figure 28-15.

I suggest you take some time to go through the tutorial. Not only will it show you how to use the software, but it will also give you practice. Speech recognition is not an exact science, so you may have to change how you talk a little bit in order for your words to be understood correctly.

When using the tutorial, you will go step-by-step through a number of lessons. In Figure 28-15, you will see the different sections of the tutorial listed. You can click these items to jump directly to that part of the tutorial. When you have completed the tutorial, you'll have an idea of how to not only use the basics of speech recognition, but you'll also know how to dictate and issue Windows commands as well.

Figure 28-15: The start page of the Speech Tutorial

Using Speech Recognition

After you've done all of the steps mentioned previously, you should be ready to start using Windows Speech Recognition. You can start speech recognition by either selecting the Start Speech Recognition link in the dialog box in Figure 28-10, or you can use the Start menu and select All Programs ➪ Accessories ➪ Ease of Access ➪ Windows Speech Recognition. When you activate speech recognition, you will see a small dialog box presented on your screen (see Figure 28-16).

This dialog box gives you the status of the Speech Recognition program. It also provides feedback on what is currently happening in the program. For example, in Figure 28-16, you can see that the speech program is active and listening. You can minimize this dialog box if you don't care to see it; however, it does provide good feedback on whether voice recognition is active, whether you were understood, and more.

Figure 28-16: The speech recognition active dialog box

If the software is listening, then the word Listening will be displayed. If it is not listening, then the word Sleeping will be displayed. To get the software to start listening, say "start listening." To get the software to stop listening, say "stop listening." You'll see the color behind the microphone icon change when the software is listening.

If you say something that cannot be understood, the software will make a noise and will display the text "What was that?" in the dialog box. You can repeat what you said at that point. If you say a command that cannot be performed, the dialog box will say "Command cannot be performed." After a second, the status will go back to listening. As you can see, it is worth watching the dialog box for the feedback it can provide.

One of the most useful commands that you can use is the phrase, "What can I say?" This provides a dialog box similar to the one in Figure 28-17 that lists the different types of commands that you can speak. This dialog box can also be displayed by selecting Open the Speech Reference Card on the Speech Recognition Options dialog box in the Ease of Access Center.

Figure 28-17: The results of saying, "What can I say?"

Tip
There are a large number of commands that you can use. One of the most beneficial is "show numbers." This command will place numbers on all items in a dialog box so that you can say a number to go to a certain location on a dialog box. You can learn the other commands by doing the tutorial mentioned earlier and by reviewing the items in the dialog box in Figure 27-17.

In general, you use speech recognition in one of two ways. The first is to give commands to Windows Vista. For example, you can issue menu commands or switch between programs. You can say commands such as "File," "Edit," "Help" to select the corresponding menu. You can also say "switch application" and you will be shown a dialog box with the current running applications to choose from. You can say "Start" to open the Start menu and then start a program by saying its name.

If Windows gets confused on a command, then numbers might be placed on the screen. You can then select the appropriate item by saying the number and then saying OK. If you find that you can't get a specific command to work, then you can say "show numbers" to tag items. For example, if you say "Start," then the Start menu will be displayed. If you then say "All Programs," windows might put this text into the search box rather than expanding the All Programs menu. To get around this, say "show numbers," and then say the number that is associated with All Programs.

The second way to use speech recognition is to do dictation. Dictation can be done in programs such as WordPad. With dictation, you can have Windows Vista write what you say. You can also use commands such as "new line," "space," and "tab" as well as commands for punctuation marks (for example, "period," "exclamation mark," "question mark"). The Speech Recognition Tutorial walks you through the key commands for using Windows Speech Recognition for dictation.

Speech Recognition Options

When you have the speech recognition software running, you should notice a small microphone icon in the notification area of the taskbar. Clicking this icon, activates a pop-up menu that displays a number of options (see Figure 28-18). Many of these options are for features you've seen described already in this chapter. Others enable you to customize additional settings.

One of the options you may want to check is Options ➪ Run at startup. This causes the speech recognition software to automatically run when Windows Vista starts. If you want to bring the Speech Recognition dialog box back to its regular size after minimizing it (see Figure 28-16), select Open Speech Recognition in this dialog box. You should note that minimizing the dialog box does not turn off speech recognition. Rather, it only hides the dialog box. You can still say Start listening, stop listening, and all the other commands. You simply won't see the visual feedback.

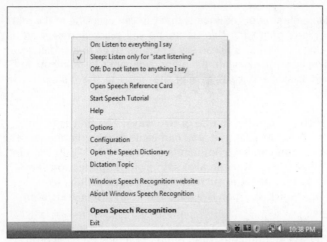

Figure 28-18: The Notification icon pop-up menu for Speech Recognition

Summary

Everyone who uses Windows Vista gets to design a unique work environment by customizing his or her desktop, Start menu, taskbar, and Accessibility Options. You also can customize a number of accessibility features. Here's a quick summary of the major points covered in this chapter:

✦ Microsoft has improved and simplified the Accessibility features in Windows. You can now access the key features from the Start menu by selecting All Programs ⇨ Accessories ⇨ Ease of Access.

✦ To configure accessibility options for sensory or motor impairments, click the Start button and choose All Programs ⇨ Accessories ⇨ Ease of Access ⇨ Ease of Access Center.

✦ By answering a few questions in the Ease of Access Questionnaire, you can let Windows Vista recommend settings that will work for your specific needs.

✦ Windows Vista provides a number of general accessibility features to make using the computer easier. These include features such as High Contrast, Toggle Keys, Sticky Keys, Filter Keys, and Mouse Keys.

✦ The Windows Magnifier enables you to magnify a portion of the screen to make it easier to see.

✦ The Windows Vista On-Screen Keyboard displays a keyboard onto the screen that you can use with a mouse or other pointing device.

✦ Windows Vista provides a very powerful speech recognition program that you can use to issue commands or do dictation to the computer.

Expanding Your System

As mentioned early on in this book, Windows Vista is computer software. Specifically, Windows Vista is your computer's operating system. Every computer needs an operating system to work, because the operating system pulls together the various components that make up a computer system. The operating system also determines how you, the user, operate the computer.

Windows Vista is also your computer's *platform* — that term comes from the fact that there are other programs that can run on top of Windows Vista. We generally refer to those other programs as *application programs, applications,* or *apps* for short. There are literally thousands of optional application programs you can purchase, install, and use with Windows Vista. There are also thousands of hardware devices you can purchase, install, and use with Windows Vista.

Learning About Hardware and Software for Windows Vista

If the whole concept of buying optional hardware and software is new to you, it wouldn't hurt to just browse around a large computer store or even around one of the large office-supply chain stores just to see what kinds of things are available to you. You can also check out many Windows Vista-compatible programs (software) and hardware devices online. Just use your web browser to go to www.WindowsMarketplace.com. When you get to the home page, click the All Software tab to view some available programs, or click the Hardware tab to see examples of devices.

Tip You can also get to the Windows Marketplace by going to the Start Menu and selecting All Programs ⇨ Extras and Upgrades ⇨ Windows Marketplace.

After you're on either of those pages, you can click any category name in the left column. Then click any subcategory name on the next page that appears. You'll see a listing of Windows-compatible products you can purchase and install.

Adding hardware to your computer is a two-step process, the second step being the biggie. The two steps are 1. Install the new program or device. 2. Learn how to use the new program or device. The information you need for both steps might be in a manual that came with the product. In the case of software that you download from the Internet, however, the Help that came with that program or the web site from which you downloaded the program will be your only sources of information.

Most companies that produce hardware and software strive to follow certain standards that make installing their products the same as installing anyone else's products. But it's not really a great idea to just assume that you already know how to install a particular device or program by some sort of birthright. You should always try to refer to whatever instructions you can find. Nonetheless, if you must wing it, you'll usually find that the general techniques described in this chapter work just fine.

Playing It Safe with Installations

When you install new hardware or software, there's always a slight risk that the product won't be 100 percent compatible with everything else that's in your computer. Unfortunately, you won't know if there's a problem until after you install the program. By then, the installation procedure has already made some sweeping changes to your system.

Setting a Restore Point

To play it safe with hardware and software installations, you can set a *restore point* just before you install the product. A restore point is a way of telling Windows to remember exactly how everything is set up right now. Windows then makes a copy of all the *system files* — files created and managed by your computer, as opposed to document files that you create and manage yourself. If you discover problems after installing a new hardware or software product, you can uninstall the product (as described later in this chapter). Then tell Windows to go back to those previous system files, where everything was working just fine.

Just before you're about to install a new product on your computer, you'll do well to set a restore point. Doing so is quite easy.

STEPS: Create a Restore Point

1. Open the Start menu by clicking on the Start button. Right-click Computer in the right column. From the pop-up menu, select properties. This displays the System window with information about your system. On the left side of the window, select System Protection from the Task list. The System Properties window shown in Figure 29-1 opens. Make sure the System Protection tab is selected. (Note that you may see a dialog window pop up that asks you for permission to continue. You'll need to click OK.)

 Note You can also get to the System Properties window by clicking the Start button and choosing the Control Panel. From the Control Panel home page, select System and Maintenance, then System. On the left side of the System Window, select System Protection from the Task list.

2. Click the Create button near the bottom of the dialog box. This button is used to create a restore point. A window opens for creating a restore point (see Figure 29-2).

3. Type a description, using your own wording, of this point (for example *Pre-Web Cam Installation Point* if you're about to install a Web cam).

4. Click the Create button. You will see a message as the restore point is being created. Upon successfully creating the restore point, a message is displayed.

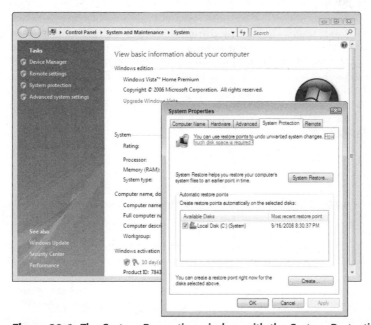

Figure 29-1: The System Properties window with the System Protection tab selected

5. Click OK. You can also click OK on the System Properties dialog box to close it.

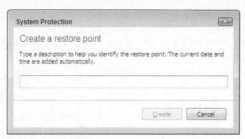

Figure 29-2: The System Protection prompt for a restore point description

That's all there is to it. Whether or not you'll ever need to revert to that restore point remains to be seen. If everything works correctly after the installation, you won't need to use the new restore point at all. Later in this chapter, you'll learn how to get back to a restore point, if the situation requires doing so.

Installing New Software

Unlike documents, which you can freely copy to your hard disk and use on the spot, any new program you acquire needs to be installed before you can use it. The installation process configures the software to work with your particular hardware and software. The process also creates an icon or program group on your All Programs menu, so you can start the new program as you would any other.

You need to install a program only once, not each time you intend to use it. After you've installed a program, you can put the disk from which you installed away for safe-keeping. You'll generally only need the original installation disk to reinstall the program if you accidentally delete it from your hard disk or if a hard drive crash damages the program.

How Do I Answer All These Questions?

Most installation programs present some options along the way, allowing you to pick and choose how you want things done. At each step along the way, there will usually be a default setting — a choice that's been made in advance for you. If you don't understand a question, don't take a wild guess as to how to proceed. Instead, just leave the current settings intact, and click the Next button to move to the next page.

Exactly how you install a new program depends on how the program was delivered to you. Programs delivered to you on a CD require one procedure, whereas programs you download require a slightly different procedure. You'll look at each procedure separately in the sections that follow.

Installing Software from CDs, DVDs, and Floppies

Programs sold through computer stores are usually delivered on CD-ROMs or DVDs, although occasionally you'll still find programs delivered on floppy disks. Installation is usually pretty simple. With programs delivered on CD or DVD, the process usually goes like this:

1. Close all open program windows on your desktop by clicking their Close buttons or by right-clicking their taskbar buttons and choosing Close.

2. Insert the CD or DVD into your computer's CD or DVD drive and wait a few seconds.

3. If you have not turned off User Access Control (UAC), then you will be asked to either Cancel a program from running or to Allow the program to run. Since you are doing the setup, you know you are the one running the program, so select Allow.

4. When the installation program appears on the screen, read and follow its instructions until the program is installed.

5. When the installation procedure is complete, remove the disk from your drive and store the disk in a safe place.

If Nothing Happens when You Insert the Disk . . .

Let's suppose that you're trying to install a program that was delivered to you on a floppy disk. Or perhaps the program was delivered on a CD or DVD. But when you insert the disk, nothing pops up on your screen automatically, or rather than a setup program, you see the Autoplay dialog box from Windows Vista asking what you should do. In either case, you need to start the program's installation process manually. If nothing happens, here's what to do:

1. Close all open program windows on your desktop by clicking their Close buttons or by right-clicking their taskbar buttons and choosing Close.

2. After you've inserted the disk and waited long enough to ensure that nothing is going to open automatically, click the Start button and choose Computer.

3. In the Computer window, double-click the icon that represents the drive into which you inserted the disk.

4. If Step 2 starts the installation program, skip to Step 6 now. Otherwise:

5. Look for and double-click the icon named Setup or Setup.exe.

6. Read and follow the instructions presented in the installation program that opens. (If the User Access Control dialog is displayed, you will need to select the Allow option.)

7. When the installation is complete, remove the disk from its drive and put it away for safe keeping.

If you get the AutoPlay dialog box from Windows, then you can select Open folder to view files. You can then continue at Step 5 above.

To start the new program, click the Start button and look around for its icon on the All Programs menu. Then just click the icon that represents the new program.

Downloading and Installing Programs

The Web is home to thousands of programs that you can download and install right on the spot. The exact procedure will vary a little from one program to the next. Typically, all the instructions you need will be available on the web page perform which you can download the program. You can print that page by choosing File ➪ Print from your web browser's menu bar or by selecting Print from the Print toolbar button if you are using Internet Explorer.

Tip   The Ultimate Collection of Windows Shareware at `www.tucows.com` is home to thousands of programs you can download and try out for free.

If you don't see any installation instructions but just a link to download the program, go ahead and click that link. Before Windows starts the download, you'll see the standard warning that appears when you download a program, as shown in Figure 29-3.

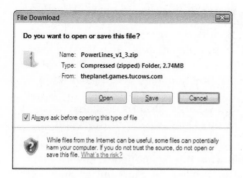

Figure 29-3: The standard warning that appears when you download a program

You always have to make a judgment call as to the safety of a program you're downloading. If you're downloading from a software manufacturer's web site, or a service like Tucows (pronounced *two cows*), you can assume it's safe to proceed. If you heard about this program through some junk e-mail or dubious web site, you're taking a risk if you proceed. If you have any doubts, you'll do well to click Cancel and forget it. Then go to a reliable service like Tucows and try to find the same program or a similar program there.

Anyway, let's assume that you trust the company providing this program enough to just go ahead and install the program. You only have to click the Open button and follow the instructions on the screen. When the installation is complete, you can start the program from your All Programs menu.

If you're not 100 percent sure about the program you're downloading, you can click the Save button, rather than the Open button, to just copy the program without installing it. After you choose Save, the Save As dialog box opens. There, you can navigate to the folder in which you want to place the file (this will default to your Downloads folder). Take a look at the file's name, too, so you can recognize it later. Go ahead and save the file normally.

Next, you can scan the downloaded file for viruses, just to make sure. When you feel confident enough to install the program, go to the folder you placed the icon in, and double-click the program's icon. Then follow the installation instructions that appear on the screen.

As always, when the program is installed, you can start it anytime by clicking its icon on the All Programs menu.

 See Chapter 10 for more on downloading files from the Internet.

Turning on or off Windows Components

As you know, Windows Vista comes with several sample programs already built in. The various programs that come with Windows Vista are generally referred to as Windows components. These programs are generally installed as soon as Windows is installed on your computer. So there's rarely any need to install such a program. Instead, just work your way to the program's icon through the All Programs menu, and click the program's icon.

If, for whatever reason, you happen to find that a component is missing, you can turn on the component yourself. You might need to grab your original Microsoft Windows Vista DVD for this job or grab whatever disk your computer manufacturer provided.

 Some computer manufacturers configure their systems in such a way that you can install missing Windows components without using a CD or DVD. If in doubt, you can try installing the component without a disk. Additionally, some components are installed by default, but turned off since you are likely to not use them. In such cases, you won't need the disk. You should have the disk handy, however, in case you are prompted for it.

1. Click the Start button and choose Control Panel.

2. In the Control Panel, select Programs, and then select the Turn Windows features on or off check box under the Programs and Features section.

3. If you have not turned off the User Account Control (UAC), then you will be asked for permission to continue. Click the Continue button. The Windows Features dialog window shown in Figure 29-4 opens.

Figure 29-4: The Windows Features dialog window

 Caution Do not clear any existing check boxes from the Windows Features dialog window; doing so will uninstall the program whose check box you cleared. You should also not change any settings, if you don't know what it does.

4. Make selections in the list for what you want to turn on. If an item has a plus sign next to it that means it contains subitems. Clicking the plus sign will expand the category so that you can choose from the individual item.

   For example, if you want to turn off Solitaire, you can click the plus sign next to Games. This expands the Games category. You can then clear the Solitaire check box. You would turn Solitaire back on by adding the check mark back.

5. Click the OK button. Wait while Windows makes your changes to the components.

6. Close the Control Panel Programs window.

The newly installed components will be available from the All Programs menu. If you uninstalled a component, then it will no longer be available; however, you can always turn it back on by following the same process.

Installing New Hardware

Installing new hardware can be complicated. First of all, there are *internal hardware devices* that you have to install inside the computer. (Or get someone to install for you, if you're not comfortable with taking your computer apart and digging through wires.) Then there's *external hardware*, which connects to your computer through a cable and a *port* (or plug) on the computer.

The exact plugs available on any given computer, where those plugs are, and how they're arranged vary from one computer to the next. The plugs are rarely labeled. You have to be able to recognize each port by its shape. The cable for any device will fit only in one of those plugs, however, so that is a good clue as to which port you need to use. Figure 29-5 shows some common ports, although your computer's ports may be arranged differently.

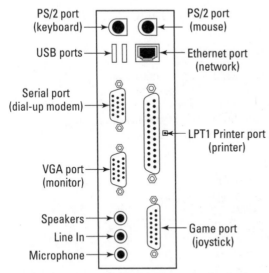

Figure 29-5: Examples of ports on the back of a computer

External devices come in two categories as well. There are *hot-pluggable* devices, which connect to a USB port. To install such a device, see the section "Installing USB Devices" that follows. Then there's everything else, which connects to one of the ports (other than USB) shown in Figure 29-5. To install one of those devices, see the section "Installing non-USB devices" that follows.

> **Note** Many digital video cameras can connect to a computer through an IEEE 1394 (also called FireWire) port. For more information on FireWire, see the section "Getting Video from Your Camcorder" in Chapter 18.

Installing USB Devices

 Universal Serial Bus (USB) is a relatively new technology that makes installing hardware simple. Many hardware devices you buy these days connect to the computer through a USB port and cable. The symbol for USB ports and devices is shown at left.

Although you should always follow the device manufacturer's instructions to install a USB device, the general procedure goes like this.

STEPS: Install a USB Device

1. Leave your computer turned on and running.

2. If the device needs to be plugged into a wall socket, plug it in.

3. If the device has an on/off switch, turn the device off.

4. Connect one end of the USB cable to the device; connect the other end of the USB cable to the computer.

5. Turn the device on using its on/off switch.

6. Keep your eye on the screen and wait a few seconds.

You should see a message, or a series of messages, pop up near the notification area. When you see a message telling you that the product is installed and ready to use, as in the example in Figure 29-6, you're done.

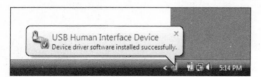

Figure 29-6: Connected USB device installed and ready to use

Installing Non-USB Devices

Hardware devices that don't plug into a USB (or FireWire) port are not *hot-pluggable*, which means that the computer must be turned off when you connect the device. Again, follow the device manufacturer's installation instructions. But in general, the procedure goes like this:

1. Close all open programs and save any work in progress.

2. Shut down windows (click the Start button and choose Turn Off Computer ➪ Turn Off).

3. If your computer doesn't shut down all the way, turn the computer off using its main power switch.

4. If your device needs to be plugged into a wall socket, go ahead and plug it in.

5. Connect the device to the computer through the appropriate cable.

6. Turn the hardware device on.

7. Turn the computer on last.

As Windows is booting up, it should detect the device. If Windows needs more information or files, you'll see instructions on the screen. Follow those instructions, and the device should be ready to use by the time you get to the Windows desktop.

Uninstalling Programs

If you have any old programs that you don't use any more and want to free up the disk space that the program is using, you can *uninstall* the program. Likewise, if the newly installed program is causing your computer to misbehave, you can uninstall it; then use System Restore to bring back your previous system files.

Keep in mind that it's never sufficient or safe to just delete the program's icons or files from your hard disk. When you install a program, it makes certain changes to your system that need to be unchanged to get your computer back to its previous state.

Caution   The terms *uninstall* and *remove* mean to get rid of it permanently. If you think there's even an outside chance you'll use the program again, don't remove it. The only way to get an uninstalled program back onto your system is to reinstall it from scratch by using the original installation disk or by downloading the file.

To uninstall a program currently installed on your computer, follow these steps.

STEPS: Uninstall a Program

1. If the program is currently open, close it.

2. Go to the Programs and Features dialog window. You can get there in one of the following ways:

    • Click the Start button and choose Control Panel. From the home page of the Control Panel, under the Programs section, select Uninstall a program.

    • Alternatively, select Computer from the Start menu. In the toolbar, click the button titled Uninstall or change a program.

    • When you are at the Programs and Features dialog box, a list of installed programs will be displayed. Figure 29-7 displays the three programs currently installed on my computer.

3. Scroll through the list of installed programs until you find the one you want to remove; then click that program's name. This changes the menu on the page to include an uninstall option as shown in Figure 29-8.

4. Click the Uninstall/Change or Uninstall button (or whatever button appears) after you click the program's name and follow the instructions on the screen to completion.

Note   If you see a message indicating that some of the files to be deleted might be shared with other programs, you can choose whichever option allows you to keep those files on the computer. They're tiny files that don't take up much space and will do no harm if left in place.

5. You can close the Program and Features window.

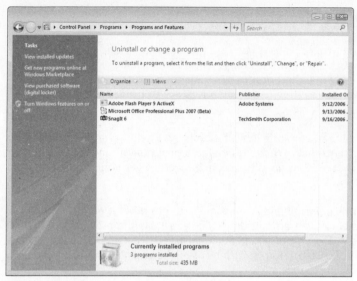

Figure 29-7: The list of programs installed

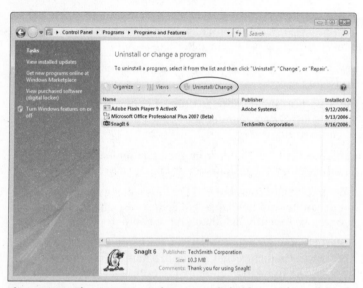

Figure 29-8: The Program and Features dialog box with a selected program

The program has been removed from your computer, and its icon(s) removed from your All Programs menu. If you removed this program because it made your computer unstable, and you set a restore point before installing the program, see the section "Restoring Your System Files," later in this chapter, to go back to your previous restore point.

Uninstalling Hardware

Uninstalling (removing) hardware is easy for USB devices — a bit more complicated for other types of hardware. But either way, you generally want to tell Windows you're about to remove the device before you actually remove it. Doing so gives Windows a chance to reconfigure your system to operate correctly without that hardware device.

Removing USB Devices

Certain types of USB devices, such as digital cameras and disk drives, transfer files back and forth to your computer. It's always a good idea to make sure any open files are closed before you disconnect the device, so you don't end up with any corrupted files. In general, if you're sure the device is not currently being used, you can simply unplug it. If you're not sure if it is in use, follow these steps.

STEPS: Remove a USB Device

1. Look for a Safely Remove Hardware icon in the notification area, as in the example shown in Figure 29-9 (the tooltip appears when you're pointing to the correct icon).

Figure 29-9: Notification area icon for removing USB devices

2. Double-click the notification icon to open the Safely Remove Hardware dialog box shown in Figure 29-10. Then . . .

   • If you see the name of the device you're about to remove, click its name and choose Stop. Click OK in the Stop a Hardware Device dialog box that opens.

   • If you don't see the name of the device you're about to remove, don't worry about it. It just means there aren't any open files, so the device need not be stopped.

3. Click the Close button in the Safely Remove Hardware dialog box.

Now you can turn off the USB device and unplug the cable.

Figure 29-10: The Safely Remove Hardware dialog box

Uninstalling Other Types of Hardware

Hardware devices that don't connect through a USB or FireWire port are a little more complicated to remove. When you uninstall a device, you won't be able to use it again unless you reinstall it from scratch. So don't uninstall any hardware devices just for practice. Know what you're removing, and why, before you do anything. Then do the following.

STEPS: Remove a Non-USB Hardware Device

1. Close all open program windows.

2. Right-click the Computer icon on your desktop or Start menu and choose Properties. The System Properties dialog box within the Control Panel opens.

3. Click Device Manager on the left side of the window. This opens the Device Manger. You may be prompted by the User Access Control (UAC) for permission to continue.

4. Click the + sign next to the icon that represents the type of device you're about to remove; then click the name of the specific device you want to remove, as in the example shown in Figure 29-11.

5. Choose Action ➪ Uninstall from the menu bar in Device Manager, or click the Uninstall button in the toolbar. Alternatively, you can right-click the item and select Uninstall from the pop-up menu.

6. Read and follow any instructions on the screen to completion.

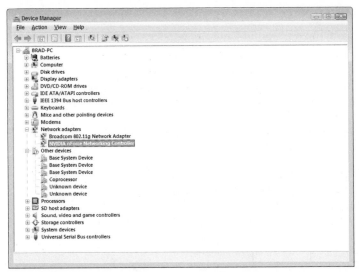

Figure 29-11: The Windows Vista Device Manager

7. Close all open dialog boxes and windows.

8. Click the Start button and choose to Shut Down the computer.

9. When the computer shuts down, disconnect the device from the computer.

10. Turn the computer back on.

The computer should boot up normally to the Windows desktop. If you set a restore point prior to installing the hardware you just removed, refer to the following section to learn how to return to your previous restore point.

Restoring Your System Files

If you set a restore point just before installing a new program or hardware device, then changed your mind and uninstalled that program or device, you can go the extra step and restore all your system files to their previous state. Make sure you uninstall the program or hardware device first. Then follow these steps to restore your system files to the most recent restore point.

Caution　　Never use System Restore as an alternative to a simple Undo (Ctrl+Z). Restoring your system files to an earlier time undoes *all* changes that you've made to your system since setting the restore point. If you installed any new hardware or software since that time, restoring your system files is likely to create a lot more problems than it solves!

STEPS: Restore Your System Files

1. Close all open program windows and save any work in progress.

2. Click the Start button and choose All Programs ➪ Accessories ➪ System Tools ➪ System Restore. You may be prompted by the User Account Control for permission to continue. When you continue, the System Restore dialog window is presented (see Figure 29-12).

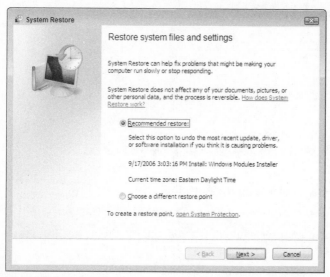

Figure 29-12: The System Restore dialog window with the recommended restore point selected

3. In the System Restore window select whether to use the recommended restore point that is displayed, or to pick a different restore point, and click Next.

4. If you chose a different restore point, then you will be presented with a list of restore points that have been set. If you named your restore point, you'll be able to find it in the list. Alternatively, you can look for the date and time you set the restore point.

 Tip   Windows Vista automatically creates restore points from time to time. You'll see those listed as System or Install checkpoints in the list.

5. Click the name of the restore point you created just before installing your hardware or software, as in the example shown in Figure 29-13; then click Next.

6. A confirmation page is displayed. Click the Finish button to start the restore.

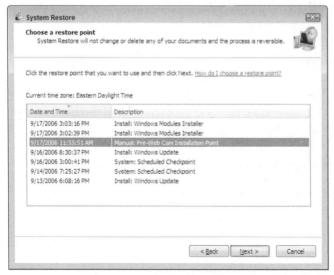

Figure 29-13: Choosing a recent restore point

Your computer will begin its shutdown procedure, and you'll see a dialog box indicating that system files are being restored. Then the computer will restart from scratch, and you'll see another message indicating that the restoration was successful. Click the OK button in that message, and you're done!

Summary

This chapter has been about expanding your computer system by adding new hardware and software. To summarize the main points covered in this chapter:

✦ Before installing new hardware or software, consider creating a restore point as a safety net, in case things don't work out as expected.

✦ To install new software from a CD or DVD, insert the disk into your drive, wait a few seconds, and follow the onscreen instructions.

✦ To download and install a program in one fell swoop, begin the download by clicking the appropriate link. When the File Download dialog box appears, click its Open button, and follow the onscreen instructions.

✦ To install a USB device, leave the computer on but the device turned off. Connect the device to the computer, turn on the device, and watch the notification area for feedback.

✦ To install non-USB hardware, turn off the computer, connect the device, and turn on the device. Turn on the computer last, and watch for any instructions that appear on the screen.

✦ To permanently remove a program from your system use the uninstall options provided in Windows Vista. Don't simply delete them from the hard drive.

✦ To safely disconnect a USB device, first double-click the Safely Remove Hardware icon in the notification area and stop the device. Then disconnect the device from the computer.

✦ To remove non-USB hardware, first uninstall the device through Device Manager. Then shut down the computer, disconnect the device, and restart the computer.

✦ To recover system files from a previous restore point, click the Start button and choose All Programs ➪ Accessories ➪ System Tools ➪ System Restore.

Disaster Prevention and Recovery

✦ ✦ ✦ ✦

In This Chapter

Dealing with error messages

Easy troubleshooting

What to do if the computer freezes up

Getting information about your computer

Fixing startup problems

Making backups

Turning off UAC

✦ ✦ ✦ ✦

Computer problems occur, especially if you're a beginner trying to figure things out as you go along. Fortunately, most of these problems are trivial, resulting in no more than descriptive error messages on the screen and a button to get back to where you left off.

Some problems can be a bit more serious. We sometimes refer to the bigger problems as *fatal errors*. The word *fatal* is a bit extreme though. Using a human analogy, I think it would be more accurate to say *temporarily unconscious* rather than *fatal*.

Then again, there are big problems, like hard drive crashes that cause you to lose all or most of the contents of your hard drive. These are extremely rare, however. But it certainly can't hurt to keep backup copies of important files, just in case. In this chapter, you'll learn strategies for dealing will all types of problems, from small to large.

Dealing with Error Messages

There are lots of little things that can go wrong when using a computer, especially for beginners who are trying to do and learn at the same time (or are skipping the *learn* part altogether). When little things go wrong, you'll see some sort of error message on the screen. There are tons of little error messages for different types of errors. Figure 30-1 shows an example of one.

Figure 30-1: A sample error message

In previous versions of Windows, most error messages were very sparse. In Windows Vista, the error messages are much better, but still can be a bit confusing. Error messages often tend to use all the official buzzwords of the computer biz, which is like Greek (or geek) to the neophyte. Nonetheless, the way to deal with them is as follows. First of all, read the message. That may seem obvious, but a lot of people just close these little message boxes without reading them first. Bad idea! The message appears for a reason: to tell you what went wrong.

If the message makes no sense to you, there are a few ways you can get more information.

✦ Some (but not all) error messages contain a Help button, which you can click to get more information about the problem.

✦ If you were trying to accomplish something by guessing, consider using Windows Help and Support to look up a better way to do the job.

✦ If there are specific technical terms in the message that you don't understand, consider looking up those terms in Windows Help and Support.

Tip   Windows Help and Support provides help for Windows only. Just about every program you use will have its own, separate troubleshooting and help advice, which you can get to by choosing Help from that program's menu bar. See Chapter 3 for more information on Help and Support.

For example, the error message in Figure 30-1 states there was an error deleting the file but offers no Help button. A good strategy is to open Windows Help and Support, search for the phrase **delete file**, and learn about different ways to delete files. Maybe you can figure out what you did wrong by reading the related search results.

Note The problem in Figure 30-1 is that we tried to delete a file that was currently being used, which doesn't really make sense. This error message is relatively descriptive. Not all messages will be.

If Help and Support is of no help, you can break out the big guns and go to `http://search.microsoft.com`. This web site contains mountains of information. So you'll want to type as many significant words as possible from your error message in your search. You'll do well to type **Vista** as the first word of your search text, to try to narrow the search to Windows Vista issues.

Still, there's no guarantee that you'll find your exact error message and simple solution. Sad but true — sometimes you just need to know what you're doing. There is no single book, or single web site, that contains *everything* there is to know, let alone a solution to every problem. But the better you're able to search for information when you need it, the more likely you'll be able to solve the problem quickly.

Tip If Windows Vista came preinstalled on your computer, your computer manufacturer's web site can also be a great resource for information. If you don't know the URL, try sticking the company name between `www.` and `.com`, as in `www.dell.com`, `www.gateway.com`, `www.hp.com`, or `www.SystemMax.com`.

There's an old saying about knowledge being of two kinds: the things we already know and the things we can find when we need it. Knowing how to use Help and Support is critical to getting the information you need, when you need it. Remember, you get to Help and Support from the Start menu.

Easy Troubleshooting

Windows Vista has some built-in troubleshooters that can help you diagnose and solve many problems on your own. To get to the troubleshooters:

1. Click the Start button and choose Help and Support.

2. From the Home page, click Troubleshooting (if you see it).

The page that is displayed lists many different types of problems, as shown in Figure 30-2. Use the scroll bar at the right side of the list to see all of your options; then click whichever option best describes your problem. Alternatively, you can click one of the categories on the right under *In this article* to go to a specific topic area.

Figure 30-2: Using Troubleshooting options in Windows Help and Support

Some computer manufacturers replace the built-in Help and Support Center with their own versions. If you don't see Troubleshooting as an option on the first page of your Help screen, there's another way to get to them. In the Search box near the top of the Help window, type **troubleshooting in Windows**, and press Enter or click the Search button to the right. Then, under suggested topics, click Troubleshooting in Windows, as shown in Figure 30-3. This will take you to the Troubleshooting options page.

Tip You should also take a look through the search results. You'll see that it lists a number of options for troubleshooting.

When you open a troubleshooting option, you'll see a question or some options. You should pick the option that most relates to your situation. You will also see suggestions on what you can try to resolve the issue. Simply follow the suggestions and you should be able to troubleshoot the issue.

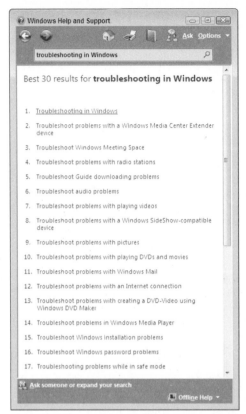

Figure 30-3: Help results for troubleshooting

What to Do If the Computer Freezes Up

Some errors are too serious to just display a simple message. Those types of errors are often caused when two or more programs running simultaneously sort of crash into each other in your computer's memory. Because Windows isn't involved in that problem, it can't solve the problem. So instead, it just displays some generic, technical error message like "Invalid page fault" or some such thing, followed by a long (and not at all helpful) memory address.

When that happens, your mouse and keyboard may stop responding as well, leaving the computer *hung* or frozen. Sometimes, you can get control of your computer again by opening Task Manager. Try pressing Ctrl+Alt+Del (even if your keyboard doesn't seem to be working, holding down the Ctrl, Alt, and Delete keys might work). From the list of options that is displayed, select Start Task Manager. If your mouse is still working, you can right-click the current time and choose Task Manager.

Tip

Most keyboards include lights that indicate if some of the keys are active. For example, a light turns on when the Caps Lock key is pressed. If your computer seems frozen, try pressing one of these keys to see if the light goes on or goes off. If it does, then it might be that you simply have an unresponsive program.

When Task Manager opens, click the Applications tab as in Figure 30-4. Read down the Status column for any program marked *Not responding*. Then click that program's name, click the End Task button, and be patient. It might take a minute, but hopefully you'll see a dialog box that offers the option to End Now. Click that button, and be patient for another minute or so.

Figure 30-4: The Applications tab of Task Manager

If Windows can close the offending program or programs, at least you'll be able to save your work in any other programs that are still open. You should save an unsaved work immediately, close all open programs, and restart the computer.

If you can't get Task Manager to open at all, your only recourse will be to restart the computer. Look around the front of the computer case for a Restart button you can push. You may have to hold the button in for a couple of seconds for the computer to turn off. If your computer has no such button, you'll need to turn the computer off using the main power switch. Then turn it back on.

When Windows says a program is *Not Responding*, that does not necessarily mean the computer is completely locked up and that the program is "dead." Rather, it may be that there is something preventing the program from continuing quickly. In many cases the program and Windows may work this out on their own. As such, you should give the program a few minutes to see if it comes out of the Not Responding state before ending it with Task Manager or restarting your computer.

Getting Information About Your Computer

If by some miracle you actually get to contact a real live human being to get help with a problem, there's a good chance the person is going to answer your simple question with a lot of complex questions. The reason goes back to the fact that there are so many different hardware and software products available. It's difficult to diagnose a specific problem without knowing some facts.

There are a few tidbits of information you can get about your computer using the System window shown in Figure 30-5. This window includes information on your processor, the amount of memory, your operating system type, and a rating for how your computer works with Windows Vista.

Many questions that you get in response to your question will require more detailed information about your computer. Few people know what brand of video card or hard disk is in their computer. But you can get all kinds of detailed information like that from the System Information program, shown in Figure 30-6. Here's how:

Note System Information is very technical and not likely to be of much use to anybody except a computer professional.

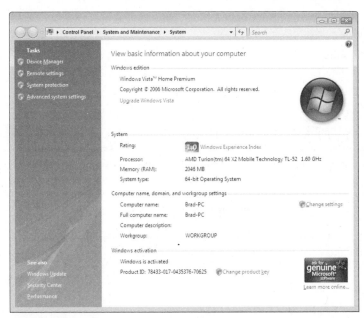

Figure 30-5: The System window containing information on your system, including Windows version and basic system configuration

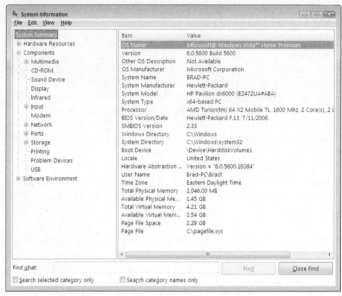

Figure 30-6: The System Information window, which contains detailed system information

STEPS: Get Detailed Information About Your System

1. Click the Start button and choose All Programs ⇨ Accessories ⇨ System Tools ⇨ System Information.

2. In the left column, click the + sign next to any category name to expand the list.

3. Click a specific subcategory name to see detailed information in the right pane.

You can search System Information for specific information using the Find what text box near the bottom of the window. For example, if you're looking for specific information about your computer's DVD drive, you can type **DVD** in the Find what box, make sure both check boxes below it are cleared, and click Find. If you don't find the information you're looking for, you can click Find Next again, until you locate the information you need.

 Tip If you need to know the version number of a specific program, open that program and choose Help ⇨ About from its menu bar.

Fixing Startup Problems

Some problems can prevent your computer from starting normally. The most common problem, and easiest to fix, is the "Nonsystem disk or disk error" message that appears before you get to the Login screen or Windows desktop. The solution to that problem is usually simple: Remove the floppy disk from your floppy disk drive, and remove any CDs or DVD from their drives. Then press the Enter key and wait a few seconds. The computer should start normally; you're back in business, and you can skip reading the rest of this section.

If that message appears even when there are no disks in any of your removable drives or if your computer begins to start up normally but stops before you get to the Welcome screen or Windows desktop, the problem might be on your hard disk. You can often get around that problem by following these steps:

1. Turn the computer off, then back on.

2. Keep tapping the F8 key as the computer is starting up. When you get to a screen with a bunch of options on it, press the ↓ key until the Last known good configuration option is highlighted.

3. Press the Enter key.

Let's hope that will solve the problem and you'll back in business. If that problem occurs every time you start the computer, however, you'll be wise to restore your system files, as described shortly.

If your computer won't start normally and you can't solve the problem using one of the preceding methods, you can usually start your computer in *safe mode*. As comforting as that name sounds, it really just means your computer will start with the bare minimum of capabilities, which makes it just usable enough to get the problem fixed. Sometimes, the computer will automatically go to safe mode if there is a problem.

If the computer won't boot up, and won't go into safe mode, turn off the computer, turn it back on, and keep tapping the F8 key. You should get to a menu of options with Safe Mode highlighted. Press Enter to select that option and start the computer in safe mode.

You'll see a text telling you that you're in safe mode. You'll also see the Help and Support dialog box describing what safe mode is. Your desktop might be a little weird-looking desktop due to the safe mode's resolution and screen settings. Despite the screen's weirdness, you can click the Start button and choose All Programs ➪ Accessories ➪ System Tools ➪ System Restore to get to the System Restore window. From there, choose the most recent restore point — or the restore point just before that one — and follow the instructions on the screen to restart the computer with the previous system files. If it doesn't work the first time, try again using an earlier restore point.

 See "Restoring Your System Files" in Chapter 29 for more information on System Restore.

The Startup Repair Program

If setting a restore point doesn't work, then you can try using the Startup Repair program. This is a program on the Windows Vista disks that can be used to try to repair some more critical issues with Windows such as damaged or missing system files (those files that are a part of the Windows operating system).

If the installation files are on your computer, then you might be able to run the Startup Repair program from the boot options. The boot options menu is the same menu you used to get to the Safe Mode earlier. When your computer is starting, keep pressing F8 until a menu appears listing Safe Mode and other startup options. You'll want to look in this menu for the Repair your computer option. If this option is there, then select it. Follow the instructions on the screen. You will eventually get to the System Recovery Options menu where you can select Startup Repair.

If you need to run Startup Repair, then you have a serious issue. If you are not very comfortable with your computer, then you are better to get a professional to take a look at the issue.

When All Else Fails

If all else fails, it could be a serious error with your hard drive. It would be best to have a professional take a look at the disk before you do anything drastic. But if the drive is damaged beyond repair, you've lost your hard drive. And since everything in your computer is stored on the hard drive, that means you've lost all your documents, favorites, settings, programs, and everything else.

 Caution   Never format your hard drive. Doing so will erase Windows, all your programs, and your documents — everything!

The only hope of recovering any data from a ruined hard drive is by sending the drive to a specialized *data recovery service*. Getting the data off the disk requires a *clean room* (like an operating room), an expert, time, and money. There's a risk, too, because there's no way to know in advance what you'll actually be able to recover from the drive.

Although such serious hard drive crashes are rare, the best defense is to have backups of all your important files. If you have backups of your important files, you can just trash the old hard drive, put in a new one (which is a lot cheaper than consulting a data recovery service), reinstall Windows, your programs, and your documents.

Making Backups

As mentioned in earlier chapters, everything in your computer, so to speak, is actually stored in folders and files on your hard disk. If your hard drive is damaged beyond repair, you'll lose everything in your computer. Although such damage is rare, you don't necessarily want to store hundreds of hours of work on one hard disk. Backup copies of your files provide the safety net you need to recover from a serious hard drive problem.

A backup is a copy of the exact original file, stored on some other disk. It doesn't matter what type of medium you use. A CD, DVD, Zip disk, another hard disk, or even tape (if you have the patience of a saint) will do just fine.

Large corporations use expensive, complex backup hardware and software to keep copies of their mission-critical data. They even have backup administrators — people whose sole job is to ensure that backups are done right and know how to recover files from the backups in an emergency. As the owner of a PC, it's unlikely that you're going to want to spend a ton of money on backup equipment, let alone a full-time backup administrator's salary.

In the past, the primary option for backing up your computer usually meant buying a third-party backup utility. There are numerous backup solutions available for purchase. Then again, depending on your version of Windows Vista, you may already have a backup program!

The Windows Vista Backup and Restore Center

If you are using Windows Vista Home Basic or Windows Vista Starter Edition, then you will need to find a backup solution. If you are using any of the other versions, then you can use the Windows Vista Backup and Restore Center to create a backup.

 Note   The value of a backup program might be worth the cost of upgrading from Windows Vista Home Basic to Windows Vista Home Premium. You can upgrade by running Windows Vista Anytime. This is available be clicking the Start button and then selecting All Programs ➪ Extras and Upgrades ➪ Windows Vista Anytime Upgrade.

Backing up Windows and Programs

Many of the files on your computer are system files and program files — those files that make up Windows Vista and all your programs. Backing up all those system and program files takes a lot of time and a lot of disks. Fortunately, there's no need to back up your system and program files over and over again, because most of them never change.

Whether or not you even want to bother making backups of those files is questionable, because of the very nature of programs and system files. Unlike documents, which you can just copy to your hard drive and use, programs (that is, system files and program files) need to be *installed* on your computer to work properly. The installation process configures the program to run properly in your particular hardware and software environment. You can't take a program installed on one computer and just copy it to another computer and expect it to work. It won't.

So consider this. Let's say you have copies of all your installed programs on CDs or some other medium. Your hard disk crashes and you have to replace it. How are you going to get all those programs that were installed on the old hard disk to the new hard disk? And how are you going to be sure that they'll work on the new hard disk without ever having been installed on that disk? (Remember, you can't just copy an installed program to another computer;

you have to install the program.) They *might* work. But there's a big difference between *might* and *will*.

 Caution Knowing how to do a backup is only a partial solution. You also have to know how to *restore* from the backup, should you ever need to.

Here's a strategy that can avoid the whole business of backing up all those tens of thousands of system and program files and living with the anxiety of really not knowing if they'll do you any good. When you buy a program, it's usually delivered on a CD. When you buy a computer with software already installed, you usually get an extra copy of all the system files and program files on one or more CDs.

In a sense, those CDs are better than backups, because the copies on the CDs contain the actual installation files needed to install the program. In other words, they're the very files you need to *install* the program. So in a sense, you already have backups of all those tens of thousands of program and system files that are on your hard disk. If you lose Windows and all your programs, you can just reinstall them from the original CDs.

 Caution Many programs require a serial number or product key to install. You should store all your original CDs, and any serial numbers/product keys, in a safe place. A fireproof safe would be your best bet, as many insurance companies won't cover software, no matter how you lose it.

Then, of course, there are programs you download for which you don't have any original CD. Probably the best solution to backing those up is to just remember where you got them. In the unlikely event of a serious hard drive crash, you could always go back to the web site and get the latest-and-greatest version of that program. Once again, you're installing from scratch, which is the proper way to do it.

Backing up Documents

Documents are files you create or download. Reports and letters you type, spreadsheets, pictures, songs, and videos are all examples of documents. You're free to open and change documents at any time. Thus, unlike system files and program files, documents can, and do, change.

You can easily back up any given document or set of documents just by copying them to a CD or some other removable disk. There's no need to use fancy backup software there. You could use the built-in copying capabilities discussed in Chapter 19.

 Caution Forget about using floppy disks to back up all of your documents. Most likely, you'd need tons of floppies and a lot of time. Use a writable CD, which can hold as much as about 650–700 floppies, or a writable DVD, which can store as much as about 4,500 floppies.

Messages and Financial Data Are Not Documents

Not all data is stored in the form of documents, settings, program files, or system files. Take, for example, e-mail messages. Search as you may, you'll never find any e-mail messages stored in documents on your hard disk, despite the fact that you may have tons of messages sitting in your e-mail program. Like e-mail messages, certain types of *data files* aren't exactly documents either. For example, names and addresses stored in e-mail program address books and financial data stored in bookkeeping and accounting programs might not qualify as documents.

To make backups of e-mail messages, names and addresses, and financial data, you are better to use the same program you use to manage the data. For example, to make backups of e-mail messages with Microsoft Outlook as your e-mail client, you have to use Microsoft Outlook, not Windows. To make backups of Quicken and QuickBooks data, you should use the Backup options contained within those programs.

For help in backing up e-mail messages, names, and addresses, Quicken, QuickBooks, or other data files, open that program's Help (not Windows Vista Help) and search for **backup** and **restore**.

If you keep all your documents in your Documents and Public Documents folders, making backups of all those files is relatively easy as well. Just copy each folder to some sort of removable disk, and you have all your backups. Again, no special hardware or software is needed. You just need enough Windows know-how to be able to copy folders. If you lose a document, or all your documents, you just copy them from the backup disk to your hard disk, again using standard Windows tools and techniques.

Using the Windows Vista Backup and Restore Center

As previously mentioned, most versions of Windows come with a Backup program that you can use. This program is in the Windows Vista Backup and Restore Center. To access the backup program, do one of the following:

✦ From the Start menu, select All Programs ➪ Maintenance ➪ Backup and Restore Center.

✦ From the Start menu, select Control Panel. From the Control Panel's Home page, select, from the System and Maintenance section, the Back up your computer option.

 Caution Remember, if you are using Windows Vista Home Basic edition, you will not have this program.

When you start the Backup and Restore Center, you will be greeted with a dialog box similar to the one in Figure 30-7.

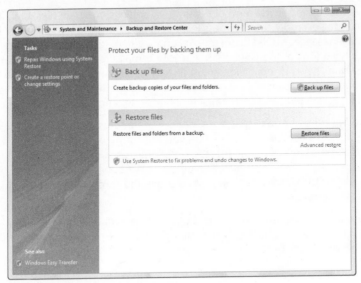

Figure 30-7: The Backup and Restore Center

From this dialog box you can begin the process of doing a one-time backup, or you can set your computer up to do a backup of files on a regular basis. You can schedule regular backups to occur at a certain time, day, and frequency. To either set up or do a one-time backup, do the following steps.

STEPS: Setting up a Backup the First Time

1. From the Backup and Restore Center, click the Back up files button. If prompted for User Account Control permission, then click Continue. You will be presented with the Back Up Files dialog box, shown in Figure 30-8.

2. In the Back Up Files dialog box, you state where you want to put the backup — the copies of the files that will be copied. If your computer is on a network, you can choose a computer; otherwise, you can select a disk drive for the backup. Any drives that are valid will be listed in the first option of the dialog box. If you plan to do an automated backup, then you will need to make sure a disk is in the drive when it is time for the backup. If the backup is too big for one disk, you'll need to be there to switch disks as well. Backup to a secondary hard drive alleviates this issue.

   In the dialog box, select your backup location and click Next. This displays the next step in the backup process shown in Figure 30-9.

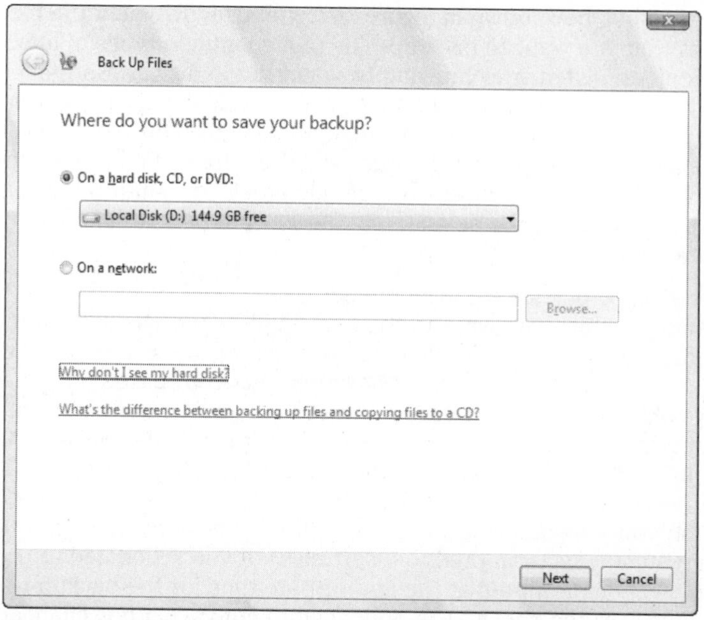

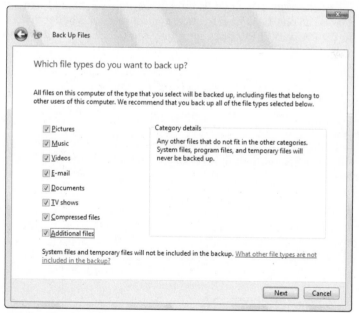

Figure 30-8: The Back Up Files dialog box: Picking a location

Figure 30-9: The Back Up Files dialog box: Selecting file types

3. In the dialog box shown in Figure 30-9, you need to select the file types that you want to back up. The most common types of files to back up are listed. You can simply select the items you want backed up. If you are using Windows Mail, you can select the E-mail option. If you are not sure what a type is, then move your mouse over it. The Categories details box on the right will then present additional information. After you have selected the file types you want to back up, click Next to go to the next step in the Backup process shown in Figure 30-10.

4. In the dialog box shown in Figure 30-10, you need to set the frequency at which you want to the backup to occur. The first time you set these values, a backup will be done immediately after as a starting point. After that time, your backups will occur based on the settings of how often, what day and what time you set in this dialog box. Set the values and then click Save Settings to start the backup. A status bar will show the status of the backup as it is occurring.

At this point, you are done with the backup. If you chose to back up to a disk drive, then you may be prompted to insert disks. If you scheduled future backup, you will be prompted at the appropriate time for the backup to happen. In many cases, the backup will only need to copy what has changed. This means that future backups may actually happen quicker than the original one.

Tip If you are using CDs or DVDs for your backup, you should remember that CD-Rs can only be written to once. In most cases, it is better to do a backup to CD-RW or DVD-RW disks since they can be used more than once.

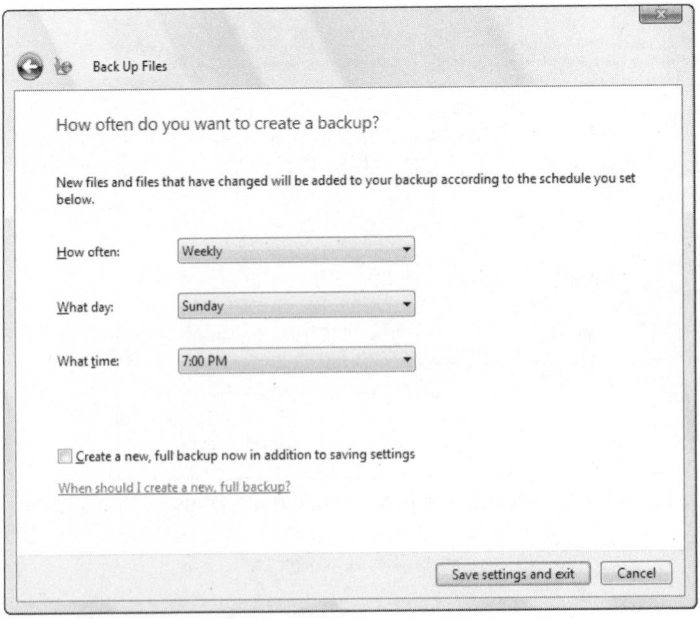

Back Up Files

How often do you want to create a backup?

New files and files that have changed will be added to your backup according to the schedule you set below.

How often: Weekly

What day: Sunday

What time: 7:00 PM

☐ Create a new, full backup now in addition to saving settings

When should I create a new, full backup?

Save settings and exit   Cancel

Figure 30-10: The Back Up Files dialog box: Frequency

Checking Backup Status and Settings

You can also use the Backup and Restore Center to check your Backup settings and to check the status of your last backup. When you return to the Backup and Restore Center (shown in Figure 30-7), you will see the time of the last backup, the next backup, and also the location where files are being saved to. You can check or change your other settings as well as get more details by clicking the Change settings link under the Back up files button. This displays the Backup Status and Configuration dialog box (see Figure 30-11).

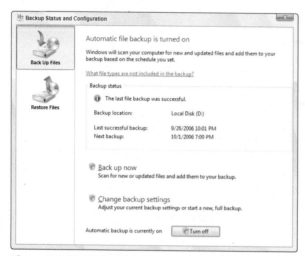

Figure 30-11: The Backup Status and Configuration dialog box on my machine

In this dialog box, you can turn off automatic backups by clicking the Turn off button. You can also run through the backup setup by clicking the link to change backup settings. When you are finished, you can close it by clicking the X button on the top right.

Restoring a Backup

Hopefully you will never need to do it, but if something should go wrong with files on your machine, you may need to restore your files. Should this happen you will need return to the Backup and Restore Center as shown earlier. There, you select the Restore files button within the Restore files section. This presents the Restore Files dialog box shown in Figure 30-12.

You need to decide whether you want to restore files from the last backup or an earlier backup. After you've selected a backup to use, you will be prompted as shown in Figure 30-13 to select specific files to back up.

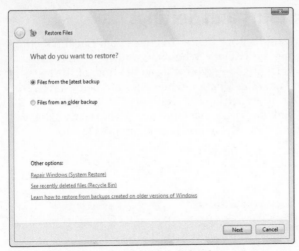

Figure 30-12: The Restore Files dialog box

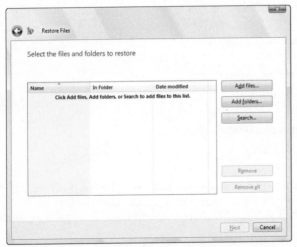

Figure 30-13: The Restore Files dialog box for listing
files and folders to restore

Within this dialog box, use the Add files, Add folders, or Search button to pull
up a copy of Explorer that can be used to select and add files that you want to
restore. Within the Explorer windows, select the files and then click the Add
button to add them to the Restore Files dialog box.

After you've selected all the items you want restored, click the Next button. You
will then be prompted for a location to place the items you selected. Enter a
location or select to have them restored to the original location. Click Next when
this is complete. The restore will start. If there are any name conflicts, then
Windows will prompt you to select whether to keep the existing file, to replace
it with the restore copy, or to keep both. Answer appropriately. When the
restore is completed, you can click the Finish button to close the dialog box.

Using Windows Easy Transfer

If you are using Windows Vista Home Basic, you do have another program you can use as a last effort for creating a backup. This is the Windows Easy Transfer program. It is actually a tool designed to help you transfer documents and settings from an old computer to a new computer that already has Windows and other programs installed on it. But there's no rule that says you can't use it to make backup copies of files on your hard disk.

To back up your settings files, follow these steps:

1. Close all open programs.

2. Click the Start button and choose All Programs ➪ Accessories ➪ System Tools ➪ Windows Easy Transfer. The Windows Easy Transfer wizard is displayed as shown in Figure 30-14.

3. Click Next. If you have programs opened, you will be prompted to close them. If not, you will be taken to a menu that enables you to choose to start a new transfer or to continue with an existing one.

4. Choose My New Computer.

5. On the next page, choose No, show me more options. This enables you to select to use disks or the network to transfer files. Before asking you which media you'll use, you will need to state whether your old machine has Windows Easy Transfer.

6. Continue to follow the direction in the dialog boxes.

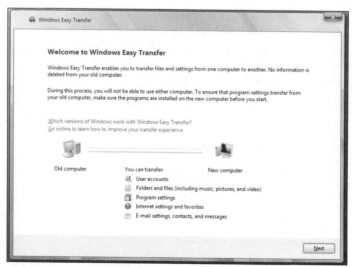

Figure 30-14: The Windows Easy Transfer wizard

When completed, you will have copies of files you can then install on a different computer. Should disaster happen, you should be able to also install them back onto your original computer as well.

Turning off User Account Control (UAC)

Throughout this book, I've referenced the User Account Control. If you haven't turned it off, then you will find it to be an annoying dialog window that pops up a lot when you are using Windows Vista. Although it can be annoying, it is actually there for your protection. If a computer virus or a bad program makes it onto your system, then if that program tries to run, the UAC will pop up asking whether you started the program. If you didn't, then you know something else did. This alerts you to the issue, plus it keeps a program from running automatically.

Consider if Restore was ran by such an errant program. If it were to run and restore your original backup, then all changes since your last backup would be gone. The UAC stops the program and waits for a response, so it prevents the program from simply running.

Even so, if you want to turn the UAC off, you can. To do so, use the following steps. You'll need to be an Administrator or have the Administrator password.

STEPS: Turning off the User Account Control (UAC)

1. Go to the User Accounts dialog box. You can do this in one of several ways:

   - Enter **user account** in the Search box on the Start Menu. Then select User Accounts when it is displayed on the menu.

   - Select Control Panel on the right side of the Start menu. From the Control Panel Home screen, select User Accounts and Family Safety, then select User Accounts.

2. From the user Account menu that is displayed, select Turn User Account Control on or off. This displays the dialog box shown in Figure 30-15.

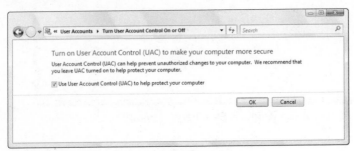

Figure 30-15: The UAC on or off dialog box

3. Select or clear the box in the dialog to turn on or off the UAC feature. Click the OK button to complete the process.

 Caution The steps for turning off the UAC are tucked at the end of this chapter and out of the way. This is because you really should leave it turned on. It is there for your protection. You should only turn it off if you have very good anti-virus software running on your computer that is up-to-date.

Summary

This chapter has been about dealing with common computer problems and steps you can take to protect yourself against data loss. The main points to remember are as follows:

✦ Minor problems and errors result in only a temporary error message on the screen.

✦ Windows Vista Help and Support includes some troubleshooters designed to help you diagnose and solve common problems in a step-by-step manner.

✦ If your computer hangs, you can often free it open by pressing Ctrl+Alt+Del and closing any programs that is not responding. Remember, just because it is listed as *Not responding* doesn't mean that it won't eventually respond.

✦ To get technical information about your computer, use System Information in the System Tools menu.

✦ If your computer won't start normally from the hard drive, restart the computer, press F8 repeatedly as the computer is warming up, and choose the Last Known Good or Safe Mode option from the menu that opens.

✦ When it comes to making backups, most versions of Windows Vista include a Backup program you can use. You can also restore files that were backed up.

✦ You have the ability to turn off the User Account Control pop-up. It is recommended, however, that you leave it turned on.

Connecting Your Computers

Warning: You are heading into the technological major
leagues. This is not recommended for slow children at
play. If you skipped Parts I, II, V, VI (and maybe III and
IV) to get here . . . well, I really don't know what to say.
Except maybe "Good luck" (snicker, snicker). Getting
two or more computers to talk to each other is not an
undertaking for the technologically faint of heart. It can
be outright ugly.

But when it works, it's great. You don't have to have a
printer for every darn computer in the house. You don't
have to have an Internet account for every computer.
You don't have to fumble around with floppy disks or
CDs to get stuff from one computer to another. You just
have to know what you're doing with *one* computer
before you start messing with lots of them. So, consider
yourself forewarned as you take a step forward into
high-tech big leagues.

We start this section with one very positive comment—
Windows Vista has made it much easier to work with
networking.

Design and Create Your Own Network

I f you have two or more computers, you may already be using what's known as a *sneaker network*. For example, to get files from one computer to another, you copy files to a floppy of CD. Then you walk over to the other computer and copy the files from the disk to that computer. Wouldn't it be nice if you could just drag icons from one computer to the other without having to use a floppy or CD?

What if you have several computers, but only one printer, one Internet connection, one DVD burner? Wouldn't it be nice if all the computers could use that one printer, that one Internet connection, and that one burner? All of these things are possible if you connect the computers to one another on a *local area network* (LAN).

What Is a LAN?

A *local area network* (sometimes referred to as a LAN or workgroup) is a small group of computers within a single building or household that can communicate with one another and share *resources*. A resource is anything useful to the computer. For example:

✦ All computers on the LAN can use a single printer.

✦ All computers on the LAN can connect to the Internet through a single modem and Internet account.

✦ All computers on the LAN can access shared files and folders on any other computer on the LAN.

In addition, you can move and copy files and folders among computers using exactly the same techniques you use to move and copy files among folders on a single computer.

Tip If your computer is already part of a LAN, you don't need to read this chapter. Go straight to Chapter 32 to learn how to use your LAN. If you're wondering how a LAN works, you can look ahead to Chapter 32 as well.

Planning a LAN

To create a LAN, you need a plan and special hardware to make that plan work. For one thing, each computer will need a device known as a *network interface card* (NIC) or *Ethernet card*. Those you can purchase and install yourself. But if you get an *internal card* (one that connects inside the computer) and you're not big on opening computer cases and fumbling around in wires, you should probably buy the cards and have them installed professionally. There are also external NIC cards, which generally just plug into a USB port on the computer. Those are simple to install.

The exact NIC you get depends on how you want to connect the computers. The traditional way of connecting computers involved using *Ethernet cables*, specifically designed for connecting computers. But in recent years, engineers have invented many new ways to connect computers using existing phone lines and power lines within the house and even without any cables at all. These more recent methods are often best for household networking, because you don't have to run cables all through the house to get the computers talking to one another.

Obviously, you're not going to find any of this specialized hardware at your local supermarket. You need to go to a computer store, one of the large office-supply chain stores, or an online vendor such as LinkSys (www.linksys.com) or Belkin (www.Belkin.com). With that in mind, let's take a look at some different ways you can create a LAN from two or more computers.

Caution We can't tell you exactly how to install your hardware, because that depends on what you purchase. Be sure to follow the manufacturer's instructions to correctly install whatever hardware you buy.

Connect Two Computers on a Traditional LAN

If you have two computers, and don't plan on getting more any time soon, you can install an Ethernet card (NIC) in each computer. Then you just need a single Ethernet *crossover* cable to connect the two computers. The cable must be a crossover, as shown in Figure 31-1, or the connection won't work.

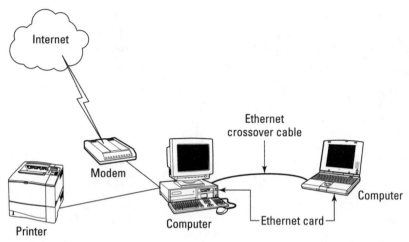

Figure 31-1: Example of connecting two computers with an Ethernet crossover cable and two NICs

Connect Three or More Computers on a Traditional LAN

If you have three or more computers to connect, and they're all in the same room and close to one another, you can use a traditional Ethernet hub and Ethernet cables to connect the computers. You'll need exactly one NIC and one traditional Ethernet cable (no crossover cables) for each computer in the LAN. Figure 31-2 shows an example of four computers connected on a traditional LAN. Notice how each computer connects to the hub only — there are no cables that run directly from one computer to another computer.

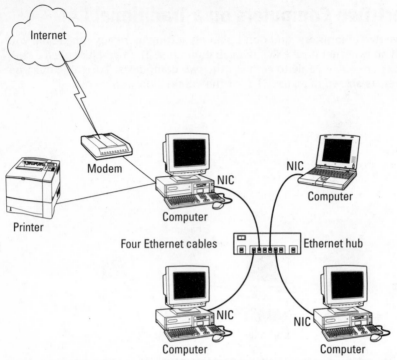

Figure 31-2: Example of four computers connected in a traditional Ethernet LAN

Connect Computers without Ethernet Cables

If you want to connect multiple computers in separate rooms, and don't want to run cables all over the place, you can use the wires already there. You can either use phone jacks (provided those phone jacks are all connected to the same phone number). Or you can use power outlets. These are actually two different technologies: the first is called *phone line networking*, the other is called *power line networking*. You have to get hardware designed for one or the other — don't try to mix and match.

For example, you can install a power line NIC in each computer and connect each computer to a traditional power plug (the same plugs you use for lamps). You'll also need one hub specifically designed for power line networks. If you prefer to use phone lines instead of power lines, you'll need a *phone line NIC* for each computer on the LAN. You also need one hub specifically designed for phone line networks. Figure 31-3 shows an example. The computers in the lower part of the figure would likely be in a different room from the computer shown in the top of that figure.

 Tip   The network interface card (NIC) used on a phone line network is often referred to as a *home phone line network adapter*, abbreviated HPNA.

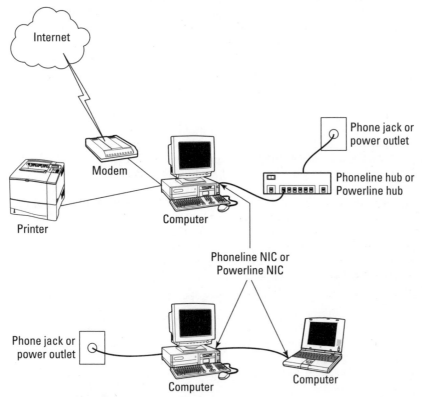

Figure 31-3: Example of three computers connected on a phone line or power line LAN

The advantage to using a phone line or power line LAN is that you don't have to run cables all over the house. The only disadvantage is that these LANS don't transfer data quite as quickly as a traditional LAN. But it's not likely that anyone would notice, because when it comes to day-to-day networking tasks, the speed difference is trivial.

Connecting Computers in a Wireless LAN

Wireless networking reigns supreme when it comes to convenience and ease of use. As the name implies, with wireless networks you don't have to run any cables anywhere. Plus, no computer is tied down to any one cable. For example, you can use your notebook computer in nearly any room in the house, or even out on the patio, and still have Internet access without being tied to a cable. Wireless networking is definitely the wave of the future.

To set up a wireless LAN, you need a wireless NIC for each computer. You also need one Wireless Access Point (WAP) that connects to one computer, as illustrated in Figure 31-4.

The advantages of wireless networking are, of course, the lack of cables and the ease of setting it all up. The only disadvantage is that wireless networking is a little more expensive than traditional Ethernet networking and might be a little slower. But again, the speed difference is trivial, and I doubt that anyone is going to complain that it's too slow. (Even the slowest LAN hardware is still a thousand times faster than a dial-up connection to the Internet!)

 Caution The speed of your LAN is independent of the speed of your Internet connection. If you have a slow dial-up Internet connection before you create your LAN, you'll still have the same slow connection after you set up your LAN. The only way to speed up your Internet access is to get rid of your dial-up account and get a broadband account such as DSL or Cable.

One other possible disadvantage with wireless is the occasional blind spot in or around the house, where a notebook computer just can't seem to get connected to the LAN. But those blind spots tend to be few and far between, as long as you're within about 300 feet of the Wireless Access Point. There are also wireless extenders you can purchase that can help to increase the distance a wireless network will work.

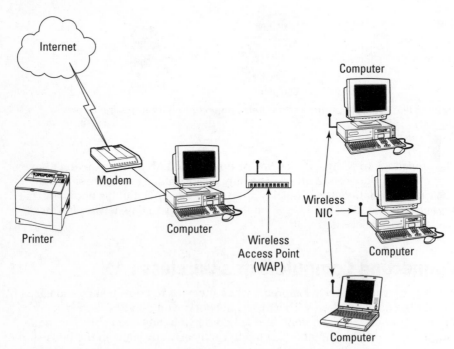

Figure 31-4: Example of four computers connected on a wireless LAN

Networking with a Router

In each of the preceding examples, we've pictured one computer as already having an Internet connection through a modem. That could be either a dial-up modem or a broadband modem that connects through cable or DSL. From the standpoint of the LAN, it doesn't matter how the one computer connects to the Internet.

As an alternative to using a modem connected to one computer, and a separate hub to connect the computers on a LAN, you can use a device known as a *router*. A router plays two roles: It's both the modem that provides Internet access and the hub that connects all the computers in the LAN together, as illustrated in Figure 31-5. Routers are available for broadband (DSL or Cable) Internet connections only and thus are often referred to as *broadband routers*.

 Tip   A router is sometimes referred to as a *residential gateway*.

The techniques you use to set up a LAN based on a router are slightly different from the techniques used when the hub and modem are separate components. As always, be sure to follow the manufacturer's instructions to a tee when setting up a network that uses a router.

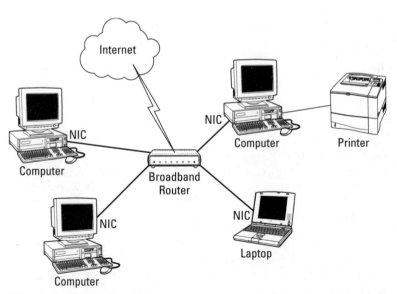

Figure 31-5: Example of four computers connected to each other and the Internet through a router

Mixed-Mode Networking

Far be it for me to complicate things, but I don't want to leave you with the impression that you can use only one type of networking equipment in your LAN. The fact is that you can mix and match to some extent. Doing so can be a real brain challenge, and I wouldn't recommend it for the technologically faint of heart. But if you already have a traditional Ethernet LAN and want to add computers to it, you can use phone line, power line, or wireless networking to add those computers.

Figure 31-6 shows an example of a LAN. The computers in the office are connected to each other in a traditional LAN. The kids' computers, which are on another floor on the other side of the house, connect to the LAN through phone lines. Then there is a free-floating notebook computer that connects to the LAN wirelessly. An Xbox 360 and a TiVo system are also connected to the LAN. Both are connected with wireless network adapters.

Everyone on the LAN shares a single 1,000K cable Internet connection and a single printer, both of which are in the office. The office computer has a collection of about 5,000 songs, which anyone can access and play from any computer in the house. One computer also has a spare hard drive, which every other computer can use for making backups (without fumbling around with removable media like CDs).

All network security is maintained from the office. Each family member has an e-mail account and .NET Passport. A single spam filter that cleans out unwanted mail from everyone's e-mail account every 30 minutes is maintained on one computer. The home network administrator also has free reign over every file and folder on every computer in the house. But nobody can get to his e-mail, work folders, or anything else he wants to keep private. In short, everyone gets to share exactly what the network administrator wants him or her to share but nothing else.

When it comes to networking, the possibilities are endless. All of the examples presented so far are just examples and aren't intended to show limitations. For example, you can have as many computers as you want on a LAN. You're not limited to three or four computers. The whole trick is getting the right hardware for your goals and getting it all installed and connected according to the instructions that came with the hardware.

 Tip If you order a new broadband Internet account, you can often get your ISP to send somebody out to the house and set up the whole kit and caboodle for you.

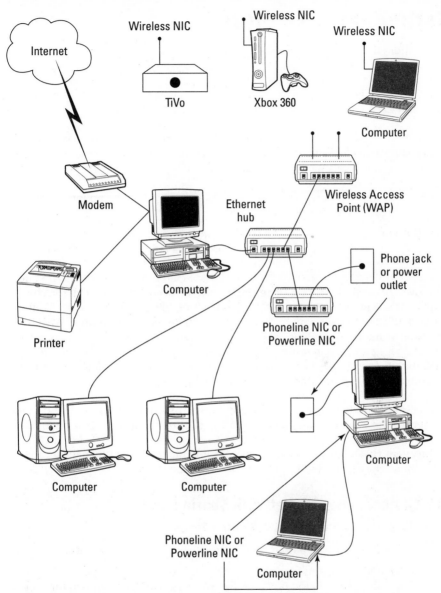

Figure 31-6: Example of a LAN that uses traditional, phone line, and wireless networking to share a printer, files, and Internet connection

Setting up a Network

As mentioned, I can't tell you exactly how to set up your networking hardware—only the people who manufactured your hardware can help with that. So I have to make a big leap here and assume you've already set up all your hardware according to the manufacturer's instructions and that all the computers are connected to a hub (or connected wirelessly).

When all the hardware is installed, and all the computers are connected, you're almost ready. With Windows Vista, Microsoft has made great strides in making the job of setting up a network simple. First:

✦ Make sure all hardware devices (computers, printers, modems) are plugged in and turned on.

✦ Restart every computer in the LAN to get to a fresh and clean Windows desktop, with no other programs running to complicate matters.

Windows Vista will take care of setting up the basics of the network for you. Really, Vista will do most of the hard work. If you are going to connect your network to the Internet, you might also need to set up your modem. With Windows Vista, however, you might be surprised and it might all set up automatically! If not, you can follow the instructions provided with the modem for setting it up as either a part of your network or as a device connected to a single computer that you then share across the network.

If you set the modem up on a single computer, then that computer will be designated as the Internet Connection Sharing (ICS) host, as described next.

In the event that your network doesn't set up automatically you can run the Network Setup wizard. First, go to the network xxx:

STEPS: Accessing the Network Sharing Center

1. From the Start menu, select Control Panel.

2. From the Control Panel Home screen select Network and Internet.

3. Select Network and Sharing Center. You'll see the Network and Sharing Center dialog box (see Figure 31-7). The icons shown for you are dependent upon your network.

With the Network and Sharing Center open, you can now click Connect to a network to start the Network Connection wizard. On the first page of the wizard, shown in Figure 31-8, you will need to indicate the type of network you are connecting to.

Select the type and then follow the remaining instructions if there are any. When the wizard is done, it indicates that the network was successfully set up. If there is an issue in the setup, then you will want to diagnose the problem as shown later in this chapter.

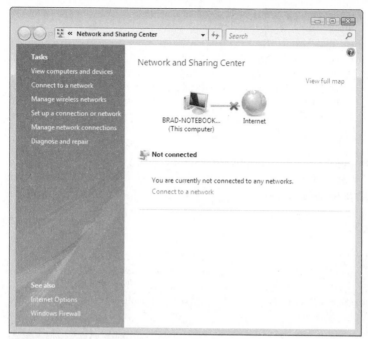

Figure 31-7: The Network and Sharing Center with a network not shown

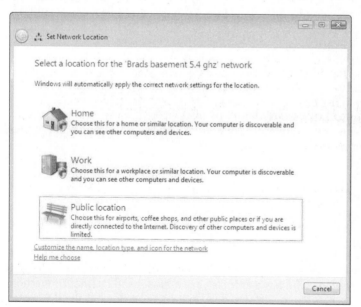

Figure 31-8: Selecting a network in the Network Connection wizard

Setting up an Internet Connection Sharing Host

If your LAN is set up like one of the examples shown in Figures 31-1 through 31-4, the computer connected to the modem will be the *ICS host* (or Internet Connection Sharing Host). In all four of those figures, the computer on the left (which has both a printer and a modem attached to it) is the ICS host. Think of the Internet as a party and the computer with a modem attached as the host of that party. Before you finalize the setup of your network, there are some things you need to know about the ICS host:

✦ Before setting up a shared connection, make sure you're sitting at the ICS host computer.

✦ Make sure that the ICS host is online, and stay online, before you run the ICS host. (If you can open a web page from the ICS host, you know you're online.)

If you're using a router, as in Figure 31-5, no computer will act as ICS host. The router itself is the host of the party. So in that case, it doesn't matter which computer you're sitting at when you start the Network Setup wizard. But since you're going to be the administrator of this network, I suggest that you start at whichever computer you use most often.

Setting up a Shared Connection

Your network should set up automatically in Windows Vista. One thing you may need to manually configure is your Internet connection or a connection to an access point. If this is the case, then you can run the Network Connection or Network Setup wizard.

Accessing the Internet from any computer on a local area network is largely a *transparent* operation, in the sense that each user at each computer should be able to just open his or her web browser or e-mail client and access the Internet normally. No extra steps should be necessary. At most you may need to run the wizard mentioned in the prior section. There are a couple of gotchas to be aware of, though:

✦ If one of the computers is acting as an ICS host, that computer must be running and online for other computers to access the Internet.

✦ If you use a router rather than an ICS to share an Internet connection, there is no ICS host, so only the computer trying to access the Internet needs to be running.

 Caution   Dial-up Internet accounts and local area networks don't mix well — just about everyone who has a LAN also has a broadband Internet connection, which is accessible to all computers on the LAN, as long as the ICS host is running. Plus, all computers on the LAN must share (split up) the available bandwidth. And with a dial-up account, there's very little bandwidth to share!

With everything else in place, as described previously, follow these steps.

STEPS: Run the Set up a Connection or Network Wizard

1. Open the Network and Sharing Center as shown earlier in this chapter.

2. Open the Network Connections icon. The Network Connections folder opens, looking something like the example shown in Figure 31-9 if your network has been set up. (Your icons will be different — don't worry about that.)

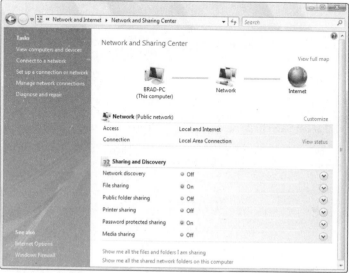

Figure 31-9: The Network and Sharing Center

3. From the Tasks list on the left side of the Network and Sharing Center, click Set up a connection or network.

4. The wizard starts. You will be prompted to select the type of connection you want to set up as shown in Figure 31-10. To set up a broadband connection to the Internet, select the first option, Connect to the Internet. Ultimately, you should select the type of connection you have. If you don't have a broadband connection, then selecting the first option will not succeed for you when you go to connect to the Internet. After you've selected the connection type, click Next to continue.

5. The next page of the wizard will depend on the selection you made on the first page. If you are setting up an ICS, then chances are you selected to set up an Internet Connection. On this page of the wizard you would then see something similar to Figure 31-11. If you don't see the type of connection you want to make, then select the Show connection check box at the bottom of the dialog box. This has already been selected in Figure 31-11. Click the option for your connection type.

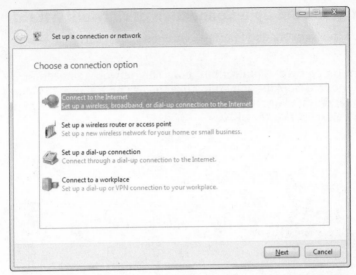

Figure 31-10: Selecting the type of connection you want to set up

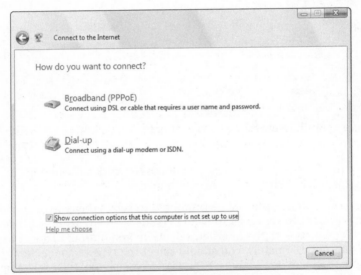

Figure 31-11: Selecting how you want to connect

6. The next wizard page looks like one of the examples shown in Figure 31-12. If you selected broadband, then you will have a dialog box similar to the one on the left. If you selected dial-up you'll have a dialog box similar to the one on the right.

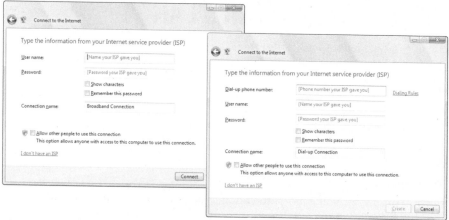

Figure 31-12: Internet connection options

On this page you need to fill in the required information:

User name: This is the user name you were given by your Internet service provider (ISP).

Password: This is the password given to you by your ISP. If you don't want to have to keep entering this, you can select the Remember this password check box.

Connection name: This is the name that Windows Vista assigns to this connection. If you have more than one connection, you'll be able to use this name to tell the connections apart.

Dial-up phone number: If you are setting up a dial-up connection, then you will also need to set up the phone number to dial for the connection.

Allow other people to use this connection: Select this check box to share the connection. If you are setting up an ICS connection, then you need to select this check box to allow others to use the connections.

7. Click the Connect or Create button to continue. With the broadband connection, Windows Vista will attempt to connect to the Internet. If it fails, you will be given the option to try again, to diagnose the problem, or to go ahead and set up the connection anyway. Choose the action you want and follow the steps to complete the wizard.

8. You can click the Close button to end the wizard when all is done. When you've completed the wizard, you'll come to its last page, where you can click the Close button. You can close the Network Connections folder as well. You're done setting up the connection.

Using the Internet in a LAN

If you can't get a computer other than the ICS host to access the Internet, you'll need to make sure the modem that provides access is shared. You can set the modem to be shared, or simply verify its settings by doing the following.

STEPS: Making Sure a Connection Is Shared

1. Go to the Network and Sharing Center as shown earlier in this chapter.

2. Select *Manage network connections* from the Tasks area on the left. This shows you a list of the connections that you have set up on your computer.

3. Right-click the Internet connection you want to confirm is shared. From the menu that is displayed, select Properties. This displays the Connections Properties dialog box for that connection. (You can also select, from the button bar, Change settings for this connection to display this dialog box.)

4. Select the Sharing tab in the dialog box. You should see something similar to Figure 31-13.

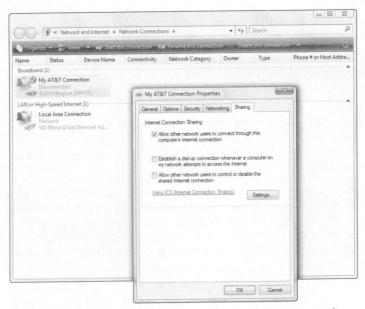

Figure 31-13: The sharing options on the Connections Properties for an Internet connection

5. Select the options you want. You may need to select the first option to allow access to the lower options. These options are only relevant if you are using an Internet Connection Sharing setup as shown earlier in this chapter. The type of sharing that occurs depends on the options you select:

- **Allow other network users to connect through this computer's internet connection:** You need to select this to allow the connection to be shared.

- **Establish a dial-up connection. . .:** If you are using a dial-up connection, then, when another computer tries to connect to the Internet, the modem will be dialed for them. Be aware that they may need to enter a user name and password to fully establish the connection.

- **Allow other network users to control or disable the shared Internet connection:** If you want others to be able to configure the Internet connection from their machines, then you should select this option. If you don't want others to make changes to the settings, then don't select this option.

In addition to the primary settings above, there are also advanced settings that can be shared. Clicking the Settings button displays a dialog box that enables you to determine what advanced settings on your network can be shared.

6. After you've set your sharing options, click OK to save them and exit the dialog box.

If anything goes wrong, Windows Vista will let you know and will generally offer to diagnose the issue for you.

Securing a LAN

A local area network connected to the Internet has the same Internet security threats as a single computer connected to the Internet. How you deal with the problem varies with different types of hardware. You may want to refer to the documentation that came with the hardware for specifics. However, the general rule of thumb is that, if you're using an ICS host, you only need to enable the Internet Connection Firewall on that one computer, as shown in Chapter 13. Doing so will block hacking attempts for all computers on the LAN.

If you enable the Internet Connection Firewall on computers other than the ICS host, you may prevent the LAN from sharing resources. I say *may* because Windows Vista lets you set sharing to just the local network.

Since hacking attempts are blocked at the modem, before they get to any computers on the LAN, it's really only necessary to activate the firewall on the ICS host — not on every computer in the LAN.

With a router, firewalls are a little trickier, because each computer on the LAN has its own connection to the Internet through the router. However, virtually all routers (that I know of) have a firewall or NAT (Network Address Translation) built right into them. So once again, hacking attempts get blocked before they reach any computer in the network. Technically, it's not really necessary to enable the firewall on any computer on the LAN when there's a router involved. However, if you're up-to-date with Windows Updates, enabling the firewall on individual computers couldn't hurt and wouldn't prevent normal sharing of resources.

Beyond Firewalls

Of course, firewalls block hackers and worms only. They don't block viruses or other malicious code sent in e-mail attachments or stored in programs you can download from the Internet. Each computer on the LAN needs its own virus protection.

Each computer on the LAN needs to be up-to-date with Windows Update to maximize its security. So you may want to enable automatic updating on each computer, as discussed in Chapter 13.

Testing and Troubleshooting Your LAN

By the time you read this, you should have already set up all of your network hardware and run the Network Setup wizard on every computer on your LAN. Now for the moment of truth (drum roll). Let's see if your computers know about each other. Here's how:

1. Go to any computer on the LAN, click the Start button, and choose Network.

2. Give the computer a second to go out and gather up all the names of other computers in the network.

You should see an icon for each computer currently turned on and part of the LAN. Figure 31-14 shows an example. The icons in your folder will reflect the names and descriptions you gave to computers on your own LAN, of course, not the icons shown in the Figure 31-14.

If icons don't appear right away, choose View ➪ Refresh from the menu bar or right-click in the content area of the window and select Refresh from the menu that is displayed. You may need to do that a few times, especially if you're walking from computer to computer to verify their connections.

If you double-click the icon for a computer on your LAN, you'll see icons representing that computer's shared resources, assuming that computer is turned on and running.

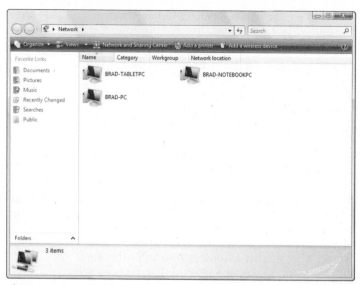

Figure 31-14: An example of computers on a LAN showing up under the Network folder

If you weren't able to see icons for all the computers on your LAN, don't panic. Sometimes a little wake-up call is all it takes. Carefully check all cables to make sure they're tight and connected where they should be. Restart each computer after verifying that its cables are snug in their plugs.

> **Tip** Any device or computer not turned on is inaccessible to the LAN. In fact, from a network standpoint, any device currently turned off doesn't even exist.

If a particular computer still won't cooperate, then it may be that the computer is not sharing any files or resources. You'll want to read Chapter 32 to learn how to set up the computer for sharing.

Network Troubleshooting

If you're fortunate, you won't have to do this. But if you tried every alternative and still can't see icons for all the computers on your LAN in View Network Computers, you have some troubleshooting to do. Fortunately, most network problems turn out to be something minor rather than some big technical brouhaha. The most common problems are:

✦ A device (computer, modem, hub, or printer) is turned off and needs to be turned back on.

✦ A cable is unplugged somewhere or isn't properly seated in its plug.

✦ A wireless networking card on a laptop computer isn't properly seated in its PC Card slot.

✦ A computer needs to be restarted, because something wasn't turned on or properly installed when the computer was first started.

If you've checked and rechecked all the connections and still can't see other computers in the network through the Network dialog box, the next step is to run the Diagnose and Repair wizard. Go to the Network and Sharing Center as shown earlier in this chapter. Select, on the left side under Tasks, the Diagnose and repair option to run the wizard. You should follow any instructions and answer any questions posed by the wizard.

If you are still having issues with your network, then you can walk through the Network Troubleshooters. Here's how:

1. Click the Start button and choose Help and Support. Select Troubleshooting. This will list a number of troubleshooters. The Networking section should list several that you can select.

2. Select the troubleshooter that most fits your situation. If you are not finding a computer on your network, then select Troubleshoot problems finding computers on a home network.

3. Follow the information in the Networking Troubleshooter (see Figure 31-15), and click Next. Answer any questions to the best of your ability.

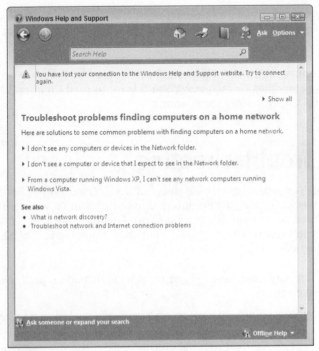

Figure 31-15: The Networking Troubleshooter

The troubleshooter might able to help you solve the problem. Don't be afraid to poke around through available resources, as described in Chapter 32. You never know — sometimes a computer that doesn't show up under View Workgroup Computers might actually be there, sharing some of its resources.

You Did It!

When you get the LAN working, give yourself a big pat on the back. Creating a LAN is no small technological feat. They should give away trophies, or at least a T-shirt, to people who accomplish this task. But, alas, the only reward is the tremendous power and convenience of having all your computers talking to each other on a LAN.

With your LAN set up, the next step is making sure you can share items. In Chapter 32 you will learn how to adjust settings to share your music, documents, and other files with those on your network.

Summary

Let's review the main points covered in this chapter before moving on to Chapter 32, where you'll learn how to use the LAN you worked so hard to create:

- ✦ A local area network enables computers in a home or building to share resources.

- ✦ A resource is anything useful, such as an Internet account, a printer, or a folder that contains files useful to everyone on the LAN.

- ✦ To create a LAN, you need to purchase and install networking hardware.

- ✦ You can connect computers using traditional Ethernet cables, phone lines, and power lines already in your house, or even wirelessly with no cables at all.

- ✦ The first step in creating the LAN is to install all the networking hardware according to the hardware manufacturer's instructions.

- ✦ When all the hardware is in place, you might need to run the Network Setup wizard on each computer on the LAN. In most cases, Windows Vista should set up the network for you automatically.

- ✦ To view all the computers on a LAN, open your Network folder on the Start menu.

- ✦ To use the Internet from any computer on the LAN, just start any Internet-related program normally (for example, a web browser or e-mail client).

- ✦ To troubleshoot a LAN, first check the most likely problems (power turned off on a computer or device, loose or disconnected cable, or firewall turned on even though the computer isn't the ICS host). Use the Network Troubleshooter to help with subtle problems.

Sharing Things on a Network

A local area network (LAN) consists of two or more computers connected through some sort of networking hardware. On a LAN, you can use *shared resources* from other computers in much the same way as you use local resources on your own computer. In fact, the way you do things on a LAN is almost identical to the way you do things on a single computer.

For example, everything you learned about printing documents on your own computer earlier in this book works just as well for printing on a network printer.

Opening a document on some other computer in a network is no different from opening a document on your own computer. Moving and copying files among computers on a network is the same as moving and copying files among folders on your own computer.

Some Networking Buzzwords

Like everything else computer related, networking has its own set of buzzwords. All the buzzwords you learned in earlier chapters still apply. But there are some new words to learn, as defined here:

- ✦ **Resource:** Anything useful, including a folder, a printer, or other device.

- ✦ **Shared or Public:** A resource accessible to all users on a computer and to all computers within a network. A shared folder is often referred to as a *share, network share,* or a *public folder.*

✦ **Local computer:** The computer at which you're currently sitting.

✦ **Local resource:** A folder, printer, or other useful thing on the local computer or directly connected to the local computer by a cable. For example, if there's a printer connected to your computer by a cable, it's a local resource (or more specifically, a *local printer*).

✦ **Remote computer:** Any computer on the network other than the one at which you're currently sitting.

✦ **Remote resource:** A folder, printer, or other useful resource on some computer other than the local computer. For example, a printer connected to someone else's computer on the network is a remote resource (or more specifically, a *remote printer*).

Figure 32-1 shows an example of how the terms *local* and *remote* are always used in reference to the computer at which you're currently sitting.

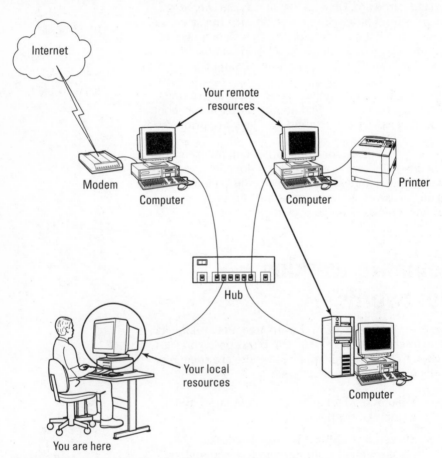

Figure 32-1: Examples of local and remote resources, from your perspective

Turning Sharing On

Whether you want to share a printer, documents, or something else, the first thing you will need to do is to let Windows Vista know that sharing is okay. You do this on the Network and Sharing Center that you saw in Chapter 31.

To access the Network and Sharing Center, from the start menu select Network. In the Network folder that opens, select Network and Sharing Center from the toolbar. This displays your Network and Sharing Center similar to Figure 32-2.

In order to find other items on your network, and in order to be found on the network, you need to turn Network discover on. Additionally, when you want to share items, you have to indicate this. In the Network and Sharing Center, you can customize your sharing and discovery settings in the lower part of the window. In Figure 32-2, you can see that Brad-PC can be discovered on the network and that the owner of that PC can share files. You also see, however, that the owner's public folders are not shared by default, nor are his printers or media.

These settings can be changed by clicking the down-arrow button on the right of each item. This expands the option and enables you to then turn the option on or off. In Figure 32-3, you can see that Printer sharing turned on. This means other computers will be able to access the printer on this machine.

These settings provide somewhat general control of sharing. In the following sections, you'll learn how to fine-tune what you share.

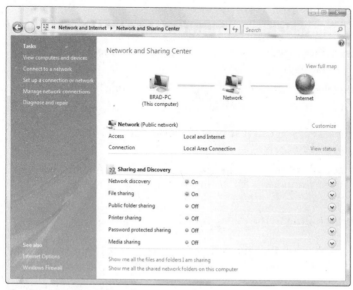

Figure 32-2: The Network and Sharing Center showing the sharing status of Brad-PC

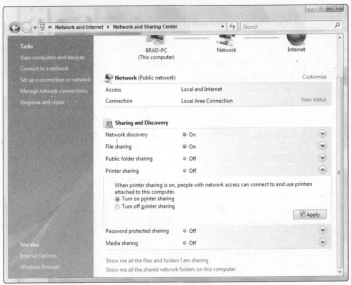

Figure 32-3: Setting up the computer so that printers can be shared

Using a Shared Printer

On a network, anybody can use a shared printer connected to any computer in the network. Printing to a shared printer is no different from printing to a local printer. The steps are the same.

STEPS: Print Using a Network Printer

1. While viewing the document you want to print, do whichever of the following is most convenient for you:

   - Choose File ➪ Print from the program's menu bar.

   - Press Ctrl+P.

   - In some cases, you can just right-click the text you want to print and choose Print.

2. Click the name of the printer you want to use, or choose its name from the Printer drop-down list, as in the examples shown in Figure 32-4.

3. Click the Print button in the dialog box to start printing.

If the document fails to print, the computer or printer you're trying to use may be turned off. You'll need to make sure both of those devices are turned on before you can use the printer.

Figure 32-4: Multiple printers available in the sample Print dialog box

If a printer on the network doesn't show up in your Print dialog box, either the printer isn't shared or your computer doesn't know that the shared printer is available. Both problems are easily fixed, as described in the next sections.

Sharing a Printer

Printers in a local area network will usually be connected to one of the computers in that network. To ensure that the printer is shared, so everybody in the network can use it, follow these steps.

Caution With the right hardware, you can connect a printer directly to a LAN without going through a computer. With that type of arrangement, you need only to make sure that the printer is turned on.

STEPS: Share a Printer on a Network

1. Go to the computer to which the printer is connected by cable. If either is turned off, turn on the printer first and the computer second.

2. Click the Start button and choose Printers. Or, if that option isn't available, click the Start button, and choose Control Panel. From the Control Panel Home screen, select Hardware and Sound, then Printers.

3. Click the icon that represents the printer you want to share.

4. Click Share from the tasks listed in the toolbar. Or right-click the printer's icon, and choose Share.

5. Click the Change sharing options button. This enables you to then change the sharing settings. If you are not an administrator, you may need to enter a system password.

6. Choose Share this printer; then type a name for the printer as in the example shown in Figure 32-5. Click OK in the dialog box.

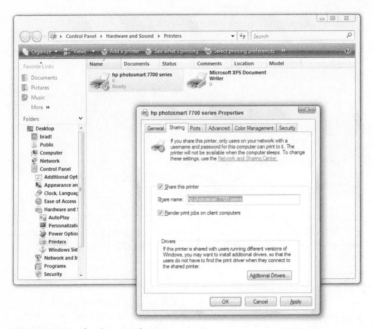

Figure 32-5: Sharing a printer

 The printer's icon will show little people on the bottom left corner, as in the example shown at left. The printer should show up automatically in all network computers' Print dialog boxes. In case the printer doesn't show up on a particular computer, the next section explains how to get it to show up.

Tip
To add a Printers and Faxes option to your Start menu, right-click the Start button and choose Properties. Click the Customize button. Select Printers in the list of Start Menu Items. Click OK.

Adding a Shared Printer to Your Computer

If you know that a printer on the network is shared, but you still can't access the printer from your computer, add the printer to your Printers folder manually. Here's how.

STEPS: Add a Shared Printer to a Network Computer

1. Make sure the printer, and the computer to which it's attached, are turned on and shared.

2. Sit at the computer that cannot access the shared printer.

3. Click the Start button and choose Printers. Or click the Start button and choose Control Panel. From the Control Panel Home screen, select Hardware and Sound, then Printers.

4. On the toolbar in the Printer folder click Add a Printer. Alternatively, you can right-click an open area in the window and select Add Printer. The Add Printer wizard opens.

5. Choose Add a network, wireless, or Bluetooth printer. If necessary, click Next. The Add Printer wizard will search for available printers and display them. This may take a few minutes.

6. Scroll through the list of available printers until you find the one you want. Click the printer's name. Click Next. If the printer you want is not listed, you can click the text, The printer that I want isn't listed. This will prompt you with a dialog window that enables you to enter the specific name and location of the printer or the TCP/IP address of the printer.

7. Follow any additional instructions that appear on the screen; then click Finish on the last wizard page.

An icon for the printer will appear in your Printers folder. If you want to make that printer your default (which means, it's the printer used automatically if you don't specify a different printer), right-click the printer's icon and choose Set as Default Printer. The default printer's icon will display a white check mark in a black circle.

Close the Printers window. You should be able to access the printer from any program's Print dialog box as described in the section "STEPS: Print Using a Network Printer," earlier in this chapter.

Using Shared Documents and Folders

Every Windows Vista computer in a network has a Public folder. If you made the change in your Network and Sharing Center shown earlier to allow the sharing of folders, then by default, the subfolders and documents in the Public folder are available to everyone on the network. Files and subfolders in your Documents folder are private, meaning they're invisible to other computers in the network and can't be accessed from the network.

If you want to share some of the documents currently in your Documents folder (or any subfolder within Documents), you can just move or copy those documents to an appropriate Public folder on your local computer. For example, moving songs from your Music folder to your Public Music folder will instantly make all those songs available to every computer in the network. You can use any of the techniques described in Chapter 20 to move and copy files between folders on your personal folders and your Public folders.

If you move a document to a shared public folder, there will still be only one copy of the document on the entire network. So, if some other user on the network changes the document, you're stuck with the changes.

If you want other users to be able to play around with the document, but not change your original, *copy* (don't *move*) the document to the Public folder instead. The copy in your Documents folder will remain invisible to other users, so they can't even see it, let alone change it. Whatever havoc other users wreak on the shared copy of the document won't affect the copy in your Documents folder at all.

Using the Network Folder

All of the public folders and documents on a network are neatly bundled together in a single folder named Network. To get to all public folders and documents on the network, open your Network folder. There are two quick and easy ways to do that as illustrated in Figure 32-6 and described here:

✦ Click the Start button and choose Network.

✦ Open your personalized folder (or any other folder that is viewed in Windows Explorer). (Click the Start button, and choose your personal folder.) Then click Network within the Folder section of the Navigation pane.

If you don't see Network on your Start menu, and want to add it, follow these steps:

1. Right-click the Start button and choose Properties.

2. Make sure Start Menu (not Classic Start Menu) is selected. Then click the Customize button next to Start Menu.

3. In the list of Start Menu Items that appears, scroll down to and select (check) Network.

 Tip   While you're in the Start Menu Items list, feel free to choose any other items you care to place on your Start menu.

4. Click the OK button in both open dialog boxes.

From now on, whenever you click the Start button, the Start menu displays all the items you selected in the Start Menu Items list. Now let's get back to networking.

Figure 32-6: Two quick routes to your Network folders

Opening Public Documents and Folders

To open, edit, or print a document on a remote computer, it's not necessary to copy that file to your computer first. You can just open it from its current location by following these steps.

STEPS: Open a Public Folder or Document

1. From your own computer, open the Network folder. The folder containing icons for all shared resources to which you have access opens, as in the example shown in Figure 32-7.

    Tip If the Network folder doesn't show everything you were expecting it to show, right-click an open area and select Refresh from the menu that displays. It may take a few seconds for all icons to appear.

2. Double-click the icon that represents the computer or folder that contains the document you want to open. If necessary, navigate through subfolders until you find the document you want.

    Tip In the Network folder, icons that look like folders represent shared folders on the LAN. Other icons might represent sites on the Internet to which you can upload files.

3. Double-click the icon for the document you want to open. Or right-click the document's icon and choose Open With and the program you want to use.

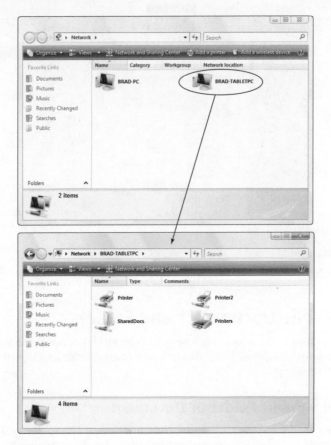

Figure 32-7: A sample Network folder (top) and the contents of one of the computers listed on it (bottom).

The document should open normally on your computer — no differently from a document stored on your own computer's hard disk. If the document won't open because you don't have an appropriate program installed on your computer, see the "What About Sharing Programs?" sidebar that follows.

If you can't even find the shared document you're searching for, there are several possible causes:

✦ The computer on which the shared resource resides is turned off. You'll need to start that computer normally to access its shared resources.

✦ The resource you're trying to access isn't shared. You'll need to go to the computer on which the document resides and move it to a shared folder or share the folder in which the document is currently stored.

✦ The folder you need to access is already shared but needs to be added to your local computer's Network folder manually.

What About Sharing Programs?

Although you can share folders and documents freely on a LAN, there's no way to share programs. You can only run programs currently installed on your computer and accessible from your All Programs menu. If you try to open a document on another computer, but don't have the appropriate program for that document type, you can't open the document.

Don't' bother trying to copy an installed program from one computer to another — it won't work. Only programs that you specifically install on your own computer will run on your computer.

The only solution will be to install the necessary program on your own computer. If the program you need is a freebie, like Adobe Reader, you can download and install the program from www.adobe.com.

Solutions to the latter two problems are described in the sections that follow. But first, there's the possibility that when you double-click a public folder's icon, the folder won't even open. Instead, you'll see an error message like the one in Figure 32-8.

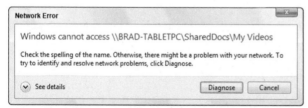

Figure 32-8: Error message that could appear when you double-click a shared folder's icon

One possible cause for the error is that the computer sharing the folder isn't connected to the network or isn't turned on. But an even more perplexing possibility is that the whole computer is being protected by a firewall. The only computer that needs firewall protection is the ICS host. A connection to a LAN really doesn't need firewall protection, because you can't *hack* one computer on a LAN from another computer on the same LAN.

So, the solution, if it's a firewall problem, is to go to the computer on which the public folder is stored and turn off its firewall as shown in Chapter 31.

Sharing Folders

All documents within a public folder — including documents within subfolders of that Public folder — are accessible to all users of the network. If you're using an older version of Windows that doesn't have a Public or Shared Documents folder, you can create a folder and share it. Or you can just share the folder as it stands. To share a folder outside of the public area, you must first turn on file sharing in the Network and Sharing Center as shown earlier in this chapter. Next, the general procedure described as follows will usually do the trick.

STEPS: Share a Folder

1. On your local computer, open Windows Explorer (or your personal or Documents folder) and navigate to the parent of the folder you want to share, so you can see the icon that represents the folder you want to share.

2. Right-click the icon of the folder you want to share and choose Share.

 Tip In some versions of Windows, you may have to right-click the icon, choose Properties, and look for the Sharing options within the dialog box that opens. If in doubt, search that version of Windows' Help for **share**.

3. On the Sharing dialog box that opens, choose from the top drop-down list who you want to share this folder with (see Figure 32-9).

4. After you've selected a person, click the Add button to add his or her account to the list of people that can access the folder. Guests include anyone without a login ID to your computer.

5. After the person or group is added, you should set their permission level in the drop-down list to the right. From this list, you can select one of the following permission levels:

   - **Reader:** This person or group can only read items in the folder. They cannot change or delete any items.

   - **Contributor:** This person or group can read your files but not change or delete them. They can also add their own files as well as change or delete their own files.

   - **Co-owner:** This person can read, add, change, or delete any file in the folder.

6. Click Share in the dialog box. The File Sharing dialog box will take a few minutes to set up the items to be shared.

7. When the sharing is set up, a dialog box will tell you that the task is completed. You can click the Done button to close the dialog box.

When shared, the folder's icon will display the sharing symbol on the bottom left corner. You'll see this symbol anywhere the folder is displayed.

To remove sharing from the folder — so network users can't get to it anymore — repeat the preceding steps and click the Share this folder on the network check box at any time. In Step 3, one of two things may happen.

If the sharing dialog box opens, then instead of adding people in Steps 3 to 5, you should click the people or accounts in the list and then change the permission level to Remove as shown in Figure 32-10. After you have removed the names or groups you don't want to have access anymore, click the Share button (see Step 6 above) to make the changes to the folder.

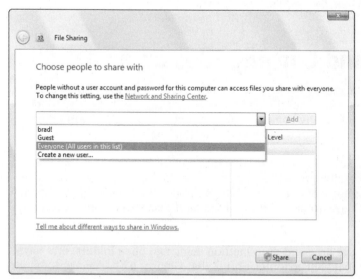

Figure 32-9: Sharing a folder and letting other people change its documents

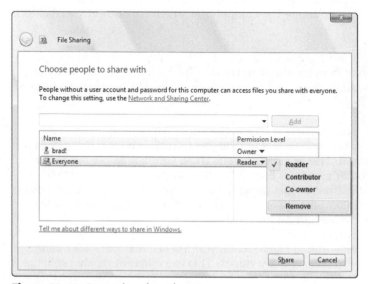

Figure 32-10: Removing shared access

The other thing that might happen is that instead of the sharing dialog box, a dialog box may be displayed asking whether you want to stop sharing the folder. Simply select that option to stop sharing.

The folder should show up within the Network folder and its subfolders on all computers throughout the network automatically. If it doesn't, there are solutions to that problem, too, as discussed next.

Moving and Copying Files on a LAN

Moving and copying files on a LAN is virtually identical to doing so on a single computer. You can use any of the techniques described in Chapter 19 to move or copy files around on any computer or from one computer to another. As always, there will be a source folder and a destination folder.

For example, let's say you have a lot of songs in your Music folder that you want to make accessible to all the computers on the LAN. But while you're at it, you decide to put them in someone else's Public Music folder, rather than in your own Public Music folder, to reclaim the hard disk space they're taking up on your computer.

If you want to do the drag-and-drop method using two open folders, first navigate to your own local Music folder. Shrink that window a bit to make room for another folder.

Next, open your Network folder and navigate to the folder to which you want to move the files. For example, in Figure 32-11, the folder in the upper-left corner is on the local computer — the computer at which I'm currently sitting as I write this.

The folder in the lower right of Figure 32-11 is the Public Music folder on a completely different computer named Homie. The folder has been opened by opening the Network folder on a local computer and just drilling down from the SharedDocs folder on Homie.

Note the address of the source folder in the upper left, as it appears in the address bar: Public > Public Music. You can tell this is a local drive because the name is standard. This is more obvious when you look at the address in the destination folder's address bar, Network > HOMIE > SharedDocs. The Network part at the front of that name tells you that you're most likely looking at a folder on a different machine. In this case, the SharedDocs file is on the computer named Homie, not on the local computer.

It is also worth noting that in Figure 32-11, you will see that the folder names are My Music, My Pictures, and My videos. This is a different naming scheme than Windows Vista uses. In this example, files are actually copied to a Windows XP machine. Although the folders are named differently, the process is simple regardless!

Figure 32-11: Source folder (upper left) and destination folder (lower right).

The rest of the copying is easy. Select the files to move or copy in the source folder, right-drag them to the destination folder, release the mouse button, and choose Move Here or Copy Here (depending on which you want to do). This is the same as moving or copying files between two folders on a hard drive. The fact that there are two separate computers involved here is irrelevant and has no bearing on *how* you select, move, or copy the files. Adios, sneaker net!

Sharing Media Files

In Windows Vista, the process of sharing media files has been given a little extra attention. When you share folders, files, and documents as shown in this chapter, it includes the sharing of any media files. With Windows Vista, however, you can get a finer level of control in sharing media. This includes the ability to add parental guidance as well as other limits.

If you return to the Network and Sharing Center, you will see that there is an option for Media Sharing that can be turned on or off as shown in Figure 32-12. When you turn on this setting, then your media files will be shared with others on the network. If you turn it off, then it won't unless it is a part of another shared folder.

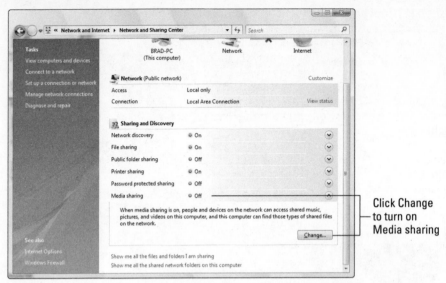

Figure 32-12: The media sharing and discover setting in the Network and Sharing Center

When you click the Change button, you will be given a dialog box that enables you to share your media. In the Media Sharing dialog box shown in Figure 32-13, click the Share my media option; then click OK.

Figure 32-13: Sharing your media is as simple as selecting the Share my media check box.

Note   If you are using a public network, then you might not be able to turn on the media sharing setting. You will need to change your network to a private network for security. Click the Networking button in the dialog box shown in Figure 32-12. You'll be able to change your network to private. After doing this, you may need to go back to the Network and Sharing Center and reset the sharing settings for files, folders, and printers. When done, you can then return to the media sharing options.

Although simply selecting the check box and clicking OK is enough to share your media, you might want to go a little further with your settings and provide some restrictions on what you allow to be shared. After clicking OK, the dialog box will be displayed again with an extra button and the ability to select individuals or groups. With the individuals and groups listed, you can allow or deny their access to your shared media by simply clicking their icon and clicking the appropriate button. If you allow them, then you will be able to customize their access by clicking the Customize button while their icon is highlighted.

Just as you can customize settings for an individual or group, you can also adjust the same settings globally. Either way, the settings you can configure are presented in Figure 32-14.

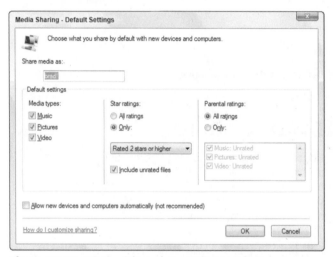

Figure 32-14: Customizing what media you share

As you can see in Figure 32-14, you have the ability to restrict the types of media you want to share. You can clear the check boxes of any types you want to restrict. You an also set whether bad music is shared. By bad, I mean both low ratings and parentally not approved. After you've adjusted any restrictions on what you want to share, click the OK button to set them.

Before saving the changes, you might want to also change the name given to the shared media. You can see that in Figure 32-14, the default name is the user account name. When you view the network icons on the Network folder, this is the name that will be seen for the shared media. Figure 32-15 shows my Network folder after turning media sharing on.

If you decide you want to change the media settings you made, go back and follow the same steps you used to turn them on and set them.

Figure 32-15: The network folder with media sharing on

Seeing What You're Sharing

You should always consider the risks of sharing resources, especially files.
If you share, it is often best to restrict your files and documents to the most
restrictive level that works. This will help protect you. For example, if you
share documents and give other people access rights to change and delete
files, then they may change or delete your document.

As time goes on, you might not remember every folder you've shared. The
solution to this is to use one of the custom searches to see what you are sharing. You can get to this by going to Windows Explorer. You can be viewing
Documents folder or any other folder. In Windows Explorer, click Searches
from the Favorite Links on the left. This displays saved searches. One of the
standard searches is called Shared By Me. Click it.

Be cautious of this search, though. Public folders, media, and global files that
are shared by using settings in the Network and Sharing Center may not be
listed in the search results.

Summary

Whew, this last part of the book has been a whirlwind tour of creating and
using a local area network. In truth, networking is one of those topics one
could easily write an entire book about. And many people have. But the basic
things you need to know to take advantage of a network for day-to-day tasks
are all summed up right here in one chapter. To recap:

✦ In a network, a local resource is something on your own computer's hard disk or a device installed on your own computer.

✦ A remote resource is any device or folder in, or on, some other computer in the network and shared so everyone in the network can use it.

✦ To use a remote printer, just print your document normally. But when you get to the Print dialog box, choose the remote printer's name.

✦ To get to a remote document in a shared folder, open your Network folder. Then open the folder (or parent folder) to the document you want to open.

✦ To move and copy files between computers in a network, use the same techniques you use to move and copy files on your own network. The remote folder can be either the source folder or the destination folder.

✦ You can share media on your computer with others. You can restrict what media is shared, based on features such as your star ratings, parental controls, and individuals.

Installing Windows Vista

If you purchased your PC with Windows Vista already installed, you need to hang a U-turn. There's nothing in this appendix for you. Go straight to the introduction, or Chapter 1, at the start of this book, and forget all about this appendix.

If you purchased an upgrade version of Windows Vista to replace your current Windows XP, and you haven't yet installed that upgrade, this is the place to be. To tell you the truth, you really don't have to read this entire appendix to install your upgrade. You really just have to do this:

1. Insert the DVD that came with your Windows Vista Upgrade into your computer's DVD drive and wait a few seconds.

2. Follow the instructions that appear on the screen to install Vista by upgrading your current version of Windows.

When the installation is complete, remove the new DVD from your DVD drive, put it in a safe place, and ignore the rest of this appendix. If these two steps don't quite get the job done, please read on.

Windows Vista System Requirements

For the more technically savvy readers who know what things like RAM and hard disk capacity are about, here are the requirements for installing Windows Vista:

+ 512 MB of system memory

+ An 800 megahertz (MHz) *x*86 or *x*64 microprocessor

+ A graphics processor that supports DirectX 9

+ A VGA or better monitor

+ A keyboard

+ A mouse or similar pointing device

+ A CD-ROM or DVD drive

The preceding requirements are considered capable of running Windows Vista. The recommended requirements start with the preceding and include the following changes or additions:

+ A 1 GHz 32-bit or 64-bit processor

+ 1 GB or more of system memory

+ 15 GB of free hard disk space on a 40 GB or larger drive

+ 64 MB Graphics card (128 MB graphics full Aero Interface) on a card that supports DirectX 9

+ DVD-ROM drive

+ Internet access capability

Preinstallation Housekeeping

If you've been using your PC for a while with an earlier version of Windows, you'll want to do some things before you begin your upgrade:

+ If your computer has any time-out features, such as the power-down features found on some portable PCs, disable those features now.

+ If you have an antivirus program handy, run it now to check for, and delete, dormant viruses that may still be lurking on your hard disk.

+ Make sure that any external devices (printers, modems, external disk drives, and so on) are connected and turned on so Windows Vista can detect them during installation.

+ To play it safe, back up the entire hard disk at this point in case something goes wrong and you need to get back to where you were.

+ If your PC is connected to a local area network (LAN), check to make sure that you're connected to the LAN so Windows Vista can see your LAN during installation.

When all that's finished, you're ready to begin the installation.

Installing Windows Vista

To upgrade an existing version of Windows, start your computer. Then put the Windows Vista DVD in your DVD drive and wait for the Welcome screen to open as shown in Figure A-1.

If you get the AutoPlay dialog window, then select Run setup.exe. If nothing appears on the screen within a minute or so, follow these steps:

1. Open Computer on your desktop.
2. Open the icon for your DVD drive. If the Welcome screen opens, skip the next step.
3. Click (or double-click) the Setup (or setup.exe) file on the DVD.

By now, you should definitely see on your screen some options for Installing Windows Vista. To get things rolling when the Windows Vista Setup wizard opens, choose *Install now*.

The installation procedure will begin. You might notice that the screen goes blank once in a while during the installation. Don't be alarmed; that's normal. If the screen goes blank for a long time, try moving the mouse around a bit to bring it back. From here on out, you can just follow the instructions on the screen.

Figure A-1: The Windows Vista installation start-up screen

The first instructions you will likely see are how to get updates for the installation as shown in Figure A-2. If your computer is connected to the Internet, then choose to go online and get the latest updates. This helps to ensure that you have the most recent copy of Windows Vista when the installation is completed.

The next dialog box you see will ask you to enter your product key for activation as shown in Figure A-3. There is also a check box you can select to go ahead and activate your copy of Vista. This step is to make sure that you are using a legitimate copy of Windows Vista and not just borrowing your friend's copy. The product key will either be on the Vista media or the packaging for the media.

If you don't have the product key with you, the installation enables you to continue. When you click the Next button, you will be asked whether you want to enter your product key now. If you click the No button, then you'll be prompted to indicate which version of Windows Vista you own. You'll also need to check the box labeled *I have selected the edition of Windows that I purchased.* You'll then be able to click Next, and the installation will continue.

 Caution   Make sure that you select the copy you really have. If you enter a product key for a different edition later, then it won't match and won't work.

Be aware that if you don't enter a product key, you will have to enter one later (within 30 days). You won't be able to activate your copy of Windows Vista without it. And, if you don't activate your copy of Vista, it will quit working after a period of time.

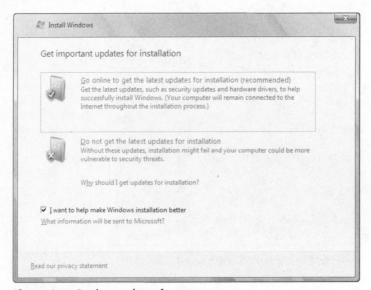

Figure A-2: Getting updates for setup

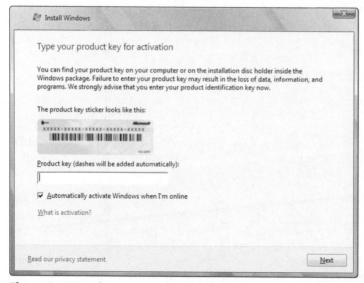

Figure A-3: Entering your product key for activation

When you are past the product code prompts, you will next be asked to agree to the licensing terms for Windows Vista. Although most people don't read this agreement, you might want to take a few minutes to read through what you are agreeing to when you install Windows Vista. You'll need to check the *I accept the license terms* box before you'll be able to click the Next button to continue with the installation.

Installation Options

The exact procedure from this point on will vary a bit, depending on the version you are installing as well as depending on whether you are upgrading or installing a new version. If you are upgrading, you'll be able to choose between upgrading and doing a custom install. If you do a custom install, you will effectively wipe off any files, programs, and other documents that you might have had on your system. They will likely be gone, never to be seen again. As such, if you want to keep files and documents, you'll need to create a copy of them to put back on after the installation is completed. Alternatively, you can choose to upgrade.

If you choose to upgrade, then the installation wizard will jump right into copying, gathering, expanding, installing, and then completing the upgrade. A dialog box will be displayed while this is happening — similar to Figure A-4. Although the installation of Windows Vista is supposed to be faster than prior editions, an upgrade may take several hours to complete.

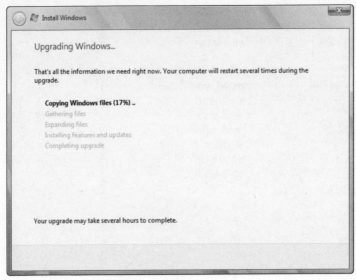

Figure A-4: The upgrading process

When the crunching is completed, you will be asked for a bit more feedback before the installation can be fully completed. You will be greeted with a request to Help protect Windows automatically. You will be given the option to use the recommended settings, to install only important updates, or to skip this question until later. If in doubt, choose the recommended settings. This turns on Windows Updates and helps keep your copy of Windows current.

After determining update options, you will likely be prompted to set the date and time along with the time zone. You can also set whether or not you want Windows to automatically adjust the time for daylight savings changes.

If all goes well, you should see a dialog box thanking you for working through the setup process. If you click the Start button, Windows Vista should be launched for the first time.

Starting the First Time (the System Performance Check)

You should expect to have to wait the first time Windows Vista actually starts. Windows Vista will check your systems performance. While it does this, you will see information displayed on the screen about some of the features that Windows Vista offers. Whether it is the checking of the performance or the desire to spend time presenting information on features, you will still have to wait. A status bar across the bottom of the screen will show you the progress of the check on system performance.

If you are doing an upgrade, then you should see the login screen after the performance check is completed. If you did a new install, you may be prompted for additional information as Windows Vista completes any setup necessary for your computer.

Note With an upgrade or a new install, you might see a number of pop-up dialog boxes that mention the installation of drivers. A driver is a program that helps the operating system and computer understand other devices such as hard drives, your mouse, and video cards. You might be asked to insert disksthat came with these devices. If you don't have the disks, you'll be able to tell Windows Vista to look on the Internet or to do the best it can. If you follow the prompts, you'll be told what you need to do.

Product Activation

The wizard may then ask that you activate your copy of Windows as shown in Figure A-5. If you have an Internet connection already, you can choose to activate your copy of Windows Vista. Alternatively, you can choose to use the computer with reduced functionality. You may also be able to choose to activate later; however, you will be prompted again later to activate, and at some point you will have to activate or go to reduced functionality.

Figure A-5: The prompt to activate your copy of Windows

Sharing the Computer

If more than one person will be using the computer, you can choose to give each person his or her own *user account*. Doing so will allow each person to have a private Documents folder, desktop, Internet favorites, e-mail address, and so forth.

If you're not so sure about the *user account* business, you can skip it for now. You can create user accounts at any time by referring to Chapter 25 in this book.

Done!

At this point, the installation should be completed. The best thing to do next is to proceed to Chapter 1 to get Windows Vista rolling.

Shortcut Key Quick Reference

Trying to use Windows Vista without a mouse or other pointing device is like trying to drive a car without a steering wheel — not easy. About the only time you need to use the keyboard is when you're typing text.

If your work requires a lot of typing, such that your hands are on the keyboard a lot, you can use *shortcut keys* to get many things done without taking your hands off the keyboard. Most of these keys are described throughout the book, but here's a quick reference to many of them.

Tip   To view shortcut keys on your screen, search Windows Help and Support for keyboard shortcuts.

General Keyboard Shortcuts

Cancel (bail out)	Esc
Close active document window	Ctrl+F4
Close active program	Alt+F4
Copy	Ctrl+C
Copy by dragging	Ctrl+*drag*
Create shortcut by dragging	Ctrl+Shift+*drag*
Cut	Ctrl+X
Delete	Delete or Del
Delete without Recycle Bin	Shift+Delete or Shift+Del

Continued

Continued

Help	F1
Menu bar (activate)	F10
Next menu bar menu	→
Open menu	Alt+*underlined letter* on menu option
Paste	Ctrl+V
Prevent CD autostart	Hold down Shift while inserting CD
Previous menu bar menu	←
Print	Ctrl+P
Rename selected item	F2
Select All	Ctrl+A
Shortcut menu for selected item (open)	Shift+F10
Start menu (open)	Ctrl+Esc
Stop task	Break
Switch to another open program	Alt+Tab or Alt+Esc
Switch to another program using Flip3D	⊞+Tab
Switch to another program using Flip3D and arrow keys	Ctrl+⊞+Tab
Task Manager	Ctrl+Alt+Del
Undo	Ctrl+Z
View properties	Alt+Enter
View shortcut menu	Alt+Spacebar

Text-Editing Shortcut Keys

Delete character to left	Backspace
Delete character to right	Delete (Del)
Down a line	↓
Down a page	Page Down (PgDn)
End of document	Ctrl+End
End of line	End
Next character	→
Next paragraph	Ctrl+↓
Next word	Ctrl+→

Previous character	..
Previous paragraph	Ctrl+↑
Previous word	Ctrl+←
Select all	Ctrl+A
Select next character	Shift+→
Select next word	Shift+Ctrl+→
Select page above	Shift+Page Up (PgUp)
Select page below	Shift+Page Down (PgDn)
Select previous character	Shift+←
Select previous word	Shift+Ctrl+←
Select to end of document	Shift+Ctrl+End
Select to end of line	Shift+End
Select to end of paragraph	Shift+Ctrl+↓
Select to start of line	Shift+Home
Select to top of document	Shift+Ctrl+Home
Select to top of paragraph	Shift+Ctrl+↑
Start of line	Home
Top of document	Ctrl+Home
Undo last edit	Ctrl+Z
Up a line	↑
Up a page	Page Up (PgUp)

Dialog Box Shortcut Keys

Cancel	Esc
Command	Alt+*underlined letter*
Display Active Items from List (when a list is selected)	F4
Help	F1
Next option	Tab
Next tab	Ctrl+Tab
Open higher-level folder (when in the Save As or Open dialogs with a folder selected)	Backspace

Continued

Continued

Previous option	Shift+Tab
Previous tab	Ctrl+Shift+Tab
Select/clear check box	Spacebar

Windows Explorer Shortcut Keys

Collapse expanded list or select parent folder	←
Collapse selected folder	Num Lock + - (on numeric keypad)
End of list	End
Expand selected list or select first subfolder	→
Favorites (show/hide)	Ctrl+I
History (show/hide)	Ctrl+H
Next folder	Alt+→
Next item	F6
Open address bar drop-down list	F4
Parent folder	Backspace
Previous folder	Alt+←
Refresh contents	F5
Search	F3
Select address bar	Alt+D
Shortcut menu (selected icon)	Shift+F10
Show all subfolders under selected folder	Num Lock + * (on numeric keypad)
Show contents of selected folder	Num Lock + + (on numeric keypad)
Start of list	Home
System menu	Alt+Spacebar

Ease of Access Shortcut Keys

FilterKeys on/off	Hold down right Shift key for five seconds
High Contrast on/off	Left Alt + Left Shift + Print Screen

MouseKeys on/off	Left Alt + Left Shift + Num Lock
StickyKeys on/off	Press Shift 5 times
ToggleKeys on/off	Hold down Num Lock for five seconds
Ease of Access Center	⊞+U

Windows Sidebar Shortcut Keys

Bring all gadgets to the front	⊞+Spacebar
Next Sidebar gadget	⊞+G
Next Sidebar control	Tab

Microsoft Keyboard Shortcuts

Minimize all	⊞+M
Computer (open)	⊞+E
Ease of Access Center	⊞+U
Mobility Center	⊞+X
Restore all	⊞+Shift+M
Run	⊞+R
Search	⊞+F
Search for computers (need to be on a network)	Ctrl+⊞+F
Show desktop	⊞+D
Start menu open or close	⊞
Switch to next program on taskbar	⊞+T
Switch programs using Flip 3D	⊞+Tab
Switch users (or lock keyboard in domain network)	⊞+L
System Properties dialog	⊞+Break
Utility Manager	⊞+U
Windows Help and Support	⊞+F1

Microsoft Help Viewer Shortcut Keys

Table of Contents	Alt+C
Connection Settings menu	Alt+N
Customer Support Page	Alt+A
End of topic	End
Help and Support home page	Alt+Home
Next viewed topic	Alt+→
Options menu	F10
Previously viewed topic	Alt+←
Print	Ctrl+P
Start of topic	Home
Search box	F3
Search current topic	Ctrl+F

Index

Continued

Continued

Continued

Continued

Continued

Continued

Continued

Continued

Continued

Continued

Continued

Continued

The books you
read to succeed.

Get the most out of the latest software and leading-edge technologies
with a Wiley Bible—your one-stop reference.

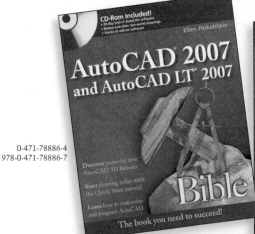

0-471-78886-4
978-0-471-78886-7

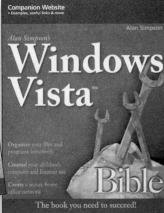

0-470-04030-0
978-0-470-04030-0

0-7645-4256-7
978-0-7645-4256-5

0-470-10089-3
978-0-470-10089-9